Bix: The Davenport Album
by Rich J. Johnson
with Jim Arpy & Gerri Bowers

Copyright © 2009 Estate of Rich J. Johnson
All rights reserved. No part of this book may be reproduced in any means, print or electronic, without consent of the author or his representative.

Project of Mississippi Valley Writers Colony
mvwc@qconline.com

Published by:
Razor Edge Press
Barnegat NJ

ISBN 978-0-9774018-5-7
Library of Congress Number: 2009930592
Printed in the United States of America by Lightning Source, LaVergne TN

BIX:
The Davenport Album

**by
Rich J. Johnson**

**with
Jim Arpy & Gerri Bowers**

In memory of Les Swanson

TABLE OF CONTENTS

Overture	1–9
Beiderbecke & Miller	10–14
Genealogy: Charles & Louise	15–25
Genealogy: Carl T. & Adele	29–37
Genealogy: Bismark & Aggie	38–47
Genealogy: Ottilie & A.J. Stibolt	48–50
Genealogy: Lutie & Max Von Binzer	51–58
Beiderbecke Ghosts	59–60
Genealogy: August Pieper	61–66
Pastor Henry	67–72
Der Demokrat	73–78
Genealogy: Hilton Family	79–85
Genealogy: Hill–Kennedy–Petersen	86–118
Aggie's Letter	119–121
Others Who Worked in the Beiderbecke Household	122–123
Genealogy: Charles Burnette	124–133
Genealogy: Mary Louise	135–141
Aggie's Church	142–145
St. Katharine's & Kemper Hall	146–150
Maternal Roots	151–157
Musical Roots	158–163
News of 1903	164–177
Leon Bismark Beiderbecke	178–201
Family Friends Remember Bix	202–204
Bix's Nickels	204–206
Tales from Tyler School	207–211
Alexander the Great	212–213
Night Out With Dad	214–215
Bix's Neighbors	218–221
QC Musical Legacy	222–227
A Date at the Garden	228–235
Burtis Opera House	236–243
Showman Charlie Kindt	244–247
Turner Hall & Grand Theater	248–253
Iowa's Gilded Lily	253–258
Davenport's Other Little Genius	258–262
On the Trail of Bix's First Piano Teacher	262–265
Music on the Mississippi	266–277
Famed QC Band on Book Cover	278–279
A Look Inside the Carlisle Evans Scrapbook	280–285

Tony Catalano & Crew	286–292
Banjo Man Lou Black	293–296
Letters to Jean	297–318
Harold Teen	319–322
Soda Jerk	323–324
Drugstore Harmonies	325–327
Meet Me at the Y	328–329
Bix Onboard	330–333
Others Who Knew Bix	334–341
Jazzman's Memories	342–346
Lorry & Lee	347–355
Karlie Vollmer	356–362
Bix Haunts	365–385
When Bix Played Knox	386–387
Story of Storyville	388–391
Brick's Place	392–395
Bix & the Shimmy Queen	396–398
Red Hot Mama Knew He Was Special	399–402
Floyd Bean, Lazy Piano Man	403–405
Linwood Raids	406–414
Remembering Linwood	414–416
Quinlan Memories	417–419
Terrace Gardens: What a Grand Place	420–423
The Guy Who Flunked Bix	424–426
Fritz Putzier	427–433
On the Hunt for a Bank and a Band	434–435
Thelma's Valentine	436–437
Scandal Finds Bix	438–454
Bix and the Future Football Hall of Famer	455
Lake Forest	456–464
Six Weeks in Syracuse	467–473
Chicago Jazz	473–480
When the Great Gershwin Played the Col	482–486
Kings of Jazz	486–488
Angela's Ring	489–494
Iowa City	494–501
I Am Not a Swan	502–510
All That Jazz	512–526
Whiteman's Boys	527–531
Bix & Red	532–533
Bix & Bing—Songbirds of a Feather!	534–536
An Interview with Bix's Old Flame	536–539

Bix in Hollywood	540–547
Bix Takes the Cure	549–556
Letter to Sis	558–562
Down Memory Lane	563–570
Satchmo Toots Bix's Horn	571–580
A Bit of the Macabre	580
Bix Tried to Get Me Up There	580–581
Sadly, the Fortunetellers Were Right	582–588
Crowd Scant at Bix's Funeral	589–593
Those Bieberbach Brothers	594–596
Tri–City Musician's Union	597
QC Chanteuse	597–602
Ted Fio Fito Presents	602–608
Music Goes Round and Round	608–619
Hoagy's Tribute	620–626
Bix Lives	627–642
Appendix	643
Charles & Louise Beiderbecke Estate	644–659
Points of Interest Then & Now	660–676
Bix Kin	677–681
Image Index	681–684
Coda	685–692
Bix Meets Louis	693–695

OVERTURE

As the magnificent whirl of the cosmos makes time, mass and population, it still cannot know what extraordinary people it is creating. They come and they go; the savants, the untalented, the brilliant and the common. Were Frank Lloyd Wright and Pablo Picasso an accident? Should we say James Joyce and Puccini and Michelangelo began as flukes or a lucky dice throw somewhere east of the sun?

Science still doesn't know what creates genius or talent or even happiness. Perhaps the Divinities, knowing we needed special handling, blessed us with prodigies and the precocious to beguile and thrill us, to make our brief tenure here meaningful and better.

Bix Beiderbecke was a common oracle with inlays of *esprit de corps*. He heard things beyond the musical clef that escaped others.

No one knows why he ignored the official and approved fingering system for cornet and trumpet and invented one of his own, or why he didn't know or care that both horns were transposing instruments until Hoagy Carmichael explained it to him.

Nor can it be explained how that tone—a crying, lyrical spurt of joy in the night, a silvered stiletto exploring and enlarging the ballroom of Jazz—that so many had tried to imitate, was manufactured inside this simple-cut Iowa boy's head.

He never became wealthy. No matter. Fame and money and élan or the lack of it never entered his mind. Bix Beiderbecke pushed that first valve down because it was all he knew or wanted or cared about. Towards the last, and with demons in his head, modest ways still remained for he was unaware that he was becoming famous as a new kind of performer. Bix Beiderbecke was a then–post modern zealot of good heart. In his short life of 28 years he had harmed no one, and showed others the way, this Orpheus with impeccable horn who celebrated America's art form of jazz with passion and fanaticism. As the horn of Bix pulsated with diminishing breath and bravery, it cried out in its final purity, *Singin' The Blues*, and the air magnified golden pear-shaped tones.

William Perry
Moline, Illinois

BRADY SREET HILL AT FIFTH, 1884—nine decades before Bix 7 runners first arrived
PERRY STREET AT SECOND, 1887—horse & wagon where River Center now stands

Bird's eye view of the Upper Mississippi Valley, showing Nahant Harbor in the foreground; Rockingham, lower left; Davenport, middle left; Rock Island opposite shore on the right; 2nd bridge, built 1873, crossing at Arsenal Island; and Moline upstream, top left of illustration from the 1875 Iowa State Atlas

Timeline

Col George Davenport robbed & shot July 4, 1845

Antoine LeClaire

1850—city population: 1,850; Scott County advertised 22,041 acres of prairie land for $1.25 an acre; George L. Davenport & Antoine LeClaire partner in city's first foundry and machine shop; Iowa College opened

1851—345 new homes built in Davenport; CRI&P RR construction began in Chicago; Upper Davenport, later known as Village of East Davenport, platted; Maine Law enacted creating the first dry state

1852—Davenport Literary Society argued pros and cons of Maine Law; city council gives downtown property owners one year to install sidewalks or face tax liens for installation cost

1853—population: 5,000; LeClaire & Davenport dissolved partnership

1854—Scott County's first fair; ex-Pres Millard Fillmore among dignitaries aboard first train to Rock Island; work began on river rapids to increase channel by 250 ft wide & 4 ft deep

1855—city marshal chased by mob with pitchforks and muskets when liquor confiscated under state prohibition; Michael Donahue buys LeClaire Foundry, builds city's first fire engine

1856—first railroad bridge across Mississippi opened between Davenport & Rock Island; Beiderbecke & Miller opened grocery store; Effie Afton Steamer crashed new bridge; East Davenport annexed

son of Col Davenport

First Bridge on the Mississippi view from Col Davenport house, Rock Island Arsenal

Timeline

1857—Burtis House hotel built; 3-year-old Mary Larned Allen is first to be buried at Oakdale Cemetery; Davenport & Moline fire engine companies lose to Rock Island in first-ever tri-city hose competition

1858—German laborers mob Cook & Sargent Exchange after Nebraska bank notes refused

1859—Odd Fellows dedicate Hibernian Hall on Brady St

1860—brothers-in-law Weyerhaeuser & Denkmann purchase first of several tri-cities lumber mills

1861—Antoine LeClaire died; Iowa Gov Sam Kirkwood established five Union Army camps in Davenport; B'nai Israel congregation formed in Davenport

1862—Schuetzenverein (shooting association) formed

1863—First National Bank of Davenport is first in the nation under National Banking Act; first of 12,000 Confederate prisoners arrived at Arsenal Island

1864—Camp McClellan commander protects convalescing soldiers by giving *sporting women* cold bath in the river; Griswold College cornerstone ceremony

1865—Iowa Soldier's Orphan Home founded by Annie Wittenmyer at Camp Kinsman

1866—Ebenezer Cook buys bankrupt Mississippi & Missouri railroad for $2.1 million; Pres Jackson ordered release of 177 Sioux prisoners at Davenport's Camp Kearney

1867—Burtis Opera House opened Dec 26

1868—Mercy Hospital opened; Schuetzen Geseltschaft (shooting society) purchased 20 acres west of Davenport

1869—Sisters of Mercy tour Scott County poorhouse before opening a hospital for sick and insane

1870—Schuetzen Park opened

1871—Academy of Science and First Presbyterian chapel built at 7th and Brady; Unitarian Church built at 10th and Perry

1872—Mississippi river stages included among records kept by newly-formed Weather Bureau; Dr. Spinney opens Linwood sulphur springs resort

1873—new double-deck bridge replaced first railroad bridge between Davenport and Rock Island

1874—Susan B. Anthony lectured at the Burtis Opera House; Phebe Sudlow became first woman school superintendent

Burtis Opera House

Griswold College
Kemper Hall to the left

Turning mechanism of 1872 bridge

Railroad deck of 1872 bridge

Timeline

1875—Beiderbecke & Miller move from West 2nd & Gaines to 100 block of East 2nd St; first high school opened at 7th between Rock Island & Iowa streets

1876—Susan Keating Glaspell born to Scott County pioneers Elmer & Alice Glaspell

1877—First Lutheran Pastor Jacob Gass uncovered carved tablets and pipes at mound dig, a hoax perpetrated by members of Academy of Science (Putnam Museum)

1878—Alice French published *Communists and Capitalists* under pen name Octave Thanet

1879—Davenport Brown Stockings first minor league baseball team west of Mississippi

1880—June 26 flood crest 18.4 ft; Beiderbecke & Miller build new 4-story structure on 2nd Street

1881—Soldier's monument on Main St dedicated July 4th

1882—Koehler-Lange Brewery wins prohibition lawsuit

1883—United Presbyterian Church moves from 11th & Scott to 11th & Brady

1884—Mayor Ernst Claussen negated state prohibition with city ordinance legalizing *new varieties of beverage* such as Seafoam and Kentucky Bluegrass; John Streckfus opened Acme Packet Co in Rock Island

1885—George L. Davenport died; Dr. William Grant performed first-ever appendectomy Jan 4th on 22-yr-old Mary Gartside at Mercy Hospital; St. Katharine & Kemper Hall established; first electric street lamps.

1886—*Northwester News* became *Davenport Daily Times*

1887— Masonic Temple built at 3rd & Brady; *Davenport Democrat* buys *Davenport Gazette*

1888—Flood 18.6 ft; nation's second electric streetcar launched Aug 11th on Brady Street Hill

1889—George Cram Cook graduated from Kemper Hall

1890—Iowa National Bank established with Charles Beiderbecke as president

1891—Brewster property sold to Davenport Outing Club

1892—canoes on 2nd St as Mississippi crests 19.4 ft on June 27; Grammar School Number 9 (Tyler) built at East High and Grand streets

F.G. Clausen, architect

Susan Glaspell

Alice French
a.k.a. Octave Thanet

Timeline

1893—Beiderbecke & Miller incorporated; Frank McCullough paid $1,200 at auction for Linwood summer resort

1894—mulct taxes collected from 286 Scott County liquor dealers

1895—magnetism healer Daniel D. Palmer began chiropractic treatment at office on 2nd & Brady; First Presbyterian cornerstone laid July 20 at Iowa & Kirkwood

1896—construction of new bridge delayed by Feb ice jam; Iowa enacted estate tax, exempting spouses and children as direct heirs

1897—long distance telephone service; St. Luke's Hospital at 8th & Main began nurse's training school

1898— Schleswig-Holstein veterans memorial stone ceremony at Washington Square Park; Saenger Fest Hall built

1899—First Presbyterian dedicated at Iowa & Kirkwood; A.W. Lee added *Davenport Daily Times* to his Lee Syndicate

1900—Griswold College purchased for new high school; Andrew Carnegie donated $75,000 for public library at Main & 4th; first concert at Central Park

1901—Maennerchor 50th anniversary; Brown takes over business college; $1 mil in losses from East Davenport fire at Weyerhaeuser & Denkmann lumber yard; CRI&P passenger rail established; Claus M. Kuehl opened Suburban Island amusement rides

1902—four students complete chiropractic training, including D.D. Palmer's son Bartlett Joshua; Burtis House became Kimball Hotel

1903—Bishop Henry Cosgrove declared Davenport the *wickedest city* in America; *Democrat* announced Mar 10th birth of son to Mr. and Mrs. B.H. Beiderbecke; wine rooms abolished & gamblers run out of town.

1904—Griswold bldg leveled to make way for new high school on Main Street; Charles Berkell leased Germania House for vaudeville theater; *Democrat* purchased *Leader*

1905—United Presbyterian disbanded; Sarah Bernhardt at Grand Theater; Eva Tanguay at Burtis Opera House; John L. Sullivan boxed at Orpheon theater; Ficke family returned from 10-month world tour; mayor ordered midnight saloon closing

Janitor Harvey Lillard claimed his deafness cured by D.D. Palmer's treatment

Schleswig-Holstein veterans
Washington Square Park
March 24, 1898

Large crowds and live bands greeted visitors arriving in Davenport by train in 1898 for the 18th annual Saengerfest

Bishop Cosgrove

Timeline

Second Street at Harrison 1907
Iowa National Bank, center left;
Harned Von Maur, far right

W.F. Cody
"Buffalo Bill"

John Looney

1906—Chiropractor D.D. Palmer jailed 105 days rather than pay fine for practicing medicine without a license; Davenport Commercial Club opened; Leo Kerker took over Saengerfest hall, renamed Coliseum; Bishop Cosgrove died of cancer

1907—Gordon-VanTine Co incorporated; new high school opened on Main St; Franco-Prussian memorial stone ceremony at Washington Sq Park; new Coliseum opened; E.P. Adler became head of Lee Syndicate, owner of *Daily Times*; first dry Sunday Dec 15th

1908—Davenport schools changed from numbers to names of presidents; Arthur Ficke joined father's law practice; lawsuits shut down 40 of 191 city taverns.

1909—Iowa's *red-light district* abatement act ended legal brothels; Brick Munro's dance pavilion closed; Iowa College moved to Grinnell; YMCA dedicated.

1910—Victor Animatograph began manufacturing amateur cameras and projectors; Acme Packet Co incorporated as Streckfus Steamboat Line in Rock Island

1911—construction of levee wall and LeClaire Park; William 'Buffalo Bill' Cody of Leclaire, IA, received loving cup after Aug 3rd farewell performance at Burtis; Diamond Jo packet boats bought by Streckfus Lines; Gordon-VonTine sold first-ever kit houses.

1912—Columbia Theatre built; Dav's Frank Kellogg died of gunshot to gut after riding trolley to watch Market Square riot sparked by RI mayor beating newspaper publisher John Looney

1913—Coliseum burned to ground, rebuilt across street from original site.

1914—aviation pioneers Oscar and Mary Solbrig exhibit and fly hand-built plane

Franco-Prussian Memorial
Washington Square Park

Timeline

1915—Columbia Theatre opened season with the Creole Band; Blackhawk Hotel opened at 3rd and Perry; beer concessions end at Schuetzen Park

1916—Connor Looney first enlistee for Pancho Villa Expedition; Victor Animatograph $3mil movie contract from NY company; Tri-City Symphony's first concert May 29 at Burtis Opera House; Harned Von Maur bought Petersen & Sons; Socialist Party won majority city council seats; A.D. Ficke launched Spectra hoax; Kimball House converted to Perry apartments

1917—Buffalo Bill died in Denver Jan 10th; *Der Demokrat* ceased publishing due to Iowa's Babel Proclamation

1918— Feb 19th federal edict: "All saloons and bawdy houses within a half mile of government installations must close within 36 hours"; Prussian memorial removed from Washington Sq; slacker drive snares 2,000; Turner Hall & Grand Theatre used as makeshift hospitals during flu epidemic that kills 2,000

1919—National Prohibition; C.A. Ficke sold land for Kahl building; Robert Karlowa broadcast first wireless radio concert; local hospitals began footprint IDs for newborns

1920—Bettendorf's Holy City neighborhood flooded; Capitol Theatre opened Dec 25th; Socialist mayor and councilmen elected in Davenport; top four-floor addition begun on Hotel Blackhawk

1921—after Mar 3rd show at Columbia, Bee Palmer wed her pianist; Vera Cox named 1of3 prettiest girls at DHS; Buckley Novelty orchestra w/Bix at Linwood Inn; Bix played aboard excursion boats *Majestic & Capitol*; Beiderbecke Five played at Haynes Dance School Aug 5

1922—Mississippi crests at 17.1 ft with flood water above Front Street railroad tracks; radio station owner Robert Karlowa sold 15-year-old radio license to B.J. Palmer; Connor Looney gunned down in Rock Island

1923—First National Bank at 2nd & Main destroyed by fire; 10-story bank rebuilt on the same site; Capitol Theatre opened; July 7th liquor raids shut down Linwood, Munro's Hollywood Inn & other Scott County roadhouses; Eagles Danceland opened New Year's Eve

1924—*Four Horseman* moniker penned by reporter Grantland Rice after Notre Dame defeated Army 13-7 in football

First Feature at new Capitol Theatre

B.J. Palmer gave daily lectures on WOC radio station

First National Bank after the fire

Timeline

Graf Zeppelin over tri-cities

Spirit of St. Louis at Moline Airport
August 19, 1927

Run on the bank at Third & Brady

1925—Notre Dame beat Stanford in Rose Bowl with four touchdowns by DHS alum Elmer Layden; nation's first municipal art gallery opened in Davenport's old armory, Isham Jones at Danceland; Spencer ferryboat business sold to William J. Quinlan

1926—fire destroyed Poppy Gardens roadhouse in rural Rock Island County; tri-cities theaters show silent movies without music due to musician's strike

1927—Pablo Casals appeared at Danceland; Carlisle Evans band played for Charles Lindbergh reception dinner Aug 19 at Arsenal; Ferd Korn invested in monocoupe airplane factory in former Bettendorf tabernacle

1928—NBC radio variety show debut included Whiteman w/Bix in NYC; Korn Bakery introduced Butternut sliced bread, first commercially produced loaves using Davenport inventor Otto Rohwedder's slicing machine; Paul Whiteman Orchestra w/Bix performed in Clinton, Nov 23; Nov. 30th police raid at E. Davenport Turner Hall netted 4,185 bottles of booze

1929—Illinois Gov Len Small* left office in January without pardoning John Looney and Anthony Billburg; Graf Zeppelin flew over Tri-Cities Aug. 28, same night Whiteman's Orchestra w/Bix broadcast from Hollywood for CBS Radio

1930—WOC & WHO synchronized & became Central Broadcasting Company; Archibald Crossley's first-ever radio listener survey ranked top five evening programs: #1 Amos 'n' Andy; #2 Fleischmann's Yeast Hour w/Rudy Vallee; #3 Atwater-Kent Hour w/ Frances Alda; #4 Lucky Strike Dance Orchestra; #5 Camel Pleasure Hour w/Bix &Dorsey brothers

1931—Municipal baseball stadium built; Mississippi Hotel/RKO Orpheum opened; Bank Panic shut down Union Bank and Trust; Susan Glaspell won Pulitzer Prize in dramatics for *Allison's House*; died: C.A. Ficke, age 81, and Leon B. Beiderbecke, age28

*Governor Small did pardon 20 communist party members convicted under Sedition Act and Chicago Southside bootlegger Ed *Spike* O'Donnell. Small later acquitted of money laundering as state treasurer, after which four of his jurors got state jobs.

Charles Edward Russell

Rock Island bricklayer Charles Correll joined Freeman Gosden to form radio's Amos 'n' Andy

Ad pages from 1898 book, *Rock Island Arsenal: In Peace and War*

BEIDERBECKE & MILLER

History of Davenport and Scott County Vol. II by Harry E. Downer 1910:
BEIDERBECKE–MILLER CO., WHOLESALE GROCERS, Established 1856, Incorporated 1893

Charles Beiderbecke, coming to America as a young man of seventeen years and his youthful training being that of a German lad, entered upon activities in the new world with no false ideas concerning the advantages here offered. He knew, however, that the path to success is open to all and that the fruits of labor are sure and certain. Therefore with the persistent energy he sought prosperity and in time came to be known as one of the leading merchants and financiers of Davenport.

Born in Westpahlia…and there attended a university, studying for the ministry. He sailed for America in 1853. He did not tarry on the Atlantic coast but made his way to Indianapolis, Indiana, and for three years was employed in the post office.

He was sent by the government to Dubuque, Iowa, where he also held a position in the post office, but not liking that city he remained for only a short time and then removed to Davenport. Here he afterward entered into partnership relations as the senior member of the firm of Beiderbecke & Miller, wholesale grocers. They were located at the corner of Gaines and Second streets and afterward removed to Second street between Main and Harrison streets. In 1880 Mr. Beiderbecke erected a business block in which he continued to carry on his commercial interests throughout the remainder of his days…. Extending his efforts to other lines, he was recognized as one of the leading representatives of financial interests, becoming president of the Iowa National Bank, which he aided in organizing in 1890, continuing as chief executive officer until his death. Mr. Beiderbecke's executive ability was furthermore called into play in connection with social and municipal interests. He was a director of the Maennorchor and also a member of the Turners Society…. He did not belong to any church but attended the services at the Unitarian and in his life exemplified a broad humanitarian spirit.

BEIDERBECKE & MILLER, wholesale grocers, 107 and 109 West Second Street, established this business as a retail grocery store in 1856. In 1865 it became a wholesale establishment. They occupy a four–story, five–floor, 150x33 feet building, with an L 33x75 feet. It is the largest establishment of its kind in this city. They handle a complete stock of imported and domestic groceries and provisions and do an annual business of $800,000.

Chas. Beiderbecke, the senior member of the firm, was born in Westphalia, Prussia, Germany, July 20, 1836. His father, Henry Beiderbecke, was a principal in the schools in Germany and married Sophia Becker, by whom he had seven children. He died October 1851; she died in March 1852. Charles attended college in Germany until 1853, when he came with an uncle to America. He located at Indianapolis, Ind., where he clerked in a grocery store some ten months and in the post office two years. He then clerked in the Dubuque, Iowa, post office until September 1856 when he came to Davenport and formed the present partnership with Mr. F. H. Miller.

Frank H. Miller was born in Hanover, Germany, Sept. 4, 1836, of Frederick and Elizabeth Miller, natives of Germany. When Frank was about seven years old his parents immigrated to the United States and located in Cincinnati, O., where his father worked in a brewery. Frank attended school until he was 14 years of age, when he went into a clothing store with his brother, A. H. Miller. After remaining with him for four years, he went to Indianapolis, Ind., and clerked in a merchant tailoring establishment there until 1856, when he came to Davenport, Ia., and formed a partnership with Mr. Chas. Beiderbecke, which still exists. He was married in Cincinnati to Miss Caroline Busch, Oct. 17, 1861. She is a native of Hanover, Germany. By this union there were eight children, six living—Bertha, Louisa, Paulina, Charles, Luella and George. Mr. Miller is a Mason and a member of Fraternal Lodge, No. 221; Davenport Chapter, No. 16, and St. Simon of Seven Commandery, A.O.U.W.; of Lessing Lodge, No. 74, and Fireman's Liberty, No. 1. Mr. Miller is one of the enterprising and representative business men of the city.

1880 Census: Frank Miller, 43; Caroline, 38; Bertha, 16; Louisa, 14; Paulina, 11; Frank, 7; Charles, 4; Luella, 2; George, 9 mo.
23 November 1888, *Davenport Tribune*: WARNEBOLD–MILLER
  Last evening at the residence of the bride's parents, 1527 Brady street, occurred the marriage of Mr. Edward Warnebold and Miss Pauline Miller. The spacious parlors were

all beautifully decorated and illuminated. The ceremony was performed by Squire Koch in the presence of a large number of invited guests and friends.... The young couple will go to housekeeping at once on Fourteenth and Main streets where the groom has a beautiful home prepared.

1900 Census: 1527 Brady St—Frank Miller, 63, wholesale grocer; wife Caroline, 58; daughter Luella, 22; son George, 20, bookkeeper; daughter Pauline Warnebold, 31; granddaughters Della, 6, and Elsie, 3

1910 Census: 1318 Main St—Frank Miller, 73; daughter Pauline Warnebold, 42; granddaughters Adalia, 16, and Elise, 13.

Obituary 29 January 1917, *Davenport Democrat–Leader*:

F.H. MILLER, CITY PIONEER, IS SUMMONED
FOR YEARS WAS MEMBER OF BEIDERBECKE & MILLER, WHOLESALE GROCERS
WAS PROMINENT IN BANKING
A MAN OF BROAD INTELLECT AND CITY BUILDER IN THE EARLY DAYS

Frank H. Miller, one of the best known of the earlier merchants of Davenport, for many years a member of the prominent wholesale grocery firm of Beiderbecke & Miller, died at 10:20 o'clock Sunday night at the home of his daughter, Mrs. Pauline Warnebold, 1318 Main street. He was in the 81st year of his age.

Until his retirement a few years ago, Mr. Miller's entire life was one of activity and usefulness. He was born in Hanover, Germany, Sept. 4, 1836, and when 7 years old emigrated [sic] with his parents to the United States, settling in Cincinnati. He came to Davenport in 1856 and entered partnership with his friend, Charles Beiderbecke, in the retail grocery business. Through the excellent business judgment and keen insight of these two partners, they soon developed into a wholesale business and as such they became one of the leading firms of the kind in the Mississippi valley.

This partnership continued for 45 years or until Mr. Beiderbecke's death which occurred in 1901. Two years later Mr. Miller retired from active business pursuit and since had led a quiet and peaceful life.

On Oct. 17, 1861, Mr. Miller was united in marriage to Caroline Busch, who preceded him in death in 1901. Surviving are six children, as follows: Mrs. Fred A. [Bertha] Lischer, Mrs. W.H. [Louisa] Weiss, Mrs. Pauline Warnebold, Mrs. W.T. [Luella] Kieschler, Charles C. Miller and George Miller of Omaha. There are also 10 grandchildren and five great–grandchildren.

Mr. Miller was a man of broad intellect and in the early days was one of the city builders. He was a member of the Fraternal Lodge No. 221, A.F.& A.M. and of Cyrene Commandery, Knights Templar. He was director and for many years served as president of the Oakdale Cemetery association. He was also prominent in local banking circles.

The funeral will be held Wednesday afternoon, with services at 2 o'clock at the daughter's home with interment in Oakdale cemetery. Friends are invited to the home. Burial will be private.

Retired Pioneer Merchant Called

FRANK H. MILLER.

Mr. Miller, prominent retired merchant, for many years member of the well known wholesale grocery firm of Beiderbecke & Miller, died at 10:20 o'clock Sunday evening at the home of his daughter, Mrs. Pauline Warnebold, 1318 Main street.

Frank Miller House—1527 Brady St

F. H. MILLER, CITY PIONEER, IS SUMMONED

For Years Was Member of Beiderbecke & Miller, Wholesale Grocers.

WAS PROMINENT IN BANKING

A Man of Broad Intellect and City Builder in the Early Days.

Frank H. Miller, one of the best known of the earlier merchants of Davenport, for many years a member of the prominent wholesale grocery firm of Beiderbecke & Miller, died at 10:20 o'clock Sunday night at the home of his daughter, Mrs. Pauline Warnebold, 1318 Main street. He was in the 81st year of his age.

Until his retirement a few years ago, Mr. Miller's entire life was one of activity and usefulness. He was born in Hanover, Germany, Sept. 4, 1836, and when 7 years old emigrated with his parents to the United States, settling in Cincinnati. He came to Davenport in 1856 and entered partnership with his friend, Charles Beiderbecke, in the retail grocery business. Through the excellent business judgment and keen insight of these two partners, they soon developed into a wholesale business and as such they became one of the leading firms of the kind in the Mississippi valley.

This partnership continued for 45 years or until Mr. Beiderbecke's death which occurred in 1901. Two years later Mr. Miller retired from active business pursuit and since had led a quiet and peaceful life.

On Oct. 17, 1861, Mr. Miller was united in marriage to Caroline Busch, who preceded him in death in 1901. Surviving are six children, as follows: Mrs. Fred A. Lischer, Mrs. W. H. Weiss, Mrs. Pauline Warnebold, Mrs. W. T. Klechler, Charles C. Miller and George Miller of Omaha. There are also 10 grandchildren and five great-grandchildren.

Mr. Miller was a man of broad intellect and in the early days was one of the city builders. He was a member of Fraternal Lodge No. 221, A. F. & A. M., and of Cyrene Commandery, Knight Templars. He was a director and for many years served as president of the Oakdale Cemetery association. He was also prominent in local banking circles.

The funeral will be held Wednesday afternoon, with services at 2 o'clock at the daughter's home, with interment in Oakdale cemetery. Friends are invited to the home. Burial will be private.

Obit 1-29-1917

GENEALOGY: CHARLES & LOUISE

CARL 'CHARLES' BEIDERBECKE, born 20 Jul 1835 in Katholisch Benningham, Wesphalia, Prussia; died 21 Oct 1901 in Macon, Missouri; Parents: Heinrich Beiderbecke & Sophie Becker.
LOUISE PIPER (LOUISA PIEPER) born 18 Jun 1840 in Hamburg, Germany; died 27 Oct 1922 in Davenport, Iowa; Parents: August Pieper & Caroline Hellmers

Married: 21 Apr 1860 in Davenport, Iowa; H. R. Claussen, J. P., officiating
09 June 1860 Census: Residence: Northwest Corner Ripley & 2nd; Charles Beiderbecke age 23 merchant, born Prussia; Louisa Beiderbecke, age 20, born Hamburg; F.L. Miller, age 23, born Hanover
    Louise and Charles had three children who died of smallpox, brought home by Louise's father, August Pieper, upon his return from the Civil War on May 24, 1865. Charles was in Germany for a visit to the homeland with friends; he left May 10. The three children were buried in the backyard by a neighbor, who also died of smallpox. Louise was pregnant with Carl at the time; he was born Christmas Eve 1865. No christening records exist for the three deceased Beiderbecke children. August Pieper and daughter Louise attended the Unitarian Church and according to church historians, Unitarians did not perform baptisms or communions; traditional rites replaced by ceremonial blessing of children and babies.
    In 1865 the Beiderbeckes were living on West 3rd between Main & Harrison; 1866 *Davenport City Directory* lists them as residing at No.74 north side Second Street between Harrison and Ripley. Charles' uncle, Frederick Wilhelm Beiderbecke, listed as living with Charles and Louise in 1866.

Library History, November 7, 1877: *The corner stone for the Cook Memorial Library was laid at Sixth and Brady streets. The members of the first Board of Trustees were Charles Beiderbecke, the Rev. A.M. Judy, Mrs. J. J. Richardson, the Rev. J. P. Ryan, Edward Kauffmann, Mrs. J. P. Van Patten, George Wolters, Judge C. D. Waterman and S. F. Smith.*
1885 Business Directory: Beiderbecke & Miller wholesale Grocers 109 W 2nd.
1870 Census: #161 Beiderbecke, Carl, age 34, Grocer wholesaler; Beiderbecke Louise, age 28, keeping house; Beiderbecke Carl, age 5; Beiderbecke Mathilde*, age 3; Beiderbecke Bismark, age 2; Beiderbecke Louis*, age 6 mos; Piper John*, age 57, Clerk in store; Soltan Anna, age 27, domestic servant. [*John is Louise's father August Pieper; Louis is Lutie, Mathilde is Ottilie]
1880 Census: Beiderbecke misspelled Beiclerleeske...Living at 619 West Sixth,

Young Charles Beiderbecke

Louise Piper Beiderbecke

Davenport: Charles, age 44, Wholesale Grocer; Louise, age 40, keeping house; Carl, age 15, at school; Othilie, age 13, at school; Bismark, age 12, at school; Lute, age 10, at school.

26 May 1881: CHAS. BEIDERBECKE'S NEW HOME What will be one of the finest residences of the city is to be erected by Mr. Charles Beiderbecke, of the firm of Beiderbecke & Miller. He has chosen as his location the attractive site at the northwest corner of Western avenue and Seventh street. The general style of architecture is to be Swiss and the building will have a frontage of 48 feet on Seventh street by 75 feet on Western avenue. This improvement will cost about $10,000, and having many new features is at this time worthy of special notice as others may desire to avail themselves of hints or suggestions.

1885 Census: Charles age 48 wholesale Grocer; Louise, age 44; Carl, age 20, clerk in grocery; Ottilie, age 18; Bismarck, age 16; Lutie, age 15.

9 May 1890 *Davenport Democrat*: The question of annexing the thickly settled districts just outside the present city limits will be voted May 30. If you are a progressive man you will vote for annexation. MR. BEIDERBECKE'S REASONS

"I am in favor of annexation," said Charles Beiderbecke. "I haven't given the matter of the proposed limits much study, but I think they are fair to all as they now stand. The act of annexation is a forward movement of the best sort, and it will increase our population by a considerable amount. Those two considerations are enough with me to induce me to give the movement my support."

People who know Mr. Beiderbecke, and every man in Davenport knows him, are well aware that he does not lend himself to schemes that work injury to the city, or that prejudice the interest of his neighbors. When he favors a thing of this sort he does so because he thinks there is merit in it. He is one among many business men of this city who think in that same way.

1895 Census: Beiderbecke misspelled Beiderlecke, Charles, age 59; Louisa, age 54; Lutie, age 24; Chas, age 30; Adel, age 21 [Carl T. & his wife Adele]

1894–1895 City Directory Davenport, Iowa The Iowa National Bank Of Davenport Capital $100,000.00. Charles Beiderbecke president, A. P. Doe vice–president, Charles, cashier. Directors, Charles Beiderbecke, W. C. Putnam, W. P. Halligan, A.P. Doe, C. A. Ficke, J. H. Hass, Henry Schroeder, M. D. Petersen, W. O. Schmidt, J. D. Brockmann, P. J. Paulsen, 2d NW Cor Harrison. 1900: Iowa National Bank 302 W. 2nd St.

1901: Telephone number for the store was 269; same number for Beiderbecke home.

22 October 1901:
BODY IS HERE–LAST JOURNEY OF LATE CHAS. BEIDERBECKE COMPLETED
Conveyed from Macon, Mo., Where Death Occurred—
Funeral to Take Place Tomorrow

The body of the late Chas. Beiderbecke, who died yesterday morning at Macon, Mo., arrived in the city this morning about 7 o'clock and were taken to the family

Charles' & Louise's first home on Scott Street next door to the fire station

24353　　　　　　　1.00　　　　　　Mch 9/91
United States of America
State of Iowa
County of Scott

I Charles Beiderbecke a naturalized and loyal citizen of the United states hereby apply to the department of State at Washington for a passport for myself accompanied by my wife Louisa Beiderbecke.

I solemnly swear that I was born at Benningham in Prussia Germany on about the 20th day of July 1835 that I emigrated to the United States sailing on board the steamer Germania from Hamburg on or about the – day October 1859 that I resided 38 years uninterruptedly in the United States from 1853 to date at Indianapolis, Dubuque & Davenport that I was naturalized as a citizen of the United States before the District Court of Scott County Iowa at Davenport on the 5th day of September 1859 as shown by the accompanying certificate of naturalization, that I am the identified person described in said certificate that I am domiciled in the United States my permanent residence being at Davenport in the State of Iowa where I follow the occupation of wholesale grocer, that I am about to go abroad temporarily, and that I intend to return to the United States with the purpose of residing and performing the duties of citizenship therein.

Oath of Allegiance

Further I do solemnly swear that I will support and defend the Constitution of the United States against all enemies foreign and domestic, that I will bear true faith and allegiance to the same and that I take this obligation freely, without any mental reservation or purpose of evasion. So help me God.

　　　　　　　　　　　　　　　　Ch Beiderbecke
Sworn to before me this 23rd day of March 1891
　　　　　　　　　　　　　　　　Wm Hoerch
　　　　　　　　　　　　　　　　Notary Public
　　　　　　　　　　　　　　　　Scott County Iowa

Age 55 years	Mouth oval
Stature 5 feet 7½ inches	Chin regular
Forehead high	Hair grayish
Eyes brown	Complexion fair
Hair straight	Face full

1898 Saengerfest committee, around the table L-R: Robert Krause, Charles Voss, Jens Lorenzen, Henry Lischer, Charles Beiderbecke, Louis Best, Henry Braunlich, C.A. Ficke, Fred Clausen, and Paul Karlowa. Lischer published *Der Demokrat*. His son married Frank Miller's daughter; architect Fred Clausen married Lischer's daughter and designed the Beiderbecke-Miller building. Best, Karlowa and Krause were brothers-in-law. Friendships between these men continued among children and grandchildren. Ficke's nephew and law partner loaned a cornet to Beiderbecke's grandson; Braunlich's son was Aggie Beiderbecke's attending physician when she died.

THE FIFTIETH ANNIVERSARY; MAENNERCHOR CELEBRATION TODAY.

Excursion Trains Will Come From Four Different Directions—History of the Society and Its First President.

Address of Welcome .. Mayor Fred Heinz
Hubertus, a Picture of the Chase......
.... Weinzierl
Solo for baritone, with chorus and orchestra. Fritz Singer, soloist, Davenport Maennerchor.
Musical Selection by Strasser's Band.
Greeting to the Home .... Cromer
All Present Singers.
PART THE SECOND.
(a) (b) Musical Selections by Strasser's

THE city will be c
tors today, th
excursion train
Clinton, Marsh
lington, and visitors
regulars from Chicago
Moline. The occasio
tennial anniversary
Maennerchor, which
celebrated at the Sc
afternoon.
The Davenport Mae
chorus, is one of the
ganizations which is
pass the golden jubi
existed without char
It was away back i
John Jordan was
Davenport had no st
tric lights; no Schue
newspaper, when the
founded by the musi
of the city. It was
similar American
thought of. The soc
ed under many dir
time, and some of
joined the majority
But God reigns a
chor still lives.
Among the old members of the society who will be present at the fete today are Gustav Schlegel and Charles Beiderbecke, both of whom have wielded the baton. The recently deceased G. Wiehle was the first director of the Maennerchor. Christian Mueller and A. Bruns are also old members, and H. E. J. Heinsen, now in San Francisco,

DAVENPORT ILLUSTRATED---SAENGERFEST SOUVENIR

BIEDERBECKE-MILLER CO.

The fame of a city is largely due to the prosperity of its merchantile houses. More particularly is this the case in relation to its wholesale and manufacturing establishments. The well-known and substantial wholesale grocery of Beiderbecke-Miller Co. deserves considerable credit in this connection. This establishment commenced from a small beginning and is identical with the growth of Davenport. It takes rank as one of the oldest and most substantial wholesale houses west of Chicago. The premises occupied are contiguous to the railway system of the city and consist of a four-story building having a frontage of

35 feet and depth of 180 feet and an additional L adjoining, 60x100 feet. The business transacted is a large one, their patronage extending throughout this and adjoining states. The officers of the company are Charles Beiderbecke, president; F. H. Miller, vice-president; B. H. Beiderbecke, treasurer; and C. T. Beiderbecke, secretary. These gentlemen are justly rated as first-class business men, while as financiers they stand deservedly high. Under their management the business has prospered, and by their well-known ability they have had the satisfaction of knowing that the trade of the house has been constantly increased.

CHARLES BEIDERBECKE

1869 the society participated in the Saengerfest at Galena, and on June 14, 15 and 16, 1870, took part in the Freeport convention under the direction of Charles Beiderbecke.
In the year 1872 the society attended the Saengerfest of the North American Saengerbund in St. Louis, and in June 1873, the Saengerfest in Dubuque.
Chas. Beiderbecke resigned his office on March 30, 1875, whereupon he was voted a resolution, thanking him for his faithful work as director. H. Braunlich succeeded him, and under his direction the concert for the twenty-fifth anniversary celebration of the society, held June 23, 1870, was held at the Schuetzen park.

*Daily Republican
May 26, 1901*

1853, Gustav Schlegel was made director of the society. Mr. Schlegel resigned in 1856, and was succeeded by Mr. Lambach, but re-elected in a short time.
In the year 1862 the dangers threatening their adopted country moved the German patriots of the Maennerchor to take up the musket for the Union. Ac-

home on West Seventh street. The news of the death was received in the city with universal sorrow. Mr. Beiderbecke was one of the old and respected citizens of Davenport and his active connection with the mercantile interests of the city made him especially prominent in all projects relating to the welfare of Davenport. The death occurred at the home of his daughter, Mrs. Von Binzer, in Macon, Mo., where Mr. Beiderbecke had gone to visit but a few days previous. In the morning he, with his daughter, had been out walking when he complained of a pain in his chest and a heavy feeling. He sat down for a few moments to rest and then walked home. He rested in armchair for awhile, but feeling tired said he thought he would lie down for a few minutes. He went to the bed and was sitting on the side when he suddenly fell backward. He was caught by his daughter and died immediately in her arms. Mr. Beiderbecke had left the city but the Saturday evening previous for a visit with his daughter. He had been at his office all day Saturday and was apparently as well as ever. No indications of an illness were apparent Sunday. The cause of death is supposed to have been apoplexy. The funeral will take place from the residence tomorrow morning at 10 o'clock. Interment will take place at Oakdale cemetery in the family lot. The funeral will be private. The death will be mourned by many Davenport citizens among whom the deceased was well known. Being in the wholesale grocery business for years in partnership with F. H. Miller, he was closely connected with the public life of the city. He was one of the conservative, yet progressive business men who have built up a flourishing business for themselves and been instrumental in the healthy growth which Davenport has enjoyed. Not only in his own line of business was he active, but also in the financial institutions of the city. He was president of the Iowa National Bank of Davenport. Mr. Beiderbecke has been a resident of this city since 1856, since which time he has been in active business in the city. He was born in Westphalia, Prussia, July 20, 1830. He was one of seven children. His father was principal of a school in Germany and Charles received a liberal High school and college education. His father died in 1851 and his mother in 1852. In the following year after finishing at college, he came to this county with an uncle and located in Indianapolis. Here he received his primary education in the business which became his life work. He clerked in a grocery store for ten months. After that for two years he was employed in the post office at that place. After a short residence in Dubuque, Ia., where he was engaged in the post office, he came to Davenport and entered into partnership with F. H. Miller, which relationship continued until his death. In January 1859, he was married to Miss Louisa Pieper [error: date is April 1860]. From this union he had seven children, four of whom are still living. They are Mrs. Von Binzer, Mrs. Albert Stibolt, Carl and Bismarck. He is also survived by his wife. During all his life Mr. Beiderbecke showed an interest in the growth of the city and its public institutions was a leader of the German choral organization, which made the city famous and was at one time a member of the school board of the city. In other ways he manifested his public spirit. When a library board was to be chosen his name was one of the first suggested, both on account of culture and business ability. His connection with the banking institutions of the city was the natural result of his ability as a business man and financier.

23 Oct 1901 *Daily Leader*: LAID TO REST
THE REMAINS OF CHARLES BEIDERBECKE
IMPRESSIVE SERVICES HELD OVER THE REMAINS OF ONE OF DAVENPORT'S FOREMOST CITIZENS—GUSTAV DONALD SPEAKS AT HOUSE AND REV. A.M. JUDY AT THE GRAVE.
The funeral of the late Charles Beiderbecke was held this morning at the residence at the corner of West Seventh street and Western avenue. The services were very impressive as was the large number of the close friends and businessmen of the city.

At the residence Gustav Donald delivered an address in the German language, and at the cemetery Rev. Arthur M. Judy spoke. Beautiful music was furnished by a male quartet composed of Wallace D. Moody, G.A. Hanssen, H.E. Downer and L.G. Susemihl.

The casket was literally covered with beautiful floral tributes, the gifts of grateful and loving friends. The pallbearers were: Honorary—I.H. Sears, A. Burdick, Fred Heinz, Jens Lorenzen, C.N. Voss, A.P. Doe, John W. Ballard. Active: H.O. Seiffert, Henry Schroeder, L.P. Best, William Friendholdt, C.E. Scholing and F.G. Claussen.

Burial: 23 Oct 1901, Oakdale Cemetery, Davenport; Funeral Home: Runge & Petersen 831 W.3rd St. Davenport
Will: Davenport, Iowa file #5153
Newspaper Notice: *Saturday July 12, 1902 Auction, The undersigned will sell their stock of goods at Auction beginning Monday July 14, at 9 a.m. and continuing until sold. Come early and avail yourself of the opportunity to buy groceries at your own price. Beiderbecke & Miller Co. 107–109 W. Second St.*

When Charles died, Louise purchased four lots at Oakdale, Section 17.
> Lot 60: Charles A. Beiderbecke, interment #5258; Leon Bix Beiderbecke, interment #13146; Bismark Beiderbecke, interment #15185; Agatha J. Beiderbecke, interment #17767; Charles B. Beiderbecke, interment #20790; Mary Beiderbecke, interment #22858
> Lot 61: Louise P. Beiderbecke, interment #10716; Carl T. Beiderbecke, interment #13687; Adele S. Beiderbecke, interment #20132; Gretchen B. Murdoch (ashes), interment #23041; Gertrude B. Washburn (ashes) interment number 23040
> Lot 2: Albert J. Stibolt interment #9770; Ottilie B. Stibolt, interment #16189 Lot 1: Carl Von Binzer, interment #5585; Fera Von Binzer, interment #5600; Max Von Binzer, interment #9321; Adolph Pieper (ashes), interment #14583; Lutie B. Von Binzer, interment #18235

Oct 27, 1922, *Davenport Democrat*:
MRS. L. BEIDERBECKE DIES AT HER HOME IN DAVENPORT TODAY Mrs. Louisa Beiderbecke, widow of Charles Beiderbecke, prominent Davenport, wholesale grocer, died at 10 o'clock this morning at her home, 532 West Seventh street, Davenport. She was in her eighty–second year. A life–long patron of the arts, Mrs. Beiderbecke never failed to give her support to all local organizations interested in the advancement of music or art. Her maiden name was Miss Louisa Piper and she was born on June 18, 1840 at Hamburg, Germany. When 13 years of age she came to America with her parents and after residing in the southern part of the country for two years, the family moved to Davenport. The deceased received education both in Europe and in the United States. On April 21, 1860, she was united in marriage to Charles Beiderbecke who preceded her in death Oct. 21, 1901. She is survived by four children; B.H. Beiderbecke, C. T. Beiderbecke, Mrs. Ottilie Stibolt, Mrs. Lutie Von Binzer; eleven grandchildren, and three great–grandchildren, all of Davenport. The funeral, which will be strictly private, both at the home and at the grave, will be held Sunday morning from the home. Relatives of the deceased request that no flowers be sent.

Burial: 29 Oct 1922, Oakdale Cemetery, Davenport, Iowa; Funeral was conducted by Hill & Fredericks—Hill's wife named Carrie, same as Aggie's mother who died in 1880.

30 Oct 1922, *Davenport Democrat*: The funeral of Mrs. Louise Beiderbecke was held Sunday morning at 11 o'clock at the home, 532 West Seventh street; Hon. Henry Vollmer officiating at the home and at the grave in Oakdale cemetery. A quartet composed of Mrs. A.P. Griggs, Miss Grace Ames, J.W. Grove, and C.T. Hale sang "Lead Kindly Light" and "Abide With Me." Pallbearers were Carl Stibolt, C.B. Beiderbecke, Leon Hass, Donald Murdoch, Otto Seiffert, and Rudolph Clausen.
Louise Beiderbecke Will: Davenport, Iowa file #10980
Dated: January 18, 1902 Listed heirs: Carl T., age 57, Ottilie Stibolt, age 55, Bismark H., age 55, Lutie L. Von Binzer, age 51, all residing in Davenport, Iowa. Louise's estate included proceeds from the estate of her stepmother Eibe Pieper. Louise's father August and Eibe were married in 1873, with Charles Beiderbecke being a witness.
31 Oct 1922 *Democrat–Leader*: BEIDERBECKE ESTATE GOES TO FOUR CHILDREN The four surviving children of the late Mrs. Louise Beiderbecke, who died Oct 27, will inherit their mother's estate, according to the will, date Jan 18, 1902, filed in probate court today. The children are: Carl T. and Bismark H. Beiderbecke, Ottilie Stibolt, and Lutie L Von Binzer, all of Davenport. Carl T. and Bismark H. Beiderbecke are named executors. Judge William Theophilus has set the probate hearing for Nov 2. Cook & Bailuff are probating attorneys.
6 Feb 1923 *Democrat–Leader*: Objections in the Louise Beiderbecke estate were filed by Carl T. Beiderbecke, Denmark [sic–Bismark] H. Beiderbecke, Ottilie Stibolt and

Lutie L. Von Binzer, owners of 199 shares of the capital stock of the Shaw Land & Timber company transferred to them on Nov. 6, 1919 by Mrs. Beiderbecke at a time when the Shaw Land & Timber company was in–process of liquidation. On Sept 2, 1920, a further payment of $3,984 was made by the company and this money was retained by the four children.

MRS. LOUISE P. BEIDERBECKE IS SUMMONED

Mrs. Louise Piper Beiderbecke, widow of the late Charles Beiderbecke, who was one of the organizers and the first president of the Iowa National bank, died this morning at 10 o'clock at her home, 532 West Seventh street, of infirmities incident to old age.

Her husband, who was senior member of the Beiderbecke-Miller company, wholesale grocers, passed away on Oct. 21, 1901.

Miss Piper was born in Hamburg, Germany, June 18, 1840, and came with her parents to America in 1852. Her marriage to Charles Beiderbecke took place on April 21, 1860. Of seven children born, three of whom died in infancy, four survive, C. T. Beiderbecke, B. H. Beiderbecke, Mrs. Ottilie Stibolt, and Mrs. Lutie Von Binzer, all of this city. Eleven grandchildren and three great grandchildren also survive.

Mrs. Beiderbecke was a patroness of the fine arts, and took an especially keen interest in music. She was affiliated with every worthwhile musical project, having been a guarantor of the Tri-city Symphony orchestra since its inception.

Private funeral services will be held at the home Sunday morning, followed by services at Oakdale cemetery, which will likewise be private. It is the expressed desire of the members of the family that no flowers be sent.

THE DAVENPORT DAILY LEADER.

LAID TO REST.

THE REMAINS OF CHARLES BEIDERBECKE.

Impressive Services Held Over the Remains of One of Davenport's Foremost Citizens—Gustav Donald Speaks at House and Rev. A. M. Judy at the Grave.

The funeral of the late Charles Beiderbecke was held this morning at the residence at the corner of West Seventh street and Westren avenue. The services were very impressive and were a large number of the close friends and business men of the city.

At the residence Gustav Donald delivered an address in the German language, and at the cemetery Rev. Arthur M. Judy spoke. Beautiful music was furnished by a male quartet composed of Wallace E. Moody, G. A. Hanssen, H. E. Downer and L. G. Susemihl.

The casket was literally covered with beautiful floral tributes, the gifts of grateful and loving friends. The pallbearers were:

Honorary—I. H. Sears, A. Burdick, Fred Heinz, Jens Lorenzen, C. N. Voss, A. P. Doe, John W. Ballord.

Active—H. O. Seiffert, Henry Schroeder, L. P. Best, William Friendholdt, C. E. Scholing and F. G. Claussen.

Above: *Democrat & Leader*
Oct 27, 1922

Left: *Daily Leader*
Oct 23, 1901

DAVENPORT DAILY LEADER.

TENTH YEAR. EXTRA.   DAVENPORT, IOWA, FRIDAY, JULY 26, 1901.   EXTRA. SIX PAGES

A MILLION DOLLAR FIRE!

Thirty Acres Swept by Flames by Last Evening's Conflagration.

Fifty Homes Are Lapped Up by Fire Fiend and Hundreds Are Without Shelter.

Weyerhaeuser and Denkmann Mills and 25,000,000 Feet of Lumber Burned.

Terrible Scenes--Mothers Screaming For Their babes and Strong Men Are Powerless.

Moline and Rock Island Depts. to the Rescue.

Firemen Fall Prostrated at Their Posts of Duty, Heroes Every One.

Aid for the Poor and Destitute Should Be Immediately Forthcoming.

THE BIG FIRE AT DAVENPORT.
This picture was taken July 25th, 1901, from the government bridge, ten minutes after the alarm was turned in.

A WARNING CRY

wells up from "Biddy's" faithful lips—"The bin is empty." It will be well for your peace of mind to heed the admonition and forthwith visit the office of the Seiffert & Wiese Lumber company, where you can procure Lehigh coal that will still the trouble mind of your domestic and bring comfort to your household.

Seiffert & Wiese Lumber Co.

TELEPHONE 321.

Second Street, below Warren.

Above: 1895 Ad
Daily Leader news brief, Jan 7, 1896: Seiffert & Wiese Lumber Company in the course of next summer will erect a big sawmill in the northern pineries. The company however will continue to make Davenport the headquarters for their business.
Right: Dec 31, 1928
Below: Nov 3, 1896

Mr. and Mrs. H. O. Seiffert Observe Sixtieth Wedding Anniversary Surrounded by Their Children

IS NOT GUILTY.

The relatives in this city of Henry Seiffert who a few months ago shot a lawyer by the name of Plattner at Spokane, Wash., have received the intelligence that a jury before whom he was tried on a charge of murder, found him not guilty. Mr. Seiffert it will be remebered shot the attorney, who grossly insulted him, dead in the court room. Mr. Seiffert was a former Davenporter and his friends in this city will be pleased to learn of his release.

1) A. J. & Ottilie Stibolt
718 Western AV

2) Charles & Louise Beiderbecke
532 West 7th ST

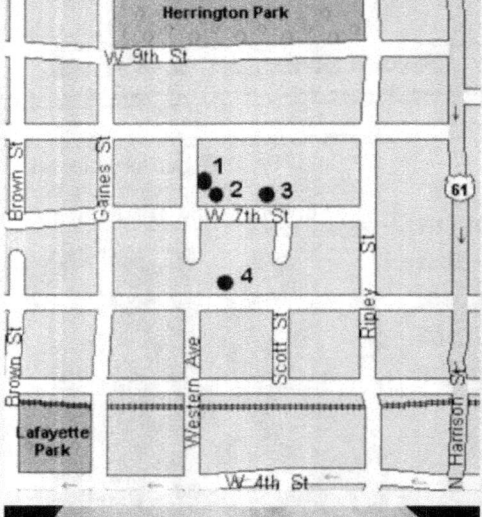

3) Carl T. & Adele Beiderbecke
510 West 7th ST

gold coast

4) H.O. Seiffert
532 West 6th ST

Genealogy: Carl T. and Adele

CARL THOMAS 'TAL' BEIDERBECKE 24 Dec 1865 – 23 Oct 1933
Spouse: ADELE SEIFFERT 25 Aug 1873 – 28 Aug 1967
Daughters : LUTIE, GRETCHEN, GERTRUDE, HELEN

Married: 09 Jan 1895: The marriage of Carl T. Beiderbecke and Miss Adele Seiffert was solemnized last evening at the home of the bride's parents, Mr. and Mrs. H. O. Seiffert, 532 West sixth street. Rev A.M. Judy performed the ceremony at 8 o'clock, in the presence of a company of relatives and intimate friends of both parties, and at the conclusion of the subsequent festivities the bride and groom departed on an eastern wedding trip. Upon their return they will take up their residence in a new home erected by Mr. Beiderbecke at Scott and Seventh streets. The groom is secretary of the Beiderbecke & Miller company and is a rising young business man, and his bride is a young lady of culture and refinement, a talented musician while possessing qualities fitting her excellently to preside over a home. Their many friends extend their congratulations.

15 August 1924 *Democrat–Leader*:
THE CHAS. BEIDERBECKE FAMILY HOUSE PARTY AT MACKINAC ISLAND
Mr. and Mrs. Charles Beiderbecke with their family of children and grandchildren left today to motor to Mackinac Island where they will spend the next two weeks at the summer cottage of Mrs. Beiderbecke's parents, Mr. and Mrs. H. O. Seiffert.
In the motor party which left for the north today were Mr. and Mrs. Donald Murdoch, Mr. and Mrs. W. D. Washburn and Miss Helen Beiderbecke.
The return home will be the first of September and Mr. and Mrs. James Seehof of Dayton, O. with their two sons Jack and Jerry Jr. will join the motorists in Chicago and return to Davenport with them for a house party at the Beiderbecke home here.

8 June 1925 *Democrat–Leader*:
SUNDAY AFTERNOON STORM CAUSES MUCH DAMAGE....A large wooden sign which hung over the entrance to Abrahams ready–to–wear store, 111–133 West Second street, was whipped from brackets and hurled into display windows during the storm. A square display window, located between windows on either side of the entrance, was broken on the side fronting street and on the east side. The large window on the east side of the entrance was smashed by the falling sign.
Goods on display were damaged to the extent of $200 and damage to display

windows estimated at $400. The building is owned by heirs of the BEIDERBECKE estate which had insurance. C.T. Beiderbecke said this morning that an adjustment had already been made by the Security Fire Insurance Co. of Davenport, which carried the risk.

CARL T. BEIDERBECKE, 68, LUMBER FIRM SECRETARY, LIFE RESIDENT HERE, DIES

Carl T. Beiderbecke, secretary of the H.O. Seiffert Lumber company, and a resident of Davenport his entire life, died last midnight at Mercy Hospital. He was 68 years old. About five weeks ago ill health forced Mr. Beiderbecke to remain at his home, 510 West Seventh street, and Oct. 11 his condition made it necessary that he be removed to the hospital. Son of wholesale grocer here, Mr. Beiderbecke had been identified with that and the lumber business his entire life. He was born in Davenport, December 24, 1864, a son of the late Mr. and Mrs. Carl H. Beiderbecke. His father was a member of the firm of Beiderbecke & Miller, wholesale grocers, and Carl, Jr. entered the business when he finished school. He was treasurer of the grocery firm when it was dissolved in 1902, and he then became associated with the H. O. Seiffert Lumber company. He was a member of the First Church of Christ Scientists. Here in 1895, he married Miss Adele Seiffert, daughter of H. O. Seiffert. Mrs. Beiderbecke survives, besides four daughters, Mrs. J. T. Seehof, Mrs. W. D. Washburn and Mrs. E. Allen Marquardt all of Evanston, Ill., and Mrs. G. D. Murdoch of Des Moines; a brother B. H. Beiderbecke of Davenport; two sisters, Mrs. Albert Stibolt of Davenport and Mrs. Lutie Von Binzer of Los Angeles, Calif.; and seven grandchildren. Funeral services will be held privately at 2 p.m. Wednesday at the Hill & Fredericks mortuary chapel, and burial, also to be private, will be in Oakdale cemetery. The omission of flowers was requested by the family.

EX–DAVENPORTER IS DEAD AT 94

Mrs. C.T. (Adele) Beiderbecke, 94, of Santa Monica, Calif.; and former resident of Davenport, died Monday in Santa Monica hospital, after a brief illness. Adele Seiffert was born in Davenport in 1873 and was married to Mr. Beiderbecke in 1893 in Davenport. He preceded her in 1933. She is survived by four daughters, Mrs. J. Seehof, and Mrs. G.D. Murdock, both of Calif., Mrs. William Washburn, and Mrs. Allen Marquardt, both of Fla.; eight grandchildren; 28 great–grandchildren; and a sister, Miss Helen Seiffert, Calif. Funeral services for Mrs. Beiderbecke were held today in Calif. Cremation followed the service and the ashes will be sent to Oakdale Cemetery, Davenport.

- LUTIE SEIFFERT BEIDERBECKE, b. 20 May 1897 at 516 W 7th, Davenport; d. 15 Feb 1970, Los Angeles, CA. Graduation: 1916, Davenport High. She married Jerome F. Seehof, born 16 Feb 1894 in Minnesota, and died 28 Aug 1967. Children: JACK SEEHOF, m. Jerri; TED SEEHOF, m. Lois; TOM SEEHOF, m. Jean.

SEEHOF–BEIDERBECKE WEDDING PARTY IS PRETTY MORNING CEREMONY

The home of Mr. and Mrs. Henry O. Seiffert, 532 West Sixth street, was the scene of a pretty wedding this morning at 10 o'clock, when their granddaughter, Miss Lutie Seiffert Beiderbecke, eldest daughter of Mr. and Mrs. Charles T. Beiderbecke of 510 West Seventh street, was united in marriage to Jerome F. Seehof of Chicago, son of Mr. and Mrs. J.J. Seehof. Very Rev. Marmaduke Hare, D. D. dean of Trinity Cathedral officiated, reading the marriage service of the Episcopal church. The wedding was very quiet and guests were confined to only members of the two families, simplicity dominating the various pretty details, and adding to the charm of arrangements. The only decorations were in baskets and bows of beautiful pink roses which were on tables and mantles in different rooms. A three piece orchestra of piano, cello and violin from the Petersen orchestra, played in the music room, giving the Bridal Chorus from Lohengan as the bride came down the stairs on the arm of her father, Charles T. Beiderbecke, who gave her away. She was met in the doorway leading to the large living room, in the west bow window of which the improvised altar had been arranged, by the groom attended by his brother Carrol Seehof of Chicago, as best man and was attended by her sister Miss Gretchen Beiderbecke. The bride was in a gown of dark blue tricolette, made with draped skirt and deep girdle. She wore as her only, ornament a string of pearls, the gift of the groom and her flowers were orchids, lilies of the valley and butterfly sweet peas. The maid of honor was in one of the new pussy willow silks of grey and white pattern, made bouffant at the hips, with square neck of lace. There were covers for 28, at the breakfast tables, which had baskets of pick roses in decoration, that of the bride, being specially trimmed with the bridal candies. Mr. and Mrs. John J. Seehof and son Carrol of Chicago were out of town guests at the wedding. Mrs. and Mrs. Seehof left for Chicago and will for the present reside at the Parkway hotel, until they go into their own home. Mr. Seehof is a copywriter with Lord & Thomas of Chicago. A cablegram of good wishes and congratulations was read from Otto Seiffert, uncle of the bride, who is in Spain on a business trip for the Moline Plow company. Mr. Seiffert sails home March 3rd. His wife, Mrs. Otto Seiffert is spending the winter with her parents, Mr. and Mrs. Frank Gates Allen at their Pasadena home and also sent her good wishes being unable to come for the ceremony.

- GRETCHEN 'GAY' SEIFFERT BEIDERBECKE, b. 27 Mar 1901, Davenport; d. 15 Oct 1983, Alameda, CA; Graduation: 1918, Davenport High; She married George Donald Murdoch, born 03 Aug 1899 in Pennsylvania, and died 03 Jan 1979 in Los Angeles. Daughter: KATHERINE MURDOCH, m. Ron Wolfman.

August 15, 1922:
MISS GRETCHEN BEIDERBECKE AND DONALD MURDOCK MARRIED "ON THE QUIET" AT WAUKEGAN

A pretty romance which had its inception within college walls terminated last Saturday in the marriage at Waukegan, Ill., of G. Donald Murdock and Gretchen Seiffert Beiderbecke, two popular and well known young Davenporters. It was a surprise wedding for all but happy young people themselves. They returned home from Chicago this morning to receive the congratulations and well wishes of their family and friends. It was several years ago that the two met while students at the University of Wisconsin. What first started as friendship quickly ripened into love and although their friends were generally aware of the fact that they were "engaged," the wedding comes as a complete surprise to them. The bride is the charming daughter of Mr. and Mrs. C. T. Beiderbecke, 510 West Seventh street. In addition to the University of Wisconsin at Madison, she was further educated at Smith's college. She is a popular sorority girl. The youthful groom is the son of Mr. and Mrs. George Cass Murdock, 928 East Sixth street. The family home was until lately at Willmette, Ill. Mr. Murdock, father of the groom, recently joined the ranks of progressive Tri–City merchants, opening a large wall paper and decorating store at 115 East Second street, Davenport and a similar establishment in Rock Island. The happy young people for the present will reside at the Beiderbecke home on West Seventh street.

- GERTRUDE 'TRUDEL' SEIFFERT BEIDERBECKE, b. 15 Feb 1903, Davenport; d. 10 Jul 1992, Santa Clara, CA; married 03 May 1923 to William Day Washburn, born 05 Nov 1896 in Illinois, died Dec 1966 in Fort Lauderdale, FL; Children: ROBERT WASHBURN, m. Suzanne; PATRICIA WASHBURN, b. 1927 in Illinois; m. Sam Chapman; children: Mike, Steve, Bill, Linda.

GERTRUDE SEIFFERT BEIDERBECKE
BECOMES BRIDE OF
WM. D. WASHBURN OF EVANSTON

A simple and very pretty home wedding of this morning took place at the resident of Mr. and Mrs. H. O. Seiffert, 532 W. Sixth street, when their granddaughter Miss Gertrude Seiffert Beiderbecke, daughter of Mr. and Mrs. Charles T. Beiderbecke, of 510 W. Seventh street, became the bride of William Day Washburn, Jr., son of Mr. and Mrs. W.D. Washburn of Evanston, Ill. Very Rev. Marmaduke Hare, D.D. dean of Trinity cathedral read the marriage service in the presence of some 40 or more relatives and close friends. The ceremony was at 10:30 in the drawing room, the large south windows being used as a setting for the improvised altar, a profusion of spring flowers in peach and lavender hues giving the colorful touch to all the rooms in gracefully arranged bouquets in baskets and vases. BIX BEIDERBECKE, the cousin of the bride, was at the piano and played the wedding march as the bride entered on the arm of he father, Charles T. Beiderbecke, who gave her away. She was in an exquisite creation of chartreuse in pearl gray made simply but in straight lines of knife–plaited skirt of the new short length, long waisted bodice of very short

MRS. WILLIAM DAY WASHBURN.

Is Holiday Week Visitor at the C. T. Beiderbecke Home

MRS. ALLEN MARQUARDT, nee Helen Beiderbecke.

Daughters of Carl T & Adele Beiderbecke, clockwise from upper left: Lutie Seehof, DHS 1916; Gertrude Washburn, wedding 1923; Gretchen Murdock, DHS 1918; Helen Marquardt, society page 1928.

sleeves with the girdle a large sash of peach taffeta which gave the touch of the color gown. She carried a bridal shower of orchids and lilies of the valley. The only attendant of the bride was her young sister, Miss Helen Beiderbecke, who was in a Landin green flat crepe frock made in girlish fashion with long waisted bodice and short sleeves. She carried lavender and peach colored sweet peas. Mr. Washburn with his brother, John Washburn of Evanston, and Dean Hare met the bridal party at the improvised altar where the ceremony of the Episcopal church was read. An informal reception followed. Mrs. H.O. Seiffert, the grandmother, of the bride who received with her was in pearl gray crepe and lace. Mrs. C. T. Beiderbecke mother of the bride wore lavender embroidered crepe. Mrs. W. D. Washburn, Sr., was in gray chartreuse beaded with steel trimmings. Mrs. John Washburn wore fawn colored crepe. Mrs. J. F. Seehof of Dayton, O., was in dark blue crepe, and Mrs. George Murdock of Cedar Rapids in grey crepe. A wedding breakfast was served after the ceremony, the bride's table being arranged in the sun parlor with covers for 24 of the young people. Decorations were arranged with a profusion of very lovely lavender and sweet peas in baskets, with the bride's cake in the place of honor to be cut by the bride. The family and other guests were served in the library, where spring flowers were also in artistic profusion on the tables in the peach and orchid arranged in large baskets and bowls. Mr. and Mrs. Washburn left on a motor trip and will be at home after June 1 at 7759 Sheridan Road, Chicago. The going away dress of blue was a gray and blue poire twill, three piece suit with small close fitting hat in gray to match. Among guests who came for the wedding were Mr. and Mrs. W. D. Washburn and Mr. and Mrs. John Washburn of Evanston, Ill., Mr. and Mrs. J. F. Seehof of Dayton, O. and Mr. and Mrs. George Murdock of Cedar Rapids, Ia. The bride comes of one of the well known old families of the Tri–Cities, being the granddaughter of H. O. Seiffert, president of the Seiffert Lumber company, and a daughter of Charles Beiderbecke, also one of the city's well known business men, secretary of the Seiffert company. She is a graduate of the Davenport High school and of the Choate school of Brookline, Mass. Mr. Washburn attended Dartmouth college and was in the late war as an aviation lieutenant. He is with the Famous Players–Lasky corporation, in the department of distribution, with headquarters in Chicago.

FAMOUS PLAYERS–LASKY was a merger between Loew's theater circuit financier and former Chicago furrier Adolph Zukor and Jesse Lasky, a New York booking agent and former vaudeville cornetist. Zukor and Lasky opened a studio on LA's Sunset Boulevard to make a film with director Cecile B. DeMille. This first–ever west coast movie studio became Paramount Pictures. Zukor and Lasky helped make Hollywood the movie capital of the world and revolutionized the industry by organizing production, distribution, and exhibition within a single company. Paramount made *Wings* in 1929, the first movie to receive an Academy

Award. It would take another two decades and Bing Crosby as its star for Paramount to win a second best picture Oscar for *Going My Way*.

- HELEN SEIFFERT BEIDERBECKE, b. 05 Aug 1906, Davenport; d. Jul 1987, Florida; married 19 Jun 1926 at Davenport Outing Club to Rueben Allen Marquardt, born 07 Mar 1898 in Illinois to George and Evelyn Allen Marquardt. Children: ALLEN MARQUARDT, m. Natalie, son: Clayton; GRETCHEN, m. David Seager; adopted Clayton Marquardt; ANNE MARQUARDT, m. James Edmondson, Children: Sarah, Susan.

19 June 1926 *Democrat–Leader*
A very lovely wedding of the late afternoon was that which took place at the Davenport Outing club, when Miss Helen Seiffert Beiderbecke, daughter of Mr. and Mrs. Charles T. Beiderbecke of 510 West Seventh street, became the bride of R. Allen Marquardt, son of Mr. and Mrs. W.G. Marquardt of 930 Bridge avenue, Evanston, Ill. The Rev. C. L. Stafford, D.D., of Muscatine, pastor of the Methodist Episcopal church and uncle of the bridegroom, read the marriage service. The ceremony was at 4 o'clock in the ball room the improvised altar being arranged beneath the gallery arch to the west reception parlor, where festoons of smilax garlanded and entwined the pillars and balcony rail, and formed a screen of greenery while on either side were the high pedestaled, statuesque seven–branched white candelabra of flaming white candles, which towered above the banking ferns and tall floor baskets filled with giant snapdragons, delphinium and roses, the flowers in soft shades of orchid blue and pink giving a touch of the bridal colors to the nuptial setting. Petersen's orchestra of strings played the wedding march as the bride entered from the east reception parlor on the arm of her father, C. T. Beiderbecke, who gave her away, the music changing to the softer harmonies of the nuptial serenade as the ceremony was read. Attending the bride were a trio of college friends: Mrs. F. L. Hinchliffe of Davenport, as matron of honor; Miss Adelaide King of Brockton, Mass., and Miss Margaret Howard of Boston, as bridesmaids. Mr. Marquardt accompanied by his brother, George Marquardt, as best man, came in from the side door meeting the bridal party at the altar. The bride was in a gown of white bridal satin trimmed with rhinestone and pearl beading, the bodice made tight and sleeveless with round neck and yoke of chiffon set on with a dainty beading in flower design of rhinestone and pearls. The full skirt was bouffant with hip–hoops and shirred at the low waist line where a half–girdle in front followed the floral design of the yoke in the rhinestone and pearls, three deep tier flounces in petal design finishing the uneven hem. The wedding veil of tulle was in a small cap effect with high coronet lace held at the back with orange blossoms. The only ornament worn by the bride was a diamond and platinum lavaliere, the gift of the groom. The nuptial bouquet was of orchids, roses and lily of the valley in shower arrangement. The bride's attendants were gowned in taffeta

and tulle fashioned alike in the colors of orchid pink and blue, Mrs. Hinchliffe wearing orchid, Miss King pink, and Miss Howard blue. Their dresses were made with tight fitting bodice and full skirt with deep bias flounces of tulle in the color in diagonal flounce trimming, velvet ribbons following the diagonal fashion from shoulder to hip where clusters of metal flowers colors held the steamers and bows. Their hats were garden models in horsehair braid to match their gowns with silver and velvet ribbon trimming to match each costume. Each carried a shower of sweet peas, roses and babies breath in the orchid, pink and blue colors. Mr. and Mrs. Beiderbecke, and Mr. and Mrs. Marquardt received with the bridal party at the informal reception which followed the ceremony. Mrs. Beiderbecke was in a biscuit colored georgette over satin trimmed with real lace, and her flowers were roses. Mrs. Marquardt wore a costume of gray georgette with roses in her corsage Bourget.

WEDDING TEA FOLLOWS CEREMONY

High tea was served in the dining rooms following the ceremony. The brides table being arranged with the wedding cake, and large silver bowls filled with roses, delphinium and pastel shades of snapdragons with two large crystal candelabra on either end. The serving table and silver baskets filled with flowers and tall princess candles in silver holders. There were 175 guests at the wedding. Mr. and Mrs. Marquardt left on a short trip and will be at home after July 15 in Evanston. The traveling dress of the bride was a sport ensemble of tan and red trimmed with monkey fur, with hat of red to match. The gifts of the bride to her attendants with evening vanity cases set with rhinestone brilliants. Among guests at the wedding from beyond the city were Dr. and Mrs. C.L. Stafford, Mr. and Mrs. Ralph Stafford and Mr. and Mrs. J. L. Geisler of Muscatine; Mr. and Mrs. H. H. Cogeshall, son and daughter Harrieson and Katherine and Mr. and Mrs. C. G. Marquardt of Des Moines; Mr. and Mrs. W. F. Elliott and son of Indianapolis; Mr. and Mrs. Jerome F. Seehof, and sons Jack and Ted; Mr. and Mrs. G. W. Marquardt, George Marquardt, Mr. and Mrs. W. C. Pool, Mr. and Mrs. John Breytspraak, Mr. and Mrs. George Traver, Mr. and Mrs. E. L. Middleton, of Evanston, Ill., Mr. and Mrs. Clarence A. Stafford of Oak Park, Ill., Mrs. Jules De Lescaille of St. Louis and Mrs. Andrew Dawson Shurr of Fort Dodge, Ia. The bride is the youngest daughter of Charles T. Beiderbecke, secretary of the H. O. Seiffert Lumber Company, and granddaughter of H. O. Seiffert, president of the company and Mrs. Seiffert. She is a graduate of the Davenport High School, and attended Connecticut college, New London, Conn. Mr. Marquardt is a graduate of Northwestern university. He was a captain in the aviation service in the late war and is a Sigma Alpha Epsilon. He is connected with the Alfred Decker & Kohn company, Chicago.

26 July 1959: Miss Anne Marquardt, daughter of Mrs. Reuben Allen [Helen] Marquardt of Fort Lauderdale, Fl., and granddaughter of Mrs. C.T. [Adele] Beiderbecke, Davenport, was married yesterday to James Paul Edmondson of Evanston, Il, son of Dr. and Mrs. Hugh Allen Edmonson, at Trinity Cathedral in

Davenport. The 4:30 p.m. ceremony was witnessed by family members including the bride's grandaunt Miss Helen Seiffert [sister of Adele Seiffert Beiderbecke], Davenport.

Her sister, Mrs. David C. (Gretchen) Seager of Big Springs, Texas, served as matron of honor. Sister–in–law Mrs. Allen C. [Natalie] Marquardt of Garden City, Michigan, and Misses Marian and Marjorie Edmonson, sisters of the bridegroom, completed the entourage.

Dr. Hugh A. Edmondson Jr. of Oak Park, Il, served his brother as best man. Ralph Smith of Rockford, Il, Jack Nicolet of Milwaukee and Jerry Rogers of Evanston were ushers.

The wedding guests were later received at the Plantation in Moline, Il. The newlyweds will tour the West Coast before returning to live in Evanston, where the bride is a senior and a Kappa Kappa Gamma at Northwestern University, and where Mr. Edmondson received his Master's degree in business administration. He is employed in Chicago.

The gowns of the bride and her attendants were selected for their summery accents. The bridal gown with its re–embroidered Alencon lace bodice, scoop neckline and short sleeves, was styled with a back–swept taffeta skirt with ended in a chapel train. The veil of French illusion was attached to a small tiara of tiny seed pearls.

The attendants' Ming blue silk chiffon sheaths were trimmed with matching satin bows. Panels of chiffon were attached to the skirt backs and in their hair they wore satin bow ornaments.

Allen and Natalie Marquardt died in automobile accident returning from the Edmondson wedding. Gretchen Marquardt Seager and her husband David raised Clayton Marquardt who was three at the time of his parents' deaths. Brothers–in–law James Edmondson and David Seager became partners in a land development company; Edmondson, president, and Seager vice president of the Great American Land Co, headquartered in Riverside, CA.

BISMARCK & AGGIE BABY PICS

Genealogy: Bismark and Aggie

BISMARCK HERMAN BEIDERBECKE 16 Mar 1868—11 Mar 1940
AGNES 'AGGIE' JANE HILTON 01 Mar 1870—05 Sep 1952

09 April 1893 *Sunday Leader*:
DELTA PHI CLUB—On Wednesday evening the Delta Phi card club met at the Gilman residence on east Locust street and were handsomely entertained by the Misses Gilman. The game played was progressive angling and everybody enjoyed the fun and excitement. Fourteen couples were present, there being seven tables in use. After the games dainty refreshments were served, an account made of the scores and the prizes awarded. Miss Harriette Berryhill and Mr. Ben Hanssen receiving the head trophys and the consolation prizes going to Miss AGGIE HILTON and Mr. BISMARK BEIDERBECKE. While supper was being served the Tourists' Mandolin club strolled around to the open windows and discoursed some very sweet music, and the evening's entertainment was greatly enjoyed in every way.

07 Jun 1893 Marriage Certificate: Bismark was 26 and Aggie was 24. Witnesses: Miss Mary Hill and Charles Beiderbecke

08 June 1893 *Democrat–Leader:* BEIDERBECKE–HILTON
At the home of the bride's aunt, Miss Mary Hill 615 East Fifteenth Street, were married Miss Aggie J. Hilton and Bismark Beiderbecke, Rev W.E. Shaw officiating. Relatives and intimate friends witnessed the ceremony and joined in congratulations afterward. Mr. and Mrs. Beiderbecke departed on one of the night trains for Chicago, intending to spend some time in the world's fair city. They will then go by boat to Duluth, then on to St. Paul by rail, and complete the trip by returning down the Mississippi to Davenport. It is an admirably planned trip and will be a happy one. The bride is one of Davenport's popular young ladies, highly esteemed in the social circle in which she moves. She is an accomplished musician. Mr. Beiderbecke is the treasurer of the Beiderbecke–Miller Co. and has business and social qualifier of a high order. On the part of many friends The Democrat tenders its best wishes for their future happiness.

11 June 1893 *Sunday Leader:* BEIDERBECKE–HILTON
On Wednesday evening occurred the ceremony uniting the lives of two of Davenport's most popular young people, Mr. Bismark H. Beiderbecke and Miss

Aggie J. Hilton. The wedding was attended by only the near friends and relatives of the contracting parties and was a charming affair, occurring at the home of the bride, No. 615 East Fifteenth street. At 8 o'clock the young couple stepped under a large and handsome canopy of flowers and surrounded by their relatives and close friends the Rev. W.E. Shaw pronounced the words which welded the two lives and hearts into one. The young couple was indeed a handsome one, standing under the floral canopy, the bride dressed in a very rich bridal dress of white satin trimmed with lace and ornamented with roses, and carrying a bouquet of bride's roses, the groom being attired in full evening dress. After the ceremony and the hearty congratulations of those present having been tendered a dainty wedding luncheon was served, and at midnight the young couple departed for Chicago to enjoy their honeymoon.

The groom is the son of Mr. Chas. Beiderbecke and is connected with the firm of Beiderbecke & Miller. He is a young man of superior abilities and talents while his bride is a charming member of Davenport's brightest social and musical circles, both having hosts of friends who will wish them joy.

After a visit to Chicago, the white city, and a tour of the lakes, Mr. and Mrs. Beiderbecke will be at home at 615 East Fifteenth street after July 15.

1894–1897: Bismark and Aggie living at 615 East 15th when Charles Burnette born.
Christmas 1895: *Mr. and Mrs. N.G. Pendleton entertained the children of their neighbors with a Christmas tree at 10 o'clock Christmas morning. Twenty four little folks gathered about the tree and were made happy.* MR. AND MRS. BIX BEIDERBECKE *did likewise for the children in the neighborhood of their home on East Fifteenth street.*

Davenport City Directory lists only three houses in 1895 on the west side of Grand Avenue: #1902, A. Vere Martin; #1912, Charles J. Von Maur; #1920, Willis B. Durfee; on the east side of Grand Avenue was School # 9, a Teacher's Training School at #1921 Grand Avenue.
1898–1907 Beiderbecke's address listed as 1933 Grand Ave; could be an error in the city directory. After 1907, address listed as #1934.
24 Sept 1900 *Daily Leader*: *Mr. and Mrs. Bix Beiderbecke will leave during the latter part of the week for New York city where they will visit friends. They will spend some time at Buffalo and at Niagara Falls, as well as visit Detroit, Mich. during their absence and will be gone about a month.*
1905 Census: 1933 Grand Ave. Bismark, Agnes, Chas. B., Mary L., Leon B., Mary Hill, (Aggie's aunt); and Annie Ramm (domestic).
1910 Census: Bismarck, Agatha, Charles, Mary, Leon B.
1920 Census: Bismarck as Bix H., Agatha H. Charles B., Mary L., Leon B.
1925 Scott County Census: Bismark, Agatha, Charles B., and Leon B. Value of home $6000; Free of mortgage; Amount of insurance carried on home $4,000.00; highest grade completed 12 (everyone), Charles B. had 2 years of college.

Bismark & Aggie with Charles Burnette,
Baby Leon Bismark, and Mary Louise

Card No. 919	Name Bismark H Biederbecker 47
Sex Male	County Scott P.O. #1934 Grand Av
Color White	Town or Township Davenport Ward 5
Married X Widowed	Occupation Mfg Fuel Co. Months in 1914 Unemployed None
Single Divorced	Total earnings for 1914 from occupation $ 2500
Months in School 1914	Extent of Education: Common/Grammar 8 High School 2 College 1
Public High	Birth Place Davenport Ia Do you own your home or farm? Yes
Private College	Incumbrance on farm or home $ None Value of farm or home $ 6000
Read Yes	Military Service: Civil War___ Mexican___ Spanish___ Infantry___ Cavalry___
Write Yes	Artillery___ Navy___ State___ Regiment___ Company___
Blind ___ Deaf ___	Church Affiliation None
Insane ___ Idiot ___	Father's Birthplace Germany Mother's Birthplace Germany
If Foreign Born are you Naturalized Y	Remarks
Years in U.S. 47	Signed Geo P Lindsay
Years in Iowa 47	

SCOTT COUNTY (IOWA) CENSUS 1915

Card No. 920	Name Agatha Biederbecker 45
Sex Female	County Scott P.O. #1934 Grand Av
Color White	Town or Township Davenport Ward 5
Married X Widowed	Occupation ___ Months in 1914 Unemployed ___
Single Divorced	Total earnings for 1914 from occupation $ ___
Months in School 1914	Extent of Education: Common/Grammar 8 High School 4 College ___
Public High	Birth Place Davenport Ia Do you own your home or farm? No
Private College	Incumbrance on farm or home $ ___ Value of farm or home $ ___
Read Yes	Military Service: Civil War___ Mexican___ Spanish___ Infantry___ Cavalry___
Write Yes	Artillery___ Navy___ State___ Regiment___ Company___
Blind ___ Deaf ___	Church Affiliation Lutheran
Insane ___ Idiot ___	Father's Birthplace Ky Mother's Birthplace Penna
If Foreign Born are you Naturalized	Remarks
Years in U.S. 45	Signed Geo P Lindsay
Years in Iowa 45	

SCOTT COUNTY (IOWA) CENSUS 1915

Card No. 921 F
Name: Chas B Beiderbecke Age: 19
County: Scott   r. # 1934 Grand Av
Town: Davenport   Ward: 5
Sex: Male
Color: White
Single
Months in School 1914 — Public: 6
Extent of Education: Common —, Grammar 8, High School 4, College 1 yr
Birth Place: Davenport Ia
Read: yes Write: yes
Church Affiliation: Presbyterian
Father's Birthplace: Iowa   Mother's Birthplace: Iowa
Years in U.S.: 19   Years in Iowa: 19
Signed: Geo P Lindsay

Card No. 922 F
Name: Mary L Beiderbecke Age: 16
County: Scott   r. # 1934 Grand Av
Town: Davenport   Ward: 5
Sex: Female
Color: White
Single
Months in School 1914 — Public: 0 High
Extent of Education: Grammar 8, High School 2
Birth Place: Davenport Ia
Read: yes Write: yes
Church Affiliation: none
Father's Birthplace: Iowa   Mother's Birthplace: Iowa
Years in U.S.: 16   Years in Iowa: 16
Signed: Geo P Lindsay

Card No. 923 F
Name: Leon B Beiderbecke Age: 12
County: Scott   r. # 1934 Grand Av
Town: Davenport   Ward: 5
Sex: Male
Color: White
Single
Months in School 1914 — Public: 10
Extent of Education: Grammar 6
Birth Place: Davenport Ia
Read: yes Write: yes
Church Affiliation: none
Father's Birthplace: Iowa   Mother's Birthplace: Iowa
Years in U.S.: 12   Years in Iowa: 12
Signed: Geo P Lindsay

Davenport Democrat–Leader Society News:

December 6, 1920 To Entertain at Tea and Luncheon at Club Mrs. B.H. Beiderbecke of Grand avenue and Mrs. Karl Vollmer of Camp McClellan have issued invitations for a tea of Friday afternoon, at the Outing Club. The hours are from 3 to 6. There will also be a luncheon of Thursday at the club given by Mrs. Vollmer and Mrs. Beiderbecke, at which Davenport friends will be guests.

December 10, 1920 AFTERNOON TEA IS BRILLIANT SOCIAL AFFAIR AT CLUB The tea this afternoon at the Outing Club, given by Mrs. B.H. Beiderbecke of Grand avenue and Mrs. Karl Vollmer of Camp McClellan, was the principal affair of Davenport's social week, over 150 Tri–City women being entertained. The Christmas season was very much in evidence in the attractive decorations, the holiday red and green being carried out in many pretty details with potted Jerusalem cherries, poinsettia and Christmas greens. The Serving table in the dining room had a large bouquet of Russell roses as the centerpiece, and lights and candles added to the pretty effect. Mrs. Vollmer and Mrs. Beiderbecke received in the south room, and assisting about the rooms and halls, and in pouring were members of their families and intimate friends: Mrs. Adolph Priester, Mrs. Henry Priester, Mrs. Oscar Priester, Mrs. A.J. Stibolt, Mrs. Leon Hass, Mrs. Malvern Iles, Mrs. M. Koehler, Mrs. Henry W. Von Maur, Mrs. W.R. Weir, Mrs. M. Von Binzer, and Miss Koehler and Gretchen Beiderbecke of Davenport, Mrs. Theo. Brown of Moline and Misses Amelie and Lillie Huber of Rock Island.

> **Real Estate Moving.**
>
> W. H. Snider & Sons are beginning to predict large sales of real estate during the coming season. They have many prospective buyers already booked, and have begun to make some good sales. A deed was placed on record yesterday to B. H. Beiderbecke for the property situated at 1933 Grand avenue, opposite the Graud avenue schoolhouse. This is one of the elegant new houses that has recently been built in Cutter's addition. The consideration was $3,600. Mr. Cutter has planned to lay out sixteen acres more and put upon the market as soon
>
> **Daily Republican March 2, 1897**

12 Mar 1940 Obituary: Bismark H. 'Bix' Beiderbecke, 71, former manager of the East Davenport Fuel & Lumber Co, a subsidiary of the H.O. Seiffert Lumber Co, died at his home, 1934 Grand avenue, at 9:50 am Monday following a lingering illness. Death was due to complications. Funeral services will be held at the Hill & Fredericks chapel at 10:30 am Wednesday, followed by strictly private burial at Oakdale cemetery. Friends are welcome at the chapel. Born March 16, 1868, in Davenport, he was the son of the late Charles and Louise Beiderbecke. He was educated in the Davenport schools and was married here to Miss Agatha Hilton June 7, 1893. When a young man he became associated with his father in the Beiderbecke and Miller wholesale grocery company as treasurer. After the dissolution of that firm, he became manager of the East Davenport Fuel & Lumber Co. He retired from active work in 1939.

B. H. Beiderbecke, Retired Business Leader Is Dead

Bismark H. "Bix" Beiderbecke, 71, former manager of the East Davenport Fuel & Lumber Co., a subsidiary of the H.O. Seiffert Lumber Co., died at his home, 1934 Grand avenue, at 9:50 a.m. Monday following a lingering illness. Death was due to complications.

Funeral services will be held at the Hill & Fredericks chapel at 10:30 a.m. Wednesday, followed by strictly private burial at Oakdale cemetery. Friends are welcome at the chapel.

Born March 16, 1868, in Davenport, he was the son of the late Charles and Louise Beiderbecke. He was educated in the Davenport schools and was married here to Miss Agatha Hilton June 7, 1893.

When a young man, he became associated with his father in the Beiderbecke and Miller wholesale grocery company as treasurer. After the dissolution of that firm, he became manager of the East Davenport Fuel & Lumber Co. He retired from active work in 1939.

Surviving are the widow; one son, Charles B. Beiderbecke, Davenport; one daughter, Mrs. Theodore Shoemaker, Suffern, N.Y.; two sisters, Mrs. Othelia A. Stibolt, Davenport, and Mrs. Lutie Von Vinzer, Los Angeles, Calif.; and five grandchildren. One son, Bix, who at one time was a noted solo cornetist with Paul Whiteman's orchestra, died in 1931. A brother, Carl, died six years ago.

Mother of Late Bix Beiderbecke Is Dead

DAVENPORT (AP) — Mrs. Agatha J. Beiderbecke, 82, mother of the late Bix Beiderbecke, one of America's immortals of jazz music, died Friday night at her Mississippi hotel apartment here after an extended illness.

Her famed son, who during his relatively short career played trumpet with top American bands in the 1920's, died in 1931. Mrs. Beiderbecke in her youth was a talented pianist and organist.

Funeral services will be Monday with burial at Davenport.

Bismark's & Aggie's marriage license 6-6-1893
Bismark's obituary: Tuesday, March 12, 1940
Aggie's obituary picked up by AP wire Sep 7, 1952

Aggie on her Grand Avenue porch before moving to the Mississippi Hotel, where she lived after Bismark died, from 1941 until her death in 1952.
The Mississippi Hotel (now lofts) on Third is home to former RKO Orpheum, named for *QC Times* publisher Philip Adler, who attended Tyler School with Bix Beiderbecke.

Surviving are the widow; one son, Charles B. Beiderbecke, Davenport; one daughter, Mrs. Theodore Shoemaker, Suffern, N.Y.; two sisters Mrs. Othelia A. Stibolt, Davenport, and Mrs. Lutie Von Vinzer, Los Angeles, Calif.; and five grandchildren. One son, Bix, who at one time was a noted solo cornetist with Paul Whiteman's orchestra, died in 1931. A brother, Carl, died six years ago.

14 Mar 1940: *Funeral services for Bismark H. Beiderbecke, who died Monday at his home, 1934 Grand Avenue, were held at 10:30 A.M. Wednesday at the Hill & Fredericks chapel with Dr. Alfred S. Nickless officiating. Burial was in Oakdale cemetery. Bearers were William K. Heningbaum, Robert McCosh, Richard Von Maur, Walter Priester, Edmund Cook and Fritz Schmidt.* [Heningbaum and Von Maur also were pallbearers for Bix]

Funeral Home: Hill & Fredericks; Interment # 15158; Will: March 1940, Davenport, Charles Burnette was 44 at the time of his father's death, Mary Louise was 41.

Iowa File # 18136 Property title transferred to Aggie on May 8, 1940. House sold May 6, 1941, to C.W. Ludtke. Charles and his family were living with Aggie on Grand Avenue at the time. They moved to 2601 Eastern Avenue, where their telephone number was 2-3462. Aggie moved to the Mississippi Hotel; she didn't need the number because at that time they had telephone operators. In 1947, Aggie got her own telephone, #7–4632. When Bix died, his parents' telephone number was Walnut 836.

Rites Monday for Mrs. Beiderbecke; Was Mother of "Bix"

Final rites for Mrs. Agatha "Aggie" J. Beiderbecke, 82, mother of the late "Bix" Beiderbecke, one of America's greatest jazz musicians, who died in her apartment in Mississippi Hotel at 8:30 P.M. Friday, will be held at 10 A.M. Monday in Hill and Fredericks chapel. Burial will be in Oakdale cemetery. Death followed an extended illness. Her famed son, who during his relatively brief musical career played the trumpet with the nation's top bands during the 1920s, died in 1931. A lifelong resident of Davenport, Mrs. Beiderbecke was the former Agatha Hilton. She was born March 1, 1870 and had attended Davenport schools, including St. Katharine's school for girls. During her earlier years she was a talented pianist and organist. She was a member of First Presbyterian church. Her marriage to B.H. Beiderbecke took place June 7, 1893, in Davenport. He died in 1940. Survivors include a daughter, Mrs. Theodore Shoemaker, Lexington, Mass., a son C.B. Beiderbecke, Davenport, and five grandsons.

Attending Physician: George Braunlich M.D.; Burial: 08 Sep 1952, Oakdale Cemetery, Davenport. Probate: 14 Oct 1952, Will: File # 24651—Charles B., her son, was Executor. Total value of Estate $59, 278.01, including $1,408.28 from Robbins Music Corporation, royalty on music compositions of Bix Beiderbecke, deceased son. Charles was 57 and Mary Louise was 53 when their mother died.

July 7, 1927

TWO AUTOMOBILES REPORTED STOLEN; ONE IS RECOVERED

Two automobiles were stolen here Wednesday when B. H. Beiderbeck, 1934 Grand avenue, reported the theft of a Ford roadster taken from the 300 block West Second street, and M. W. Hes, 2404 Pershing avenue, notified police that his Buick coupe was stolen from its parking place on the levee.

Patrolman Otto Kuehl found the Hes car at Second and Main streets late Wednesday night.

BEIDERBECKE COUSINS, L-R: Carl 's & Adele's daughter Lutie; Bismark's & Aggie's son Charles; Tillie & Albert's children Otie, Victor and Carl.

GENEALOGY: OTTILIE & A.J. STIBOLT

OTTILIE SOPHIA BEIDERBECKE
25 Oct 1866 – 18 Sep 1944
Married: 20 Sep 1888 to Albert Julius Stibolt, son of John and Carolina Stibolt

On September 12, 1888, Beiderbecke Charles & Wife sold lots to Albert J. Stibolt, 586 Forrest & Dillons Addition to Davenport, part of Lot 5 block 1; papers were filed October 1, 1888. Warranty Deed.

21 September 1888: ORANGE BLOSSOMS
The Marriage of Ottilie S. Beiderbecke, daughter of well known merchant, Charles Beiderbecke, and Albert J. Stibolt, civil engineer, occurred at 8 o'clock last evening. The handsome and spacious mansion was beautifully adorned and illuminated for the occasion, and large number of friends of the family and of the groom gathered therein. With the betrothed at the nuptial alter were Miss Clara Krause, Miss Thekia

Speidel, Carl Beiderbecke and Bismarck Beiderbecke as attendants. The Rev. A. M. Judy officiated. Bride and groom were born and reared in Davenport and the friendship which led to love and betrothal commenced in early childhood. Mr. and Mrs. Stibolt go to St. Paul and vicinity for a bridal trip. On their return they go into their own house opposite the bride's parental home.

Census 1910: Ottilie & A.J. living with Louise at 532 West Seventh Street.

02 Aug 1919, *Democrat–Leader*:
A.J. STIBOLT DIED AT HOME THIS MORNING
PROMINENT LOCAL MAN, U.S. ENGINEER, PASSES AWAY TODAY.
The death of Albert J. Stibolt, one of Davenport's most respected citizens, occurred at his home, 532 West Seventh street, at 2:30 o'clock Saturday morning. Mr. Stibolt was operated upon one year ago and seemed never to have recovered. Mr. Stibolt had been connected with the United States Engineers, Rock Island, for almost 30 years. He was born Nov. 6, 1857, at Galena, Ill., in the other half of the house occupied by General Ulysses S. Grant. He came to Davenport at a very early age and received his education here. On Sept., 20, 1888, he was married to Miss Ottilie Beiderbecke, by the Rev. Arthur A. Judy, of the Unitarian church.

He was especially loved by all the younger children who knew him. The survivors are his wife, Mrs. Ottilie, one daughter, Mrs. Leon H. Hass, of Davenport, and two sons, Carl B. and Victor A. Stibolt. Two sisters also survive. They are Mrs. Olga Marten, of Minneapolis and Mrs. Emily Hoffman, of Davenport. Mr. Stibolt was the son of J.P. Stibolt, of Galena, Ill., who came to this county from Denmark, and who was the editor of Der Demokrat during the Civil War. Funeral services will be held Monday morning at 10 o'clock from the home, 532 West Seventh street. Services at the home and the grave in Oakdale cemetery will be private.

Burial: 04 Aug 1919, Oakdale Cemetery, Davenport, Iowa

19 Sep 1944 *Democrat–Leader* Obituary:

Mrs. Ottilie B. Stibolt, 77, life resident of Davenport, died at 7:30 p.m. Monday in the home of her daughter and son–in–law, Mr. and Mrs. Leon Hass, 129 Ridgewood avenue, following an extended illness. She was born Oct. 25, 1866, daughter of the late Mr. and Mrs. Charles Beiderbecke; received her education in local schools and later married Albert J. Stibolt in 1888.

Surviving are one daughter, Mrs. Leon Hass, and son Carl Stibolt, Saratoga, Calif.; one sister, Mrs. L. Von Binzer, Los Angeles, Calif.; five grandchildren and two great–grandchildren. Her husband and two brothers preceded her in death. Funeral services will be held at 10:30 a.m. Thursday in the Hill & Fredericks chapel. Burial will be in Oakdale cemetery.

- VICTOR ALBERT STIBOLT, b. Sep 1889 in Davenport; graduated 1907 Davenport High; m. Helen Davis, daughter of T.B. Davis and Appolonia Denkmann; 1930 Census: Rock Island Plough Company, Vice President;

address: 559 Twenty–Sixth Street Rock Island, Illinois; children: Victor D, 01 Mar 1924–04 Jan 1965; Thomas B., b. 1926; Richard A, b. 1928

- OTIE CAROLINE STIBOLT, 02 Jun 1891–27 Nov 1969; graduated: 1910, Davenport High; m. 01 May 1914 to Leon Hass, 15 Apr 1890–07 Sep 1962; 1908, Davenport High; Children: Peter Hass, 26 Aug 1916–02 Aug 1988; Elenora Hass, b. 1919.
- CARL B. STIBOLT, born 06 Aug 1896, Davenport; Graduation: 1915, Davenport High; m. 24 July 1926 to Martha J. Morse, divorced 1932; m. Donna; died Jan 1977, Honolulu, Hawaii. Donna Stibolt died May 1987 in Honolulu.

HELEN DAVIS STIBOLT was the granddaughter of F.C.A. Denkmann of Weyerhaeuser & Denkmann Lumber Co. Her mother was Appolonia Denkmann. Her father, T.B. Davis with his brother Samuel—who was married to Appolonia Weyerhaeuser—founded and co-owned People's Power Co. and the Tri-Cities Street Railway. Later, T.B. Davis took over Rock Island Plow, owned by Weyerhaeuser. The company manufactured cultivators, riding and walking plows, etc. The plant later was sold to J. I. Case and Victor Stibolt transferred to Louisiana.

LEON HASS was the son of John Hass, cashier for the Iowa National Bank where Otie Stibolt's grandfather, Charles Beiderbecke, was president. Leon became head cashier for the Scott County Bank. His sister Clara was married to Walter Kruse, a partner in the Clausen–Kruse architectural firm. Leon and Clara invested in several Davenport commercial properties.

MARTHA MORSE STIBOLT was the granddaughter of Chicago industrialist Charles Hosmer Morse. Carl and Martha met when he was working for the Fairbanks–Morse Co at their Indianapolis headquarters. The couple married at the home of the bride's parents in Lake Forest, IL. Carl and Martha divorced in 1932 and six months later she eloped with a German baron and moved to Munich.

STIBOLT KIDS

Victor's job Jan 1, 1927

Carl's Wife July 25, 1926

Ex –Mrs. Stibolt Jan 13, 1933

VICTOR STIBOLT TAKES POSITION WITH R. I. PLOW

Well Known Tri-City Man Assumes Leading Executive Position.

The Rock Island Plow company, established in 1855, is effective Jan. 1, taking what it considers to be one of the most important steps in recent years in promoting its growth in the implement industry, and assuming a place of greater importance in its field. On that date, Victor A. Stibolt assumes the duties of executive vice president with headquarters in the general offices at Rock Island.

May 7, 1922
Leon Hass, husband of Otie Stibolt

Hass-Kruse Building Job Nearly Done

From February 16 to June 1 seems a comparatively short period of time, yet these dates will mark the beginning and the completion of the new Hass-Kruse $100,000 office building on Brady street between Second and Third streets.

The building is being erected by Leon Hass and his sister, Mrs. Clara Kruse, and is one of the most important real estate improvements of the year.

BECOMES BRIDE OF CARL STIBOLDT AT GARDEN CEREMONY

MRS. CARL B. STIBOLT

At a beautiful garden ceremony performed yesterday afternoon at 4 o'clock at "Fairmore," Lake Forest, Ill. home of the bride's parents, was solemnized the wedding of Miss Martha Jeannette Morse, youngest daughter of Mr. and Mrs. Charles Hosmer Morse, to Carl B. Stibolt, youngest son of the late A. J. Stibolt and Mrs. Stibolt of 322 East Seventh street, Davenport.

Heiress Elopes With Baron

Genealogy: Lutie and Max Von Binzer

LUTIE LOUISE BEIDERBECKE was born 30 Jan 1870 in Davenport and died 08 May 1955 in Los Angeles, California. She married MAX MORITZ CARL WILHELM VON BINZER on April 14, 1897, in Davenport. He was born 1858 in Switzerland and died 17 Apr 1918 in Birmingham, Alabama.

Children:
- WERNER F. VON BINZER, b. 24 Feb 1899, Davenport, Iowa; d. 12 Jan 1977, Los Angeles, CA; Occupation: financial officer with Pacific Finance Corporation and played banjo with St. Francis Orchestra; m. Alma Barman, 27 Dec 1927, Los Angeles, CA; 29 Jan 1899–04 Mar 1990.
- FRIEDEL 'FERA' VON BINZER, born 1901 in Macon, Missouri; died 07 July 1903, Alton, Illinois. Burial: 09 July 1903, Oakdale Cemetery, Davenport.
- CARL VON BINZER, born 1902 in Macon, Missouri; died 20 Jun 1903 in Alton, Illinois. Named after his grandfather, Carl (Charles) Beiderbecke, who died while visiting Lutie in Macon just before Carl was born.

19 Feb 1893 *Davenport Daily Leader*:
The Northwest Davenport Turnverein has engaged Max Von Binzer as turning instructor. Mr. Albert Petersen acts as leader of the singing section of the organization. Very favorable results are to be expected under two such capable leaders.

25 May 1893 *Davenport Tribune*: WILL CHANGE HANDS TODAY
The trustees of Griswold College will today make a lease of the Kemper hall property to J.B. Hamilton and Max Von Binzer who will conduct the school under the general supervision of the Episcopalian church. A business branch will be added, otherwise the scope of the institution will be much the same as heretofore. Instead, however of being run distinctively as a church school, by a board of trustees and no particular boss, it will be conducted as a purely business venture by Messrs Hamilton and Von Binzer, who are both teachers of experience and ability. The change is one that will undoubtedly be for the better as business methods are what talk nowadays.

29 November 1893 *Davenport Leader*: KEMPER CLOSED
THE SCHOOL HAD TO QUIT FOR WANT OF CASH
All loyal Davenporters will be sorry to learn that Kemper hall, a school of which the town has taken pride, has been closed up.
In brief, the school didn't pay expenses. Messrs Hamilton and Von Binzer leased the property at the beginning of the year and began to carry on the school as a private

Lutie Beiderbecke can be seen standing on the second deck of the Beiderbecke porch with her mother Louise leaning against a pillar on the ground-level porch and father Charles Beiderbecke standing at the front gate.

military academy. Major Von Binzer was formerly a teacher at Kemper and had done well both as a teacher and disciplinarian. Mr. Hamilton was formerly principal of the German English school in Rock Island and is a capable teacher and thorough gentleman.

These men simply started in on altogether too large a scale. No expense was spared to make the school attractive and when the bills began to come in they could not be paid. The attendance was very small, only about twenty students being in attendance and most of them being day scholars. The expenses were unusually large.

Major Von Binzer has accepted a position with the Upper Alton, Illinois, Military academy and has made arrangements whereby the boys who wish can go with him with no additional expense.

Arrangements have been made with most of the creditors to give Messrs. Hamilton and Von Binzer time to liquidate their debts.

8 December 1893 *Alton Telegraph*:

Lieut. George R. Barnett, U.S. Army, tendered his resignation as commandant at Western Military Academy. Notice has been sent to the War Department, which is expected to take early action to fill the vacancy. For the interim, Major Max von Binzer of the German Army has taken charge of the military department of the school. He is rated an able instructor in tactics and will likely be retained by the academy as assistant to whomever the War Department appoints to succeed Lieut. Barnett.

February 1897, *Ladies' Home Journal:* A PAGE AT THE BERLIN COURT

INTRODUCING AMERICANS TO AN ANCIENT AND CURIOUS GERMAN WEDDING CUSTOM

In the Ladies Home Journal, Max Von Binzer writes of his experience as a page at the Berlin Court upon the occasion of a double royal wedding and of the preceding and succeeding festivities. Describing an ancient and curious custom, he writes: "And now—after the wedding, dinner and ball—came the 'Fackeltanz.' Several of the highest officials entered the hall with flaming torches. A procession was formed, with the bride in the midst. A number of complicated polonaise figures were then executed after which the line closed about the bride and groom and marched out as escort to the bridal chambers.

"As the doors of the bridal apartments closed upon the happy pair we found ourselves immediately next to the entrance. We waited expectantly for the next feature, holding our advantageous position with some difficulty. In a few moments the doors flew open, and half a thousand silken garters, with the monograms embossed on the gold buckles, were thrown out by the ladies of honor. Court etiquette was for the nonce forgotten. Generals, courtiers, chamberlains and state ministers scrambled and fought with one another for these mementos. But we pages, rest assured, got the lion's share. I have several of these souvenirs now, although many were given away by me that night to beseeching dignitaries."

15 APRIL 1897 *Davenport Daily Republican*: MARRIED MIDST FLOWERS

Miss Lutie Beiderbecke and Max Carl Von Binzer Quietly Married

At the home of the bride's parents at 532 West Seventh street, at 5 o'clock yesterday

BRIDAL FAVORS.

An Ancient and Curious German Wedding Custom.

In The Ladies' Home Journal Max von Binzer writes of his experience as "A Page at the Berlin Court" upon the occasion of a double royal wedding and of the preceding and succeeding festivities. Describing an ancient and curious custom, he writes: "And now—after the wedding, dinner and ball—came the 'Fackeltanz.' Several of the highest officials entered the hall with flaming torches. A procession was formed, with the bride in the midst. A number of complicated polonaise figures were then executed, after which the line closed about the bride and groom and marched out as escort to the bridal chambers.

"As the doors of the bridal apartments closed upon the happy pair we found ourselves immediately next the entrance. We waited expectantly for the next feature, holding our advantageous position with some difficulty. In a few moments the doors flew open, and half a thousand silken garters, with the monograms embossed on the gold buckles, were thrown out by the ladies of honor. Court etiquette was for the nonce forgotten. Generals, courtiers, chamberlains and state ministers scrambled and fought with one another for these mementos. But we pages, rest assured, got the lion's share. I have several of these souvenirs now, although many were given away by me that night to beseeching dignitaries."

Max Von Binzer
Top: FEB 1897
Right: APRIL 18, 1918

MAJ. MAX VON BINZER DIES IN SOUTH

WAS ON WAY HOME

WELL KNOWN INSTRUCTOR AT WESTERN MILITARY ACADEMY SUCCUMBS TO BRONCHIAL ATTACK AFTER LONG ILLNESS.

Maj. Max Von Binzer, for twenty-one years a member of the faculty of the Western Military Academy and for six years military commandant of that institution, died at Birmingham, Ala., Wednesday, from bronchial troubles, after a long illness. He had been in poor health for a few years and continued to look after his duties up to last Christmas, when he found it necessary to go South. He spent the winter in the South and was so far improved that he was on his way home, expecting to resume his duties at the Western Military Academy May 1. He was taken worse on the train and was obliged to stop at Birmingham, Ala., where his death occurred.

Major Max Von Binzer was born in Switzerland in 1858, and was graduated from the Royal Military Academy in Berlin in 1878. For ten years he was an officer in the Prussian Infantry, resigning there in 1888 when he came to America to make his home. After coming to this country he became commandant at the Ohio Military Academy, leaving there in 1891 to go to Griswold College, at Davenport, where he remained until 1893. After leaving Griswold he came to Western Military Academy where he remained until 1899, holding the post as commandant. When the Bleese Academy at Macon, Mo., was opened, Major Von Binzer was placed in full charge, remaining there until 1903, when he returned to Western where he held the position of Quartermaster and Instructor of German and Spanish.

In speaking of Major Von Binzer, Major George D. Eaton of the Western Military Academy said that the school feels keenly the loss of such a faithful and loyal employee. His death will be learned with regret throughout the country by the old boys of the school, who knew and loved the well known and popular instructor.

Western Military Academy this morning had received no word as to funeral arrangements, but it is understood that Mrs. Von Binzer is on her way to Davenport, Iowa, with the body, where services and interment will take place. Major Von Binzer is survived by his wife and one son Werner Von Binzer of Cornell.

afternoon occurred the marriage of Mrs. Lutie Louisa Beiderbecke to Major Carl Von Binzer. The ceremony was preformed by Rev. Arthur M. Judy of the Unitarian church. None but the immediate relatives of the contracting parties were present. The ceremony was a simple one and was preformed in the spacious parlors of the Beiderbecke home in the midst of flowers and palms. The bride was attired in a gown of cream colored satin and carried roses. Shortly after the vows were pronounced the happy couple were driven to the C. R. I. & P. depot in Rock Island, where they boarded the 6:15 train for the south where they will spend a honeymoon of several weeks duration. The bride is the daughter of Mr. and Mrs. Charles Beiderbecke and one of Davenport's accomplished young ladies. The city has always been her home and her friends who are numbered by the score join with those present at the ceremony in extending their congratulations and hopes for the future. Mr. Von Binzer is a talented gentleman well known here from his connection with the Kemper hall several years ago, where he was military instructor. He has served with great credit in the German army, as well as in her majesty's service. At the present he is commandant at the Western Military academy at Upper Alton, Ill., where himself and bride will make their home. Among the many handsome presents received by the couple was number of valuable articles from Mr. Von Binzer's parents and relatives in Germany. Many of these gifts have been in the Von Binzer family for many generations and are doubly prized on that account. After the ceremony came a social evening at which PETERSEN'S ORCHESTRA entertained with well rendered selections of concert music.

11 June 1901 *Davenport Republican*: Commandant Max Von Binzer of the Bleese Military academy at Macon, Mo., is visiting with his family at the home of Mr. and Mrs. Chas. Beiderbecke.

6 June 1903 *Moberly Evening Democrat*: Major Max von Binzer, who is well known to a large number of our citizens by reason of having been commandant at Bleese Military Academy at Macon, and wife are mourning the loss of their little son, Carl, who died Saturday morning in the Alton hospital of cholera infantum. Shortly after their arrival in Alton on Thursday Mrs. Von Binzer and two children were taken ill and were removed to St. Joseph's hospital, where their 12–month–old son died Saturday night. The remains will be buried in Davenport, Iowa.

Daily Republican: Friends will be sorry to learn of the bereavement of Mr. and Mrs. Max Von Binzer, nee Beiderbecke. They were on their way home last week from Macon, Mo., where Major Von Binzer is commandant of the military school. At St. Louis they were stopped by the flood, but secured passage by boat to Alton. Before they were able to leave by rail their little son Carl, 14 months old was taken down with cholera infantum, and expired Saturday evening. Another of the children is very ill from the same trouble. Carl Beiderbecke, his mother and Mrs. A. J. Stibolt went to Alton on Sunday and the remains of the little one were brought home, with the older Von Binzer child, leaving the parents and other relatives with the other child too ill to be brought here. News of its improvement will be hoped for by many Davenport friends of the afflicted parents. The funeral of the deceased child will be private from the Beiderbecke home 532 West Seventh street at 10 o'clock Tuesday morning.

Cholera, a disease marked by severe vomiting and dysentery, was often fatal and epidemic. Harriet Beecher Stowe and Robert Frost both lost children to it. President James Polk contracted it in New Orleans and President Millard Fillmore's daughter died of it in 1854, the year a London physician confirmed its cause being contaminated drinking water. Improvements in water sanitation alleviated epidemics but outbreaks recurred in times of floods, particularly in low–lying neighborhoods and riverfront towns.

Baby Carl Von Binzer was buried at Oakdale on June 23, 1903. Two–year–old Fera died two weeks later, July 7, 1903. If Oma Louisa and Aunt Ottilie had not brought Werner home with them, he may also have died.

10 June 10 1913 *Alton Telegraph*: Graduation exercises of Western Military Academy occupied the forenoon of the second day of its commencement observance. Diplomas were presented and honors awarded following an address in the drill hall by Dr. Leon Harrison of St. Louis. F.W. [Werner] von Binzer of Alton, one of 30 cadets, was recipient of a medal award of highest in scholarship. John B. Heagler received a silver cup as the academy's best all–round athlete.

In 1918, the Von Binzer family resided at 2732 Bostwick Street in Alton, Illinois

18 April 1918 *Alton Telegraph*: MAJ. MAX VON BINZER DIES IN SOUTH WAS ON WAY HOME WELL KNOWN INSTRUCTOR AT WESTERN MILITARY ACADEMY SUCCUMBS TO BRONCHIAL ATTACK AFTER LONG ILLNESS

Maj. Max Von Binzer, for twenty–one years a member of the faculty of the Western Military Academy and for six years military commandant of the institution, died in Birmingham, Ala., Wednesday from bronchial troubles after a long illness. He had been in poor health for a few years and continued to look after his duties up to last Christmas when he found it necessary to go South. He spent the winter in the South and was so far improved that he was on his way home, expecting to resume his duties at Western Military Academy May 1. He was taken worse on the train and was obliged to stop at Birmingham, Ala., where his death occurred.

Major Max Von Binzer was born in Switzerland in 1858, and was graduated from the Royal Military Academy in Berlin in 1878. For ten years he was an officer in the Prussian Infantry, resigning there in 1888 when he came to America to make his home.

After coming to this country he became commandant at the Ohio Military Academy, leaving there in 1891 to go to Griswold College [Kemper Hall] where he remained until 1893. After leaving Griswold he came to Western Military Academy where he remained until 1899, holding the post as commandant. When the Bleese Academy at Macon, Mo., was opened, Major Von Binzer was placed in full charge, remaining there until 1903, when he returned to Western where he held the position of Quartermaster and Instructor of German and Spanish.

In speaking of Major Von Binzer, Major George D. Eaton of the Western Military

Academy said that the school feels keenly the loss of such a faithful and loyal employee. His death will be learned with regret throughout the country by the old boys of the school, who knew and loved the well known and popular instructor.

Western Military Academy this morning had received no word as to funeral arrangements, but it is understood that Mrs. Von Binzer is on her way to Davenport, Iowa, with the body, where services and interment will take place. Major Von Binzer is survived by his wife and one son, Werner Von Binzer of Cornell.

18 April 1918 *Davenport Democrat–Leader*: Word has been received here of the death of Major Max Von Binzer of Alton, Ill., who passed away yesterday at 3 o'clock in the south, where he had been spending the winter for his health. He is survived by his wife, formerly Miss Lutie Beiderbecke of this city, and one son, Werner, who is a student at Cornell University. Major Von Binzer was connected with the military academy of Alton, Ill. The funeral, which will be private, will be held Saturday afternoon at 3:30 o'clock from the home of Mrs. Von. Binzer's mother, Mrs. Louise Beiderbecke, 532 West Seventh street. Interment will be made in Oakdale cemetery.

21 April 1918: Funeral services for Major M. Von Binzer, who passed away at Birmingham, Ala., Wednesday afternoon, were held Saturday afternoon at 2:30 o'clock from the home of his mother–in–law, Mrs. Louise Beiderbecke, 506 West Seventh street. Reader F. L. Ray officiated, Mrs. A. P. Griggs sang a beautiful hymn. The remains were laid to rest in Oakdale cemetery. Those who acted as pallbearers were Louis Hanssen, J. H. Hass, Leon Hass, C. E. Hanssen, Walter Kruse, and Gustav Hasse.

WESTERN MILITARY ACADEMY (1879–1971)

In addition to Werner Von Binzer graduating from Western Military Academy in Alton, IL, notable alumni include B–29 pilot Paul Tibbetts, Class of '33, who flew the infamous Enola Gay that dropped the atom bomb on Hiroshima; and Medal of Honor WWII fighter pilot Butch O'Hare, Class of '32, for whom Chicago's O'Hare International Airport is named. His father, Edward J. O'Hare worked for Chicago gangster Al Capone and was gunned down by Capone's men after providing the evidence that convicted him. While Werner's father was still on the WMA faculty, Charles Ellsworth Russell attended the school but was expelled after thirteen months. Russell had trained on piano, drums and violin but became fascinated with the clarinet after hearing jazz musician Yellow Nunez play at an Elks Club dance when Russell went there with his dad. At age fifteen, Russell was hired by Herbert Berger for his Coronado Hotel Orchestra. It was Berger who gave Russell his nickname: *Pee Wee*.

22 December 1922 *Alton Telegraph*: MRS. VON BINZER BEING HONORED BY FRIENDS
Many small and informal social events are being given this week in honor of Mrs. Max Von Binzer, who is the guest of Mrs. George D. Eaton of the Western Military Academy. Mrs. Von Binzer is visiting in Alton, enroute from her former home in Davenport, Iowa, to Los Angeles, Calif., where she will live with her son, Werner Von Binzer. Mrs. Von Binzer will depart for the West on Tuesday. Werner Von Binzer is

with Max Fischer's orchestra at Los Angeles. The orchestra is said to be one of the very best on the Pacific Coast....

10 January 1926 *Davenport Democrat–Leader:*

VON BINZER–BARMAN WEDDING LOS ANGELES The marriage is announced of Miss Alma Barman, daughter of Mr. and Mrs. Barman, of Los Angeles, and Werner Von Binzer of Los Angeles, son of the later Major Max Von Binzer and Mrs. Von Binzer, formerly of this city. The wedding was Dec. 27, in Los Angeles at the All Saints Episcopal church. The Rev. J. A. Evans, the rector officiated. The couple spent the honeymoon at Del Monte, Cal. and will reside in Los Angeles. Mr. Von Binzer's father, the late Major Von Binzer, was for a time military instructor at Kemper Hall, Griswold college of this city.

21 September 1928 *Davenport Democrat–Leader:* MRS. VON BINZER OF LOS ANGELES HERE ON BRIEF VISIT WITH HER SISTER Mrs. Ottilie Stibolt of 323 East Seventh street has as her guest for an autumn visit, her sister, Mrs. M. von Binzer of Los Angeles, Calif., who will be remembered here by many old friends as Miss Lutie Beiderbecke. Mrs. von Binzer is the sister of Charles T., and B.H. Beiderbecke of this city. She was prominent in musical circles and socially when her home was here, and was a member of the Music Students and other clubs until her removal to the west. She plans to spend the month of October in Davenport and already there have been a number of informal affairs in her honor among Tri–City relatives and friends.

W. VON BINZER
ST. FRANCIS HOTEL ORCHESTRA
SAN FRANCISCO, CAL.

BEIDERBECKE GHOSTS

Of all that has been written about the Beiderbecke family, no stories are as bizarre or as heartbreaking as what is to follow. Some who have privately and reluctantly testified to what they have seen have refused to be identified publicly. Others have spoken out.

True or false? Judge for yourself.

The year was 1860. The nation was in the throes of the great Civil War. In Davenport that year, Charles Beiderbecke married Louise Piper. Charles, anglicized from his given name of Carl, was senior partner of Beiderbecke–Mueller Wholesale Groceries. By war's end in 1865, they had three children, with another on the way in December. But their happiness was to be short–lived.

Louise's father, August Pieper, had enlisted in the 37th Regiment of Iowa Volunteer Infantry and served from 1862–1865. Iowa's 37th Volunteer Infantry was known as the *Graybeard Regiment* because its members were 45 and older. Exempt from military duty because of his age, 49–year–old August Pieper chose to serve by guarding prisoners and military garrisons so younger soldiers could be on the frontlines.

According to Jean Seehof, wife of Pieper's great–great grandson Tom Seehof, in an interview with Phil Evans for *Bix: The Leon Bix Beiderbecke Story* (1998) when August returned to Davenport he brought smallpox with him and as a result, all three children contracted the disease and died.

"A neighbor came to the home, said he knew they had dead children, and offered to bury them in the backyard, which he did," Mrs. Seehof said, adding the neighbor then died of smallpox as well.

Evidently backyard burials were common practice back then. Burying victims quickly, often in mass graves, was deemed one way to halt the spread of deadly disease.

Julie Craighead, fellow Bix researcher, questioned in which backyard the Beiderbecke children might have been buried. So we did some research at the Davenport Public Library. Charles and Louise Beiderbecke lived at three residences after their wedding before building their showplace at 532 W. Seventh St, now the Beiderbecke Inn.

The first Beiderbecke home, located next to the fire station on Scott Street, had long ago been demolished; but the other two houses are still in place and no more than two blocks apart from each other. Both are large, two-story structures with ample backyards that slope down to a dirt alley. As we walked about the neighborhood, we wondered if the bones of the three Beiderbecke children lay buried nearby.

Weeks later, in conversation with a friend, I learned that folks living in one of the former Beiderbecke houses, unaware of the story of the buried children, had said that on numerous occasions they had witnessed what they took to be ghosts of young children in the house. They were said to be considering asking a priest to conduct the rites of exorcism in hope of getting the specters to leave. Stories of Beiderbecke ghosts don't end there.

Lutie Beiderbecke, the last of seven children born to Charles and Louise and sister to the three who were said to be buried in a backyard, moved with her husband Maj. Max von Binzer to Missouri. They later got a house in Alton, Illinois, across the river from the military academy where Maj. Max von Binzer taught. Lutie and Max had three children: Werner, Friedel and Carl. In 1901, while visiting his daughter Lutie, Charles died in her arms. Two years later two-year-old Friedel and one-year-old Carl died of cholera.

While talking with some Missouri folks attending the Bix festival, Julie Craighead asked if they ever journeyed over to Alton, Illinois. They replied that on occasion they would make the drive. Having obtained the von Binzer family's Alton home address, Julie asked if they would check to see if the house was still there. She later received word that the original house is, indeed, still standing.

The current owner's family had bought the house 40 years earlier and he grew up there. He married and was raising his own two children in the home. Julie could hardly believe her ears when her Missouri contact told her that the owner claimed his children had reported seeing strange things neither he nor his wife had seen.

Both children, on separate occasions, told of having seen a large dog in one of the rooms, and neither knew the other had seen it. Both reportedly were frightened to go into that room. They also claimed to have seen a telephone where no phone hung on the kitchen wall. Even stranger, the owner's wife said she has seen what she believed were the ghosts of an older man, a younger man, and a small child.

The city of Alton is well known for its ghosts and offers annual tours for the brave of heart. Perhaps for the Alton branch of Beiderbecke ghosts there's comfort in numbers in that specter world.

GENEALOGY: AUGUST PIEPER

AUGUST PIEPER
Born 12 Aug 1813 in Hamburg, Germany; died 16 Dec 1895 in Stockton, Iowa.
Parents: John Peter Pieper and Catarina Maria Dorothea Sass.
Married CAROLINE HELLMERS PIEPER, daughter of ELISABETH, 1836 in Hamburg, Germany. LOUISA, their only surviving child born in Germany emigrated with August and Caroline from Hamburg to New York, August 11, 1853, aboard the vessel *George Canning*. Their fifth child, ADOLPH PIEPER, was born 1855 in Davenport. Caroline died in 1856, before Louisa married, and before August enlisted during U.S. Civil War. August then married EIBE WOHLENBURG VOLLMER, daughter of Peter and Eibe Leiderman Wohlenburg 05 Nov 1878 in Davenport, Iowa. She died 25 Apr 1916 in Germany.

1856 Scott County Census: August, age 43, carpenter; Caroline, age 41, Louisa, age 17
1860 Directory: Billiard Maker, Phoenix Co, Billiard's & Chess Room, Brady & Ninth.
1860 Census: Davenport Household #1065 Piper, August, age 48, Adolph, age 4, Augusta Drunkhort, age 30
1861 Davenport Directory: Gaines between Front & 2nd St.
Field and Staff of the 37th Iowa Volunteer Infantry Company K: Piper, August, Age 49; Enlisted/Mustered: 11 Oct 1862; Promoted Eighth Corporal, 10 Nov 1864; Seventh Corporal, 03 Dec 1864; Mustered out 24 May 1865, Davenport, Iowa.
1866 City Directory: Boarding with E. Lemme
1870 Census: Living with Charles and Louisa, listed as John [middle name perhaps; age matches 1813 birth date]
1870–1871 City Directory: Clerk, residing at Scott South East, first house on Fourth
1875: partnered with fellow Davenport store clerk Louis Bennewitz in Stockton, Iowa; Bennewitz moved to Walcott, Iowa, in 1876
1880 Census: Stockton, Muscatine, Iowa, Merchant Dry Goods Grocer; wife Eibe Vollmer, age 42, clerk in store
1885 Census/ Lot 5, Block 9 A: Piper, August, age 71, County Store Keeper; Eibe, age 46, keeping house
Soldiers Living in Iowa 1885: Piper, August, Private, Company B. Stockton, Iowa. 37th Inf. K, Rank Corporal, Enlisted 11, Oct. 1862. Discharged May 25, 1865, Davenport, Iowa

Portrait and Biographical Album 1889
Biographies for Muscatine County Iowa Page 192

AUGUST PIPER, dealer in general merchandise in Fulton, Iowa, is a native of Hamburg, Germany, born Aug. 12, 1813, and is a son of John Peter and Catherine Dorothea Sass Piper. His father was a native of Germany, and died in that country in 1833, at the age of fifty–three years, while his mother, who was also born in that country, departed this life in 1835, at the age of fifty–six years. One son died the previous year. They had but one child that grew to manhood, August, of this sketch. In 1853 he left his native country, embarking on a sailing vessel from Hamburg, and after a long and tedious voyage of sixty–seven days landed at New York. He then went to Philadelphia, Pa., where he remained two months, when he went to Nauvoo, Ill., working in that town for two years at the carpenter's trade, which he had previously learned in the old country. From Nauvoo he continued his journey until reaching Davenport, Iowa, where he made his home for seventeen years, working for a time at his trade, but later clerking in different stores where a salesman who could speak the German language was needed. Having in that way gained the experience in mercantile business, he came to Fulton, Jan. 1, 1872, and opened a store of general merchandise, in which he was quite successful, building up an extensive and lucrative trade. His stock consists of groceries, dry–goods, boots and shoes, crockery, china, glassware, hardware, oils and hats.

In 1836 Mr. Piper was united in marriage with Miss Caroline Hellmers, and by their union five children were born, three of whom are deceased. Those living are: Louisa, wife of Charles Beiderbecke, a baker [banker] residing in Davenport, and Adolph, who is at present in Davenport, Iowa. In 1856 Mr. Piper was called upon to mourn the loss of his wife, who in that year was called to her final home. He was again married in 1878, becoming the husband of Mrs. Aibe Volmer, a daughter of Peter and Ebe Leiderman Volenburg, who were the parents of eight children, five of whom are yet living: John, Gaser, Margaret, Anna and Mrs. Piper.

Like so many of his countrymen, our subject responded to the country's call for troops to put down the Rebellion, and enlisted in 1862, serving until the close of hostilities. He was assigned to Company K, of the 37th Iowa Infantry, and during most of his term did garrison duty. In his political sentiments he is a supporter of the Republican party, and religiously, is a member of the Lutheran Church. He was appointed Postmaster by President Hayes in 1879.

Stockton, Iowa at one time was called Fulton. It is now Fulton Township, Stockton, Iowa.

1884–1885 *Iowa Gazette and Business Directory: Stockton, village called Fulton on the railway time cards, is on the C.R.I. & P. railway in Fulton Township, Muscatine county, 160 miles southeast of Des Moines, 18 miles northeast of Muscatine, the county seat, and 9 miles east of Wilton Junction, the nearest banking point. Settled in 1856, it ships grain, live stock and produce. Population 200. Telephone connection. Express U. S. Mail daily. August Pieper is postmaster. August is also owner of the General Store.*

Davenport Daily Times 18 Dec 1895:
Word was received in the city yesterday afternoon announcing the death of August Pieper, a well known former Scott county resident, which occurred at his home in Stockton Monday evening. The deceased was born in Hamburg in 1813 and before leaving the Fatherland, he joined the Icarian* community which settled near Nauvoo, Ill., but a couple of years later he left the settlement because of some dissensions and after a short stay at St. Charles, Mo., he came to Davenport in company with his wife.

While here he was connected with the Washburne hardware store for a time and later with the Beiderbecke–Miller establishment. Mr. Pieper was one of the founders of the Davenport Maennorchor and an active member of the Turner Society.

During the civil war Mr. Pieper enlisted in the "gray beard" regiment but never saw active service as they were not sent to the front on account of the advanced years of some of its members.

For several years past he has resided in Stockton where his death occurred. In 1858 his first wife died but he remarried and the present Mrs. Pieper survives him with two children, Mrs. Charles (Louise) Beiderbecke of this city and a son, Adolph Pieper. The remains will be brought to Davenport for incineration in accordance with the expressed wish of the deceased, and the funeral will take place from the B.C.R. & N. depot Thursday morning going directly to the crematorium.

* ICARIANS were followers of French philosopher Etienne Cabet's utopian society as he described in his book, *Voyage en Icarie*. Their goal was to eliminate social classes and poverty by providing for basic needs with the belief that if everyone contributed the same and removed the same there would be equality for all. Cabet and his followers fled France due to political pressures of the day. The Icarians settled first in Texas and in 1849 moved to Nauvoo, IL, which had been abandoned by the Mormons. They built homes, shops, stores, and a school made from the stones of the Mormon Temple. A later dispute among the colonists forced Cabet and those loyal to him to relocate to St. Louis. The rest stayed in Nauvoo until 1860. A vineyard begun in 1857 grew to eventually encompass 500–600 acres. Nauvoo became famous for its wines; even prohibition did not slow down production or decrease its popularity.

Obituary: The death of August Pieper at Stockton Monday evening removed a Scott county resident of ripe years and rich experience—a valuable man in any community at which his lot was cast. As may not have been generally known, Mr. Pieper came to America as one of the original members of the Icarian community that settled, in 1853 near Nauvoo, Ill. He was born in Hamburg in 1813, and was married in the Fatherland. In 1855, when dissentions broke out among the Icarians* he left the colony, and after a short visit at St. Charles, Mo., came to Davenport with his wife. Here he clerked in the Washburne hardware store for a time and later was

former home & store of AUGUST PIEPER in Stocton, IA
hospital where LOUISE BEIDERBECKE's brother ADOLPH lived

ST. JOHN'S INSANE BUILDING FOR MEN, MERCY HOSPITAL — DAVENPORT.

connected in a clerical capacity with the Beiderbecke–Miller wholesale house. He was one of the founders of the Davenport Maennorchor and an active member of the Turner society.

At the outbreak of the Civil War Mr. Pieper enlisted as a member of the "graybeards" regiment that, while it was never sent to the front on account of the advanced age of most of its members, did valuable service within the continues of the state. Since then he moved to Stockton, where he bought a store that he run successfully, and where he founded a library that was generally used throughout that neighborhood, and also held the office of postmaster. His first wife, died in 1858, and in 1887 Mr. Pieper was again married to Mrs. Eibe Wohlenburg. The wife survives, and a daughter Mrs. Charles Beiderbecke of Davenport and Adolph Pieper. The remains will be brought to Davenport for incineration, in accordance with the desire of the deceased, and the funeral cortege will leave the B. C. R. & N. depot at 10:30 a.m. Thursday for the crematorium.

Cremation: 16 Dec 1895 Hill & Fredericks Davenport, Iowa
Will #2052, Muscatine County, Iowa: Witness to signing of will T. F. Broders & J.H. Broders. He gave all his estate to his wife Eibe for her life time, and then it was to be divided equally among his children. Notice of Administration, Notice is hereby given on February 15, 1896, that Eibe Pieper, wife is administrator. Papers were dated February 17, 1896, by Heinz & Fisher Lawyers, 226 and 228 West Third St. Davenport, Iowa. Heirs: Eibe Pieper, wife, living in Stockton, Iowa, age 59, Louise Beiderbecke, Davenport, Iowa age 57, Adolph Pieper, Davenport, Iowa, age 47. Legal description of real Estate: Lot 6 & west 22 feet of lot in block 3, Stockton, Iowa, formerly Fulton, Muscatine, Iowa. Household goods were exempt. General Assets: 1. one half of a mortgage, John E. Como for $1250; 2. one half of mortgage, John Ott for $2,000; 3. one half of mortgage C. Kimball for $400. The will was closed May 5, 1897. Charles Beiderbecke had to see a Notary and swear that August Pieper, late of Fulton Township, Muscatine County, Iowa departed this life at said township on the 16th day of December 1895 and said deceased was born in City of Hamburg, Germany, on or before August 12, 1813. This was done on December 20, 1895.

Eibe took August's ashes back to Germany and stayed; she died April 25, 1916. After Louise's death in 1922, her children—Carl T, Bismark, Ottilie and Lutie—got the money.

ADOLPH PIPER (PIEPER), b. 1855 in Davenport, Iowa
1860 Census: House on Gaines bet. Front & 2nd St; Living with his father August and Augusta Drunkhort, age 30, born in Hamburg.
1870 Census: Living with W. J. Speer family; Speer, retailer; Adolph, age 14, store clerk
1870 City Directory (03 Aug): Clerk in store, Fulton, Muscatine County

1876: Student at Brown's Business School
1877 City Directory: Living with Charles and Louise, clerk at the store.
1885 Census: living in hotel—Stockton, Iowa.
1894–1937: Inmate, Davenport Mercy Hospital, Insane Department
Died: 18 Jul 1937 Burial: 28 Jul 1937 Oakdale Cemetery

Charles Beiderbecke and his brother-in-law Adolph Pieper

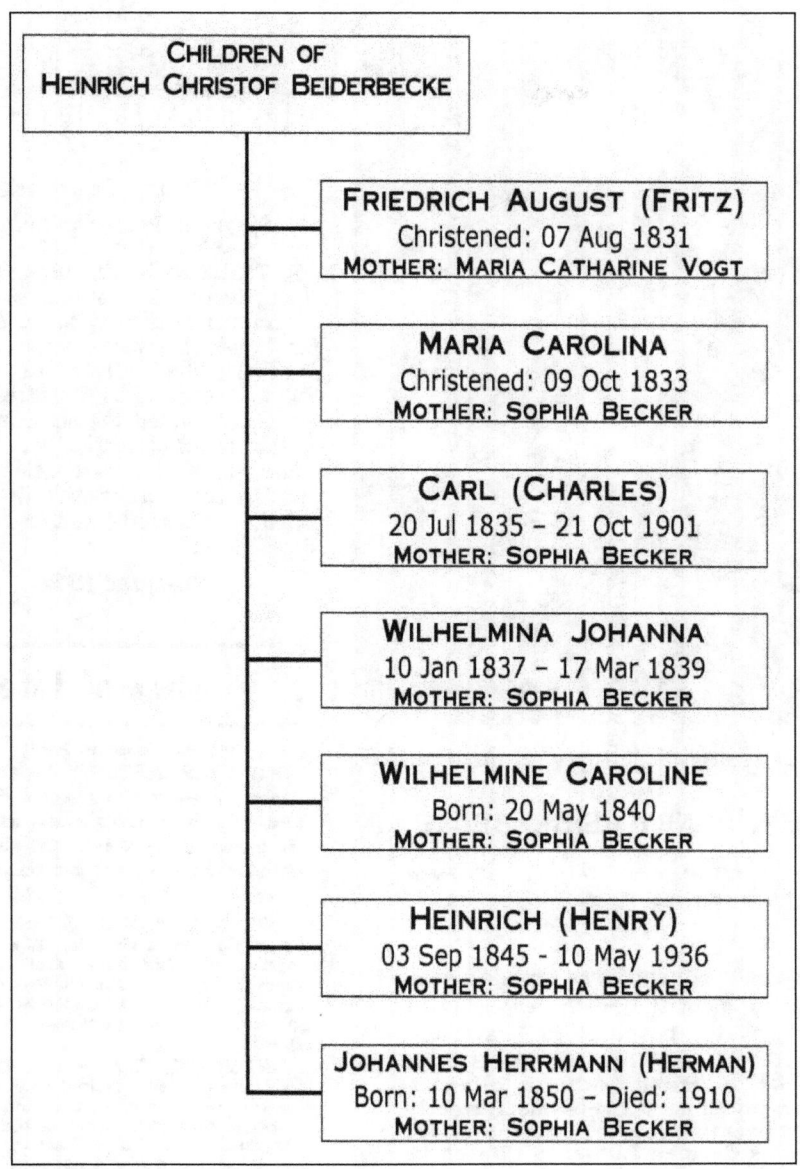

HEINRICH 'HENRY' BEIDERBECKE Jr. married MARGARITA HAHN 06 Jul 1875 in Germany. Children: EMMA MARQUERITA 1876–1970; FRED 1877–1965; HENRY JR. 1879–1924; HUGO 1880–1883; MARQUERITA 'GITA' 1882–1933; MAGDALENE 1883–1906; SOPHIA 1886–1982

EMMA MARQUERITA BRAREN, born in Otjozondjupa, Africa; died in Florida.
Children: MARQUERITA 'GITA' BRAREN LOWE, sons: GEORGE LOWE, JAMES LOWE, and JOHN LOWE; WALTER BRAREN, sons: WALTER and RALPH; GEORGE BRAREN; HERBERT BRAREN, son: VICTOR; RALPH BRAREN, b. 1897, sons: HOWARD, WARREN, KENNETH

Pastor Heinrich 'Henry' Beiderbecke

MARKS 60 YEARS IN CLERGY.

The Rev. Henry Beiderbecke, 86, Speaks in Paterson Church.

PATERSON, N. J., Aug. 16.—The Rev. Henry Beiderbecke, 86 years old, former missionary in Africa and for twenty-five years pastor of St. John's German Lutheran Church at Fulton Avenue and 169th Street, the Bronx, celebrated the sixtieth anniversary of his ordination here today. Special services were held at St. and Mr. Beiderbecke spoke from the pulpit. Mr. Beiderbecke lives in Glen Rock.

August 1936

REV. HENRY BEIDERBECKE

Retired Lutheran Minister Served 25 Years as Pastor in Bronx.

Announcement was made here last night of the death yesterday in a private hospital in Paterson, N. J., of the Rev. Henry Beiderbecke, a retired Lutheran minister and missionary, who was formerly for twenty-five years pastor of St. John's German Lutheran Church in the Bronx. He was 90 years old.

A native of Germany, Mr. Beiderbecke was ordained there in 1871. He spent ten years in Africa as a missionary and then came to the United States.

May 11, 1936

Flashes of Life

(By the Associated Press)

WOLVERHAMPTON, England — Troop Sergeant-Major John Stratford, 102, is Britain's oldest soldier. He joined 85 years ago. On his last birthday the king sent him congratulations.

OCEAN CITY, N. J.—John N. Rigby of Cornwells Heights, 72, a paymaster, who has been shot seven times by robbers, has cheated death again. Caught in an undertow when in swimming, he was rescued by surf guards.

PATERSON, N. J. — Rev. Henry Beiderbecke, 86, retired Lutheran clergyman, returned to the pulpit for a special service in honor of the 60th anniversary of his ordination. He has preached in four languages, German, Dutch, English and African dialect. He formerly was a missionary. He still writes for religious magazines.

August 17, 1931

Pastor Henry

The same year Bix died his granduncle Henry Beiderbecke retired from the New Jersey church where he had served as a Lutheran minister. Rev. Beiderbecke and his wife worked as missionaries in Africa for a decade and then moved to New York. After Henry's wife died, he lived with his son Fred, daughter–in–law Catherine and three grandchildren while writing a memoir of his missionary work. At the time of the book's publication, Henry's son Fred worked as a musician at a bowling alley. Fred had previously co–partnered a theater production company in the early 1900s but it went bankrupt.

Excerpts from
Among the Hereros in Africa:
The Experiences of H. Beiderbecke, Lutheran Minister.
Dedicated to the memory of his devoted wife and faithful helpmate
Margarita Beiderbecke, née Hahn
Born July 6, 1850 in Rehoboth, Nama–land, Africa
Died November 6, 1906, in New York City.

FOREWORD

Old people live in the past. I like to think of the labors of my first years as a missionary. And it was a great pleasure to me to utilize my leisure–hours by recording my experiences of that time.

These reminiscences refer particularly to the first years of my activity in Africa. To me, they are the most delightful, and I am sure, that to the friends of missions they will be the most interesting.

My purpose, however, is not only to entertain but to give a vivid portrayal of the joys and sorrows of a missionary, and to awaken and deepen the interest in behalf of those who still sit in darkness and in the shadow of death.

H. BEIDERBECKE

Glen Rock, N.J. January 6th, 1922

It was in the fall of 1871 that I bade farewell to my dear relatives and my beloved native country, Germany, to set out upon my journey to South–West–Africa, where I was to labor among the black Hereros as a missionary of the Rhenish Mission Society. Two brides of Herero–Missionaries and a young Christian merchant accompanied me.

We first proceeded to England by way of Holland. We remained in London a short time and then, at Southampton, embarked on an English ship for Cape Town.

...

At this time, there lived at Otjimbingue, Missionary Hugo Hahn, who is known not only as the pioneer of the Herero–Mission, but also as an explorer, and discoverer of the Herero–language. When he arrived in Africa in 1844, he did not understand the Hereros neither did they understand him. There were no books written in their language. There was nothing left for missionary Hahn to do, but to make note of as many of the words as possible that he heard, and to indicate their probable meaning. It was very difficult to determine the grammatical rules, according to which the words were changed and formed into sentences.

My first task was to learn this language. After having given 10 months of study to it, I preached my first sermon in it, not however, without much fear and trembling. Up to this time, I only had employed the Dutch language.

...

I was at the station only a short time, when I ventured to go out, after it had become dark. I met a Herero*....He stepped right close up to me, and when he recognized me, he grinned and said: "Ngu morro, ngu morro." I thought to myself: What does he want? and was glad when he moved on. The next morning I asked missionary Hahn the meaning of the words "ngu morro." He said with a smile: "That is not Herero; that is German." "German!" said I. "Yes," he continued, "it is the German for Good Morning." "But how strange," said I, "to use such an expression. Why it was a pitchdark night." That can very easily be explained. Formerly, the Hereros had no form of greeting. One day, they heard how we greeted one another by saying: Good Morning and since that time, they have adopted these words "ngu morro" as their universal salutation.

*Rev. Beiderbecke explained that the English called them Damru and that they are not related to tribes of Sudan, as is the case with African Americans but rather to the Bantu tribe.

Missionary Dr. Hugo Hahn.

Mrs. Margarita Beiderbecke, née Hahn.

Henry Beiderbecke's book about his missionary work in Africa; his father-in-law and wife.

Every two months a messenger brought me my mail and papers. It took my wagon 3 weeks to make the journey to Walfish Bay to call for the provisions that were delivered there from Cape Town. There was only one delivery a year.

I was indeed extremely happy when two years a faithful helpmate and co–worker in the person of the daughter of Missionary Hahn....

...One morning, we were shocked to see a snake lying next to our young daughter in her bed. The child was only a few weeks old. The night was cold, and the snake crept there in search of a warm place. I killed a large number of these reptiles. Time and again, I saw how they charmed small birds by their gaze, causing them to jump into their fangs to be devoured. Spitting–snakes, which eject their venom into one's eyes, and boa–constrictors, which crush their prey, also abound.

...

The religion of the heathen Hereros is ancestor–worship. They have no real idols. But each priest has a bundle of sticks in his home, and each stick represents an ancestor. The priest takes two of these ancestors i.e. sticks and rubs them against each other, till the friction produces fire. In this manner, they have again received fire from their ancestors. In case of marriage or removal, each member of the tribe receives a fire–brand from the sacred fire–place and with this he ignites the fire in his new settlement.

In this manner, every evening, each tribe surrounds the fire, which was received from the ancestors. In case the whole tribe changes its place of residence, the fire is born by the vestal...

...Makuani was the guardian of the sacred fire. Soon after the opening of the school, I examined the children concerning my sermon, of the previous Sunday for they attended services regularly. Finally, I said to them: "Children, at the conclusion of my sermon, you heard a word which was strange to you. I refer to the word: Amen. What does that mean?" Makuani raised her hand and said: "I think Amen means: Enough has been said, and it is time to go home!"

...

Missionary Hahn's name had become known in scientific circles as a result of his linguistic studies, and his ethnographical observations and researches...In 1859, he returned to Germany for the purpose of supervising the printing of his translations and the publishing of his grammar and dictionary of the Herero–language. In recognition of his labors, the University of Leipsic honored him with the doctor–title.

DER DEMOKRAT

Jens Peter Stibolt, father–in–law of Ottilie Beiderbecke Stibolt and editor of *Der Demokrat*, 1862–1887, shared his strong opposition to Iowa's Temperance movement regularly in his newspaper columns. The following excerpt is translated from its original German text for coverage of the June 1883 Davenport Schuetzenfest:

> ...Sunday morning bright and early the marksmen assembled in the Turner Hall, headed from there toward the house of last year's king, Mr. Alfred Steffen, picked him up and marched with music back past the Turner Hall, where the Turners joined them following the program's established route to the corner of 3rd and Fillmore Street from which they took streetcars to the Schuetzen Park. There the arrivals, many of whom had already had a good bit to drink, were welcomed by the President of the Schuetzen Society, Mr. John C. Boehl, with the following words: ...A little over a year ago, as we gathered here to enjoy our annual King Celebration, there was a major stumbling block on the minds of all free–thinking citizens of this land. With an insolent hand they tried to attack that inalienable right of every person to individual liberty; yes, it went so far that on the 27th of June it was successfully achieved to threaten us with a ban on holding all Sunday celebrations here. Thank God a provisional stop to the irrational machinations of these fanatics was accomplished through the common sense of the people....

In an 1872 editorial, Stibolt took on the Temperance movement in a column he headlined: *Something is wrong here, for it's not Christianity*.

> ...What they call the Christian religion are rules partly taken from Jewish and Islamic sources, and the teachings of the New Testament, which should be the source of all Christianity, they throw away....The "Christian" religion around here, that is the "American Christian religion," reveals itself and expresses itself in sanctifying the sabbath, prayer and temperance agitation....
>
> Paul explicitly stated: "Therefore do not let anyone judge you with respect to food or drink, or in the matter of a feast, new moon, or Sabbath days; these are only the shadow of the things to come... but you should confirm Christian freedom." Thus, here the apostle Paul equates the ban on eating pork and the command to sanctify

the sabbath and repeals both of them. The Christian church in Europe, both before and after the Reformation, recognized no sabbath and no sabbath service until an English sect introduced them, principally because of the secular interests and the imperiousness of the clergy and because of "Christian propaganda."

...Wine was first valued as a gift from the divinity. According to the New Testament Christ participated in many happy drinking parties and at Canaan's wedding, at the end of a jolly bout when all the guests were drunk, he turned water into the famous wine and treated the guests. ...America's pious have lifted the ban on wine from the Koran and enacted it as a church rule. They have thereby taken on a teaching in view of the fact that they must declare that Jesus and the apostles were all drinkers.

...People still want something to take away their cares. ... Mohammedans seem to have given into the enjoyment of opiates.... many church conventions of Presbyterians, Methodists, etc. that have sworn off wine but at the same time refused to declare the enjoyment of opium as sinful...we should cite the words of the Christian authors, which states: "I give you a new law, that you should love one another."

American Christians seem to know little about this Christian law, for their church and their pious people persecute with hate and meanness all who do not subscribe and live according to the just–mentioned Jewish and Islamic teachings. Yes, they consider it Christian to join up with loafers, rogues, and riffraff (see the new temperance law)...That's how American Christianity looks under the spotlight.

As far back as 1869, Editor Stibolt railed against those who would do away with the separation of church and state:

Iowa's Puritans are once again doing their favorite work. They'd like to establish a state church or church state with the 'Lord Almighty,' who suffers no other gods, and with a Christ Almighty, who curses all who displease him, at the head.

On the twelfth of this month our Senator Harlan put before the Congress a petition with the following contents:

"That the introduction of the U.S. Constitution should be changed so that 'God Almighty' is the source of all force and power of the civil government and that Jesus Christ is the sovereign of mankind and his revealed word is recognized as the highest authority in all things."

What such a modification of the U.S. Constitution would signify is evident to everybody. It would exclude from their civil rights all Jews and 'infidels' and all educated Europeans. It would exclude them and all Americans free of religion from serving in government, leaving it in the hands of a Puritanical and hypocritical autocracy. We don't fear that this petition submitted by Mr. Harlan will have a fate any different from that of similar petitions that, since a number of years, have annually been presented to the Congress and then silently thrown into the junk room....

It's odd that the Des Moines Standard and other prohibitionist papers from our state support the above–mentioned petition. For wasn't it in the Bible the Lord Almighty himself who gave Noah the grapevine, and the Lord Christ who changed the insipid water into strong wine for the thirsty and faithful guests in Canaan? Wasn't it also Paul, who suggested gallons of wine to his son Timothy to strengthen his stomach?

SUNDAY LAWS: November 8, 1859—special ordinance passed by the city council of Davenport that the city marshal be hereby ordered to prevent the unlawful assemblage on the Sabbath day at dance houses, beer houses, grog shops and drinking saloons, etc.

Davenport Gazette Nov 15, 1859
SUNDAY LAWS MEETING—the meeting of the German citizens on Sunday evening to which we alluded yesterday was attended by at least two hundred persons. Mr. H. Ramming was Chairman, and Mr. Cha. Kaufman, Secretary. The following report of the committee appointed at the meeting held on Sunday evening previous was read as per motion by Mr. Charles Asmussen in German and English, and unanimously adopted:
1. WHEREAS, The City Council of the city of Davenport, on the 2d day of November instructed the City Marshal to enforce Sec. 22, 23, and 24, of Chapter 41 of the revised ordinances of the city of Davenport, commonly called the "Sunday Ordinance;" and
2d. WHEREAS, We, as citizens of this glorious Union, have certain absolute rights granted to each of us by the Constitution of these United States and the Constitution and laws of the State of Iowa, among which rights are, to–wit:
1. That we may peaceably assemble; an absolute right, of which we are deprived by said ordinance on each first day of the week.
2. That no person shall be taken or imprisoned or deprived of his life,

DAVENPORT DAILY GAZETTE.

VOL. VI.   DAVENPORT, IOWA, TUESDAY MORNING, NOVEMBER 15, 1859.   NO. 26.

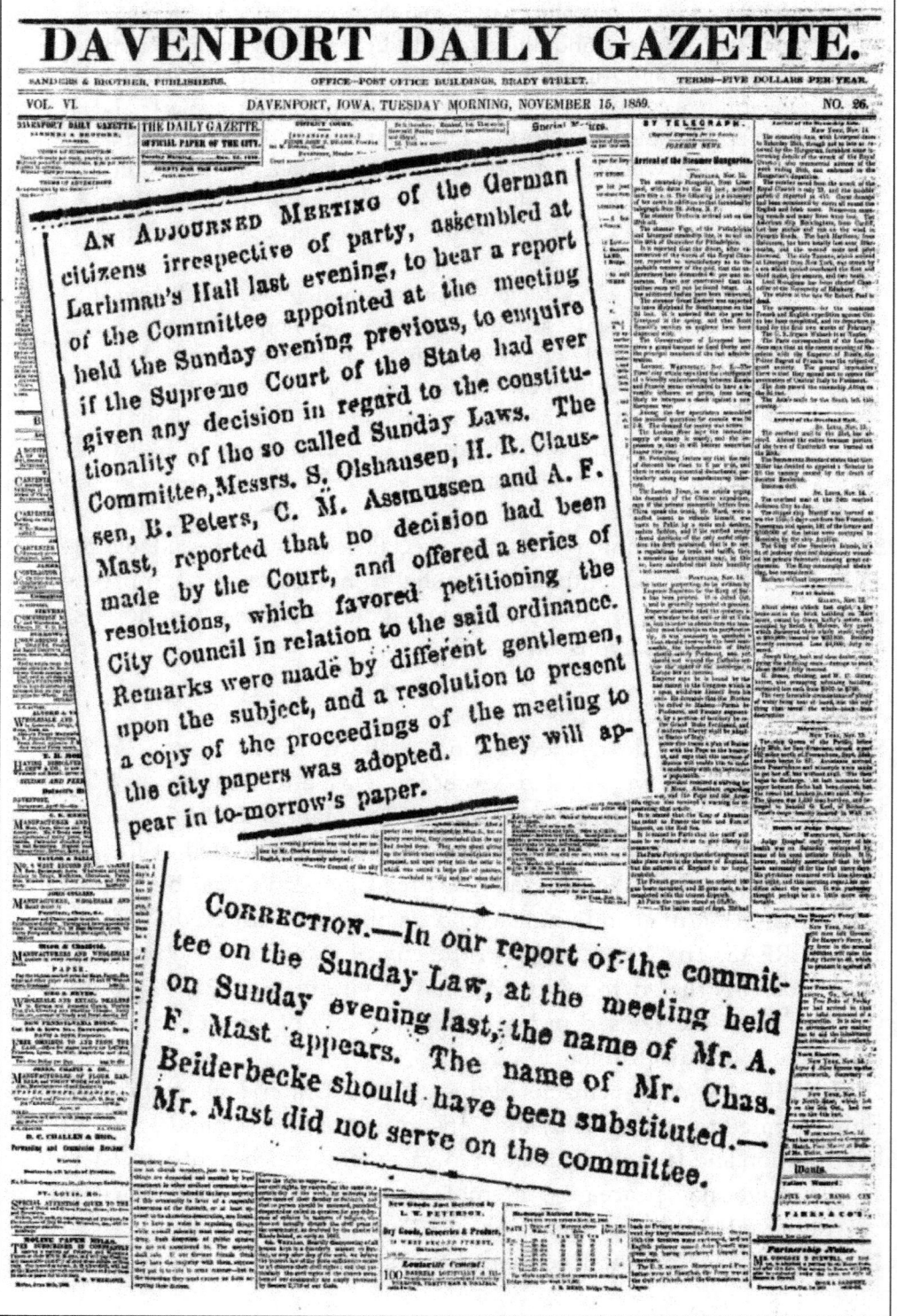

AN ADJOURNED MEETING of the German citizens irrespective of party, assembled at Lachman's Hall last evening, to hear a report of the Committee appointed at the meeting held the Sunday evening previous, to enquire if the Supreme Court of the State had ever given any decision in regard to the constitutionality of the so called Sunday Laws. The Committee, Messrs. S. Olshausen, H. R. Claussen, B. Peters, C. M. Assmussen and A. F. Mast, reported that no decision had been made by the Court, and offered a series of resolutions, which favored petitioning the City Council in relation to the said ordinance. Remarks were made by different gentlemen, upon the subject, and a resolution to present a copy of the proceedings of the meeting to the city papers was adopted. They will appear in to-morrow's paper.

CORRECTION.—In our report of the committee on the Sunday Law, at the meeting held on Sunday evening last, the name of Mr. A. F. Mast appears. The name of Mr. Chas. Beiderbecke should have been substituted.— Mr. Mast did not serve on the committee.

liberty or property without due process of law; and that while the Code of Iowa provides that the powers of a magistrate in a criminal proceeding are to be exercised on Sunday, and that a person arrested is entitled to an immediate examination of his case; the city ordinance infringes upon the liberty of the citizens by the provision that persons taken into custody by the Marshall shall be held by confinement until the ensuing day, thus depriving perhaps entirely innocent citizens of their liberty without the process of law, by the arbitrary power of an executive officer, who has no cognizance of criminal cause.
3. That no law shall be made respecting or establishment of religion, and government shall not grant to only citizen or class of citizens privileges or immunities which upon the same terms shall not equally belong to all citizens; to the contrary of which the Christian Sunday is enforced, while there is no provision for the Sabbath of the Jews; and while the Sabbath Law of the State of Iowa exempts Jews from the observance of the Sabbath, the city Ordinance applies not to Jews or any other people not belonging to any Christian denomination.
4. That each of us may acquire and enjoy properly if not injuring the rights of others, to the contrary of which although Government has the power to declare certain taxes, matters and conditions of distribution, it has no power to declare the absolute abstinence exclusively on Sundays for reasons of being offensive to a religious denomination, though not infringing upon religious liberty; and yet being no such nuisance the other six days of the week.

3d. WHEREAS, We as citizens are fully satisfied that a great portion of our American fellow citizens are induced by honest and religious motives to be in favor of such laws, and we respect them as such, nevertheless religious liberty being as dear to us as civil liberty, we believe no religious sect, be it Christians, Mohammedans, Jews or any others, have the right to suppress or encroach upon our civil rights by suspending the same on a certain day of the week, for enforcing the observance of their Sunday or Sabbath, and that no person should be molested, punished, disquieted or called in question for any difference of opinion to matters of religion, who does not actually disturb the civil peace of the community, as declared by the charter of Rhode Island, as early as 1068.

4th. Whereas, Heartily disapproving of all houses kept in a disorderly matter on Sunday or any other day of the week, we believe the law of the State sufficient to return to all citizens their civil rights and that particularly the civil rights of the church members of our community are amply protected by Section 2.718 of our Code.

Be it therefore Resolved: 1st That we believe said Sunday Ordinance unconstitutional and illegal. 2d That we request our City to rescind said resolution and to repeal said ordinance. 3d That we shall use all legal and honorable means to effect a repeal of said ordinance. 4th That a copy of these resolutions be presented to the City Council by the Chairman of this meeting. 5th That a copy of these resolutions be delivered to the city papers, by the Secretary of this meeting with the request to publish the same.

On the question which had been suggested at a previous meeting, "would not the teaching of the German language in those of our district schools where a majority of the scholars are of German parentage be advantageous?" Prof. Riepe read quite a lengthy article prepared by him in favor of such action, which was listened to with much attention, as were the remarks made by Messrs. O. Asmussen, T. Olshausen, H. Ramming, Dr. Wunderlich and B.L. Peters. On motion, a committee of four were appointed to take the subject into consideration, and report at a future meeting….

Davenporters taking their daily constitutional, c. late 1880s

Genealogy: Hilton Family

James Hilton & Fannie Mason married 1834 in Chautauqua County, New York.

1850 Census: James, 40, merchant; Fanny, 34, wife; Ann, 18; Helen, 14; Beriah, 12; Edmond, age 5; all from New York, Chautauqua, Pomfret.

1856 Iowa County, Troy Township, Iowa: James, 46, farmer; Fanny, 40; Beriah, age 18; Edmond J., age 12

1860 Census: James, 53; Fanny, 42; Ann, 26; Beriah, 22; Edmond, 14. Beriah listed as laborer on father's farm.

1863 City Directory: E. J. Hilton, cabinet maker, 2nd & Rock Island, Davenport. John Hill worked as a cabinet maker in 1869; possibly how Carrie and Beriah met.

1870 Census: James, 62, farmer; Fannie, 53; Real Estate value $8,000.

1870 Census: Davenport Ward 3, Scott Co, Iowa. Beriah living with in-laws John, Adam and Mary Hill at 615 E. 15 Street—Briar [Beriah] Hilton, 28, steamboat engineer; Carrie, 22; Aggie, 4 months. B.L. Hilton, 29, shows up later that census year as a carpenter in Missoula, Montana.

1876 City Directory: Hilton's Meat Market, Perry St. N.W. Corner 11th St; E. J. Hilton, stock dealer, 1709 Harrison St. [livestock from the family's cattle farm]

1880 Census, District 268 Scott: James, 69, farmer, b. Connecticut; Fannie, 60, wife, b. New York; Edmond, 34; Rachel, 30; Fannie, 7, Marie [Mary] age 2; James, 7 Months; and Thomas King, 63, Edmond's father-in-law.

1882 Scott County/Davenport Township No. 78 N. Range No. 3 & 4 East of the 5th Meridian Section 4: Hans Claussen, D. Dehn, John Littig, James Hilton, John Carlin, Joachim Thoeming, and Stephen G. Braybrook.

1886 Directory: James Hilton and Edmond Hilton, both farmers; James, property owner. Postal Address: Green Tree or Green Tree Tavern located about six miles northwest of Davenport, 6 miles south of Eldridge at the Corner of Northwest Blvd. and 76th Street in Davenport Township. Established as Green Tree Tavern April 4, 1878; name shortened to Green Tree 20 June 1883, name removed 1903.

1895 Census: Edward [Edmond] 49, Rachel S, 46, Fannie D, 22; Mary, 17; James R, 15, Annie L, age 10.

1908 City Directory for Colorado Springs, Colorado: Beriah living with sister-in-law Rachel and her family at 529 N. Weber [Edmond died Aug 27, 1907]

1909–1910 Census: 626 E. Boulder, Colorado Springs, CO. Beriah living with sister-in-law Rachel and her children.

1910 Census: Colorado Springs, CO. Beriah Hilton, 72, widower [Carrie died in 1880] living with his sister-in-law Rachel S. Hilton, widow of Edmond James Hilton

1911 Census: 231 N. Institute, Colorado Springs, CO. Beriah living with sister–in–law Rachel; died Sep 17 and body returned to Davenport for burial.

JAMES HILTON Obituary
December 1890: At his home in Davenport Township Tuesday morning occurred the death of James Hilton, who came to this county in 1850 and has been a well known farmer in that vicinity ever since. He was 80 years old at the time of his death and old age was the only assignable cause of the fatality. The Deceased was born in Montgomery county, New York, August 26, 1810. In 1834 he was married to Miss Fannie Mason in Chautauqua county of the native state and after 56 years of most happily spent married life she is left to mourn his death. Three of the four children born to them are still living—Mrs. L. F. Sheldon of Sedalia, Mo., Beriah L., of St. Louis and E. J. Hilton of Scott county. The funeral will take place Thursday morning at 9 o'clock from the late residence with interment in Oakdale.

FANNIE MASON HILTON Obituary
November 1893: At 10 o'clock Thursday evening occurred the death of Mrs. Fannie Hilton, widow of James Hilton, at her home in Davenport township. Her illness was not of long duration and her death was an occasion of general sorrow in her large circle of friends and acquaintances. Mrs. Hilton's maiden name was Fannie Mason, and she was born in Chautauqua county, N.Y., in 1815. In 1834 she was married there to Mr. Hilton, and came with him to this county in 1859, and has lived here ever since. The farm was always the family home, and a pleasant home it was, and a favorite place for the meeting of many friends in the country and the city as well. Mr. Hilton died Tuesday, December 2, 1890, aged 80 years. Four children constituted the family. Two are now dead. Those who survive are Beriah L. and E.J. Hilton, both of this county. The funeral will be held at 1 o'clock Sunday afternoon from the family residence.
Burial: 12 Nov 1893 Oakdale Cemetery, Davenport

FANNIE HILTON'S WILL #3599 Edmond J. Hilton, Executor
First, I direct that all claims against my estate be paid and a suitable tombstone be placed at my grave at an expense not to exceed two hundred and fifty dollars. Second, I hereby give and bequest unto my son Edmond J. Hilton the sum of One Thousand dollars in trust for the uses and purposes following, to wit, to invest during the life time of my son Beriah L. Hilton, by loaning unencumbered and improved farming lands, security of at least twice the value of the mount secured, at the annual interest, and to collect the interest accruing there on, and after defraying the expenses of making said loans and collecting said interest to pay the remainder as collected to my said son Beriah L. Hilton, to have to hold in his own right. Provided however, that if on account of ill health or infirmity of my said son Beriah L. Hilton, a sum of money larger than the annual interest derived from said investment is necessary in the

opinion of said son Edmond J. Hilton for the comfortable support of said son Beriah L. Hilton, then and not otherwise, my said son Beriah L. Hilton from time to time such portions of the principal of said trust fund as his judgment shall be necessary therefore. Third, On the decease of my said son Beriah L. Hilton, my said son, Edmond J. Hilton, shall dispose of said trust fund or what shall remain thereof together with any accrued interest there may be, if any, as follows, that is to say, shall pay into my granddaughter AGNES HILTON, daughter of said son, Beriah L. Hilton, or to her issue, if she shall depart this life before the decease of her said father, leaving her surviving issue 1/2 thereof, to have and to hold forever, and he shall appropriate the remaining half to his own use, to have to hold in his own right. Provided however, that in the event my said granddaughter, AGNES HILTON, shall have departed this life before the decease of her said father, leaving no issue surviving, then my son Edmond J. Hilton, shall on the decease of said son Beriah L. Hilton appropriate to his own use all there shall be then remaining of said trust fund, and interest accrued thereon, to have and to hold in his own right.

Fannie's will also bequeathed a gold watch to granddaughter Fannie D. and a diamond ring to granddaughter Anna L, both daughters of Edmond; one hundred dollars to granddaughter Jennie H. (Seldon) Phillips; and twenty–five dollars each to Edmond's minor children, James R. and Mary G. To Edmond and his daughter Anna, she left her silverware to be divided as they chose. All of her clothes were to be divided among granddaughters Fannie D., Mary G, and Anna L. The farm and the rest of her estate she left to Edmond. He made payments to Beriah almost annually. Signed receipts record the following: $50 paid 23 July 1894; $55 paid 04 March 1895; $50 paid 29 April 1897 and 01 April 1898; $58 paid 08 April 1899; $40 paid 18 April 1900; $40.40 paid 01 April 1901; $39 paid 01 April 1902; and $33.37 paid 24 April 1903 for a total of $415.37. Beriah signed all the receipts either as B.L. Hilton or Beriah L. Hilton.

ANNA HILTON, daughter of JAMES & FANNIE Hilton, was born 1833 in New York, and died in Missouri. She married Lemuel F. SHELDON, born 1834 in Ohio. 1880 Census shows Anna and her family living in Sedalia, Pettis, Missouri, where Lemuel worked as a railroad paymaster. They had a daughter JENNIE H. SHELDON, born 1860 in Illinois; m. PHILLIPS.

BERIAH L. HILTON married CAROLINE HILL September 20, 1868, in Rock Island, IL.

1911 Obituary: B.L. Hilton, brother of the late E. J. Hilton died Sept. 17 at the family home in Colorado Springs after an illness of several weeks following a stroke of

paralysis. The funeral services were held at the late home and the Body will be brought to Davenport for burial in Oakdale cemetery.
Burial: 20 Sep 1911 Halligan Funeral Home
The Body of B. L. Hilton, formerly a resident of Davenport, was brought to Davenport this morning from Colorado Springs, Colo., and buried in Oakdale cemetery. The funeral occurred this afternoon at 2 o'clock. Mr. Hilton died Sunday morning. Mr. Hilton lived in the city for many years.

EDMOND JAMES HILTON married RACHEL SUSANNA KING Nov 22, 1871 in Davenport.

Wednesday, August 28, 1907 *Daily Times:*
E.J. Hilton, formerly of Davenport, and at one time supervisor for Scott county, died yesterday at Colorado Springs. The Body will arrive in Davenport Thursday noon. The funeral announcement will be made later.

Thursday, August 29, 1907 *Daily Times:*
The Body of the late E.J. Hilton whose death at Colorado Springs, Tuesday, was recorded in The Times yesterday, arrived in Davenport at noon today and was taken to the home of his daughter, Mrs. W.M. Dougherty, No. 6 Grand Court. The funeral will be held tomorrow afternoon at 3 o'clock from Grace Cathedral with interment in Oakdale Cemetery. Mr. Hilton died of mitral insufficiency from which he had been suffering for about eight months. The death was not unexpected and his final illness was of two week duration. He was born in Fredonia, N.Y., Jan. 9, 1845, and came west to Iowa county at the age of 11 years. He lived there until 15 years of age, when the family came to Scott County, settling five miles north of Davenport, where his home was until five years ago. At that time he moved to Davenport. About a year and a half ago, he moved with his family to Colorado Springs. He leaves besides a devoted wife, one son and three daughters. They are James R., Mrs. W. M. Dougherty, Mary G. and Anna L. Mr. Hilton was at one time a supervisor for Scott county.
Thursday, August 29, 1907, *Democrat–Leader*
REMAINS OF E. J. HILTON HERE
Funeral Will Take Place from Grace Cathedral on Friday
E.J. Hilton, a former supervisor of Scott county, prominent farmer of Davenport township for years and more recently a Davenport business man, expired at Colorado Springs Tuesday. His remains arrived here this noon and were taken to the home of his daughter, Mrs. Wm. Dougherty of No. 6 Grand court. The funeral will be held Friday afternoon at 3 o'clock, with services at Grace Cathedral, Rev. Sherwood of Rock Island officiating. Mr. Hilton was in his 62d year. He was born in Fredonia, N.Y., Jan. 29, 1845, coming to Iowa with his parents at the age of 11 years. They settled near Iowa City, where they remained for four years, when E.J. came to Scott county, locating five miles north of Davenport. He continued to be one of the

prominent residents of Davenport township until five years ago, when he came to Davenport. A year and a half ago he went from here to Colorado Springs where his death occurred. He is mourned by a devoted wife, one son, James R. Hilton, and three daughters, Mrs. Wm. Dougherty of Davenport, and Mary G. and Anna L. of Colorado Springs.
Burial: 30 Aug 1907 Oakdale Cemetery, Davenport, Iowa
03 Sep 1907 Edmond Hilton Will lists heirs as his wife Rachel S. Hilton, children: Fannie D. Dougherty age 34,;Mary G. Hilton age 30; James R. Hilton age 27; and Anna L. Hilton age 23. Inventory of Real Estate: land at Seventeenth and Perry.
RACHEL SUSANNA KING, daughter of Thomas King, born 1849 in Baltimore, Maryland; died 28 Sep 1917 in Colorado Springs, Colorado.

Sep 1917 Obituary: Mrs. William M. Dougherty, who resides on the Dubuque Road near Eldridge, Ia., has received word of the death her mother, Mrs. R.S. Hilton, pioneer resident of Scott county, which occurred at her home in Colorado Springs Friday morning. Death followed an illness of but one week's duration. Mrs. Hilton had made her home in Colorado Springs since she moved from Scott county 12 years ago. She made many friends while residing in Scott county who will grieved to hear of her death. She was 69 years of age when summoned. Deceased leaves to mourn her demise, besides her daughter, Mrs. William Dougherty, three other children. James, Mary and Ann, all of Colorado Springs and four grandchildren. Her husband Mr. E. Hilton, preceded her in death 10 years ago. The remains will arrive in Davenport this noon over the Rock Island lines. The funeral will be held from the home of Mr. and Mrs. Wm. Dougherty, Monday afternoon at 2 o'clock. Interment will be made in Oakdale cemetery.
Burial: 01 Oct 1917
FANNIE D. HILTON, daughter of Edmond and Rachel Hilton, born 1873 in Scott County, Iowa; died 21 Feb 1960 in Rock Island, IL. Married 20 Jan 1900 to WILLIAM M. DOUGHERTY, born 25 Feb 1873 in Scott County, Iowa; died 15 Feb 1933 in Davenport.

Agnes Jane Hilton
age 15

Caroline Hilton obit, gravestone & Hill Family plot at Pine Hill Cemetery, Davenport

GENEALOGY: HILL–KENNEDY–PETERSEN

ADAM M. HILL, born 1806 in Mercer County, PA; died 1882 in Davenport, IA; wife Anna (Hannah?) Pollock 1795–1851. Children: Jane, b.1827; David, b.1829; Nelson, b.1831; Sarah, b.1833; John, b.1838; Mary, b.1839; Elizabeth, b.1841; Emily, b.1843; Caroline, b.1844; Wallace, b.1849; Addison, b.1851

1856 Scott County Census #210 household: Adam Hill, 50, widower; Caroline, 12; Jane, 25; John, 20; Mary, 18; Nelson, 25; Sarah, 23. #602 married household: David Hill, 26; Amanda, 20. Nelson Hill's residence 1858–1859: boarders at 40 E. Front St., Davenport, Iowa.

January 11, 1860 *Davenport Daily Gazette*: ARRESTED FOR HORSE STEALING—On Wednesday of last week, a young man named John Bowman hired a horse and cutter from the stable of Thompson & Brown, of this city, for the purpose of going to Blue Grass, and returning the next day. As he failed to make his appearance at the stable on the ensuing day, MR. DAVID HILL started to hunt him up, visiting Blue Grass and vicinity without getting any clues to the team. Upon returning to the city, he heard of such a turn–out being seen on the road to Muscatine. Mr. H. immediately started down and found the horse and cutter there, but not the driver. Returning home, business again called him to Muscatine on Saturday, when he met the "fast" young man. He had him arrested, and night before last lodged him at the Ackley (late Graham) House in this city. Bowman is a young man, of about 25 years of age, and hails from the vicinity of Dubuque, but was formerly from Rochester, New York.

1860 Census for Scott County: Adam, 53, boardinghouse keeper; Nelson, 26; John, 22; Mary, 20; Caroline, 16; Addison, 10. Household includes nine boarders.
#2136: A. Kennedy, 32; Sarah, 24; Mary, 1. #2192: Benedict Kennedy, 30; Jane, 27.

August 7, 1867 *Davenport Daily Gazette*: Sale of Real Estate—Mr. Wm. Harlburt has sold his residence on West side of Harrison street near Sixteenth to Mr. BEN KENNEDY for $1,540. The lot is 72x120 feet, upon it is a two story frame dwelling.
Oct 3, 1866 *Davenport Daily Gazette*: MORE IMPROVEMENTS—Mr. David Hill purchased on Monday of Mr. Bailey Davenport the lot 51x94 feet on the south side of Third, west of Main street, for fifteen hundred dollars, and yesterday commenced the erection of a brick livery stable which is to be 50x90 feet, and a one story and a half building, with all the modern improvements known to livery stable men for the convenience of their help and the health of their stock. Mr. Franklin Kirk has taken the contract for the building

Woodcut of the tri-cities when the Hill clan arrived; below is a *Daily Gazette* ad for Newcomb House where Mary Hill worked as a cook and the ad for her millinery shop on Main Street.

NEWCOMB HOUSE,

(LATE LECLAIRE,)

DAVENPORT, IOWA:

THIS HOTEL SITUATED IN THE centre of the business portion of this city and but one block from the

FERRY AND STEAMBOAT LANDING,

Will be opened for the reception of Guests on

Wednesday, the 15th of April, 1868.

It has recently undergone thorough repairs and extensive additions; among which is a Dining Hall 46x76 feet, an office 24x40; large pleasant Parlors Sample rooms for Agents, and ample accommodations for over Two Hundred Guests. It being furnished complete with

New Modern Styled Furniture, and Steam Cooking Ranges.

The Proprietors feel warranted in offering to Families, Tourists and the traveling public an attractive desirable stopping place; one of the best in the West.

PENNIMAN, SIGLEY & CO.,
[Proprietors.

apl 14 d&tf

DAILY GAZETTE.

Official Paper of the City.

WEDNESDAY MORNING, OCT. 17, '66.

LOCAL ITEMS.

OTTO KLUG, No. 52, West Second, between Main and Harrison streets, has just received a large lot of fashionable ladies' sacques, cloaks, shawls, nubias, merinos, and all other dry goods of the latest style. He also keeps constantly on hand the homemade flannels, plaids, wool yarn, socks and mittens, of the Amana Society.

oct17-d1w.

NEW MILLINERY GOODS.—Just opened, a handsome stock of millinery goods of the latest styles, and all the late novelties in bonnets and hats. The Castilian, Sylphide, Ristori, and Dexter. Feathers, flowers, and ribbons of the very best quality.

Also just received, Mme. Demorest's new and elegant winter patterns of the latest and most reliable Paris and New York fashions for ladies' and childrens' dress, at Miss M Hill's, No. 25, Main street.

oct17 d&w1tew4w.

GIVE the hour to folly and you set back

and expects to have it completed in thirty days. The stone masons commenced laying the foundation yesterday. Mr. Hill is one of our experienced horsemen, and has lots of friends who will be glad to hear of "Dave's" success.

November 26, 1867 *Davenport Daily Gazette*: INGRATITUDE—A homeless fellow who was kindly permitted by Mr. David Hill to sleep in his livery stable Sunday night, rose yesterday at an early hour and left the premises, having a carriage robe, a pair of driving gloves and other articles in his possession that did not belong to him. Mr. Hill says he never lives to see a man suffer for a place of shelter but does object to having to pay for furnishing accommodations to such chaps.

1870 Census for Scott County: Ward 3: Household #389: Alexander Kennedy, 45; Sarah, 35; Mary 11; Sarah, 7; Carrie, 3. #434 John Hill, 30, grain buyer; Adam, 62; Mary, 27; Carrie, 22; Briar Hilton, 28; Aggie Hilton, 4 months. #435: Benedict Kennedy, 42; Jane, 39; Emma, 9. Ward 4: David Hill, 41, livery stable; Amanda, 35; Clarence, 13; Edward, 10; Ida, 9; Rebecca Dornan, 20.
1870 Census for Marengo, IA: Nelson Hill living with wife Sarah A, 26; son George, 6; daughters Carrie, 3, and Jane, 5 months.
July 25, 1875 *Davenport Daily Gazette*: A "FAST ONE'S" CAREER. HISTORY OF LITTLE FRED—HOW AND WHEN HE CAME TO DAVENPORT—AN "OLD SCRUB" SOLD FOR EIGHTY DOLLARS. The victory of the Davenport horse, Little Fred, in the 2:29 race at Dexter Park on Friday created a sensation in our city—or rather his best time, 2:25, did. This horse has a history remarkable as that of Dexter. Two years ago he was sent to a prominent citizen by a relative in Clinton, Iowa, with instruction to "sell him or keep him just as you please." The gent kept him a few weeks, and then got tired of the "old scrub," as the neighbors called the nag, and sold him to DAVID HILL for $80. Mr. Hill discovered the horse possessed unusual qualities of speed—and six months after sold him to Fisher & Hebert, Fred Schulenberg, and two other gents for $2,400. The "scrub" was put in training. He appeared on the turf last summer and made his record for the season at Peoria—2:30½ . The owners were offered $5,000 for him. His pedigree isn't known.

20 May 1880 *Davenport Democrat*: In this City, Thursday, June* 20th, at 9 A.M. Mrs. CARRIE HILTON, daughter of Adam Hill, aged 36 years. Funeral tomorrow (Friday) afternoon, at 2 o'clock, from the residence of Mr. John Hill, 228 West 18th street.
*newspaper error—other obits published same day correctly state month as May
1880 Census for Scott County—220 W. 13th Street: Hill, John, age 40, Real Estate agent; Hill, Adam age 73, father/retired farmer; Mary, age 37, sister/keeping house; Hilton, Aggie, age 10, niece/at school. [Census taken June1st; Caroline died May 20th]
1518 Harrison St: B.T. Kennedy, 57; Jane, 50; Emma, 19. [Alexander & Sarah and their children not found in Scott County census records but are living at time of John Hill's death.]

88

Davenport Directory. 85

HILL & THOMPSON,
LIVERY STABLE.

THE BEST CARRIAGES AND BUGGIES AND GOOD HORSES
Will always be found at this stable.
Second Street between Main and Harrison,
DAVENPORT, IOWA.
N. B.—A number of fine Carriages kept for Funerals.

DAVID HILL'S LIVERY STABLE
Below:
dissolution of partnership with James Thompson

NOTICE.—THE CO-PARTNERSHIP heretofore existing between James Thompson and David Hill is hereby dissolved by mutual consent. James Thompson has purchased the entire interest of his late partner and is alone authorized to settle the business and sign the name of the firm in settlement.
Dated Davenport, March 28th, A. D. 1859.
JAMES THOMPSON,
DAVID HILL.

Livery Stable.

THE SUBSCRIBER WILL CONTINUE THE

Livery Business

AT THE

Old Stand of Hill & Thompson,
No. 55 West Second Street,

Where he can furnish

HORSES, BUGGIES AND CARRIAGES

To parties or funerals at the shortest notice. Horses and buggies always to hire on the most favorable terms. Grateful for the patronage to the old firm he hopes by strict attention to business to still have their custom.
Horses boarded by the day, week or month.
mch30-dtf   JAMES THOMPSON.

To-day's Advertisem'ts.

For Sale at a Bargain,

A SECOND-HAND, EIGHT HORSE
Massillon Threshing Machine.

Apply to   DAVID HILL,
At Thompson's Livery Stable, 2d st. near Harrison
jy24 d1m

Above: July 24, 1862
Below: runaway horses up for auction
June 22, 1865 —JOHN HILL replaced
David Hill as Thompson's partner

MARSHAL'S SALE.

THE UNDERSIGNED, MARSHAL OF the City of Davenport, will offer at public sale, at the Livery Stable of Hill & Thompson, on Second street, between Main and Harrison streets, in said city, on Monday the 26th day of June, 1865, at 2 o'clock P. M. of said day, one GREY MUSTANG HORSE, marked C on the left hip, about 10 years old, and one SORREL MARE, about 3 years old, found running at large in said city and, by me taken up on the 16th day of June, 1865, in pursuance of the city ordinance in such cases made and provided, to pay expenses of taking, keeping and selling the same.
Davenport, June 20th, 1865.
je13-d5t   WM. POOL, City Marshal.

According to the 1882 *History of Scott County*, James Thompson, who partnered with David Hill in a livery stable at Third & Main until 1867, also came to Davenport from Pennsylvania. He started a farm in Liberty Township and moved on to land speculating, acquiring 30,000 acres in four states. Thompson eventually owned twelve properties in Davenport, both commercial and residential. He established the First National Bank of Davenport, the nation's first chartered bank. James and Mary Moke Thompson had six children and lived at 805 Brady St.

1880 Arapahoe Census, Denver, CO: Hill, David, 60; Amanda, 45; Clarence B., 23; Edward E., 21; Ida M., 19.

1880 History of the City of Denver, Arapahoe County, and Colorado:
> Mr. [David] Hill was born in Mercer County, Penn., in 1829. At the age of seventeen, he engaged in running a canal–boat and such was his industry and economy that before he had attained his majority, he was the captain of his own boat. At twenty–one, he sold out and emigrated to Davenport, Iowa, when that city contained a population of but 1,500. The first seven years, he was successfully engaged in buying and selling stock, after which he followed the livery business for fifteen years and was identified with the growth of the city to a population of 25,000. In 1873, failing health compelled him to visit Colorado, where he derived so much benefit, that he twice returned to his old home in Iowa, confident that his health was sufficiently re–established to admit of his remaining there, but was as often obliged to return to Colorado. He has contributed to the upbuilding of Denver by the erection of several buildings, including the Denver transfer barn. In the spring of 1878, he bought out the Transfer Company and continued to run the transfer and livery business until May, 1879, when he sold out to Marrs & Brown, by whom it is still continued. Since then, Mr. Hill has confined his attention to general business and looking after some real–estate interests, which he has at Leadville. He was married in Davenport, Iowa, in 1854, to Miss Amanda J. Blair, of that city and has three children.

23 Oct 1882 Obituary, *Davenport Gazette*:
Yesterday afternoon at 4:30 o'clock death closed the career of Mr. Adam Hill, who had been a sufferer for several years. The deceased had reached the mature age of seventy–six years and four months. He died at the residence of his son John Hill, No.1 Clinton Place, Brady street, from which place the funeral will be held tomorrow afternoon at 2 o'clock. Mr. Hill came to Davenport in 1853 from Greenville, Mercer county, Pa., of which State he was a native. For some time after

coming to Iowa he engaged in farming, but for some time his home has been with his son. He was a well known and much respected citizen, though for a few years past his appearances on the street have not been frequent.

23 Oct 1882 Obituary, *Davenport Democrat*:

The long–time and well known resident of Davenport, Adam Hill, died at the resident of his son John, No 1 Clinton Place, at half past four o'clock yesterday afternoon after weeks of confinement to his bed. He had been a citizen of Davenport for twenty–nine years. Mr. Hill was born in Mercer county, Pennsylvania in 1806. His father was a pioneer, and he was raised on a farm, pursuing the vocation until 1853 when he and his children came to Davenport; Mrs. Hill having died in 1851, a sad event which caused the husband to leave the old home. Mr. Hill invested in two or three farms in Scott county and while his home was in the city with his sons David or John, he spent a good deal of his time up to eight years since in supervening them. He posed great physical strength and energy, and a versatile mind. He was member of the United Presbyterian church for more than forty years and lived up to his religious belief. His memory was wonderful, and he had the Bible at his tongue, a fact which made his arguments felt when he was engaged in a religious discretion. He leaves seven children—David of Denver, John of Davenport, Mrs. Jane Kennedy in Davenport, Nelson in Brooklyn, Iowa, Mrs. Lizzie Kidd in New York City, Mrs. Emma Harshaw in Brady Bend, Pa., and Miss Mary in Davenport. The funeral takes place from John Hill's home No. 1 Clinton Place at 2 o'clock tomorrow afternoon.

[Sarah, Wallace and Addison are omitted from list of Adam's children for reasons unknown; all are listed as heirs to John's estate in 1886; Sarah a.k.a. Sallie Kennedy lived in Davenport until her death in 1901; her husband Alexander died 1890. Wallace farmed in Mercer Co, PA, and died in 1908; Addison lived in Pittsburgh.]

11 Sep 1886 Obituary, *Davenport Democrat*:

The Death of Two Well–Known Citizens—JOHN HILL....

At 10 o'clock yesterday forenoon Mr. John Hill who was very well known in the city, died at his residence, No. 615 East Fifteenth street. Mr. Hill was engaged in the livery business for a number of years and very well known in the county. He was born in Mercer county, Pa., in 1838 and came to Scott county when he was 13 years of age. For the last two years he suffered from meningitis, which caused his death. The funeral will occur Sunday afternoon at 2 o'clock.

Nelson Hill, b.03 Jun 1831 in PA, died 10 Mar 1898 in Bear Creek, Poweshiek County, Iowa. Wife: Sarah A., born 1843. Children: George Hill, b. 1864; Jane Hill, b. 1865; Carrie Hill, b. 1867; Nelson listed as farmer in 1880 census. Burial: I.O.O.F. Cemetery, Bear Creek, Iowa [I.O.O.F—Independent Order of Odd Fellows; Finnish–British Society]

22 Feb 1916 Obituary, *Democrat–Leader*:

Miss Mary Hill passed away at 11:45 Monday night at the home of her niece Mrs. B.

H. Beiderbecke, 1934 Grand avenue, following a short illness. The deceased was born in Pennsylvania on Sept 12, 1839. In 1853 she came to Davenport and has resided here ever since. One sister, Mrs. Harshaw of Grove City, Penn., and three nieces, Mrs. B. H. Beiderbecke, Mrs. M. R. Fort and Mrs. Albert Petersen who reside in Davenport are the only survivors. The funeral will be held Wednesday afternoon

NELSON HILL CLAN, Poweshiek County, Iowa

at 2 o'clock from the home of B. H. Beiderbecke, 1934 Grand avenue with interment in Pine Hill cemetery. Services at the home and grave will be private.

ALEXANDER KENNEDY
Died: 14 Oct 1890 At his home, 1324 Harrison street, the death of Alexander Kennedy occurred this morning. The deceased was well known here, having been a resident of this city for more than 40 years. He was born in Butler county, Pa. in 1828, and 20 years later, while still unmarried, came to this city, and it has been his home ever since. The funeral will be held from the late residence at half past 2 o'clock tomorrow afternoon.

SARAH HILL KENNEDY
Born 1833; Died 17 Feb 1901 Mrs. Sarah Kennedy, widow of the late Alexander Kennedy, died at 5 o'clock Sunday afternoon at her home, 1324 Harrison street, aged 68 years. She was born in Mercer county, Pa., but came to Davenport in 1850. She was the mother of four children, of whom three are living; Mrs. J. W. [Mary] Woodward of Delphos, Kan., and Mrs. Albert Petersen and William Kennedy of this city. A brother and three sisters are also left....

The funeral services over the remains of Mrs. Sarah Kennedy were held at 2:30 o'clock this afternoon from the late home 1324 Harrison St., Rev. Meloy officiating and interment at Oakdale.

CAROLINE 'CARRIE' MAY KENNEDY
Parents: Alexander Kennedy & Sarah Hill
Born 25 May 1867; Died 02 Jul 1949
18 Feb 1891 PETERSEN–KENNEDY At the home of the bride, at 1324 Harrison street, Wednesday evening at 8 o'clock, occurred the marriage of Albert J. Petersen and Miss Carrie M. Kennedy, Rev. G.W. Snyder officiating. The ceremony was performed in the presence of numerous friends and relatives and was followed by an elaborate supper. The groom is a musician, who is a member of one of best bands, popular with his fellows and deserving of the bride he has won. She has been for some time a clerk in the Steffen store and is a young lady who will make the home circle a bright one wherever her lot may fall.
DIES AT AGE 82 Mrs. Carrie M. Petersen, 82, wife of Albert L. Petersen, well known musician, died at 6:30 a.m. Saturday in Mercy hospital after an extended illness. The body was removed to the Runge mortuary where services will be held in the chapel at 1:30 p. m. Tuesday. Burial will be in Memorial Park cemetery. Mrs. Petersen was born in Davenport, May 25, 1867, and had resided here her entire life. She was married here Feb. 18, 1891. Surviving, in addition to her husband, are three sons, Arthur A. and Victor H., both of Davenport, and Harry A., of Moline; a daughter, Mrs. Dale Besse, Indianapolis; four grandsons and a great granddaughter. A son Ceno, died in January.

ALBERT L. PETERSEN 04 Sep 1865 to 25 Feb 1951
Parents: Peter Ingvard Petersen 1818–1874 & Maria Catharina Johanna Selken 1834–1914
[ed note] Previous historic references to *Uncle Olie* are unknown and unsupported by Albert Petersen's descendants. Given that in taped interviews, Burnie Beiderbecke spoke only of *Uncle Albert*, that is the name used throughout this book.

1880 Census/Ward 2 # 312: Maria Petersen, 46; Margita, 23, store clerk; Adolph, 21, compositor; Gerhart, 19, compositor; Wolfgang, 18, painter; Albert, 14, at school.
1900 Census/1514 Ripley St: Albert, 34, musician; Carrie M, 32; Vinceno, 8; Arthur, 7; Harry, 2.
1920 Census/704 W. Locust: Albert, 55, music teacher; Carrie M, 52; Arthur, 27, co–owner electric supplies; Harry, 22, co–owner electric supplies; Helen, 18; Victor, 11.
History of Davenport and Scott County, 1910:
...In instrumental music also Davenport has achieved brilliant results. More than nine–tenths of the professional musicians here have at all times been Germans. This proportion holds when a tri–city musical organization is formed, as of the 170 members of the Tri–City Musical Society, 150 are Germans. Among the directors of

recent times who have won especial prominence are Ernst Otto and Albert Petersen. These came to the front after the already mentioned pioneer leader of instrumental music, Jacob Strasser had retired on account of advanced age.

12 May 1895 *Daily Tribune*: The management of Strasser's Second regiment band and orchestra has changed hands, Mr. Albert Petersen having been selected for that position. The band is to be congratulated upon having secured Mr. Petersen, having been a member of the band for 15 years, he has consequently obtained a great deal of experience which will be of great benefit to the organization. He may be found at his residence, 1514 Ripley street or by calling him up at phone 463, where he is prepared and empowered to make all engagements.

17 July 1898 *Davenport Daily Leader*: Tomorrow, Monday evening, Albert Petersen's orchestra will give its fourth promenade concert at Black Hawk's Watch Tower. It has been the custom to give these concerts Thursday evening, but owing to numerous engagements the management of the orchestra was forced to change the date. The orchestra will give a delightful program that evening including such selections as from Kerker's comic opera, "Little Christopher," and "The Standard Guard" by Ellenberg. A feature of the program will be a duo for flute and clarinet by Messrs F.G. Fick and Fred Otto and a quartet for cornets, alto and trombone by Messrs. C. Eckhart, F. Seiffert, WILLIAM BIEBERBACH and Henry Sonntag. They will play a double number, "Devotion in the Forest" by F. Abt, and Mendelssohn's "It is God's Design."

ALBERT L. PETERSEN | CARRIE KENNEDY PETERSEN

10 July 1900 *Davenport Daily Leader*: CENTRAL PARK CONCERT
The second Central park concert of the season was given last evening, the music being furnished by the Albert Petersen full military band of 30 pieces. The delightful event was largely attended and from every point of view was a grand success.

The night was an ideal one for an open air concert and it would have been almost impossible to have secured a pleasanter evening for such an event. The park was well lighted and presented a very attractive appearance. It was certainly an enjoyable place for the large numbers of persons to spend an evening. The band last evening was on an elevated platform which had been erected special for the occasion.

The music was of a high standard and was of a nature quite complimentary to the band. The program was not only well arranged but every selection was admirably played. The well known organization rendered its selections under the able direction of Albert Petersen....

The park commissioners are to be congratulated upon the success of the free open air concerts at Central park. That they are being appreciated goes without saying. The concerts undoubtedly will in time be a great factor in educating many people up to an appreciation of first class music.

30 Aug 1900 *Daily Republican*: ORPHANS HOME ORCHESTRA
    THE BOYS WILL SOON ORGANIZE ONE UNDER ALBERT PETERSEN'S DIRECTION
The Orphans' home boys will soon turn out something better than the drum corps, as they are now being instructed in music, and will organize an orchestra soon. Albert Petersen of the Petersen band of this city will be temporary director, and hopes to have the boys in harmony soon. Various different string and brass instruments will be used, they being furnished by the institution. Miss Glenny, music teacher at the home, is having large classes under her care.

17 May 1902 *Davenport Republican*: THE ALBERT PETERSEN SUBSCRIPTION CONCERT
Manager Sonntag of Albert Petersen's orchestra has just announced the programs for the opening subscription concerts to be given this month at Schuetzen park and Black Hawk's Watch Tower. The subscription lists for both series have filled rapidly and the fact is very gratifying to the manager and the director of the orchestra. This is the sixth series of the subscription concerts at the Watch Tower and it is due to the popularity of these concerts and the repeated requests of friends that the Schuetzen park concerts are to be inaugurated this season. The opening concert at Black Hawk will take place Monday, May 21....The first Schuetzen park concert will take place on Thursday, May 29....

29 Oct 1904 *Tri–City Evening Star*: BIG CONCERT AT CLAUS GROTH HALL
    With Albert Petersen wielding the baton, the big Strasser–Petersen band concert at Claus Groth hall Sunday afternoon will give an interesting program. Some fine

numbers have been arranged and this, the second concert of the season, will be one of the best ever in Davenport.

7 July 1924 *Democrat–Leader*:
>ALBERT PETERSEN COMPOSES MARCH WITH CATCHING TUNE, SNAPPY WORDS
>Ta–Rum. Ta–Rum–TE Dum–Dum–Dum!!

Here comes the band playing Albert Petersen's latest composition "The Mississippi Valley Fair Boosters March" which will be featured on the booster trips to neighboring towns this month. The new selection was played for the first time in the concert at Fejervary Park Sunday afternoon and was heartily applauded.

Both the words and the music are the work of Mr. Petersen who has directed the bands on the booster trips for the past two years. The song will be practiced at the meetings of the civic clubs for the next two weeks and will also be placed on sale at local music stores and in towns that the fair boosters visit.

A very attractive title page was prepared by Frank A. Free, local photographer, containing pictures of Mr. Petersen and also of Al Thomas and Tom Dougherty, the Fair Booster Twins, and Secretary C.R. Miles of the Chamber of Commerce. There is also a picture of the main entrance to the fairgrounds and the Petersen Band.

13 Feb 1925: The famous Mississippi Valley Fair March, written expressly for the use of the big Davenport fair and exposition held every year, will be played as one of the encore numbers by the Tri–City Symphony orchestra in their concert to be given at the Masonic temple, Davenport, at 3 o'clock Sunday afternoon.

This march was written by Albert Petersen, a member of the viola section of the orchestra—one of the best known musicians in the Tri–Cities. Mr. Petersen, at the request of the board of directors of the Symphony orchestra, has written a special arrangement so that it could be played at this time as a special means of helping to add interest to the campaign now being conducted for the support of the fair.

Nearly everyone in the Tri–Cities is familiar with the swinging march air of Mr. Petersen's composition and its rendition by the Symphony orchestra will be watched with interest.

Several other encore numbers have been promised in accordance with the orchestra's announced policy of offering more encores on their popular programs this year.

01 March 1926 *Democrat–Leader*: NEW SCHOOL OF MUSIC IS BEGUN BY E. SWINDELL
>12 INSTRUCTORS TO TEACH MUSICAL ART AT DOWNTOWN STUDIO

A musical conservatory aimed to satiate the musical needs of Davenport and boasting a versatile staff of instructors, has been inaugurated by Erwin Swindell, he disclosed today. The new studio is located in the Whitaker building.

Mr. Swindell, who is director of the institution which will be known as the Swindell School of Musical Arts has engaged the services of 12 musicians looked upon in musical circles as leaders in their particular departments....

In addition to courses in horn, string, and band instruments and piano and voice, courses in teaching, history of music, orchestra conducting and ensemble, professional accompaniment, classical dancing, dramatic art, and motion picture playing will be offered. Harmony, counter points, and composition also will be taught, Mr. Swindell said.

Mr. Swindell, who is director of the school...is now organist at the Sacred Heart cathedral; director of the musical department of the Villa de Chantal of Rock Island; director of the piano department of the St. Ambrose college and musical director of WOC.

...ALBERT PETERSEN, head of the local band which bears his name, and a versatile musician, will instruct in band and string instruments and orchestra conducting besides ensemble work.

ARTHUR PETERSEN, a recognized teacher of the cello of long standing, will have charge of cello pupils.... Howard Snyder, former pupil of Mr. Swindell and now first organist at the Capital theatre, will teach motion picture organ playing.

30 July 1928 *Democrat–Leader*: BAND CONCERT ON THE LEVEE WELL ATTENDED
The largest crowd of the season was in attendance at the LeClaire park on the Davenport river front last night for the Petersen's Band, directed by Albert Petersen, presented another of the Max D. Petersen Memorial programs in the park pavilion. Trumpet solos by B.F. Tabor were very well received. A new composition of Albert Petersen, the Station WOC March won a tremendous outburst of applause.

ALBERT L. PETERSEN, VETERAN LEADER IN MUSIC HERE, DIES FUNERAL SERVICES SET TUESDAY, FOR DIRECTOR, 85
Albert L. Petersen, 85, 704 West Locust street, well–known Davenport musician and leader of the Petersen band here for many years, died at 5:58 a.m. Sunday in Davenport Osteopathic hospital after an eight–week illness. Before organizing his own band, which he directed in Max D. Petersen Memorial concerts in LeClaire park, Mr. Petersen was a member of Strasser's orchestra and band. He also organized and directed St. Ambrose college's first band and he organized the band at St. Vincent's home. In addition, Mr. Petersen was an organizer and charter member of Tri–City Symphony orchestra; and he was a past president of the American Federation of Musicians local here. At the age of 17, he directed an orchestra in the former Burtis Opera house, playing for many of the most notable actresses and actors in show business. He also directed an orchestra which provided a background for silent films in the former Grand theater. Mr. Petersen was born in Struxdorf, Schleswig–Holstein, Germany, September 4, 1865, and he came to America, directly to Davenport, when he was two years old. He married Carrie May Kennedy here Feb. 18, 1881. His wife died in July, 1949. He was a 50 year member of Central Davenport Turner society. Surviving are three sons, Arthur A. and Victor H., Davenport and Harry A., Moline; one daughter, Mrs. I.D. Besse, Indianapolis; four grandsons and one great granddaughter. One son Ceno,

preceded him in death. Funeral services will be held Tuesday at 4 p.m. in Runge chapel, with burial in Memorial Park.

A BATON IS STILLED

Davenporters of all ages, and particularly those who have lived in the community for four or more decades, will note with sadness the passing of a lovable man and a fine musician, Albert L. Petersen. This fine old gentleman, who for almost 65 of his 84 years served as a professional musician, played baritone horn, trumpet and violin well, directed college and school groups, was a charter member of the Tri–City Symphony orchestra, and headed a band which for many decades played in local Parks and concert halls. Albert Petersen loved music, and gave his long life to teaching and playing. In the slang phraseology of the day, he could well be called Davenport's "Mr. Music." From the time he became a member of the then famed Strasser's orchestra of Davenport at the age of 16, until he directed his final public concert in LeClaire park last July, he enjoyed both performing and teaching. St. Ambrose college, the Immaculate Conception academy, Villa de Chantel and Annie Wittenmyer home all utilized his teaching skill at various times. For many years he was director of theater orchestras, first at the old Burtis, and later at the Capitol. Thru the summer months, however he led his band in concerts at Vander Veer and Fejervary parks and at Black Hawk Watch Tower. He trained four sons and one daughter to be very capable musicians too, so that the name Petersen became one of the community's best known names in the field of music. Though his baton is now stilled, many will long remember him standing proud, erect and earnest among his musicians in a park pavilion, ready to give the signal for some featured number he hoped would please his audience.

Children of ALBERT L. PETERSEN and CAROLINE 'CARRIE' MAY KENNEDY
- Vinceno 'Ceno' Albert 07 Dec 1892–10 Jan 1949; Marriage: 16 Sep 1916 in Davenport; Spouse: Antoinette Virginia Moetzel, Aug 1895–May 1983; Son: Vincent Petersen, b. 09 Nov 1920; m. Winnifred Adelanine Tyerman
- ARTHUR ALEXANDER 13 May 1893–15 Mar 1968; Spouse: DOROTHY ELIZABETH GRIFFIN 15 Feb 1899–08 Apr 1962; Sons: ALBERT ALEXANDER, 18 Oct 1923–27 June 2003; wife: Ana Garcia–Nunez; children: Michael, Howard, Joseph, David, Dorothy; DONALD GRIFFIN, 08 Aug 1927–25 April 1998
- HARRY ALONZO PETERSEN, 21 Sep 1897–Mar 1964; Spouse: DOROTHY SWAN 1900–25 Nov 1960
- HELEN MARGARET PETERSEN 15 Oct 1901–28 Jun 1982; Spouse: IRA DALE BESSE 17 Jul 1893–Oct 1981
- VICTOR HERBERT PETERSEN 19 Jul 1908–12 Apr 2005; Marriage: 28 Aug 1937; Spouse: VIOLET HIRL, b. 1912; Son: JAMES VICTOR PETERSEN 15 Jan 1945; m. SUE M. SCHWARTE; sons JERALD J. PETERSEN, SCOTT M. PETERSEN

16 Sep 1916 MOETZEL–PETERSEN WEDDING SOLEMNIZED THIS AFTERNOON

A quiet wedding of today that calls forth the good wishes of the wide circle of friends of both young people will be that of Miss Antoinette Virginia Moetzel, daughter of Mr. and Mrs. Ernest A. Moetzel of 1511 Harrison street, Davenport; to Mr. Ceno A. Petersen, of Davenport, son of Mr. and Mrs. Albert L. Petersen of 704 West Locust street. The event will be solemnized at four o'clock this afternoon at the parsonage of St. John's M.E. church, Rev Frank Cole to officiate. The bridal couple will be attended by Mrs. Lawrence E. Beckwith, a cousin of the bride, as matron of honor and Mr. Arthur Petersen, brother of the groom as best man. The bride will be gowned in a handsome dark brown broadcloth tailored suit, trimmed in black fur. The blouse is of white Georgette crepe and hat is a brown velvet model. Her flowers will be a corsage bouquet of bride's roses. The matron of honor will wear a black taffeta coat suit, with a pink Georgette crepe waist and a pink hat. She will wear a corsage bouquet of pink roses. The wedding dinner for the bridal party will be served at the home of the bride's parents. This evening a reception will be held at the Moetzel home for relatives only, the company to number about forty–five. The rooms are prettily decorated with pink and white asters in bouquets and with ferns and tropical plants. A buffet supper will be served, the table being done in asters in the wedding colors. Mr. and Mrs. Petersen will leave on a late train for Chicago and will go thence to St. Louis for their honeymoon trip. They will be home after Oct. 1 at 1510 1/2 Harrison street, Davenport, where the groom has a cosy apartment in readiness for his bride. Miss Moetzel is an attractive young Davenport woman, a graduate of the high school and has a host of friends. She has a sweet soprano voice and has sung on several occasions before the Davenport Women's club of which she is a member. Her father, Mr. E.A. Moetzel, is a prominent druggist. Mr. Petersen is a well known musician and successful music teacher of the city. He comes of a musical family, his father Mr. Albert Petersen, being the leader of the Petersen orchestra. The groom is a member of the Hotel Blackhawk orchestra and of the orchestra of the Har–Cen–Art* theatre. Mrs. W.T. Doak of Chicago is an out of town guest here for the wedding.

*Har–Cen–Art, 1814–20 Harrison Street, named for and operated by Petersen brothers Harry, Ceno & Arthur

14 Oct 1926 *Democrat–Leader*:

CENO PETERSEN NAMED HEAD OF BERKELL BAND

LOCAL MUSICIAN WILL MANAGE ORCHESTRA AT THE GRAND THEATER

Ceno Petersen, well known Davenport musician has been named director of the new Berkell players orchestra at the Grand theater it was announced today by Charles Berkell, manager of the theater. The new orchestra will be composed of six pieces.

Mr. Petersen, who is the son of Albert Petersen, director of Petersen's band has had considerable experience in orchestra work and is an accomplished musician.

Capacity houses are greeting the Berkell players this week in their presentation of "The Four–Flusher" Caesar Dunn's three act comedy. For next week Mr. Berkell announces the attraction will be "The Best People" by Avery Hopwood and David Grey. "The Best People" enjoyed a long run in New York and was acclaimed by the critics to be a big laugh producer. The story has to do with the jazzy proclivities of the younger generation, particularly the offspring of the so called "best people." The daughter of an aristocratic family causes the family to go into hysterics when it is discovered that she's fallen in love with the family chauffeur. About the same time the son falls in love with a chorus girl and there are more hysterics. But everything turns out as it should although there is a surprise just before the final curtain.

11JAN1949—CENO PETERSEN NOTED DAVENPORT MUSICIAN, DIES Ceno Petersen, 56, 711 Farnam street, prominent Davenport musician and lifelong resident here, died at 11 p.m. Saturday in Mercy hospital following and illness of several months. Mr. Petersen was born in Davenport on Dec.7, 1892, and was educated in the schools here. He was married to Antoinette Moetzel in Davenport in 1916. Surviving are the widow; a son, Vincent; a granddaughter, Lora Beth Petersen; his parents, Mr. and Mrs. Albert Petersen; three brothers, Arthur, Harry and Victor, all of Davenport and a sister, Mrs. Dale Besse, Indianapolis, Ind. The body was removed to the Runge mortuary. Funeral arrangements will be announced.

CENO PETERSEN FUNERAL SET FOR TUESDAY; WAS WELL–KNOWN MUSICIAN
Funeral services for Ceno Petersen, 56, of 711 Farnam street, a member of one of Davenport's prominent musical families, will be held at 2:30 p.m. Tuesday in Runge chapel. Burial will be in Oakdale Cemetery. Mr. Petersen died at 11 p.m. Saturday in Mercy hospital following an illness of several months. A lifelong resident of Davenport, he was born Dec. 7, 1892, and was educated in the schools here. He married Antoinette Moetzel in Davenport in 1916. Mr. Petersen, well known as a musician, was a member of the Tri–City Musicians society, Local No.67, and the American Federation of Musicians. Survivors include his wife; a son Vincent Petersen; his parents, Mr. and Mrs. Albert Petersen, all of Davenport; three brothers, Arthur and Victor Petersen, both of Davenport, and Harry Petersen, Moline, and a sister, Mrs. Dale Besse, Indianapolis, Ind.

ARTHUR PETERSEN, Q–C MUSICIAN, DIES
Arthur A. Petersen, 74, a prominent Quad–City musician died this morning at Mercy Hospital after a brief illness. He resided at 3025 Brady St. Davenport. Mr. Petersen was a charter member of the Tri–City Symphony, from which he retired two years ago. He had been a principal cellist with the symphony. He had been president of local 67, American Federation of Musicians. He was a member of the Davenport Eagles Lodge. Mr. Petersen's father, the late Albert Petersen was also a well known musician and had conducted river front concerts at LeClaire Park for more than 35 years. He had also been a member of the St. Ambrose College music faculty. Mr. Petersen was born in Davenport. He married the former Dorothy Elizabeth Griffin in Muscatine. The couple came to Davenport after their marriage.

Mrs. Petersen preceded him in death. Survivors include sons, Albert A., El Paso, Tex., and Donald G., New York City; six grandchildren; a sister, Mrs. Ira (Helen) Besse, Ambia, Ind. and a brother, Victor, Davenport. The body was taken to the Runge Mortuary.

ARTHUR A. PETERSEN, president of Local 67, Davenport, Iowa, for thirty years, passed away on March 15 at the age of seventy–four. Joining Local 67 on March 4, 1910, Mr. Petersen had served as a member of the executive board and as vice president before being elected President of the local on April 5, 1937. He had attended the conventions of the Federation twenty–six times. A charter member of the Tri–City Symphony Orchestra, Mr. Petersen played cello with that organization for fifty–two years. In the 1920s he performed with the Hawkeye String Ensemble over radio station WOC, Davenport. He also performed locally with the Gisela Weber Trio for a time.

20 Nov 1924 *Democrat–Leader*:
PICTURE SHOW, VAUDEVILLE, AND DANCING COMPRISE FINE PROGRAM
It is doubtful if a roll call of members of the Davenport Advertisers' club taken at the club's party at the Fort Armstrong theater in Rock Island on Wednesday night would have revealed the absence of five people. The membership was augmented by friends and ladies to the extent of approximately 300.

The entertainment commenced with the second showing of Zane Gray's "The Border Legion," the Fort Armstrong feature of the week and the Charles Novelty orchestra with Dicksey Mason...dance numbers were sandwiched between solos by Miss Mason, whose caroling is reminiscent of that of the beloved Sophie Tucker.

A supper was served at midnight at the Johnson cafeteria after which a program was given in the theater auditorium by the Ad club quartet: Miss HELEN PETERSEN, soprano, accompanied by Mrs. Amelia Schmidt Gobble; Jack Glasgow, pianist; and Miss Mason, whose "I'm Nobody's Sweetheart" set all the male hearts aflutter. Dancing was resumed until 2 o'clock.

10 April 1925 *Davenport Democrat–Leader*:
[photos of] These women were riding in a Cadillac sedan which got beyond control of the driver, Mrs. J.J. Ryan, 716 West Locust street, and backed down a steep embankment more than 100 feet long at Sixth and Scott streets at 2:45 Thursday afternoon. According to first reports Mrs. Ryan was the only passenger who stayed in the car, but later information is that Mrs. Ryan and Miss Helen Petersen, well known in musical circles in this city jumped from the front seat as the car plunged backward toward Sixth street.

Mrs. A.C. Feddersen, prominent in musical and social circles, who was riding in the rear seat us unable to get out of the machine and remained in the car. The women were on their way to attend a meeting of the Etude club at the Richard

Haak home at 625 Scott street when the accident happened. Miss Petersen and Mrs. Feddersen were to appear on the program and Mrs. Ryan was to be a guest. Mrs. Ryan was taken to the Haak home and a physician was called. She was later removed to Mercy hospital. She was not seriously injured. Miss Petersen's knee was injured when she leaped from the car. Mrs. Feddersen was not injured.

Those who witnessed the accident declare it was nothing short of a miracle that the women were not killed. The car scraped an iron railing set in concrete steps which leads north from Sixth street and this is thought to have prevented the machine from tipping and rolling down the steep bank.

27 AUGUST 1925 *Davenport Democrat–Leader*:

DAVENPORT GIRL LEAVING ON LONG TRIP

MISS HELEN PETERSEN OFF FOR 14–WEEK SCENIC CHAUTAUQUA TOUR

Miss Helen Petersen, daughter of Mr. and Mrs. Albert L. Petersen and one of Davenport's talented singers, leaves Monday on a Chautauqua tour of 14 weeks which will take her thru the states of Colorado, Utah, New Mexico, Arizona, California, Oregon, Washington, Montana, Idaho, Wyoming and Nevada. The Ellison–White circuit, on which she is booked, calls it their scenic tour.

Miss Petersen will be a member of the Artisan Novelty Trio, the other members being Miss Betty Luce, violinist, and Ira Dale Besse, basso. Both ladies are accomplished pianists, and Mr. Besse is a well–known entertainer, and the clarinet, saxophone and other instruments, and readings, figure in their programs. They will meet at Lincoln, Neb., for rehearsals, and open their tour at Denver. Miss Petersen has an offer of a year's bookings if she cares to prolong the tour.

Her engagement came about thru the visit here last winter of the Leake Entertainers, who played at the Moline High School. Mr. Leake is a cousin of Miss Petersen, and an organizer of Chautauqua companies. Visiting at the Petersen home, he was struck with Miss Petersen's talents, and has since urged her to seek a wider audience than she had here at home.

Miss Petersen was a pupil of Mrs. Amanda Schmidt–Gobble, has had various piano instructors, and has been a popular member of local music circles for some time.

January 1925:   MALE QUARTET ON CHAUTAUQUA

HIGHLY POPULAR PROGRAM IS PROMISED BY K. OF P. COMPANY

That the program to be given by the Troubadour Male Quartet on the K. of P. entertainment course, January 5 at the High School Auditorium is of a highly popular nature, is indicated by some of the numbers which are to be offered as ensemble selections, including "Hello Prosperity," "I Love a Little Cottage," "The Hunting Scene," "Close Harmony," "An Old–Fashioned Town," and many other favorites. Their entertainment is featured not only by vocal numbers, but also by all instrumental combination consisting of saxophone, banjo, cornet, violin and piano. One of their specialties is a group of negro spirituals, such as "I'll be Ready When the Great Day comes" and "De Ol' Ark's A–Movein'."

MOCRAT AND LEADER — APRIL 10, 1925

Society Women Who Narrowly Escaped Death When Car Went Over Scott Street Embankment

MRS. J. J. RYAN.

MISS HELEN PETERSEN.

MRS. A. C. FEDDERSEN.

These women were riding in a Cadillac sedan which got beyond control of the driver. Mrs. J. J. Ryan, 716 West Locust street, and backed down a steep embankment more than 100 feet long at Sixth and Scott streets at 2:45 Thursday afternoon. According to first reports Mrs. Ryan was the only passenger who stayed in the car, but later information is that Mrs. Ryan and Miss Helen Petersen, well known in musical circles in this city jumped from the front seat as the car plunged backward toward Sixth street.

Mrs. A. C. Feddersen, prominent in musical and social circles, who was riding in the rear seat was unable to get out of the machine and remained in the car. The women were on their way to attend a meeting of the Etude club at the Richard Haak home at 625 Scott street when the accident happened. Miss Petersen and Mrs. Feddersen were to appear on the program and Mrs. Ryan was to be a guest. Mrs. Ryan was taken to the Haak house and a physician was called. She

was later removed to Mercy hospital. She was not seriously injured. Miss Petersen's knee was injured when she leaped from the car. Mrs. Feddersen was not injured.

Those who witnessed the accident declare it is nothing short of a miracle that the women were not killed. The car scraped an iron railing, set in concrete steps which leads north from Sixth street and this is thought to have prevented the machine from tipping and rolling down the steep bank.

MALE QUARTET ON CHAUTAUQUA

Highly Popular Program is Promised By K. of P. Company

That the program to be given by the Troubadour Male Quartet on the K. of P. entertainment course, January 8, at the High School Auditorium is of a highly popular nature, is indicated by some of the numbers which are to be offered as ensemble selections, including "Hello Prosperity," "I Love a Little Cottage," "The Hunting Scene," "Close Harmony," "An Old-Fashioned Town," and many other favorites. Their entertainment is featured not only by vocal numbers, but also by an instrumental combination consisting of saxophone, banjo, cornet, violin and piano. One of their specialties is a group of negro spirituals, such as "I'll be Ready When the Great Day Comes" and "Do Ol' Ark's A-Moverin'."

Ralph Russell, director, baritone and pianist, is well known through many years' experience as a lyceum entertainer. Ira Dale Besse, basso with the singing quartet, also is an expert on saxophone and clarinet. Edgar Geise, tenor, cornetist and banjoist, formerly toured with the Scotch Highlanders Band. Mark Cook, first tenor, also is an exceptional violinist, one of his feature numbers being "Perpetual Motion."

Top:
4-10-1925

Left:
Jan 1925
Ira Dale Besse

Right:
Aug 27, 1925
Helen Petersen joins her future husband on tour

DAVENPORT GIRL LEAVING ON LONG TRIP

Miss Helen Petersen Off for 14-Weeks Scenic Chautauqua Tour.

Miss Helen Petersen, daughter of Mr. and Mrs. Albert L. Petersen and one of Davenport's talented singers, leaves Monday on a Chautauqua tour of 14 weeks, which will take her thru the states of Colorado, Utah, New Mexico, Arizona, California, Oregon, Washington, Montana, Idaho, Wyoming and Nevada. The Ellison-White circuit, on which she is booked, calls it their scenic tour.

Miss Petersen will be a member of the Artisan Novelty Trio, the other members being Miss Betty Lucas, violinist, and Ira Dale Besse, basso. Both ladies are accomplished pianists, and Mr. Besse is a well-known entertainer, and the clarinet, saxophone and other instruments, and readings, figure in their programs. They will meet at Lincoln, Neb., for rehearsals and open their tour at Denver. Miss Petersen has an offer of a year's bookings if she cares to prolong the tour.

Her engagement came about thru the visit here last winter of the Leslie Concertizers, who played at the Madise High School. Mr. Leslie is a cousin of Miss Petersen, and as organizer of Chautauqua companies, visiting at the Petersen home, he was struck with Mrs. Petersen's talents, and has since urged her to seek a wider audience than she had here at home.

Miss Petersen was a pupil of Mrs. Amanda Schmidt-Gobbin, has had various piano instructors, and has been a popular member local musical circles for some time.

Ralph Russell, director, baritone and pianist, is well known through many years' experience as a lyceum entertainer. IRA DALE BESSE, basso with the singing quartet, also is an expert on saxophone and clarinet. Edgar Geise, tenor, cornetist and banjoist, formerly toured with the Scotch Highlanders Band. Mark Cook, first tenor, also is an exceptional violinist, one of his feature numbers being "Perpetual Motion."

ALBERT ALEXANDER PETERSEN, 78, passed away Friday, June 27, 2003, in El Paso, Texas. Services were held in El Paso, Texas. Survivors include his wife of 48 years, Ana Maria Petersen; sons, Michael Petersen, El Paso, Texas, Howard Petersen, Fort Worth, Texas, Dave Petersen, El Paso, Texas, and Joseph Petersen, Frisco, Texas; a daughter, Dorothy Cummins, Sandia Park, Minn.; 10 grandchildren; nieces; nephews; cousins; and many friends. He was preceded in death by his PARENTS, ARTHUR AND DOROTHY PETERSEN. He is survived by a brother Donald Petersen; an uncle Victor Petersen and his wife Violet, cousins James and Vincent Petersen, both of Davenport. Memorials may be made to St. Labre Indian School or the Leukemia and Lymphoma Society. Albert was born in Davenport, Iowa on October 18, 1923, the son of Arthur Petersen, principal cellist for many years at Tri–City Symphony Orchestra. He attended St. Ambrose College, Davenport, and held bachelor's and master's degrees in music from the University of Iowa. He served in the U.S. Navy in the Pacific Theater during World War II, participating in the invasion of Saipan. Descending from a family of musicians, he joined the El Paso Symphony Orchestra and was principal bassist for more than 30 years. He also taught orchestra in El Paso Independent School District for more than 30 years, with many pupils going on to prominent music careers. He was choir director for Blessed Sacrament Church, ushered at St. Luke's and served as a music librarian. He also was the family genealogist, and avid reader, a bird lover, a regular blood donor, a loving husband and father and a good man.

VICTOR H. PETERSEN, 96, of Davenport, passed away Tuesday April 12, 2005, at Davenport Lutheran Home. Funeral services will be Friday in The Runge Mortuary Chapel. Visitation will be 10–11:30 a.m. Friday at the mortuary. Burial will be in Davenport Memorial Park Cemetery. Memorials may be made to Our Lady of Victory Catholic Church, Davenport. Victor was born July 19, 1908, the son of Albert and Carolyn (Kennedy) Petersen. He married Violet Hirl on August 28, 1937, in Grand Rapids, Mich. He had been employed by DRI and NW Railroads for 24 years, retiring in 1964. Victor was very involved in the Quad Cities music scene. He had repaired and built violins most of his adult life and operated his own violin repair and rental business for 24 years after retiring from the Railroad. He had played the cornet in the Petersen Band and played violin with the Tri–City Symphony. He was a former member of Davenport Moose Lodge and an avid golfer. He enjoyed spending time with his family especially his grandchildren and great–grandchildren. Survivors include his wife, Violet; and son and daughter–in–

law, James (Sue) Petersen, of Davenport, stepdaughter, Jean Stoffer of Dewitt, Iowa; grandchildren Jerry Petersen (Kay Winder), Scott (Julie) Petersen and Jay (Charity) Stoffer; and great–grandchildren, Sean, Rebecca and Christopher. He was preceded in death by his parents, three brothers and one sister.

JOHN HILL ESTATE

PETITION FOR LETTERS OF ADMINISTRATION

To the Circuit Court of the County of Scott:

The Petition of *Nelson Hill* of the *State of Iowa* in the County of *Dickinson* respectfully showeth: That *John Hill* of the *State of Iowa* in the said County of Scott, died in the *City* of *Davenport* on or about the *10th* day of *September* in the year of our Lord one thousand eight hundred and *Eighty Six* that at the time of his death he was an inhabitant of the County of Scott; that he left no will, as far as your petitioner has heard, or been able to discover; that he left *Personal property worth between Six and Ten Thousand Dollars and left no widow or children or parents surviving him.*

And your petitioner further showeth: that all the goods, chattels, and credits of the said deceased do not exceed in value the sum of *Ten Thousand ($10,000)* Dollars, and your petitioner prays that Letters of Administration of the goods, chattels, and credits of the said deceased may be granted by the Circuit Court to *David Hill, eldest brother of the deceased.*

Dated *Sept. 13th* 1886 *Nelson Hill* petitioner

STATE OF IOWA, SCOTT COUNTY

On this *13th* day of *September* 1886, personally appeared before me, *Nelson Hi*ll the above named petitioner, and made oath that the matters set forth in the above petition are true, to the best of the knowledge, information, and belief of said petitioner. *Hadley M. Henley, notary public Scott Co. Iowa*

TO THE CIRCUIT COURT OF SCOTT COUNTY, IOWA:

The undersigned Administrator of the Estate of *John Hill* Deceased, would respectfully report, in compliance with Chapter 71, Acts of the 9th General Assembly of Iowa, as follows, to–wit:

NAME OF DECEASED John Hill

DATE OF DEATH Sept 10th 1886

NAME OF WIDOW AND HEIRS/AGE/RESIDENCE: No widow or parents surviving; David Hill, 57, Denver, Colorado; Nelson Hill, 55, Spirit Lake, Iowa; Jane Kennedy, 57, Davenport, Iowa; Sallie Kennedy, 51, Davenport, Iowa; Mary Hill, 47, Davenport, Iowa; Lizzie Kidd, 45, New York City; Emily Harshaw, 43, Pittsburgh, Pa; Agnes Hilton, 16, Davenport, Ia; Addison Hill, 35, Pittsburgh, Pa; Wallace Hill, 37, Mercer Co. Pa

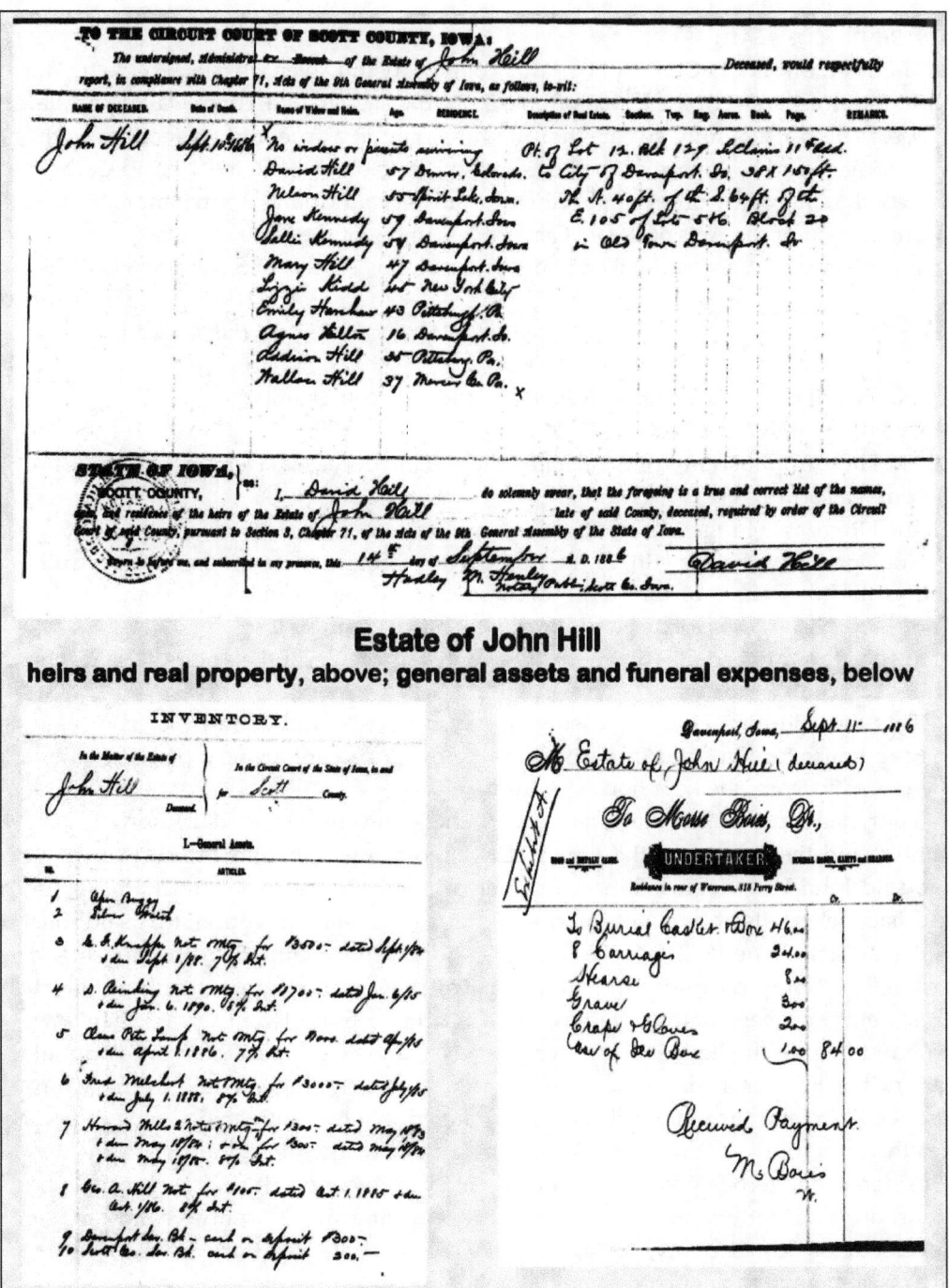

Estate of John Hill
heirs and real property, above; general assets and funeral expenses, below

DESCRIPTION OF REAL ESTATE

Pt of Lot 12, Blk 129 LeClaire's 11th Add. To the City of Davenport, Ia. 38x150 ft. The N. 40 ft of the S. 64 ft of the E. 105 of Lots 5 & 6 Block 20 in Old Town Davenport, Ia.

I, *David Hill* do solemnly swear, that the foregoing is a true and correct list of the names, ages, and residence of the heirs of the Estate of *John Hill* late of said County, deceased, required by order of the Circuit Court of said County, pursuant to Section 3, Chapter 71, of the Acts of the 9th General Assembly of the State of Iowa.

Sworn to before me, and subscribed in my presence, this *14th* day of *September* A.D. 1886

David Hill
Hadley M. Henley Notary Public, Scott Co. Iowa

In the Circuit Court of the State of Iowa, in and for Scott County:
Mary Hill, Plaintiff vs.
David Hill, Administrator of the Estate of John Hill, deceased, Defendant
December Term 1886
To the Honorable Judge of said Circuit Court:

Your petitioner, Mary Hill, of the County of Scott and State of Iowa, respectfully shows that the Estate of John Hill, deceased, is indebted to her in the sum of Six Thousand ($6,000.00) Dollars, and for cause of such claim states:

That she is an unmarried woman, forty seven years of age, and a sister the said John Hill, deceased.

That the said John Hill, deceased, was never married and that in 1865 she began to keep house for him, and from that time up to his decease, being a period of more than twenty years, she kept house for him.

Your petitioner states that one year of that time they resided in Rock Island, Illinois, and the balance of the time in Davenport, Iowa; that about fourteen years ago said John Hill, deceased, had a sun stroke, and he was never well afterwards and had sick spells at frequent intervals requiring constant attention; that said John Hill was sick from 1882 to 1886, and was an invalid confined to the house and unable to do any business, and from time to time needed great attention, which your petitioner personally gave him; that during all those twenty years there was no hired help in the house, except for one week, and she did all the work and took care of her brother at the same time when he was sick; that she had to dress him and feed him and lift him until she was broken down in health, and is now in poor health on account of this; that there were many works at a time when he was considered dangerously sick and not expected to live, and during such times the strain on your petitioner was very great; that during these twenty years she was never out of Scott County, Iowa, except when she lived in Rock Island County, Illinois, and gave constant attention to the house and her brother.

Your petitioner further states that during this period of twenty years she never received any compensation from said John Hill, for the reason that he told her that whatever was his would be hers at his death, and that he intended to leave what

Mary Hill
vs
Estate of John Hill
24 September 1886

In the Circuit Court of the State of Iowa, in and for Scott County;

Mary Hill, Plaintiff

vs

David Hill, Administrator
Of the Estate of John Hill, deceased,
                                                        ...ant.

December Term A.D., 1886

Petition.

To the Honorable Judge o...

Your petitioner, ...
of Iowa, respectfully ...
is indebted to her i...
and for cause of s... against the Esta[te]
                                    Six Thousand ($6[000.00])
That she is   suit.
a sister of the ...
That the ...
in 1865 she b...   STATE OF IOWA
his decease[d]   SCOTT COUNTY
house for ...
Your ...   I, Mary Hill
in Rock ...   the plaintiff named in
wort,   same read, and that the [facts con]-
had   tained are true as I ver[ily believe.]
spe ...
...

Subscribed and sworn t[o this]
...24th... day of ...

people that he intended to leave his property to your petitioner.

Wherefore your petitioner claims that she is entitled to at least Three Hundred ($300.00) Dollars a year, ($6000.00) Dollars in all ...

time needed great attention, which your petitioner personally gave him; that during all those twenty years there was no hired help in the house, except for one week, and she did all the work and took care of her brother at the same time when he was sick; that she had to dress him and feed him and lift him until she was broken down in health, and is now in poor health on account of this; that there were many weeks at a time when he was considered dangerously sick and not expected to live, and during such times the strain on your petitioner was very great; that during those twenty years she was never out of Scott County, Iowa, except when she lived in Rock Island County, Illinois, and gave constant attention to the house and her brother.

Your petitioner further states that during this period of twenty years she never received any compensation from said John Hill, for the reason that he told her that whatever was his would be hers at his death, and that he intended to leave what property he had to her to repay her for her devotion to him; that she did not receive from him more than $10.00 or $15.00 a year, and lived in a very economical way, and was the means of helping him accumulate a large part of the property which belongs to his Estate; that one of her other brothers, David Hill, was in the habit of giving her $75.00 or $100.00 a year as a present; that one of her sisters, Mrs. Lizzie Kidd of New York, was in the habit of giving her clothes, &c., as a present each year; that said John Hill, deceased, was perfectly willing to give her all the money she wanted, but she did not take it, for the reason that, as he claimed and as she believed, he could take better care of it for her and invest it to better advantage than she could, and that at his death it would be more valuable to her; that he told a number of

Agnes J. Hilton vs Estate of John Hill

In the Matter of the Estate of John Hill Dec'd } *In Probate No. 2474 Claim of Agnes J. Hilton*

And now on the [...] A.D. 1887, to wit at [...] A.D. 1887 of the [...] State of Iowa in the above entitled hearing on the cl[aim] By her Guardian De[...] court having heard of said claim, and was no objection to part of the heirs to [...] It is hereby or[dered] against said Esta[te] [...] in favor of Agnes [...] same is hereby al[lowed] of Eight Hundred ($[800]) per annum interest [...] day of May A.D. [...]

In the Circuit Court of the State of Iowa, in and for Scott County:

Agnes J. Hilton, by her Guardian, David Hill, plaintiff,

vs

David Hill, administrator of Estate of John Hill, deceased, defendant.

December Term A.D., 1886.

Petition.

To the Honorable Judge of said Circuit Court:

Plaintiff states that in May 1880 she inherited Eight Hundred ($800.00) Dollars from the Estate of her mother, who had died a short time previously; that Six Hundred ($600.00) Dollars of this money was loaned to James Thompson at 8 % interest, and Two Hundred ($200.00) Dollars of it was deposited in one of the Savings Banks in Davenport, Iowa; that after consultation with her Uncle, the late John Hill, and David Hill, another Uncle of hers, it was decided that said John Hill should take charge of said Eight Hundred ($800.00) Dollars to hold in trust for her; that said John Hill did collect the money, and since 1880 has had possession of the said Eight Hundred ($800.00) Dollars and has paid her no interest on the same.

WHEREFORE, plaintiff claims that this Estate is indebted to her in the sum of Eight Hundred ($800.00) Dollars, with interest thereon at the rate of 8 % per annum from May 1st., 1880, and asks for judgment against said Estate for the said Eight Hundred ($800.) Dollars with interest from May 1st., 1880 at the rate of 8 %, together with costs of this suit.

David Hill
Guardian

property he had to her to repay her for her devotion to him; that she did not receive from him more than $10.00 or $15.00 a year, and lived in a very economical way, and was the means of helping him accumulate a large part of the property which belongs to his Estate; that one of her brothers, David Hill, was in the habit of giving her $75.00 or $100.00 a year as a present; that one of her sisters, Mrs. Lizzie Kidd of New York, was in the habit of giving her clothes, etc., as a present each year; that said John Hill, deceased, was perfectly willing to give her all the money she wanted, but she did not take it, for the reason that, as he claimed and as she believed, he could take better care of it for her and invest it to better advantage than she could, and that at his death it would be more valuable to her; that he told a number of people that he intended to leave his property to your petitioner.

Wherefore your petitioner claims that she is entitled to at least Three Hundred ($300.00) Dollars a year, or Six Thousand ($6,000.00) Dollars in all, and asks for judgment in her favor against the Estate of said John Hill, deceased, for the sum of Six Thousand ($6,000.00) Dollars, together with costs of this suit.

[signed] Mary Hill

Subscribed and sworn to before me by the said Mary Hill this 24th day of September A.D., 1886.

[signed] Hadley M. Henley
Notary Public, Scott Co. Iowa

ORIGINAL NOTICE
In the *Circuit* Court of the State of Iowa in and for *Scott* County
December Term, A.D. 1886
Mary Hill, Plaintiff vs.
David Hill, Administrator of the Estate of John Hill, Deceased

To *David Hill, Administrator of Estate of John Hill, Deceased, David Hill, Nelson Hill, Mary Hill, Mrs. Lizzie Kidd, Jane Kennedy, Sallie Kennedy, Emily Harshaw, Agnes Jane Hilton, Addison Hill and Wallace Hill*...Defendants

You are hereby notified that a petition of *Mary Hill is now on* file in the office of the Clerk of the *Circuit* Court of the State of Iowa, in and for *Scott* County, claiming the sum of Six Thousand ($6,000) & 00/100 Dollars and costs of this suit for services rendered by said Mary Hill from 1865 to 1886 for John Hill, keeping house for him, attending him day & night through many years of sickness, etc. For full particulars reference is here made to the Petition now on file and that unless you appear thereto and defend before noon of the second day of the *December* Term, A.D. 1886 of said Court, which will commence at *Davenport* in said County, on the 6th day of *December* A.D. 1886, default will be entered against you and judgment rendered thereon.

Mary Hill plaintiff

ORIGINAL NOTICE
In the *Circuit* Court of the State of Iowa in and for *Scott* County
December Term, A.D. 1886

Agnes Jane Hilton by David Hill Guardian vs.
David Hill, Administrator of the Estate of John Hill, Deceased

To *David Hill, Adm. Est. John Hill, Dcd,* [sic] *David Hill, Nelson Hill, Mary Hill, Mrs. Lizzie Kidd, Jane Kennedy, Sallie Kennedy, Emily Harshaw, Addison Hill and Wallace Hill*…Defendants

You are hereby notified that a petition of *Agnes Jane Hilton by David Hill, Guardian is now on* file in the office of the Clerk of the *Circuit* Court of the State of Iowa, in and for *Scott* County, claiming the sum of *Eight Hundred ($800) & 00/100 Dollars with Eight per cent per annum interest from May 1, 1880, & for costs for funds in said amount belonging to said Agnes Jane Hilton which said John Hill held in trust and used as his own and so held at the time of his decease. For further particulars reference is here made to the Petition now on file* and that unless you appear thereto and defend before noon of the second day of the *December* Term, A.D. 1886 of said Court, which will commence at *Davenport* in said County, on the 6th day of *December* A.D. 1886, default will be entered against you and judgment rendered thereon.

David Hill, Guardian plaintiff

In the District Court of the State of Iowa in & for Scott County
Sept. Term 1887
Report of Administrator David Hill
In the Matter of the Estate of John Hill Deceased
To the Honorable Judge of said District Court:

Your petitioner, David Hill, Administrator of the Estate of John Hill, Deceased, respectfully shows unto the court that since the date of his appointment as such Administrator, he has duly qualified and filed his Bond, which has been approved, and also filed a full and complete Inventory; That appraisement of the personal property has been duly had and that the annexed statement shows all the receipts and disbursement, together with property in hand, since the date of his qualification as Administrator and up to Sept. 14th 1887….

Your petitioner further asks that this, his first annual report be approved.

Your petitioner further states that the year in which claims can be filed against the Estate has expired and that one claim in favor of Mary Hill for the sum of Six Thousand ($6,000) Dollars and one claim in favor of Agnes J. Hilton for Eight Hundred Dollars with 8% interest from May 1st 1880 has been allowed against the Estate under order of court; that no other claims have been filed and none are pending; that Agnes J. Hilton is entitled to a two eighteenth interest in this Estate; that Mary Hill by purchase and inheritance is now entitled to a Nine Eighteenth (9/18) interest in said Estate; and that David Hill by purchase and inheritance is entitled to a Seven Eighteenth (7/18) interest in said Estate; that the assignments of the interests purchased by the aforesaid parties have been filed and spread on the records of this court. [no additional text or pages]

In the District Court of the State of Iowa in & for Scott County
No. 2474
In the Matter of the Estate of John Hill Deceased
To the Honorable Judge of said District Court:

The undersigned David Hill, who owns an undivided one third interest in the above estate, and Mary Hill who owns and undivided five ninths (5/9) interest in the same, and Agnes J. Hilton, a minor seventeen and one half years of age, who owns an undivided one ninth interest in the same, all unite in consenting that the Administrator of said Estate, with the approval of the court, allow in full the claim of Mary Hill now on file against said Estate for the sum of Six Thousand ($6,000) Dollars.

David Hill
Agnes J. Hilton
Davenport, Ia. Sept 20th 1887

In Probate No. 2474
In the Matter of the Estate of John Hill Deceased
Claim of Agnes J. Hilton

And now on this 20th day of September A.D. 1887 to wit: at the September Term A.D. 1887 of the District Court of the State of Iowa in and for Scott County, the above entitled cause coming on for hearing on the claim Agnes J. Hilton by her Guardian David Hill, and the court having heard the evidence in support of said claim, and it appearing that there was no objection to said claim on the part of the heirs to said Estate,

It is hereby ordered that said claim against said Estate of John Hill, Deceased, in favor of Agnes J. Hilton be and the same is hereby allowed in the sum of Eight Hundred ($800) Dollars with 8% per annum interest thereon from the 1st day of May A.D. 1880. *N.F. Brannan* Judge

In Probate No. 2474
In the Matter of the Estate of John Hill Deceased

And now on the 22nd day of September A.D. 1887 to wit: at the September Term A.D. 1887 of the District Court of the State of Iowa in and for Scott County, the above entitled cause coming on for hearing on the first annual report of David Hill, Administrator of said Estate, which report is in words and figures as follows, to wit: (Here insert report in full)

And it appearing to the Court that said report is true & correct,

It is hereby ordered that the said Report be and the same is hereby approved and the Administrator is hereby ordered to distribute the estate among the parties entitled thereto according to their shares as set out in the aforesaid Report.

N.F. Brannan Judge

In the District Court of the State of Iowa in & for Scott County

Above: 615 E. 15th St—Aunt Mary's house

Below: 12th & Scott—former home of David Hill, granduncle of Bix

In the Matter of the Estate of John Hill Deceased
Receipt of Agnes J. Hilton by David Hill Guardian

Received of David Hill, Administrator of the above Estate the sum of Twelve Hundred Seventy ($1270) & 00/100 Dollars in full for my claim allowed against said Estate; and also the further sum of Three Hundred Eighty Seven ($387.40) 40/100 Dollars in full for my share viz. one ninth, in and to said Estate as Heir and I hereby consent to the approval of the final report and discharge of said Administrator.

Witness my hand this 22 day of September A.D. 1887.

David Hill Guardian

PETITION FOR GUARDIANSHIP
State of Iowa,
Scott County
TO THE CIRCUIT COURT OF SAID COUNTY

Your petitioner *David Hill* states that *Caroline Hill* late of *Davenport* in said County, died on or about *May* 1879* without having appointed by Deed or Will any Guardian for her children; that she left *one* child under the age of 14 years, to–wit: Agnes Hilton born Mar 1870 all of whom are residents of said County; said child is seizin** of real estate not exceeding $500 in value, and the annual rent thereof does not exceed $50. And said child is entitled to personal property not exceeding the value of $900.

That the father of said minor has not been heard from for over ten years and his whereabouts are unknown.

That your petitioner is the *Uncle of said minor*.

Your petitioner asks that *he* be appointed Guardian of the property of said child.

Your petitioner further states that *he* is a suitable person for such appointment, and consents to act as such, and to give the requisite bond.

Wherefore, your petitioner asks that he be appointed such Guardian.

Dated this *13th* day of *September* 1886

David Hill Petitioner.

Notarized by Hadley M. Henley, Scott County attorney

*Caroline died in 1880 **meaning full title to real property

24 September 1886
In the Circuit Court of the State of Iowa, in and for Scott County:
Agnes J. Hilton, by her Guardian, David Hill, plaintiff vs.
David Hill, Administrator of Estate of John Hill, deceased, defendant
December Term A.D. 1886 Petition
To the Honorable Judge of said Circuit Court:

Plaintiff states that in May 1880 she inherited Eight Hundred ($800.00) Dollars from the Estate of her mother, who had died a short time previously; that Six Hundred ($600.00) Dollars of this money was loaned to James Thompson at 8%

Estate transfer letters from Emily and W.J. Harshaw, 10-27-1886; Addison Hill, 7-11-1887; Nelson Hill, 9-20-1887:

In Probate No. 2474
For a valuable consideration the receipt of which is hereby acknowledged, I hereby sell, assign and transfer unto Mary Hill, of Davenport, Iowa, all my interest in and to the Estate of said John Hill, deceased; and hereby authorize and empower her to collect and receipt for my share as one of the heirs of said Estate.

interest, and Two Hundred ($200.00) Dollars of it was deposited in one of the Savings Banks in Davenport, Iowa; that after consultation with her Uncle, the late John Hill, and David Hill, another Uncle of hers, it was decided that said John Hill should take charge of said Eight Hundred ($800.00) Dollars to hold in trust for her; that said John Hill did collect the money, and since 1880 has had the possession & use of the said Eight Hundred ($800.00) Dollars, and has paid her no interest on the same.

WHEREFORE, plaintiff claims that his Estate is indebted to her in the sum of Eight Hundred ($800.00) Dollars, with interest thereon at the rate of 8% per annum from May 1st, 1880, and asks for judgment against said Estate for the said Eight Hundred ($800) Dollars with interest from May 1st, 1880 at the rate of 8%, together with costs of this suit.

[signed] David Hill, Guardian

In the Matter of the Guardianship of Agnes J. Hilton, minor # 2475

And now on this 24th day of March A.D. 1887, to wit—at the September Term A.D. 1887 of the District Court of the State of Iowa in & for Scott County, the above entitled cause coming on for hearing of the report of the Guardian, David Hill, which report is in hands of jurist as follows to wit: (Here insert report in full)

And it appearing to the court that said report is true & correct,
It is hereby ordered by the court that said Report be & thus same is hereby approved.

[signed] N.F. Brannan, Judge

In the District Court of the State of Iowa in and for Scott County
In the matter of the Guardianship of Agnes J. Hilton, Minor
September Term A.D. 1887
No. 2475 First Annual Report
. To the Honorable Judge of said District Court:

Your petitioner, David Hill, Guardian of the said Agnes J. Hilton, a minor, respectfully shows that since his appointment as such Guardian, he has duly qualified and filed his Bond which has been approved by the court; that during this period he has expanded money for the benefit of said minor as shown by the statement hereto annexed; that a claim in the sum of Eight Hundred ($800.—) Dollars with 8 % interest from May 1, 1880 has been allowed by this court in favor of said Agnes J. Hilton and against the estate of John Hill, deceased, and has been collected by your petitioner.

Also that the one ninth interest of said Agnes J. Hilton in the Estate of John Hill, rcvd as an heir has been collected by your petitioner in the sum of Three Hundred Eighty Seven ($387.40) & 40/100 Dollars; that said minor has an undivided one ninth interest in the real estate of said John Hill, deceased, which real estate is about to be partitioned by order of court.

Wherefore your petitioner prays for an order approving this report.

[signed] David Hill, Guardian
Notarized by Hadley M. Henley, attorney, September 27, 1887

In the District Court of the State of Iowa in and for Scott County
In the matter of the Guardianship of Agnes J. Hilton, Minor
February Term A.D. 1888
No. 2475 Final Report of Guardian
To the Honorable Judge of said District Court:

Now comes David Hill, Guardian of Agnes J. Hilton, a minor, and submits to the court this his final report in the above entitled cause:

He states that he received as Guardian of said minor about Twenty Four Hundred Dollars; that he has paid said money, or transferred notes and mortgages to said Agnes J. Hilton, in the above amount since March 1st 1888; that said Agnes J. Hilton arrived at the age of Eighteen years on the 1st day of March A.D. 1888; that he has settled in full with said Agnes J. Hilton since she attained her majority and her written consent for the approval of this final report and the discharge of said David Hill as Guardian is hereto also marked "Exhibit A" and made a part hereof; that said David Hill has expanded various sums for sending said minor to school during the time of this Guardianship, but he makes no charges or claims of any kind therefore or for any other services as such Guardian; that his duties as Guardian of said minor are now fully discharged.

Wherefore said David Hill asks the court to approve this his final report without any further notice or publication and that he and the sureties on his Bond be released and discharged from any further obligation herein.

[signed] David Hill
Notarized by Hadley M. Henley, March 7, 1888

In the Matter of the Guardianship of Agnes J. Hilton, minor
No. 2475 Exhibit A

On the first day of March A.D. 1888 I arrived at the age of Eighteen years and I hereby consent that David Hill, Guardian in the above entitled claim be discharged & that his final Report be approved & that the Administrator be excused from giving notice of his final report Mar. 8th 1888 [signed] Agnes J. Hilton

And now on this 8th day of March A.D. 1888, to wit—at the February Term A.D. 1888 of the District Court of the County of Scott and the State of Iowa the above entitled cause coming on for hearing of the final report of David Hill, guardian, which report is in hands of jurist as follows to wit: (Here insert report in full)
And it appearing to the court that said report is true & correct.

It is hereby ordered that said report be & is hereby approved and that said David Hill, Guardian, and the sureties on his Bond be discharged from any further obligation.

N.F. Brannan, Judge

AGGIE'S LETTER
[7 pages/c. October 1900]

Dear Aunt Mary,

We arrived here last night at six o'clock, after a lovely trip down the Hudson. Found Blanche and Frank waiting to meet us. They are all well. Auntie looks so nice and is a little fleshier, Aunt Lizzie is just as she used to be.

After supper, or rather dinner, Bix and Frank went downtown, Burnette went to sleep, and we sat up and talked till ten o'clock.

We are all well, your letter arrived before we got here and I was afraid to open it, but when I did was so glad to find you all doing so nicely.

I was homesick for Louise, now they would like to have you both here. But Aunt Lizzie said she knew it would not do, for you would have had all the care of both.

Aunt Lizzie has it all planned to take full charge of Burnette while we four bum.

They have two girls now and so we have nothing to do, the second girl likes children so well. She met us at the door with white cap, collar and apron. Waits on the table so lovely and has the table set with candles on the corners.

Frank and Blanche are so nice. Now don't write anything about this, but Aunt Lizzie thinks they will go to Greenville to live next Spring.

Auntie knows nothing of this so don't dare write about it.

I bet you enjoyed yourself at Oma's and the baby, too. I have seen so many little velvet cloaks and all have that little vest in front just like Sister's. All I have to do is put some lace on the collar. The little bonnets are gorgeous. The little girls wear their hair cropped so funny. I'll have to start that in Davenport.

Bix was a little sea sick on the boat yesterday, and I had a spell of it Friday and Burnette threw up a little.

Be sure and write right away, all about the "Sweetie Que."

Tell Annie not to work too hard, and don't either of you starve. I had the most elegant plum pudding on the boat yesterday that I ever tasted, cost twenty cents a slice. Oh, the boats are grand on the river and the scenery is

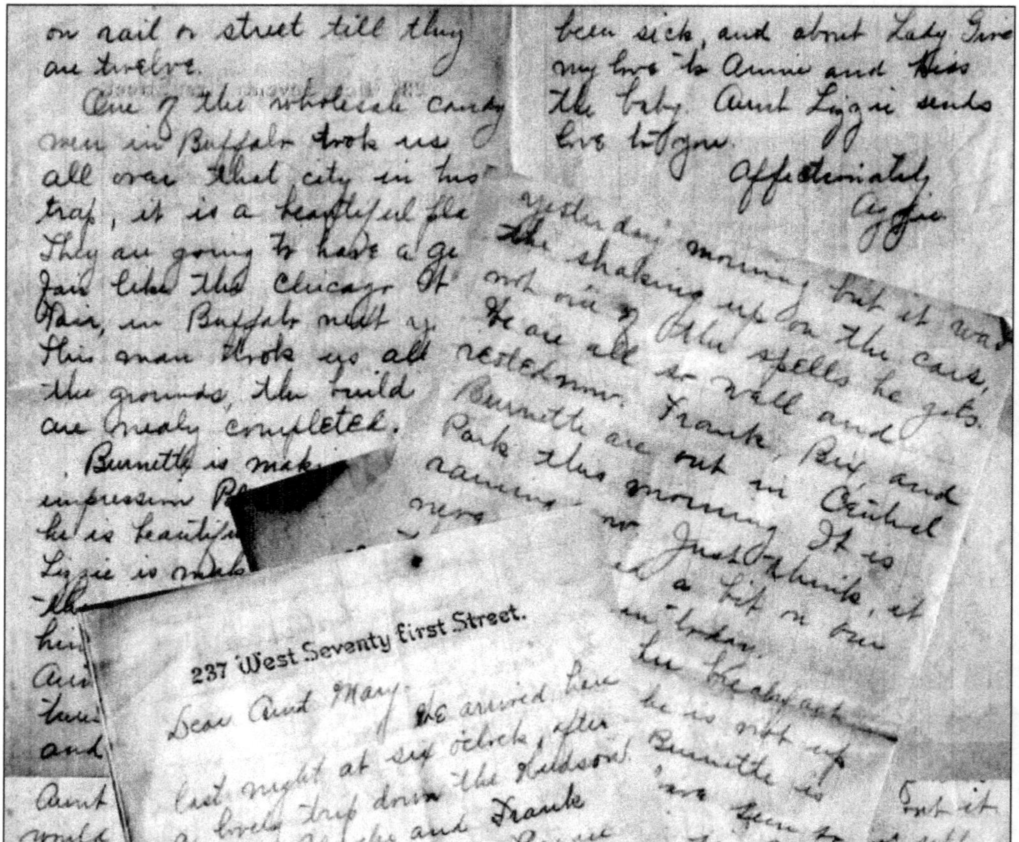

[Overlapping handwritten letter fragments; partial transcription follows.]

Letter 1 (background):

...on rail or street till they are twelve.

One of the wholesale candy men in Buffalo took us all over that city in his trap, it is a beautiful pla[ce]. They are going to have a g[reat] fair like the Chicago [fair] in Buffalo next y[ear]. This man took us all [over] the grounds, the build[ings] are nearly completed.

Burnette is maki[ng an] impressive [...] he is beautif[ul ...] Lizzie is [...]

...been sick, and about Lady [Give] my love to Annie and kiss the baby. Aunt Lizzie sends love to you.

Affectionately,
Affie

Letter 2 (middle):

Yesterday morning but it wa[s] the shaking up on the cars, one of [...] spells he gets. We are all so well and Burnette, Frank, Bix and [...] are out in Central Park this morning. It is raining — no Just think, it [...] a bit [...]

Letter 3 (front):

237 West Seventy first Street.

Dear Aunt Mary,

We arrived here last night at six o'clock, after a lovely trip down the Hudson. Found Blanche and Frank waiting to meet us. They are all well. Auntie looks so nice and is a little fleshier, Aunt Lizzie is just as she used to be. After supper, or rather dinner, Bix and Frank went down town, Burnette went to sleep, and we sat up and talked till ten o'clock.

We are all well. Your letter arrived before we got here and I was afraid to open it, but when I did was so glad [...] anything. Burnette threw up a little

lovely, great mountains rising up, right out of the river. I never paid one cent for Burnette from home to the house except of course, his meals. When at home he has to pay to go downtown. They do not charge car fare or rail or street till they are twelve.

One of the wholesale candy men in Buffalo took us all over that city in his trap, it is a beautiful place. They are going to have a great fair like the Chicago World's Fair, in Buffalo next year. This man took us all over the grounds, the buildings are nearly completed. Grand!

Burnette is making a fine impression. Blanche thinks he is beautiful and Aunt Lizzie is making him toe the mark. You ought to see him this afternoon he is in Auntie's room cutting out pictures. Now write immediately and tell me if you have been sick, and about Lady. Give my love to Annie and kiss the baby. Aunt Lizzie sends love to you.

      Affectionately,
      Aggie

[*Bix* refers to Aggie's husband Bismark; *Aunt Lizzie* is Lizzie Hill Kidd of New York; *Frank & Blanche* are Lizzie's children—about the same age as Aggie; *Auntie* is Jane Crowder, Adam Hill's sister. *Louise* and *Sister* refer to daughter Mary Louise; Lady is possibly Aunt Mary's dog.]

In 1988, Marjorie Kuehl of Davenport shared the following story about her mother, whom Aggie referred to as Annie in her letter to Mary Hill:

I knew Bix briefly because for about three years my mother, Anna Rauch Wiese, was a domestic helper for the Beiderbecke family. She also took care of his brother, Charles, and sister, Mary Louise.

His parents came to our house for dinner on occasion and we were invited to supper there. I remember a meal when Bix was there, but the thing I recall most about it was not Bix, but they scooped out cantaloupes filled with ice cream. I've never forgotten how grand that seemed.

Bix must have been about 14 or 15 then and I was six years younger. He ate with us, and I don't remember anything out of the ordinary about his conversation. He was just a normal–looking teenager.

But toward the end of the meal, he got up, put on a navy blue jacket, picked his horn off the piano and walked out the door. I guess he had a job to play. That was the last time I ever saw him.

OTHERS WHO WORKED IN THE BEIDERBECKE HOUSEHOLD

I am happily enjoying my 94th year. The following incident occurred probably in the year I was 14 or 15 and still in high school, when one evening I received a phone call from Mrs. Beiderbecke. She explained, one of her friends had suggested I might help her in a time of need. She explained, her son Bix, would be coming for a visit—she would have extra company and would need some help. Since I was free, I arranged to be there to help.

I remember setting a large table. I also remember Mrs. Beiderbecke said, "If anyone asks you to open that lower cupboard in the dining room, just say it's locked."

However, no one asked me to do so, so I had no problem. There was a large table set in the dining room for many guests, including the son, Bix. It was a jolly and talkative group who enjoyed the meal. Bix ate little but drank wine. There was no problem at any time. He was jolly and talkative and enjoyed some wine but ate very little. He seemed very nice and pleasant and glad to be in his home town.

—Jennie McDermand, letter dated 10 March 2003

The late Elvina Youngberg, Davenport, thought she might have inadvertently conned Bix Beiderbecke into taking his first drink.

No, it wasn't in some Roaring '20s honky-tonk and Bix didn't know a horn from a rattle since he was all of two years old and the only bottle he yearned for was full of good old milk. Elvina was fourteen years old and babysitting the future musical prodigy.

Bickie, as he was called by his family, was just being taken off the bottle and kept wailing for it. "I kept telling him I'd broken his bottle and he had to drink from a glass. He wasn't easily convinced, but finally I fooled him and he took the glass just fine," she remembered. AI know that was his first drink from a glass and I was the one who gave it to him."

Emma Doering Offerman was nanny to three-year-old Bix. In a 1997 interview with Jim Arpy, Emma's granddaughter Catherine Bealer said: "I grew up hearing all about Bix, not so much that he was a famous person,

Nanny Emma, age 16

but rather what a special loving child he was." Catherine said her grandmother "spoke of having such a loving, close relationship with Bix that she named her third child, and only son, Leon Bix Offerman. One of the stories Grandma told was of Bix being ill and no one could comfort him because he wanted her. Mr. Beiderbecke sent the car for her and she returned to the house to care for Bix."

I knew Bix well and loved him to death as a dear friend, though I was five years younger and he was about 23.

I used to do maid work for his mom and dad, who entertained a lot, and later for his brother, Burnie and his wife.

Bix would come to his brother's house a lot. I was crazy about Dixieland music and anytime I'd say, "Bix, why don't you play the piano," I wouldn't have to coax him. We'd sit together on the bench and he'd play for me.

I felt like we were sweethearts, though, of course we were just good friends.

He came home during the last year of his life and I felt so sorry for him. He'd had pneumonia in New York and he'd have to lift his legs up with his hands when he first got up and then he'd just shuffle along.

I used to read and hear things about him that I knew weren't true. He was so handsome and nice. I was going steady then with the man who became my husband, but I'll tell you...I sure could have gone for Bix.

—Lillian Leonard, Davenport 1988

Charles Burnette Beiderbecke

Mary Louise Beiderbecke

Genealogy: Charles Burnette

CHARLES BURNETTE 'BIX' or 'BURNIE' BEIDERBECKE, 11 Aug 1895–Mar 1972; Graduation: 1914, Davenport High; He married Mary Dennison Neelans [misspelled as Neelan in newspapers] b. 22 Apr 1904 Onslow, IA, d. 22 Jan 1990, Jacksonville, IL.

3 November 1912, Davenport *Democrat–Leader*: The battle between Davenport high school and Coe College freshmen came down to an intercepted forward pass in the last minutes of the game. The score was 10 to 9 with Coe's Knapp grabbing victory with a fifty–five yard touchdown. Davenport's opponents admitted that this squad is the fastest bunch of football players in uniform. Indeed, for three years Davenport has maintained a championship team. Two years ago they won the state championship and last year came mighty close to claiming the honor again. The game yesterday was their first defeat this season. Davenport scored on a touchdown and a safety.
The lineups for this game were:
Davenport—Koch c, Thompson lg, Duley rg, BEIDERBECKE rt, Hagenboech lt, Roch re, Langwith le, Noth q, Day rhb, Hannssen lhb, Crosby, captain, fb.
Coe freshmen—Dunlap c, Spencer lg, Wills rg, Brannaman lt, Morton rt, Peschan le, Russett le, Lighter re, Skein q, Park rhb, Hedges, captain, lhb, and Knapp fb.

November 1913, Davenport High School Bulletin, *The Picayune*
   The fellows went to Dubuque on the 25th of last month and it is little wonder they ever came back, so engrossed were they with the city and its environs. In fact they were so pleased that souvenirs in the way of school pins and the like can be seen on some, while others have about them candy, and notes, all from the up–river town.
   Of course everyone knows the attraction. Dubuque is full of girls and they so affected the heads of the fellows that all played rotten ball the first half with the exception of Sears who, not being troubled with tender feelings for the opposite sex, simply put the opposing line to rout, stopping end runs and breaking every kind of interference.
   Then while the fellows were getting their wind, Coach Nixon had a little to say; quite a little, in fact, to judge from the change that came over the fellows when the second half opened. It may be well to state here that Tomson came out of his trance once in the first half, making a single touchdown, the try for goal failing. In the second half, however, the fellows woke up and added 26 points, making a final score of 32 to 0.

The second half is worth the telling. Almost immediately after the beginning of play Rhodes made a touchdown after a thirty yard run by Tomson. Rhodes was soon taken out and Kelly substituted. Later after the ball had seesawed back and forth for some time, Tomson crossed the line but fumbled the ball. Kelly was there, however, and covered the pigskin, giving another touchdown.

Rhodes went into Kaufmann's place in the last period. BEIDERBECKE made his first touch–down this year on a tackle–back formation worked from the ten yard line. Brownlie kicked the goal. Soon after the Sheldon Special was worked with effect, but the score was not counted as the boys were conveniently penalized. The fun came, however, when the same play was worked around the other end, immediately after.

Rhodes carried the ball and Brownlie kicked the goal, making a total of 32 points for Davenport. The most effective plays used by Dubuque were spread for formations which were at first hard to handle.

9 June 1924 *Democrat–Leader*:
BEIDERBECKE NEW MANAGER FOR HARNEDS
Purchases Victrola Department at Local Department Store
C. B. "Bix" Beiderbecke, popular young Davenport life underwriter, has taken over the management of the Victrola Department of the Harned & Von Maur store, it was announced today. He purchased the control of this department from the Murray co., which was managed by W. J. Murray. The new department manager at the local store enters upon his duties at once. He will continue the old policy of carrying a large stock of both popular and classical records. Leon B. Beiderbecke a younger brother of the department manager and also known as "Bix" will become associated with his brother in the Victrola Department in the near future. He is well known as a musician as he is now playing with the Wolverines Recording Orchestra of Chicago. A line of hand instruments will be added to the stock of the department.

29 July 1924 *Democrat–Leader*:
DICK VON MAUR DOPED TO TAKE SINGLES TITLE
Defaulting to Douglas Ludington to save himself for the men's doubles, Oliver Murray, favorite in the Outing club's annual tennis tournament, lifted Dick Von Maur into the position of favorite Monday afternoon. Von Maur, who has been displaying remarkable form for the past several weeks, is now looked upon to come thru his remaining matches and cop the singles championship without much difficulty. Monday L.R. King fell before the new favorite in straight sets, 6–1; 6–1....Results of other matches Monday follow:
Robert Fox defeated BURNETTE BEIDERBECKE, 6–3, 6–2....

13 Aug 1924 *Democrat–Leader*:
BECHTEL–HILL BEAT VON MAUR AND BEIDERBECKE
Harold Bechtel and Laurence Hill defeated Dick Von Maur and Bix Beiderbecke in the men's doubles of the Outing club tennis tournament in the only match played yesterday, 6–4; 6–2. Both Bechtel and Hill played in fine form. This afternoon Robert Fox and W.P. Kimball meet in the finals of the men's singles.

01 Dec 1925 *Democrat–Leader*:
ORTHOPHONIC VICTOR WILL SHOW MONDAY
DEMONSTRATION GIVEN AT HARNED & VON MAUR VICTROLA DEPARTMENT

Simultaneously with other Victor Talking Machine company dealers all over the United States, Harned & Von Maur will demonstrate to the public for the first time Monday in the Victrola department the orthophonic Victor talking machine, which has been the topic of discussion in the musical world for the last two months.

The exterior of the instrument has undergone no fundamental change, being enclosed in a handsome walnut cabinet of period design; the interior, however, is altogether different. One of its striking features is a great horn six feet in length, which is ingeniously folded and out of sight within the body of the cabinet. Above it is the usual record turntable and tone–arm, the later of new and improved construction. The sound box is completely changed, a unique diaphragm of duralumin being substituted for the old mica disc.

"The entire instrument, from needle to horn opening, has been carefully designed according to a mathematical formula based upon the principle of matched impedance," C.B. Beiderbecke, manager of the Victrola department at Harned and Von Maur, says. "Thus by perfect coordination of the various working parts one to another, it has been made possible to take the sound impulses from the needle and to conduct them smoothly and without distortion into the air. The result is music undiluted and undefiled."

Mr. Beiderbecke explains that heretofore there have been three chief defects in the talking machine—limited range, limited volume, and failure to bring out clearly the tone color of the sounds recorded, that indefinable quality by which it is possible to distinguish between the various instruments or voices even when playing notes of the same pitch. These difficulties have now been removed, he says. Thus the Orthophonic talking machine is capable of producing sounds as high as the highest not of the piccolo or as low as the deepest tons of the base viola. It can reproduce them in such a way that you can readily identify the notes of the violin, cornet, flute and every other variety of instrument, or voice.

For the first time a drum sounds like a drum, the harp like a harp, and the piano, one of the most difficult of all instruments to record, comes into its own at last with absolutely faithful and meritorious reproduction.

A varied and comprehensive musical program has been arranged to demonstrate the capacities of the new instrument in every field. The selections range from vocal

SOCIAL HAPPENINGS

A Maquoketa, Ia., wedding of this morning which is of unusual interest to Tri-City friends, is that of Miss Mary Dennison Neelan, daughter of Mr. and Mrs. John Neelan of Maquoketa, and Charles B. Beiderbecke, elder son of Mr. and Mrs. B. H. Beiderbecke of 1934 Grand avenue, Davenport.

The wedding took place at 10 o'clock at the residence of the bride, the Rev. Archibald Finden, pastor of the Congregational church at Maquoketa, officiating. Miss Ruth Neelan, sister of the bride as bridesmaid and Leon Beiderbecke, brother of the groom as best man attended the couple.

The bride was in her traveling suit of dark blue poirre 'trill and her flowers were roses. There was a wedding breakfast after the ceremony — only members of the two families being guests of the day, the yellow chrysanthemum and ferns with the wedding cakes and candles being used in decoration.

Mr. and Mrs. Beiderbecke left on an eastern trip and on their return to Davenport will reside on east High street.

Mr. and Mrs. B. H. Beiderbecke and Leon Beiderbecke, the parents and brother of the bridegroom went from Davenport for the ceremony.

The bride comes of a well known family of Maquoketa. She is a graduate of the schools of her home city and was for a time a student at Mercy hospital training school for nurses.

Mr. Beiderbecke is a member of a well known old family of Davenporters, being a grandson of the late Charles Beiderbecke, for whom he is named, and who was one of the founders of the well known pioneer firm of Beiderbecke & Miller.

Mr. Beiderbecke is manager of the music and victrola department of the Harned & Von Maur store of which he has been in charge for the past year or more.

MAQUOKETA GIRL WEDS WELL KNOWN DAVENPORT MAN

MRS. C. B. BEIDERBECKE.

Nov 12, 1926
Bix stood up for us at our wedding... he came from Detroit where he was playing with Goldkette... Bix played at our wedding on a sit-in basis.
—Burnie to Phil Evans, 1959

solos to full band and orchestral ensembles, with the plentiful mixture of dance and specialty selections.

Mr. Beiderbecke will be glad to play any selection of your own choosing and to show the difference between the reproduction of the superseded Victor models and the new Orthophonic machine. The Victrola department is located on the mezzanine floor.

10 Nov 1926 *Democrat–Leader*:

MAQUOKETA GIRL WEDS WELL KNOWN DAVENPORT MAN

A Maquoketa, Ia., wedding of this morning which is of unusual interest to the Tri-City friends, is that of Mary Dennison Neelan, daughter of Mr. and Mrs. John Neelan of Maquoketa, and Charles B. Beiderbecke, elder son of Mr. and Mrs. B. H. Beiderbecke of 1934 Grand avenue, Davenport. The wedding took place at 10 o'clock at the residence of the bride, the Rev. Archibald Finden, pastor of the Congregational church at Maquoketa, officiating. Miss Ruth Neelan, sister of the bride as bridesmaid and Leon Beiderbecke, brother of the groom as best man attended the couple. The bride was in her traveling suit of dark blue poirre trill and her flowers were roses. There was a wedding breakfast after the ceremony, only members of the two families being guest of the day, the yellow chrysanthemum and ferns with the wedding cakes and candles being used as decoration. Mr. and Mrs. Beiderbecke left on an eastern trip and on their return to Davenport will reside on east High Street. Mr. and Mrs. B. H. Beiderbecke and Leon Beiderbecke, the parents and brother of the bridegroom went from Davenport for the ceremony. The bride comes of a well known family of Maquoketa. She is a graduate of the schools of her home city and was for a time a student at Mercy hospital training school for nurses. Mr. Beiderbecke is a member of a well known old family of Davenporters, being a grandson of the late Charles Beiderbecke, for whom he is named, and who was one of the founders of the well known pioneer firm of Beiderbecke & Miller. Mr. Beiderbecke is manger of the music and victrola department of Harned & Von Maur, store of which he has been in charge for the past year or more.

22 December 1925 *Democrat–Leader*:

Quite the most interesting Christmas benefit ball which has ever been undertaken as a holiday event in the three cities is the holiday weekend dance St. Katharine's School Alumnae association is giving at the Davenport Outing club the evening of Dec. 29.

People far and near have a personal desire to make the affair an outstanding success, having the feeling of a close association with the school, either as patrons or students. All are desirous of buying tickets, not so much with the thought of going and having a delightful time themselves but rather cherishing the thought of helping the association and incidentally an institution which is one of the finest of its kind in the country.

Every committee has its activities outlined and is busily engaged in looking after its work so that the ball promises to be not only the social even but a financial success as well.

The floor committee, composed of Miss Josephine Von Maur, Mrs. Burton Forrester and Miss Eleanor Harned, will be assisted by a group of men in the following:

From Davenport—Richard Von Maur, John Van Patten, R.J. McKinney, BURNETTE BEIDERBECKE, Charles Duncan, Herbert Lohmiller, George Von Maur, Herbert Ruhl, Burton Forrester, E.C. Mueller, Charles Wilson and C.M. Cochrance. From Rock Island—Leon Mitchell, John Potter and Ben Potter. From Moline—Albert Crampton.

14 March 1929 *Democrat–Leader*: LOCAL RADIO SALESMEN ON CHICAGO TRIP

Seven members of the radio department of the Petersen Harned Von Maur store left last evening for Chicago where for two days they will be guests of the Griggsby–Grunow company, makes of the Majestic radio.

They are winners in a six week's sales contest. In Chicago they make daily trips to the factory where they will thoroughly familiarize themselves with the manufacture of the Majestic in all its details. Aside from business hours they will be entertained socially by the company.

The Davenporters joined the special train of Majestic dealers and salesmen at Clinton and from there continued the journey to Chicago.

Those making the trip from Davenport were Roy Fude, manager of the radio department at Petersen's and the following salesmen: C.B. BEIDERBECKE, Harold Wiese, Ben Curtis, R. Wiedenhoeft, August Schultz and Ralph Rynet.

30 March 1972: C.B. BEIDERBECKE; JAZZMAN'S BROTHER

Charles B. Beiderbecke, 77, brother of the late Leon Bix Beiderbecke, the legendary jazz trumpet player died Thursday at St. Luke's Hospital. Services for Mr. Beiderbecke, 601 1/2 Scott St. Davenport, will be 1 p.m. Saturday in the Hill & Fredericks Chapel, Davenport. Burial will be in Oakdale Cemetery. Visitation is from 7 to 9 p.m. today at the mortuary. Memorials may be made to the American Heart Assn. or to St. Luke's Hospital. Mr. Beiderbecke was formerly secretary–treasurer of the Oakdale Cemetery Co., Davenport and was elected president of the Iowa Cemetery Officials Assn. in 1943. In 1966, forced to retire from the Oakdale position by severe eye problems, he became the official host at St. Luke's Hospital, the only such position in the Quad–Cities. He was born in Davenport. He married Mary Neelans in 1926 in Maquoketa, Iowa. Mr. Beiderbecke is survived by his wife, sons Charles, Denver, Colo., and Richard, Decatur, Ill., five grandchildren, and a sister Mrs. Theodore Shoemaker, Lexington, Mass.

MARY BEIDERBECKE, 85 JACKSONVILLE, ILL. Mary N. Beiderbecke, 85, formerly of Davenport, died Monday at Passavant Hospital, Jacksonville. Mrs. Beiderbecke was the sister–in–law of Bix Beiderbecke, Davenport jazz musician. Memorial services will be 1:30 p.m. Wednesday at First Presbyterian Church, Jacksonville. Memorial services will be 2 p.m. Friday at First Presbyterian Church, Davenport. Burial of the cremains will be in Oakdale Cemetery, Davenport. Cody and Son Memorial Home Jacksonville, is in charge of arrangements. She was a registered nurse. Mary Neelan married Charles B. Beiderbecke. He died in 1972. She was a graduate of the former Mercy Hospital School of Nursing, Davenport. She was a member of the church. Memorials may be made to American Cancer Society. Survivors include sons, Charles H., Denver, and R. Bix, Jacksonville; five grandchildren; two great-grandchildren; and sisters, Ester Dahlberg, Moline, and Ruth Onken, Morrison.

Burial of Mary N. Beiderbecke: 26 Jan 1990 at Oakdale Cemetery, Davenport
Sons of C. Burnette & Mary Neelans Beiderbecke: Charles Hilton and Richard Bix.

CHARLES HILTON BEIDERBECKE, m. Eilene; Children:
- CHARLES MICHAEL, m. Susie
- STEPHEN RICHARD, m. Angela; children: Bix Alexander and Troy Marcus
- ANN WEIR, m. Scott Rush; children: Erik Paul Rush and Kristin Rush

DENVER—Charles H. Beiderbecke, 71, of Denver, formerly of Davenport, died Nov. 1, 1999, in Denver [Arvada, Colorado]. No services were held. The Body was cremated. Mr. Beiderbecke was employed in sales management. He was born Aug. 23, 1928, in Davenport. He was the nephew of jazz musician Bix Beiderbecke. During the Korean War, he served as a staff sergeant in the 48th Cavalry. Survivors include a daughter, Ann Weir Rush, Meridian, Idaho; sons, Charles M., Nashville, Tenn., and Stephen R, Lakewood, Colo., and a brother, Richard Bix Beiderbecke, Jacksonville, Ill.

RICHARD BIX BEIDERBECKE, m. Arlene; m. Judith Andrews; Burial: 29 July 2005 at Oakdale. Children of Richard and Arlene:
- CHRISTOPHER BIX BEIDERBECKE, b. 1958; son: James
- ELIZABETH ANNE 'LIZ' BEIDERBECKE, b. 07 March 1960, m. Carl Hart; daughters: Lauren Hart, b. 20 Mar 1991; Olivia Hart, b. 24 Oct 1994

Jacksonville, IL—Richard Bix Beiderbecke, 73, of Jacksonville, Ill, passed away peacefully Sunday afternoon, Sept. 5, 2004, at Passavant Hospital in Jacksonville after a lengthy battle with cancer. His family was with him throughout his ordeal. Bix was born Dec. 11, 1930, in Davenport, the son of the late Charles Burnette and Mary Neelans Beiderbecke. He is survived by his wife, Judith (nee Andrews), daughter Elizabeth (husband Carl) Hart, of Springfield, son Chris, of Moline, Ill.; and three granddaughters, Jana, Lauren and Olivia Hart. He was preceded in death by a brother, Charles Hilton Beiderbecke. Bix, nephew of the legendary jazz musician Bix Beiderbecke, attended the University of Iowa where he received his B.S. in psychology. He was a member of Beta Theta Pi social fraternity and captain of the Iowa Fencing Team for two years. During the Korean War he severed as a

Sergeant with the 25th Infantry Division. He worked in advertising and marketing for several years for John Deere in Davenport and Mexico City, Mexico for Massey Ferguson in Toronto, and Allied Farm Equipment in Chicago, where he met his future wife, Judith. He then went to work for Lundia–Meyers, in Decatur, Ill., Davenport, and then to Jacksonville in 1975. In 1981 he went to work for DEA with the State of Illinois, retiring in 1991. Bix's wit was unchallenged and his friendships legion. He attended a stag weekend for approximately 45 years in the Ozarks every June with a group of friends who had been in kindergarten together. He almost made it all the way to appear on the TV show "Jeopardy!" if he had only known something about "hard rock." He loved people, cacti, stamp collecting, reading, traveling, the stock market, his animals, and above all, the Iowa Hawkeyes. He and his wife had traveled extensively since his retirement. A celebration of his life will be held at 2 p.m. Saturday, Sept. 11 at the First Presbyterian Church in Jacksonville. The family will meet friends following the service. His cremains will be interred in Oakdale Cemetery in Davenport. Memorials are suggested to Jacksonville Theatre Guild. Cody and Sons Memorial Home is in charge of arrangements.

1937 photo taken by Ted Shoemaker of Bix's nephews with their parents—front row, L-R, Julien & Charles Bix Shoemaker; Richard Bix & Chuck Beiderbecke; back row, L-R: Ted Jr. & Mary Louise Shoemaker; Mary & Burnie Beiderbecke

Charles 'Burnie' Beiderbecke

YEARBOOKS

DHS Class of 1914
C. BURNETTE BEIDERBECKE "Bix"
Football, D., '11, '12, '13
Class President, Spring, '13
Class Track
Kappa Delta

J. Armitage—We know nothing to reduce height, but fasting for a few months will prevent further growth.

Bix—No, it is not disloyal to encourage girls in towns in which the team visits, because all's fair in love (and war).

Parker W.—We do not know whether the manager of the American has an opening for you or not, but we wish you luck.

No, girls, we know of no way to keep hairpins in their place, but by forcing them in by hydraulic pressure.

No, Miss B., we know of no way to make Harry G. stop arguing in 12B Latin, except to gently but firmly invite him to leave the room.

DUM TEMPUS FUGIT

Some Wants.

WANTED—A date with Otto. Dolly Kuehl.

WANTED—A new school room for teaching algebra, by a young man, with three or four large windows, a good blackboard and seating space to accommodate twenty. Apply first floor, D. H. S.

WANTED—To buy, rent, or borrow a nice new puppy. Medium sized ones preferred but tall and long ones will do in a pinch. Please apply in person. Mary Louise Beiderbecke.

WANTED—A good foot reducer. Have tried small shoes. Don't do any good. Apply with your ideas to Vic Maehr.

WANTED—Some good curly hair. I am now using the false kind, so don't send any more of that. Apply to Dolly Kuehl.

WANTED—A return ticket to Illinois, where the rest of the suckers live. Apply in person with the ticket to Beulah Schultz.

WANTED—A good long winded, twelve-cylinder telescope with which to equip a certain young lady, otherwise known as Mary Bird (we leave out the middle name for spite) so that she may see the little freshies of the school and not tread upon them.

WANTED—An efficient dog catcher to guard Study Room A door to keep that horrid brute of a dog from entering therein. Mr. Breeden

DHS Class of 1917
MARY LOUISE BEIDERBECKE "Sis"
"My character may be my own, but my reputation belongs to any old body that enjoys gossiping."
Class Will Committee
Social Committee '16-'17
Class Treasurer '16

GENEALOGY: MARY LOUISE

MARY LOUISE BEIDERBECKE was born 20 Oct 1898 in Davenport, Iowa, and died 12 Dec 1984 in Lexington, Massachusetts. Graduation: 1917, Davenport High School. She married THEODORE SHOEMAKER, son of William Toy and Mabel Warren Shoemaker, on 08 Nov 1924 at Davenport Outing Club; He was born 04 Oct 1899 in Philadelphia, PA, and died 11 Jul 1962. Children, all born in Atlanta, GA: TED SHOEMAKER JR. 08 August 1926; CHARLES BIX SHOEMAKER, 14 Feb 1928; SUSAN, twin sister died at birth; JULIEN SHOEMAKER, 21 Mar 1931.

23 June 1924, *Democrat–Leader*:
Mr. and Mrs. B. H. Beiderbecke of 1934 Grand avenue announce the engagement and approaching marriage of their daughter Mary Louise to Theodore Shoemaker, son of Dr. and Mrs. William Toy Shoemaker of Philadelphia, Pa. The announcement of the engagement was a surprise of this noon at a charmingly appointed luncheon at which Miss Beiderbecke entertained at the Davenport Outing club as a pre–nuptial courtesy for Miss Sara Murdock whose marriage to Coleman Clark is to be an event of Saturday. When the names of the hostess and Mr. Shoemaker were discovered in the dainty place cards at each plate the shower of good wishes was turned upon the new bride–to–be and everyone naturally wanted to know all about it and when the wedding was to be. The luncheon table was arranged with a basket centerpiece of blue delphinium, corn flowers and pink rose buds and the budded pink and blue colors were carried out in various pretty details of decoration. The afternoon was enjoyed with Mah Jong, and there were favors for high score and for the guest of honor. There were 26 in the party. Miss Katherine Miller of Martinsburg, W. Va., who is visiting Miss Mary Louise Bird, was an out of town guest. The wedding of Miss Beiderbecke and Mr. Shoemaker will be some time in the early fall, the home to be in the east. Miss Beiderbecke is the only daughter of B. H. Beiderbecke, manager of the East Davenport Fuel company and the East Davenport Branch of the H.O. Seiffert Lumber company of this city and is a graduate of the University of Chicago in the kindergarten department. Mr. Shoemaker attended the University of Pennsylvania, and is a civil engineer with Warren Brothers of Boston, an asphalt contracting and paving company.

6 November 1924 *Democrat–Leader*:
ENTERTAIN AT DINNER FOR BRIDAL PARTY
C.B. Beiderbecke and L. B. Beiderbecke entertained at dinner at the Outing club Friday

Mary Louise 'Sis' Beiderbecke

evening in honor of their sister, Miss Mary Louise Beiderbecke and Theo. Shoemaker, whose wedding was Saturday night at the club. The guests were members of the bridal party and rehearsal followed the dinner hour.

Saturday, 8 November 1924 *Daily Times*:
The Marriage of Miss Mary Louise Beiderbecke, daughter of Mr. and Mrs. B.H. Beiderbecke of 1934 Grand Avenue, Davenport, to Mr. Theodore Shoemaker, son of Dr. and Mrs. William T. Shoemaker of Philadelphia, Pennsylvania, will take place this day at the Davenport Outing Club. The ceremony will be performed at 3 o'clock by Dr. L.M. Coffman of the First Presbyterian Church in the presence of about 150 friends and relatives.

Leading the bridal possession will be the ushers, Messrs. John Hamilton, Joseph McCarthy, and brothers Charles B. Beiderbecke and Leon B. Beiderbecke.

The brides attendants, walking singly, will be Misses Persis Williams, Bernice Hanssen, Mrs. Donald Murdock, and Barbara Shoemaker of Philadelphia, a sister of the groom. Little Miss Nora Hass will be scattering rose petals in the path of the bride.

They will be met at the altar by the groom and his best man, Mr. Ralph Powell of Chicago, a fraternity brother from the University of Pennsylvania.

A reception will follow the ceremony and there will be dancing in the ballroom to ALBERT WRIXON'S ORCHESTRA. At 10:30 o'clock, supper will be served in the dining room.

The bridal couple will leave on a wedding trip, the destination of which is not announced. The bridal couple expects to be in Philadelphia for the Christmas holidays.

Sunday, 9 November 1924 *Democrat–Leader*:
SHOEMAKER–BEIDERBECKE WEDDING
One of the very lovely fall weddings in which special interest centers because of the prominence of the young people was the marriage Saturday evening at 8 o'clock at the Outing club of Miss Mary Louise Beiderbecke, only daughter of Mr. and Mrs. B. H. Beiderbecke of Grand avenue, to Theodore Shoemaker of Philadelphia, son of Dr. and Mrs. William Toy Shoemaker of Philadelphia.

Rev. L. M. Coffman of the First Presbyterian church officiated, using the single ring service.

The ceremony was in the main hallway on the first floor, the west door being concealed with an elaborate canopy as a nuptial bower of southern smilax banked with ferns and palms, with the background arranged as an altar with a large candelabra bearing the slender white Princess candles. The tall cathedral floor candle sticks were on either side bearing white wax tapers.

Erwin Swindell at the piano, played before the ceremony and gave the Bridal Chorus from Lohengrin as the bridal party came down the wide stairway, "To a Wild Rose" being played during the ceremony and later the Mendelssohn march as the recessional.

EVENING——THE DAVENPORT DEMOCRAT

Their Engagement is Announced as Surprise at Noon Luncheon

THEODORE SHOEMAKER.

MISS MARY LOUISE BEIDERBECKE.

Mr. and Mrs. B. H. Beiderbecke of 1934 Grand avenue announce the engagement and approaching marriage of their daughter, Mary Louise, to Theodore Shoemaker, son of Dr. and Mrs. William Toy Shoemaker of Philadelphia, Pa.

The announcement of the engagement was a surprise of this noon at a charmingly appointed luncheon at which Miss Beiderbecke entertained at the Davenport Outing club as a pre-nuptial courtesy for Miss Sara Murdock whose marriage to Coleman Clark is to be an event of Saturday.

When the names of the hostess and Mr. Shoemaker were discovered in the dainty place cards at each plate the shower of good wishes was turned upon the new bride-to-be and every one naturally wanted to know all about it and when the wedding was to be.

The luncheon table was arranged with a basket centerpiece of blue delphinium, corn flowers and pink rose buds, and the budded pink and blue colors were carried out in various pretty details of decoration.

The afternoon was enjoyed with mah jongg, and there were favors for high score and for the guest of honor. There were 26 in the party.

Miss Katherine Miller of Martinsburg, W. Va., who is visiting Miss Mary Louise Bird, was an out-of-town guest.

The wedding of Miss Beiderbecke and Mr. Shoemaker will be sometime in the early fall, the new home to be in the east.

The wedding will take from Davenport one of the very popular members of the younger set.

Miss Beiderbecke is the only daughter of B. H. Beiderbecke, manager of the East Davenport Fuel company and of the East Davenport branch of the H. O. Seiffert Lumber company of this city and is a graduate of the University of Chicago in the kindergarten department.

Mr. Shoemaker attended the University of Pennsylvania, and is a civil engineer with Warren Brothers of Boston, an asphalt contracting and paving company.

SUNDAY MORNING — THE DAVENPORT DEMOCRAT AND LEADER — NOVEMBER 9, 1924
Bride and Attendants at Shoemaker-Beiderbecke Wedding

Mary Louise (#2)
Wedding attendants:
#1 Gretchen Murdoch
#3 Barbara Shoemaker
#4 Bernice Hanssen
#5 Nora Hass
#6 Persis Williams
Hanssen & Williams were high school classmates

Below: cousin Gretchen 'Gay' and Bix standing at left with Burnie behind Ted Shoemaker (seated) Flower girl Nora Hass is granddaughter of Aunt Ottilie Stibolt

The ushers, John Hamilton, C. B. Beiderbecke, brother of the bride, [Leon B. also an usher but not listed] and Joseph McCarthy of this city led the way, the bride's attendant being Mrs. Donald Murdoch, cousin of the bride, of Davenport, Miss Barbara Shoemaker, sister of the groom, of Philadelphia, and Misses Bernice Hanssen and Persis Williams of Davenport, girlhood chums of the bride. Little Miss Nora Hass, the 6-year-old daughter of Mrs. Leon Hass, the cousin of the bride, was flower girl and dressed in a dainty frock of lace and white net over flesh pink silk, scattered rose petals in the pathway of the bride who came last on the arm of her father, B. H. Beiderbecke, who gave her away.

The bride was in a gown of white crepe-back satin made in straight lines with wraparound skirt and wide pearl girdle, caught to one side with a fur ornament from which was arranged the side train. The bodice was sleeveless with boat neck, finished with riffled collar of Duchess lace. The wedding veil was in coronet in front with appliqués of lace and orange blossom rosette-clusters trimming the sides and back.

She carried a shower of lilies of the valley and orchids tied with lace ribbons.

The bride's attendants were dressed alike in gowns of georgette, Mrs. Murdoch in pea green, Miss Hanssen in shell pink, Miss Shoemaker in orchid and Miss Williams in maize, their dresses being made in full skirts having panels of taffeta petals of the same color as the gown, the bodice trimmed with taffeta petals and made sleeveless and round neck.

Each carried pompom chrysanthemums in the bronze orchid and pink shades tied with ribbons to match their gowns.

Following the ceremony there was a reception to the bridal couple in which Mr. and Mrs. Beiderbecke and Dr. and Mrs. Shoemaker received the bridal party.

Mrs. Beiderbecke was in powder blue georgette trimmed with silver and margot lace and her flowers were lavender and pink sweet peas, orchids and lilies of the valley tied with orchid and silver ribbon.

Mrs. Shoemaker was in black lace robe over silk embroidered in Chinese gold embroidery and her flowers were orchids, lilies of valley and sunset roses tied with gold ribbons.

The reception was in the parlors with dancing later in the ball room where supper was served at 10:30. Pompom and button chrysanthemums were used in tall floor baskets everywhere in all the shades of pink, orchid and yellow, and a mound of pink roses and white chrysanthemums were used on the bride's table with the wedding cakes and candles. There were 150 guests, among those from out of town being Dr. and Mrs. William Shoemaker and Miss Barbara Shoemaker of Philadelphia, Beard and Ralph Powell of Chicago, Leon B. Beiderbecke of Detroit, Mich., and Miss Nettie Day of Chicago.

Mr. and Mrs. Shoemaker leave on a wedding trip and plan to spend the Christmas holidays in Philadelphia at the groom's home.

The traveling dress of the bride was a three-piece suit in rose color with ribbon trimmed hat of felt to match.

The bride attended the local schools and St. Katharine, graduated from kindergarten department of the University of Chicago. Mr. Shoemaker is a graduate of the Philadelphia schools and attended the University of Pennsylvania where he was a Kappa Epsilon fraternity member.

He is now special representative inspector of the technical service department of Warren Bro. Paving Road Construction Company of Boston, Mass.

Dedication reads: *To the Sweetest sister in the world from her brother—Bix Beiderbecke*

Aggie's Church

21 October 1883 *Davenport Daily Leader*:

The people of the UNITED PRESBYTERIAN CHURCH, northeast corner of Brady and Eleventh streets, expect to occupy their upper room on Sunday, Oct. 28, one week from today, with services appropriate to the occasion of their first meeting in the new audience room. This congregation was organized in October 1854 as the Associate Reformed Presbyterian Church, with ten members and was in connection with Rock Island under one pastoral charge [Rev. J.R. McCalister] for a number of years. In 1856 they erected their building on the corner of Scott and Eleventh streets, which they continued to occupy until July 1st when they purchased their present location [Brady & 11th]. In 1858 by a union with the Associated Presbyterian Church they assumed the name and title of United Presbyterian.

Since July 1 last the congregation has been occupying their lecturing room under the pastoral care of Dr. S.B. Reed, and during that time had the building repaired and painted and the auditorium frescoed and furnished in a neat and tasteful manner.

Tri–City United Presbyterians first worshipped together as a Covenanters congregation in the public school house at Rock Island's Union Square. It was a plain frame building with a dry goods box for a pulpit and a nail keg with a board across it for the pastor's seat. The pews were planks laid across nail kegs or boxes. The lights were plain tallow candles.

When Caroline Hill married Beriah Hilton in Rock Island in 1868, the United Presbyterian Church was on the southwest corner of Third Avenue and 14th Street in Rock Island. Caroline's sister Mary Hill stated in her claim against her brother John's estate that she had lived a year in Rock Island. Possibly, Beriah was living there at the time and Mary went to stay with Caroline while Beriah was working on the riverboat, perhaps during the time she was pregnant with Aggie. No records have been located beyond Mary's reference in the probate records of John Hill.

United Presbyterian's Davenport congregation disbanded in 1905. They reorganized a year later under new leadership but Aggie Beiderbecke had transferred to Davenport's First Presbyterian, where she remained until her death. Bix was confirmed at First Presbyterian in 1916 but he likely was baptized, as his brother and sister had been, at United Presbyterian.

First Presbyterian's congregation began with about ten members meeting in a small building belonging to Thomas S. Hoge in the alley on Ripley between Front and Second. They built a log cabin in 1840 at the southwest corner of Main and Third streets.

When Antoine LeClaire laid out the town of Davenport, he set aside lots for each of the religious denominations. The lot LeClaire designated for the Presbyterians was on the river bank, but with $150 of their own funds and a $50 donation from LeClaire, they chose an alternative site on west Third between Harrison and Main. In 1844 they built a brick chapel at 222 W. Third, expanding to two stories with a steeple in 1854. First Presbyterian was one of two churches in the territory to have a bell at the time.

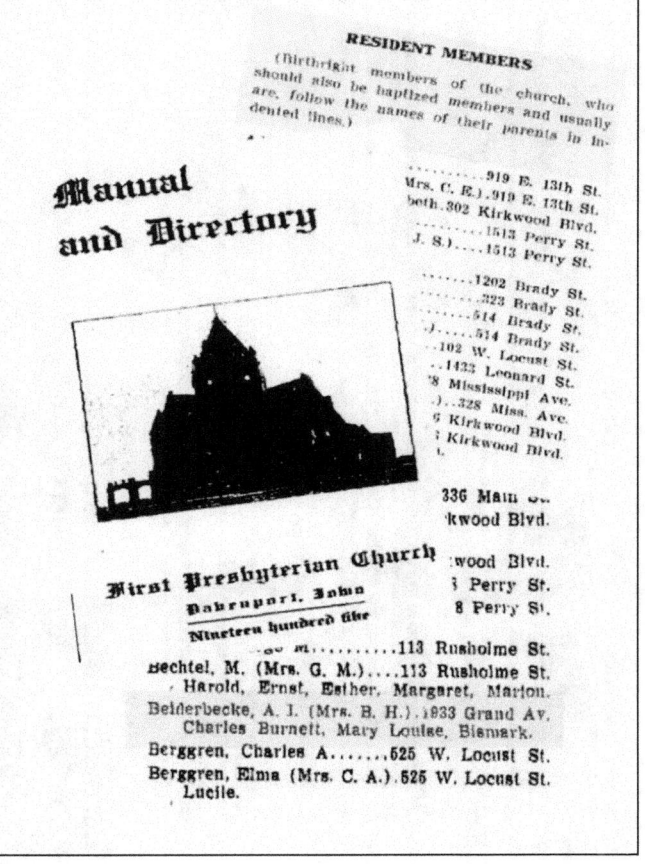

Rev. J.B. Donaldson, shared the history of the two bells in a story in the *Davenport Daily Leader* on July 24, 1899:

A bell was counted then of great importance. So the ladies held a fair in the courthouse in 1846. They secured two cannon and the artillery Company to fire salutes, and the discharge broke the windows of the courthouse and made a hole in their profits. But they made $150 and purchased a fine bell. It was one of the first bells to cross the Mississippi and was afterward sold for the courthouse in Clinton.

The twin pioneer bell went to Iowa City and had an eventful history that makes it known as Hummer's bell. This eccentric genius could not collect his salary. So he levied on the bell. But the congregation rallied, took away the ladder from the belfry before the preacher could get down and hid it in the river. It was afterward sold to the Mormons.

The sight of Hummer in the church tower thundering angry imprecations on his

Top Left: 1st Presbyterian at 7th & Brady next door to the Academy of Science

Bottom Left: Kirkwood & Iowa site under construction in 1898

Top Right: dedicated on December 17, 1899

Center Right: $200,000 remodel with Bible School addition, 1924

Bottom Right: view from Kirkwood Blvd, circa 1900

former charges moved a young artist to sketch the scene. The caricature is still preserved in the library at Des Moines and it had such merit that a legislator sent the young man to Paris to complete his education in art.

In 1864, Davenport's First Presbyterian bought at auction for $20,000 the former St. Luke's Episcopal Church at Seventh and Brady. Rev. J.B. Stewart was the minister in 1873 when an organ was built for the church.

In 1898, with 240 adult members and 400 Sunday schoolers, the congregation had outgrown the Seventh Street building. It was sold to the Academy of Science—today's Putnam Museum, which used the building until April of 1907 when it was torn down to make way for new Masonic Temple, now Palmer College auditorium.

The new church building at Kirkwood and Iowa was built of Marquette brown stone with a magnesium stain, known as the *rain drop* marking. Its Romanesque architecture features carved oak leaves and foliage in the gables. The ceiling of the octagonal interior has a Maltese cross and a Greek cross. It was a very expensive building for its time, costing $86,000.

Ground was broken March 18, 1898, and the church was dedicated December 17, 1899. The old Third Street church was torn down in April 1907 to make way for a business block.

At the laying of the cornerstone on July 20, 1898, Rev. Robert F. Sample of New York, father-in-law of then-minister Rev. J.B. Donaldson, paid tribute to Presbyterian founder John Knox in his keynote address:

When quaint Thomas Chalmers stood behind St. Giles' church in Edinburgh, looking at a stone bearing two initials, "J.K." and a date, set in the granite pavement over which the wheels of traffic and travel daily rolled, he said: "Underneath that stone lays a man whom Scotland heard with the marrow of her bones. For her liberties she owes more to him than to David II, to Robert Bruce, to Mary, beautiful Mary, Queen of the Scots, or all her crowned heads combined.

LeRoy M. Coffman became pastor in 1908 and led the effort to pay off the church's remaining $10,000 debt. Over the next two decades the membership grew to 1,338 adult members and 56 Sunday school classes with an enrollment of 1,256. A new Bible school, built for $178,000 opened June of 1924. Remodeling of the main church that year cost an additional $22,000.

St. Katharine's Hall

Renwick Mansion—St. Margaret's Hall

ST. KATHARINE'S & KEMPER HALL

St. Katharine's Hall—now senior apartments—stands on a bluff overlooking the Mississippi River at Tenth Street and Tremont Avenue. It originally was called Cambria Place, homestead of former city mayor and lumber capitalist John L. Davies. The mansion was designed by Rock Island–born architect George O. Garnsey, who designed the State Capital building in Springfield, IL, in 1869. Garnsey re–designed many of the buildings destroyed by the Great Chicago Fire of 1871.

St. Katharine's preparatory school for girls opened September 24, 1884. Christian academies for girls and boys had been endowed in 1883 and established in Davenport through the Episcopal Diocese of Iowa. St. Katharine's first headmistress, Mary Buffington stepped down after the 1902 school year to marry *Davenport Democrat* publisher J.B. Richardson.

America's first Episcopal Order, the Sisters of St. Mary took over St. Katharine's in 1903. Under the nuns, a chapel and gymnasium were added and the campus expanded from five to twelve acres with the purchases of adjoining Renwick and McCandless properties. The former home of William Renwick—also a lumber manufacturer whose father had been mayor—became St. Margaret's Hall in 1907.

Mary Louise Beiderbecke took music lessons at St. Margaret's Hall during the 1913–1914 terms. Her mother had studied piano and violin at St. Katharine's Hall its first year in operation. A school brochure for boarding students in Mary Louise's day stated: Each girl signs up for two school periods a week of Red Cross work, under the direction of the Red Cross Chapter in town. She also signs up for personal efficiency, sufficient exercise, eating food in sufficient quantities and less eating of candy, ice cream and between meals, proper care of the body, erect posture, etc., and for all that prevents waste and makes for economy.

When the nuns fell on hard times after the Great Depression and WWII, the school passed into private ownership and became non–denominational in 1943. It continues as Rivermont Academy in Bettendorf.

Kemper Hall, the boy's preparatory school on south–east corner of Griswold College campus was named for the fist Episcopalian bishop in the Northwest Territory. The school was dedicated on St. Andrew's Day, Nov 30, 1885. Its final year of operation was as a military academy run by Max Von Binzer, husband of Lutie Beiderbecke. The Von Binzer's moved to Alton, IL, where Max became military instructor at Western Military Academy.

When Griswold and Kemper closed in 1893 the property was purchased for Davenport's new public high school. From 1875–1907, the city high school stood between Iowa and Pershing, 6th and 7th Streets. Before 1875, high school courses were held in grade schools. When the public high school moved to former Griswold College campus at Main and 11th Streets, the east end building became Lincoln Grammar School—today's Lincoln Fundamental School at 318 E. Seventh.

Kemper's military drill instructor **Max Von Binzer** and his wife Lutie

Above: **Kemper Hall** on SE corner of Griswold College campus became home economics building for the public high school in 1907

Below: Mississippi River view from **St. Katharine's Academy** at Tremont & 10th

Right: **Sisters of St. Mary** with St. Katharine's Academy students

Top: **Bix's mom graduated from City High School at 7th & Pershing**
Below: **Bix attended the Main Street campus from 1918-1921; Burnie & Mary Louise graduated from what now is Davenport Central High**

Above: Business College, 1895
1908 postcard of Second Street looking west
B&M wholesalers across from Martin Cigar Store;
Brown's Business College, end of block

Street cart vendors were the fast food stops in Bix's day

MATERNAL ROOTS

While the Beiderbeckes were of German origin, Bix's maternal roots trace back to Northern Ireland. His great–grandfather Adam Hill was the son of Richard and Sally Hill. Richard was born 1772 in county Manahan, Ireland. He emigrated from Londonderry in May of 1789 to Wilmington, Delaware, and then to Mercer County, Pennsylvania.

Mercer County's Grove City in the northwestern part of Pennsylvania is about 25 miles from the Ohio border. That is where Bix's grandmother Caroline Hill Hilton was born in 1844.

Caroline's mother, Anna Pollock, died in 1851 after giving birth to Addison, the youngest of eleven Hill siblings.

Caroline was nine when her father took her and five of her siblings to Scott County, Iowa, in 1853, following eldest brother David and his wife Amanda to Davenport. The two youngest boys, Wallace and Addison, were left behind with Caroline's sisters Emily Hill Harshaw and Elizabeth Hill Kidd. Emily and Lizzie had married cousins.

Emily, a.k.a. Emma, married jeweler William James Harshaw. He was the son of Andrew Harshaw and grandson of Irish diarist James Harshaw, a wealthy farmer and Presbyterian elder who kept a daily journal spanning a quarter century of Irish life during the potato famine and rising animosities between Protestants and Catholics.

The six–volume Harshaw Diaries passed down to Emily's son Edwin. He put them in a basement vault at the Grove City Bank where he was the head cashier. During a remodeling of the bank in the mid–1980s the Harshaw Diaries were rediscovered. They now are archived in Belfast at the Public Records Office of Northern Ireland.

Emily Harshaw sent young Addison Hill to live with his father in Davenport for a time but Addison eventually returned east and settled on a Pittsburgh farm, as did Wallace Hill.

When the Hill clan—Adam and his children Jane, Nelson, Sarah, John, Mary and young Caroline—first arrived in Davenport, eldest brother David co–owned a livery stable on Second Street between Main and Harrison. He sold out to partner James Thompson in 1859 and invested in farmland and horses. In 1866, he opened another livery stable at Main and Third.

Adam operated a boarding house and with his son John farmed land on the northern outskirts of Davenport. Later, John worked as a land agent for David's former partner, James Thompson before partnering in David's livery stable.

For health reasons, David Hill moved his family to Denver, Colorado, in 1873. He returned to Davenport to handle family matters after John's death in 1886. When his health again deteriorated David returned to Denver.

Nelson Hill married and moved to Marengo near Iowa City and eventually to Poweshiek County. Jane and Sarah married brothers; Jane to Benedict Kennedy and younger sister Sarah a.k.a. Sallie to older brother Alexander. The Kennedy men were plasterers by trade in Davenport.

Mary Hill graduated from the Davenport Business College and became a milliner. She also worked at the Newcomb House and later operated a catering business at 2226 Grand Avenue.

Caroline, or Carrie, was twenty-four when she married B.L. Hilton. Rev J.R. McCalister of the United Presbyterian Church officiated at their ceremony in Rock Island, Illinois. They lived briefly in Rock Island, along with Carrie's sister Mary.

Beriah L. Hilton was born 1838 in New York and came west in 1856 with his father James, mother Fannie Mason Hilton, brother Edmond, sisters Helen and Ann. The Hilton family settled on a farm in a place called Green Tree in rural Scott County, Iowa. The 1860 census shows Beriah working as a laborer on his father's farm.

Carrie gave birth to daughter Agnes Jane on March 1, 1870. Beriah was listed in that year's census as Briar Hilton, a steamboat engineer, living with Carrie and 4½ month-old Agnes, a.k.a. Aggie at 220 W 13th, the home of Carrie's brother John. Adam Hill and Aggie's Aunt Mary also lived there. Neither John nor Mary ever married.

Beriah left his wife and infant daughter behind and went west. He shows up in census records as a carpenter in Missoula, Montana, and with his brother Edmond at a Colorado Springs mine. He was in St. Louis when his father died in 1890 and in Davenport three years later when his mother died. Tennessee shows him as an eligible voter in Lincoln County in 1891. Later records show him dividing his time between Colorado Springs and Davenport.

Fannie Hilton's will set up a trust fund for "my granddaughter, AGNES HILTON." It also provided annual stipends for Beriah. He signed for them every year from 1893 until 1903—the year his grandson Leon Bismark

Beiderbecke was born. Beriah died in 1911 while living in Colorado Springs. His brother Edmond had died four years earlier and Beriah was living with Edmond's wife Rachel and her children. His body was returned to Davenport, for burial in the Hilton family plot at Oakdale cemetery.

Meanwhile Aggie grew up with the Hill family in her Uncle John's home. She was only nine when her mother died in 1880. Two years later Aggie's grandfather Adam died and her Uncle John four years later. At the time, they lived at 615 E. 15 Street.

John had been in poor health since Aggie was about two. Aunt Mary kept house for him, providing round–the–clock care during the last couple years before he succumbed to meningitis. For her steadfastness, Mary had been promised by John that she would inherit his money and property. He died without a will.

Nelson handled John's legal matters until David could be made executor of the estate. It was then that David filed for legal guardianship of Aggie, stating in the court document that her father had been absent at least ten years, whereabouts unknown.

As Aggie's guardian, David got back the money his niece had inherited from her mother but used by John for his own business investments.

Mary, too, got David's help in securing title to the Fifteenth Street house. The rest of the siblings signed off on claims to John's estate. In total, Mary received $7, 743.30, including the house. Agnes J. Hilton received $1,657.40, including a parcel of land, sold later to Louisa Beiderbecke. As executor, David received $1,355.90.

David had set up a trust fund for Aggie. When she turned eighteen, she received $2,400 while still living with Mary at the Fifteenth Street house.

Aggie's parents had been married by the minister who served United Presbyterian congregations both in Rock Island and Davenport. In her grandfather's obituary, it said Adam Hill "was a member of the United Presbyterian Church for more than forty years and lived up to his religious beliefs. His memory was wonderful and he had the Bible at his tongue's end, a fact which made his arguments felt when engaged in a religious discretion."

While sharing their origins in Scot–Irish Protestantism, Davenport's First Presbyterian and the Hill family's United Presbyterian Church were separate organizations until merging in 1983 as the Presbyterian Church USA.

Aggie and Bismark married on June 7, 1893, with her Aunt Mary and Bismark's dad as their witnesses in a service officiated by Rev. W.E. Shaw at

STATE OF IOWA)
)   IN THE DISTRICT COURT
SCOTT COUNTY)

....
IN THE MATTER OF THE ESTATE

          OF   FINAL REPORT

MARY HILL, DECEASED
....

TO SAID COURT:

      Comes now, Agnes J. Hilton Beiderbecke, Executrix of the Last Will of Mary Hill, deceased and respectfully makes this her final report. She advises the court that she should be charged with the following:

Cash in Scott County Savings Bank as per inventory	$400.00
Cash in German Savings Bank as per inventory	180.00
Interest from Scott County Savings Bank	23.00
Interest from German Savings Bank	6.88
	$609.88

That as against said receipts she is entitled to credit for the following disbursements:

Paid O.C. Hill, undertakers bill	147.50
Paid Schricker Marble & Granite Co.	10.00
Paid Bill for court costs of Lane & Waterman	83.60
	241.10

      Recapitulation

Receipts	$609.88
Disbursements	241.10
Balance	$368.78

      She further advises the court that under the terms of the Will of Mary Hill, all of her estate was bequeathed to the Executrix and her children, Charles Burnett Beiderbecke, Mary Louise Beiderbecke and Leon Bismarck Beiderbecke, share and share alike; that she has made settlement and paid one-fourth (1-4) of the said estate to herself, one-fourth (1-4) to Charles Burnett Beiderbecke, one-fourth (1-4) to Mary Louise Beiderbecke both being of legal age; that she has paid the one-fourth (1-4) due to Leon Bismarck Beiderbecke to Agnes J. Hilton Beiderbecke his mother and natural guardian, he being now near fourteen years of age and she shows the receipts hereto for all of said distributions.

She further reports to the court that on account of the size of the estate, there was no liability for collateral inheritance tax; that administration has now been open for more then one year and no claims have been filed against said estate; that all debts known to the undersigned have been paid. She, therefore, asks that this report be approved, the estate closed and the Executrix discharged from further duty and liability.

Respectfully submitted

Agnes J. Beiderbecke
Executrix

STATE OF IOWA)
) SS
SCOTT COUNTY)

I, Agnes J. Hilton Beiderbecke, being duly sworn on oath depose and say, that I am the person making the foregoing report, that I have read the same and the statements therein contained are true as I verily believe.

Agnes J. Beiderbecke

Subscribed and sworn to before me this 23 day of May, 1917.

J. R. Lane
Notary Public, Scott County, Iowa.

the Fifteenth Street house. Rev. Shaw served the Davenport United Presbyterian Church, located at the corner of Brady and Eleventh streets. That congregation disbanded in 1905—the same year Aggie and her children show up in First Presbyterian's membership directory. Even after the city's United Presbyterians reorganized in 1906, Aggie remained with First Presbyterian. Mary Hill apparently switched over to First Presbyterian, as well. She had moved near her niece Aggie, to a house at 1920 Grand Avenue.

Both Charles Burnette and Mary Louise were born before the family moved to Grand Avenue in 1900. On March 10, 1903, Aggie and Bismark welcomed their third child, Leon Bismark Beiderbecke, the name recorded on First Presbyterian's cradle roll.

When she signed up for old age assistance, Aggie listed her father's name as *Breigh* Hilton. Her parents' wedding certificate showed his name as B.L. Hilton. He signed his initials or as *Beriah* on receipts for the inheritance money from his mother's estate. Census records show these and *Briar* as variable spellings for Aggie's father.

Aggie is not mentioned as a surviving child of Beriah Hilton in his obituary. His funeral arrangements and those of his brother Edmond were handled by Edmond's daughter, Fannie Hilton Dougherty of Davenport. She had married in the Catholic faith, probably because her mother Rachel King Hilton was Catholic.

As for Aggie's name, it is *Agnes* according to legal documents—everything from guardianship papers and probate documents for her Uncle John to the wills of her grandmother Fannie Hilton and Aunt Mary.

She married as *Aggie Jane* but 1915 census card lists her as Agatha. First Presbyterian membership rolls list her under the initials A.J. or as Mrs. B.H. Beiderbecke. Her name on Bix's death certificate was written as *Agatha* by the undertaker. And it was her children, Charles and Mary Louise, who buried her as *Agatha*.

How she got from Agnes to Agatha is a matter of speculation. Aggie is a nickname both for Agnes and Agatha, names for saints but of different origins and meanings. Perhaps someone somewhere along the way mistook the formal form of her nickname and addressed her as Agatha. Having heard it, she might have preferred Agatha. Nevertheless, she could not legally sign that name. It appears she consistently went by *Agatha* as an adult but formally signed as Agnes or Mrs. B.H. Beiderbecke.

Three generations—Bix, his mother, and his grandfather—confounding future historians by their names.

ESTATE OF MARY HILL
Filed: April 26, 1916

May 23, 1917
Agnes Hilton Beiderbecke signed on behalf of her minor son, Leon Bismark

"PUBLIC FRIDAY."

Our Rising Generation Today Will Entertain the Public at the Various Schools.

This day closes the winter term in our public schools and for a short time the children will be free from their studies and school duties only to return to them with renewed energy. The different schools have prepared programs which will be executed this afternoon. The following is the program for the high school, which begins at 2:30:

Opening address .... Mr. Kellogg
Music quartet.... Messrs. McGlashon and Edgar, Misses Kulp and Pierce
Essay.................... Walter Eagal
Music, instrumental ....
    Messrs. Scott and Spelletich; Eagal and McGlashon.
Recitation with music............
.... Blanche Chambers
Vocal solo............. Alma Hanssen
Piano duet.. Misses Frisius and Hilton
Oration............... Claus Ruymann
Vocal solo............. Jessie Hopkins
Essay............... Louise Middleton
Piano solo............. Mary Brunton
Recitation........ ...... Aggie Helbig
    Critic's Report.

Aggie's high school days. Top left, March 1892; bottom left, Feb. 1891; right, March 1889

PERSONAL.

O. G. Murray left last night on a business trip to Chicago.

Mrs. J. P. Van Patten is visiting in Kansas City, St. Joseph and Lincoln.

Mrs. Geo. V. Knostman and children left yesterday for Peoria to visit her great-grandmother.

Mrs. Valentine left for her home in Denver last evening after a pleasant visit with her son, George Valentine.

Misses Agnes Hilton and M. Hill have gone to New York City for an extended visit with friends and relatives.

Lecture on Astronomy.

A very large audience assembled at the Baptist church last evening to hear Prof. H. G. Sedgwick's lecture on "Astronomy," and they were more than repaid. The exercises of the evening were opened by a piano duett by Miss Aggie Hilton and Miss Annie Maxwell, followed by a vocal duett by Miss Alice Collins and Miss Rosa Lamb, this being followed by a piano solo by Miss Hilton. Prof. Sedgwick was then introduced, and described, in a glowing manner, the things pertaining to the world's celestial, filling the hearts of his hearers with a desire to to study and know more about other worlds. He led them, step by step, up from this sleeping world of ours, taking first, in his journey through the starry firmament those planets nearest us, then on and on, till his audience was fairly wild with enthusiasm and delight. Davenport may well be proud to to claim such a man as Prof. Sedgwick. He knows whereof he speaks, having acquired, by long study and use of astronomical instruments, a vast knowledge of things relating to worlds above us. The audience had an opportunity to walk home under as bright a star lit sky as it is one's privilege to see and no doubt each one viewed the heavens with a new interest, awakened by Prof. Sedgwick's lecuure on "Astronomy."

Musical Roots

A newspaper account of the wedding of Bismark Beiderbecke and Aggie Hilton noted that "the bride is one of Davenport's popular young ladies, highly esteemed in the circles in which she moves. She is also an accomplished musician."

Aggie's formative years were filled with music—music that she passed along to her children. She studied piano and violin at St Katharine's School at a cost of $375 for two years for non–boarding students. Aggie sent her daughter Mary Louise there to study music in 1913. After graduating from Davenport High School in 1888, Aggie continued her musical studies through private lessons. She became the church pianist and organist at United Presbyterian.

It was through music that Aggie first became acquainted with the Beiderbecke family at their German music soirees. Louise Piper Beiderbecke was also an accomplished pianist; Bismark's father Charles was a composer and director of a men's chorale society, the *Maennorchor*.

Without a doubt it was Aggie who first shaped her children's musical passion, especially her youngest boy. From his cradle days right through adolescence, Bix heard the music of his mother's piano. Whether it was a Debussy piano suite, or a Chopin serenade, or a Stravinsky sonata, Bix listened and learned.

Big brother Burnie told of how their mother held Bix on her lap, while she played *Mr. Dooley* on the piano to him. Bix would kick his feet to the rhythm. At about three, he slipped out of his high chair, escaped to the parlor and made his way to the piano. Family members rushed in and were astounded to find that Bix was playing *Mr. Dooley* with one finger, exactly as he had heard his mother play it.

That precociousness continued in kindergarten, according to his first teacher, Alice Robinson: "when we sang, Bix would wander over to the piano and pick out the tune we had just sung. He had perfect pitch even then. I have never had another child who could do what Bix did."

Who but Aggie would have first placed Bix's tiny fingers on the piano keys? Who corrected his mistakes and encouraged his progress? And would it

MUSICALE.

Vocal and Instrumental Concert Last Night.

The musical entertainment given last evening at the Baptist church called out an audience that comfortably filled the auditorium. It was one of a series of concerts that have been given for the benefit of the pipe organ fund. The amount previous to last evening's receipts approached one thousand dollars; so that those who have the affair in charge are making satisfactory progress toward giving that congregation an instrument that will be a credit to the church.

At 8 o'clock Misses Florence Jorden and Lillie Woodward at the piano, Prof. Ernst Otto and Mr. Gustav Foehringer with violin and violincello opened the evening's entertainment with the familiar chords of Mendelssohn's "Wedding March." It was given with correct tempo and a dash of brilliancy that placed the audience in pleasurable expectation of the remaining numbers.

Prof. Ernst Otto - Geb. Schoenwalde, Schleswig/Holstein 1865   Gest. Davenport, IOWA 1939

Miss Aggie Hilton

Mr. Ernst Otto next came forward with his violin and with Miss Jorden as accompanist, played De Beriot's Concerto in G. Major, a selection whose intricacy called for the nicest and most delicate execution. The professor won many admirers by his rendition of a selection which is part of the repertoire of the best violinists. Prof. Otto acknowledged the encore which followed by bowing his thanks.

**Davenport Daily Gazette
February 21, 1885**

Miss Aggie Hilton then gave a piano solo, "Movement Perpetual" by Weber with telling execution. She was followed by Misses Laura Mitchell and Norma Allen who closed the entertainment with a duet, "Rondo Brilliant," Weber. The audience who were beginning to appreciate the length of the programme would gladly have heard the young ladies again.

The concert was given under the direction of Mrs. Norman Jordan and her daughter Miss Florence, and the performers with with the exception of Prof. Otto and Mr. Foehringer were the pupils of these ladies. The entertainment may certainly be considered an artistic success, combining in the programme both classical and popular selections.

not be a mother's desire to expose her children to all things cultural, gathering up the Beiderbecke brood for family outings to park concerts and social events where bands, such as that under the baton of Uncle Albert, performed *old school* music? Yes, Bix was exposed early on to a rich variety of music.

Sometimes it's easy to forget that Bix was a piano prodigy, mainly because his virtuosity with a cornet was what earned him legendary fame. But Bix loved playing the piano. His friend, Les Swanson, often told how Bix would "sit and doodle at the piano, experimenting with ninth and thirteenth chords." These were chords then unheard of in jazz, that Bix had learned by listening to classical compositions played by his mother.

True, he possessed perfect pitch and instant recall, but it was Aggie who played the piano tunes Bix heard and fell in love with. When Aggie hired Professor Grade to give all three of her children piano lessons, the professor may have given up on the youngest of them but Aggie certainly did not.

She allowed young Leon to learn things on his own terms. The classical music she shared with him came back to her in the altered chords, the whole-tone scale and other nuances Bix frequently inserted into his jazz soloing.

When Bix played at Linwood Inn, Floyd Bean remembered his mom helping him read some lead sheets for new songs the band was adding to its program. "Bix took them to where his family was sitting and his mother would help him figure out the melody," Bean recalled.

Bix never did well at sight reading. But he could score music, according to trumpeter Max Kaminsky in his autobiography, *My Life in Jazz*:

> I was seventeen and in my third year of high school when the Goldkette band came to town. I introduced myself to Bix and told him I played trumpet so he invited me to his room after rehearsal, where we talked about music. I asked him if he would write out a hot chorus of *Blue Room* for me to practice, and he obligingly fished a piece of manuscript paper out of the pile of sheet music on the littered table next to the bed and wrote out a thirty-two bar chorus in about three minutes.

New Orleans piano man Armand Hug was nineteen when he met Bix while on tour with Paul Whiteman in 1928. Shortly before he died, Hug shared with jazz scholar John Paul Perhonis what Bix had said about his creative methods:

> I asked Bix how he went about working out his solos. He told me he liked to work alone. He would be playing a few chords and then he would jot them down. He worked a lot of things out on paper. He could write things down, you know. He told me he worked a

>lot of cornet solos out on piano first. He thought things out through the piano. That's where he got lots of his harmonic ideas.

Hug told historian Phil Evans that he was at a private gathering with some other New Orleans musicians and a few of Whiteman's guys and got a chance to play piano accompaniment to Bix's cornet. Hug asked Bix to show him some chord progressions for *In a Mist*. "He stood in the back of me and put his hands over my shoulders and played the parts for me. Believe me! I shall never forget that piano lesson."

But where does such a generosity of spirit begin? Without a doubt for Bix it came from the unconditional love of his family and a mother's nurturing of his unique gift. Throughout Bix's life, it was Aggie who appreciated and encouraged his musical talent.

In a local newspaper article Aggie acknowledged that she and the family listened to the Paul Whiteman radio broadcasts, saying, "We can always tell when Bix's horn comes in. We know every time Paul Whiteman's orchestra is on the air and Leon knows we'll be listening in. The melody is carried by another cornetist but the sudden perky blare and unexpected trills—those are the jazz parts and they are Leon's."

New Orleans trumpeter Joe 'Wingy' Manone, whose 1929 *Tar Paper Stomp* later became Glenn Miller's *In the Mood*, gave an interview to the *Quad–City Times* in July 1972, recalling his days rooming with Bix:

>He slept with his horn. He'd play it before he went to bed and when he got up in the morning. Why, he'd get up at any hour of the night and start playing if he thought of something. He got kicked out of more hotels for doing that. But it didn't bother me... Hell, I loved it. That was music.

Davenport trumpeter Wayne Rohlf recalled that Bix rarely went off the staff, and still:

>Bix was probably the greatest improviser the world has ever known—his style of licks, chords and progressions were years ahead of their time...There are many who can play ten times as much cornet as he could. But there isn't a man, living or dead, who could improvise the beautiful solos Bix did. Technically, he wasn't a great musician but, my God, what glorious music he played. He really was ahead of his time. And after he was gone, many of us who knew him went and played over his grave. To some that may sound irreverent but Bix would have liked it. Only thing he would have asked of us is that we play it good.

Contrary to what some would have us believe, Bismark and Aggie

Beiderbecke appreciated the tributes to their son. Bismark lived to proudly read music critics' praises of his son's original compositions, including the following review by Jeff Davis in 1938:

> The record year is ending in a blaze of glory, the blaze being the downright genius of the late and great Bix Beiderbecke as a composer and the glory being that of Bunny Berigan and an inspired band. There is a cycle of three records, five of the sides being Bix compositions: *In the Dark, Candlelights, Davenport Blues, Flashes*, and, of course, the immortal *In a Mist*. If I were selecting the ten best records of 1938, I would unqualifiedly include at least four of these numbers in the group. Bix, thought of usually as a brilliant trumpeter—or rather, he played the cornet most of the time, emerges here as one of the abiding composers of our time.

Kind of makes you wonder what it felt like for Bix's mom and siblings to sit down at the Beiderbecke piano, open the sheet music to a piece that bore their family name and play it.

NEWS OF 1903

When Leon Bismark Beiderbecke came into the world on March 10, 1903, Davenport was a city known far and wide as a refuge for the drinking man. Saloons dominated. Seven years earlier Mayor Henry Vollmer had dedicated a new city hall, declaring a promise kept by building it "without issuing a single bond and without increasing the rate of taxation by a single mill or the fraction of a mill."

City Hall's doors opened in 1896 with $50,000 of its $80,000 cost already covered by way of liquor taxes. Republicans called them sin taxes and tried making the sale and consumption of alcohol a political issue. Democrat Vollmer won a second term by a comfortable margin.

Between the Gay '90s and the Roaring '20s came a decade when Davenport's burlesque theaters and shimmy queens, gambling dens and sporting women earned it a reputation as *the wickedest city in America*.

January 14—*Daily Republican*: THAT INCIDENT OF ANITA RAY AND THE IOWA
 NO OCCASION FOR SURPRISE AT SUCH OCCURRENCES IN THIS CITY

Those whose thoughts are so wholly centered on the things that make for sweetness and light that they have no glances to cast at what is going on in the great, crude, heedless and reckless world about them, may find a revelation of existing conditions in the story of Anita Ray, who complained of the toughness of the Iowa theater. But to the individual who is about town and keeps his eyes peeled and his ears open for the facts of the varied life about him; who is aware of the fact that there are probably as many as 500 and possibly as many or 1,000 wine rooms, or stalls, in nightly operation in the city; who is cognizant to the indisputable fact that there are as many bacchanalian revels west of Perry street as there are east of it; to such a person the idea of Anita's story being in the nature of a revelation has its humorous side. Assuredly, to the thinking part of the population, who has any knowledge of existing conditions, Bucktown is depraved, deeply depraved.

Has anyone ever suggested that Bucktown set up a high standard of morality, and has anyone any reason to be surprised if he learns of naughty things being done in Bucktown? And the Iowa theater? Has it been the thought of any adult person in the city that the Iowa was a nice, quiet, decent family resort? The Iowa is a variety theater of the low type, does not profess to be anything else. It is fitted up with boxes, four on a side, with a number of girls who work the boxes, selling liquor to "suckers." The stage productions are not bad, and when the performance is over there is a big dance in which the box girls and the actresses are required to take part.

The theater of the sort of the Iowa is not new to Davenport, and the report of its existence should occasion no surprise. What is surprising is that some people profess to be shocked and amazed at things which are commonplace in this city.

Mayor Becker talked with Anita Ray at his office for over an hour and cross-questioned her closely regarding her experience at the Iowa. He did not find her to be a tender, innocent thing. On the contrary, he discovered quickly that she was a rough talker, and that she had an extensive and intimate acquaintance with the seamy side of life.

January 18—*Daily Republican*: The Rt. Rev. Henry Cosgrove of the Roman Catholic diocese of Iowa has taken to the pulpit this day to call forth all citizens to join in a crusade against gambling, prize fighting, all-night and Sunday saloons and their social evil.

"I have heard enough and I have been sufficiently told by men who travel and have the chance to know to convince me that we have a city here with worse conditions of immorality than any other in America. I believe from what I have heard that Davenport is the wickedest of them all. I don't like to sit still while it is going to the devil."

The bishop said that the story of Miss Anita Ray, a 17-year-old music hall singer from Chicago, should be of sufficient enough evidence for the need to take immediate action. "Alas, the mayor has been trifling and quibbling with the situation while the entire city degenerated," the bishop declared. "This is a strike for better morals. It is set to arouse the conscience of Davenport. Let us do something about it."

To that end, the bishop has petitioned Davenport's civic authorities to take immediate action against the proprietors of wine rooms. "The door that is worst of all is the door to the wine room. It is a gate to perdition," said the bishop.

Rev. George Giglinger, secretary to Bishop Cosgrove, called upon other church leaders to join in the bishop's crusade against the wine rooms. "The most insidious and destructive forms of vice are cloaked by the seclusion of these wine dens. They are the most active and efficient of all the recruiting stations for the army of the fallen. Young, upstanding women are here lured to sin and to follow the course of the flesh and the devil."

The generality of the people don't know much about these places. The unskilled observer might enter the saloon that contains them and see no evidence of them. He might go to the Iowa theater or some other resort of that kind, where the wineroom flourishes in its highest development, and think he has seen all there was about the place, when as a matter of fact he had seen nothing but the small show of goods in the front window.

However there are not lacking stories of the work of the winerooms, and they are not pleasant stories, either, nor are they stories that can be turned away with a laugh. Bishop Cosgrove hits the winerooms a particularly hard blow and the things that are related of its work justify even more than he says. The moral lascivious and destructive forms of vice are cloaked by the seclusion of these dens. They are the most active and efficient of all the recruiting stations for the army of the fallen. And who knows of a heavy hand laid on a wineroom in this city, at least within recent times?

January 21 — *Daily Republican*: Mayor Becker returned at 8 o'clock last night from his trip as a member of the special committee of the city council on the question of water rates. From the depot he went to his office in West Second street...took up pen and paper and wrote out an order for tearing out the stalls in saloons and providing that the doors must be taken off the wine rooms so that an officer any other person walking through the building might see the occupants of the minor apartments. Soon after the mayor finished writing this order and had placed it in an envelope to leave at the station, he was found by a representative of the Republican. The mayor showed the reporter the order and explained his reason for issuing it.

"I have been keeping in touch with municipal matters here while I was away as far as convenience would permit. I noted the statements of the press regarding the winerooms and the notoriety the city was gaining throughout the country. I was surprised by the assertions made in the papers and in the pulpit and took steps to acquaint myself with the facts. I discovered that the privileges accorded certain people were being abused, and that where an inch had been given in interest of the general desire for liberal government, a mile had been taken in many instances. This thing has got to stop and no one is more desirous of regulating the wineroom than I, now that I have convinced myself that it is really a menace to the people of the city, particularly to the young people.

As for gambling, that had already been restricted as much as could be expected. Craps, roulette, wheels of fortune, and faro had been prohibited and the gambling rooms broken up and only games of cards were allowed and these only to a limited extent.

On the subject of saloons that are open all night, Mr. Becker said he believed it would be against the wishes of the majority of the people to enforce any order regulating the hours at which a man should open or close his place of business.

January 22 — William Randolph Hearst's *Chicago Record Herald*:
STORY OF ANITA RAY AS TOLD BY HERSELF, SHE HAVING LEFT
DAVENPORT FOR HER HOME AT 15 LANE PLACE, CHICAGO,
AFTER THE INCIDENT WHICH CAUSED THE CRUSADE OCCURRED

"I was very glad to get the engagement to sing at the new opera house at Davenport," she said, "because I was very much in need of employment. When I saw the place I was fearful, and after events proved the justice of my fears.

"The trouble came exactly as I feared. A number of rich young fellows from about town came to the theater to see the new singers from Chicago. They were drinking wine and were quite boisterous. They had two or three women with them. After one of my turns they sent a note to the manager asking him to send me to the box in which they were sitting.

"Go up to the box with that crowd," said the manager to me.

"I looked up at the crowd. They were drinking and roistering and women and all were smoking.

"I won't go," I said.

"You will go," he said.

"I was firm and he grew very angry."

"If you do not go to that box and drink a bottle of wine with that party I will turn you into the street," he cried.

"I did not have a cent of money, but when I still refused to obey the summons of the men in the box I was turned out of the theater and told to go.

"I had no money and no way of getting back to Chicago. At last I went to the police station and finally found the chief. I told him my story and he informed the mayor. Mr. Kindt, the manager of another theatre—a good one—got me a ticket back to Chicago. The next day the mayor ordered an investigation of the new Iowa opera house and had the manager arrested. That place will never run again," he told me. "All girls are not as strong as you and you probably have saved many a girl from ruin."

January 22—*Davenport Democrat*:

The growth of gambling here is a thing that not so many people can see. The prize ring is open to the eye and ear, but the poker game, the roulette wheel, the faro box and other paraphernalia of the tiger's lair are better concealed. And yet, while the games have not been openly advertised, as have the ring events, the community is pervaded by the absolute assurance that you can get into almost any kind of game you want right here in the heat of the city. The feeling is general that these games have much increased in number, that the professional gamblers here have much increased in number, and that the men of the city who have been beguiled into these games, young and old, have increased in number....The gambler, in magnificence of attire and emblazonment of jewelry, puts up a swell front on the principal streets of the city as though he owns the town. The green table and the dealer's box have been inside and out of sight but everything else has been plain on the surface. There has been no effort to minimize even the appearance of evil...peddled in stores, offices, streets and alleys, hotel lobbies, and possibly even in homes.

* * *

If Anita Ray is half as good as she is pictured by the Chicago papers, her proper home is certainly in the celestial city. The wonder is she could abide the atmosphere of the Iowa theatre for a moment, and it is a wonder too she should refuse champagne when it is a conceded fact she had been drinking beer. However, it is a blessing that she is safe in Chicago, far from the contaminating influence of this modern Gomorrah. One may be truly good in Chicago, but not in Davenport, if some of the Chicago papers are to be believed. Hearst's Chicago American tells how Miss Ray "rather than drink a bottle of champagne with the son of Davenport's wealthiest men and his roistering companions, defied her manager and was turned penniless into the street at midnight."

Anita is credited with saying: "A weak girl in the clutches of those men is lost. I am fortunate. I am thankful to be safely back in Chicago, with that horrible experience behind me."

In an editorial yesterday morning the Chicago Record–Herald got funny and under the heading of "The Worst Town in America," gave utterance to the following:

"The title of 'worst town in America' has been snatched from the brow of proud, imperial New York. No longer can the metropolis of the East boast of her supremacy in the matter of abundant and variegated forms of vice and crime. She is no longer a top–notcher in the lurid allurements of sin. She is just a plain, ordinary, quiet milk station, not even on the main line to Perdition. If the satanic through "flyer" stops at the New York water tank some one will have to flag it. The town is off the schedule.

"The center of vice and crime has moved from New York to Davenport, Ia. This is the testimony of Bishop Cosgrove, a respected citizen of the Iowa town, who knows whereof he speaks. He declares he has traveled all over this land and he unhesitatingly gives Davenport the palm for all–around wickedness. In fact he assures the citizens of Davenport that they are living in the 'worst town in America.'

"When Tammany went out of power it soon became evident that the center of municipal vice and debauchery was drifting westward. It passed over Goshen, Kalamazoo and Aurora and settled upon the benighted town of Davenport....They will now be printing Davenport in larger letters on the railroad maps."

January 22—*Davenport Daily Republican*:
THE NAUGHTY THINGS THE ALDERMEN FOUND

Intent on finding out for themselves whether or not Davenport is the wickedest city in the world, Alderman Lunger and Klauer made a little pilgrimage into Bucktown Tuesday night and rounded up the more notorious places of the district. ...In one place they found some women drinking at a bar. In another they report that they found cash slot machines going in full blast. Withal the journey was said to have been a very interesting one and to have opened the eyes of these gentlemen to the true situation.

MAYOR BECKER'S ORDER WITH REGARD TO WINE ROOMS

The town read the Republican at the breakfast table yesterday morning and noted the action of Mayor Becker with regard to the suppression of wine rooms, and the town spent the rest of the day talking about it...in all parts of the city there was haste on the part of saloonkeepers to comply with the requirements of the new order of the mayor. Some took the matter complainingly and others philosophically. Some blamed Bishop Cosgrove and some blamed Mayor Becker.

One of the best known bartenders in the city, a man who has many friends among people of all classes, declared yesterday that he was not surprised when he heard of the order by the mayor, for the reason that he knew the mayor to be right in saying the wine room privilege has been abused. In many places it had been terribly abused. No restraint was placed upon the conduct of patrons, and "chair–warmers," as women are called who sit around wine rooms for hours waiting to be entertained at the expense of men who drop in, were allowed to be regular attaches of the place, in many cased being furnished by means when suffering from financial stringency. These "chair warmers" became adept in working for the interest of the resort were encouraged to remain as long as they would. In at least two places no women were allowed to come with escorts, no females being allowed on the premises except the "chair warmers."

In reference to the third point for which we are fighting, viz: the closing of the all –night saloon, the mayor does not think that there is a strong demand for it. All classes of people, of American as well as of German descent, have, however, expressed to us a strong desire of having the saloons closed some time during the night. If the saloons be allowed to run all night as heretofore, the rough and tough element of the town will soon try to have the history of the wine rooms repeated under another name. If the saloons close at a certain hour there will be less drunkenness, less staying away from the family circle, and less occasions for our youth to gather for immoral purposes. It is the law that orders the closing of saloons, and it ought to be called the police–hour, aft which no saloon dare keep open. The Iowa law fixes the hours of closing from 10 o'clock at night until 5 o'clock in the morning and all day on Sunday, etc.

January 23—*Davenport Democrat*: The crusade for morality and the action of the mayor in ordering stalls to be torn out of saloons and doors to be taken off of wine rooms continued to be the chief topic of conversation in the city yesterday.

Bishop Cosgrove's plan of attack on vice and immorality was praised on all hands, and the tact and evident good sense he exhibited in dealing with the situation were described as being an example to other clergymen, who are apt to defeat their own ends by an exhibition of immoderation, making demands, the granting of which would be entirely out of the question.

But perhaps the most interesting opinion being expressed is that hiding behind the moral wave, concealed in the generous shelter it provides are those who would like to see the scalp of Waldo Becker dangling in their wigwam.

Mr. Becker was a new figure in politics when he consented to accept the nomination for mayor. That he was an unknown quantity to the leaders of his party, and was universally conceded to be a good fellow had much to do with his election. It was a cold day indeed for the Republicans when they did not hear that some Democrat had tried to play the foster father to that political orphan, Waldo, and had got the marble heart for his pains....

The town had been wide open for a time and although the mayor had shut down the slot machines and gambling rooms, wine rooms were flourishing and were being abused to an alarming extent. The youth of the city were being encouraged to live the life of the bohemian and the libertine. Young girls were being dragged down by drink and loose company. Indecent dances had been introduced and were being used at masquerades in many parts of the city.

When Bishop Cosgrove did call a halt, Mayor Becker was out of the city and if he would have acted at once he could not do so. When he did return and was advised of the demand for reform, he acted instantly.

Men who had said nothing when the hoochee–koochee was being danced as far west as Brady street now stood on housetops and piously proclaimed that the city was so vile it smelled to heaven. They did not forget to emphasize that the mayor was to blame.

That part of the press which is notoriously serving certain corporate interests left none of the recourses of the dictionary unemployed to pain the moral degradation of the city. From one of these offices emanated the specials to Chicago papers which have given the town such an unenviable reputation. The almost forgotten incident of Anita Ray was dug up and the knockers sought to hide behind the figure of this frail female.

When interviewed by a Republican reporter yesterday, the mayor said he had ordered the suppression of the stalls and the regulation of the wine rooms because he felt he had followed public sentiment in the matter. He wished to do what the public desired him to do. He would not make the saloons close at the hours in compliance with the mulct law until he thought the Davenport public desired such closing. He would continue to keep gambling within bounds as far as possible, so as to prevent it from being a menace. As to his course in all these matters he would use his own judgment and would stand pat on it, no matter what happened.

January 24—*Daily Republican*: SLOT MACHINE ARRESTED IN BUCKTOWN

That Alderman Lunger and Klauer visited the Iowa theater on their slumming tour has been demonstrated by the fact that one of the two slot machines Mr. Lunger says he saw paying money was arrested in that place by Officer Sandford, was hauled to the police station in the patrol wagon and was booked by Desk Sergeant Tilebein as "Lunger's slot machine."

...Another happening in Bucktown yesterday was the order received by Jock Manwaring and the Iowa theater to shut up shop at once. The mayor ordered this. He said the Hackman's ball the night before had been advertised some days previously and rather than work a hardship he had not closed the place until it transpired.

January 28—*Chicago Record Herald:* LIKENED TO HADES
GIRL WHO STARTED REFORM CRUSADE TELLS OF DAVENPORT
SAYS TOWN IS A "LITTLE HELL"
TOUGHEST PLACE IN AMERICA, ACCORDING TO ANITA RAY

Miss Anita Ray, the concert singer who is responsible for the reform crusade instituted by Bishop Cosgrove, says Davenport is a veritable hell hole of iniquity, that Chicago is a paradise when compared to the Iowa town....

"If it is true that God has forsaken Chicago, then He has never even visited Davenport, Iowa. For to one who experienced what I did in that Iowa city there can be but little doubt that religion and the Divine hand never touched Davenport. The technical name for Davenport is "Little Hell." Nothing else will fit it exactly. For a town of its size there is more vice than in any other city in the country. Why do I say it? Because I have seen it; I have experienced a week of it. And nothing that has ever happened in my life will ever again make such an impression on me as did this one week.

"I have traveled in the concert halls of the Ghetto, the saloons of Lake View and the music dives of the West side but nowhere was there such vice as I saw in one concert hall in Davenport, Ia. In Chicago the frequenter of a music hall is the workman who goes to see the show, spends a little money for beer for himself and perhaps friends, and then leaves. The Chicagoans go to the music hall for the mere purpose of seeking recreation and such enjoyment as a vaudeville and musical show can afford. But not so with the Davenport man. The Davenport music halls are patronized by the sons of the wealthy houses, who carouse and spend money for the special purpose of getting the young girls drunk. They spend hundreds where the Chicagoans spend one dollar. They spend their nights in carousal, their days in slumber. Work they know not. Their unbridled debauchery goes on unhindered by police or authorities. The police make no attempts to stop it. They know that girls are ruined and their lives busted every night, but they do not interfere.

"Wickedness in Chicago? Let my good ministerial friends visit Davenport and never again will they assail the name of Chicago. They will see what a real wicked city is like. They will see what real vice is."

February 2—*Dubuque Telegraph–Herald*: OPERA HOUSES ARE USED FOR PLACES OF CAROUSAL

Since the agitation which began several weeks ago in regard to the evil influences which exist about the city of Davenport, much good has been done and the general tendency of the mayor and the civic authorities has been to move with utter impartiality in their efforts to eradicate some of the most crying evils. When it was seen that opening the doors of the wine rooms alone did not entirely accomplish the results aimed at in the crusade against these temptations to crime, orders were issued for the tearing out entirely of the partitions of the rooms.

Not only the saloons, which are operated as such alone were bereft of their wine rooms but the Iowa theatre, concerning which there has been much comment, was closed entirely and the performances were prohibited. The action was greeted with satisfaction by the respectable portion of the community.

The new Orpheon theatre, however, which has been running under various names for the past three or four years and which has been a by-word in the community, has remained un-assailed.

While the closing of the Iowa has met with almost universal approval, the conditions at the Orpheon are just as bad. The doors of the wine rooms at the Orpheon have been removed and the faces of the men and women who frequent these apartments are revealed to all but under another name rooms with a greater degree of secrecy are to be found in the building. The boxes on the sides of the house have the level of the first floor and screened with curtains afford a privacy as great as that of the average wine room before the crusade put an end to them. The boxes have openings facing the stage which can be screened from the rest of the house by means of the curtains.

Liquors are served here. Men and women congregate in couples. The difference between these and the wine rooms is one only in name. They have the added attraction of a vaudeville performance, the greater part of which is far from being conducive to clean thoughts.

February 4—*Clinton Herald*: It is strange the element when driven out of Clinton knew so well where to go to find protection. However, it is not strange that Davenport should follow the example of Clinton, as this city always leads its sister at the foot of the rapids. Clinton people feel no uneasiness over Davenport driving any of her evil-doers to this city. It will require many years for Davenport to catch up with Clinton and most other Iowa cities from a moral standpoint.

When Bishop Cosgrove declared in the pulpit that Davenport was the wickedest city in the United States, he gave expression to views long held by outsiders, but which were withheld from the public as a matter of courtesy. Clinton don't want any of the riff-raff from Davenport, and is in no danger of being invaded by the lawless from Scott's metropolis. Their present pastures are too verdant to seek new fields.

...Every city is the architect of its own fortunes, the maker of its own reputation. When the objectionable citizens were expelled from Clinton why did they not strike for Oskaloosa, Decorah, Cedar Falls, Mt. Vernon, or some of the other towns of the state under similar influences? Why did they think of Davenport as a haven? Not altogether for the reason that it was downstream and floating would be easy.

Davenport has persistently advertised its condition and had asserted that it would not be ruled by the laws of the state. The gamblers and the fallen women had no expectation that the state would be allowed to molest them there. They regarded the city as the city had regarded itself, as an experimental station for vice and a school for the violation of state law. Davenport is reaping just as all the other cities or all the other villages and country places will reap as they have sown. There is a seed time and a harvest. The river cities might have had good esteem from the better element of the people had they so chose. They deliberately selected their associates and planned their associations.

No city is free from these reflections. There are places in Cedar Rapids, a few as low and as vile as were the larger number of the same kind in Davenport. There are not in the whole world more degraded men than are a small and select band in this city, and their villainies have sunk below the plane of morality in the animal kingdom. There are probably but a few of them, but they are here, and when an ex-convict or other bad character reaches the city he knows where to go. When men and women have arrived at a certain stage of degradation as men and women they can go no lower, and every city has its specimens who have struck rock bottom, it is for the cities to say whether they will in all cases and to the best of their abilities observe the law or whether they will make excuse in the case of those for whom the law was made.

February 6—*Cedar Rapids Evening Gazette:* The Davenport newspaper reports that the visitor in that city will have some difficulty in finding his bearings, especially if he should arrive after midnight. This, of course, refers to the fact that the saloons have been ordered closed after midnight, and that Davenport has officially proclaimed that she is within two hours of Iowa. The difference of two hours time would indicate a difference of thirty degrees longitude, but if Davenport keeps moving this way at the recent rate of travel we may hope for eventual reunion and annexation.

February 7—*Tri-City Star*: CLAIMS HE WAS FLEECED AT THE ELDORADO

A Japanese acrobat who is at present performing in an act at the Orpheon theater yesterday attempted through his attorneys Hubbell & Hubbell to have a warrant served on the proprietors of the El Dorado on East Third street for running a gambling resort contrary to the laws of the state. [Justices asked] to sign the warrant, but both refused. They stated that he must first show that his intentions are good and that he is attacking the El Dorado because it is contrary to the law....They say that they have experienced cases of this kind before, in which the warrant was issued and then the case dismissed after the defendant had settled the debt. They do not propose to be made the tool of a collecting agency.

Kalnatura Namba claims he lost $325 and a diamond ring worth $150 at the El Dorado gambling rooms between the house of 12 and 4 o'clock Saturday morning... He is or was engaged as a performer at the Orpheon with his two sons....The law gives him no civil remedy—that is he cannot bring an action to secure a judgment for the amount of his loss. His only remedy is a criminal action under the laws of the state of Iowa, as laid down in the statutes. ...The justices believe Attorney Hubbell is simply seeking the warrant in order to use it as a "big stick" to force settlement. Louis Martens of the El Dorado has stated he believed the extent of [Namba's] losing to have been $4.50. He stated that he never advanced the ring for paying a gambling debt, but understood he had loaned money on it from a private party. He also said that he had heard [Namba] had lost money in other resorts beside the El Dorado.

March 10, *Davenport Republican*: WORLD'S LAST DAYS ARE HERE

The Rev. J.A. Earl, who ran for congress last fall in the Third district on the Prohibition ticket, declared to a crowd that packed the First Baptist church to the walls that according to his interpretation of scripture we are now living in the last days, as referred to in Timothy iii, 18. He said there are indisputable evidences that the verses refer to present time, and as proof he referred to the disobedience of children to parents, the utter disregard for law, both human and divine, and many other vices that are rampant in every section. His sermon has created considerable commotion, and is much talked about all over the city.

March 23—*Dubuque Telegraph–Herald*: From being what was termed by Bishop Cosgrove of the Catholic church, "the wickedest city in the world," Davenport has been transformed into a model of civic and moral purity, which according to the test it has withstood, will last, and the city will continue to be good.

A wave of moral reform probably never swept quicker and cleaner than did what has swept over this city. All wine rooms have been abolished from the saloons, the saloons are closing at midnight; bawdy dance halls and indecent exhibitions in theaters are closed or restricted; slot machines are abolished; fourteen gamblers have been indicted by the grand jury and thirty–nine women and young girls have been arrested and either sentenced to jail or shipped out of the city for being on the streets at unreasonable hours of the night.

Such, in brief, is the result of the work of Mayor Waldo Becker, enforced by Chief of Police Henry Martens, and egged on by Bishop Cosgrove, the greater part of the Protestant clergy, and a couple of persistent newspapers. In the list might also be noted the fact that prize fights have been "cut out," for Davenport was becoming famous as a boxing center.

Although the mayor was forced into the reform business, he has gone into it with a characteristic energy, and has accomplished more than all the other mayors of Davenport have been able to do in the seventy–odd years the city has been such.

July 22—*Iowa State Press*: For a little while Davenport enjoyed the reputation of being the wickedest city in the United States. By the efforts of Bishop Cosgrove and Rev Giglinger it lost that marked distinction for a time—but only for a time, and the clergy now propose taking the matter in hand again and acting with a set purpose for arousing public sentiment to where some of the more notorious resorts shall be compelled to come under the regulations which belong to and control the vicious. There is considerable excitement in the tenderloin district and a general public belief that it is time the red light be ordered to close before midnight.

November 6—*Tri–City Star*: Samuel Treiten, who came all the way from Alberta, Canada, in search of his daughter who ran away from home to go on the stage, found her at the Orpheon theatre where she was paid $7 per week to sing and encourage the generous purchase of drinks by the male patrons of the place. The girl was taken home yesterday.

November 7—*Tri–City Star*: A few nights ago the Star presented to its readers a discussion of the man who will be bought by a drink. It met the approval of all parties. Men of different political opinions told the Star it was the truth and it worked for good.

This evening the Star desires to say a word about the candidate.

Like the voter, the candidate is often led astray. He not only treats, but he frequently drinks with the man he treats. And sometimes he does this with frequent regularity, much more than a candidate for office should. Slumming has been a habit in Davenport for some time.

What is slumming?

Ask the candidate. He will tell you that in order to be elected he will have to make the rounds of all the saloons in that disreputable part of Davenport known as Bucktown.

Yes, it is a hard word. The Star would rather *not* use it. And yet, the truth often hurts, so that we shut our eyes to it and pass over it. And yet the truth is there, and when you open your eyes again it looms up bigger than ever.

It has been customary a few nights before election for candidates to make the rounds of this part of the city. They forget for the time being that they have families, that they are respectable, and that they are running for a respectable office, created by respectable people.

There are a great many candidates who do no slumming. Still they are elected. There are a great many candidates who do slumming and yet are defeated. This may be the exception, or the rule.

But it is to the candidate who does indulge in this kind of political work that these remarks are intended.

Are you going to blow a hundred dollars in that part of the city tonight?

Are you going to get beastly drunk with the boys tonight?

Are you going to forget that the office is decent, and that these means are not decent?

Don't do any slumming. Cut out the booze. Brace up. Be a man.

November 30—*Cedar Rapids Evening Gazette*: It seems that the devil has so firm a hold on Bucktown that even the grand jury bends its knees to him and shirks its duty.... So declared Dr. George Giglinger, the energetic young priest who has led the moral crusade in Davenport since Bishop Cosgrove first delivered his philippic on Davenport's wine rooms, dance halls, and brothels and declared it "the wickedest city in America." When interviewed by a reporter, Dr. Giglinger told a remarkable story of attempted bribery and neglect of duty by public officials, and declared his intention to continue the moral crusade to its bitter end.

December 6—*Davenport Daily Leader*: SERVE NOTICES OF INJUNCTION
SEVEN SALOONKEEPERS ARE NOTIFIED TO APPEAR IN COURT
PETITION STATES THAT THEY ARE VIOLATING
THE STATE LAWS AND ASKS THAT THEY BE CLOSED UP

Notices against seven of the Davenport saloonkeepers were served yesterday and the fight against the wine room is now on in earnest.

The notices were given to Sheriff McArthur at five o'clock Friday night and yesterday morning the saloonkeepers were all notified...proceedings are filed against those running the saloons and the owner of the property and are as follows:

H. Clay Woodward, who conducts the Iowa Theatre and the Davenport Malting Co

August Sandholm, who is proprietor of the Slate house and Maria A. Beauchaine the owner

Christian Brubaker, Miles Brubaker who conduct the saloon at Brady and Fifth street and the Davenport Malting Co

Oscar Raphael, who conducts the Orpheon theatre and Johanna Rapheal

James A. Munro, who conducts Brick's pavilion at 229 East Second street and Chas. Lienhardt owner of the property

Harry Manwaring, who runs Jock's dance hall at 307–309 East Second street and J.H. Manwaring

Robert Theleman and Albert Smith, who conduct the Senate saloon at 127 East Third street

Rev. George Giglinger appears as the plaintiff in each case and the petitions are brought under the state laws and the injunctions are asked for violating the state statutes.

The notices state that the person is to appear in the district court and show reason why he is not conducting a saloon contrary to the law.

...The petition invokes the statutes against the saloon men but whether it refers to the prohibitory law or the mulct law is not known. The prohibitory law forbids the sale of intoxicating liquor of any sort except in drug stores, but the mulct law which was passed later forbids saloons having blinds at the front windows, backdoors, chairs or tables in the room, that the saloons must close on holidays and Sundays and at ten o'clock at night.

Should this sweeping statute be put into effect it would bring every saloon in the city against the law. As a matter of fact these strict regulations have never been observed in the city and those who are prosecuting the cases state that it is not the intention to start any sweeping move, but simply to close those places where wine rooms exist and women congregate....

Brick Munro was at the court house yesterday morning inquiring into the nature of the petition filed and he stated that he intended to fight the case. He stated that he had engaged an attorney and that he was going to make a test battle of it. He said that if it was brought on the grounds of his place being a nuisance he could prove that it was not and he was going to see whether it could be closed or not.

STATE LAWS STRINGENT

The republican state liquor laws are very stringent. They consist of prohibitory law, which is the ruling enactment, and the so-called mulct law, which provides exceptions under certain conditions. These mulct law conditions are radical and it is said not a single saloonkeeper in Davenport or Scott county observes them.

December 10—*Davenport Daily Leader*: Davenport's moral crusade, started by Bishop Cosgrove and kept simmering by Rev George Giglinger, the bishop's secretary, made its first real showing when Rev Giglinger filed suits against the Iowa and Orpheon theaters and five saloons for maintaining wine rooms contrary to law. The owners of the property were made co-defendants among them the Davenport Malting Co, which owns and operates about sixty of Davenport's two hundred saloons.

Dr. C.H. Preston, former city physician, said, "Whether or not Davenport is exceptionally bad—and I doubt if such is the case—yet it cannot be questioned that the drinking and gambling resort and the brothel are and have long been working fearful havoc among the young in our midst...Until human nature can be largely made over, through the slow processes of education, I doubt the wisdom of attempting prohibition of either evil...

December 11—*Davenport Daily Leader*: Six more injunction proceedings were filed in the district court...against the following parties: Linsey Pitts, colored, 120 East Fifth street; William Ranson, colored, 310 East Second street; Saratoga Saloon, Mrs. Fard, proprietress, 322 East Second street; Eldorado, Louis Martens, proprietor, 116 East Third street; Palace Hotel and Saloon, Brick Munro, proprietor, 115 Brady street; Jennie York's resort, 330 East Front street

DAVENPORT GOES ON THE WATER WAGON

On New Year's Day 1908 there were 191 saloons in Davenport and 49 outside city limits in Scott County. Two years the Civic Federation had reduced that by sixty-six through permanent injunctions. Gambling houses and brothels had gone underground but the remaining saloons operated by rules of the Mulct law. By then new state law compelled all cities to reduce the number of saloons to one for every 1,000 of population. This measure was in process in Davenport when the state wide prohibition law, effective Jan. 1, 1916, was passed.

BIX AT AGE FOUR all decked out in a sailor suit for this studio photograph. Other photos on the opposite page show Bix modeling popular boy's fashions of the era. Clockwise from top left: wearing a Buster Brown outfit and standing beside Miss Beeson for the kindergarten class photo from Tyler School; age three in a belted smock and Buster Brown haircut that hid his big ears; looking dapper for Tyler School's seventh grade group shot in a tweed Norfolk jacket and newsboy cap; and an outfit so popular with the moms of the era that both Bix and future pal Hoagy Carmichael posed in their belted Russian peasant shirts.

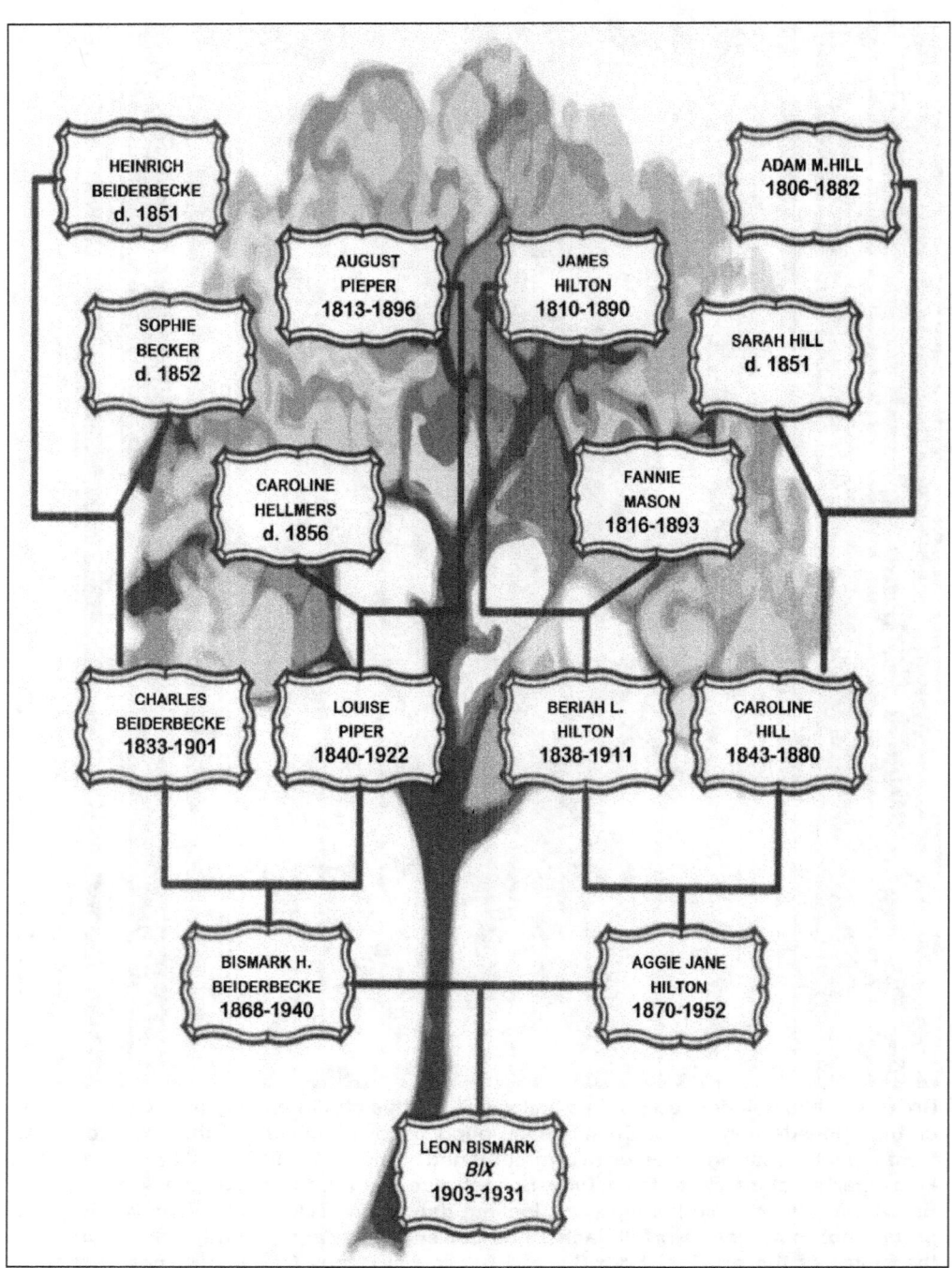

On Tuesday March 10, 1903, the forecast called for rain and colder temperatures. Next day the *Davenport Democrat* society column announced: *Mr. and Mrs. B. H. Beiderbecke welcomed a little son to their home last night.*

LEON BISMARK BEIDERBECKE

First Presbyterian Church **1905** member directory: Resident Members *(Birthright members of the church, who should also be baptized members and usually are, follow the names of their parents in indented lines.):* Mrs. B. H. Beiderbecke, Charles Burnette, Mary Louise, **Bismark**.

Davenport School Records for **1909** include the name of **Bismark Beiderbecke**. All grade school records show **Bismark**, sometimes spelled **Bismarck**. These records may be seen at 1616 Brady Street in Davenport, Iowa.

Name listed as **Bismarck Beiderbecke** on **June 1912** Sabbath School certificate. First Presbyterian Church Record of Confirmation: **Beiderbecke, Leon Bix** Apr 20, **1916**, first legal document with his name as *Bix*. These records may be seen at First Presbyterian, 1702 Iowa St, Davenport, Iowa.

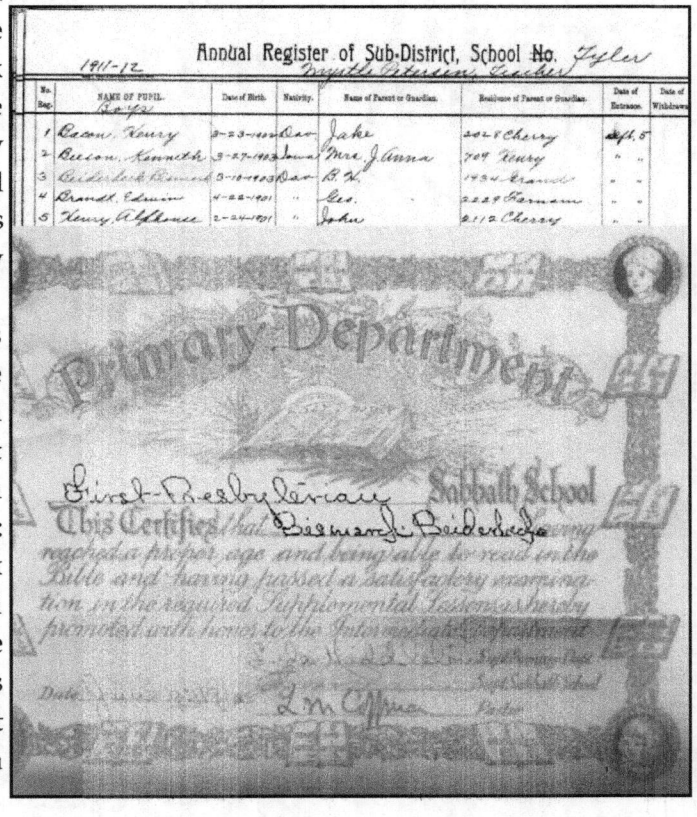

May 23, 1917: Aggie Hilton Beiderbecke signed Mary Hill's estate documents on behalf of her minor child, Leon **Bismark** Beiderbecke.

New York death certificate records name as Leon Bix Beiderbecke. Scott County birth records amended November 19, 1962, to **replace middle initial 'B' with 'Bix.'** Officials in Des Moines said it would have had to have been a family member who altered Scott County's record. A birth certificate

For the Year 19 10-11   A. I. Nauman Principal.
Carrie Brouse, Teacher.

#	NAME OF PUPIL	Date of Birth	Nativity	Name of Parent or Guardian	Residence of Parent or Guardian	Date of Entrance	Date of Withdrawal	GRADE Began	Left
	Adler, Philip		Dav.	E. P.	629-14th.	Sept. 6		2B	
	Brandt, Edwin		"	2229 Farnam	George	" "		2A	
	Bacon, Henry		"	Jacob	2025 Cherry	" "		2A	
	Bartness, Earl		Ia.	Elmer	2023 LeClaire	" "	Oct. 24	2B	2B
	Beck, Albert		Dav.	Fred	2404 Farnam	" "		2B	
	Beeson, Kenneth		Ia.	Henry	709 Henry & Grand	" "		2B	
	Bismarck-Biederbeck		"	B. Biederbeck	1934 Grand	" "		2B	
	Brandt, George		Dav.	George	2229 Farnam	" "		1B	
	Burns, Leland		Ill.	Ralph	2128 "	" "		2B	
9	Carson, Bruce		Ia.	Joe	1029 Kent	" "		2B	
1	Cozens, George		Ill.	George	2136 Grand	" "			
2	Dickerson, Armand		Ia.	C. E.	2326 "				
3	Feney, Loras		Dav.	John	"	" "			
4	Fennell, Joe		"						
5	God...							2A	
								2A	
						Rock Island	" "	2B	
					835 Kirkwood			2A	
			Dav.	Sydney	1625 Iowa			2B	
1			Dav.	Geo. R.	418 - 15th St.	" "		2B	
2	McStern, Harry		"	Paul	607 E. 14th	" "		2B	
3	Osborn, L.		Ia.	Lee	1935 Bridge	" "		2B	
4	Pohl, Wilbur		"	John	Central & Arlington	" "		2A	
5	Ramick, Richard		Dav.	"	1524 Eastern	" "		2B	
6	Henry, Alfonse		"		2112 Cherry	" "		2B	
7	Shantz, Harry		Ia.	Harry	720 E. Locust	"	7	2B	
8	Swaby, Leo		Dav.	Lewis	2312 Farnam		6	2B	
9	Yunker, Wegner		"	Oline Hartman	1922 College	"	" Sept. 13	2A	2A
0	Wren, Bobs		Ia.	Walter	2002 Tremont	" "		2A	
1	Cumming, Willis		Neb.	A. C.	706 Kirkwood	"	12 Nov. 20	2B	2A
	Cook, John		Ohio	Harry E.	2021 LeClaire	Jan. 15		2A	
1	Ackerman, Clara		Dav.	Adolph	1923 Iowa	"	6	2A	
2	Bailey, Elizabeth		Mich.	Joe	742 E. 15th	" "		2A	
3	Brainard, Ruth		Ky.	Stanley	2007 R. I. St.	" "		2A	
	Bacon, Irene		Dav.	Jacob	2025 Cherry	" "		2A	
	Brandt, Alberta		"	Al.	313- E. 14th	" "		2A	
5	Case, Corrine		"	Bert	2020 LeClaire	" "		2A	
	Cook, Isabel		"	R. P.	"	" "		2A	
	Cozens, Violet		Ill.	Geo.	2136 Grand	" "		2B	
7	Fish, Doris		Mass.	James	2022 LeClaire	" "		2A	
0	Gillian, Marie		Dav.	James	1619 Iowa	" "		2B	
1	Hearn, Iney		"	Wm.	2421 Bridge	" "		2A	
2	Johnson, Alice		"	George	810 E. Locust	" "		2B	
3	Meyers, Harriet		"	H. C.	2222 Cherry	" "		2B	
4	Ramick, Beatrice		"	John	1524 Eastern	"	May 13	2B	2A
5	Stacy, Alice		"	Byron	426 E. Clement	" "		2B	

Top: Bix's birth certificate on file in 1953.
Center: Scott County Recorder's Office log noting amended birth certificate issued Nov 19, 1962.
Right: reissued birth certificate.

from State of Iowa, Division of Vital Statistics, reissued February 1963, shows name the way Bix signed it as an adult: **Leon B. Beiderbecke**.

3 March 1908 *Davenport Daily Times*:

BIRTHDAY CELEBRATION AT NO. 9 KINDERGARTEN

Yesterday was the fifth birthday anniversary of Master Leon Bix Beiderbecke, the bright little son of Mr. and Mrs. B.H. Beiderbecke of 1934 Grand avenue, Davenport, and the event was celebrated at Miss Alice Robinson's kindergarten in school No. 9 by his little classmates. A handsome birthday cake with lighted candles sent by Mrs. Beiderbecke was brought into the kindergarten room by Master Bix, while the little folks sang with a will "Happy Birthday to You." Then with the extra candle "to grow on" left lighted, the cake was cut and distributed. Master Bix received many pretty gifts as remembrances of the day.

School No.9, a teacher's training school, was built in 1892 at 1921 Grand Avenue; addition to the north side of the building was built in 1902. All Davenport elementary schools renamed for U.S. presidents on July 1, 1908. School No. 9 named for tenth president, John Tyler.

7 July 1910 *Davenport Daily Times*:

7–YEAR OLD BOY MUSICAL WONDER

LITTLE BICKIE BEIDERBECKE PLAYS ANY SELECTION THAT HE HEARS

Leon Bix Beiderbecke, aged 7 years, son of Mr. and Mrs. B.H. Beiderbecke, 1934 Grand avenue, Davenport, is the most unusual and the most remarkably talented child in music that there is in this city. He has never taken a music lesson and he does not know one key from another, but he can play in all completeness any selection, the air or tune of which he knows.

Little "Bickie," as his parents call him has always had an ear for music. When he was two years old Mrs. Beiderbecke says that the child was able with one of his chubby fingers to play the tune of "Yankee Doodle." It was not as distinct by any means, as he can play, but even then the tune could be detected as it was running through the child's mind.

It must not be understood that he still plays with one finger and one hand. He plays every selection that he learns as completely in the bass and treble clef as it is written. In fact, so acute is his ear for music that if his mother plays a piece in another key than that in which Bickie has always played it, the child, will sit down and play the piece in exactly the same key with proper bass accompaniment.

Bix with Sunday School class; birthday news 3-11-1908; and holding hands with cousin Trudel on steps of the Outing Club

Society

HAROLD BAUER OF PARIS TO GIVE RECITAL AT CLINTON

Davenport lovers of the best in music will be greatly interested in the announcement that Harold Bauer, the noted pianist of Paris, will give a recital at the Clinton Opera house, Clinton, on Tuesday evening, April 14. Mr. Bauer, who is considered the best teacher of the piano in Paris today, was the instructor of Miss Gertrude Brannigan of Davenport during her studies abroad last year. He is a pianist of brilliant attainment; an Englishman by birth. He has been in America on several tours, but has never before been in this vicinity. No doubt a large number of tri-city people will go to Clinton to attend his recital.

BIRTHDAY CELEBRATION AT NO. 9 KINDERGARTEN

Yesterday was the fifth birthday anniversary of Master Leon Bix Beiderbecke, the bright little son of Mr and Mrs B H Beiderbecke of 1934 Grand avenue, Davenport, and the event was celebrated at Miss Alice Robinson's kindergarten in school No 9 by his little classmates. A handsome birthday cake with lighted candles sent by Mrs Beiderbecke was brought into the kindergarten room by Master Bix, while the little folks sang with a will "Happy Birthday to You." Then with the extra candle "to grow on" left lighted, the cake was cut and distributed. Master Bix received many pretty gifts as remembrances of the day.

HARMONY CIRCLE MEETS WITH MRS ELLIS

Mrs. J. S. Ellis, at her home, 601 LeClaire street, Davenport, was hostess to the Harmony Circle of King's Daughters yesterday afternoon at its

V. CHRONOLOGICAL ROLL.

No.	NAME IN FULL	RECEIVED BY Month Day Year	Month Day Year	I. B. R. INDEX
1480	Strom, Chas H. B.		Apr. 18-1916	
1481	Miller, Harry E.		Apr. 18-1916	
1482	Moorhead, Samuel H.		Apr. 19-1916	
1483	Moorhead, Amelia (Mrs. Sam'l)	—	Apr. 19-1916	
1484	Clark, Ben H.		Apr. 19-1916	
1485	Georgian, Alphonso A.		Apr. 19-1916	
1486	Goddard, Austin J.		Apr. 19-1916	
1487	Salter, Chester Day		Apr. 19-1916	
1488	Bills, Lucille		Apr. 19-1916	
1489	Bills, Virginia		Apr. 19-1916	
1490	Lepper, Charlotte		Apr. 19-1916	
1491	Bender, Edna May		Apr. 19-1916	
1492	Berger, Frederick E.		Apr. 20-1916	
1493	Berger, Mrs. Agnes J.	Apr. 20-1916		
1494	McDonald, Donald	Apr. 20-1916		
1495	Davenport, M. C.		Apr. 20-1916	
1496	Cameron, Mary Elizabeth		Apr. 20-1916	
1497	Hoffman, Ruth		Apr. 20-1916	
1498	Hoffman, Donald		Apr. 20-1916	
1499	Rueffel, Bessie May Mrs Schoor		Apr. 20-1916	
1500	Davis, Hazl		Apr. 20-1916	
1501	Hays, Willis		Apr. 20-1916	
1502	Beiderbecke, Leon Bix		Apr. 20-1916	
1503	Moorhead, Flora Mrs Donald		Apr. 21-1916	
1504	Wall, Mary		Apr. 21-1916	
1505	Worthington, Lillian F. (Mrs Carl)		Apr. 21-1916	
1506	Goddard, Frank M.		Apr. 21-1916	
1507	Goddard, Ellwicka (Mrs. F. M.)		Apr. 21-1916	
1508	Goddard, Florence Adell		Apr. 21-1916	

Bix's confirmation at First Presbyterian recorded April 20, 1916

As a rule, however, if he hears and learns the air of a piece he will play it in one or two, and sometimes three or four flats.

The child has a love for music. It is such a satisfaction and delight to him that if he is a little out of sorts, as any child occasionally is, his spirits are always brightened by a suggestion from his loving mother that they go to the parlor and play a little on the piano.

When Bickie is playing the piano, he never looks at the keys; he never watches his hands. To one watching and listening to the child playing the piano, it might seem that the child's mind was not on what he is playing, because his eyes are centered upon objects about the room or he is looking into space with apparently no thought of the piece he is playing. But a careful observation of that gaze and of the child indicates that his mind is absorbed in the music, in the melody that he is playing.

Bickie attends the Tyler school on Grand avenue, across from the Beiderbecke home, and whenever Prof. Otto comes to the school he plays the violin and calls upon Bix to play the accompaniment on the piano.

Mrs. Beiderbecke is a gifted pianist and the child hears and has always heard music at the home. His mother is contemplating engaging an instructor, even at the child's tender age, for the reason that she fears his playing will become too mechanical and that he will never fancy playing by note.

Mr. and Mrs. Beiderbecke are very proud of their little son, and they have reason to feel proud of him.

20 April 1916: Confirmation as member of First Presbyterian under the name: Leon Bix Beiderbecke
28 January 1918: Enrolled spring term at Davenport High School as Leon Bix Beiderbecke; attended seven semesters—spring & fall 1918, spring & fall 1919, spring & fall 1920, spring 1921
1919: six cornet lessons from Julius Paudiet who lived at 618 Warren Street in Davenport.
September 1921: enrolled at Lake Forest Academy; expelled May 21, 1922
1921: *The Bix Beiderbecke Five*: Bix, 1934 Grand Ave; Fritz Putzier, 2124 West Second Street; Bob Struve, 2819 Iowa Street; Erskine C. Albright, 1222 Pershing—born same year as Bix, brother of Dorothy Albright; Dick Woolsey, 815 East Fifteen Street.
May 3, 1923: Bix plays piano at the wedding of his cousin Gertrude 'Trudel' Seiffert Beiderbecke to William Day Washburn.
February 2–20, 1925: Bix briefly attends University of Iowa

DAVENPORT HIGH SCHOOL RECORD

Name: Beiderbecke, Bix Leon
Date of Birth: March 10, 1904
Place of Birth: Davenport, Iowa
Entered: January 28, 1918
From: Tyler School
Graduated: _____ Course: _____
Remarks: _____

Bix's not-so-stellar academic career. G=Good; P=Pass; F=Fail. After six semesters at Davenport High School, he transferred to Lake Forest Academy. The telegram below was sent to his mom after he'd been expelled. Instead of taking the train home, as Headmaster Richards wrote, Bix went to Chicago and the rest, as they say, is history

---

WESTERN UNION TELEGRAM

May 21, 1922

To: A. Beiderbecke
Street and No.: 1934 Grand Ave.,
Place: Davenport, Iowa

Bix leaving Chicago one o'clock today for home. Letter following

Jnoj Richards

Davenport Democrat–Leader stories:
March 5, 1925:

THE DAVENPORT BLUES IS LATE POPULAR PIECE COMPOSED BY BIX BEIDERBECKE OF THIS CITY; RECENTLY RECORDED

Very prominently displayed on one of the most recent releases of the Gennett Record Co. is "The Davenport Blues", a recent blues number composed by Leon "Bix" Beiderbecke of Davenport and recorded by his own orchestra, "Bix and His Rhythm Jugglers."

A pianist and trumpet artist who has a musical history which would occupy pages and pages to do it justice, Bix is a Davenport product and in deciding on a name for his latest hit, chose that of his old home town. Besides directing his own orchestra he is also in the ensemble of Jean Goldkette's Victor Recording Orchestra of Detroit.

Any of the Gennett records made by Bix and his orchestra or any of the Goldkette Victor records can be heard at the Harned & Von Maur victrola department, which is managed by C.B. Beiderbecke, who proudly boasts that he is Bix's older brother.

March 13, 1927:
Word from Bix Beiderbecke, Davenport's wonder musician in the popular music field, indicates he has been offered a position in Paul Whiteman's brass section. Bix, who is a pianist and trumpet artist, as well as an arranger and composer, is at the present time playing with Gene Goldkette's Victor recording orchestra in Detroit.

At the same time that he received the Whiteman offer he was approached by Vincent Lopez with an offer to become first trumpeter in that organization. In a letter to his parents, Mr. and Mrs. B.H. Beiderbecke, 1934 Grand avenue, he stated that he was not certain in which direction he would jump, or whether he would jump at all, because he was completely sold on Goldkette and his organization.

In the same letter he announced that "Davenport Blues," his own composition will be released on Victor, Brunswick, Okeh, and Columbia records in the very near future. Two Victor records, soon to be released, for which the music was arranged by Bix, are "Lane in Spain" and "Meet My Sweetie." Other records, now in the finishing process, which he contributed to the making of, are "Four Leaf Clover," "Sunny Disposish" and "Stampede."

November 23, 1927: DAVENPORT BOY WILL TOUR WITH PAUL WHITEMAN'S ORCHESTRA
L. Bix Beiderbecke, son of Mr. and Mrs. B.H. Beiderbecke, 1934 Grand avenue, composer of popular numbers and regarded as the finest cornet player of popular selections in the country, will tour the world with Paul Whiteman during the later winter, spring and summer.

Whiteman's orchestra is now playing at the Tivoli theater in Chicago after completing engagements at the Chicago and Uptown theaters. Next week the organization moves on to Pittsburgh and then New York for six weeks at the Paramount theater.

Then the orchestra will sail for Europe, where concerts will be presented in London, Paris, Berlin and other large cities. The itinerary will continue thru southwestern Europe and Asia, the plans calling for a circling of the globe before the return to American shores. It is expected that at least eight months will be spent in the globe tour.

The only 24–year–old Bix, as he has always been known to his local associates and as he is known today in musical circles, is an artist with the cornet. He was for a long time associated with Gene Goldkette's celebrated orchestra.

He is also known as a composer and recording artist. The Okeh records company has just issued his latest composition, "In a Mist," played by Mr. Beiderbecke himself at the piano. One of his compositions which attained considerable popularity was "Davenport Blues."

April 25, 1928:
"Bix Beiderbecke, perhaps the finest trumpeter in the country, will now play for you his composition, In a Mist." This simple announcement in the Paul Whiteman orchestra broadcast in the midnight program over the national networks from New York Tuesday night electrified the Davenport listeners tuned in and most of a small little family group in the B. H. Beiderbecke home, 1934 Grand avenue. Their son, Leon was that same "finest trumpeter". But six months ago he joined Paul Whiteman's orchestra after repeated requests from that famous jazz leader. His reticence was due to the

fact that he played by ear and scarcely knew one note from the other. Now he is a soloist and a composer, this latter with the aid of a fellow musician who wrote the score as he played it. "In a Mist" he played on the piano in this featured broadcast. "Bix" as he was known by the gang, and there always was a gang of "fellers" with him in his boyhood days, has displayed his jazz tendencies since earliest youth. He went to the local schools, went 3 years to the Davenport high school and one year to the Lake Forest academy at Lake Forest, Ill. He was known as a jazz artist in every school he attended but beyond that, school had little appeal and he had no inclination to go on to college. Music lessons too were too much like a grind. He took piano lessons for a time from two local instructors, not more than a score in all. He had wonderful promise, his teachers said, but he veered away from the labor of learning. What was the use of droning "one, two, three, four" when you could rattle off the latest jazz tune thru a magic sense entirely apart from mathematics? So ran his youthful reasoning. He exhibited the same attitude toward a business career. During the summers he assisted his father in his coal office, but for a life work he had other plans. For the past three years he has been cornetist with the Jean Goldkette orchestra of Detroit and was on one of the musical tours with that organization that Paul Whiteman heard him play. He is now 25 years old. "We can always tell when Bix's horn comes in," says his mother. "We know every time Paul Whiteman's orchestra is on the air and Leon knows we'll be listening in. The air is carried by the other cornetist but the sudden perky blare and the unexpected trills—those are the jazz parts and they are Leon's."

February 10, 1929:   'JAZZ IS MUSICAL HUMOR,' SAYS
DAVENPORT COMPOSER AND
CORNETIST OF WHITEMAN'S BAND
Believes Humor of Jazz is Many–Sided; Classifies
Catch–as–Catch–Can Music as 'Sweet' and 'Hot',
but Prefers the 'Hot' More Than Purring
Respectability of the 'Sweet'

PLINKY–PLANK! Blooey moans! Crooning tones!
Ear–ticking, toe–inciting, soul–wrenching melodies
—that's jazz!
Put them all together and what have you?
"Musical humor," says the world's hottest cornetist of Paul Whiteman's orchestra, Leon "Bix" Beiderbecke, who is convalescing from a recent illness

at the home of his parents, Mr. and Mrs. B. H. Beiderbecke, 1934 Grand avenue. And "Bixie" as his friends all call him should know. For a year and a half he has played with the king of jazz orchestra on Whiteman's special concert tour and filled every little niche and cranny with a catch–as–catch–can tricks of melodic figures and spent hours in the recording library of phonograph and music companies recording his own compositions. "Jazz is musical humor," he says. "The noun jazz describes a modern American technique for playing of any music accompanied by noise called harmony, and interpolated instrumental effects. It also describes music exhibiting influence of that technique which has as its traditional object to secure the effects of surprise, or in the broadest sense, humor."

Those "Barrel–House" Tones!

Tracing the origin of jazz back to the gay nineties when Dixieland musicians played negrotic "barrel–house" tones into "bowlers" and blew moaning saxophones into jugs and lengths of gas pipe, Mr. Beiderbecke pointed to the date Feb. 12, 1924 when Paul Whiteman gave the first jazz concert ever given in Aeolian hall, New York, and by cacophonic combinations proved what change came over the face of Melusina and Terpsichore in a decade.

"The jazz band's chief stimulus, of course was the rise of the negro 'blues' and their exploitation by the negro song–writer, W. C. Handy," the cornetist stated. "They at once were melancholic and humorous, and dealt exclusively with the singer's own emotion and philosophy. Their experiments were covert. In today's jazz they are open. The visual effect of comic instruments and bodily contortions of the musicians is, tho dispensable, a part of jazz itself."

Mr. Beiderbecke classifies jazz as "sweet" and "hot." He likes the "hot" which slightly modifies the original pandemonium of the "Livery Stable Blues," more than the purring respectability of the "sweet", whose hush and muffled throb is heard behind a balustrade of potted palms at debutante dances.

Humor "As You Like It"

"The humor of jazz is rich and many–sided," he said. "Some of it is obvious enough to make a dog laugh. Some is subtle, wry–mouthed, or back–handed. It is by turns bitter, agonized, and grotesque. Even in the hands of white composers it involuntarily reflects the half–forgotten suffering of the negro. Jazz has both white and black elements and each in some respects has influenced the other. Its recent phase seems to throw the light of the white race's sophistication upon the anguish of the black." "Bixie" as his boyhood gang called him, practically grew up with music. His grandfather, the late Charles Beiderbecke, was a composer and pianist of no little fame, and his mother, before her marriage was organist at the First Presbyterian church in Davenport. Music was in the air at the Beiderbecke home! "Bixie" took piano lessons for a time from two local instructors, not more than a score in all. When he arrived at prep–school at Lake Forest, Ill., he was dripping arpeggios and mooning over Chopin's nocturnes like any mere high–brow.

Goodbye Grieg and Liszt!

At 17 he became interested in certain insidious and perverse inflections which crept into popular music, so he bought himself a cornet and laid aside his Grieg and Liszt.

"The boys told me to put more American punch into melodies," he said, "A copy of 'Yes We Have No Bananas' was put before me and I was told to play like a he–man."

He did. Figuratively speaking, he taught the cornet to laugh by unexpected thrills, to moan by sudden perky blares, to do stunts, and to hold its head up high. He emphasized exact tempo and decisive rhythm. After completing his course at Lake Forest, he enrolled in the school of music at the State University of Iowa. Here he droned, "one, two, three, four" on the piano while he transposed and translated notes and melodies into orchestral scores. With his "huddle system," came the desire to start an orchestra and in the fall of 1925, he organized a motley crowd of ex-collegiate and called them the "Wolverines." From Chicago to New York the itinerant orchestra played. Later looking for new and lucrative fields to conquer, "Bixie" played for six months with Charlie Straight's orchestra in Chicago, and three years with Gene Goldkette's band in Detroit, which broadcast programs over station WGN.

We Want More

It was on one of the musical tours of that organization that Paul Whiteman heard him play and urged him to join the orchestra. But contracts are contracts and not until his contract was up did he make the change. Since joining Whiteman's orchestra "Bixie" has played one of the three concert pianos besides being cornetist, and director of one of Whiteman's orchestras. Among the most recent compositions recorded are "Thou Swell, Tu Tan Elegante," and "In A Mist," in which "Bixie" is feature in a piano solo.

"We have great times traveling about," he said—the "boys" are airplane crazy and movie–shy. We have a new Travelair plane and several are learning to pilot.

"Might come in handy sometime," he laughed, "in case we oversleep and miss the train, but we're generally on time. In fact, one time we were a bit ahead of the Uptown theatre in Chicago and curtain went up without warning. 'Be nonchalant' was employed and we picked up our instruments and started to play."

December 15, 1929: BEIDERBECKE VISITS HERE WITH PARENT
Leon B. "Bix" Beiderbecke, son of Mr. and Mrs. B. H. Beiderbecke, 1934 Grand avenue, who has attained national fame as a trumpet player with Paul Whiteman orchestra, is visiting his parents in Davenport. He will spend a short vacation here over the Christmas holidays and rejoin the orchestra again in the east about the first of the year.

Daily Times, 7 Aug 1931: "BIX" BEIDERBECKE, DAVENPORT BOY AND FORMER STAR CORNETIST WITH PAUL WHITEMAN, DIES IN NEW YORK.

Democrat–Leader, 7 August 1931: DAVENPORT YOUTH, FAMED AS MASTER OF TRUMPET SUCCUMBS TO PNEUMONIA
DIES WHILE MOTHER AND BROTHER ARE SPEEDING TO BEDSIDE
While his mother was speeding to his bedside, word was received here Thursday night of the death in New York City of Leon "Bix" Beiderbecke, Davenport youth who became nationally known as star cornetist of Paul Whiteman's orchestra and son of Mr. and Mrs. B. H. Beiderbecke, 1934 Grand avenue. Death occurred Thursday at 9:30 P.M., following a short illness of pneumonia. Friends of the youth telephoned Mr. and Mrs. Beiderbecke here Thursday Morning that he was seriously ill. His mother, accompanied by his brother, Burnette, left for New York City Thursday afternoon at 3:40 o'clock. During the night Mr. Beiderbecke received a telegram stating that his son had died. Due to the fact that the train bearing Mrs. Beiderbecke will not reach New York until late this afternoon it is assumed that she is unaware of her son's death.
BODY TO BE RETURNED HERE (*Times*)
FUNERAL HERE (*Democrat*)
Although details have not been arranged the body will be returned here for funeral services and burial. Besides the parents and the brother, Burnette, of this city he is survived by one sister Mrs. Theodore Shoemaker of Atlanta Ga. His father is manager of East Davenport branch of H.O. Seiffert Lumber Co. here.

Young Beiderbecke was for three years a featured star with Paul Whiteman's original orchestra and was described by America's "jazz king" as the finest trumpeter in the county. For about the same length of time he was also cornetist with the Gene Goldkette orchestra in Detroit and did considerable recording and radio broadcasting. He was also composer of several numbers which became generally popular including "Davenport Blues" and "In a Mist." Becoming early an exponent of modern "jazz", young Beiderbecke deserted a conventional musical education when still a boy and played thereafter largely "by ear."

<p style="text-align:center">BORN IN 1903 (Times)
STARTED CAREER IN SCHOOL (<i>Democrat</i>)</p>

"Bix"* as he was known to a large number of friends here and in other sections of the country, was born in Davenport, March 10, 1903. He attended the public schools here and was a student for a time at Forest Hill academy near Chicago. After spending some time in the music department of the University of Iowa, he launched his musical career by organizing an orchestra of his schoolmates. While with Goldkette's orchestra the famous Whiteman heard him play, and it was only after repeated invitations that Beiderbecke joined the Whitman orchestra. For a time he was director of one of Whiteman organizations. The peculiar style that characterized his playing became familiar to Davenport radio listeners through broadcast over a national network from New York. He also attained fame as a pianist, making several records of original compositions. About two years ago he left the Whiteman band and had organized an orchestra of his own in New York. He visited here for several months a year ago with his parents while he recovered from an illness. He returned to New York in March of this year and had been spending much of his time in composition.

*"*Bixie" instead of "Bix" used by the Democrat. The Times and Democrat stories are nearly identical but for sub–heads and with the same incorrect spelling for names of Charles Burnette and Jean Goldkette, and misidentification of Lake Forest as Forest Hill academy. Since 1915 Davenport–based Lee Syndicate owned both the Daily Times, a morning newspaper, and the Democrat, an evening edition, except on Sundays. The papers maintained independent editorial staffs but the report of Bix's death likely was written by the same Democrat reporter who did the 1929 Bix interview.*

UNSUCCESSFUL RACE WITH DEATH DAVENPORT, IA., AUG 8—(UP)—A race with death ended unsuccessfully for Mrs. B.H. Beiderbecke who left here for

THE DAVENPORT DEMOCRAT
AND LEADER

SEVENTY-SIXTH YEAR—No. 258 DAVENPORT, IOWA, FRIDAY EVENING, AUGUST 7, 1931 TWENTY-EIGHT PAGES PRICE FIVE CENTS

CATHOLIC ORDERS FACE BAN IN SPAIN

Harry Steeb, Moline Student Flyer, Hurt in Crash

PLANE FALLS 200 FEET AT LOCAL FIELD

Accident Occurs Soon After Take-Off in Home-made Ship.

RECOVERY IS EXPECTED

Fracture of the Left Leg and Internal Injuries Received.

DEAD IN NEW YORK

SEEK TO PIN MANY CRIMES ON WINKLER

Pal of Fred Burke in Hospital as Officers Gather To View Him.

AFTER FIRE HAD DONE ITS WORK

SEIZURE OF PROPERTY IS POSSIBILITY

$6,000,000 Worth of Holdings Reverts to State Under Bill.

CHURCHMEN BLAME 'REDS'

Abolishment of Official Religion of Nation Is Also Advocated.

Davenport Youth, Famed As Master of Trumpet Succumbs to Pneumonia

U. S. CHAMBER TO PUSH PLAN TO HELP IDLE

Dies While Mother and Brother Are Speeding To Bedside.

Urges Quick Action Necessary to Forestall Dole Legislation.

$24,000 Suit Outgrowth of Lake Tragedy

OUR WEATHER MAN

DUBUQUE COUNTY TREASURER FREE ON $10,000 BOND

Want Ads

CRAMER OFF FOR ISLANDS

PLAYS WITH OLD PISTOL, IS SHOT

DEMOCRAT WANT ADS

DEAD IN NEW YORK

LEON "BIX" BEIDERBECKE

Davenport Youth, Famed As Master of Trumpet Succumbs to Pneumonia

U. S. CHAMBER TO PUSH PLAN

Dies While Mother and Brother Are Speeding To Bedside.

New York when she learned that her son was seriously ill there with pneumonia. The son was Leon Bix Beiderbecke who had become widely known as a cornetist in Paul Whiteman's orchestra. Yesterday after Mrs. Beiderbecke left for her son's bedside but before she could reach New York, word came of the musician's death.

Bix died 9:30 pm Thursday evening. His mother and brother did not arrive in New York until Friday afternoon. Bix was probably put on the train Saturday, August 8; arrived in Davenport on Sunday, August 9 at 10:30 pm. Visitation was held Monday, August 10. Tuesday, August 11, was the funeral and private burial at Oakdale Cemetery.

Daily Times August 8, 1931:
STATION WOC PAYS TRIBUTE TO MEMORY OF BIX BEIDERBECKE
Stations WOC and WHO paid a brief tribute to Leon Bix Beiderbecke, who died Thursday night in New York City, during the broadcasting of the Valley dance program this noon, when Bert Sloan, pianist, played one of his compositions, "In A Mist," and the announcer read the following statement.

We are saddened at the untimely death of Leon "Bix" Beiderbecke, Davenport boy who made himself famous as one of the leading trumpet players of the United States.

Bix passed away last Thursday at 9:30 p.m. in New York City after a brief illness of pneumonia. Recognized as a musical genius while still in his home town, Leon Beiderbecke went to the cities where for three years he acted as trumpet soloist, playing for "The King of Jazz," Paul Whiteman, who recognized Bix's ability and termed him "the finest trumpeter in the country." He was connected for about the same length of time with Gene Goldkette's orchestra in Detroit, during which he did considerable recording and broadcasting.

It was quite natural that anyone so talented should turn to the work of composing music, and among the many numbers which he brought out, one stands forth as a fine example of modern rhythm.

In memory of Leon "Bix" Beiderbecke, Bert Sloan will play as a piano solo this young genius' outstanding composition, "In A Mist."

Hill & Fredericks Funeral Record: No. B   Date August 6, 1931
Name of Deceased: Leon Bix Beiderbecke, Resident: New York, N.Y., Birthplace: Davenport, IA. Day of Birth: Mo. Mar. / Day 10/ Year 1903; Date

of Death: Mo. Aug. / Day 6/ Year 1931; Age: Years 27/ Months 10/ Days 3; Place of Death: New York City; Sex: Male; Color: White; Single; Occupation of Deceased: Director of Music; Cause of Death: Lobar Pneumonia; Certifying Physician: Dr. G.W. Lynn, Register Address: New York, N.Y.
Name of Father: Bismark Beiderbecke; His Birthplace: Davenport, Ia.
Maiden name of Mother: Agatha Hilton; Her Birthplace: Davenport, Ia.
Informant: Bismark Beiderbecke, Address: Davenport, Ia.
Insurance: x; Charge to: Mr. B.H. Beiderbecke
Place of Burial or Removal: Oakdale Cemetery; Date of Burial or Removal: August 10, 1931 Funeral Services: at Chapel; Date of Services: Aug. 10, 31; Hour: 11 A.M. Name of Minister: Dr. Leroy Coffman; Casket [checked but no detail so likely his body shipped from New York in a casket; Re–

Embalming: 15.00; Auto Hearse: 15.00; Service 35.00; Limousines: 1 x 10.00, Sedan 10.00, Hearse No. 2 15.00, Flower Car; Cemetery Fee 15.00

1931 City Directory: Bix listed as residing at1934 Grand Ave.; occupation: Musician. Bix's Pallbearers: Louis Best, #37 Glenwood; William Henigbaum Jr., 2526 River Drive; Dr. John M. Wormley, #22 Kenwood; Karl Vollmer Jr., #2 Hillcrest; Richard Von Maur, #18 Glenwood; George Von Maur, 2516 River Drive.

Louis Best—1956

Louis Phillip Best, 55, a former resident of Davenport, died unexpectedly at 10:30 a.m. Monday in his home at Chevy chase, Maryland. Services will be held at 2 p.m. Thursday in Washington, D.C. at the Gawlers Funeral Home. The body will be cremated and the ashes will be brought to Davenport for burial in Oakdale cemetery. Mr. Best was born in Davenport, July 23, 1901. He attended schools here and was graduated from the State University of Iowa Law School and from Harvard School of Business Administration. He married Miss Sabia Lewis in Indianapolis, April 26, 1927. He was a manufacturer's representative in Washington. Survivors include his widow; three sons, Lt. J.C. Louis Phillip Best Jr., with the U.S. Navy in Panama; Steven and Schuyler, at home; one sister, Mrs. Herbert M. Lowry of Rock Island, and one grandson. Friends who wish may make donations to the heart fund or to local charities.

William Henigbaum—1979

Services for William K. Henigbaum, 82, of 34 Hillcrest Ave. Davenport will be 3 p.m. Wednesday at Weerts/Hill & Fredericks Funeral Home, Davenport. Burial will be in Oakdale Cemetery, Davenport. Visitation is 7 to 9 p.m. Tuesday. Memorials may be made to the Tri–City Symphony Orchestra. Mr. Henigbaum died Sunday at Americana Heath Care Center, Davenport after a brief illness. He was a member of the Tri–City Symphony Orchestra Association more than 20 years and served as its treasure many years. He was the father of William Heningbaum, who has been a violinist with the symphony since 1935. He married Helen K. Gobble* widely known Davenport pianist, in 1920 in Davenport. She died in 1951. Mr. Heningbaum retired in 1952 from Huebotter Furniture Co., Davenport after 30 years with the firm. He was an avid golfer and a member of the Rock Island Golf Club. Survivors include sons William, with whom he resided and John, Atlanta, Ga., five grandchildren, a great–grandchild and sisters, Mrs. F. J. (Margaret) Curtis, Delray Beach, Fla., and Mrs. E.L. (Elizabeth) Mills, Boca Raton, Fla.

*Helen Gobble was the daughter of Amalia Schmidt Gobble, who partnered with Charles Grade in music schools both in Davenport and Muscatine. Professor Grade gave piano lessons to Bix, his brother Burnie and sister, Mary Louise.

RICHARD VON MAUR—1985

Richard Von Maur, a prominent Davenport business executive and community leader, died Saturday at St. Luke's Hospital in Davenport. He was 89. Von Maur, 2915 Middle Road, Davenport, played an important role in charting the growth and development of Petersen Harned Von Maur into Iowa's largest independent department store chain. He served for several years as chairman of the board and president of the company. Von Maur, the son of C.J. Von Maur who was co-founder of Harned & Von Maur was "a good solid highly respected, citizen," said Henry Hook, former publisher of the Quad–City Times. "He never really was in the lime–light, but played a key role in the company's development, said Hook. Von Maur was active in the retail merchants bureau of the Davenport Chamber of Commerce and in 1966 was named a charter member of the Downtown Davenport Hall of Fame, which organizers said included, "some of the most famous names in retailing in this part of the country and probably from coast to coast." Von Maur was also known for his extensive involvement in other community affairs, including fund drive work for the American Red Cross during World War II, the Davenport Community Chest, and the American Cancer Society. Memorial services will be 11 a.m. Monday at Trinity Episcopal Cathedral, Davenport. Private burial will be in Oakdale Cemetery, following cremation rites. Weerts/Hill & Fredericks Funeral Home, Davenport, is in charge of arrangements. Memorials may be made to Davenport Family Y or the cathedral, both of which he was a member; or Quad–City Symphony Orchestra. Von Maur married Elsie Wood in 1927 in Philadelphia. Survivors include a daughter Mrs. Donald (Alice) McDonald, Pleasant Valley; sons Charles, Pleasant Valley, and Richard Jr., Davenport; 10 grandchildren; a great–grandson; a sister. Mrs. Albert (Josephine) Crampton, Moline.

Telephone interview on July 29, 2004 with the late Elsie (Richard) Von Maur, living on Middle Road in Davenport: She was 103 years old, very friendly and more than willing to share what she remembered about Bix. When Bix was born, her father–in–law Charles Von Maur was living at 1912 Grand Ave. The Von Maur family later moved to 1800 East River Drive. At the time of Bix's funeral, she was out of town, visiting family in Philadelphia. Her husband Richard served as a pallbearer for Bix, and for his father Bismark. Elsie did not attend Bix's funeral but is listed with her husband among those who sent flowers. Bix broke his mother's heart, Elsie added.

KARL KOEHLER VOLLMER—1985

No obituary published, only a death notice. He was born 30 Oct 1902 in Davenport, Iowa, and died June 1985 while residing in St. Louis, Missouri.

DR. JOHN WORMLEY—1992

Bettendorf—Dr. John M. Wormley, 91, of 1350 Kimberly Ridge Road, died Wednesday at St. Luke's Hospital, Davenport. Services will be 11 a.m. Saturday at Weerts Funeral Home, Davenport. Burial will be in Memorial Park. Visitation will be 4–8 p.m. Friday. Dr. Wormley was a Davenport dentist. He retired in 1974 after 48 years of dental practice. He married Ester Wulff in 1937 in Keokuk, Iowa. He was a graduate of the University of Iowa Dental School. He was a life member of American Dental Association and Iowa State Dental Association. He was a member of St. Paul Lutheran Church, Davenport; and the Outing Club, Short Hills Country Club and Davenport Moose. He was a former member of American Prosthetic Society and American Academy of Physiogical Dentistry. He was past president of Scott County Dental Association and Hills Hunting Club, a charter member and past president of the Davenport Club and one of the founders of the Friendly House Dental Clinic. Memorials may be made to the church or a favorite charity. Survivors include his wife, a daughter, Kitty (Mrs. Daniel) Schmitt, Davenport, a son Dr. John H., Midway Ga., 11 grandchildren, 14 great grandchildren, sisters, Francis (Mrs. Bruce) Clark, Ida Grove, Iowa, and Sue (Mrs. William) Sanborn, Scottsdale, Ariz., a brother Dr. Charles, Davenport.

GEORGE VON MAUR—1995

George Karl Von Maur, 93, died Friday at his home, 2516 E. River Drive. Services will be noon Monday at the family home. Entombment will be at Oakdale Mausoleum, Davenport. Visitation will be 3–5p.m. Sunday at Weerts Funeral Home, Davenport. Mr. Von Maur was born Dec. 3, 1901, to Henry and Dorothy Vollmer Von Maur. He attended Davenport High School and graduated in 1924 from Yale University, where he was a member of the boxing team. He returned to Davenport after graduation and worked in his father's store on Brady Street. When the store closed during the Great Depression, he entered the investment banking business, eventually retiring from Beyer and Company, Davenport. As a youngster, he often was exiled to the garage with his pal, Bix Beiderbecke, on Sunday afternoons. While their elders played bridge. Bix practiced his horn, accompanied by George on harmonica. They remained friends for the rest of Bix's life. Together they visited many a New York and Chicago speakeasy. Mr. Von Maur married Antoinette Sollo in 1931 in Davenport. Although the early years of their marriage was shadowed by the Depression, they endured and prospered for 59 years together. They enjoyed frequent trips to Jamaica and various European cities. He boxed for sport for many years and played a lousy game of golf. Mr. Von Maur was born and died in his family home. He enjoyed walks in his neighborhood until his death. It was his wish to spend his remaining years at home. Survivors include a son Henry, Coinsins, Switzerland; three grandchildren and nieces, Anne Rueffel (Mrs. Jack) Gilbert, Davenport, and Shirley Taylor, Aspen, Colo.

Family Friends Remember Bix
Stories told to Jim Arpy for the *Quad City Times* in July 1988

HE SAT ON A BIG DICTIONARY TO PLAY THE PIANO
I was three years older than Bix and knew his older brother, Charles Burnette, and sister, Mary Louise, better than I did Bix. But I can still remember Bix as a little boy, so small that he sat on a big dictionary to play the piano. He was a cute, dark–haired little kid and very talented. He looked just like the pictures you see of him at that age. I'm sure that even then Bix must have been considered a prodigy. And when he was perched on top of that piano, why he could really rattle it off. We called the brothers Bix and Bix2.
— Mae Steffen (1900–1992) Mae's father–in–law owned the store where Carrie Kennedy worked before marrying Albert Petersen

HE'D MAKE A BEELINE FOR THE PIANO
Bix was younger than I was, but my parents knew his folks. His parents would take Bix along when they went to parties in various houses. I can remember them bringing him to our house on many evenings. He'd make a beeline for the piano. It was a fine piano and Bix loved to play it. And he'd do it to everyone's confusion. He knew what he was doing, but that sure didn't help the card games. But even if his music tended to spoil them, Bix would keep playing— even if no one wanted to hear it. I don't recall his parents telling him to stop.
— George Von Maur (1901–1995)

HIS PARENTS TRIED TO SET HIM ON THE RIGHT PATH
I was older than Bix, who was then of high school age. I heard him play the piano while I was in his parents' home and always thought he might have quite a career ahead of him if he was physically able to handle it. By that, I mean overcoming the temptations he'd face. I always thought Bix was a fine young man and never a shoddy individual. He certainly came from a fine family and I'm sure his parents encouraged him and tried to set him on the right path.
— Alma Maehr (1898–1996) Maehr's Confectionery

WE KIDS NEVER REALIZED HE WAS THAT GOOD

In his younger days, I probably knew Bix better than anyone. His grandmother lived at Seventh and Western in Davenport and we lived at Seventh and Scott.

He and his grandma were great buddies. Her piano was one of the big attractions for Bix. When we'd go to the silent nickel movies, Bix didn't care about the plot. He just wanted to hear the guy who played piano accompaniment. As soon as the show was over, he'd hurry back to his grandma's to play on her piano what he'd just heard.

He was just as crazy then as he was later, not afraid of anything. He was quite a character even as a kid.

His grandma was quite a character, too, and a good piano player. She was always ready to have him play the piano and I guess she was quite proud of him. But we kids never realized he was that good.

Bix was an all–around boy and had a lot of friends. I remember one Halloween night that he came to our neighborhood. There was an old maid sourpuss everybody was scared to death of. We dumped ashes on her porch and then rang the bell. Bix was the last one to jump away as the door opened. The old maid reached out, grabbed Bix and yanked him into the house.

Well, we didn't know what would happen. We all sat across the street staring at the house and wondering what she was going to do to Bix. After about ten or fifteen minutes, the door finally opened and out came Bix carrying two big bags of cookies.

That's the kind of guy he was. He could win anybody over. He was a charmer.

Later, at any Davenport High School dance where there was an orchestra Bix was there, always borrowing an instrument so he could sit in.

A lot of times Bix would take a date and just forget about her if someone let him play the trumpet or piano. It didn't really bother him to leave the girl alone all night. He wasn't really that gung–ho about going out with girls anyway.

We weren't close the last few years before I moved away. Even in high school he'd been on the road playing for some time. And even then he'd want to have a drink, but I wouldn't call him a drunk. Everyone was always offering him drinks, but he held them very well.

If I look back at Bix, I see him as a sloppy dresser. He just didn't give a damn how he looked. But he had the talent even then.

We always marveled at how he could remember all that music from having heard it. I never could understand it; it was kind of uncanny. He'd just sit at the piano, and God, he could run up and down the keys!

I've thought about Bix many times over the years. We always called him a rounder. He had a style all his own. I see articles and think how much I lived through the things in them with him.

He always just wanted someone to ask him to play. He had the rhythm and was a natural.

—Leon *Skis* Wernentin, Rock Island (1902–1989)

Leon Wernentin with photo inset of Louise Beiderbecke

Left: steamboats heading to Clinton, IA. One Beiderbecke family story has Bix stowed aboard a Clinton-bound riverboat. The captain returned him home that night and told how Bix had entertained the passengers playing piano.

Below: I&I interurban trolley stopping at Brady St Depot. This line traveled to suburban areas between Davenport & Muscatine so Burnie might have rode it regularly while courting his future wife, Mary Neelans.

BIX'S NICKELS

By the tender age of six, Bix had become quite the entrepreneur. "He used to go to the neighbors' houses and play little ditties for which he received candy, fruit, and nickels," recalled his brother Burnie. "He did like those nickels. He quickly learned that fellows visiting their girls would try to impress them and gave Bix lots of nickels and dimes."

Carl & Adele's daughter Helen—front center and to the left of Bix, recalled the family holiday gatherings where all the grandchildren performed and she, being the only one younger than Bix, always had to go last. "Bix was a hard act to follow," she said, recalling he usually played piano.

BEIDERBECKE CHRISTMAS 1912
Matriarch **LOUISE** (14), **CARL T** (13) his wife **ADELE** (4) daughters **LUTIE** (17) **GAY** (12) **TRUDEL** (18) **HELEN** (19); **BISMARK** (15) wife **AGGIE** (9) daughter **SIS** (16) sons **BURNIE** (21) and **BIX** (20); **TILLIE** (6) husband **AL** (5) sons **VICTOR** (3) **CARL** (11) and daughter **OTIE** (2) son-in-law **LEON** (1); **LUTIE** (7) husband **MAX** (8) son **WERNER** (10)

Famed for playing music by ear, Bix also spelled that way, like in this note at age nine to Aggie:

> *My Dear Mother I hate to ask you but do you Mind if you give me a nickel becaus I need one of those things That Takes marks off paper you know what I mean I cand spell it how are you this is a fine dinner gime some more. Well I guess I will ring off so good by*
> *frome your Leon Bix
Beiderbecke not
Bismark Remember*

> *Dear papa how are you if mama has not got a nickel as i said in her letter I know you wont mind giving me one Well My hand is teired and I am going to ring off so good by.*

At age nine, Bix attempted to mimic his dad's dunning reputation for bill collecting:

> *Davenport Iowa*
> *June 22. 1912.*
> *My Dear father will you please excuse me for taking that nickle from Edward Goff I tried to give a nickle to him but he said we will have that for a treat and I said no I have to give it to you so fineley I got it out of him and he has it now and papa please let me and Bill go to a moving picture show I have been diging weeds I dug 5 five baskets full a penney a basket so that is 5¢ you will have to give me*
> *Well I guess I will ring off now*
> *well good by*
> *from Bickie*
> *and I am very sorry I took it from him and so let me to a moving pic-ture show and I will never do it again and if I do you can make me stay in all the time*
> *well I will go now so good By*

TALES FROM TYLER SCHOOL

Leon Beiderbecke and Larry Andrews grew up in houses separated by a field where the neighborhood kids played. "My dad was a hardware salesman, and while he was a good provider, we never dreamed of having the money available that Bix's folks had," Larry said.

"Nevertheless, when I first went to kindergarten, I wore the same kind of suit as Bix, velvet Lord Fauntleroy, with collar and flowing tie, etc. We immediately struck up a friendship that was really to endure...we had to stick together. We were odd sheep in the lot and there is strength in numbers."

Larry's dad, Howard Andrews, was a traveling salesman for Rascher, Schricker & Rascher Hardware Co of Davenport. His mom, Ada Nutting Andrews, was an art teacher.

As with Bix's relatives on his mom's side, Larry's family belonged to the United Presbyterian Church. Larry later helped raise funds for the former Mt. Ida congregation to build what now is McClelland Presbyterian.

Recalling their early days at Tyler, Andrews said, "At the start of morning class, we all met in the school lot and marched into class as Miss Robinson played a tune on her piano. After school I went to the Beiderbecke home to await my parents. Bix would crawl up on the Beiderbecke piano stool and play the same tune Miss Robinson had played that morning. Bix even duplicated any mistakes she had made."

Larry's most indelible memory of Bix was of him sitting at the Beiderbecke family piano "He would play—yes, I said play—band numbers and other songs from school as best as his hands could follow on the big keys. We would sing them until his mother would kick us out of the house. This was a usual practice winter, summer, rain or shine. Bix wanted to stay in and play his own gramophone or play the piano and sing. His mother wanted him to grow up big and strong."

Larry said that Bix did not come by his nickname by birth. "He liked the name, yet his brother was also called Bix. "So he became Bickey, and it was not until he started high school that he became Bix instead of Bickey."

When Bix came home to Davenport, Larry was playing banjo with Trave O'Hearn. Later, he became owner and president of the Eastern Iowa Radio

Tyler School seventh graders; Bix standing on the far right.

Bix, Larry Andrews and Vera Cox had speaking parts in Tyler's 1916 Christmas Play with Bix singing lead on a ditty called *Messenger Boy* and doing double duty as a carpenter.

Bix's mom must have thought he looked good in sailor suits since so many early photos had him decked out that way, including the one below astride a mule on Grand Avenue when Bix was about nine.

& Electronics School, and engineering contractor for some thirty-two Midwest broadcasting stations.

He served as president of the Quad-City Radio Technicians Association and as secretary of the Chicago IRE professionals group. Throughout the 1940s, he helped secure operating licenses and guided start-up owners through FCC regulations. Early on Larry began collecting tributes to Bix Beiderbecke through oral histories and taped interviews with former teachers and school chums. He was a supporter of efforts for an annual Bix tribute but died of a heart attack before seeing that dream become reality.

Larry W. Andrews (1903-1961) is buried at Oakdale where now each July the sounds of jazz rise in the distance, just across the field at the Beiderbecke place.

Miss Alice Robinson (1878-1940) was the niece of Edward Russell, a noted abolitionist and editor of the *Davenport Gazette*. Her famous cousin, Charles Edward Russell, published thirty books on American history and received the 1928 Pulitzer Prize in biography. As an investigative reporter, he exposed Wall Street corruption in New York and political corruption in Washington D.C. Theodore Roosevelt called reporters like Russell muckrakers. "There is no such thing in this world as a wasted protest against any existing evil," Russell would claim.

In 1909 he co-founded the NAACP. He also was an early advocate of a Jewish homeland in Palestine. As a member of the Socialist Party, he ran twice for governor of New York State and once for mayor of New York City but turned down the party's presidential nomination in 1916. He was tossed out of the party by Eugene Debs when he supported Woodrow Wilson.

Alice Robinson continued her family's tradition of social activism but from a more conservative stance. After her widowed mother died, Alice shared their house at 1207 Pershing Avenue with fellow teacher Ella Carry.

Alice graduated from St. Katharine's School in 1896. After completing a year of teacher's training at Public School No. 9, she opened a kindergarten class at the People's Union Mission, 207 W Second St in Davenport.

The mission was founded in 1895 by Rev. Edward *Ned* D. Lee for the benefit of disadvantaged children, particularly those living among the saloons and brothels of Bucktown. With financial backing from Bucktown dancehall owner Brick Munro, People's Union Mission opened Friendly House in 1903 at 313 E. Second.

In her early years of teaching, Miss Robinson went door to door soliciting students for her kindergarten classes. She told parents that education was what separated the haves from the have-nots, and that the sooner children got started the greater the opportunities for success.

"There is good in every child," she said. "Every child has a natural–born gift. Modify the bad tendencies so that good habits begin to develop and you put that child on the right footing for a life of purposefulness and fulfillment."

That earnestness made Miss Robinson equally successful when she solicited for students among the families of Public School No. 13, opened in 1900 at Fulton and Christie streets in the Village of East Davenport. She taught at what would later become Pierce School until the end of the 1907 term and then transferred to School No. 9, where she had first trained as a teacher. It was in her first year at the later–named Tyler School that young Master Leon Bismark Beiderbecke came under Miss Robinson's tutelage. Bix started school with the spring term of 1908. "When he came to my class he was a very normal little fellow with beautiful brown–green eyes. He loved music!" she recalled in a taped interview she gave another of her former students, Larry Andrews.

School No. 9 kindergarteners with Bix in the back row, far right standing beside teacher's aid Judith Beeson, her face partially obscured by the hair ribbon of the girl to Bix's left. Miss Robinson can be seen in the back row, center.
Note the girl with the her Steiff bear in the front row. These German-made jointed teddybears debuted in America after the March 1903 Leipzig Toy Fair after a savvy buyer placed an initial order for 3000 of them.
By 1907 Steiff bears with their trademark button in the ear reached nearly a million sales in America.

"In kindergarten there was play, work, and music and it was going on all the time," Alice Robinson said. "When Miss Beeson would play, he would stand by her and then he would play what she played, exactly, only an octave higher."

Judith Ann Beeson (1877–1966) was the widow of telegraph operator Henry Beeson, who died in 1909. Bix became classmates with her son Kenneth after being held back a grade level due to his bout of scarlet fever. Mrs. Beeson often played piano at social gatherings and was one of many parent volunteers at Tyler School, which had formed the school district's first parent–teacher club, forerunner of the PTA, in 1898. Miss Robinson had previously gotten mothers of her mission school kindergarten active in volunteering through the West End Mother's Club.

Carrie Brown, Bix's second grade teacher, told Larry Andrews that she had only happy memories of Bix. "He used to play *Pretty Little Glow Worm* on the piano with all the accompaniments. I inquired if he could play *We have a Little Fairy*. He replied, 'I almost can.'"

Miss Mildred Colby told Andrews that a teacher doesn't forget pupils as charming and cooperative as Bix Beiderbecke. "Whatever you were doing, he would help you and went with the stream."

She taught seventh and eighth grade music where the curriculum first introduced students to harmony parts. "Most of them couldn't keep up with the melody. Bix could sing second or third parts even though they were not written."

Miss Colby recalled that Bix's sister also had a talent for the piano. Mary Louise's oldest son, Ted Shoemaker Jr., attended kindergarten at Tyler School. He told jazz historian Phil Evans that his dad's construction business got hit hard by the Stock Market Crash of '29 so the Shoemakers moved in with his grandparents for awhile.

Miss Robinson was still kindergarten teacher. But the schoolyard that had been nothing but an open field when Ted's mom and uncles attended was newly equipped with swing sets and a merry–whirl, purchased by the city and installed over summer break. A baseball field and volleyball court also had been added in 1929.

Tyler's teacher training school had been discontinued after 1913. By 1942, the school, itself, had vanished and the entire lot became a city park, which it remains to this day.

Bix, second row far right, wears his class ribbon on the right side while fellow Tyler School eighth grade graduates have theirs on the left, all but Lucile Sorrowfree on the top far left. Miss Sorrowfree—great name—was a neighbor on Kirkwood Blvd to Carlisle Evans' cornet player Harold Oerman. Larry Andrews stands left of Bix and Vera Cox, the girl who first stole his heart, is seated in the middle of the front row with her lovely long dark hair draped over her right shoulder as she holds the broadside of the school pennant.

ALEXANDER THE GREAT

A ten–year–old's Christmas list: Dec 4\13: *...a box writing paper movie picture machine if its nots expensive and Foot ball and Dollar and book aouiji board extre a box of tools and a Box of Candy and a little writing desk and Macceno Set no 1 and that's all dad From Bixie*

The camera Bix wanted was made in Davenport by Victor Animatograph Company. Victor cameras and projectors were introduced in 1912 and sold locally at Petersen & Sons department store in Davenport.

In a career that spanned more than half a century, Alexander F. Victor (1878–1961) made more than 150 different models of picture–making and projection equipment.

Victor summarized his early life by saying that he had been an "exhibitor, cameraman, producer, studio owner, script writer and twice an actor." He neglected to mention that he also was an inventor with 86 patents to his credit.

Born near the Arctic Circle in Sweden, Victor became a magician's apprentice at age 16 and toured Europe, performing sleight-of-hand with cards and coins. While in Paris in 1896, he saw the first European exhibition of a motion picture and convinced Lumiere Freres to sell him a movie projector and a 15-minute film that he then incorporated into his performances. In Cairo, Egypt, later that year, Victor's mentor died and he carried on as the *Boy Wonder of Magic and Illusion*. When he came to the United States in 1900, he brought along his Lumiere projector and toured the Eastern U.S., billed as *Alexander the Great*.

Victor's props were destroyed in a 1909 warehouse fire in Toledo, Ohio, ending his showbiz career. He took a job with the Toledo branch of Davenport-based White Lily Washing Machine Company where he developed the first-ever motor operated washing machine.

All those years tinkering and repairing his Lumiere projector had developed Victor's creative skills in mechanical engineering. He had some ideas for improvements that would expand the use of commercial movie-making equipment. With help from a Toledo machine shop and Edison Laboratories in New Jersey, he made a prototype for a non-theatrical movie camera and projector intended for use by amateurs. Sam White, owner of Davenport's White Lily Washing Machine Co., provided start-up funding for the Victor Animatograph Company and manufacturing operations began February 16, 1910. In 1916, the company got a $3 million contract to make films for a New York firm.

Alexander Victor was named posthumously in 1964 to the Society of Motion Picture Engineers Honor Roll. The Victor Animatograph Corporation headquarters at 527 W. Fourth St., Davenport—the Ferd Haak Building—was added to the National Registry of Historic Places in 1983.

Among work applicants at the Davenport-based Victor Animatograph filmmaking division was a young illustrator named Walt Disney. He didn't get hired, so moved on to Hollywood. The rest, as they say, is history.

Bix's night out with his dad in May 1920 included supper at the Commercial Club, Main & W. 4th, above, and a movie at the Liberty Theater, 217 Perry St, where they saw *The Great Redeemer*, advertised at left.

NIGHT OUT WITH DAD

While Aggie was in Chicago visiting Mary Louise at school in May of 1920, Bix wrote the following:

6th Period, Davenport H.S.
Seat 461–Room 6

Dearest Mother & Sis,

Well Ill bet you're having the time of your young? Life. I sure wish I was there with you as I'm going to have a huge test in French and Ive been studying like Abe Lincoln and am sure Ill have it down so don't let it worry u. Last night dad met me at the Commercial club where I ate the best meal I have ever eaten and I sure was hungry as I hadn't eaten since morning; It consisted of Baked lake trout with tartar sauce, roasted spuds and some swell lettuce salad with mayonnaise on it. 1st course we had my favorite soup real thick and creamy not tomato 3 glasses of milk 4 pickles celery & a sq yrd of apple pie. That held me for a while. We then participated in a game of billiards at which I earned a much needed 2 bits from dad if I beat him. That 2 bits went for dinner—forgot money, lot of good it did.

We then went to the liberty where we saw a picture that made you cry, laugh, yell, whisper, creep, cheer and pray—The redeemer with wonderful accompaniment. On the whole the bunn was superb—as good as any I ever had in Chicago thanks to dad, then I was in bed at a quarter to ten and am feeling fine. Well mom & Sis that picture has changed me and for about a month Ill be good; it contains good and bad and from the picture I prefer the good—Amen.

Write me a card both of u.
Love to Sis & Ma. Regards to John.
Bickie.
Sis—Heard any good music?
The reason I wrote this is to Congradulate Sis and forgot—many kisses & good wishes sis.
    Bick.

Bix was congratulating his sister for completing her courses at the University of Chicago. She had only two terms of practice teaching still to complete; one term she did in Indiana and the other in Davenport, receiving her teaching certificate in 1922.

TOBACCO.
Chew MATCHLESS WOOD TAG Plug Tobacco!

IT IS THE

Finest In the World.

The Pioneer Tobacco Company,
NEW YORK   BOSTON!
CHICAGO.

BEIDERBECKE & MILLER,
Wholesale Grocers,
Agents. . . . . Davenport, Iowa

DANCING
EVERY SUNDAY EVENING AT PARISER GARDEN

Otto's full band. Free hack from Jack Frost's, Blackhawk.

Every Sunday evening.

J. F. MARTIN, Prop.

Merchant Tailors AND CLOTHIERS.

The undersigned have this day formed a partnership under the firm name of **WINECKE & PERRY,**
For the purpose of Manufacturing
Clothing for Gentlemen's Wear,
AT 224 BRADY STREET.

And propose to keep constantly on all of the best makes of CLOTHS, DOESKIN, BEAVER COATING, SUITINGS, &c., that are produced in Europe and America. We also have very arrangements made with leading Importers, so that all Novelties of the French, English, German and American Markets will be placed in our counters that hours are bought, for CASH, thereby inducing us the largest discount, and in order to give our Patrons the full benefit, we propose to sell, FOR CASH ONLY, and avoid all possibility of loss from any cause and the annoyance and delay of collection. We solicit an examination of our goods and prices and would be pleased to have your order. We propose making up our goods in the LATEST STYLES known to the trade, and in all cases guarantee satisfaction.

We are, very respectfully,
W. F. WINECKE,   WINECKE & PERRY.
Ezra Perry.
Davenport, Aug. 1st, 1870.

Learn the **One-Step Hesitation** and **Tango** at home

Book of Instructions—FREE

Just received from the Victor Talking Machine Company, book of "Three Modern Dances" with 8 pictures of Mr. and Mrs. Vernon Castle and 28 moving picture photographs showing steps of the dances with complete instructions for each step.

Come in and get a copy of this very unique booklet. Come soon as we have only a limited supply and they won't last long.

Harned & Von Maur

Don't Hang Up Your Wheel!

Fit it up with the

Ice Cycle Attachment

It is the only device ever made which can be successfully used with your bicycle on ice. More sport than you ever dreamed of. On exhibition and for sale by

Rascher, Schricker & Rascher
Hardware Co.

After the Stork
has made his visit, there is a two-fold need of
ANHEUSER-BUSCH'S
Malt-Nutrine

It contains just the food properties needed for mother and child.
A predigested food with unequaled strengthening properties.
Invigorating, sustaining, not intoxicating.

Sold by Druggists. Prepared by
Anheuser-Busch Brewing Ass'n
St. Louis, U.S.A.

Do not fall to include the Anheuser-Busch Brewery in your trip to St. Louis.

You'll Say—
They All Say—
"It's Delicious"

Griffin's Chocolate Fudge
40c Per lb.
20c Per Box
TAKE HOME A BOX TODAY

Griffin's
"That Delightful Place"
THIRD AT HARRISON
Ice Cream   Steaks   Lunches

Otto's Music Studio
HICKEY BUILDING
205 Brady Street, Room 308-309

ERNST OTTO
Graduate Leipzig Conservatory

Academic Instruction Voice, Piano, Violin and Harmony
RES. PHONE: DAV. 6887
DAVENPORT, IOWA

DR. KARL VOLLMER
DR. HARRY H. LAMB
Suite 1021

PRACTICE LIMITED TO
EYE — EAR — NOSE — THROAT

Ingersoll Watches

SALES 8,000 A DAY

This is the Ingersoll Dollar Watch, which sells at the lowest price, carries the strongest guarantee and has a larger sale than all other watches. Perfect in accuracy, size and style. Other Ingersolls at $1.50, $1.75 and $2.00. Sold by dealers everywhere or postpaid by us for $1.00. Booklet free

Robt. H. Ingersoll & Bro.
Dept. 3, 51 MAIDEN LANE, NEW YORK

the HUB

"RADIO" Jumbo Peanuts

The peanuts the radio fans heard crack in Boston, Canada and Texas.

Roasted Fresh Every Day.

When out riding stop and try them.

BOLDT'S GROCERY
Locust and Harrison Sts.
Phone Dav. 2007

ICE SKATES PRECISION MACHINE SHARPENED
WHILE YOU WAIT!
Hockey and Racers, 25c
Figure Skates, 50c

KUNKEL SPORTING GOODS
315 W. 2nd Street

Shredded Wheat

ADVERTISEMENTS

1. 1872 AD—major supplier to R.I. Arsenal
2. Bix played here at the Broken Blossom Café
3. 1879 AD—Mr. Winecke wrote reference letter on Bix's behalf to Lake Forest Academy
4. 1903 AD—local brewers tried to keep them out
5. 1914 AD—instructions for dancing to ragtime jazz
6. 1910 AD—Larry Andrews' dad worked here
7. 1920 AD—Bix hung out here with Thelma Griffin
8. 1916 AD—Bix's grade school music teacher
9. 1900 AD—Karlie Vollmer's dad
10. 1919 AD—Bix first heard live jazz here
11. 1903 AD—Glenn Sears agreed to play Hibernian Hall for this
12. Bix shopped for clothes here
13. Bix's favorite snack
14. First floor—skates; 2nd floor—Bucket of Blood
15. Bix's favorite cereal

Roger & John Hostetler used composites of themselves and Frank Goddard's baby son Austin with the line, "We never fail to catch 'em" to advertise their Davenport photography studio.

Bix with Nora, wife of Louis Lasher—head of Iowa National Guard during WWI

W.F. Winecke's obit, Jan 7, 1927; six years earlier he'd written a letter of reference for Bix's application to Lake Forest Academy

Bix, second from left, between Howard Andrews and his son Larry with Charles Simpson in 1914

BIX'S NEIGHBORS

The year Bix was born, Charles and Mary Von Maur—parents of Burnie's pal Dick Von Maur—sold their beautiful home at 1912 Grand Avenue to W.F. Winecke.

William Winecke was a tailor by trade. He started with a partner but struck out on his own in 1890, eventually buying the building he occupied on the northwest corner of Third and Brady. The original two-story structure was damaged by fire in 1901, same year Winecke's only brother died of pneumonia and left him soul heir to a large sum of money from his bachelor brother's successful cigar manufacturing business and real estate investments in Minneapolis.

Winecke replaced his original building with a three-story brick structure that had retail shops on the ground level with storerooms in the back, offices on the second floor and rental flats on the third floor.

He and his wife Ada had no children of their own so they donated much time and financial support to the Unitarian Church. Among their circle of church friends was Bix's Aunt Tillie. That friendship proved quite valuable to Aggie Beiderbecke when she needed a letter of recommendation to enroll Bix at Lake Forest Academy. Mr. Winecke wrote a glowing character reference on Bix's behalf.

Just before going off to the academy in the fall of 1921, Bix had a gig with the Ralph Miedke Orchestra for a bank opening in Moline. According to Fritz Putzier, the two of them had their photographs taken in their tuxedos before heading across the river.

Fritz recalled the photo studio was in Whitaker building in downtown Davenport.

The studio was owned by brothers John and Roger Hostetler. Another brother, Eugene, was the engineering division superintendent at the Rock Island Arsenal. Eugene Hostetler was also Bix's neighbor.

The 1921 photo of Bix in a tuxedo borrowed from his Uncle Carl has yet to surface. But there's another image of Bix that has a connection far as neighbors go. It's the one of Bix at age eight standing beside a lovely lady sometimes misidentified as Bix's mom. The woman actually is Nora Lasher, wife of Louis G. Lasher. They owned the house that Eugene Hostetler bought at 1936 Grand Avenue.

Louis Lasher graduated from Kemper Hall back in the days when it was a military school run by Bix's uncle, Max Von Binzer. Lasher fought in the Spanish–American War, serving in Company B, 50th Iowa Volunteer infantry. He then signed on with the 12th U.S. Infantry and served in the Philippines from 1899–1902.

After his military discharge, he worked for a military provisions company in Pennsylvania and returned to Davenport in 1905 to open the Lasher Manufacturing Co. He then became general manager of the C.O.D. Dyeing and Cleaning Co, which specialized in military uniforms.

In 1915 Lasher was appointed by the governor to the post of lieutenant colonel of the Iowa Guard. This required moving his family to Camp Dodge in Des Moines, thus selling the Grand Avenue house to Hostetler. Through a rapid series of promotions, Lasher eventually made brigadier general and adjutant general in 1918, serving at that post until 1927. Lasher's leadership of the Iowa Guard came at a time when the very existence of state militias was being scrutinized by federal legislators.

President Woodrow Wilson's call for Americans in April 1917 "to make the world safe for democracy," soon revealed a lack of sustainable troops to have much impact on behalf of allied forces. They had to initiate the draft.

Meanwhile, among the first U.S. regiments in France was Iowa's 168th which served with the 42nd Infantry Division under Chief of Staff Douglas MacArthur. He named his unit: Rainbow Division.

The National Defense Act of 1916 brought state militias under federal control with a mandatory designation from that time forward as National Guard. Iowa Guardsmen had to be deactivated from their state militias and then re-activated for overseas service.

Rainbow Division saw 164 days of actual combat with 700 killed and 3,100 wounded. Those who came home after the war found their military records listed them as draftees. It took a concerted effort by State officials to change Guardsmen's WWI designation to volunteer rather than draftee status on their service records.

In his post-war reports to Gov. Harding, Lasher voiced concern for the future of the state militia. He'd managed to get Iowa National Guard enlistments up to about 3,500 but complained about "bad relations with the War Department."

Lasher noted delays in supply shipments and payments to soldiers, as well as federal policies that hurt the Guard's preparedness. Lasher was not alone in interpreting the policies of the U.S. War Department—forerunner of the Department of Defense—as advocating against state militias. Nevertheless, under his leadership, the Iowa National Guard reached its peak post–war strength of 6,335 men by 1924.

A footnote on local history leading up to America's entry into WWI: When the president called for volunteers after Pancho Villa's border raids led to rumors of a German–Mexican alliance, the first enlistee in Davenport was John Connor Looney, son of Rock Island attorney and newspaper publisher John P. Looney, who owned a ranch in New Mexico. The Looney gang pretty much ran every vice operation in Rock Island and Scott counties. Connor Looney was shot dead during a Tri–Cities turf war in 1922.

Bismark Beiderbecke, seated front left in the surrey being pulled by *Democrat* publisher Jennis Richardson's *Davis Locomobile* for Davenport's July 4th parade, 1901. Richardson, in white coat, recalled the auto had its quirks, such as the chain drive jumping off its sprocket at 15 mph. Its brakes were no match for Brady Street hill and with only a rear axle band, no reverse. It had a 6 hp z-cylinder marine-type engine. Original cost: $700. After three years, he sold it for $300.

QC Musical Legacy

Jim Petersen, grandson of Albert Petersen, shared a tale about Bix coming to his dad's rescue. It happened when Victor Petersen followed some older kids one day to a baseball game at the Tyler School grounds across the street from Bix's boyhood home.

Seems it started to lightning and thunder and the wind came up, rain pouring down hard. In fact, a twister had hit just north of town.

"Dad was about seven at the time," Jim said. "All of the other kids, startled and afraid, scattered and ran, leaving him alone.

"He was at least two-and-a-half miles from home, scared and crying under a tree. He didn't know his way back and huddled there, trying to stay out of the pelting rain.

"But then along came Bix, who was 12 at the time. He was on his way home on his bike. He stopped in the downpour and offered to take dad home on the handlebars. It would have been easier and smarter for Bix to invite him into the Beiderbecke house just across the street, but take my dad all the way home he did."

Jim said it left a very strong impression on his dad far as how warm and caring a person Bix Beiderbecke really was.

Victor Herbert Petersen, youngest child of Albert and Carrie, passed away in 2005. Jim, second cousin once removed to Bix Beiderbecke—shared more about the Petersen family's musical legacy.

"Bix fans know my grandfather as *Uncle Olie*. To me, he was *Bopa*. He first worked with Bix teaching him to play and read music. As we know, that wasn't the easiest of tasks, but *Bopa* always had a great affection for Bix."

Jim said his grandfather came to America at the age of three from the Schleswig-Holstein province of Northern Germany.

"My dad played cornet in Grandpa's band, and violin in the symphony; he also sang. His sisters and brothers all played musical instruments. Uncle Art played cello. Uncle Ceno was a pianist and also played the viola. Aunt Helen sang and played the piano; and Uncle Harry was a violinist who once played with the Lawrence Welk Orchestra."

Jim's dad was born in 1908 and married Violet Hirl in 1937 at Grand

Rapids, Michigan. Victor had been employed by DRI&NW Railroad for twenty–four years, retiring in 1964. He had repaired and built violins most of his adult life and operated his own violin repair and rental business for 24 years after retiring from the railroad.

"My most–prized possessions are the last violin Dad crafted—he made a total of fifteen—and Grandpa's baton, given to him by his band members in 1912," Jim said.

He recalled with fondness the summer park concerts when his grandfather conducted the band and Uncle Art was the program announcer. "After Albert passed on in 1951 at age 85, Uncle Art conducted and my dad announced the numbers." Jim added that every concert ended with John Phillip Sousa's *The Stars and Stripes Forever*.

"I had the pleasure of singing from the LeClaire Park band shell stage in the early 1960s, with my high school choir, directed by Mr. Milton Anderson."

He had his younger son Scott and his granddaughter Rebecca with him at the Bix Afterglow party… "when Rich Johnson received his much–deserved Jean Golkdette award," Jim said. "There could be two more Petersen generations loving the Bix sound in the future if the chatter on the way home is any indication."

Jim Petersen with family photos and his granddad's baton.

Strasser band at Schuetzen Park

In a 1941 *Davenport–Leader* article, Albert Petersen shared his observations on the public's changing musical preferences:

> "When I began in music, the public taste was for what we today call the 'old music,' the classics. Then something new was introduced and called 'ragtime music.' It swept through the country and was the kind of music in demand, but it didn't last. Along came 'jazz,' which was only a variation of the so-called ragtime tunes, and all the people wanted to hear was jazz music. That was worked over to become swing music, but today that type of music is on the way out, and the people are going back to the fundamental music, the old beloved tunes from the great operas, the catchy musical comedy compositions, and the sound, intelligent early American classics."

Ceno Petersen's son Vince said that his grandfather began violin lessons at an early age and was proficient on several instruments. "At age 16, Albert played violin and baritone horn for the Strasser band and orchestra, a respected musical organization in Davenport's early days."

Jacob Strasser, an accomplished musician and disciplinarian of the old school, appointed Albert his assistant director in 1895. The Strasser–Petersen band performed at local festivals, parades and other social functions.

Albert headed orchestras at Davenport's Burtis Opera House, Rock

JACOB STRASSER, FIRST VIOLINIST ON LEFT
ERNST OTTO BAND AT SCHUETZENPARK BANDSHELL

Island's Harper Opera House and the Illinois Theater, as well as Moline's Wagner Opera House. For seventeen consecutive seasons the Petersen band played Davenport's Vander Veer, Credit Island, and LeClaire parks. His concerts attracted large crowds at Schuetzen Park, Watch Tower, and Campbell's Island.

He was principal viola in the Tri–City Symphony Orchestra, and was on the faculty of the Swindell School of Musical Art in the former Whitaker Building in Davenport when it opened in 1926.

Albert was founder and president of Local 67 American Federation of Musicians. His son Arthur held the presidency for some thirty–plus years. Ceno Petersen directed several area theater orchestras.

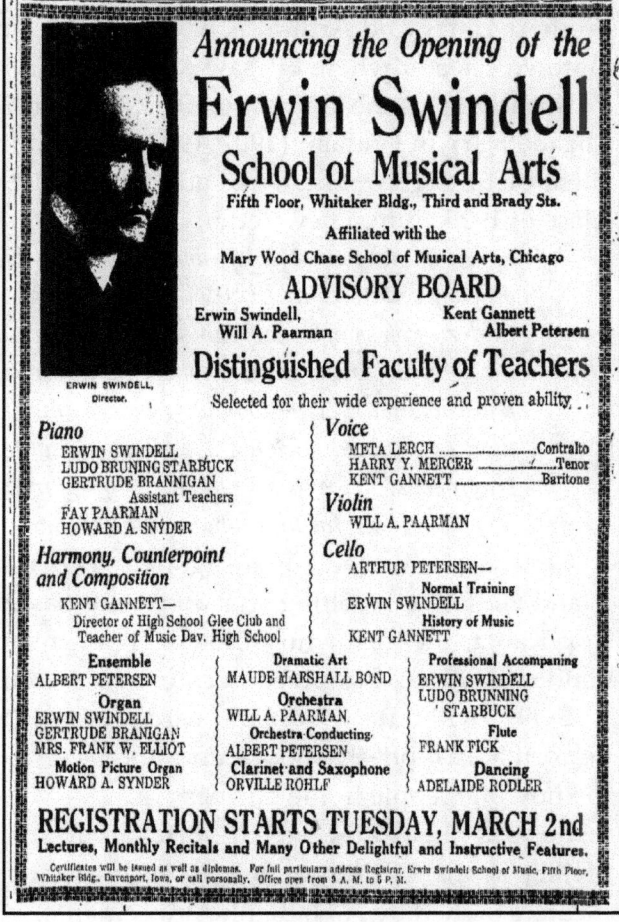

Vince, himself, performed more than half a century as a violinist. During World War II, while serving in Special Services, Vince played with the Calcutta Symphony Orchestra in India. Like his father and grandfather before him, Vince served as an officer of the musician's union.

Albert's wife Carrie was the namesake of her Aunt Caroline Hill Hilton—Aggie Beiderbecke's mother, hence the family connection to Bix.

Vince recalled stories Albert told about Bix. "Grandpa said that Bix wasn't interested in taking lessons on the cornet. He just wanted to play it," Vince said with a laugh. "Grandpa could see that Bix had a special talent, but it was difficult to harness, as he put it. He agreed that musically Bix was ahead of his time."

Vince said he sort of remembered that Albert even hired Bix to play at the Grand Theater, but added he couldn't confirm it.

A Date at the Garden

Bix's cousins operated a movie theater near Locust on Harrison, up the street from the drug store owned by Ceno Petersen's father–in–law. The theater's name, Har–Cen–Art, came of combining his name with that of brothers Harry and Arthur. A block down from Moetzel Drug Store was the Uptown Theater where Bix saw *King of Jazz*. It later became the Coronet.

But it was at the Garden on Third Street between Brady and Main that Elizabeth Irwin Gadient (1907–1997) recalled hearing Bix play piano for the silent picture show. She wrote about it in a 1990 letter for Davenport High's Class of 1925 alumni newsletter:

> *Remember the old Garden Theatre in Davenport? I had my one and only date with Bix Beiderbecke there. He was studying piano under Professor Grade and so was I. One day at the studio he asked me to come to the theatre where he was playing (by ear) and I sat a few rows back. This was long before sound movies, and there were many standard melodies to play—wild for the Indian raids and stampedes, "Hearts & Flowers" type for the love scenes. I thought he was wonderful to be able to play without music.*

Elizabeth's husband Frank golfed with Dick Von Maur at the Arsenal Island Golf Club. Golfing was a favorite pastime for Charles Grade and for Roy Kautz, the guy who flunked Bix on his musician's union exam. Both Grade and Kautz competed in country club tournaments.

Even without a union card, Bix managed a few impromptu performances, off–the–books and on–the–QT at local movie houses thanks to knowing people in the business.

Besides the Har–Cen–Art, Bix sat in sometimes with his friends Ed Meikel at the Garden and Romy Alford at the Casino, both organists in theaters owned by A.H. Blank Amusements.

Abraham Blank operated a chain of movie houses between Omaha and the Quad Cities. In Davenport he started out with the Family, the Casino, and the Garden in 1915. Adding Rock Island's Spencer and Fort Armstrong theaters and Moline's Majestic in 1924, Blank's Des Moines–based company became Tri–State Theatre Corp.

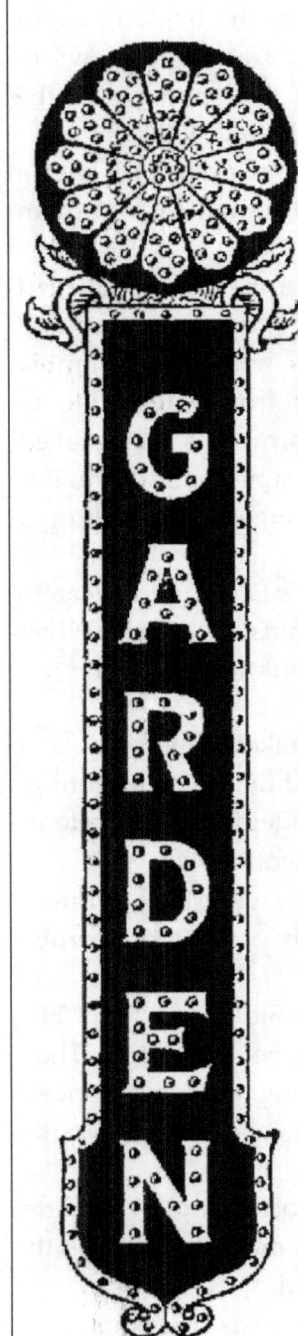

A. H. BLANK

THIS MACHINE ALMOST HUMAN IN ITS WORK

What do you think of a machine which automatically pops and butters popcorn, then sorts out the unpopped grains and at the same time, with the other hand so to speak, it roasts peanuts. This machine is run by electricity. Its base is 23¼ by 21¼ inches. It works like a charm. A. C. Nicolet, agent for the Holcomb & Hoke Manufacturing company of Indianapolis, Ind., has installed two of these machines in Davenport, one in Ray Achley's "Smallest Store in Town" at the Masonic Temple and the other in the Olympic theatre on West Third street.

EDWARD MEIKEL & ROMELLE FAY began their musical careers with A.H. BLANK Amusements, operators of the Garden and three other Davenport theaters plus two in Rock Island and one in Moline. All Blank theaters had organs but Davenport's Olympic was first to sell popcorn to QC movie audiences, beginning in October 1922.

Bill Washburn, husband to Bix's cousin Trudel, was the booking agent for Famous Players–Lasky Corp, which licensed its Paramount shows to Davenport's Garden Theatre. Paramount's *Peter Pan* was playing at the Garden when Bromo Sulser's Iowa Collegians played there in 1924.

For a time Davenport's Third Street was known as the *theater loop* with a dozen movie theaters within walking distance of each other, four of them operated by Tri–State Theatre.

The grandest of them was the 2,500–seat Capitol, which opened Christmas Day 1920.

Six years later A.H. Blank agreed to swap leases with the Columbia across the street, converting that 1,500–seat theater from vaudeville to movies. Upside for Columbia's Orpheum circuit performers is they played to a larger house at the Capitol. The Columbia later became the Esquire. But when he first took possession, Blank's only major change was installing a screen and an organ. All Blank's theaters had organs.

Son–in–law Sam Greenebaum was managing Blank's Davenport theaters when 18–year–old Ed Meikel hired on as an organist in 1915. When Greenebaum died at age 38, Abraham's son, Ralph Blank took over the tri–cities operations.

During his ten years with A.H. Blank theaters, Ed Meikel garnered quite a reputation as an organist. But he tipped his hat to the kid five years his junior, with little formal training who played remarkably adept improvisations, jazzing up riffs to Ed's organ accompaniments for the silent movies.

Ed's and Bix's lively keyboard duets would later entertain summer crowds at White Lake, Michigan, where they spent July of 1922 in a combo put together by Bix's Lake Forest pal Sid Stewart.

At the White Lakes Yacht Club, they were billed as Sid Stewart and His Boys. Sid played sax. Ed played piano. Bix played cornet *and* piano. They had a drummer and xylophonist and when not playing weekend dances, the guys hung out together at a boathouse owned by Stewart's grandparents.

After that summer break, Ed returned to Davenport's Capitol Theatre where he continued playing organ until 1925 when he moved permanently to Chicago. In 1929 he married Davenporter Helen Gadd.

She worked as a private secretary for a Chicago bank president. Ed played organ at Chicago's Harding Theatre.

Also in Chicago at the time was former Casino organist Romy Alford, playing Chicago's State–Lake theatre.

July 1922 at White Lakes Yacht Club with SID STEWART AND HIS BOYS; L-R: Sid, sax; Bix (face obscured by his hat & hand); Ed Meikel, piano; and drummer Ed Shears.
Bix and Ed Meikel in a canoe on Lake Michigan

Julia Romelle Alford was named for her grandmother. She preferred to go by her middle name. Romelle—*Romy* as Bix called her—began musical training with Amalia Schmidt–Gobble and by age sixteen was studying piano and organ at Augustana College in Rock Island.

Female theater organists were not uncommon in the era of silent movies. Romelle played the organ at the Casino when Ed Meikel was next door at the Family.

She recalled Bix as a shy and mannerly boy who ingratiated himself with a keyboard style Romelle could only describe as "avant–garde," adding "it worked for him and thoroughly entertained anyone within ear shot."

Born September 15, 1901, Romelle was the only child of Clarence and Christine Alford. Her parents met while her dad worked as a telegraph operator in Christine's hometown in Wisconsin. When Clarence's father died, he moved his family to Davenport. Clarence then worked for the CRI&P telegraph office. Romelle grew up in her grandmother's house at 526 W. Sixteenth Street.

Julia Johnson Alford was a devotee of Iowa–born Helen Van Metre Anderson's Church of the Higher Light. Grandma Julia led Sunday services at Davenport's Nienstedt Hall, Third and Marquette streets.

Congregates mostly discussed their founder's books. She wrote under the name of Helen Van Anderson. To cover publishing expenses, Anderson's books had ads for astrology, psychic/spiritual powers, and palmistry. Of the dozen titles Anderson published between 1894 and the early 1920s, the one that remains in print and still popular is *The Mystic Scroll: A Book of Revelation*.

Grandma Julia's congregation practiced a religion that was part Christian Science, part Unitarian, and part feminism. Julia visited with the sick and taught youth classes on healthy habits for body and mind, particularly in overcoming *habits of the secret and evil type*.

That might explain the hours Romelle's dad spent alone in the garage painting circus scenes on the walls. He told a newspaper reporter in 1929 that as a little boy he wanted to run away and join the circus.

He'd even written to Charles Ringling inquiring about a job and showed the reporter the letter he'd received in response, stating that there were no openings available for ticket–takers in Ringling's company. But the item Clarence most cherished among his circus memorabilia was an 1867 letter written by P.T. Barnum.

Clarence said he got it from a neighbor whose uncle did landscaping for Barnum's Connecticut estate.

RADIO STATION KOAM

Above: Kansas, 1940s; below, left: Montana, Sep 1968; right: *Democrat-Leader* story on CLARENCE ALFORD's garage circus, April 14-1929

Guest soloist

Romelle Fay Mekar will be guest soloist Sunday with the Helena Symphony Orchestra. Mrs. Mekar is one of Butte's most talented organists. She has had extensive training and study with some of the most famous artists, including Clarence Eddy, Leo Podolsky, Rachmaninoff and Pietro Yon. She plays a fluent style of the French school of organ. The "Champagne Pops Concert" will be held in the Placer Hotel at 3 p.m.

Clarence Alford Re-Enacts Noah's Ancient Role, Parading Painted Animals on Humble Garage Wall

Clarence E. Alford Putting the "Finishing Touches" on His Troupes for the "Big Parade."

YOO HO, SKINNAY, com' on over!

The circus has come to town!

Out on West Sixteenth street, the neighborhood juveniles are having the gay moments of their young life, ballyhooing within hearing and running distance of blocks around.

Yep! Honest to goodness, the circus is here. And believe it or not, it's here to stay. It took Clarence E. Alford, 526 West Sixteenth street, seven months to bring his show troupe to Davenport, but now

enough to use in docking the Lusitania.

Three weeks later, it was a wide-open eye lad whose school books eagerly tore a letter open bearing the name Charles Ringling of the Ringling Brothers' circus. The reply read:

Thanks Anyway, Charles!

"Dear Sir: Your letter of the seventh instant: We have all the ticket sellers engaged for this season and therefore cannot offer you an engagement. Signed, Charles Ringling."

ent stature than in most shows. The young lady, who has eight chins and no knees, tips the scale at 4,500 pounds. If a correct estimate can be made from the painting. She's a hippopotamus!

Old Gray Mare Collegiate!

Then came a snarling lion, a growling puma, a couple of spotted leopards, a camel with a fourteen inch yarn, and an old gray mare with "steel" shaded slippers that colorfully click along in the procession with more noise than collegiate heels—the animals "on parade" in Mr. Alford's circus.

Leaving behind her reverend grandma and doodling dad, Romelle married Arthur Fay in 1922. He was a chemist from Bettendorf who worked at the Rock Island Arsenal.

The wedding was held at the Fay family's church, Bettendorf Tabernacle which later was converted to a factory for the monocoupe airplane. Romelle's maid of honor was her best friend Bernice Rosenberg, who also was Arthur's next–door neighbor.

When Bernice married Jacob Strasser's son Henry two years later, Romelle played for their wedding.

Romelle and Arthur moved to Evanston, IL, where Richard Melvin Fay was born on Christmas Day 1926. Romelle continued her piano and organ studies at Chicago's Sherwood Music School under the tutelage of Russian–born virtuoso Leo Podolsky, renowned for his Rachmaninoff interpretations.

When WLS–Chicago went on the air in 1928, Romelle had a weekly half–hour program of organ music that aired in the Quad Cities on Sundays between the Major Bowes program and concerts from Radio City Music Hall.

In the mid–30s she was in Lincoln, NE, and married to Ed Cummins, sales manager for stations KFAB–KFOR. Romelle played organ concerts on the radio at noon each day from the Lincoln Theater. At night, she played jazz organ at Lincoln's Varsity Theater. In the 1940s she was working for Station KOAM in Pittsburgh, Kansas.

Since she always used *Romelle Fay* as her stage name, it's uncertain when she stopped being Mrs. Ed Cummins and became Mrs. Muri Mekar.

By 1968 Romelle and her third husband, E.R. Muri Mekar, were living in Butte, MT, where they did music therapy at the state hospital and played together in local nightclubs.

Muri Mekar became symphony director in Helena. He previously had conducted orchestras in Dallas, Philadelphia, Arizona and New York. After his death, Romelle retired to Orlando, Florida, where her son Rick Fay played with the Davey Jones Orchestra at the Floridian Hotel. She lived to be eighty–five.

THEATER TOPICS
By BARNEY OLDFIELD.

Organ slapper at the Varsity is Romelle Fay professionally, otherwise Mrs. Ed Cunniff, who was sales manager for KFAB-KFOR. Romelle, considered in the stamping grounds of Milt Herth, in Chicago, as being as fast as he is on the swingy electric organ, will come over KFAB on World Broadcasting System records starting Oct. 4. When the Varsity opened, she had the audience wild about her tunes, and she'll kick them out daily for the remainder of the week.

BOX OFFICE MAGAZINE
Oct 1, 1938

Lincoln—General Manager Howard Federer for the Nebraska Theatres Inc. has signed for a nightly broadcast via KFOR featuring MRS. ED CUNIFF at the organ. This puts both theater circuits here on the radio. The Lincoln Theatres are also renewing Barney Oldfield's chattering.

- Chicago jazz organist MILT HERTH introduced the Hammond electric on the radio in 1935.
- Nebraska-born Hollywood reporter Arthur 'BARNEY' OLDFIELD was named for the pioneering race car driver.

TONIGHT 9:15 P. M.
ROMELLE FAY
(Popular N.B.C.-C.B.S. "SWING" Artist)
at the Console of the
SCHMOLLER & MUELLER
Hammond Electric Organ

The Independent Record

Butte musician will head Helena Symphony Orchestra

DR. MURI MEKAR

Dr. Muri Mekar, a Butte artist who gained national recognition for performances and original composition with the Philadelphia and Dallas Symphony orchestras and the Long Beach Opera Co., has been named musical director and conductor for the Helena Symphony Orchestra. His contract calls for directorship in the 1960-63 season.

He is now doing work in music therapy at Warm Springs State Hospital, playing at night clubs, and with his wife, Romelle, has several concerts scheduled for January.

He did extensive orchestral work under Ossip Gabrilovitch and Sir Henry Wood in London, and with Alfred Hertz in San Francisco. He was a conductor for the West New York Civic Chorus and the Long Beach Opera Co., and the Amarillo Symphony.

His preparation for a career as a pianist, violinist, conductor and composer included work with Remy and Hewitt in Fontainebleu, France, and as a protege of the late May Peterson of the Metropolitan Opera in New York.

Above: **Kimball House** lobby after 1881 renovation. Charles and Louise Beiderbecke stayed here while their West 7th St house was under construction. Below: exterior of **Kimball House**, former Burtis House, 4th & Perry (now a vacant lot)

Burtis Opera House

Before building what was considered the finest hotel in the west when Davenport was *where the west began*, J.J. Burtis, a dentist originally from New York came to Iowa from Missouri where he had served two terms as a state legislator. After leasing LeClaire House, he built his namesake hotel in 1857 at a cost of $150,000. It originally stood on the southeast corner of Iowa and Fifth streets.

Burtis House served as headquarters for military officers stationed at Arsenal Island during the Civil War. When the officers wanted to erect a flag pole on the hotel roof, Dr. Burtis informed them that the property was in his wife's name, so permission had to come from her.

Mrs. Burtis had heard rumors that her brother in Missouri had been shot by a Northern sympathizer. She would agree only to allow officers to hang their flags out the windows of their rooms, warning that if a Union flag was hoisted atop the Burtis House she would burn the building to the ground.

Burtis House faced Davenport's Fifth Street railroad tracks. Passengers stepped off the train at the hotel's entrance. When the railroad changed its thru–line over the newly constructed bridge, the hotel ended up in the switch yard. The property was then purchased for $7,500—less than one twelfth its original worth—by Abel Kimball, general superintendent of the Chicago, Rock Island & Pacific Railroad.

A new hotel was built in 1876 next door to the Burtis Opera House at Perry and Fourth streets on the new CRI&P railway line, again with its entrance at the arrival point for travelers by train to Davenport.

Howard Burtis took over the hotel and after his uncle's death renovated both properties in 1881. At the suggestion of local businessmen, the hotel was renamed Kimball House. Until construction was completed on their West Seventh Street house, Charles and Louise Beiderbecke rented rooms at the Kimball House—later the Perry Apartments and later still the Vale, where Ronald Reagan lived while working at WOC radio in Davenport.

Since 1867 the Burtis Opera House had been said to be the finest theater between New York and San Francisco. During a stage show on January 29, 1869, theatergoers were introduced to a new contraption called the bicycle.

For the theater's reopening on September 1, 1881, the featured performers were Sprague's Georgia Minstrels. Largest of its kind at the time, the all-black choral group entertained an audience of 1,300.

Howard Burtis turned over theater operations to Fluke & Mann, who later hired Charles T. Kindt as manager. Kindt started out booking acts for the Grand Theater when it opened August 1888 in the new TURNER HALL. This was where Bix Beiderbecke performed with his high school glee club in 1920.

The Grand and Burtis competed for the best acts on the circuit. "In those days, Davenport had only 26,000 people—hardly enough to support two large theaters," reported the *Democrat* newspaper. "Competition was so keen and attendance so great that Davenport became one of the great show towns in the nation. No booking agent would think of setting up a road company route without playing Davenport."

Even after enlarging the Burtis stage, Fluke & Mann lost out to Kindt for the Davenport premiere of 1889's theatrical production of *Ben Hur*. The rival theaters called a truce. The *Democrat* reported: "It was agreed that Mr. Kindt would operate both houses. The Burtis would be used during weekdays and the Grand open only on weekends. The agreement was a wise one. Both theaters prospered and the city was never without good entertainment."

Edwin Booth's first appearance in Davenport was 1882 in *Richelieu*.

> Saturday April 21, 1888: Though the top price was a steep $5.50, it was worth it to see the great Edwin Booth and Lawrence Barrett, together with their excellent company, perform Shakespeare's grandest tragedy, "Julius Caesar." Booth was Brutus, Barrett was Cassius. The Burtis was filled for the play.

Booth had performed the part of Brutus to his older brother's Marc Antony and younger brother's Cassius in a benefit that raised funds for the Shakespeare statue in New York's Central Park. It was the one and only time the Booth brothers appeared together on stage—the year before younger brother John Wilkes Booth assassinated Abraham Lincoln. Edwin, coincidentally, saved the president's son by pulling him up onto a train platform after Robert Lincoln had fallen.

The Divine Sarah, otherwise known as Parisian-born Sarah Bernhardt, brought Sardou's *Fedora* to the Burtis stage on June 7, 1887. Bernhardt's protégé Lilly Langtry, nicknamed the *Jersey Lily* for her British birthplace, appeared here the following year during her American stage tour.

> The great strongman Sandow is at the Burtis, flexing his muscles and thrilling the ladies. Every inch of him is muscle. He is managed by a man named Flo Ziegfeld. Sandow is carrying with him a full troupe of athletes,

Richard Mansfield as Beau Brummell

Lilly Langtry

Sarah Bernhardt

Eugen Sandow

BOOTH & BARRETT
Playbill for
Julius Caesar 1888

Edwin Booth, circa 1888

> *whose muscles are so enormous that it appears they could lift up the whole Burtis building on their backs and carry it to Rock Island.*

Eugen Sandow performed to sold-out shows during his week at the Burtis. Born Frederich Wilhelm Müller in Königsberg, Prussia, Sandow's interest in muscle-building came of viewing Greek and Roman statues. Florenz Ziegfeld hired Sandow for his carnival. The crowd showed more interest in Sandow's bulging muscles than his weight-lifting fetes so Ziegfeld had him pose like a statue. Flo Ziegfeld, the carnival barker who later would become synonymous with Broadway showgirls, had thus made his first star.

In 1905, Kindt purchased the Burtis Opera House from the Burtis estate. He and partner Frank Chamberlain booked acts for a dozen or so theaters in Illinois and Iowa, including Rock Island's Illinois Theater where Bix Beiderbecke later would attend a high school play with pals Vera Cox and Karl Vollmer.

When Kindt booked Clyde Fitch's *Sapho* in April 1900, the show's lead actress Olga Nethersole was under indictment for public indecency in New York for having performed the show there. Kindt operated under the adage that all publicity was good publicity. Still, he maintained a reputation as *legitimate theater* for his opera houses.

Neighboring variety theaters such as the Standard, the Bijou, Orpheon and the Iowa theaters operated wine rooms on their premises and required that their female entertainers sit with patrons while not onstage. That was the line Kindt refused to cross.

Still, he introduced the locals to a Québec-born singer whose risqué repertoire included *It's All Been Done Before But Not the Way I Do it* and *Go As Far As You Like*. Titillating? Yes, but Eva Tanguay earned as much as $3,500 a week with her so-so voice and brassy style.

Known as the *I Don't Care Girl* after her most famous song, Tanguay performed before an audience of Iowa lumbermen at the Burtis House in February 1907. During an earlier appearance in *Sambo Girl*, a newspaper reviewer said Tanguay "danced like a whirlwind gone mad. She traversed until the audience screamed with laughter. She acted but it was always farce. Her songs will no doubt be the talk of Davenport all this winter of 1904 and into 1905."

Al Jolson, who sang at Brick Munro's dance pavilion in 1905, returned to Davenport in 1908 with Lew Dockstader Minstrels at the Grand Opera House, and then in 1917 as the star of the touring company for *Robinson Crusoe Jr.* at the Burtis.

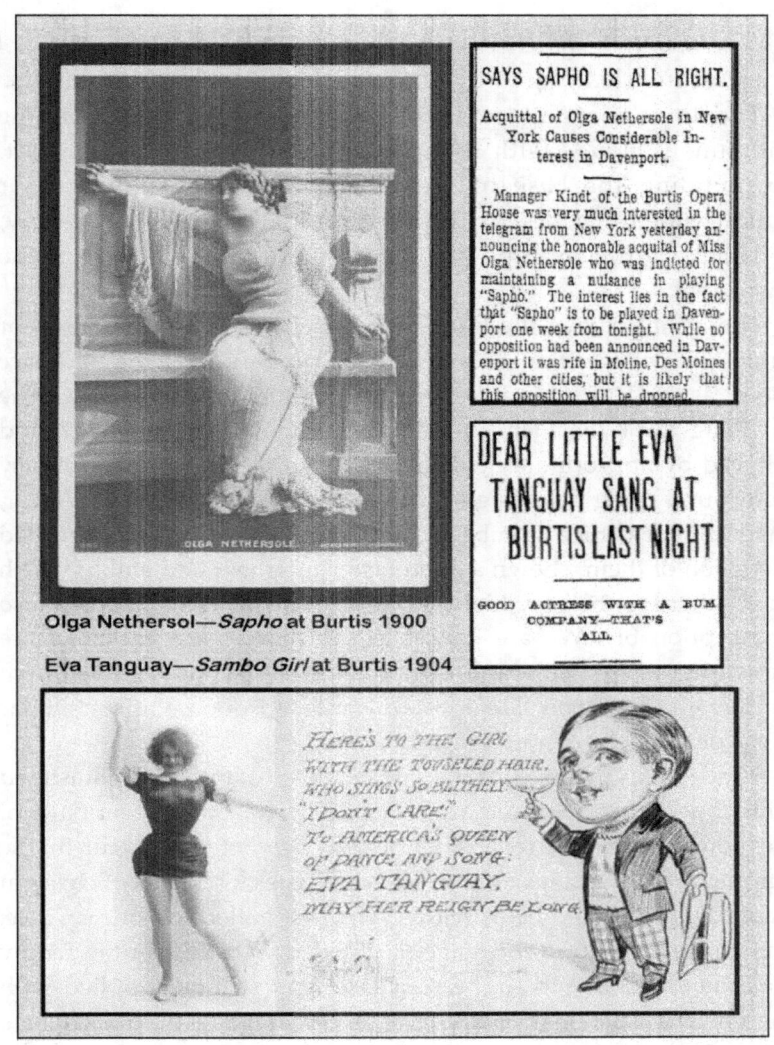

Olga Nethersol—*Sapho* at Burtis 1900

Eva Tanguay—*Sambo Girl* at Burtis 1904

Besides national touring companies, tri–city audiences saw the finest of homegrown talents on the Burtis stage including Clinton–born Lillian Russell and Davenport's own violin prodigy Florizel von Reuter. In 1916 the opera house hosted an inaugural performance of the Tri–City Symphony Orchestra—today's QC Symphony. Albert Petersen and his sons were among the musicians in the symphony's early decades.

Although the twelfth municipal symphony orchestra founded in the U.S., member musicians mostly came from Jacob Strasser's band, formed in 1856.

Interior details for the original three–story Burtis Opera House at 415 Perry Street were provided in the December 20, 1867, edition of the *Daily Gazette*. The opera house had reception rooms on the second and third floors, a lecture/dance hall in the basement, and stairways to the left and right of the entrance leading to the main auditorium. Further details:

The dome bears a handsome design, representing azure blue and sun–lit clouds with flying cupids disporting in the midst. Surrounding the base of the dome are eight "sunlights" or double cone reflectors, J.P. Frink's patent, which shed a mellow, soft light, sufficiently powerful to illuminate every part of the vast room.

The ceiling above the large arch panel is divided into deep or sunken panels, adding to the acoustic properties of the audience room, as well as agreeably breaking a monotonous surface. The frescoing is of the Flemish–Venetian school, airy and light, and relieved by appropriate fields in colors, painted with rare delicacy from purely original designs. The artists, Messrs Ficke & Winzer, have in their choice of subjects, and with the elegant and finished execution of them, shown a good taste, judgment and ability which entitle them to the very highest praise. Their work in stucco is also unexceptionable. We are happy to say that these gentlemen are Davenport artists; although their skills were acquired in Southern Germany where their talents were employed upon edifices similar to the one they have now so well adorned.

The seats in this part of the house are substantially upholstered with dark crimson red and are arranged here as in all other parts of the house with due regard for a full view of the stage. In the Parquet are 726 sittings; in the five wide aisles by means of chairs at least 200 more could be provided. The first gallery or Dress Circle, immediately fronting the stage, is divided into thirty–nine family boxes holding four to six persons each and will be supplied with comfortable cane–seat chairs. The boxes are safe from intrusion, being entered by means of small doors. On the sides of this gallery are five rows of upholstered seats raised above each other and accessible by separated aisles. The sittings in the gallery are 400 with the same susceptibility of increase as in the Parquette. The second or upper gallery is set back somewhat from the projecting frontage...and will seat 300 persons without using chairs or considering standing room.... There is a full view of the stage afforded from any seat in the entire house. The...house...has a capacity to accommodate about 1,900 people....

The Proscenium is one of the largest in the United States... private boxes, two on either hand, are sumptuously furnished and draped with rich Brocatelle and lace curtains. Immediately over the proscenium is a painting by Mr. Fick, the artist, representing the bust of Shakespeare surrounded by the chubbiest and freshest looking imaginable cupids....

Dr. Burtis was fortunate in securing the services of Messrs. Bird & Simons, scenic artists of New York....The drop curtain is a splendid specimen of scenic art, done in imitation of the Gobeline Sevierj Tapestry. The act drop alone cost over two thousand dollars and is a classical production of rare beauty: subject, Carthaginian Ruins.

Every precaution has been taken to provide against accident by fire...galleries...lead up by two passages with wide landings. The steps are of easy tread...it would almost be impossible for these stairways to be blocked...There are wide doors and stairways on either side of the Proscenium, in Parquette and Dress Circle, which would aid materially in emptying the House. The doors all open outward.

Fortunately no one was inside when a fire broke out in the early hours of Monday, April 25, 1921. An escaped mental patient torched the Burtis Opera House along with three other buildings within a one–block radius.

Alexander, crystal gazer, who was playing at the Burtis this week, sustained a loss at $15,000 when paraphernalia in his dressing room was destroyed. He salvaged several trunks filled with equipment. Alexander entertained a big crowd at the Burtis the night of the fire, telling the audience what the future held in store for them—everything except that there was going to be a fire about two hours later that would destroy the stage on which he was standing. He even told how he once moved from one hotel to another because he knew there was going to be a fire there. And there was. Alexander claimed afterwards that he had a hunch there would be a fire in the Burtis.

After the Burtis fire, the building never again served as a theater. Kindt converted the first floor to offices for Cusack Advertising Co., makers of large outdoor signs. Kindt became corporate director and district manager for the Chicago–based company. He also founded the Tri–Cities Advertisers Club, which continues to this day as the QC Ad Club. The Cusack building later became home to Tri–City Electric.

SHOWMAN CHARLIE KINDT

The following excerpts are from a series of articles by former theater owner Charles T. Kindt for the *Davenport Democrat–Leader* in 1929:

Do you remember the first horseless carriage which came to Davenport? Well, if you don't I'll tell you it was Hi Henry's Minstrels that brought it here and Hi drove it himself up and down Perry street. It had been announced and Perry street was lined with hundreds of people on both sides from Fifth street down to Front street.

William F. Cody a.k.a. Buffalo Bill was born in Scott county on the banks of the Mississippi near LeClaire. After he became famous and had gain the reputation of being the greatest scout of the American frontier he drifted into show business and perhaps very few of you may know that the first performance he ever gave was staged at the old Burtis theater. His manager at that time was Josh Ogden and the name of his first play was *The Scout of the Plains*.

Pat Campbell was a temperamental English artist and wired me to have the Rock Island railroad cease running trains during her performance as she had heard that the depot was adjacent to the Burtis.

My friend Leon Allen could not very well stop trains from running on schedule but agreed that the clanging of bells, blowing of steam, etc., would be prevented.

[note: your humble author had a similar experience with Rock Island–born vaudeville singer Maureen Englin back when we were part of the newly formed Writer's Studio, a Quad Cities critique group that gathered weekly to share manuscripts. In a member's backyard, Maureen was reading out loud from her latest story when a train passed. She asked David Collins, the youngest of our group, to run after the train's conductor and insist he stop blowing the horn.]

"I considered myself very fortunate when I first booked Richard Mansfield [March 23, 1894] in his wonderful performance of *Beau Brummel* [co–written with Clyde Fitch.] I had learned of his temperamental nature in Milwaukee where we had played him in *Dr. Jekyll and Mr. Hyde*." [performance on the London stage so convincing, Mansfield became a suspect in the infamous Jack the Ripper murders.]

"I went to quite an extensive expenditure in preparing his dressing room...entirely renovated, re–carpeted, and redecorated. In bringing in the trunks some transfer man dropped a very heavy piece of baggage on the floor just above Mansfield's dressing room, jarring it with such force that it knocked the entire plaster from the ceiling. We cleaned it up as best we could and when Mr. Mansfield arrived in the evening and saw the condition...refused to go on. I left his presence with these words: "The curtain goes up at 8:15 and if you do not go on then and give your performance you had better be out of this town."

Mansfield was onstage and on time and later made up to Kindt for his financial loss on the show by returning for a benefit performance of *Prince Karl* in April that same year. He was back in 1898 in *A Parisian Romance*. When he performed at the Burtis in 1901, he brought along two horses because he liked to spend his free time riding. He requested they be kept at the Kimball House because they had wearied of the train car.

When Eddie Foy headed the touring company of *The Crystal Slipper or Prince Prettiwitz and Little Cinderella,* Kindt recalled, "It was a beastly hot night and after the show the performers parked themselves in the proximity of the old Kimball House bar and proceeded to irrigate their thirsty souls."

Among the performers was ballet master Giovanni Novissimo. "It seems that he and the dispenser behind the bar got into a heated argument over wine which resulted in a fistic combat that proved rather disastrous to the suds distributor. So serious in fact that he had to be transported to his home in an express wagon." Signor Novissimo and others from the cast were taken to police headquarters in the patrol wagon.

"I used all the arguments and explanations that I could to have the bunch released. Meanwhile they were creating the biggest disturbance ever occurred in the police station. George Broderick, who had a tremendous baritone voice was singing, 'Farewell my love, light of my life farewell. For crimes unknown I am placed in a dungeon cell,' the Ralph Rackstraw lines from *H.M.S. Pinafore*. Douglas Flint with his wonderfully low range was singing *Down in the Deep* and the others were contributing their share."

The company was to leave on the 6:30 train for Des Moines so Kindt promised Chief Frank Kessler that he'd get them on that train and out of town. "All right, Charlie. Take your howling menagerie of wild animals and see that they don't miss their train, and never book another bunch like this in Davenport."

Eddie Foy kept a Chicago audience from panicking by remaining onstage when a fire broke out at the Iroquois Theater on December 30, 1903. A malfunctioning spotlight caused the blaze that killed six hundred, leading Davenport's city council to order the Burtis and other theaters to be updated with steel curtains. Kindt argued his theaters were safe with their asbestos-lined curtains and said he'd shut them down rather than spend hundreds of thousands of dollars installing and operating steel curtains.

During the season of 1910–1911, I insisted on playing Minnie Maddern Fiske on our circuit the week before Christmas. Her manager husband said that there was no chance of doing a good business during that period but in my enthusiasm and confidence of the drawing power this little lady had in our section of the country, I offered him a guarantee.

I bought the week for $4,500 and it looked to me like stealing money. We had never before played Mrs. Fiske in any of our towns for less than $1,300 or $1,400 a performance.

The biggest night's receipts we had to my recollection was in Davenport and the gross was just $120…total receipts on the week were about $2,300 and little Charlie took a jolt in the jaw for the losses.

Mrs. Fiske's performance at the Burtis as *Tess of D'Uberville* was a role she later played on film, shot by Thomas Edison.

Only a short time ago I witnessed Al Jolson's performance of *The Jazz Singer* at the Columbia [4–27–1928]. When Al was discovered jazz singing was not even thought of. I recall his engagement at the Burtis opera house when I was just crazy to have him meet my pals who were members of the Pocahontas club. I arranged to have a dinner…of ravioli and pork chops.

It being Good Friday and pork not being kosher made it a tough meal for Al and a little worse for Paul, Al and Joe Lagomarcino. [The Lagomarcino family owned a Davenport wholesale fruit company; descendants still operate the family soda fountain and confectionary shop in Moline and Davenport.]

…Al Jolson's career actually happened in Davenport and the place was run by Brick Munro. On many occasions I took my managerial friends down to see him. Al admitted to this old–time connection in Davenport at the performance given at the Burtis.

He was given a terrific ovation after the second act and was called upon for a curtain talk and came out, planted his feet on my Steinway and there and then thanked the audience for his reception.

"I am not singing so well tonight," he said, "and I doubt if any of you could sing if you were as full of ravioli as I am."

Later on in his talk he kidded them and thanked them for paying $3 a seat to see his act when only a few years ago they could have witnessed his performance for the price of a glass of beer at Brick Munro's.

CHARLES T. KINDT.
Burtis Opera House

CHARLES BERKELL.
Grand Theater

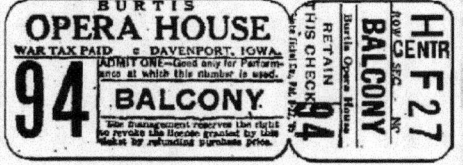

LEFT: First and last tickets from the Burtis Opera House. These belonged to Edgar Stafford who acquired the 1867 ticket from a relative of Antoine LeClaire. The opening night program featured speeches and music. The 1921 ticket was an unsold seat for Alexander the Magician.

Above are Burtis owner Charles Kindt and Grand Theater Players manager Charles Berkell, who also operated the Elite, the city's first vaudeville theater.

TURNER HALL & GRAND THEATER

Davenport's Turner Society goes back to 1852 when thirteen young German –American citizens, trained in their fatherland, established a *turnverein* here.

Early drills were held in the open air at Christ Mueller's property near the vinegar factory at Second and Fillmore. That winter they moved to the upper floor of a flour mill at Front and Warren streets where snow and rain came thru cracks and crevices, *adding pep* to their gymnasium work.

The *White Jackets* as Turners came to be called because of their white uniforms, were subject to attacks by the *Know–Nothings* who hated everything foreign, it is said. Blue laws forbidding meetings and entertainments on Sunday forced Turners to abandon their exercises in the open and to seek a hall.

They leased Lahrmann's Hall on west Fourth between Brown and Warren streets. In the fall of 1853 members began building their own hall, collecting two dollars from each member to help pay for the materials. They did the work themselves, building the hall on their free time. In 1857, they purchased a lot on the south side of Sixth Street between Gaines and Brown.

When the Civil War brought need of volunteers in April 1861, Iowa Gov. Kirkwood's first enlistees organized in the Davenport Turner hall. All but three were German–born. At war's end, Davenport Turners resumed their club activities at Third and Scott streets where Jacob Strasser had founded a German Theater Verien. The Turner's bought the theater property in 1870 and added a gymnasium.

In 1888 a new Turner Hall was built with a second–floor opera house, the Grand Theater. The Grand's original manager, Charles Kindt, purchased the Burtis House and booked acts exclusively for his circuit of Midwest theaters. The Turner Society remodeled the Grand in 1905 but still failed to turn a profit. It went mostly unused until Charles Berkell took it over in 1921.

Berkell got his start in Davenport with comedy partner Nate Blossom. In 1905, they opened the Elite, Davenport's first vaudeville theater, leasing the ground floor and basement of the Germania House on Brady near Third Street. Vaudeville was promoted as family–friendly entertainment without the dancing girls in risqué outfits. Burlesque became striptease but vaudeville evolved into the comedy and variety shows of radio and early television. Berkell's success at the Grand Theater was hailed that first season by *Billboard*, a national theater magazine:

> Last September when industrial conditions were at their worst, when the unemployment situation was most critical and business men everywhere pessimistic, Charles Berkell, a veteran in theatrical circles opened the Grand Theater, offering stock shows.
>
> Davenporters never dreamed the old Grand would house an audience again. Close friends shook their heads and exclaimed, 'Charlie can never make a go of that place!' Many warned him he would go broke. Today the Grand Theater is one of the best paying houses in Davenport. The caliber of shows offered by the Grand Players soon made Davenport play lovers forget that the theater was an old out–of–date house; that it was one of the few second–story theaters remaining in the country.
>
> Business came slow at first. Money was lost the first week and the second. The third week business got better and the fourth week the receipts paid expenses. Davenporters were quick to realize Mr. Berkell's company was offering something quite out of the ordinary at an extremely low price and the fifth week the receipts helped pay the loss of the first three shows. Capacity houses turn out several nights a week and now the wise ones are saying: 'I told you so—I knew he could do it.' It has taken good attractions to turn the trick but Mr. Berkell from the start brought the best productions which could be obtained. Mr. Berkell's feat is all the more remarkable considering Davenport has seven downtown theaters, all first–class houses.

Bix partnered with Raymond Moore, son of Rev. Steward and Maria Moore of Davenport's Bethel A.M.E. Church, for a musical dance number. Glee Club, back row L-R: Moore, Boyd Ellis, Paul Krasuski, George Summers, Bix; middle row L-R: Erwin Sindt, Loring Pollock, Richard Petersberger, LeRoy Evans, Francis Curley; front row, L-R: Oscar Pries, Vincent Klauer, Victor Kloppenburg, Hugh McGovern

·P·R·O·G·R·A·M·

(A)
Mandolin Club
Primrose March .... Hauser
Early Dawn Waltz .... Brunover

Saxophone Specialty
My Isle of Golden Dreams .... Blaufuss
    VIRGINIA BRADFORD, NATHAN CITRON
O Solo Mio .... di Capua

(B)
Boys' Glee Club
(1) Winter Song .... Bullard
    More and More .... Seifert
(2) Ferrera .... Bullard
    One, Two, Three—Hawaiian Melody ....
    The Owl and the Pussy Cat .... Ingraham

(C)
Girls' Glee Club
Allah's Holiday .... Friml
Serenade .... Strauss

(D)
String Orchestra
Happiness .... Trinkaus
Evening Chimes .... Kriens
Cinderella March .... Papini

(E)
Exhibition Drill
D. H. S. Unit, Reserve Officers' Training Corps, under the command of Captain J. W. Peyton, U. S. A.

(F)
Miss Kier and Her "Black Jazz Babies"
Far Away in the South .... Adams
A Toast

Jazz Specialty
Moores and Beiderbecks
Ma Punkin Sue .... Webster

(G)
Toy Symphony .... Haydn

(H)
Segnori Toni and Toby
Famous Acrobats, in Over and Under

(I)
Isle of Capri
(An Italian Carnival)

Characters:
Rosa (a singer) .... Elizabeth Sala
Lolita (a dancer) .... Anne Downer
Maria .... Marie Struve
Carmencita .... Adelaide Rodler
Victorini .... Helen Kohrs
Pedro (a serenader) .... Francis Curley

Chorus of Villagers
Members of Glee Clubs and Girls' Chorus

Musical Selections
Isle of Capri .... Bassett
Row, Comrades, Row—Italian Folk Tune
Tick-a-tock—Italian Folk Tune
Funiculi, Funicula—Italian Folk Tune
La Zingara .... Bohm
O Solo Mio .... di Capua
Barcarolle, "Tales of Hoffman" .... Offenbach

Story
Capri! The very name suggests love, laughter and song. Who can think of Capri and not picture its beauty. The rose tipped mountains, the blue grotto, fair skies and sunny waters.

Synopsis
The scene opens on a bright festival day with Rosa and her friends gathered around her singing praises to the beautiful Isle of Capri. At the conclusion of this Pedro and his friends are heard strumming their guitars in the distance. They arrive on the scene singing a boating song. They are cordially greeted and the festivities continue, all joining in the carnival, singing and dancing until evening approaches. They then disperse but the spirit of the serenade moves Pedro to seek the Villa of Maria and sing beneath her window.

Concert--Vaudeville

Given by the
MUSICAL ORGANIZATIONS
of the
DAVENPORT HIGH SCHOOL

Under the General Direction of
MISS ALICE ROGER

Assisted by
MISS IREN KIER, Accompanist
& MRS. ERNST JACOBSEN,
Stage Manager

GRAND · OPERA · HOUSE
Friday Evening, 8 o'clock, May 28th
1 · · · 9 · · · 2 · · · 0

1920 DHS music program at Grand Opera House; glee clubs included Bix and Albert Petersen's daughter Helen.

MANDOLIN CLUB
MRS. MARTIN SILBERSTEIN, Director

FIRST MANDOLIN
Arthur Temple
Robert Brown
Helen Sass
Florence Berrigan
Richard Toll
Reginald Duggleby
SECOND MANDOLIN
Alvord Boeck
Leo Ely
Harold Tinton

Margaret Craig
Clara Eckermann
Evangeline Boettger
Marcia Caverly
FIRST BANJO
Waldo Dimond
SECOND BANJO
Erna Eckert
VIOLIN
Harry Shapiro

GUITAR
Edna Soehren
CELLO
Marcus Miller
SAXOPHONE
Virginia Bradfield
Nathan Citron
TRAPS
Herbert Silberstein

BOYS' GLEE CLUB

FIRST TENOR
Francis Curley
Victor Kloppenburg
Paul Krasuski
Raymond Moore
SECOND TENORS
Boyd Ellis

Hugh McGovern
Oscar Pries
Richard Petersberger
Loring Pollock
BARITONES
Earl Bertuliet
Bix Beiderbecke

LeRoy Evans
George Summers
BASSES
Robert Hender
Vincent Klauer
Richard Le Buhn
Erwin Sindt

BLACK JAZZ BABIES

Raymond Moore
Hugh McGovern

Bix Beiderbecke
Vincent Klauer

Earl Bertuleit

GIRLS' GLEE CLUB

FIRST SOPRANOS
Velma Blair
Helen Canniff
Anne Downer
Margaret Doud
Naomi Earhart
Margaret Frank
Dorothy High
Helen Kohrs
Geraldine Norton
Ella Smith
Harriet Schmid

Elizabeth Sala
Virginia William
SECOND SOPRANOS
Florence Benton
Laura Freund
Lonnie Houvenagle
Phyllis Headlee
Bernice Krieger
Phyllis Kreul
Carol Keller
Lillian Mesecker
Lucile Miner

Helen M. Petersen
Georgia Shaffer
CONTRALTOS
Vernice Albrecht
Irene Loy
Adelaide Rodler
Miriam Miner
Marie Struve
Helen Warner
Mildred Wood
Pearl Weaver

STRING ORCHESTRA
MISS ANNA JOHANNSEN, Director

FIRST VIOLIN
Richard Le Buhn
Amy Soyster
Doris Martyn
Marie Deppe

SECOND VIOLIN
Henry Kruz
Elmer Debus
Gladys Thompson
THIRD VIOLIN
Dorothy Kasten
Alvord Boeck
Berthella Skelley

FOURTH VIOLIN
Bernard Leemhuis
Israel Barr
CELLO
Marcus Miller
PIANO
Laura Freund
Eleanor Mueller

TOY SYMPHONY

TRIANGLE
George Summers
HORN
Richard Toll

QUILL
Florence Berrigan
CYMBALS
Victor Kloppenburg

DRUMS
Howard Makeever

MEMBERS OF GIRLS' CHORUS
In "The Isle of Capri"

Margaret Archibald
Dorothy Brainard
Edna Citron
Elizabeth Conant
Dorothy Craven
Doris Cunningham
Helen Coleman

Lila Harrington
Rosalie Heible
Helen Myers
Genevieve McGee
Alma Ruth McCrorie
Eleanor Nebergall
Kathryn Naumann

Marguerite Naumann
Viola Nelson
Mildred Sharp
Helene Shanley
Marie Spencer
Emily Van Patten

EXECUTIVE STAFF

Tickets and Advertising—W. R. Baker   Costumes—Miss Maude Firth
Assistant—L. E. Keller   Ushering { Ray McClellen
                                                 { J. W. Underwood.

Grateful appreciation is due the following for their valuable assistance and co-operation:
Behind the Scenes
Miss Bess Hall   Miss Minnie Johns
Miss Mabel Long   Irene Parno Holliday
Miss Anne Downer—Staging dance
Mrs. Agnes Montanus—Dramatization of "Isle of Capri" and assistance in staging two numbers.

May 21, 1922 *Democrat–Leader*:

When the Grand Players close their season at the Grand theater on the night of May 20 that famous old theater will have run for a full season for the first time in its 40–year history.

Sometime in 1888 the doors of the then–palatial Grand were thrown open to the public. It was erected by the Davenport Turners and big things were planned for the *wonder theater* as it was called by old Davenporters. But the dreams of the owners received an awful shock in the years that followed, for not once until the fall of 1921 did the Grand run a full season.

Years passed and everything from opera to movies was tried in an effort to make the theater a paying proposition. Everything failed until Charles Berkell, known as the mastermind of Iowa theater men, took over the lease in July 1921. 'What's Berkell going to use that place for, certainly not a theater?' was heard from business men who long respected Charlie's ability as a theater man. They waited three weeks to learn what Berkell wanted with that *hay loft* as they termed the place. Then one day came an announcement that a stock company had been secured and that the Grand's doors would be reopened on Sept. 4. And the doors of the old building did open on that day. Furthermore they stayed open for 37 weeks.

After the first two weeks the Grand Players drew tremendous throngs for every performance and Charlie's bank account has been considerably fattened by his impossible venture. Charlie has often been asked how he happened to take a chance on such a place as the Grand. "Give people the best and they'll climb a flight of stairs. Davenporters wanted stage plays, and they wanted good stage plays. If I had brought in a cheap company and put on cheap shows, engaged a cheap scenery artist, was cheap in my advertising, I would have fallen down the same as others have. I always try to give theatergoers the best that money can buy and I believe the policy is the best in the long run."

Feb 1923—Charles Berkell's Grand Players, the popular organization which for two seasons has entertained Tri–City theatergoers at the Grand Theater, will give its final performance here March 24 and will open in Indianapolis a week later. Regarded as one of the leading stock companies in the country, the fame of the Grand Players spread from coast to coast and theatrical managers everywhere had been watching. Many cities tried to secure the company but Manager Berkell rejected all offers. However, the Indianapolis offer was so attractive that it was impossible to turn it down. Many famous actors who have visited

Davenport in the last two years have praised the work of the local company, declaring it to be one of the most remarkable stock companies ever organized. Only a short time ago a trade paper said the following: "We wonder if Davenport and vicinity realizes what a wonderfully artistic and capable stock company it has. The plays are produced and mounted with all the finish and care of a big road show." During the past two seasons the company has presented many of the biggest and most recent hits offered on Broadway.

After a season in Indiana, the stock company returned to Davenport and Berkell hired Ceno Petersen as his orchestra conductor at the Grand. Two years earlier Ceno's sister Helen had performed with the girl's glee club at the Grand. The boy's glee club included cousin Bix singing baritone, a talent inherited from his Opa Charles.

But it was Bix's first public performance on cornet that impressed Vera Cox when he played a minstrel song for a dance routine by fellow glee club member Raymond Moore, son of the minister at Bethel A.M.E. Church.

Iowa's Gilded Lily

Mark Twain coined it the GILDED AGE, that era between post–Civil War Reconstruction and the Panic of 1893. The term came from Shakespeare's *King John*: "To gild...the lily is wasteful and ridiculous excess." *Gilding the lily* characterized America's industrialist *robber barons* with their opulent displays of excess wealth. The Gilded Age's poster girl was none other than Iowa–born Lillian Russell.

She made her entrance on the world stage a few miles upriver from Davenport in Clinton, IA, on December 4, 1861. Parents Charles and Cynthia Leonard named her Helen Louise but she went by the nickname Nellie.

Her father published the *Clinton Weekly Herald* until 1865 when he moved the family to Chicago. Nellie's love of performing began there in convent school and by eighteen she was on the New York stage in the chorus of *H.M.S. Pinafore*.

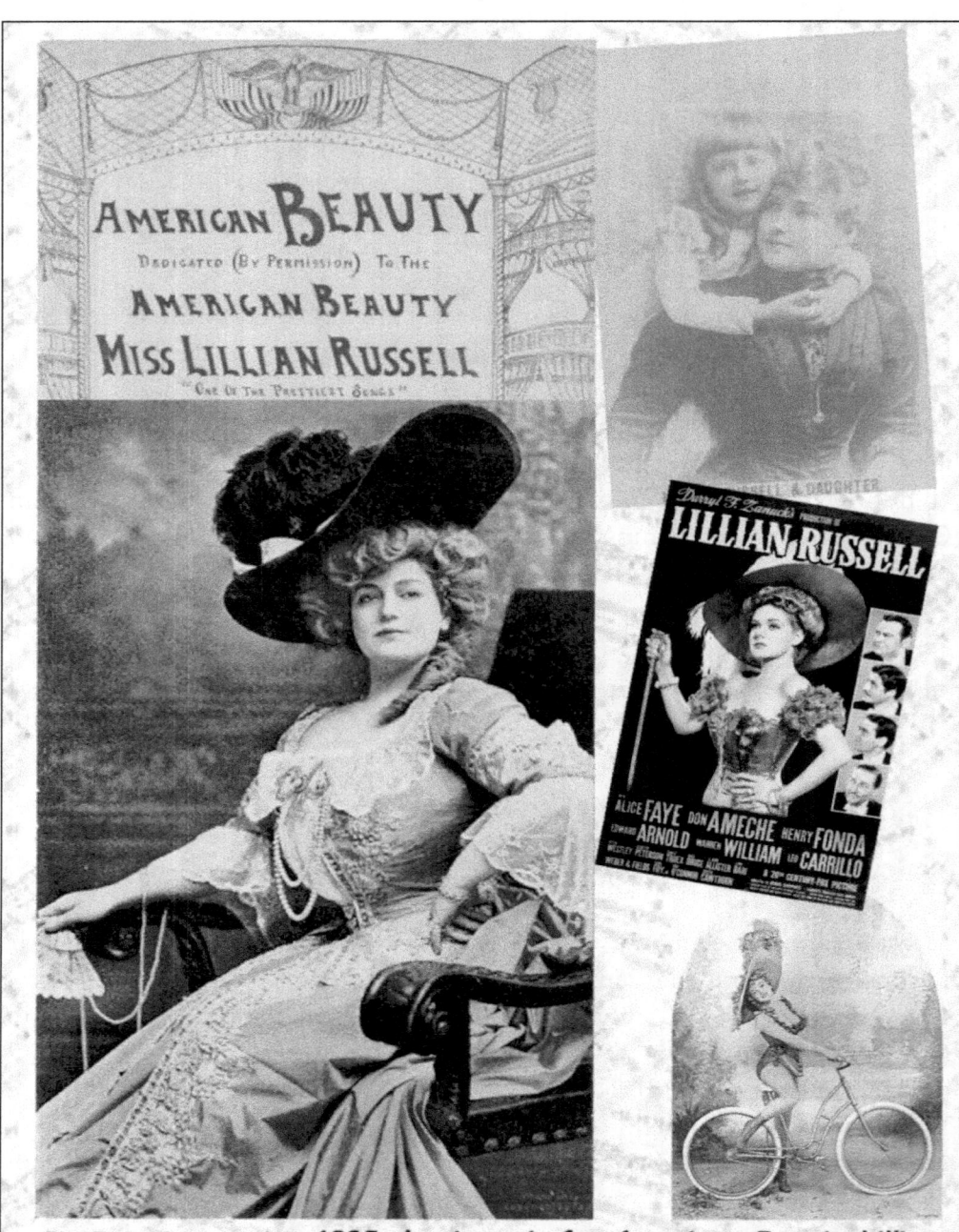

Clockwise from top left: **1895 sheet music for *American Beauty*, Lillian with daughter Dorothy; 1940 movie poster; 1958 Marilyn Monroe homage; Lillian Russell, c.1900**

At Tony Pastor's Music Hall, she was hired for a burlesque version of *Pirates of Penzance*, which premiered February 7, 1881. Pastor gave her the stage name of Lillian Russell. The story goes that he liked how all those "Ls" looked on the marquee.

From Pastor's shows, she moved on to New York's Casino Theatre where she met and married English composer Edward 'Teddy' Solomon. A second marriage for Lillian but for Teddy it was a second wife. He was charged with bigamy and Lillian got an annulment. They had a daughter, Dorothy. Lillian also gave birth to a son who died in infancy. While still with Solomon, she performed on the London stage in comic operas, several written especially for her by him.

In 1890, she helped Alexander Graham Bell launch the first long distance hookup, singing Offenbach's *Sabre Song* by telephone from New York to Boston and Washington, D.C.

> *Davenport Tribune, 8–30–1892: Last evening a special train containing Lillian Russell and her troop, in all 125 persons, passed through the city enroute to San Francisco. The train stopped here long enough to let the people take supper with Landlord Sommers of the Kimball.*

Lillian traveled the country in a private Pullman car. It stopped twice, 1896 and 1906, for performances before the hometown fans in Clinton.

Prior to her arrival In Davenport for an appearance at the Burtis Opera House in *Lamb's Gambol*, Lillian had requested an entire floor at the Kimball House for her private use. She also asked that the cook prepare Welsh rarebit for her after–show dinner.

Early on she'd been described as a "china doll of teacup grace" but soon enough the fickle press was calling her *Airy–Fairy Lillian*. Willa Cather wrote in 1894: "To be as beautiful as Lillian Russell is enough to make a fool of any woman." Among fans, she was *the American Beauty*, title song of her 1896 show at the Casino Theatre. After three failed marriages and taking up with Diamond Jim Brady, she was dubbed *Queen of the Dudes* by one magazine.

Diamond Jim was said to have given her stockings encrusted with jewels and a bicycle with diamonds on the wheels. She also was said to have worn a diamond–studded corset and had a diamond collar for her pet spaniel. But her real passion was for hats, the bigger the better to accentuate her hourglass shape.

New Yorker magazine's A.J. Liebling would later write that his father's ideal woman was the voluptuous Miss Lillian. "She was a butterscotch sundae of a woman, as beautiful as a tulip of beer with a high white collar,"

Liebling wrote. "If a Western millionaire, one of the Hearst or Mackay kind, could have given an architect carte blanche to design him a woman, she would have looked like Lillian. She was San Simeon in corsets."

By the turn of the century Lillian was earning $2,500 a week on stage. Her repertoire included 1892's *After the Ball*, the first song to sell a million copies of sheet music. But her trademark song, *Come Down Ma Evenin' Star*, came from Weber & Field's 1902 burlesque show *Twirly Whirly*.

The song became a bestselling record in 1903 both for Mina Hickman on Victor Records and Henry Burr on Columbia. Lillian did not record any of her songs. It was her personality, not her voice that sold tickets.

She was once asked if it embarrassed her to be followed by crowds and gawked at in traffic. She answered, "When they cease to do so, it will be very embarrassing."

In 1899 Lillian went to work for Joe Weber and Lew Fields. She remained through the 1904 season, after which Weber and Fields broke up. Lillian returned for a farewell engagement with the comedy duo the year before their music hall closed in 1913.

Her fourth husband, Alec Moore, was a Pittsburgh newspaper publisher. They married in 1912. Lillian became active in Republican politics and the suffrage movement. In 1922 she traveled to Europe on behalf of President Harding. A fall aboard ship on the return trip led to complications that ended in her death on June 6th.

Lillian's husband later became ambassador to Spain. TIME magazine characterized Alexander Moore as having a Will Rogers' approach to diplomacy. Upon meeting Spain's Queen Victoria Eugenie, he reportedly said to her, "Gosh, you're beautiful! You remind me more than anybody else I ever knew of my wife."

When Moore died in 1930, his will included a bequest of $100,000 to "the queen who reminded him of Lillian Russell." His stepdaughter Dorothy Solomon received only $1,000.

Dorothy had followed her mother into acting, using the stage name Dorothy Russell. She had far more notoriety off-stage, having married six times. In a letter to TIME, published Oct. 29, 1934, Dorothy attempted to set the record straight about her mother's famous bicycle.

> Sirs:
>
> In TIME, Oct. 8, there appears on p. 50, an article under the caption Art. In the second paragraph it states: "A bicycle–shaped stud was reminiscent

the gold–plated, diamond–studded bicycle he [Diamond Jim Brady] gave to Lillian Russell.

That is an absolute untruth as are many of Mr. Parker Morell's anecdotes in his story of "Diamond Jim." . . . My mother, Lillian Russell, was not even acquainted with Mr. Brady during the bicycle era. As for the vehicle itself, it had a gold–plated handlebar with mother–of–pearl grips, no diamonds. The pedals were also gold–plated. The bicycle was a gift from the Columbia Bicycle manufacturers in appreciation of the vast amount of publicity they derived from her using their product and because she had purchased so many of them, one for each member of the family. . . .

DOROTHY RUSSELL

To Dorothy Russell Solomon de Castiglione Einstein O'Reilly Calvit, who won fame of her own by upsetting the will of her stepfather, the late Alexander Pollock Moore (TIME, May 4, 1931), thanks for a description of her mother's bicycle. Confronted with it, Author Morell sticks to his story. His silent collaborator, "Diamond Jim's" longtime Secretary Herbert Haberle, testifies that he attended to procuring the case for a gold–plated, jeweled bicycle given by his employer to Miss Russell. Moreover, says Secretary Haberle, Brady met Lillian Russell in 1881 or 1882 when she was entertaining at Tony Pastor's Music Hall and he dropped in every day from Tammany Hall next door.—ED.

After renovations to the *City of Clinton Showboat* in 1980, the theater was renamed in Lillian Russell's honor.

Forty years earlier, Clinton residents turned out en masse for the movie premiere of *Lillian Russell*, starring Alice Faye. Co–starring in the role of Edward Solomon was Don Ameche, who grew up in Dubuque, IA, and is buried there, upriver from Clinton.

A year before Alice Faye played on–screen's Lillian Russell, she had starred in *Rose of Washington Square*, a movie loosely based on the career of Ziegfield Follies star Fanny Brice and her gambler husband Nicky Arnstein. Brice sued the production company for invasion of privacy but the same subject matter earned a 1969 Oscar for Barbra Streisand in *Funny Girl*.

Alice Faye's version of the Fanny Brice story co–starred Al Jolson and William Frawley. Best known for his roles in TV's *I Love Lucy* and *My Three Sons*, Frawley grew up in Burlington, IA, downriver from Davenport. He spent several seasons on the vaudeville circuit before launching a movie career and was the first singer to introduce audiences to *My Melancholy Baby* and Al Jolson's signature song, *My Mammy.*

New York fashion photographer Richard Avedon paid homage to the Gilded Age's leading lady by posing Marilyn Monroe as Lillian Russell. Avedon set the scene with a vintage backdrop and dressed Marilyn in an elaborate hat, scanty burlesque costume and sat her atop a bicycle. Avedon's photos of Monroe personifying five decades of beauty icons were published by LIFE magazine in 1958.

DAVENPORT'S OTHER LITTLE GENIUS

After their mother played *Mister Dooley* for young Bix, he repeated it note for note according to Burnie. The novelty tune originated on Broadway in 1902 with the musical, *A Chinese Honeymoon.* Lyricist William Jerome and composer Jean Schwartz later featured it in their original production of *The Wizard of Oz.*

Bix made his Broadway debut in 1924 with the Wolverines. He was in Michigan playing with Goldkette's band at the Blue Lantern casino when Davenport newspapers hailed the return of violinist Florizel Reuter with a special hometown performance, July 20, 1925, at the Burtis Opera House.

Given their prominence in Davenport's music society, it's likely some of the Beiderbecke and Petersen clans attended Reuter's concert. Whether or not Aggie and Bismark did, they had their own rising star in the family.

The Beiderbecke's record collection was expanding to include tunes featuring Bix on cornet and piano. One of the first was a test pressing for *Tiger Rag*, recorded by the Wolverines the summer of 1924. Eventually the collection would include original compositions by Bix. Aggie would receive royalties for those songs.

Meanwhile Florizel Reuter's much-heralded U.S. concert tour had likely stirred Aggie's memories of being pregnant with her third child. The big news of 1902 was an original opera composed by 11-year-old Reuter for Romania's Queen Elizabeth.

Does King of Jazz trump Queen of Romania?

Aggie still had her sights set on classical music when she hired Professor

Grade to teach her son the proper way to play. Seeing Bix hailed a *boy wonder* at age seven must have drawn comparison to stories of Jacob and Grace Haddox Reuter's son giving his first concert at age four in Chicago. "He is the wonder of the age," one Chicago paper declared of Florizel Reuter. "You cannot afford to miss the opportunity of hearing this little genius."

A little genius with Lyman Gage for a benefactor! Better known for saving America's banking system by establishing the gold standard for U. S. currency while treasury secretary under McKinley, Gage was the leading force behind Chicago's 1893 World's Fair. That's where blond-curled Reuter was first discovered, playing a violin small enough for his two-year-old fingers.

A *Davenport Democrat* reporter, who interviewed Florizel when he was four, found him so studious that he didn't care to play with toys.

"When indoors, he divides his time between books, slate and his violin," the reporter wrote. "When outside, he often piles his little wagon full of chips and pulls it to the cookstove woodbox. He continually wants to accomplish something."

Had Aggie let Bix doodle *Mr. Dooley* too long?

By age ten, Reuter had graduated with top honors from the Conservatory of Music at Geneva, Switzerland. Two years later he performed at Carnegie Hall and gave command performances for McKinley and Theodore Roosevelt.

A year later Reuter was in Athens, Greece, to perform a series of concerts with the royal orchestra. "They wanted me to be their permanent conductor, but of course, I refused," said the 13-year-old.

He next traveled to Constantinople to play for Turkish sultan Abdul Hamid and later confessed he had stage fright performing for the sultan's 283 wives and 220 children. Abdul rewarded the young violinist with a sack of gold coins worth $500.

Reuter's friendships with European nobility included England's Queen Alexandra, whose Danish heritage accounted for her anti-German sentiments in the Schleswig-Holstein conflict. Bulgaria's Czar Ferdinand appointed Reuter his director of the Vienna Conservatory of Music. There Reuter worked with Strauss, Grieg, and Ravel.

The First World War sent Reuter fleeing to Switzerland where he met and married a cellist. At war's end, Ferdinand abdicated the throne to his son, who would die mysteriously two years later, shortly after meeting with Adolph Hitler. Meanwhile, Reuter regained prominence and by age 32 was rich and living in a castle in Berlin. Gone and all but forgotten back in Iowa, Reuter fell off the radar when war again came to Europe.

FLORIZEL REUTER HAS COME HOME

Will Give Violin Recital Next Thursday.

Music of Masters Will Be Interpreted By the Most Wounderful Violinist of the Century, Through Not A Dozen Years Old.

AT THE BURTIS—

Tonight—A Cavalier of France.
Tuesday—Ten Nights in a Bar-room.
Thursday—Florizel Reuter, Violinist.

FLORIZEL REUTER

Eleven-Year-Old Violin Virtuoso, Author and Composer.

that *other* Davenport boy wonder
FLORIZEL REUTER 1890-1985

Music is enough for a lifetime, but a lifetime is not enough for music.
~Sergei Rachmaninov

It was around that same time Aggie opened her Grand Avenue home to jazz historian Marshall Stearns. She didn't live to see the publication of his book, *The Story of Jazz* (1958, Oxford University Press) or to read: *The contrast between the lyrical and precise cornet of Bix and the wild and dramatic trumpet of Louis reflects the middle–class Davenport, Iowa, background of Beiderbecke and the uptown New Orleans of Armstrong's childhood. Later horns would be even more wild and dramatic than Armstrong's, but none could be more controlled and tasteful than Beiderbecke's.*

Aggie must have sensed from Mr. Stearns' questions that something of historic worth had come of Bix's all–too–brief life.

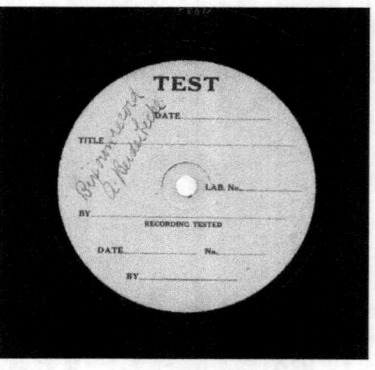

She entrusted to Mr. Stearns that original test press of *Tiger Rag*. At his request for authentication of its provenance, Aggie wrote on the otherwise blank record label: *Bix own record A. Beiderbecke* before turning the test press over to Marshall Stearns. That test press is now in the archives of the Institute of Jazz Studies at Rutgers University.

Florizel Reuter resurfaced in the 1950s, impoverished and pleading for a job in the States so he could bring his Swiss–national wife with him. He still was an American citizen but had to be investigated thoroughly to make certain he was not a Nazi sympathizer. Turned out he had been persecuted by Hitler's regime, stripped of property and opportunity to earn a living because he had helped Jews to escape Berlin.

Eventually Reuter and his wife were offered positions at the Wisconsin Conservatory of Music. News of Reuter's return to America went unnoticed in Davenport. Instead, some local musicians focused on launching an annual tribute to Bix. Only one musical genius from Davenport whose name still garners international recognition and that name is Beiderbecke.

ON THE TRAIL OF BIX'S FIRST PIANO TEACHER

Bix entered the third grade in 1911 at Tyler School in Davenport, already showing signs of becoming a musical prodigy. Just one year earlier, the *Davenport Daily Democrat* ran a featured article on Bix entitled: 7 YEAR OLD BOY MUSICAL WONDER,

7-YEAR OLD BOY MUSICAL WONDER

Little Bickie Beiderbecke Plays Any Selection That He Hears.

Leon Bix Beiderbecke, aged 7 years, son of Mr. and Mrs. B. H. Beiderbecke, 1934 Grand avenue, Davenport, is the most unusual and the most remarkably talented child in music that there is in this city. He has never taken a music lesson and he does not know one key from another, but he can play in all completeness any selection, the air or tune of which he knows.

Little "Bickie", as his parents call him, has always had an ear for music. When he was two years old Mrs. Beiderbecke says that the child was able with one of his chubby fingers to play the tune of "Yankee Doodle." It was not as distinct, by any means, as he can play now, but even then the tune could be detected as it was running through the child's mind.

It must not be understood that he still plays with one finger and one hand. He plays every selection that he learns, as completely in the bass and treble clef as it is written. In fact, so acute is his ear for music that if his mother plays a piece in another key than that in which "Bickie" has always played it, the child will sit down and play the piece in exactly the same key with proper bass accompaniment.

As a rule, however, if he hears and learns the air of a new piece he will play it in one or two, and sometimes three or four flats. In fact, he plays most of his pieces in flats.

The child has a love for music. It is such a satisfaction and delight to him that if he is a little out of sorts, as any child occasionally is, his spirits are always brightened by a suggestion from his loving mother that they go to the parlor and play a little on the piano.

When "Bickie" is playing the piano, he never looks at the keys, he never watches his hands. To one watching and listening to the child playing the piano, it might seem that the child's mind was not on what he is playing, because his eyes are centered upon objects about the room or he is looking into space with apparently no thought of the piece he is playing. But a careful observation of that gaze and of the child indicates that his mind is absorbed in the music, in the melody that he is playing.

"Bickie" attends the Tyler school on Grand avenue, across from the Beiderbecke home, and whenever Prof. Otto comes to the school he plays the violin and calls upon Bix to play the accompaniment on the piano.

Mrs. Beiderbecke is a gifted pianist and the child hears and has always heard music at the home. His mother is contemplating engaging an instructor, even at the child's tender age, for the reason that she fears that his playing will become too mechanical and that he will never fancy playing by note.

Mr. and Mrs. Beiderbecke are very proud of their little son, and they have reason to feel proud of him.

Left: *Democrat* 7-7-1910

Right: C.F. Grade

Below: Schmidt Music Co 1922 Ad

Amalia Schmidt-Gobble, partner in Gobble-Grade Music Studio

C. F. GRADE

FLOAT-"MUSIC HATH CHARMS" AWARDED FIRST PRIZE
TRI-CITY FLORAL PARADE- JUNE 21ST 1916.

Schmidt Music Company

Invites You and Your Friends to Visit Their Music Store on

Thursday Evening

During the Hours from 7:30 to 9:30 P.M.

The Occasion of—

Davenport Merchants Combined Spring Opening and Style Revue

A Musical Treat in Store for You

MRS. AMALIA SCHMIDT-GOBBLE
Musical Director WOC.

LITTLE BICKIE BEIDERBECKE, PLAYS ANY SELECTION THAT HE HEARS.

According to Bix's brother Burnie, Bix began taking piano lessons in September 1911 from Professor Charles Grade [pronounced GRAH–DAY]. The story goes that Professor Grade, although residing in Muscatine, visited the Beiderbecke family each week to give Bix piano lessons.

After a lesson or two, Bix asked the professor to play the next week's assignment so he could hear how it should sound. When the professor returned the following week, he was surprised how well Bix could play the assigned composition.

This pattern continued for a couple of weeks until Professor Grade discovered, to his dismay, that Bix was actually memorizing the professor's rendition. Even worse, Bix included the professor's mistakes. Needless to say, Professor Grade abruptly terminated the lessons.

With help from Muscatine musician Anne Olson, the following is learned: Charles Grade, son of German immigrants Ferdinand and Elizabeth Gabel Grade, was born January 9, 1870. He attended Muscatine High School, graduating in the class of 1888. Mr. Grade went to Berlin in 1889 to study piano for three years. At the end of this period, he returned to Muscatine where for 50 years he successfully followed his chosen profession of teaching. Also, for 35 years he operated a studio in Davenport, in addition to a residence studio in Muscatine.

Professor Grade's original Davenport studio was located at 118½ W. Third St. In 1925, he partnered with Amalia Schmidt Gobble in Gobble–Grade Music Studios. In 1937, the Gobble–Grade studios moved into room 301 of the Whitaker Building, 228 Brady Street. In 1951, Mrs.Gobble added her daughter, Helen Gobble Henigbaum and son–in–law William Henigbaum to the music studio faculty. William Henigbaum was a pallbearer at Bix's funeral.

Charles Grade died July 19, 1942. The cause of death was listed as pancreatic cancer. His obituary noted that Mr. Grade was an instructor of remarkable ability, having started many students on successful musical careers. Among them were brothers Earl and Wayne Rohlf.

Professor Grade was a conductor of the Muscatine Union Orchestra for a number of years, and also was organist of the Congregational Church during a considerable interval. He was affiliated with Iowa Lodge No. 2 AF&AM, and the Washington Chapter No. 4 AF&AM. Professor Grade never married.

Wonder if the professor kept tabs on his former short–term student, noting that Bix became a world–renowned jazz cornetist and at all pleased to hear him playing his original piano composition at Carnegie Hall?

BAND CONCERT THIS AFTERNOON FEJERVARY PARK

9-7-1924

Program to Be Rendered by Petersen's Band at 3 O'Clock.

A public concert under the auspices of the park board will be given this afternoon at 3 o'clock at Fejervary Park by Petersen's Band. The program follows:

March—"The Nash"
   (H. L. Booth)
Melodies from "Foxey Quiller"
   (DeKoven.)
(A)—Somewhere a Voice is Calling;
(B)—Smiling Thru—Arthur Tate.
Solo for Trumpet—Wayne Rohlf.
Waltz—"On the Beautiful Rhine."
   (Keler Bela)
Fantasie—"Portuguese Reveille"
   (Meyerells.)
Intermission.
Fantasie from "Carmen."
   (Bizet.)
Overture—"Fra Diavolo".
   (Auber.)
(A)—Popular—"Arcady".
   (Al Jolson.)
(B)—"Linger Awhile."
   (Owens.)
Selections from "High Jinks."
   (Hauerbach.)
Elks' Reunion.
   Wm. E. Slater.

GREAT CROWD AT CONCERT ON LEVEE SUNDAY

Solos by Peter MacArthur and Wayne Rohlf Made Fine Impression.

A crowd of several thousand people heard the Sunday evening concert given by Albert Petersen's band at LeClaire park last night. Peter MacArthur, popular local musician and song writer who has been crippled for the past year, made a decided hit when he was carried to the bandstand and sang "The Mississippi Valley Fair Boosters' March." Mr. MacArthur was forced to repeat the song several times.

Wayne Rohlf, son of Orville J. Rohlf, musician, was warmly applauded when he played a trumpet solo number during the concert by Petersen's band at LeClaire park on the river front yesterday. The number was "The Charmer" by Ross. The young musician's fine expression and good attack were particularly evident. He responded with the encore number "Emilia Thru."

His brother Earl, member of the Augustana College Male quartet, leaves next Saturday on a concert tour thru northern Iowa and Minnesota. The quartet recently toured thru Illinois and Iowa and made a hit at its various concerts.

One of Soloists School Concert

1924

WAYNE ROHLF.

The son of O. J. Rohlf, a member of the Tri-City Symphony orchestra, and a brother of Earl Rohlf, who has made a favorable record as a pianist, Wayne Rohlf will be one of the soloists from the High school in the second annual concert of the Davenport Public School orchestras at the new Masonic temple next Wednesday.

Wayne plays the trumpet. He is a member of the Tri-City Symphony orchestra.

DANCING COLISEUM

Good music, good order and a good time always.

Saturday 1927

Wayne Rohlf
and His Orchestra

Gents 50c   Ladies 25c

Sunday

Burke-Amidon

Original Steamer Capitol Orchestra

Playing that wierd steamboat music.

Dancing till 1 o'clock

Gents 75c   Ladies 25c

DAVENPORT'S YOUNG ARTISTS WIN HONORS

3-18-1925

Junior Orchestra Makes Hit of Afternoon on Convention Program.

Davenport young artists and junior pianists captured five out of the six honors in the artist, student and junior music contests held at the annual state convention of the Iowa Federation of Music clubs at Iowa City Tuesday, which was Junior day at the convention.

Nine students and young professionals competed for honors.

Miss Jeannette Brewbaker, Davenport's lovely voiced young singer, a pupil of Miss Grace Ames, carried off the first honors in the voice contest for young professionals; Earl Rohlf, a pupil of Charles F. Grade of this city, was first in the pianoforte contest for students from 15 to 18 years of age; Beatrice Struck first, with Evelyn Siem and Gordon ____er, all ___ city, as ____ second ___ in the ___ pianoforte work. The junior pianists are pupils, respectively, of Miss ___

Grand Family Dance
Saturday, April 28
Maysville, Ia. 1928

Music Furnished by
O. J. ROHLF'S ORCHESTRA
Dancing from 8 p. m. to 2 a. m.
Gents. 75c; Ladies. 25c.
Come and dance the old-time as well as the new dances. A good time is assured.

ALBERT ROEHLK, Prop.

1922

Wayne Rohlf, accompanied by his brother Earl Rohlf, presented a cornet solo, "The Charmer," by Louis Ross, and Earl Rohlf played "Prelude in C Sharp Minor" by Rachmaninoff. Both boys are excellent musicians, and their solos were among the most pleasing of the entire program. The readings which were to have been given by Mrs. Faye McCarthy of Rock Island, were omitted as Mrs. McCarthy was unable to be present.

The sing yesterday was under the auspices of the Van Buren school Parent-Teachers' club, and a committee from the Scott county council of Parent-Teachers' clubs. The Van Buren committee comprised Mrs. O. Rohlf, Mrs. R. Baker, Mrs. C. Volrath, Mrs.

Streckfus Line boats harbored near Credit Island, a summer resort known earlier as Grand Isle and Suburban Island; reached by trolley while Bix was a boy.

Diamond Jo's SIDNEY packet boat, built in 1880, was converted by Streckfus Lines to an excursion boat operating between St. Louis and St. Paul. After extensive renovations in 1921, it was renamed the WASHINGTON. The boat was decommissioned in 1937 and dismantled the following year.

MUSIC ON THE MISSISSIPPI
by Jim Arpy

The big white paddlewheel dipped and splashed as the steamboat *St. Paul*, venerable granddaddy of them all, lazed upstream toward Davenport. Echoing across the muddy waters was the solid Dixie beat of *High Society*, so sweet and toe–tapping good that it was already drawing crowds to the city's riverside docks.

There was nothing sweet and serene in the mien of Captain Joe Streckfus, master of the *St. Paul* and a growing fleet of showboats that made up the Streckfus Line.

"Get that idiot off the bandstand. If he's too damned bashful to stand up and sing, get him clear off the boat," the leather–lunged captain boomed. This one among his frequent outbursts was remembered by some because there was something a bit special about that particular poor, shy so–called–idiot, who seemingly had reached the end of his career in mid–river.

The young man bowing his head during the tirade would in time overcome his timidity to become America's beloved roving musical ambassador of good will, Louis *Satchmo* Armstrong!

Captain Joe, whose hometown was Rock Island, just across the

NEW STYLE DANCE STOPPED ON BOAT

CAPT. STRECKFUS OF STEAMER "J.S." CREATES SENSATION

SHOWS TOO MUCH HOSIERY

Well Known Riverman Appears in the Role Of Reformer—Mustn't Show Stockings on Boat

Above is the J.S. Deluxe, 1928; restored from the original steamer seen below two decades earlier.

Year: 1908. Dance that raised Captain John Streckfus' ire: Turkey Trot.

Mississippi from Davenport, was a fussy martinet when it came to the manner in which music was played aboard the Streckfus excursion boats. Still, he had a direct hand in molding the careers of many fine and famous musicians. It was said he had a good eye and ear for a winner, and no desire to have a loser aboard his boats.

He wasn't always right, though. He once threatened to fire a whole band if it didn't get rid of one cornet player. Captain Joe just considered it a prime sin that the young man couldn't read music. He banned the hapless youth and his horn from both the steamboats *Capitol* and *Washington.*

This momentary setback didn't end the career of that lean cornet man from Davenport, one Bix Beiderbecke, who went on to carve his own niche in music in general and jazz in particular.

I'll always remember the late Davenporter Wayne Rohlf at earlier Bix Festivals, always spiffily decked out, his wide-brimmed Panama hat at a jaunty angle, always near the tent where then Bix Society President Don O'Dette presided over a group of musicians, many whose names can still be found on old Dixieland records.

Wayne, a fine musician, who could recall times of playing with Bix and other celebrities, was also an extraordinary jazz historian with a musical collection larger than those of most museums. It was great to sit alongside his canvas chair while Festival bands played and he spun stories of the very same kind of music filling the air around us.

He had compiled an extensive history of the bands and boats that delivered music and entertainment to the Quad Cities.

Most of the excursion boats Rohlf remembered operated under the banner of the Streckfus Line: the *J.S.,* the *Washington, Capitol, St. Paul,* and the mighty *President,* biggest and most posh of the showboats plying the Upper Mississippi River. The Streckfus Line's *Admiral* was even larger, but was confined to the lower river since it was too husky to squeeze through the Keokuk Locks. It operated mostly on the Illinois River circuit.

"One of its regular bandsmen was Fritz Putzier, who contributed to musical history when he sold a much-used old cornet for $35 to a fellow Davenport High School music lover named Bix Beiderbecke," Rohlf said.

In a later interview Fritz laughed and said that Bix made only a down-payment and never did pay him the full amount.

Rohlf recalled the *W.J. Quinlan* ferry also featuring many great local musicians. "People think the bands on the boats played Dixieland jazz, but this isn't true," Rohlf said. "Most of them had from eight to ten pieces and

CAPTAIN JOHN STRECKFUS alone on top deck while moored at Nahant Marsh. Below center, with his sons, Roy and Joe to his left; Verne and John Jr. to his right.

were too big for jazz bands, which originally had five or six men. They played somewhat in the Dixie style, but it wasn't the same. I don't recall seeing one Dixieland band aboard a boat."

Rohlf said showboat season usually extended from the beginning of May to Labor Day. Bandsmen were expected to play for daytime excursions and again for moonlight cruises. "Anybody who played on a boat really earned his money because it was a long, hard grind."

Among the early bands Rohlf remembered were Charlie Creath, Pirone's Syncopators, and the Fate Marable Band, which in addition to Louis Armstrong and Baby Dodds, included an outstanding banjo player named Johnny St. Cyr.

"It wasn't unusual in those days for bands to change their names from year to year, or even in mid–season. If they weren't drawing well they would change the band's name and hope to attract more customers. Also, musicians were always going from band to band and there was a lot of turnover.

Among some of the great bands featuring black musicians, Rohlf named the Creath, Pirone and Marable bands. White bands included the Burke–Leins Orchestra, Al Knappe, Doc Wrixon, Tony Catalano and Carlisle Evans bands.

"After Leins broke up the partnership, the group with which he had played became the Burke–Amidon Band, and a season later it was the Burke–Webb Band," Rohlf said. "I was a kid about twelve when I took my first excursion boat ride. That was about 1918. From Davenport, the boats would take you up the river to Clinton or down river to Muscatine. Most people would take along a basket lunch and make a day of it, though they did have sandwiches and soda pop aboard, but no liquor. Most of the daytime excursions were sponsored by public schools or Sunday schools.

"All of the time the boat was moving the band would be playing, except for the twenty minutes they got off every hour. You'd go out in the morning and come back around 4 p.m. Then around 7 p.m. the boat would leave again for the moonlight excursion. They'd go six or seven miles up or down river and anchor in midstream. People would dance until 10:30 or 11 p.m. then the boat would head back. The bands slept aboard the boats."

Most of the big boats had three decks, with a ballroom on the second deck, cabins on the third, and the crew's dining and galley areas on the main deck. The excursion boat era continued up to about 1946. By that time people were drawn to more sophisticated entertainment and had the greater mobility of the automobile. "But even in the forties such bands as Morrie Bruckmann's were swinging aboard boats like the *Washington*," Rohlf said.

His files bulged with photos and typed histories of other bands of an earlier era, including many studded with still famous personalities, though not all necessarily had served apprenticeships aboard the showboats.

Rohlf noted among them were the Original New Orleans Jazz Band and the Mound City Blues Blowers, also out of New Orleans, as was Muggsy Spanier who made fans sit up and take notice wherever his band played.

Jelly Roll Morton

"I fondly remember Rock Islander Les Swanson at the keys of the steam calliope aboard the riverboats. The calliope made so much noise that the musician playing it had to plug his ears. Musicians referred to it as the whooper because of the volume of sound it produced.

"I remember the Jelly Roll Morton Band of the '20s and Louis Armstrong when he played with King Oliver in Chicago. Also the Original McKinney's Cotton Pickers. It's amazing how many of those bands would later be household words," Rohlf said.

He cited, as an example, the band headed by Heavy Elder that included

Davenport's Columbia Theatre opened in 1915 with the Original Creole Orchestra as its opening program. L-R: Eddie Venson, Dink Johnson, Freddie Keppard, Jimmie Palao, George Baquet, Bill Johnson, and W.M. Williams. Joe 'King' Oliver replaced Keppard in 1918 and was bandleader by 1921.

King Oliver and His Creole Jazz Band L-R: Ram Hall, Honore Dutrey, Joe 'King' Oliver, Lil Hardin, David Jones, Johnny Dodds, Jimmie Palao, and Ed Garland

March 5, 1925

King Oliver to Return Sunday

King Oliver and his Creole Jazz Band after playing to an attendance of over 2,000 at the Coliseum last night, proved to be one of the most wonderful jazz bands, was finally induced to cancel his Sunday night engagement at Gary, Ind. and again appear at the Coliseum Sunday night.

King Oliver with his cornet proved to be a real artist when it came to jazz music when he played the "St. Louis Blues" as he is a cornet player that a great many musicians sit and listen to by the hour.

THE GALENA DAILY GAZETTE

"Jelly Roll" Morton Brings His Marvelous Colored Orchestra to Royal Palais

The man who made jazz! The man who plays jazz on the piano, on Victor records and Q. R. S. piano rolls, as no other pianist in the world can do! The man who composed more "blues" and "stomps" than Verdi wrote operas! The man who leads the most quaking, quivering, shaking, shivering colored orchestra on the face of the globe (or below it)!

That's "Jelly Roll" Morton, composer par excellence, originator of jazz and stomps, the most striking modern musical figure of his race. And he's bringing his superb syncopating dance orchestra, the Red Hot Peppers, to the Royal Palais next Tuesday, August 30.

It is generally conceded that true jazz with its sweeping rhythms, weird harmonies and mournful moods, originated in the South. And it was "Jelly Roll" Morton who more than any other individual has developed this style of music into an art, which has attained a vogue not only in this

1927 NEWSCLIP & POSTER
for
composer/pianist

FERDINAND 'JELLY ROLL' MORTON
(1890-1941)

Claude Thornhill on piano and Wendell Mayhew, later a trombonist with Paul Whiteman's Orchestra.

Many years ago, as a reporter for the *Quad–City Times*, I had the privilege of interviewing the late C.W. Elder, one of the last and most colorful steamboat captains. He brought back those days of steamboats and Dixieland as he spun tales of his life aboard the Streckfus boats.

Clarence *Heavy* Elder began working for the Streckfus Lines in 1922 and moved up the ranks from purser to captain. He also was a musician and bandleader.

Capt. Elder recalled what a musical taskmaster Joe Streckfus was. "He left nothing to chance and would regularly attend rehearsals, holding his watch in his hand and tapping his foot. Woe to someone if the band failed to keep the proper tempo—70 beats a minute for fox trots and 90 beats for one–steps. If it happened too often there were bound to be new faces aboard."

Yet, as Capt. Elder recalled, "It was Captain Joe who gave so many musicians their start. He insisted on regular rehearsals and always strove for perfection. Dixieland music was born in New Orleans, of course, but it was the Streckfus steamboats that carried the happy sounds up from the bayou country to make devotees in the North. Many of the bands featured black musicians."

Louis Armstrong, in his autobiography, *Satchmo*, recalled starting the season in Davenport, strolling along the city's levees and polishing his virtuosity on his golden horn under Capt. Joe's critical eye.

Capt. Elder happily recalled how the new music from Dixieland was a hit on the Upper Mississippi. Huge crowds pushed aboard when the Steamer *Sidney* docked at Burlington and Muscatine. Most of the musicians aboard, he said, came from New Orleans, St. Louis, and what was then the Tri–Cities: Davenport in Iowa, Rock Island and Moline in Illinois. Today, with Bettendorf included on the Iowa side, we're known as the Quad–Cities.

One pioneer performer still well–known among jazz buffs today was Fate Marable, who Capt. Elder deemed "the most colorful riverboat musician in the country." In addition to leading his own all–black bands, he also performed on a Tangley Air Calliope, incidentally made in Muscatine by Norman Baker's firm. Though Marable had many attractive offers to play on other riverboats, he remained loyal to Captain Joe.

Louis Armstrong is one of many musicians who prospered under Marable's wing.

Others included Charles Creath and Dewey Jackson, both of whom eventually had their own bands and cut records. There was also Jimmy

CLARENCE *HEAVY* ELDER selling tickets aboard Streckfus Line's *Washington* excursion boat in 1939. Below is a 1927 ad from the *Davenport Democrat-Leader*

Blanton, later a featured soloist with Duke Ellington, George *Pops* Foster, and James *Zutty* Singleton.

The prime test for every musician who tried out on a Streckfus boat was for one of Capt. Joe's favorite tunes, *High Society* and if the applicant didn't bobble on it, he presumably could play anything.

"None of the other excursion steamboats at that time could compare with the Streckfus Line as far as its Dixieland bands were concerned, though many tried," Capt. Elder said. "On Streckfus boats the laggards couldn't help but improve, what with the coaching of Marable and of Capt. Joe. They either got good or they were dropped out."

Playing on the boats was a grueling way to make a living, though. "The hours were terrible with the long all–day trips, where you played almost constantly, and when it got dark you played into the night for the moonlight excursions. In later years, Capt. Joe was obliged to use two bands, one smaller one for the day trips, and a big one for the evening.

"On the tramping trips, all bands played until its musicians were virtually unconscious," Capt. Elder remembered. He chuckled about one occasion when he had to tune a calliope in zero weather aboard the *I. Lamont Hughes* steamer.

"We went out on the Ohio River, fighting ice, and me playing, of all things, *In the Good Old Summertime.* The steam from the whistles froze on the keys almost on contact, so in order to keep playing I had to pour black engine oil all over the keys. I went on playing while wearing white canvas gloves."

Capt. Elder said one of the heading–for–fame musicians he helped train was jazz composer Claude Thornhill, who came aboard the *Washington* at Wheeling, Virginia, on June 1, 1925. "He was just 17 years old and wearing short pants. But was he good!

"Boat orchestras in my time played no popular ballads as a rule. We played four–beat Dixieland. The standard tunes then were *Dixieland One Step*; *Milllenburg Joys*; *High Society*; *Panama*; *Clarinet Marmalade*; *At the Jazz Band Ball* and *Muskrat Ramble.*"

He explained that "many times the captains begged band leaders to slow the tempos because they were afraid the dancing crowds might tear the boats apart." Despite Capt. Joe's strictness where music was performed, Capt. Elder liked and admired him.

"He was the guiding force behind all of this music on the river, a tough, wise prophet helping to spread the gospel of Dixieland jazz. He was the daddy of it all."

CALLIOPES ON THE MISSISSIPPI

Left: Les Swanson aboard the Streckfus Line's *Washington*.

Below: Fate Marable aboard the *St. Paul*

St. Louis Blues

VOLUME 100

100th

Traditional Dixieland Classics

Play-A-Long Book and CD Set
For ALL Instrumentalists and Vocalists

Jamey Aebersold Jazz

FAMED QC BAND ON BOOK COVER

When members of the Carlisle Evans Orchestra posed for their publicity photo in 1921 they couldn't have imagined that nearly a century later they'd grace the cover of one of a series of popular music instruction books.

Julie Craighead, Rock Island music teacher and Quad–Cities musician, first saw the cover of Jamey Aebersold's 2004 100th *Play–A–Long*, which her students use, she was sure the unidentified bandsmen on the cover were familiar. "I just knew I'd seen that picture before and that it had strong Quad–City connection," she said.

Entitled *St. Louis Blues*, the book offers students sixteen musical pieces from the early jazz age. Most of the musicians pictured were well–known locally; some had key roles in the evolution of jazz.

The original photo features all seven members of Evans Original Jazz Band: Evans, piano; Leon Roppolo, clarinet; Louis Black, banjo; Myron Neal, saxophone; Jack Willett, drums; Emmett Hardy, cornet; and Tal Sexton, trombone. Several jazz buffs have the same photo in their collections. Wayne Rohlf loaned his copy to *Down Beat* magazine and their credit line included Jack Willett's name. Willett likely wouldn't be thrilled that he and Sexton were cropped out for the music book cover.

Aebersold's sheet music books span the evolution of jazz from classic to modern styles. Each book is accompanied by a CD that allows the student to feel he is playing along with the professionals.

Jamey Aebersold was born July 21, 1939, in New Albany, Indiana. He attended college in Indiana and graduated in 1962 with a Masters Degree. He played saxophone, piano and bass. In 1989 the International Association of Jazz Educators voted him to their Hall of Fame. With this award he joined other jazz luminaries such as Count Basie, Duke Ellington, Charlie Parker, and Louis Armstrong.

Jazz historians argue whether or not Bix's playing style was influenced by Emmett Hardy but all seem to agree Hardy was a cornet virtuoso in his own right, based on what others had to say about his playing. He had switched to playing banjo when tuberculosis robbed him of breath to play his horn. Hardy died at age 22.

EVANS ORIGINAL JAZZ BAND: Jack Willet, drums; Myron Neal, sax; Carlisle Evans, piano; Emmett Hardy, cornet; Leon Ropollo, clarinet; Tal Sexton, trombone; Lou Black, banjo

A LOOK INSIDE THE CARLISLE EVANS SCRAPBOOK

Exploring jazz history is similar to working a 5000–piece jigsaw puzzle. A key component might turn up when you least expect it. For example, trumpet player Bill Kramer called one day to ask, "Did you know that Carlisle Evans' sister lives in Rock Island?"

CARLISLE EVANS
1892-1944

THERESA EVANS BEYER & BILL KRAMER in 1990

Had he lived, Carlisle Evans would have been nearly 100 years old at the time. Bill laughed off my astonishment. "I went to school with her so she isn't *that* old," he said and agreed to arrange a meeting with Theresa Evans Beyer.

At her tidy home on a quiet street, Theresa Beyer (1911–2003), a widow, greeted and directed us to the dining room.

She said her brother was nineteen when she was born. "But we were very close," she added, opening a time–worn scrapbook on the table. "That's Carlisle with his band. Look how young he was." Asked about the other musicians in the photos, she pointed out Lou Black, Emmett Hardy and Leon Roppolo.

"You knew Roppolo?"

"Knew him…he lived with us. I remember many a night waking up and hearing him play the clarinet," she said. "He couldn't read or write music, but boy, could he play. The only thing," she paused a moment as if deciding whether to go on, "the only bad thing…he smoked muggles, I think they called it. My brother tried to get him to quit but he never did."

"How about Emmett Hardy, did you hear him play?"

"Of course," she answered. "He was with Carlisle for about six months when Leon played. He had a beautiful tone. I do remember that, plus being a very nice guy."

Other musicians who played in the Evans band included Leon Prima, Tony Catalano, Tal Sexton, Jack Willett and Myron Neal. Theresa also knew Bix and Esten Spurrier and heard them play many times.

She recalled the days when her brother's band played aboard the Streckfus line steamboats. "I can tell you a story that sticks in my mind more than anything," Theresa said. "I was just a little girl and we lived in a house in downtown Rock Island, where the YWCA is now. Carlisle was the oldest and there was another sister, Mary and their parents, John and Mary Evans.

"When my brother's boat would hit the railroad bridge downriver, he would start to play *Mother O' Mine* on the calliope. My mother, who had cooked for two or three days knowing that he would be coming in, gathered the food in whatever she could carry it in—including my little red wagon—and head for the levee. The entire band would be standing along the rail grinning and waving, because they knew that they were in for one big meal."

As the scrapbook pages turned, memories came forward and Theresa talked. "I remember sitting alongside of Carlisle on the piano bench sometimes when he played," she said. "And there's the ferry boat *Quinlan*. His band played a long time on it.

DANCE TONIGHT
At The Beautiful
POPPY GARDENS
On the Geneseo Paved Road, One Mile From Colona.

Music by

Evans Jazz Orchestra

Admission 75c per couple, extra lady 25c

If you have not been out to this beautiful spot, come today. It is the talk of the Quad-Cities.

Don't forget our Tuesday and Thursday night dances.

Catch bus at the Silvis garage on Eighth street. Will return passengers to Warner's Crossing.

The place to Eat, Drink and Dance.

"NATURE'S BEAUTY SPOT"

Dancing · Dancing
EAGLES AUDITORIUM
TONIGHT

Carlisle Evans

AND HIS INCOMPARABLE ORCHESTRA

Exalted Rulers

OF

Entertaining

DANCE MELODY AT

IOWA'S MOST BEAUTIFUL BALL ROOM
FOURTH AND SCOTT STREETS EVERY
TUESDAY, THURSDAY, SATURDAY AND SUNDAY

TUESDAY—T. P. A. & U. C. T. DANCE
THURSDAY—SCOTT ZEDOKA JOLLY BUNCH DANCE

DANCE TONITE

Capitol Gardens
KAHL BLDG.

John H. Davies, Mgr.

The Coolest Place in the Tri-Cities.

Never over 70 degrees.

Capitol Garden Orchestra

Under Direction of Carlisle Evans

Playing a Dance Program of Speedy, Soothing Syncopation As You Like It.

REFRESHMENTS SERVED

DANCING
Coliseum Ball Room

Saturday, Sunday

Come Hear Lewis Black With Evans Orchestra

Mardi Gras Dance

TUESDAY, JAN. 13

Novelties for Everybody

CARLISLE EVANS ADS: Poppy Gardens, June 1923; Danceland (Eagles) 4-12-1924; Coliseum with Lou Black, 1925; Capitol Gardens, Sep 1927

"The radio programs..." she continued, turning the page, "Carlisle's band on WOC in the '20s when crystal sets were common."

Sure enough, there were newspaper clippings from the Davenport Daily Times that even listed songs such as *Weary Blues, Too Tired, Copenhagen,* and *Mandy Make Up Your Mind* to name a few.

Theresa also shared the letters her brother received from listeners. One from Howard Way of Niagara Falls, New York, March 19th, 1924, said:

...this morning at 2:15 am I was listening to your program on my 3 tube radio set. I use a Victor Victrola for a loud speaker and your orchestra selections are louder than records. Carlisle Evans has a very fine orchestra, much better than the Vincent Lopez Orchestra of Buffalo.

Another excerpt came by way of Columbus, Ohio, dated November 17, 1924:

We happened to be turning at random and hit your special program last night, or rather, this morning, and were pleasantly surprised. We are all students at Ohio State University and are regular bugs of the dance music game, but must admit that we never heard a hotter outfit than the Carlisle Band. It is seldom that a dance band is so good at both sweet and hot stuff. Give us more of the same. We like it.

It was signed: the Boys of Charley Mobley's Orchestra.

Other letters in the scrapbook included one from Leon Prima in New Orleans who was thinking about coming up north to play with Carlisle again. One from Little Jack Little praised the band for a time when he played with them in Minneapolis. Another, from Mr. J. McCloskey of the Marigold Gardens in Minneapolis, extended an open invitation to play there any time that Evans band could fit it in their schedule.

Theresa's scrapbook had news clippings from when her brother played for a banquet honoring Charles Lindbergh at the Rock Island Arsenal on August 19th, 1927. Also, a story about the opening of the Greyhound Race track at Moline's 53rd Street and 23rd Avenue, where Evans' band was the featured entertainment. Theresa emphasized that Carlisle was known for his rhythm, not his solo work. "His piano rhythm carried the band," she said.

Maybe we didn't need that scrapbook his sister Theresa so cherished to remind us that Carlisle had a great band, but it crystallized for us just how popular he was.

Carlisle Evans died in 1944. At the time, his 19–year–old son, Carlisle 'Ki' Evans was a U.S. Marine, serving in Guam during WWII. He was injured in battle in July of 1944.

First reference to *Quad Cities* came with Charles Lindbergh's visit after historic transatlantic flight in 1927. Arriving at the Moline airport, the aviator then rode in a motorcade through the streets of East Moline, Moline, and Rock Island before crossing the Mississippi by way of the Arsenal bridge, traveling to Davenport's Central Park and back again to Arsenal Island where later that evening Lindbergh gave the keynote address and received a platinum ring, inscribed: QUADCITIES GIFT TO LINDBERGH, AUG. 19, 1927. He stayed overnight at Quarters One, residence of Arsenal commander, thus avoiding any show of favoritism among the host cities. Welcoming committee, above L-R: Col David King, RI Arsenal commander; John H. Siesken, East Moline mayor; Claud W. Sandstrom, Moline mayor; Lindbergh, *Spirit of St. Louis* pilot; Louis Roddewig, Davenport mayor; Chester Thompson, Rock Island mayor.

TONY CATALANO & CREW

As Wayne Rohlf recalled it, Bix grabbed any opportunity that came along to play with local musicians. "He used to sit in with Carlisle Evans, Tony Catalano, Bill Greer, and Doc Wrixon any time they would let him."

Clarinetist Leon Roppolo, just a year older than both Bix and Emmett Hardy, joined in on a couple sessions with the Neal Buckley Novelty Orchestra.

But trombonist Santo Pecora admitted to having been annoyed with Bix for always showing up at their Rock Island boarding house when the band practiced.

Years later when Pecora heard Bix on tour with Whiteman in New Orleans, the two reportedly greeted one another in a friendly hug. "Remember when you thought I couldn't play?" Bix asked. Pecora answered, "You sure can now."

Missouri-born pianist Jess Stacy was a Bix fan from the get-go. Stacy later earned international acclaim for an extended piano solo on Benny Goodman's *Sing, Sing, Sing*—first performed at Carnegie Hall. He recorded Bix's piano compositions: *Flashes, In the Dark,* and *Candle Lights.*

In his 1946 journal, Stacy wrote about Bix's piano technique. "He sat down at the piano and played the kind of stuff I'd always had at the back of my mind but had never been able to express."

He recalled during his last riverboat excursion gig, before moving to Chicago in 1924: "Bix came on board in Davenport, his home town. At that time he had just recorded *Riverboat Shuffle* with the Wolverines. Jimmy Cannon and Lyle [Tal] Sexton greeted him by singing his chorus on that record.

"Bix picked up Tony's cornet—he had his own mouthpiece—sat in and played *Eccentric* and *Skeleton Jangle* with us. He used the first valve most of the time and did the work of the other two valves with that wonderful lip. Of course, he knocked everybody stiff. And then, when he finished, he took over my bench at the piano, played *Give Me a June Night, Baby Blue Eyes,* and *Clarinet Marmalade,* and assassinated everyone all over again."

During the winter, while the *Capitol* excursion boat was on its Lower Mississippi route, Tony Catalano played QC venues like Davenport's Col ballroom.

NEAL BUCKLEY'S NOVELTY ORCHESTRA

JESS STACY

Catalano made Rock Island his home. He had come from an Italian family of classically-trained musicians. His older brother Emil, a violinist, died Christmas Day in Fort Wayne, IN, while playing for the *Follies of 1914* touring company. The Fort Wayne musician's union buried Emil without his family present—they were all still living in Italy.

When he finally made his way to his brother's grave in Indiana, Catalano was on tour with Illinois bandleader Eura Stroud. His fellow musicians went with him to the theater where Emil had died. The brass section performed one of Emil's favorite songs, according to the local newspaper: *Not content with this recognition, the musicians went in automobiles to the Catholic cemetery where Tony for the first time stood beside the grave of his brother. Tears coursed down his cheeks as beautiful memorial services were followed by the band music and hymns which Emil loved. Many people witnessed the impressive scene.*

Tony Catalano left Stroud to work aboard the newly launched *St. Paul* excursion boat out of St. Louis, owned by the Streckfus Steamer Line. There he met a violinist who shared his brother's name—Emil Flindt. Catalano and Flindt played at least one season aboard the same excursion boat with Fate Marable.

Emil Hugo Flindt (1887–1961) was born in Davenport and moved to Clinton, Iowa. Along with riverboat gigs, Flindt toured the Upper Mississippi with his own ragtime band. When the U.S. entered WWI, Flindt and fellow members of the Clinton Citizen's band enlisted together in the army. Another QC band that enlisted *en mass* was the Augustana College varsity band in Rock Island.

The Clinton band served as the 126th Field Artillery Band. Flindt was director. Prior to his unit being sent to France, Flindt had composed the music for what he would later call *Waltz of the Poppies*. The name was inspired, said Flindt, by the flowers that grew among the graves of U.S. soldiers buried in Flanders Field.

After the war Flindt organized his own band back home in Clinton. He later moved his wife Leah and son Jack to Madison, WI. Among the musicians who toured the Midwest with Flindt was Wayne King of Savannah, IL. With added lyrics, Flindt's waltz became King's theme song: *The Waltz You Save for Me*.

Meanwhile Catalano had acquired a shared affinity with Fate Marable for a new kind of music coming out of New Orleans. Once he'd heard jazz, Tony Catalano pretty much abandoned classical music.

Streckfus Lines enacted segregation among its excursion bands so

EMIL FLINDT, far left, and TONY CATALANO, far right with Fate Marable, center, aboard the *Sidney*, c. 1917; below: Flindt, far right, with the Rag-O-Maniacs, c. 1919

DEMOCRAT AND LEADER — SEPTEMBER 21, 1924

TONY CATALANO WITH THE ORCHESTRA AT COLISEUM

TONY CATALANO.
Dancers at the Davenport Coliseum this year will keep step to the music of Tony Catalano's cornet. Tony is playing with Evans' orchestra at the local dancing palace.

Top Right: *Capitol Deluxe* 1927
Center Right: *J.S. Deluxe* 1935
Bottom Right: *President* 1940
Bottom Left: 1927

Danceland BALL ROOM

Saturday Nite
Always a Big Time
Greer's Orchestra
At Danceland
Gents, 50c   Ladies, 25c

SUNDAY NITE'S SPECIAL
TONY'S IOWANS and
BILL GREER'S ORCHESTRA
DAVENPORT'S TWO LEADING DANCE ORCHESTRAS
IN CONTINUOUS DANCE MUSIC TILL 1 A. M.

GENTS, 75c   LADIES, 25c

Marable and Catalano both went looking for jazz musicians on behalf of their boss.

Fate Marable's early recruits are well known by now: Pop Foster, Baby Dodd, Johnny St. Cyr, and, of course, Louis Armstrong.

Catalano did a pretty good recruiting job, too: Emmett Hardy, Leon Roppolo, George Brunies, Santo Pecora, and Paul Mares. He added to that New Orleans roster several QC–based musicians, including Carlisle Evans and Lou Black. Later in Missouri, he met and hired young piano player Jess Stacy from Cape Girardeau.

Like Marable, Catalano lost many of those early recruits to Chicago. Lou Black and Jess Stacy headed to Chicago's Loop. Catalano tried the Chicago scene himself in the early 1920s, playing in a trio with drummer Earl Wiley and clarinetist Roy Kramer at the Arsonia Café. But he seemed to have preferred his associations with tri–cities musicians. More importantly, perhaps, he had steady employment with Streckfus.

Carlisle Evans played only two seasons on the excursion boats. Catalano then formed Tony Catalano and His Commanders. On shore, they went by Tony's Famous Iowans. With Catalano on cornet and mellophone, original members included Elmer Blankenfeld, saxophone and clarinet; Andy Anderson, saxophone and cornet; Verle Glick, banjo and guitar; Pat Patterson, bass and violin; Earl Peters, piano; Tal Sexton, trombone and slide cornet; and George Jones, drums and xylophone.

The *Capitol* underwent one last remodeling before being decommissioned. On Upper Mississippi excursions, Streckfus Lines replaced it with the *J.S. Deluxe*. In 1934 the *President* replaced the *J.S. Deluxe* in 1934. In 1941, Streckfus moved home port from St. Louis to New Orleans. Catalano seems to have disappeared from the QC region after that.

The *President* returned to Davenport as a casino boat, Iowa's first after riverboat gambling legislation passed in 1991. It has since been replaced by the Rhythm City Riverboat Casino.

Above: 1922 Below: 1923

Fate Marable was bandleader of several Streckfus Line bands, including a group made up of musicians from his hometown of Paducah, KY, and his famed Capitol Revue which featured Louis Armstrong, 3rd from right below; that's Marable at the piano.

NEW ORLEANS RHYTHM KINGS, L-R: George Brunies, trombone; Paul Mares trumpet; Ben Pollack, drums; Leon Roppola, clarinet; Mel Stitzel, piano; Voltaire 'Vollie' DeFaut, clarinet, saxophone; Lou Black, banjo; and Steve Brown, bass fiddle. Mares, Brunies, and Roppolo had been childhood friends in New Orleans and worked with Black aboard the *Capitol* excursion boat. NORK began at Chicago's Friar's Inn in 1922; the name originated with Roppolo's former outfit that traveled the vaudeville circuit with Bee Palmer.

BANJO MAN LOU BLACK

Rock Island–born Lou Black was the original banjoist with the New Orleans Rhythm Kings, a seven–piece band that made jazz fans sit up and take notice in the 1920s.

Lou began playing banjo at age seven and by 16 was working professionally in a band led by Moline dentist–turned–drummer Albert Wrixon.

In 1919, he joined the Carlisle Evans Band aboard the *Capitol* on excursions between St. Louis and St. Paul. He then moved on to Chicago, where the Rhythm Kings made several hit records, including six songs in 1923 with composer/pianist Jelly Roll Morton.

"We were at the Friar's Inn for a couple of years, and when we'd finish work or there were no customers, we'd go over to the Dreamland and sit in with Pop Oliver and Louis Armstrong. Nobody ever matched Pop Oliver except Bix Beiderbecke, who sat in with us when he was in town.

"Once, someone wrote out one of Bix's solos, note for note and without letting on, put the transcription in front of him and asked him to play it. Bix, who was a grand kid, looked at the music and looked at him and said, 'Hell, I can't play that fancy stuff!'"

Bix first heard the Rhythm Kings while attending Lake Forest Academy. There, he'd formed the Cy–Bix Orchestra with classmates Walter 'Cy' Welge on drums and Samuel 'Sid' Stewart on saxophone. Their style was greatly inspired from hearing Dixieland played by the Rhythm Kings.

In an era when the banjo was a solid rhythm instrument, Lou Black was a star. A friend once said of Lou, "He's got paws like a bear, but he picks that banjo with a feather." A music critic wrote, "He's a Dixieland man first, last and always. It comes out no matter what he plays."

Black next joined the *Original Memphis Melody Boys* but returned to the Carlisle Evans band. And then, in the prime of his career, he put down the banjo, disgruntled about where he saw the music heading. He saw the banjo replaced by guitars and string bass and his beloved instrument laughed off center stage to become, as he put it, "a taxi driver's instrument."

He took a job in 1926 as assistant program director at WHO radio station in Des Moines and moved there with his wife Natalie, their son and daughter. Natalie Hart Black of Clinton, IA, was a state beauty pageant runner–up when she and Lou met. They married in 1921.

After B.J. Palmer bought WHO in 1930, Black moved his family back to his hometown of Rock Island and worked briefly for WOC but the station was shut down because it shared the same frequency as the Des Moines station.

It was also during this transition period that sportscaster Ronald 'Dutch' Reagan from Dixon, IL, was moved from WOC Davenport to the WHO Des Moines. The Davenport station was back up and operating by 1933 but Lou Black had dropped off the radar.

He was 62 and selling building materials at Moline Consumers Co, when rediscovered while playing weekends at the Moline Holiday Inn. A local reporter interviewed for a story that ran under the headline: *No Comeback, If You Please*.

"One thing I can't stand is a has–been who tries to make a comeback," Black said in the interview. But the story got picked up by newspapers

LOU BLACK
1900-1965

Noted Banjoist Joins Evans'
Coliseum Orchestra Tonight

LOUIS BLACK
Mr. Black, who is one of the best banjo players in the country, will appear with Evans' orchestra at the Coliseum tonight.

Top Right: *Democrat-Leader*
12-31-1924

Bottom Right: Lou & Natalie
at home in Rock Island 1963

nationwide and Black was back in the spotlight, getting offers to play in New York and London.

He had been reluctant even to pick up his dusty banjo. But in early 1962 the daughter of an old family friend begged him to teach her to play. He agreed. He had to loosen up his cramped, aging fingers, he said, so he started practicing.

"I realized that something had gone out of my life and now it was coming back. I really liked those old-time tunes that sound good only when played on a banjo. So I bought another banjo, this time for about $1,000. Then a couple of guys my age joined me and we called ourselves the Dixie Lads."

They played only Friday and Saturday nights "because we have daytime jobs," Lou said.

His sidemen were Lee Stoeterau on piano and reedman Bert Kell.

"I'm getting a tremendous kick out of this," said Black. "But sometimes it makes me want to cry. I can't help but think of the fellows who can't be here to play again. My fingers don't move the way they used to, but my mind knows more."

At the urging of his hunting buddy, Vance Bourjaily, an assistant professor of English at Iowa State University, Black went to New York and made oral history tapes for researcher Tobert J. Mantler.

"The banjo has been maligned for a long time and I wanted to prove it doesn't deserve that. A lot of years in my life went to waste. I don't suppose I could have kept the banjo alive, but I didn't help things by quitting.

"When I first started to play the banjo I had an insatiable desire to be the best. I suppose now I'd just like to prove I can still do it."

His story made it to the *New Yorker* magazine and fans kept him onstage at NYC's Bourbon Street till four in the morning. But other than a couple records for Columbia, he turned down offers that would have returned him to full-time career on the road.

"I'm happy in my selling job, with my little part-time music job and living with my wife in Rock Island," he told a reporter.

On November 3, 1965, Lou was in a car crash that left him with a broken leg and broken rib. While still recuperating at St. Anthony's Hospital in Rock Island, he suffered a heart attack and died Nov 18.

He is buried in Rock Island's Memorial Park Cemetery, just across the Mississippi from fellow QC jazzman Bix Beiderbecke.

When Muscatine's Harold Waldo Oerman passed away at age 74 in 1979, the family followed his instructions and scattered his ashes on the Mississippi River while a five-piece band played Dixieland jazz. Harold graduated from Davenport High and played cornet with several QC bands, including Carlisle Evans, shown in the photo inset above from an unidentified locally-published sheet music used for the cover of his 160-page journal. He wrote it for his daughter, Jean Yelle, providing a first-hand account of the QC jazz scene in the 1920s and what it was like to play with musicians like Bix Beiderbecke. Following are excerpts from *LETTERS TO JEAN*.

LETTERS TO JEAN
by Harold W. Oerman

In 1919 we moved from Walnut to Davenport, Iowa. It was here that my musical talent really developed, although for about a year and a half I lost interest and sort of let my horn blowing lapse. Then I took it up once more, really in earnest, and at the start of the 1920 fall term, I tried out for the High School Band and was assigned 1st chair, solo cornet. Mr. Miller, the band director, had a much higher esteem of my abilities than was deserving, as I wasn't really that good. He was quite a guy, a fine musician and an excellent Director. He had a stunt which had everybody puzzled and it took some doing to figure it out because he was very secretive about telling how it was done. He could play a duet on the trombone. After much pondering over this feat, I finally figured out how it was done. He would play the melody in conventional manner with his lips and slide. The harmony he would hum into the horn. The two would merge together inside the horn and out the bell would come the duet. The pitch of a trombone and a man's voice is just right for this kind of thing, but it does not work too well on a cornet with its higher pitch, which I learned when I tried it.

Seated next to me in the band was Wayne Rohlf. His ambition was to dump me from the first chair. I was equally determined that he wasn't going to. He would show up at rehearsal, and then for the benefit of Mr. Miller and me, spin off an intricate solo of a sort. The next week I'd be ready with one bit more difficult. Back and forth this went, week after week, each of us trying to show the other one up. Mr. Miller, I'm sure was fully aware of the feud but did nothing about it as I continued to hold down the first chair.

Then one week Wayne showed up with a new gimmick. His next-door neighbor had started a Jazz Band. Wayne learned a few of the so-called licks and when he showed up at the next band rehearsal he gave off with a few of them. Poor as they must have been, that stopped me cold. Up until then, I was what would be called a "Long-haired" musician and looked with scorn upon this new thing called "jazz". But I was not about to let Wayne Rohlf outdo me, even if it meant forsaking my principles as regarded jazz vs. orthodox music.

The next day I went down to Petersen's record department. I had no idea of what to ask for, so all I said was that I wanted a "jazz" record. Charles Beiderbecke, big brother of Bix, could not have made a better selection. He sold me the

Original Dixieland Jazz Band's recording of "Clarinet Marmalade" on one side and "Mournin' Blues" on the other. I must have driven Mom, Dad, Orey and the neighbors to distraction. I played that record over and over and over, ad infinitum, then played along with it until I had mastered the cornet part of each tune note for note. Now it was my turn to show up Wayne Rohlf, and show him up I did. More importantly though, it started me off in a new direction in music which would not only prove to be profitable, but was also to provide me with some of the happiest days of my life.

It soon got around that I could play Jazz, although really, I was very much of a neophyte. One day Lawrence Andrews, a classmate, who played a longneck banjo, asked me if I would be interested in starting a little band. I was. We got Louie Bruhn on piano, Wallace Bowlby on a C-melody saxophone, and Vance Young on drums for a five-piece combination. I'm sure it must have been pretty bad, but we had fun, especially when we played the tune "Hot Lips". I had copied Henry Busse' chorus from the Paul Whiteman recording, something I now realize was pure corn.

We called ourselves the Radio Jazz Band. We did not belong to the Musician's Union, but we managed to get a few scab jobs the summer of 1921, mostly on a percentage of the gate and share expenses. One night at Propstei, Iowa, we got rained out and it cost us each a dollar for our share of the expenses. Only six couples showed up.

Once or twice a week on a Tuesday or Thursday night, after the fall term of school had started, we would practice till about 9:30 P.M. in the second-story room above the music store in Rock Island which Wallace Bowlby's dad owned. On the way home, Lawrence and I would stop by the Coliseum dance hall on 4th Street in Davenport and stand out in the foyer listening with awe to the fabulous Carlisle Evans band. This was the finest band anywhere around outside of New Orleans, St. Louis, or Chicago. It was the acme of achievement and the envy of all Tri-City musicians to become a member of this great little outfit. Bob Struve, who was in my trigonometry and physics classes, played trombone with the Evans band. He was superb, as was everyone else in the organization. Little did I dream, as I stood there enraptured by that marvelous music, that in a little over a year I would be playing with that wonderful band.

Our little group was not destined to be together too long. First, Louie Bruhn, then Wallace Bowlby joined the Musician's Union to join an outfit being formed by Tracy Mumma to be called the Capitol Syncopaters. With them gone, our little outfit folded. I did manage to keep going, getting a job here and there with pickup outfits, but they were all pretty low caliber jobs and we were lucky to get $3 a night. Some of the boys I played with were Len Esterdahl, banjo; Joe Stroehle, piano; Chuck Lospitch, piano; Leo Barr, saxophone/clarinet;

Harold Waldo Oerman

The Oerman family in their Maxwell automobile in 1913

Doc Wrixon, drums; and many more I can't recall. Every one of these were reasonably good musicians, except Doc Wrixon, and after a few years experience went on to good bands....

Before I forget, one of the side effects of playing with Lawrence Andrews was that it got my brother Orey into the jazz band business. I bought a cheap banjo at a second-hand store for $5. Lawrence taught me some chords and I made some effort to show him how to blow a cornet. I, in turn, taught Orey the banjo chords I had learned and he went on to become one of the best banjoists in the Middle West. He still does a good job of it.

One day in midsummer of 1922 I got a call from Louie Bruhn asking me if I would be interested in joining the Capitol Syncopaters. This was a good little outfit which got a couple of weekend jobs and occasionally during the week, just enough for a kid still in High School. Besides I had played with Louie and Wallace Bowlby in the Andrews band and knew I would fit in. It meant joining the Musician's Union, but this I was sure would be no problem.

The first order of business was to apply for membership in the Union and to be accepted. One afternoon after school I went down to the Union Headquarters, which were then in the German Turner's Building on the south side of West 3rd Street just west of Ripley Street. There I made my wishes known to Roy Powell who was Secretary of the Union. He took my application and said that I would probably be accepted if I could pass the examination because the Union was at the time a bit short of cornet players.

In those days, the Musician's Union was practically a closed corporation holding its membership to a bare minimum, just enough to supply the demand, and requiring that every applicant pass an examination before a board of three. They did not want a surplus of members crying for work and they wanted only those who could demonstrate their musical ability.

About a week after I made application, a notification came by mail to appear at Union Headquarters on the following Friday afternoon to be examined. I was quite shaky when I showed up as I heard sordid tales of how tough the examiners were, especially old man Schmidt, who was President of the Union and an ornery old bird. Fortunately, Mr. Schmidt was engaged somewhere else, so it was decided by the other two examiners, after a half-hour wait, to go ahead without him. I had no difficulty with the music placed before me and passed the test to the satisfaction of the two examiners. But luck ran out on me. Just as I was being told I could put my horn in its case and go, who should stalk into the room but old man Schmidt. The first thing he wanted to know was "Did he play the marsch?" "No, he had not played the marsch." "Veil, I vant to hear him play the marsch." The "marsch" turned out to be "Under the Double Eagle"…It was one of the marches we played often in the High School Band and I sailed right through it. All old man Schmidt did was to grunt and say that he was satisfied.

In less than a week I received a notification of acceptance by the Union and soon after became a member of the Capitol Syncopators. Louie Bruhn was on piano, Leroy Johnson, drums, Wallace Bowlby, saxophone, Tracy Mumma, saxophone/clarinet, and yours truly on cornet. The name derived from Tracy Mumma's having played on the Capitol Excursion boat the year previously. The Capitol Syncopators was a pretty good little outfit and we had three and four jobs a week, a little more than I really wanted, as I was still in High School. . .We shared, with a couple of other bands, the jobs left over after the Carlisle Evans band was booked up. Our favorite spot was the Davenport Outing Club where the elite of Davenport hung out, the large pavilion in Watch Tower Park, The Rock Island Arsenal Country Club, Davenport Country Club and Moline Elks. We did play in some crummy places too, such as the Bucket of Blood on the southeast corner of 2nd and Ripley Streets in Davenport and the Odd Fellows Hall in Moline.

It all happened one fateful night the first week in January 1923. We were playing at the Poultry Show in the exhibition hall on the north side of 5th Street just east of Main Street, Davenport. If you can, just try to imagine the pandemonium associated with an affair. When the band was not playing, the ducks, geese, chickens, pigeons, turkeys, and guinea hens were cackling for all they had in them. As soon as the band started up, they would cease immediately, and we would fill the hall with jazz. I would not want to make any judgment on which was the worst. I'd say it was a toss-up. The job started on a Tuesday night and lasted until the following Saturday. We started at 7:00 pm and played until 10:00, in ten to twelve minute sets, three to four sets an hour.

The fateful night which I mentioned was on the Friday of this engagement, a night on which the Carlisle Evans Band, surprisingly, was not booked. About 9:00 I happened to look up and who should I see coming into the hall but Bob Struve... I immediately turned around and told Louie Bruhn that Struve had come in so he would be sure we played our best tunes on the next set. I had expected that Bob would stick around for only one or two sets and then leave. But the bugger kept hanging around till 10:00, quitting time. We were all hoping he would get the hell out, as our repertoire was limited and we were running out of good tunes to play.

While I was packing my horn away Bob was saying the band sounded good and which way did I go home. I told him I took either the LeClaire Street or Mount Ida street car, whichever came along first, as it made little difference because at the end where I got off each was less than a block from home. He asked if I would mind taking the Mount Ida that night so I could ride up Brady Street with him...No sooner had we gotten seated than he told me that Chet Ogden, Evie's cornetist, was leaving the band to start the second semester at the University of Iowa in mid-February. Evie had asked Bob to talk to me to see if I was interested in the job...To believe that such a thing as being invited to become a member of that fabulous band was happening to me was beyond comprehension. And to think that I even had to think it over was the height of stupidity. By the time I got up on Saturday morning, after a sleepless night, my mind was made up. The first thing I did was to call Tracy Mumma and tell him about it and to see if he was going to insist on the Union rule that required a two-week notice when anyone left a band. He said he would be the last to stand in anyone's way of such an opportunity. Then I called Bob Struve and told him "yes".

... So on Sunday night, January 14, 1923, I got into my Tuxedo, picked up my cornet and headed for the Coliseum. I got there a little after 7:30, about a half-hour early, and Carlisle "Evie" Evans had just gotten there. He was laying music out on the piano. Surprisingly, he was the only one who played from music. He never made a move to come over and introduce himself or to welcome me to the band, so I just stood around until Bob Struve and some of the other boys showed up. Bob was the only one I knew. He introduced me around after everyone was on hand. The personnel of the band was Carlisle Evans, piano and director; Wade Foster, saxophone/clarinet; Bob Struve, trombone; Richard Miller, drums; Bob Sheerer, violin; Penny Pennington, bass horn; Heavy Elder, banjo; and, of course, yours truly, cornet. Heavy Elder left the band a few weeks later and was replaced by Fred Flick, a real lady's man, a dead-ringer for Rudolf Valentino and a top notch musician. He played a long-neck banjo rather than the conventional tenor banjo.

Here was a collection of the top musicians in the Tri-Cities, although I could never exactly figure out why a jazz band needed a violin. I expect it was because Bob Sheerer was a feature writer for the Moline Dispatch and Evie got a lot of free publicity, well worth more than what he paid Bob. Besides, Bob's wife had some rather potent social connections which didn't hurt when it came to landing some of the better jobs at the elite spots in the Tri Cities.

... The Coliseum, in which Evie's band was engaged...was decorated with Japanese lanterns and streamers of all colors. In the middle and hanging from the ceiling was a large rotating ball about three feet in diameter onto which was glued mirrors about one inch square completely covering the ball. Whenever a waltz or romantic tune was played, all the lights in the hall were turned out and colored spotlights were played on the rotating ball to give an unusually pleasing effect, the mirrors reflecting the colored lights in all directions, somewhat like colored snow falling.

I seemed to be the center of attraction that night as everyone wanted to have a look at the new cornet. There was always a jam around the band stand which was at an elevation of about four feet above the dance floor. It was gratifying and reassuring to receive a round of applause when I would take a chorus, as I don't mind admitting that I was pretty jittery that first night.

To this day, whenever I hear many of the tunes popular at the time, I am transported back to that never-to-be-forgotten night... one of the biggest thrills of my life. Here are some of the tunes popular at the time: Runnin' Mild, Alice Blue Gown, Tiger Rag, Panama, Jada, Way Down Yonder in New Orleans, Yes We Have No Bananas, Bugle Call Rag, Japanese Sand Man, Nobody's Sweetheart, Hot Lips, Angry, Mr. Gallagher and Mr. Shean, Clarinet Marmalade Blues, Mournin' Blues, Wish I Could Shimmy Like My Sister Kate, Maple Leaf Rag, Nobody Lied when They Said I Cried Over You, Jazz Me Blues.

We played four nights a week at the Coliseum: Tuesday, Thursday, Saturday and Sunday. Besides that, there was rarely a week that Wednesday and Friday were not booked and occasionally we would get a Monday. This was far more than I wanted, as I was still in High School and it was an awful grind to get home anywhere from 1:00 A.M. to 2:00 A.M. and have to get up at 7:00 A.M. to get to school on time.

... There was one stretch when we played forty-six nights in a row, had one Monday off, and then had another stretch of thirty-eight nights in a row. I will put all modesty aside at this point and say that I was a shot in the arm for the band, because before I joined it, the one thing the band was weak in was the cornet.

We made many excursions out of town to Peoria, Galesburg, LaSalle, Woodhull, Stockton, Freeport, and Monmouth, all in Illinois, and to Clinton, Iowa City, Des Moines, Dewitt, Dubuque, Burlington, and Cedar Rapids, all in Iowa. I make mention of this to indicate how wide-spread was our popularity.

The trip to Peoria was perhaps the hardest, especially on a bitterly cold winter night. It was 125 miles from Rock Island...we had to leave in mid-afternoon to get there in time to get thawed out and to eat before the job started. This was the annual Masonic Winter Ball and ran from 8:00 P.M. until 2:00 A.M. Coming home was the worst, as everything was closed at that ungodly hour, and we could not stop in anywhere to get a cup of coffee and thaw out. We went in a caravan of two automobiles which only had side curtains to keep out the cold and a grill plate over the exhaust pipe to let in some heat... what a wonderful sight it was, around 4:30 to 5:00 A.M., to get back to Moline and see Vic's hamburger joint which stayed open all night. There we would stuff ourselves with hamburgers, home-baked beans, and cups of steaming hot coffee.

OREY OERMAN on banjo and HAROLD OERMAN on cornet with Carlisle Evans

Some of the other out-of-town places were further than Peoria, but these jobs were all in the summer and it was a breeze.

Evie was not only a good man when it came to running the band, but he was also responsible when it came to paying his men. In the whole year and a half that I played with him, there was not one night in which he did not pay us off, in cash, before the last dance. Union scale was $6.00 for the four hours, or any part thereof, from 8:00 P.M. till 12:00 midnight, even if we didn't start until 9:00 P.M. or later. Any time before 8:00 P.M. or after midnight, and on holidays, it was time-and-a-half, except New Year's Eve, which was double time. Evie always paid from one to three dollars more than scale. It was nothing at all to make $50 to $60 a week, and in those days that was big money. Each night when I got home I would put my money in a silk bag with draw strings which hung on my dresser. Mom had used this bag at one time for collecting the loose hair which came out when she combed it. It was surprising how fast that bag would fill up with bills and how often I would have to make a trip to the bank to deposit it. When I left the band to go to the University of Illinois in 1924, I had over $3,000 in the bank.

The Coliseum's season ran from Saturday of the Labor Day weekend until the last Saturday of May. After that it was too hot to hold dances there, as there was no air-conditioning at that time.

During the summer months, dances were held in pavilions open on all sides, with a roof to protect from rain. For the summer of 1923 and 1924 we played at a new place about twelve miles east of Moline called Poppy Gardens. In fact, it was

DANCING

The Beautiful Poppy Gardens

On Geneseo Paved Road—Regular Tuesday Evening Dance
Music Is Furnished by the Popular Jazz Orchestra

75c Per Couple.   Extra Lady 25c.

Catch the Bus at Silvis Garage, Eighth Street. Passengers Are Returned to Warner's Crossing.

DANCE TONIGHT

At The Beautiful POPPY GARDENS

On the Geneseo Paved Road, One Mile From Colona.

Music by

Evans Jazz Orchestra

Admission 75c per couple, extra lady 25c

If you have not been out to this beautiful spot, come today. It is the talk of the Quad-Cities.

Don't forget our Tuesday and Thursday night dances.

Catch bus at the Silvis garage on Eighth street. Will return passengers to Warner's Crossing.

The place to Eat, Drink and Dance.

"NATURE'S BEAUTY SPOT"

JUST A NICE RIDE—
—and then, oh! what fun you have after you get to the
POPPY GARDENS
On the Geneseo Highway
DANCE
'Til Your Heart's Content
CARLISLE EVANS
And His 9-Piece JAZZ ORCHESTRA
Will Keep You on the Go
CHICKEN DINNERS
Served Daily from 6 p.m. to 9 p.m.
Phone M. 1074 for Reservations
DANCING Tuesday, Thursday, Saturday, Sunday

HAVE YOU BEEN OUT to the beautiful POPPY GARDENS

on the Geneseo Paved Road

DANCING

TONIGHT and Every Tuesday, Saturday and Sunday Night

MUSIC BY THE PEPPY

EVANS' JAZZ ORCHESTRA

DINNERS—Excellent chicken, roast or steak. Phone Moline 2545 and make reservations before 2 p.m.

SODA FOUNTAIN—In charge of experienced people—stop in and enjoy a real cool and refreshing drink.

FREE Admission to Grounds **FREE**

JUST A NICE RIDE—
—and then, oh! what fun you have after you get to the
POPPY GARDENS
On the Geneseo Highway
DANCE
'Til Your Heart's Content
CARLISLE EVANS
And His 9-Piece JAZZ ORCHESTRA
Will Keep You on the Go
CHICKEN DINNERS
Served Daily from 6 p.m. to 9 p.m.
Phone M. 1074 for Reservations

newspaper ads for Carlisle Evans at Poppy Gardens—Summer 1923 & 1924

completed just in time for the beginning of the 1923 summer season, the first Saturday in June. Our band opened the place.

Poppy Gardens was a pretty rough and tumble joint and there was hardly a Saturday or Sunday night but what there were at least a couple of brawls or fights by some guys who had had a bit too much moonshine or spiked beer under their belts. To handle the situation, there was a fellow by the name of Rocky who was the bouncer and it didn't take him long to break up any disturbance. He was a big six-foot-two specimen of a man, hard as nails, afraid of nothing or anyone, but at heart one of the nicest persons I've ever known. Normally he wouldn't hurt a fly, but when it came to breaking up a disturbance he was right in there. His real name was Rockefeller and he did indeed belong to the famous John D. Jr. clan, but as he said, the wrong side of it. He had a day-time job as a line foreman for the Bell Telephone Company working out of the Davenport Headquarters.

When we first started at Poppy Gardens I would meet Bob Struve downtown about 7:15 P.M. and ride out with him. He had a 1922 Dodge Coupe. But then, in mid-summer he got married and that ended that. So I took to riding with Rocky who lived on Bridge Avenue just four doors from our house. Little did I realize how in those thirty-minute rides each way he was to shape my future.

It seems that everyone has at least one experience in a lifetime that is never-to-be forgotten, even though it may not be of that great importance or significance. Mine has to do with that great tune "It Had to Be You".

I was a real nut about railroads as a boy and my highest aspiration was to be a locomotive engineer on a fast passenger train. I have never out-grown the desire, although it's just as well that I never went on the railroad. Dad would not stand for it anyway. By the time I would have had the seniority to be an engineer, the Diesel locomotive had replaced the old steam engine. That was like running a street car. The thrill of operating the fascinating steam locomotive went with its demise. Many old-time steam locomotive engineers retired early rather than to have to take over a Diesel engine when their beloved steam locomotives were replaced.

There was a man by the name of Jim Williams who used to come to Poppy Gardens whenever he had time off. He was a locomotive fireman on a freight train that ran between Silvis and Blue Island, Illinois. I got to know him quite well, and it was not long before he learned of my intense desire to be a locomotive engineer. One night he invited me to take a ride with him up in the engine. I was not able to make the entire route, because Evie's band was so heavily booked, but I could go to Bureau, about one-third the way, get off there, and catch a passenger train back to Davenport getting in around 4:00 P.M. This would give me plenty of time to clean up and meet my ride out to Poppy Gardens.

... I caught the passenger train for the ride back to Davenport right on schedule. We got as far as Princeton, Illinois, about halfway, then sat there and sat there... The connecting rod on the right side of the locomotive had broken and we were not able to budge an inch... Around 7:00 P.M. temporary repairs were completed, and the train got underway at about half-speed. I was in a quandary about what to do... Carbon Cliff, was just three miles north of Poppy Gardens, but it was not a scheduled stop. I explained my predicament to the conductor and he stopped the train there to let me off. I made a bee-line for U.S. Route 6, hoping to catch a ride, but had no luck, so just ran down the road as fast as my legs would carry me. It was by now going on 9:00 p.m. It seemed forever, but the lights of Poppy Garden at last showed up. As I rounded the bend for the last 1,000 yards, what should I hear but the delightful lilting strains of "It Had to Be You"....

I was greeted with a roar of laughter as I dashed to the band stand and took up my cornet. During intermission I went to the washroom to get rid of as much of the soot, grease, and grime as I could. Evie and the band never got over ribbing me. To this day, whenever I hear "It Had to Be You" I am transported back to that night on Route 6 as I was dashing madly for Poppy Gardens.

During the summer of 1923 the Davenport Eagles Club built a new four-story building on the south side of 4th Street a block west of Ripley Street. On the second floor was an elaborate hall named Danceland. Evie was offered the job of playing there four nights a week; Tuesday, Thursday, Saturday and Sunday, the same as the Coliseum. He had had a couple of run-ins with old man Peterson, who owned and operated the Coliseum, and the opportunity to play in a brand-new hall as elaborate as this was too good to pass up. Labor Day weekend 1923 we opened at Danceland. It was a beautiful hall, but only about half the size of the Coliseum. With the following the band had, we packed them in so thickly it was hardly possible to dance on Saturdays and Sundays, the two big nights. We practically ran the Coliseum out of business.

... I have used the word "Play" in reference to the many jobs for which we were engaged. Most musicians would say that they had worked so many nights, or had worked at such and such a place. With me, it was never work, and the word play is exactly what it meant to me. I am sure that I was having much more fun than the people out there on the dance floor, and the irony of it all was that I was being paid big money for having a good time.

A frequent visitor to our band was Bix Beiderbecke who would "sit in" on cornet and hold us all spell-bound.

As much fun as it was to be playing with that marvelous Evans Band, I could see after about a year of it, that music was not a career for the long haul... First of all, looking around, it was obvious that most musicians were "burned out" by the time they got to be around thirty and wound up in the pit orchestra of a vaudeville house or theater. Secondly, I did not like the night hours... Thirdly, and probably the most important consideration of all, I was not at all happy with the environment of a public dance hall. While a lot of nice couples came for the pure pleasure of dancing, particularly on Tuesday and Thursday nights, there was a lot of riff-raff of unaccompanied guys and gals who came just to be picked up. Most of these were very unsavory characters, real tramps, and there were a lot of them. Don't misunderstand that just because a boy or girl came stag it meant that they were no good, because there were a lot of nice kids, who came single. But, by and large, the majority of them were no good....

By early spring of 1924 I started to do some serious thinking about what I might want to get into. And you will be surprised who it was who influenced me. None other than Rocky, the bouncer. I rode back and forth to Poppy Gardens with Rocky. It was a thirty-minute ride each way, and every night I would listen to him moan and groan, which went somewhat as follows: "By god, if I wasn't married, with a wife and five kids, I'd go to Boston Tech and take up Electrical Engineering". Then he would launch into a big dissertation about how they actually ran tests on street cars, how they were experimenting with artificial lightning, how much money a good Electrical Engineer made once he got on his way ($5,000 to $7,000 a year), what a magic place General Electric Company was... Rocky really knew what he was talking about because his job as a line foreman for the Telephone Company brought him in contact with engineering problems. After hearing this twice a night, four nights a week, I began to get the impression that there was all the magic in Electrical Engineering that he portrayed. So, off to Boston Tech (Massachusetts Institute of Technology) and to Iowa State College at Ames I sent my high school credit record. Boston Tech was out immediately because the tuition was completely out of reach, $800 a year as I recall... So the die was cast and I decided to go to Ames. As soon as I had made up my mind, I told Evie that I was leaving the band to go to college, but if it was all right with him, I would like to stay on till the season at Poppy Gardens was over, the Thursday before Labor Day weekend. He agreed.

And then, still another event took place which changed the whole business and sent me off in another direction. One night in early mid-June, Paulie Freed, a top-notch pianist, came out to Poppy Gardens. I had not seen him for some time as he was attending The University of Illinois. He had just gotten home for summer vacation. During intermission he sought me out and said, "I hear you are leaving the band to go to college." ...He asked if I intended to continue playing the cornet and I told him I had to in order to meet the expense of going away to school. He said that in that case I ought to go to the University of Illinois as there was so much more opportunity to play there because it was twice the size of Ames. Besides, the pay was much better, $10 a night as compared with $6 to $7 at Ames. And if I had any doubts about the quality of Illinois, it was considered to have one of the best Engineering Schools in the country. So the next day I went over to the High School and had them send my credit record to Illinois at Urbana. About ten days later I received an application blank, and in another ten days I had been accepted... It was a real satisfying and financially rewarding one to play with the Carlisle Evans band and it was with deep regret and the shedding of tears that I left that fine organization that last night of the Poppy Garden season.

***

I first met Bix in the fall of 1921 when I was a junior in High School... At that time he was playing the piano only, and insofar as I am aware had not yet touched a cornet, the instrument on which he was to gain such World-Wide fame. I would bump into him in the hall between classes and then he'd inveigle me into coming over to his house after school, as he put it, "to do a little jamming". Or he'd meet me downtown on Saturday or Sunday afternoon on my way to a show and the same thing would happen. Bob Struve was also always included. The three of us would fool around with one tune after another. Bix would teach Bob and me runs and breaks by playing them on the piano, but it was not too easy because Bix could rarely play the thing the same way the second time. Anyhow, Bob and I got the general idea. Then we'd put it together and it was surprising how good it all came out. Bix was as adept at coming up with a good trombone part as he could for the cornet. Bob and I learned much of what we played throughout our musical careers from these little jam sessions.

It was very difficult to play with Bix. He played mostly up on the black keys of the piano which put the rest of us in the most ungodly keys, three and four sharps or flats. Later, Bob Struve told me that Bix had started picking tunes out on the piano when he was in the second grade. Bob was in grade school with Bix and used to go to his house after school. Bix had a set of drum sticks and would get pots and pans out of the cupboard and beat out crazy rhythms. Then he would go to the piano and pick out tunes with weird harmonies. His fingers were too short to work well back and forth between the black and white keys and when he found it was easier to use mostly the black keys, he just stayed with them. He was completely self-taught and could not read a note. Yet, by the time he was twelve years old he had mastered the piano almost completely. He could play anything from popular through classical music. He had a style unlike anyone else. He would play a lot of

Davenport 1920s
Top: Second St at Brady
Below: Parking on the Davenport Levee

crazy runs with his right hand and accompany this with a rolling bass with his left. His chord formations were quite weird and unorthodox and his timing and rhythm very much off-beat and syncopated. In later years, probably about 1927, he recorded, off the cuff, a tune called "In a Mist". A top-notch pianist... copied it from the record as closely as he could and made a score of it. I bought a copy and found that many of my friends who were accomplished pianists had great difficulty in playing it because of the weird chord progressions and crazy rhythms.

The first I heard about Bix playing a cornet was in the fall of 1922 when I was riding in a car on my way to a rehearsal with Wayne Hostetter, a violinist who played some pretty fancy stuff on the fiddle. I made some comment about Louis Panico, who was at the time playing with Isham Jones at the Canton Tea Gardens in Chicago, and mentioned what a hot chorus I thought he had played in a tune called "Nobody Lied When They Said I Cried Over You". Wayne said that was pure corn. He also made the remark that the hottest cornetist in the country was Bix Beiderbecke. I wasn't even aware that Bix had taken up the cornet. But it was not long until I learned differently and that Wayne was absolutely right.

I was playing with Doc Wrixon one week in the Garden Theater while the comedy was being shown, when who should come in but Bix. He had just gotten off an excursion boat. He sat down beside me, took my cornet and started to play. It was absolutely unbelievable and I just sat there in a daze.

After this, I got to see and hear Bix a lot whenever he stayed around Davenport any length of time. He was gone from home more than he was home and his family never knew half the time where he was. It was a big worry to his mother.

Bix attended Lake Forest Academy for a while but was dismissed when he was found missing from his bed while he had slipped away to go into Chicago to listen to Pop Eye Oliver and Louis Armstrong at Lincoln Gardens. He also attended the University of Iowa for a while but it did not take. He was a musician and was happy only when he was in a band or was listening to one. He was not in the least bit academically inclined.

When he would be in town...Bob Struve and I would pick him up on 2nd and Brady Streets where he would generally wait for us on our way out to Poppy Gardens. If he missed us and we had to go on without him, he would hitch a ride out with someone else. I had a 1900-vintage short, stubby cornet which I would use sometimes for kicks or, when for variety, the band would put on a German band number. Bix would sit in with this horn. He liked it particularly for its round full tone, the ease with which it could be blown, and the smooth responsive valve action. Bix held us all spell-bound, all, that is, except Evie and Bob Sheerer, who did not understand or appreciate his genius. Bob, the violinist, stood up when he played and had a sort of bird's eye view of the hall and surrounding area. If Bix would show up unannounced at some place where we were playing and Bob spotted him coming, he would turn around and yell to me, "Hey String, hide the cornet, here comes that goddamn Beiderbecke." When Bix sat in with us, I would just put my horn down and absorb as much of that wonderful playing as I could. Besides, it would have been nothing short of downright sacrilegious to have played my kind of stuff in the presence of anyone as great as Bix.

Bix had a tone the likes of none which, in itself, would have been the envy of any cornetist. A tone, you might say, with a tear-drop in it. And his style of playing was unmatched. Most cornetist would play a jerky, disconnected succession of two to four-measure phrases throughout the chorus or main strain of a tune, play a wow-wow style, or go wild with cramming as many notes into a measure as they could manage, meaningless hodge-podge of nothing, one measure after another. Not Bix. He played an uninterrupted, easy-going, relaxed, continuous flow of runs consisting of only a few, but sometimes many notes throughout the chorus or strain. With him it was quality not quantity that counted, although in instances he would come up with a most tricky, very-difficult-to-execute run of many notes. To illustrate, I'll refer you to the interlude before the last strain of his recording of Clarinet Marmalade Blues. I was never able to copy that run of those last three measures and have never come across anyone who could, although, I'd hazard a guess that Esten Spurrier could. And there were never empty spots or holes in a tune when Bix was in a band. He could anticipate one coming and would just plug it with maybe one or two notes, but what notes these would be!

Bix shunned a mute like so much poison and said that the only thing it did was to spoil a cornet's clear round tone or to mask a lousy player's goofs. He always played with an open horn, until he was forced later in the Whiteman Band to use a mute. It galled him no end and was one of the things that made him so unhappy with the Whiteman outfit. Bix abhorred wow-wowing of any kind or form, a popular style of many cornet and trombone players of the period.

Bix never played anything the same way twice. Although there was some similarity in a chorus of the same tune from one playing of it to the next, there were very definite differences in concept which were quite evident. There is a recording of this to illustrate where the published version of the record and another cutting made at the same sitting clearly reveal the marked difference in successive playing...two of the tunes on it that demonstrate this aspect of Bix are "Lonely Melody" and "From Monday On", both from Whiteman recordings.

Bix taught me almost everything I knew about playing and I developed a style somewhat simulating his, but very inferior. I was able to play a lot of his runs and develop choruses of my own, but sooner or later I would get into a rut and wind up playing one chorus after another exactly the same.

...Bob Struve told me about the time a little group of musicians tried to slip Bix into the Musicians Union in Davenport.... The examiners passed out a tune with a part for each member and requested them to play it. The cornet, clarinet and trombone parts were written to hold a chord of four whole notes tied together for four measures for sixteen beats. The drum was to sustain a roll for the sixteen beats. Meanwhile, the piano part called for four measures of arpeggios. In case you are not sure of what an arpeggio is, it is the playing of the notes of the chord in very rapid succession up and down the scale instead of holding the notes of the chord simultaneously. Bix had no more idea than the man in the moon that all he had to do was just to sit there and hold one note for sixteen beats. When he heard that piano start up and down the scale, he took off in hot pursuit and followed the piano note for note. The examiners were too straight-laced and hide-bound to recognize the genius and talent they had just witnessed. ...How proud they are now that his name appears on their roster of musicians. In fact, they actively help to sponsor the Bix Beiderbecke Festival held annually in Davenport on or near the anniversary of his death.

Another peculiarity of Bix's playing was his use of the third valve instead of the first and second for a lot of notes. Many have pondered over this and have even tried to tie it into some psychological bent of his, as if there was some great mystery associated with it. That is a lot of hog-wash and there is no mystery to it at all. Remember, Bix was self-taught and found out quite by accident that the third valve would give the same note as the first and second, middle A, for example Besides, the third valve imparts ever so slight discordance to the note, and this Bix liked. In fact, he often used the first and third valves instead of open, such as middle G, for this very reason. It sounded better to him. I frankly believe that no matter what valve or combination of valves he used, the right note would have come out.

As an individual, Bix was very humble, retiring and shy. He never put on any airs in his playing, like holding his horn in one hand and putting the other on the nape of his neck, or pointing his horn toward the sky, or hunching up a shoulder, or swaying back and forth. He would just pick out a spot on the floor, keep his eyes glued to it and play. He was always belittling his own playing...

I remember when The Benson Orchestra of Chicago, with Don Bestor directing, came to Davenport. As each section of the band was featured, the men in that section would stand up. Bix and I were there listening and I asked what he thought of that. His only comment was that they were a bunch of guys who stood up with horns. Perhaps his biggest fault and the thing that in part led to his early death, was that he did more drinking than he should have, but I will have to admit that I never saw him when he had had too much. It was also rumored that he smoked muggles (marijuana cigarettes), but again, I must have to admit to never having seen him do so.

Bix played with many bands and made a lot of recordings...but in my own mind, those made with "Bix and His Gang" or "Bix and Tram" would stand the acid test. Tram was Frankie Trumbauer, an outstanding man on C-Melody saxophone. Bix's recordings with Paul Whiteman are not at all good, with the possible exception of "From Monday On" and "Lonely Melody". If I really had to come up with what I consider to be his best efforts, they would be: Jazz Me Blues, Clarinet Marmalade Blues, I Need Some Pettin', River Boat Shuffle, Royal Garden Blues, Singing The Blues, Since My Best Girl Turned Me Down, In A Mist (piano solo), Clementine (recorded with the Jean Goldkette Band when they were engaged in the Book-Cadillac Hotel in Detroit), I'm Coming Virginia, Tijuana, and Davenport Blues.

Whiteman had a large organization of I'd hazard a guess, at least twenty to twenty-five musicians. He played some fancy arrangements scored by Roy Bargy, Ferdie Grofe and George Gershwin, and toured the country putting on jazz concerts. Bix had by this time learned to read music to a limited degree, but the Bargy-Gershwin-Grofe arrangements were a bit too much for him, so he just sat back waiting the time when he was supposed to take off with a hot chorus. Well, this just does not work with a guy like Bix who had spent a lifetime improvising. Also, as any musician who plays Dixieland will attest, it is necessary to run through several tunes to warm up and to get into the swing; somewhat akin to a baseball pitcher going through his warm-up in the bullpen. It was sheer folly and completely unfair to expect Bix to come up with anything good simply by pointing the finger and saying "now it's your turn". The Whiteman Band put on one of these concerts in Orchestra Hall in Chicago in the early part of 1929. Merle and I were living in Oak Park and Len Esterdahl and his wife were living in Chicago, so the four of us went to the concert. At intermission, Len and I went backstage to visit with Bix. He seemed to be quite discouraged and unhappy and told us that had he known what he was getting into he would never have joined the band. In spite of this, he stuck it out with Whiteman until near the end of 1930.

Having left the Whiteman band, Bix knew he had to get back into the swing once again, so he organized a band of his own. I can't recall any of the members with absolute certainty, although I'm sure one of them was Benny Goodman, another possibly Gene Krupa, and on reflection, I think maybe Bill Rank played trombone. One of the last recordings Bix made, and it was with this new band, was "I'll Be A Friend With Pleasure". The chorus he took is a most plaintiff one, and if you listen closely, it seems almost as if it is a farewell.... Merle and I had just gotten home for vacation on the day the Davenport Democrat carried the headline "Bix Beiderbecke Is Dead".

...Mrs. Beiderbecke, his mother, was a grand person and one of whom I was extremely fond. She said to me, "Well, Harold, now at least we know where Bix is". The sister never recognized Bix as anything more than a wastrel of a brother who hung around with such low-brows as dance-hall musicians. But after he had gained renown as the greatest of all cornetist, became a member of the famous Whiteman Band, and then passed away so suddenly at such an early age, they broke down and realized finally what he really was.

Radio Station WOC put on several memorial broadcasts commemorating his life, played many of his recordings, particularly "In A Mist", "Candle Light", and "Davenport Blues".... For the funeral, Paul Whiteman sent a huge floral display with a tag "From Paul Whiteman and the boys". Bix was laid out clad in a light gray tweed suit with a colorful necktie, the first time I had ever seen a corpse clothed in anything other than somber black. It was most befitting.... Bix was buried in the family plot in Oakdale Cemetery, Davenport, not more than one-hundred feet from the German plot where Robert, Merle (your mother), Dad and Mom are buried.

While we are on the subject of Bix, let us not pass over or forget another cornetist, also a Davenport boy and still living there, who is the closest thing ever to Bix, Esten Spurrier. Put them in separate rooms as a blind-fold test, let them play alternately and I have doubts if anyone would be able to tell which was which, even down to the tone. In fact, for my part, there are things "Spur" does that I like better than what Bix did, although in the overall picture, Bix undoubtedly has to be considered the best. Spur grew up with Bix and learned his style to perfection, yet he never really copied Bix like so many of us did. Everything he plays is original and he is like Bix too, in that he never plays anything the same way the second time. If I remember correctly, the only thing that kept Spur from becoming big-time is the fact that he had a weak lip and there was nothing he could do to strengthen it. By the time a night's work was a little more than half over, his lip would give out and that took care of that.

There is lots of talk about musicians who played like Bix, such as Jimmy McPartland, Bobby Hackett, Red Nichols, Bob Scobey, Paul Mares, and Bunny Berigan to name a few. While these were all exceptionally fine musicians in their own right who did indeed play some things resembling Bix, they did not begin to come anywhere near as close to Bix as does Spur.

   Hoagy Carmichael is another musician of great fame with whom I was well acquainted. He was going to the University of Indiana at Bloomington studying law at the same time that I was going to the University of Illinois in Urbana. He would bring a hot little band over to Urbana to play at fraternity or sorority house dances. On a Saturday night, following a dance, it was the custom of many musicians to gather at a pre-designated fraternity house and "wood-shed" until day-break, groups of five to seven at a time taking their turns playing. Hoagy always joined in on these sessions. He would even stay over until late Sunday afternoon to hear the Illini Rhythm Kings, of which I was a member, play at Paul Prehn's Confectionary. Fraternities and sororities did not serve meals on Sunday evening and this was the gathering place for those who wanted a snack to finish off the day. Hoagy played the piano beautifully with a style very much like that of Bix. He had already written "Wash Board Blues" and took great delight in listening to our rendition of it, which I had been taught by Bix late in the summer just before I took off for school. He was to compose "River Boat Shuffle" the next spring. But it was several years later before he wrote the most famous and popular piece of music anyone has ever written, "Star Dust".

   I also had an acquaintance, but not as close as the others, with Jimmy and Tommy Dorsey, Benny Pollock, Benny Goodman, Elmer Shoebel, Ben Bernie (the Old Maestro), Bob Crosby, Jack Brunis, Paul Mares, and Gene Krupa.

   I became acquainted with Louis "Satchmo" Armstrong in the summer of 1923 when he was playing at the Lincoln Gardens in Chicago with Joe "Pop-Eye" Oliver. We had an open Wednesday which Evie had deliberately left unbooked and left Poppy Gardens for Chicago immediately at the end of Tuesday night's engagement... We made the rounds of the Chicago dance halls and wound up at Lincoln Gardens about 2 A.M. and stayed until the band quit playing at day-break. You can't possibly imagine what a terrific band old Pop Eye Oliver had. The only members of the band I can recall are Oliver and Louie on cornets, Kid Ory on trombone, and Lil Armstrong, Louie's wife, on piano.

   Orey and I had a marvelous time in Chicago. We soon learned how to get around by street car, bus and the elevated railway. On Saturday night we took off for Midway Gardens to hear the Elmer Shoebel band, a hot little outfit. After a couple hours there, we went over to the Trianon, but stayed only a short time because the band was so mediocre. It was only 10:30 P.M., so I suggested we head for Lincoln Gardens to hear Pop-Eye Oliver and Louis Armstrong. This was a pretty daring thing for a couple of young Iowa country boys to do, as Lincoln Gardens was in a very tough, dangerous neighborhood. That didn't deter us, we were so anxious to hear Pop-Eye and Louie. When we got to Lincoln Gardens, the ticket man refused to sell us a ticket. Said we were not old enough. But luck was with us. Louie happened to be close-by during the break between dances, saw what was going on, and came over to the ticket man and said "It's OK. I know this boy, you can let them in". Orey and I sat on the platform right next to Louie sopping up that out-of-this-world music.

From this first meeting with Louie, he and I developed a close bond of friendship that lasted until he passed away in 1971. ...Louie was such a great show-man and his "Scat" style of singing became so popular that he became what has to be the greatest jazz musician that ever lived. Louie stumbled onto the "Scat" singing quite by accident.

He was making a recording of "Heebie Jeebies" and was supposed to sing a chorus. He did not know the lyrics by heart so had had them typed on a sheet of paper. About a third way through the chorus he accidentally dropped the sheet of paper. Rather than interrupt the recording, he started to sing a sort of mumbo-jumbo while he picked up the paper, then resumed the words after he had retrieved the paper. If you will listen to the record you can hear his voice gradually fade and then come back as he stooped over to pick up the paper. The record became a phenomenal success and started Louie off on this inimitable style of singing. His style on cornet was outstanding and he had an upper range of C above high C. There was no apparent limit to his stamina and he could play for hours upon hours without seeming to wear down.

He sweated profusely and always kept a stack of handkerchiefs nearby with which to mop his face and brow. Whenever I went to hear Louie play, I would take him half a dozen handkerchiefs with his initial in one corner. Louie became renowned as an Ambassador of Good Will, gaining an enviable reputation the world over.

Jack Teagarden, the trombonist, was also a close friend of mine. I would class him the Bix of trombonists. He had the smoothest, easiest, sweetest style imaginable. He could not read a note but carried a 3" x 5" card of chord formations around to refresh himself from time to time. He was part American Indian. He played for many years with Louie Armstrong and I am sure that one of the greatest bands ever assembled played one season in the old downstairs Blue Note on East Madison Street in Chicago.

The band was composed of Louie Armstrong, cornet; Jack Teagarden, trombone; Earl "Father" Hines, piano; Arville Shaw, bass fiddle; Barney Begard, clarinet; Sid Catlett, drums; and the incomparable Velma Middleton, vocalist. She must have weighed three hundred pounds. She and Louie would bring the house down when they vocalized "That's My Desire" together or when she would go through the motions of a high-kicking dance. This band was Dixieland jazz at its very best.

Jean Yelle did not identify the gentleman in the bowtie but that's her dad, Harold Oerman on the far left and Bob Struve beside him at their table with Jack Teagarden on a break from performing at Rock Island's Horseshoe Club.

HAROLD TEEN

Ray Eisele and I drove my *Harold Teen Ford* to Chicago to visit with Bix....
—Larry Andrews

Many on the Illinois side of the Quad Cities remember Vic's hamburger joint. It was a converted streetcar on 14th Street between 4th and 5th Avenues in Moline and served hamburgers between two slices of bread, in lieu of a bun. The old comic strip, *Harold Teen*, often featured Vic's in its storyline.

Long before America ever heard of Archie, Harold Teen was the quintessential American teenager. The strip was created in 1919 by Moline-born Carl Ed—rhymes with *feed*, not *fed*.

His full name was Carl Frank Ludwig Ed. He entered Augustana College at age fourteen and through the encouragement of his college art teacher, submitted and published his first political and sports cartoons in the Rock Island *Argus*. The pay wasn't enough to live on, so while working at night on comic strips, he pulled day shifts at various local factories—as a trimmer in a buggy shop, then a riveter of railroad cars, later as an automobile test driver. When he met and married Ellen Schwack of Rock Island, he was working as a timekeeper at the Rock Island Arsenal. That was followed by a billing clerk job for Moline People's Power Company.

Without Carl's knowledge the *Argus* editor had submitted samples of his work to the World Color Syndicate in St. Louis. He was hired at $15 a week to draw his *Big Ben* strip about a baseball fan. After two years of producing six strips a week, Carl asked for a raise but didn't get it, which meant moving back to Rock Island in 1913 to live with his wife's parents.

Soon after, he was offered full time work as a cub reporter at the *Argus*. That eventually led to being a sports editor and eventually city editor for the Rock Island paper. But he never abandoned his cartooning, having developed a new baseball strip called *Luke McGluke, the Bush League Bearcat* that was distributed by World Color Syndicate.

In 1918, he was offered a job at the *Chicago Evening American* newspaper and it was while working there that he met silent screen star Harold Lloyd, his inspiration for Harold Teen, a comic strip about teenagers.

Carl successfully pitched his strip to *Chicago Tribune* co–owner Captain Joe Patterson and *The Love Life of Harold Teen* premiered in February 1919 and went national as *Harold Teen* in May of that same year through the Chicago Tribune Syndicate. At the height of its popularity in the '20s and '30s, Harold Teen shared the comics section in more than 300 newspapers with the likes of *Little Orphan Annie, Gasoline Alley, The Gumps,* and *Alley Oop*.

Harold drove a beat–up Ford he called the *Leaping Lena* and popularized teen slang such as *Yowsah* and *pantywaist*. Harold and the gang hung out at Pop Jenk's Sugar Bowl and the *gedunk* sundae, a favorite of Pop's customers became a cultural phenomenon.

WWII Marines and sailors adopted the term *gedunk* for sweets or candy. Pronounced gee–dunk with a hard G, its use extended to slang for greenhorn sailors.

The Sugar Bowl, where Harold and girlfriend Lillums Lovewell and sidekick Shadow Smart hung out, was based on a sweet shop near Carl's house in Evanston, IL.

Harold Teen also popularized bell–bottom pants and his signature yellow raincoat would be identified a generation later with Dick Tracy.

Sheiks and shebas, honeybuns and twerps, twits and drips—educators complained but kids loved that Harold spoke their language. Carl kept up with

HAROLD TEEN GETS JAZZED —FEB 1924

the ever-changing teen vernacular through his daughter, Donna Jean—who later married RCA Victor recording director Fred Reynolds—and her friends.

In a 1931 interview Carl told of the origins of his popular strip. He said that shortly after World War I, the idea of a prolonged adolescence, whereby a person hovered between childhood and adulthood instead of going to work by age 14, hadn't yet completely penetrated mainstream consciousness. Comics themselves were only a couple of decades old. "There was no comic strip on adolescence," he said, "I thought every well-balanced comic sheet should have one."

Toys and merchandise tie-ins with popular breakfast cereals made Harold Teen the Harry Potter of his day. Along with a Whitman *Big Little Book* and a couple of Dell comic book features, Carl Ed's characters made it to the big screen in 1928. The strip's title character was played by Arthur Lake, who later played Dagwood to Penny Singleton's Blondie. Song-and-dance-man Hal LeRoy took over the lead role in the 1934 musical comedy.

Harold, Lillums, Shadow, Pop Jenks and the rest of the Sugar Bowl gang were laid to rest after Carl's death at age 69 on October 10, 1959.

Carl Ed (1890–1959)

Gramps and Shadow head to Vic's Diner

SODA JERK

For all of you young whippersnappers out there, back in the 1920s–1940s, soft drinks were referred to as *soda pop* and those who worked behind the counter dispensing such drinks were called *soda jerks*, which was the shortened form of soda jerker.

Mr. Webster defines a soda jerk as a person who prepares and serves sodas and ice cream at a soda fountain. Smart guy, that Mr. Webster.

In the 1920s, E.A. Moetzel owned a drug store and soda fountain at 1511 Harrison Street in Davenport. Post Office station No. 2 had a space in Moetzel's store and his family lived in an apartment above the store. Across the street was the J.M. Bowling and Billiards. Today, the building that once housed the Moetzel drugstore still stands and currently is Lumpy's Tavern.

Moetzel's daughter Antoinette married Bix's second cousin, Ceno Petersen.

The store was just three blocks north of the high school, no doubt a popular place with students. A young 17–year–old Bix Beiderbecke, struggling through his junior year at Davenport High, now Central High School, worked at the soda fountain after school and on weekends, when he didn't play a gig somewhere.

Moetzel Drug, 1509 N. Harrison—Now: Lumpy's Tavern

Eipper's Drug, 312 E. Locust—Now: Cy's Rental

DRUGSTORE HARMONIES
from the journal of Helen Eipper Giltner, 1982
with permission from her daughter Marie Smith

My acquaintance with Bix Beiderbecke was when I was in high school. I graduated in 1921. My father August Eipper, a pharmacist, had his drug store and soda fountain on East Locust Street in Davenport. He was the type of person who drew young people, especially boys, to him, just to visit and many, many times for help and advice.

We were very close and for many years I helped him at the store, even before I entered high school. Daddy was very musical and played the guitar and mandolin. When it was quiet, especially on a rainy evening, we would go to the prescription department where there was a window seat in a bay window. From there, we could see the customers as they came in the store. Daddy kept his guitar back there so we could sing and play together.

AUGUST EIPPER

One night Bix wandered in while we were harmonizing. He motioned for us not to get up and hurried back to where we were. He listened a while and then asked if he could join us. After that night he came quite often, especially on rainy nights, and the three of us would harmonize, sometimes for several hours at a time. *Play a Simple Melody* was a favorite song. Of course, there were many interruptions to take care of customers, but we had lots of fun.

Bix would come to the store on school holidays, weekends, and vacations during the day so we visited quite a lot when I wasn't busy. We'd compare classes and social activities of our schools mostly. He went to public high

Two interior views of Eipper Drug Store, c. 1920s

school and I attended Immaculate Conception Academy as a day schooler in a girl's boarding school. The I.C.A. is now the co–ed Assumption High School in Davenport. I think Bix had a hard time comprehending an all–girl's school, as he would laugh at some of our affairs such as girls dancing together. We both played the piano, he by ear, and I by note. I lived across the street from the store so one evening we went over and tried very hard to teach each other how to play *our way*. Needless to say, it was hopeless but fun.

He seemed to be a *loner*, not lonely, but just alone. He'd talk about going to parties but I don't remember ever hearing him mention dating. One night he came in all dressed up. On inquiring why, he answered, "Oh my brother and sister are having a party. I had to get dressed up to greet the guests but I couldn't stay around...all that stuff and smooching." They were several years older than Bix.

His main interest was music. I remember him being quite concerned one spring. He wanted to play with a band on an excursion boat and the requirements were very strict. His worry was about playing so much by ear. But somehow he managed it as I can remember being on a one–day excursion and he was playing. Another interest we had in common was we both played horns in our school bands.

HELEN EIPPER

I finished high school before he did and went on to teach school the next year. That summer was the last time I saw him. He went on to play in bands, but when he came home for visits he'd go to the store and ask daddy about me. This pleased me very much, especially since he stopped on his last visit home.

Davenport YMCA, c. 1918

Martin Cigar Store, 2nd & Brady

MEET ME AT THE Y

Jim Stroehle is a prominent Quad–City drummer whose dad used to hang out with Bix when both were kids. "My dad, Joe Stroehle, played piano and said that Bix knew chords that weren't even invented yet so Dad tried to meet Bix wherever there was a piano. He wanted to learn some of those neat chords.

"The YMCA at Fourth and Harrison had a piano so Dad would set up a meeting with Bix there. Then Dad, who attended Harrison School a short distance away, would wait for his teacher to leave the room, which she frequently did late afternoons. As soon as the door closed behind her, Dad would open a window, jump out, and head for the YMCA. Somehow, he never got caught.

"Dad said that back then Bix was playing 9ths, 13ths, and other exotic chords that local piano players had never heard of. His only regret was when Bix left Davenport to attend Lake Forest Academy. That ended his piano lessons with Bix."

Jim's dad went on to be one of the Quad–Cities' first–class pianists and bassists until his death in 1986.

Joe Stroehle on bass with Paul and Curly Licata, photographed by Les Swanson on Feb. 9, 1941

BIX ONBOARD
by Les Swanson

There's an old notion that one did not become a bona fide jazz musician until he had served time on the Mississippi riverboats.

Bix did this in two rather short stints on the *Majestic*, and the *Capitol*. He was eighteen in 1921 when the musician's union intervened and ordered him off the *Capitol* because he was "just a kid who couldn't read a note of music." He lasted thirteen days with the Majestic Plantation Orchestra, and just ten days with Doc Wrixon's Capitol Harmony Kings.

D.W. Wisherd's *Majestic* was a popular excursion boat and major competitor of the Streckfus Line excursions on the Upper Mississippi.

Bix was recruited on June 21st for the *Majestic's* round–trip from Davenport to St. Paul. He replaced trumpet player Chet Ogden, who was called home to Geneseo because of a family emergency. Bix thoroughly enjoyed the gig, brief as it was.

The Plantation boys loathed written music, playing everything out of their hats. Band members were Romie Siemon, piano; Wade Foster, violin; Al Woodyatt, sax; Pee Wee Rank, drums; and Bob Strove, trombone.

Anticipating trouble with their local musician union moguls, the entire band joined in Missouri. However, the Davenport union refused to recognize that affiliation and they were pulled off the job when they got back here.

Only Siemon was allowed to stay on the *Majestic* when the captain explained that he was sorely needed for playing the calliope.

I played with most of these jazz men in the 1920s and in the '30s. I took some lessons from Siemon when he became program director of radio station WHBF in Rock Island. He later moved to California where his drawing skills led to a couple of syndicated comic strips in the early '50s.

After the *Majestic* band was unceremoniously kicked off the boat, Bix's second job came by way of some sort of a musician's mutiny on the Steamer *Capitol*.

Some of the hottest jazz men of their day were in that band, including George Brunies, Emmett Hardy, Leon Roppolo, and Santo Pecora. It was said that they became bored with dentist–turned–drummer Albert Wrixon's stock arrangements.

Steamer Capitol and the band Bix had to quit in 1921 below, l-r: Bobby Watson, John Sheppard, Hal Conger, Omer van Speybroeck, Byron Webb, Vic Sell, Grant Harris, and Albert 'Doc' Wrixon

Steamer Majestic docked at Fort Madison, IA, one of the stops during Bix's June 1921 gig with musicians illustrated below by Rome Siemon for jazz historian Phil Evans

When they left, Doc Wrixon had to recruit eight more musicians in twenty-four hours, including Bix on cornet and Omer *Spy* van Speybroeck on sax.

Spy told me that it was just after July 4th that he and Bix sat on their instrument cases for two hours at the Davenport levee while waiting the arrival of the *Capitol*.

The new band struggled through Wrixon's old arrangements fairly well and Bix played along with his usual counter-melody licks. According to Spy, Wrixon wasn't too happy with Bix's inability to read the charts.

When the boat returned to Davenport from its cruise between Hannibal, MO, and Winona, MN, the union reception committee was there to order Bix off the job once more. Wrixon apologized to both the union men and Bix, and promised to obtain a card-carrying replacement immediately.

Spy told me that Bix had the time of his life on the boat. Bix took a liking to the calliope music. He and Spy would ham it up playing duets, Spy on the bass notes while Bix played the higher keys.

As a calliope player on eight different boats, I imagine it must have been quite crowded with four hands on a keyboard of two and a third octave.

Spy said they got to hear Fate Marable's band on the Streckfus sister excursion boat *St. Paul*. He also remembered that Bix spent his leisure time at the *Capitol's* ballroom piano experimenting with spread formations and chord progressions.

Bix would never play a complete number, according to Spy, but concentrated on intricate chords and phrases. Some of these chords are probably in his composition, *In a Mist*.

I remember on the dates that I played with Bix, he doodled with what he called his *M.F.* or *Mist Feeling* chords. He often remained on the stage during intermissions working out things on the piano while other band members headed for the bar.

On one occasion, he showed me a progressive spread ending, which I still occasionally use. I asked if he had used it in his compositions and he replied, "Not yet."

He never finished it because the end came only a few months later.

OTHERS WHO KNEW BIX

HEAD FULL OF MUSIC

Bix and I joined the band on the excursion boat, Capitol, together. No it wasn't our idea when we joined the boat to become great musicians. It was just a good job, a girl in every port, we thought, a sailor sort of thing.

We were just kids who'd both played a little with local bands. We all knew how good Bix was, but he wasn't on the boat very long. He wasn't too good at reading music and Doc Wrixon, who had the band on the boat, was pretty strict. You had to do things just the way he wanted them.

Anyway, after Bix left the boat he immediately got a better job with another band.

We musicians thought Bix was marvelous. He could sit at the piano and come up with ideas and beautiful chord changes.

I never knew Bix to do any drinking, at least not while I was around him. He always went right on and played, and played very well too.

I became a professional saxophonist, playing mostly in Chicago, and saw him backstage there once when he was with Paul Whiteman.

One time on the boat, Bix and I played a calliope duet, maybe the only time and surely the first time he'd ever played a calliope. I played the melody and Bix the chords. Worked out pretty well, too.

I liked the guy. He wasn't rowdy. His head was just full of music. Sometimes on a long haul on the boat he'd sit on the dance floor alone and play.

Bix had a knack for playing rhythm. Some trumpet players tried to copy him back in those days and still do today.

When I heard Bix was dead, I was shocked. I never knew he was such a rounder. I think he just wasn't able to take the drinking and sickness.

—Omer van Speybroeck, East Moline (1901 –1991)

D=A=N=C=I=N=G COLISEUM
TONIGHT, SUNDAY and TUESDAY

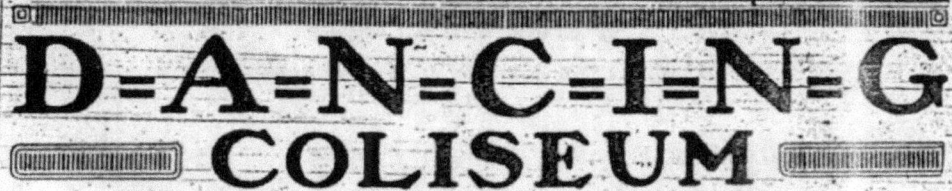

COME TO THE BIGGEST PLACE

WRIXON AND HIS 7---Piece Orchestra---7

Always the Latest and Best—20,000 Feet of Floor Space

1,000 Electric Lights   Always a Good Time

WRIXONS COLISEUM "JAZZ" ORCHESTRA

DID NOT KNOW BIX THE LEGEND
Excerpts from WARREN POSTEL'S 1985 letter
to the Davenport High School Class of '23 Secretary

I knew Bix the person. I did not know Bix the legend.

Bix and I knew each other in DHS before he was kicked out in 1921 and after failing most of his studies for the second time around. He was sort of shy, rather quiet, nice looking and a good sand lot ball player. I never heard him play a horn until I bought some records the Wolverines cut for [Gennett] Records after he had been kicked out of Lake Forest Academy. He played the piano at parties, could not read a note but had a perfect ear, and now and then he played with a small combo for the Friday dances in the DHS gym. I remember his house on Grand Avenue and his mother telling me Bix had taken piano lessons from Professor Ernst Otto* who for many years led the Davenport Orchestra and Otto's Band which played in the two parks.

I saw Bix again in the mid–1920s in New York when he was with the Goldkette Band and once in Los Angeles when he was with Paul Whiteman. He was at the height of his all too short jazz career. The last time I saw him was late in 1929 in Davenport. He had just returned from a month at the [Keeley] Institute where Paul Whiteman had sent him to dry out. I remember he was pudgy, and did not look at all well. He seemed cheerful and planned to rejoin Whiteman in 1930. He was playing at Danceland and the LeClaire Hotel in Moline and I recall the Kappa Delta dance at the Black Hawk Hotel and he was in the band. At times he was brilliant and at other times he was not. He looked like death warmed over. I remember seeing Vera Cox and her husband Ferd Korn that night. Bix dated Vera a few times but I suspect she saw a better future being married to Ferd who was with the family bakery. His brother Chuck was in my class. As you know Bix did not rejoin the Whiteman Band and that less than two years later on 6 October [sic August] 1931 he was dead, His legacy was some records, most with very short solo parts, and three piano compositions which were set down to music by Bill Challis who had been an arranger for the Goldkette and Whiteman organizations and who was Bix's friend and really tried to take care of him. That Bix had elements of greatness is possible. That he chose to throw it all away is fact....

*Although violinist Ernst Otto did head up the school's orchestra for a time, likely Mr. Postel meant Charles Grade as the piano teacher mentioned by Aggie Beiderbecke

WEDNESDAY EVENING — THE DAVENPORT DEMOCRAT AND LEADER — MAY 16, 1923

SELECTED FOR THE CAST OF "THE COUNTRY COUSIN"

 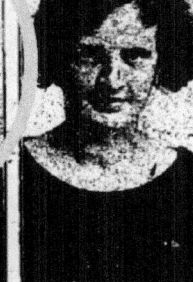   

WARREN POSTEL — ONALEE DAWSON — RUTH BODE — ALDENE PARSONS — MAX WEAVER

"The Country Cousin" is Play Selected to Be Presented by Davenport High School Seniors

"THE Country Cousin," a four-act comedy by Booth Tarkington and Julian Street, has been selected by the faculty as the play to be presented by the Davenport high school seniors this year. The faculty committee is composed of Principal Marshall, Miss Johnson and Miss Esther Russell.

Miss Aldene Parsons and Miss Ruth Bode have been chosen for the leading feminine roles. Miss Parsons is an active member of her class and has done excellent work in the English department of the school. She will carry the part of Eleanore Howitt, a flapper-like daughter, who is highly amusing on account of her "little girl" troubles. Miss Bode has been a member of the staff on both the school paper and annual. Her work in forensics has also been excellent. She will have the role of Nancy Price, the best-looking, intelligent girl in the United States, who is just bubbling with humor.

The leading male roles were awarded to Warren Postel and Max Weaver. Postel is active in the English department of the school and is a captain in the R.O.T.C. unit. He has been selected to carry the part of Sam Wilson, the college boy, who is deeply in love with Eleanore. Max Weaver will carry the role of George Tewksbury Rey-holds, another chap who falls for the good-looking country cousin, Nancy Price.

Miss Onalie Dawson, who has been selected for the heavy role of Mrs. Maud Howitt, is a prominent member of her class and a member of the annual staff. Much of the success of the play is based on her part.

Other members of the cast are as follows:

Miss Howitt .... Lois Klenze
Stanley Hewitt .... Dale Tullis
Abigale Wainwright ....
.... Bernice Pollock
Mrs. Jane Kinney ...... Lois Duvall
Cyril Kinney .... Frank Hodgdon
Archie Gore .... Charles Korn
Pruitt .... Roy Fletcher
Blake .... Edward Jones

The selecting of the play and the cast covered a period of several weeks. Many plays were read by the faculty committee and "The Country Cousin" was believed to be the best for a high school production. Altho four acts are rather long for high school artists to present, the cast that has been selected are so capable that the committee has no doubt that the play will be a huge success.

At the present time no definite time has been set for the presentation of the play. It will, no doubt, be given in a downtown theater. Last year the play was presented at the Columbia theater during the last school week in June. Most likely, the play will be presented at the same time this year.

Student committees who will have charge of the production of the play will be announced by class president, James Camp, in a few days.

The first rehearsals will be held the first of next week. Miss Johnson, instructor of public speaking at the school and a well-known amateur play producer, will have charge of the play.

WARREN POSTEL
DHS Play 1923
DHS alumni letter: 20 Nov 1985

96 Dublin Drive,
Pleasant Hill, Ca. 94523,
20 November 1985.

Dear Ruth:

Thank you for the October Newsletter. There are still a few faces that I am able, in my mind's eye still associate with a name. Of course it is not the same face that now exists but the one I knew 62 years ago. Marie Bretcher, Jacque McCool, Chuck Warner and Fritz "Putsie" Putsier whose trumpet like Bix Beiderbecke's became a legend. Fritz, Wayne Sheliff, Eaton Spurrier should have been Pallbearers at Bix's funeral but were not asked for some reason or other by the family. There were no jazz musicians. My father sent me a clipping from the Davenport Democrat and the only mention that associated Bix with this new art form was a mention that Paul Whiteman has sent a 6 foot tall cornet done in roses. I knew Bix the person. I did not know Bix the legend.

Bix and I knew each other in DHS before he was kicked out in 1921 after failing most of his studies for the second time around. He was sort of shy, rather quiet, nice looking and a good sized lot player. I never heard him play a horn until I bought some records that the Adverts cut for Gennet Records after he had been kicked out of Lake Forrest Academy. He played the piano at parties, could not read a note but had a perfect ear, and now and then he played with a small combo for the Friday dances in the DHS gym. I remember his house 1964 Grand Avenue and his mother telling us Bix had taken piano lessons from Professor Ernst Otto who for many years led the Davenport Orchestra and Otto's Band which played in the two parks.

I saw Bix again in the mid-1920s in New York when he was with the Goldkette Band and once in Los Angeles when he was with Paul Whiteman. He was at the height of his all too short jazz career. The last time I saw him was late in 1929 in Davenport. He had just returned from a month at The Keely Institute where Paul Whiteman sent him to dry out. I remember he was puffy, and did not look at all well. He seemed cheerful and planned to rejoin Whiteman in 1930. He was playing at Danceland and the LeClaire Hotel in Moline and I recall the Kappa Delta dance at the Black-Hawk Hotel he was in the band. At times he was brilliant and at other times he was not. He looked like death warmed over. I remember seeing Vera Cox and her husband Ford Korn that night, Bix dated Vera a few times but I suspect she saw a better future being married to Ford who was with the family bakery. His brother Chuck was in my class. As you know Bix did not rejoin the Whiteman Band and that less than two years later on 6 October 1931 he was dead. His legacy is some records, most with very short solo parts, and three piano compositions which were set down to music by Bill Challis who had been an arranger for the Goldkette and Whiteman organizations and who was Bix's friend and really tried to take care of him. That Bix had elements of greatness was possible. That he chose to throw it all away is fact. That he was born in Davenport gave the city a legend. Bix probably would have said "Oh Shit".

Howard Brandenburg and Bernice "Bunny" Pollock were in my class. Bunny was in the cast of our class play "The Country Cousin" by Booth Tarkington, a comedy in four acts written I think in 1917. She played the part of Athalie Wainright. The other members of the cast were Lois Klenze, Aldene Parsons, Ruth Bode, Max Weaver, Dale Tullis, Lois Duval, Frank Hodgdon, Onalee Dawson, Charles Korn and myself in the lead role of Sam Wilson, The Country Cousin. Most of us had been in the Women's Club

BUSTED IN PEORIA

Yet another chapter with Bix and the excursion boats, this by way of Mildred Otto who told of Bix having signed on for a job aboard the Steamer *Julia Belle Swain* in Peoria. The original *JBS* paddle–wheeler offered excursions on the Illinois River between Peoria and St. Louis during the 1918–1924 seasons and then transferred to Pittsburgh where it operated on the Ohio until being destroyed by fire in 1931.

Without ever having blown a note, Bix had to cancel his gig on the *JBS* because his parents ruled that he was too young at age sixteen to be working with a jazz band on a steamboat. Before leaving Peoria, Bix recommended Mildred's husband, Ray Otto of Davenport, for the job. Bix and Ray had often played together in youth bands.

Ray served as secretary of AFM Local #67 from 1930 to 1936. He played trumpet with the Tri–City Symphony Orchestra and several big bands. While union secretary, Ray frequently filled in with out–of–town bands that were short a man in their brass sections. He was a terrific sight reader but seldom took solos on improvised tunes, Mildred said, adding that he was one of maybe a dozen musicians back then who played with the symphony one day and a jazz band the next.

Mildred Otto rattled off names of QC's '20s–era big bands including Carlisle Evans, Tony's Iowans, Bill Greer, Jimmy Hicks, Trave O'Hearn, Harry Rathjen, Art Kurth, Herb Heuer's Whiz Bangs—a 12–piece band that frequently played over radio station WOC; Ralph Miedke's Society Orchestra, I.M. Ross, Thompson's Melody Boys, Art Whalen, Heavy Elder, Emil Flindt, Rome Siemons, Bernie Schultz, Johnny Day, Larry Drew's Ambassadors, and Doc Wrixon's Capitol Kings.

Wrixon had abandoned his dental practice to lead his band. Les Swanson recalled having rubbed elbows with Ray Otto in both the Trave O'Hearn and Doc Wrixon units. The pay scale for dance bands in the 1920s was six

WAYNE ROHLF

Bernie Schultz and Orchestra to Go on Tour

Davenport's Crescent Organization Will Record for Victor.

'It will be all aboard for Canada: for Michigan and for Florida, too, when Bernie Schultz and his Crescent orchestra from station WOC at Davenport, Ia., push out from the old home town next Thursday to show the world' that Iowa produces real musicians as well as tall corn.

For Bernie Schultz, who played for 18 months with the world-famous Paul Whiteman orchestra, and who was well known in the East for his work on the Keith circuit and with various orchestras of note, is taking his 10-piece Davenport orchestra on a tour that he expects will reflect considerable credit on the home city.

The Crescents will go first to Erie Beach, Ontario, Canada, for a four-weeks engagement and will then move to Paw Paw Lake in Michigan where they will spend the next 12 weeks at the famous Michigan resort. About the middle of September they will head for Coral Gables, Fla., and a winter in the Southland.

On Sept. 1 the Schultz orchestra will record its first record for the Victor people under the name of the Crescents from WOC of Davenport.

The ten-piece Crescent orchestra is composed entirely of Tri-City musicians. The young men who will accompany Mr. Schultz on the tour are Wallace Bowlby, Rock Island, Eddie Anderson, Moline, and Omar Haugland, Davenport, all saxophone players; James Ross, banjo; Wayne Rohlf, trumpet; Art Wunder, trombone; Vic Carlson, piano; John Day, drums, and Al Waffle, tuba. Mr. Schultz plays the trumpet and violin and is also the director.

Schultz Orchestra: John Day, drums; Vic Carlson, piano; Omar Haugland, Eddie Anderson and Wallace Bowlby, saxophone; director Bernie Schultz and Wayne Rohlf, trumpet; Al Waffle, tuba; Art Wunder, trombone; and James Ross, banjo and violin.

Davenport Democrat & Leader May 26, 1926

Above: Wayne Rohlf Orchestra at Danceland in 1928

dollars a man for the 8–midnight engagements plus $1.50 for each hour of overtime. The union adhered to that scale even during the Depression although some outfits would occasionally take a job for $4 per man.

At one point, Tony's Iowans merged with Carlisle Evans. The band included Tony Catalano on trumpet, Bob Struve, trombone, a sax section of Wade Foster, Nate Marblestone and Dick Hoffmeister; Carlisle Evans on piano, Louis Black on banjo, and Rich Mueller on drums.

Many local groups simply faded into oblivion when the Great Depression reached its depth in 1931. Evans and Hicks were among the first that folded. Trave O'Hearn and Heavy Elder bands survived through the early 1930s.

Mildred said her husband Ray spent a few years playing with the Harry Brondel Orchestra in Rock Island. He left the secretary's post to take a position with the U.S. Corps of Engineers at the Clock Tower on Arsenal Island, but continued playing his horn on weekends.

Mildred recalled that winter of 1929–30 when Bix was back home. She chatted frequently with him while he had gigs with Jimmy Hicks, Leo Bahr and the Danceland Orchestra. She said that Bix seemed in good spirits and expressed confidence that he had licked the alcohol problem.

WHITEMAN COMING TO HEAR BIX PLAY

I was from Welton, Iowa, and then moved to Davenport, though I didn't know Bix there. But my sister, Cora Neels, went to Davenport High School with him.

It was in Detroit, Michigan, that I first met Bix. I used to go to the Greystone Ballroom in Detroit where he was playing.

Bix was glad to see someone from home. We had a good time one night. I went with him and arranger Paul Mertz on a sleighing party out to Island Lake after a big snow storm. It was very pretty. We all piled in a big horse drawn sled. It was maybe 1927.

I don't know of any hard–drinking on Bix's part. Oh, it was the era of raccoon coats and on the sleigh ride everyone had enough bottles that were passed around. I didn't notice Bix drinking, though maybe he did. I didn't see much of him after that night.

Bix was not a womanizer, just a nice kid, always a gentleman. One night he told me that Paul Whiteman was coming to listen to him play. That was a big thing. Whiteman was very important. It could be a tremendous break for Bix, the top of the musical ladder. "Are you going to go with Whiteman?" I asked.

Bix said, "No, I like to play with this gang." Later, though, he joined Whiteman.

There were two bands at the Greystone and when his wasn't playing and I was there Bix would dance with me. He was a good dancer, too. He had the rhythm.

Around 1930 or 1931 I ran into Bix back in Davenport. He said to call him sometime and we'd go out. Well, we never did.. He told me, "You know, I'm not drinking anymore." It was just a few months later that he was dead.

—Cletis Sparks, Clearwater, FL (1914–1991)

ONE DRINK GOOD AS 400

I first met Bix in the early '30s when I was playing cornet at the Blackhawk Hotel with the Trave O'Hearn Band.

When I first heard Bix was going to play with our band, I'd thought I'd get to the hotel a half hour early and try to meet him. So, I got to the Gold Room and there was a man there already on the stand, smoking a pipe.

He stuck out his hand and said, "Bix Beiderbecke's my name."

Prohibition was on then, so I delicately asked Bix if he'd like a drink. He looked at me and replied, "No, if I have one drink, it's as good as 400."

I played with him then, too, on the Jimmy Hicks band, and later at the Fort Armstrong Hotel in Rock Island. I sat down next to Bix and he said, "I don't read, so will you play first cornet?" I knew he played by ear. After playing the cornet for a while, Bix switched over to piano. At the end of the dance it was pretty late, but Bix came over and asked if I had a car. When I said I did, he said, "good, then let's go out to the Bluebird," which was a joint out on the edge of town.

I told Bix that I couldn't go, that I had to get up in the morning to go to my regular job. Bix was pretty incredulous. He couldn't imagine anyone wanting to do anything but play music.

—Mervyn J. *Bus* Howe, Davenport (1908–1988)

JAZZMAN'S MEMORIES
by Jim Arpy

Drummer and vaudeville veteran Glenn Sears rifled through a jazzman's deck of memories for this 1991 interview. Bix Beiderbecke turned up, King Oliver, Louis Armstrong, Wingy Manone, and Leon Roppolo, too. "Benny Goodman and Pete Fountain had nothing on Roppolo," he said.

As if their notes still echoed off the walls at the Col Ballroom in Davenport, Sears remembered savoring the sounds of Roppolo and Emmett Hardy and other New Orleans musicians.

"I can't exactly remember what some of the boys looked like, but who could forget the way they played! Emmett was a terrific trumpet player. So was Wingy, even though he only had one arm," Sears said.

Was Bix influenced by Emmett Hardy's trumpet styling?

GLENN SEARS 1903-1994

Sears, elegant at 86 and saber –honed, reached back some seventy decades while contemplating the question. "Not really, though I can't personally recall Bix meeting Emmett but he must have because he used to go down to the Col once in a while."

This nudged another thought from the past. "Bix was a different sort of person. An annual festival in his memory...Oh dear God, don't let Bix know about it 'cause he'll flip and flop in his grave.

"Bix wasn't outgoing; he stayed more or less in the background.

"If you asked Bix whether he'd rather go see Marilyn Monroe or sit in with some band there was no question but what he'd rather play all night, the hell with the girls."

"Still," Sears chuckled, "he took my girl away from me...Vera Cox."

Shy, retiring Bix?

"Yes. I guess he must have liked her a lot. He went out with her quite a few times. I liked her, too. I used to buy those little boxes of chocolate, four pieces to a box, and sit in front of her house on Bridge Avenue near Locust, just waiting for her to come out.

"Even though I was about fourteen or so, my mother would let me drive our big long 448 Packard and I'd pick up several girls just because I thought I was so darned smart. When Vera was along she was the one I'd take home last and first we'd go for a little ride. I'd just look at her and think how beautiful she was."

Was he upset when Bix took out his girl?

Sears pondered the question. "Well, no. I guess I figured Bix was harmless. That might be a heck of a thing to say. But it was true. If it had been some others I knew, I'd have worried, but Bix was never a girl-crazy kind of guy.

"I used to like to have Bix play with my band. I often played with Jimmy Hicks, who had a bigger band than mine. Les Swanson played piano most of the time when I played with Jimmy's band.

"But Bix—people just didn't understand him. I'd go on one of the boats with him once in a while and he always wanted to stand back or sit where he could watch the orchestra. All the time it was always music, music, music.

"When we'd leave the boat, we'd usually stop at Hamburger Pete's. Pete had a horse and wagon near Hickey's Cigar store at Second and Brady Streets and sold hamburgers, six for a quarter. Bix wasn't usually a big eater but he did love those hamburgers," Sears laughed.

"My brother played on the steamer *Washington* and I think they did hire Bix, but he only lasted a couple of weeks as I remember. Heck, that's been seventy years ago. It's pretty hard to remember now. But I can remember my telephone number from 1923— Kenwood 4134."

Sears got his first dance job at the age of eight or nine. "My folks took me down in the horse and buggy to the Hibernian Hall. I carried my bass drum upstairs and several of the other musicians they'd take it and hollered, 'get away from it, kid!' I protested: 'that's my drum,' and they said: 'Oh yeah, sure' and I guess I got slapped a few times before they finally realized that I was telling the truth."

Sears eventually led a succession of his own bands; among them the Dixielanders, Dixie Ramblers and Memphis Melody Boys. "The way I learned to play the drums was that my brother Hal played piano and Charlie Bates, a friend of ours, played violin. I had an old birdhouse and a couple of sticks and when the two of them would play, I'd beat on the birdhouse," Sears recalled.

"Later, Charlie Herzog, a musician, made a set of drums for me with a foot pedal of brass so I could hit the cymbals and bass drum. At first, they wanted to chase me away from the dance, but we played all the old tunes like *Everybody's Doing It* and it was a lot of fun. But about 11 pm I would get tired and I'd fall off the child's chair I was sitting on, onto the floor. I was little enough that the women wanted to pick me up and kiss me and I'd run and hide behind the piano."

At first Sears turned down his brother's offer of two dollars a week to play the Hibernian Hall dances with him, since he was too young to appreciate money. What finally won him over was his brother's Ingersoll dollar watch that he had long coveted.

"We played at the hall every Saturday night and eventually we added a clarinet. They hadn't even made saxophones yet. I'm talking about before anybody was born," Sears chuckled.

He remembered back when he was attending Tyler School, Bix was getting help from his brother Hal to read and write music. But apparently the lessons didn't last long. "Bix could play anything on the piano. But it was kind of ghastly stuff nobody could understand.

"He played with a different style. When I sang with my band, I sang more or less in counter harmony. Bix played quite a bit of counter melody on the trumpet," Sears said. "When Bix played with a bandleader like Jimmy Hicks, there might be three trumpet players, maybe Esten Spurrier and someone else and Bix out on the side playing the counter melody for all of the off–tunes that a lot of musicians didn't understand. Esten did. He had played a lot with Bix."

Sears explained, "Bix had a different way of slurring. Guys would listen to it and ask each other, 'what in the hell is that?' They'd turn him down for jobs. How surprised they all were when he died and Whiteman and some band members came here and there was so much fanfare.

"I guess we all about fainted when we learned Whiteman had hired Bix. We were booked at a theater in Trenton, New Jersey, when we learned where Whiteman was rehearsing and went to watch. It was a huge building and way down front was a half circle of about 25 seats for the Whiteman band. Then, so high up you'd almost need a stepladder to reach it, was one vacant seat.

"Whiteman came out, hit the stand with his baton and murmured, 'Well, well, well, again we always have one missing. Could it be there's anybody here who could sit in that seat?'

"Pretty soon a head we recognized as Bix's, and then a body materialized up there and he sat down, cracking, 'Yes, could it be me?'

"After Bix left Whiteman and came home, he'd go with me to Ma Henning's boarding house at Sixth and Main. Ma was a wonderful woman who had a piano slightly out of tune. She'd make cookies and Bix would play for her, though it used to kill him when she'd demand tunes like *In the Shade of the Old Apple Tree* to which she'd sing along. But Bix would try his best to jazz it up," Sears remembered.

Sears worked in the amusement business dealing with pinball machines, bowling alleys, juke boxes and the like. He also played on the ferryboat *W.J. Quinlan*. Later, he was on the road as a drummer in the Bernie Schultz band, playing presentation for the various acts.

He thinks he quite possibly gave Vaudeville's Ole Olsen and Chic Johnson the idea for the act that made them famous. Getting someone to sit in on drums, Sears would slip into a jumpsuit with oversized buttons and take a seat in a box, or at the rear of the theater. Chomping a banana, monkeylike, he'd make remarks about the adagio dancer's beauty. An usher would warn him, and finally begin to chase him with Sears winding up on stage, doing a fancy buck and wing and exchanging quips with the dancer.

Olsen & Johnson

In his early days, Sears was friends with Neil *Moon* Reagan and his brother, the future president Ronald *Dutch* Reagan, who was then a radio announcer at WOC. Sears was with the WOC Cardinals Orchestra for a while and used to chat with the Reagan brothers in the Palmer College cafeteria. He remembered *Dutch* Reagan as a bit of a smart aleck.

Harking back to Bix, Sears said, "He was just born too soon. I had a lot of Bix's records, including *In a Mist* and my wife sold them for a dime apiece at a garage sale.

"I remember times when Bix seemed lost in thought and I'd ask him what he was thinking about. He'd say something like, 'Oh, I'm in a cloud.' I often wondered if that was where the title for *In a Mist* originated.

"If you were around Bix and could have read his mind, you'd probably have seen that he was always trying to figure out some phrase on the cornet dial that would go in between a break. It was always music. He just loved it. I wish he could come back but just like then, I doubt many would understand him."

Sears recalled a night that his band was playing for a party at the Davenport Outing Club, "and who should show up to sit in but Louis Armstrong and Jack Teagarden, both taking a break from a gig at the Horseshoe in Rock Island. We played several of those old rag tunes and I was just loving myself beating those drums. Afterward the guy who sponsored the party came over and asked, 'who in the hell were those guys?' 'Just two of the greatest musicians in the world, I said and was told, 'well, don't let them sit in with you again. They stink.' See, he didn't understand them either."

In 1935, Sears was playing at Moline's LeClaire Hotel for performers who had won the Major Bowes Amateur Hour. Bowes signed the more talented of his contestants to six month vaudeville tours. "There was this one skinny kid with a golden voice and I played while he sang. Later I saw him backstage and said, 'Kid, you're darned good' and he said, 'Well, that's what they tell me.'

"I told him, 'if I weren't so busy I'd take you on as manager because I really think I could do something with you.' He thanked me and said he really could use a manager, though he expected to have one soon. Wasn't long after that he recorded with Tommy Dorsey and everybody knew his name—Frank Sinatra!"

Sinatra in the QC: 1935 Major Bowes Amateur Hour tour; with Tommy Dorsey at the Col in 1940; 1994 at the Mark with Frank Sinatra Jr. as his conductor

Ruby Keeler & Al Jolson

He said, I think trying just a bit to impress me, that he'd dated Ruby Keeler, but that he'd lost out to Al Jolson.
—Vera Cox Korn
in a 1967 interview for *Storyville* magazine

LORRY & LEE

Vera Cox had been voted one of three *most beautiful* in her high school class. She loved the stage. In a review of her performance in an amateur production at Immaculate Conception Academy in 1923, a reporter stated, "Miss Cox is very happy in her part of the petite French maid who is coy and very Frenchy and vivacious…" Vera might well have pursued an acting career but opted instead for marriage and family.

She was born Aug. 22, 1904, in Vermont, IL. The middle child of John and Mary Cox, Vera had one brother, Charles, who was six years older and a sister, Helen, five years younger. The family lived on Bridge Avenue in 1910 but moved to Iowa Street, living at three different addresses between Vera's grammar and high school years. Grandma Cox lived with them at 2815 Iowa St, according to the 1920 census record.

Bix lived three blocks away. He and Vera became classmates in the fall of 1921 when he had to repeat third grade after his bout with scarlet fever.

Vera was Bix's first girlfriend. "He regularly visited," Vera said. She recalled that he had a peculiar way of playing piano. With his fingers stiff on the keys, he spent hours playing chords, engrossed in his music. "His mother would have to call on the phone to ask that Bix be sent home for dinner."

Recalling Vera's stories about Bix, John Cox Korn told Phil Evans in a 1996 interview that his mother recalled Bix regularly coming to her house to play piano for them. "Both my mother and grandmother remember having to shake Bix while he was playing on the family upright. He was not asleep but apparently in whatever kind of reverie musical geniuses get in when they're playing."

It is a description of Bix's behavior told in similar terms by others who observed him at the piano. A neurologist might have considered the possibility of petit mal seizure.

VERA COX

**Davenport High School
1922 Yearbook**

**Cox House
1709 Bridge Avenue**

Vera at 17

There's been a number of suggested causes for his struggles at school. Seemed no matter his determination to do well, Bix fell behind as each school term progressed. Yet he demonstrated extraordinary retention of information. One of his New York musician friends recalled that Bix won all bets when it came to reciting verses from the Gideon Bibles in their hotel rooms on the road.

Even geniuses can be poor spellers, lousy at sentence structure and punctuation. These flaws made for a unique letter–writing style, as Vera described it. She said she regretted not keeping more of Bix's letters. But one that did survive was sent by him while she was visiting her mother's family in Vermont, IL:

Davenport High School's 1918 play cast, front row, L-R: Jack Shaefer, Merrill Lyons, Tiny Bechtel, Kenneth Emanuelson, Bix Beiderbecke; middle row, L-R: Blair Johnson, Ann Jennings, Gertrude Beiderbecke (Carl T's daughter), Karl Vollmer; back row, L-R: Tootsie Bechtel, Deborah Drury, Herb Buck, Lee Hohrs, and Vera Cox.

say yes
Davenport, Ia
July 10, '20
Dear Vera,
I'm sorry to say that I was asked at three parties at which I was take you one has passed, Doddy Dow's, at which I had to take Bunny Hansen at the last resort but I was filled with disappointment, emotion & beer at not being able to take you. Next Thursday is Hillie Kohler's* party at which I'm bound to take you, now Very, getting down to brass tacks will you come Wednesday and meet me at Galesburg or someplace and I'll bring you home, then Friday I'll take you to Geo. Von Maurs party. For the love of all good things wire one word yes and then I'll write all arrangements to meet you then if desired I'll take you back to continue your visit, please wire Yes. I might be able to beat fates time by having you here anyway if you'll only consent of all bad luck this is the worst to have all these partyies while your away. hurry & wire.

Tell your grandmother that old friendship is the best and you've decided that I'm about as good as anyone which I hope is true, —tell her you're coming back to me.
Well Lorry must close please answer. Yours Anxiously
Lee.
Say yes

*Hildegard Koehler, daughter of brewer Oscar Koehler was a cousin of George Von Maur and Karl Vollmer

Bix called Vera by her middle name. "He thought 'Lee' after Leon and Lorry went nicely together," Vera told Art Napoleon, who interviewed her for a *Storyville* magazine article, DAVENPORT DAYS, VERA COX REMINISCES (Issue #12, Aug–Sep 1967)

In that interview, Vera recounted the first time she watched Bix play the cornet in public. She said he hadn't had the horn very long and she was afraid he was about to embarrass himself. It was during their school vaudeville night at the Grand Theatre. All the kids were astounded at how good he'd become, Vera said. "He really thought he didn't have any talent, and was honestly surprised when he got to be famous," she added.

In a letter dated May 7th '20, written by Bix to his mom while in class at Davenport High:
Tonight I'm taking Vera L. C. to the R.I. class play with Karlie Vollmer

The play, A PAIR OF SIXES, was performed at the Illinois Theater by the 1920 senior class of Rock Island High School. Above, top left, is a billboard advertising the play; top right is a Watch Tower yearbook cast photo; bottom photo is the Illinois Theater.

Still standing on Second Avenue, the Illinois was used as a furniture store for many years before being converted to apartments on the upper floors and an art gallery on the main level. It was one of several Quad Cities theaters where Bix's uncle, Albert Petersen, conducted orchestras. Next door, left edge of the photo, is the Bowlby Music Store owned by the family of saxophonist Wallace Bowlby. Now a café, the upper floor at Bowlby's is where Harold Oerman was among the musicians who played with Bowlby before he joined the Capitol Syncopators.

'MISS SOMEBODY ELSE' CHARMS CLUB AUDIENCE

Comedy Is Most Cleverly Put on by Local Talent at the Academy.

"Miss Somebody Else" with Mrs. Edwin J. Bettendorf in the leading part and Robert McGregor as the hero and leading man, supported by a cast of unusually good local talent composed of: Mrs. A. C. Feddersen, Miss Deborah Silber, Weston Harris, Miss Vera Cox, Mrs. R. J. Smith, Mrs. Carl Richter, Mrs. Irwin Naeckel, Mrs. C. R. Miles, Miss Venita Koch, Mrs. Harold Bendixen, Hank Moeller and Earl Fries, put on the best performance of the kind the Davenport Woman's club has ever attempted, and one of the best local talent plays ever given in the Tri-Cities, at the program for Monday's general meeting of the club at the Immaculate Conception Academy.

There was keen anticipation over the theatricals on which club players have been working hard for many weeks.

St. Cecelia Auditorium was filled with an audience of 440 enthusiasts who became a laughter-swept, applauding, delighted throng of admirers as scene succeeded scene and one heard on every side evidence of keen enjoyment in: "Isn't is splendid?", "This is the best ever," "We sure have lots of talent right here in the club", and kindred sentiments, vocal of appreciation.

Mrs. Bettendorf in the leading role made a bewitching "Nora O'Brien". Disguising her personality of "Constance Darcy" the mining magnate's daughter, she becomes the waiting maid in a tea room, dons a servant's ruffled cap and frilled apron and incidentally plays the fairy god mother to the old friend of her mother who is in financial difficulties. She is really hunting for a young crook who has robbed her father—but that is "subrosa."

Robert McGregor as Cruger Blainwood, son of the society leader of the town is the gay and happy lover of Constance Darcy and discovers Nora's disguise. The scene was especially appealing in which he sings a love song to Nora as she plays in the twilight at the piano. Mr. McGregor was in fine voice and the scenes were so well liked they had to be repeated before the audience was satisfied.

Mrs. Smith as "Susan Ruggs," the maid servant of Mrs. Delevan was the hit of the afternoon. Her entrance brought a riot of hilarity; her "get up" convulsed the audience and her acting was something that kept the house in a spasm of laughter.

Susan's idea of a perfectly gorgeous time was reading the daily "obits", and she feels like a "wicked daughter of Babylon" amid the festive gaity of Mrs. Delevan's tea garden. Her final exit from the scene to become the bride of the undertaker is the climax of the most humorous line of incidents in the play.

Miss Cox is very happy in her part of the petite French maid who is coy and very Frenchy and vivacious but whom Susan scorns as a "Jezebel".

Mrs. Feddersen as the financially embarrassed tea room proprietor, Miss Deborah Silber, her young daughter; Mrs. Carl Richter the society leader; Mrs. Erwin Naeckel, her debutante daughter; Mrs. Harold Bendixen, Miss Venita Koch, and Mrs. C. R. Miles as pretty, fascinating society girls add charm and vivacity and color to the scenes of society life which are incidental to the play, while Weston Harris as Ralph Hastings brings to his part of the intriguing villian who dabbles in the affections of three pretty maids, considerable force and successfully meets the exacting demands put upon him in playing the care free happy lover, on all trying occasions.

Hank Moeller and Earl Fries as the awkward, but much in demand society men are excellent and combine in splendid support of the principals.

Miss Irma Dorgan was the graceful dancer who at the opening of the second act in the tea house garden scene, gave a Spanish dance dressed in a Spanish red heavily fringed crepe shawl. Mrs. Leo Wynes of Rock Island playing her accompaniment at the piano.

Club women are elated over the success of the play and the clever presentation the club players assisted by friends have gone to so much time and hard work in presenting.

Mrs. E. J. Bettendorf, chairman of the program committee of the club has been the inspiration in the undertaking, and the splendid support and assistance she has had from all who have taken part in the play is most gratifying.

The play will be given this evening at 8 o'clock in the Academy auditorium, before a sold out house, and its second evening presentation will be Wednesday.

Tickets will be sold at the door tomorrow night. Any one holding tickets this evening may use them Wednesday, but tickets for Wednesday evening will not be accepted tonight as every seat in the house is already sold.

4-10 1923

Miss Cox is very happy in her part of the petite French maid who is coy and very Frenchy and vivacious but whom Susan scorns as a "Jezebel".

Vera's son, John C. Korn, said his mother always got irritated with people who claimed Bix's middle name was not Bismark.

He liked repeating the story his mother told of when he was fifteen months old and Bix brought him a bag of peanuts. That was New Year's Day 1930. The night before, Vera and Ferdinand Korn had gone to the Rock Island Elks dance where Bix played with Jimmy Hicks band. Bix was on his twelfth week of sobriety.

Larry Andrews was playing banjo with the band that night. He drove Bix to the club and home again. "During intermission, he stayed on the bandstand because he wasn't drinking, and the place was loaded with drinkers," Andrews recalled, adding that Bix asked about the old gang, especially Vera.

Larry said she had married one of the Korn boys—the family owned a bakery. "When intermission was over, and we were playing our first number, Vera and her husband danced by. Bix and I looked at one another and laughed," Andrews said.

During the next set, Bix went over to talk to his old girlfriend and her husband. Vera recalled that "he, Bix that is, insisted on seeing our baby. He said, I think trying just a bit to impress me, that he'd dated Ruby Keeler, but that he'd lost out to Al Jolson."

Vera and Ferd lived in Pella, Iowa, and were spending the holidays with relatives in Davenport.

Besides their family's bakery, Ferd Korn and his brother Tom had been members of the Davenport Flying Club. The brothers were original investors in the *monocoupe aeroplane*. They served on the board of directors of Central States Aero Inc (CSA) which was charted October 12, 1926.

Don Luscombe, owner of an advertising company and a registered pilot, started CSA by convincing the Korns and other local businessmen of the need for a private plane they could fly while dressed in a business suit without the usual helmet, goggles, and flight overalls—arriving for a meeting as neatly as when they boarded their private plane.

Tom Korn was CSA's vice president. Ferd pitched the monocoupe to potential buyers. Luscombe's brother Robert also served on the board, as did Frank C. Wallace who owned an airfield in Bettendorf where the prototype monocoupe was tested. The plane was built in a former Bettendorf tabernacle.

Luscombe's design innovation was a cockpit styled like an enclosed two–seater motorcar. Passenger and pilot sat side by side instead of behind or in front. Luscombe hired Clayton Folkerts to engineer a working model of his design. Folkerts was later renowned for his champion racing planes.

The monocoupe made its inaugural flight from Moline airfield on April 6, 1927. Soon the company was getting worldwide requests, producing one plane a week with orders backing up quickly.

Moline–based automaker Velie Motors Co bought CSA and incorporated as Mono Aircraft Inc in February 1928. In October of that year, W.L. Velie died and within four months his son also died.

The monocoupe was sold to a St. Louis firm at Lambert Field and remains popular among collectors. Folks arriving at the QC International Airport pass beneath a Velie monocoupe, hanging from the lobby ceiling.

A mutual affinity for airplanes would have made for good conversation between the husband and old beau of Vera Cox.

It could have smoothed away any awkwardness over Bix offering a gift of goobers to their infant.

Planes and peanuts—ahead of his time there, too?

SOCIETY

Ferd Korn Tells Quota Members Why "Monocoupe" Is Popular with Flyers

Ferd Korn, one of the directors of the Central States Aero company, manufacturers of the Monocoupe, with factory in Bettendorf, spoke before Davenport Quota club members Thursday noon at the luncheon hour meeting at the Chamber of Commerce, and gave a most interesting and entertaining talk on the building of the miniature plane, which has become a great favorite with flyers.

Mr. Korn described the good points of the plane, its strong endurance, power and advantages over larger models.

"We have the advantage of the experiences of big plane manufacturers in building our model, and the ground we cover in consequence has comparatively little of the experimental, for we are building along the practical and utility lines which appeal and can be appreciated by every one who knows anything about flying," said Mr. Korn.

There was a description in detail of the various essential parts of the air machine, and circulars illustrating the miniature plane were handed about. Mr. Korn stated the factory was being enlarged; that other cities were after the company with inducements of money and factory sites; that the company which was first putting out a machine in three months or so now could turn out a perfectly finished, fully equipped Monocoupe in a week, that this would be doubled probably in a short time, and orders were coming in thick and fast, and the demand far exceeded the supply.

**Davenport Democrat & Leader 10-28-1927
Top photo:
Pilot Don Luscombe
Right: CSA's Monocoupe Aeroplane at Cram Field, Bettendorf 1927**

KARLIE VOLLMER

VERA COX
KARL VOLLMER
BIX BEIDERBECKE

Tonight I'm taking Vera L.C. to the R.I. class play with Karlie Vollmer....

Karl Koehler Vollmer—*Karlie* as Bix called him—was a cousin of George Von Maur and the son of Dr. Karl and Paula Vollmer. Dr. Vollmer was an eye, ear, nose and throat specialist and had an office in the Kahl building.

Uncle Henry Vollmer served three terms as Davenport mayor. He was 27 years old when first elected, youngest to serve the City. In 1914 he became a U.S. Congressman but lost the next term election after joining in on a legislative effort to enact an embargo while the U.S. remained neutral in Europe's Great War. Another uncle, Fred Vollmer, was charged with espionage in 1917.

Karl Vollmer's maternal grandparents were Henry and Ottilie Koehler. Henry Koehler Sr. worked at Arsenal Brewery before the Civil War. Located at River Drive and Mound Street in East Davenport near the coal company where Bix's dad had his office, the brewery became Koehler–Lange after 1871 when Henry Koehler and Rudolph Lange, sons–in–law of owner George Schlepp, took it over.

Uncle Oscar Koehler studied at Germany's famed Worms' academy for brewers. When Oscar returned to Davenport, he merged several small local breweries into the Davenport Malting Company. In 1894 he took over Koehler–Lange and married Rudy Lange's daughter Matilda. Their youngest child, Hilda 'Hillie' Koehler also was a schoolmate of Bix.

Oscar's company vied with its main competitor, Ernst Zoller's Independent Malting Co for exclusive distributorships among Scott County tavern owners.

Rather than alienate the drinking customers, both breweries bid on the expired leases of tavern keepers who didn't sign contracts with them.

With these properties sub-leased on a monthly basis and the tenant responsible for weekly, sometimes daily mulct tax payments, taverns fell into the hands of what other business owners deemed an *undesirable class of citizens*. This turf war is said to have been what led to the decline of East Second Street. Where Bix's grandfather had operated a successful wholesale grocery store became a neighborhood of brothels and bars.

Oscar Koehler's brewery sold malt liquor through druggists for medicinal purposes. When Iowa enacted full prohibition in 1884, Koehler-Lange introduced its Mumm beverage.

July 1884, *Davenport Democrat*:

> Messrs Koehler & Lange, the largest brewers of this city report that their new drink, Mumm, is meeting with success. Mr. Koehler said: "It is thoroughly non-intoxicating and contains, in place of the usual percentage of alcohol, different ingredients of a most excellent nature. With a pleasant pungency of flavor, and the quality of satisfying natural thirst quickly, it is perfectly pure, and thus becomes, from a sanitary view, especially commendable."
>
> This reporter tried a glass for himself and found it to be amber in color and sparkling, and its top was foamy. It was delicious to the tongue and palate, and indeed the whole system, for the weather was very, very sultry—and the long ride through the dust had created thirst. The *mumm* was delicious. It was as agreeable as lemonade—delightful as a mint julep and one could sip many glasses as he pleases and feel no more effected in the head than from good coffee.
>
> The firm feels jubilant over their success and thinks that they certainly have a drink equal to be but non-intoxicant. The beverage cannot be placed under the ban of law anymore than cider or coffee can—though the fact is the people may be deprived of these beverages yet. Any teetotaler, any radical prohibitionist can test it; if he or she could imbibe a dozen glasses of it, they would be no more intoxicated from it than from a dozen glasses of lemonade. It is the coming drink in Iowa. The firm will sell it by the keg and it will be bottled for sale. The firm has applied for patent. The ingredients are known to the proper officials—and of course there will be no objection to shipment of it by rail or river.

JULY 17, 1884.

"MUMM."

Something About the Unintoxicating Substitute for Beer.

The Davenport *Democrat* sent a reporter out the other day to interview Messrs. Koehler & Lange, the largest brewers of that city, as to their success with their new drink to take the place of beer. The reporter was told that the new drink was called "Mumm." Mr. Kuhler said: "It is thoroughly non-intoxicating, and contains, in place of the usual percentage of alcohol, different ingredients of a most excellent nature. With a pleasant pungency of flavor, and the quality of satisfying natural thirst quickly, it is perfectly pure, and thus becomes, from a sanitary view, especially commendable." The reporter was invited to try a glass for himself and he describes it as follows: It was amber in color and sparkling, and its top was foamy. It was delicious to the tongue and palate, and, indeed, the whole system, for the weather was very very sultry—and the long ride through the dust had created thirst. The "mumm" was delicious. It was as agreeable as lemonade—delightful as a mint julep and one could sip as many glasses as he pleased and feel no more effected in the head than from good coffee. The firm feel jubilant over their success and think that they certainly have a drink equal to beer, but non-intoxicant. The beverage cannot be placed under the ban of law any more than cider or coffee can—though the fact is, the people may be deprived of these beverages yet. Any teetotaller, any radical prohibitionist can test it; if he or she could imbibe a dozen glasses of it, they would be no more intoxicated from it than from a dozen glasses of lemonade. It is the coming drink in Iowa. The firm will sell it by the keg and it will be bottled for sale. Of course there will be trouble about shipping it. The firm have applied for a patent. The ingredients are known to the proper officials—and of course there will be no objection to shipment of it by rail or river.

Davenport Malting Company

Office 2d/Taylor   Brewers and Bottlers
Davenport, Ia.

Above: Oscar Koehler's brewery

Left: Koehler-Lange introduces its new drink, Mumm

Below: customers celebrate outside John Hill's tavern (not Aggie's uncle) after the state supreme court overturned the 1882 Iowa prohibition law

August 1884, *Davenport Gazette*: "Mumm"

>No doubt many of our readers think this is a new word, coined by the brewers, and is equivalent to lager beer. Not so, however. The word is found in Webster's dictionary, spelled "mum" (German *mumme*) and is defined as a malt liquor much used in Germany, made of malt, oatmeal and ground beans.
>
>It is said to have originated in Hamburg, Germany, and so renowned was its reputation for intoxication that the eighteenth century book printer John Playford included a popular drinking song of the ribald variety in his book of musical companion:
>
>>There's an odd sort of liquor
>>New comes from hamborough
>>T'will slick a whole wapentake
>>Thorough and thorough;
>>Tis yellow, and likewise
>>As bitter as gall,
>>And strong as six horses,
>>Coach and all
>>As I told you 'twill make you
>>As drunk as a drum;
>>You'd fain to know the on't
>>But that for my friend, mum.

While Oscar looked after the family business in Iowa, his dad and three brothers—Hugo, Max and Henry Jr.—operated American Brewing Company (ABC) in St. Louis, MO. In July 1903, Henry Jr. joined with Chicago brewers Edward Wagner and son to incorporate Wagner Brewing Company of Granite City, IL. Wagner was the last brewery to open in southern Illinois prior to towns there going dry in 1904.

Wagner advertised its beer as *liquid bread*, citing a *famous German chemist* for their brand's healthy quality. Wagner's ad claimed its beer contained the *"highest food value and the lowest percent of alcohol, therefore it is a genuine temperance drink."* The ad further claimed *"Temperance workers realize that by encouraging the use of beer they discourage the use of intoxicating liquors."*

In 1907 Wagner's and ABC became part of a St. Louis syndicate, the Independent Breweries Company (IBC) with Hugo Koehler as treasurer. IBC's president, Henry Griesedieck Jr., was the brother of Joe Griesedieck, who bought Lemp Brewery and its Falstaff trademark.

War restrictions on coal and barley in the summer of 1918 led to IBC producing soft drinks. Still sold today, IBC root beer is now owned by Dr. Pepper–Seven Up Inc., a division of Cadbury–Schwepps.

The Koehler fortune came of a product that cost about a dollar a keg to produce and sold for seven times as much. After thirteen years under the Volstead Act, they revived Falstaff with government permit #1, selling beer by the caseload the first day Prohibition ended—July 7, 1933.

Bix's pal Karlie Vollmer graduated from Cornell and Harvard. He first worked as secretary–treasurer for Midwest Fox Co, later Ramsey Advertising in the Kahl building before joining the family business in St. Louis as Falstaff's vice president of marketing. He married Jane Chandler Jones of Kansas. Their daughter, Patricia Jane graduated from Vassar.

Karl was among Falstaff executives on hand for the St. Louis Brown's American League 50th anniversary celebration in 1951. In *Veeck—As In Wreck: The Autobiography of Bill Veeck*, with Ed Linn, the Brown's owner recounted the day his team made history with the shortest guy ever to play professional baseball:

>...The day we chose was a Sunday doubleheader against the last-place Detroit Tigers, a struggle which did not threaten to set the pulses of the city beating madly.
>
>...Up on the roof behind home plate we had a special box with a connecting bar and restaurant for the care and feeding of visiting dignitaries. By the time I got up there to join Bud Griesedieck and the rest of the Falstaff executive force, the cake had already been rolled out onto the infield grass. Along with the cake came Sir John Falstaff or, at any rate, a hefty actor dressed in Elizabethan clothes....
>
>... Sir John tapped the cake with his gleaming cutlass and, right on cue, out through the paper popped Eddie Gaedel. There was a smattering of applause from the stands and a light ripple of laughter....
>
>Karl Vollmer, their advertising manager, was plainly disgusted. "Aw, this is lousy, Bill," he said. "Even the cake gimmick, you've used that before in Milwaukee and Cleveland. You haven't given us anything new at all."
>
>...The gloom in that box was so thick that our Falstaff could have come up and carved it into loaves with his cutlass. (That didn't seem like a very good idea at the moment, however, because Vollmer looked as he was just about ready to grab the cutlass and cut my throat.) "This is the explosive thing you couldn't tell us about," Vollmer

muttered. "A midget jumps out of a cake and, what do you know, he's a real live Brownie."

But the big surprise was still to come. Wearing the number 1/8 on a Brown's jersey made to fit his 3–foot–7–inch–65–pound frame, Eddie Gaedel stepped to the plate to pinch hit for Frank Saucier. Again from Veeck's autobiography:

> By now, the whole park was rocking, and nowhere were there seven more delirious people than my guests in the rooftop box. Veeck the jerk had become Willie the wizard. The only unhappy person in that box was me, good old Willie the wizard. Gaedel, little ham that he was, had not gone into the crouch I had spent so many hours teaching him. He was standing straight up, his little bat held high, his feet straddled wide in a fair approximation of Joe DiMaggio's classic style. While the Falstaff people were whacking me on the back and letting their joy flow unrestrained, I was thinking: I should have brought that gun up here. I'll kill him if he swings. I'll kill him, I'll kill him….

Gaedel swung. Three times! He got the walk and a pinch runner took the base while Gaedel got a standing ovation from the 18,000 fans in the stadium.

Both the Browns and the St. Louis Cardinals were under exclusive broadcasting rights to Griesedieck Brothers Beer, cousins of Falstaff's owners. After each inning, millions of radio listeners over ninety stations were reminded by 25–year–old Cardinal's announcer Harry Caray that "GB" meant "Good Beer," even after its competitor, Anheuser–Busch, took ownership of the team in 1953.

The GB brand folded into Falstaff and Carey followed his sponsor to the Chicago White Sox where his tag line became: "Holy Cow! Have another Falstaff, folks!" Carey kept the "Holy Cow" when he switched brands and leagues.

As for Karl Vollmer, Falstaff had him pinch hitting for them a couple years later during boycotts against corporations supporting the NAACP. Segregation ruled the South when *Time* magazine featured the company in its April 2, 1956 issue:

> …The Falstaff Brewing Corp. of St. Louis got into trouble late last year, after it bought for one of its Negro salesmen a $500 life membership in the N.A.A.C.P. on the theory that it would help him in his dealings with Negro customers. The White Sentinel, a sewer sheet published in St. Louis by John

Hamilton, an ex–Communist, printed a photograph of Falstaff's Vice President Karl Vollmer handing the check to an N.A.A.C.P. official.

Later that year, Vollmer led a promotional campaign for the Falstaff brand in the western United States. He had negotiated a TV contract, reported in the *Nevada State Journal* on May 16, 1957:

...Falstaff last January launched a new television series based on actual cases from the files of Nevada State Police...

The series, called "State Trooper" stars Rod Cameron as a lieutenant in the State police, headquartered at Carson City. The outdoor scenes in the series were filmed on location here and in other Nevada localities.

On the same page as the news story and a photo of Falstaff executives, Karl among them, there's an advertisement for Jack Teagarden's show at Reno's Nugget Casino. Teagarden had played on the last recordings Bix made. Wonder if Bix's old school chum caught the show?

SUNDAY MORNING—THE DAVENPORT DE

Milady Davenport Now Smoking Pipe In Response to the Latest Decree of the World's Arbiters of Fashion

working gal, jazz baby, modern millie—just don't call them sportin' women!

MONDAY EVENING—THE DAVENPORT DEMOCRAT AND LEADER—DECEMBER 3, 1923

Here They Are, Bobs and Long Tresses-- Take Your Choice

 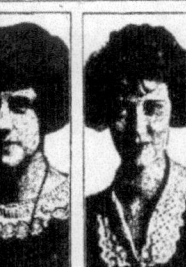     

| Only a Few Girls With Bobbed Hair Are Good Looking | OPEN HOUSE AT KAHL BUILDING TO BE TUESDAY | Portals Through Which 1,800,000 People Pass in the Course of a Year | ELEVATORS GO 16,348 MILES IN ONE YEAR | Girls With Long Hair Are Afraid to be Beautiful |

Above: LeClaire Park 1920; Below: Flood of 1922 when 17-ft crest passed the guard shack on Front Street (River Drive)

BIX HAUNTS

Bix Beiderbecke lived and died under Prohibition. Iowa had enacted its first liquor law soon after gaining statehood, outlawing saloons or what then were called dram shops. An 1855 State law restricted sales of intoxicating liquors to druggists. Iowa became a dry state in 1882, prohibiting all sales and manufacturing of liquor within its borders.

Davenporters challenged the law and won. Legislators reworked the language the following year and Davenport ignored it.

In 1893 local option taxes or mulct tax law was enacted. Davenport's city assessor recorded 180 liquor licenses issued under the law.

A reporter for the *Corning Free Press* in Corning, IA, (birthplace of Johnny Carson on the Iowa–Nebraska border) wrote of what he observed during an evening's entertainment at the Coliseum in July 1907:

> Families could be seen grouped around the tables and enjoying their beer in true German style. This was all in supposed prohibition Iowa. The same thing in Corning would create quite a stir, but in Davenport nothing was thought of it and it was considered highly proper.

Iowa State Treasurer's Mulct Tax Official Record 10–07 to 9–08 showed that Davenport collected $1,670 in taxes from 170 saloons. By comparison, Des Moines, the state capital, collected about $64,000 in taxes from 113 taverns during the same period.

In 1909, the State passed the Moon Law—named for Sen. Edwin Moon—which limited towns to one tavern per one thousand residents. Davenport ignored that law by citing its home rule charter.

Ten years later the State passed stricter enforcement of prohibition, three years ahead of the Volstead Act. On January 1, 1922, *Democrat–Leader* columnist W. L. Purcell reflected in his *Them Was the Good Old Days*:

> Remember when the Davenport brewers went on strike because the bosses wanted to limit 'em to 40 glasses of beer a day—during workin' hours? Cruel—wasn't it? ...Remember the time of President Garfield's funeral—when saloonkeepers scouted all over this City Beautiful for keys to lock their doors for two hours during the services? Them joints hadn't never been locked after the day they were first opened...

Davenport, Iowa, 24 Oct 188[?]

To J. H. HARRISON, Registered Pharmacist, No. 469:

I am not a minor, am not in the habit of becoming intoxicated, and hereby apply for

AMOUNT — KIND OF LIQUOR.

1 pint Whisky

Which is to be used "only for the actual necessities of medicine."

Emma Adelia Rice, Purchaser

J H Harrison, Reg. Ph. No. 469

Above: whisky prescription

Right: 1888 news story

Looney's *Rock Island News*
May 6, 1922

NO LIQUOR FROM THE DRUGGISTS

DAVENPORT, Iowa, April 30.—All the druggists of this city have united in giving formal notice that after today they will not sell or dispense any alcoholic liquor of any kind, for any purpose whatever. The action taken is not from choice. Competent legal authority has advised the pharmacists that the conditions of the prohibitory law passed by the last General Assembly are such that business cannot be done without violating it. Representatives of wholesale drug houses at Chicago and in the East who have recently visited interior towns between the Missouri and Mississippi Rivers say they have found but one druggist who will take out a permit under the new law, and he has a contract to furnish a State institution with the proscribed articles. There are, however, some 200 saloons openly doing business in Davenport, besides some wholesale liquor houses.

The Rock Island News

VOLUME ELEVEN—NUMBER TWELVE. ROCK ISLAND, ILLINOIS, SATURDAY, MAY 6, 1922. PRICE FIVE CENTS

DRUGGISTS CAUGHT

BUCKET OF BLOOD RUN WIDE & WET UNDER THE NEW ADMINISTRATION

This Notorious Resort Is Hangout For Very Lowest Creatures Of Underworld

E. MOLINE C. OF C. IS SHOWN UP

Selling Booze In Other Places As They Do In Davenport, Under Nose Of The New Administration

MUELLER HAD BETTER CLEAN UP DRUG HOUSES

They Are Worse Menace to the Public than the Soft Drink Parlor With Its "Hard" Drinks Ever Was And If Mueller Is Really Trying to Enforce the Law You May Look For Immediate Action

Talk about bein' sociable! It was always fair weather at the Bucket of Blood, the Double Elbow and the Blue Goose. They wasn't none of them sneaky stickup guys moochin' around on the dark, lookin' to sap a live one for the price of hooch. None of this miserable gizzard–grindin' moonshine was bein' dished out in the homes neither. The women folks was playin' the washboards and 'tendin' to their knittin' and not learnin' to be distillers...if every dame that's operatin' a home–hooch factory was sent up, they'd have to put sideboards on the big house out at Anamosa. In the old days you could get a quart of real likker or a bottle of wine for one berry at Roddewig's...or any of them wholesale joints. They wasn't no hip–oil in them times, nor no doctor's pint prescriptions at three bucks a throw....when the big brewery guys...Oscar Koehler, Charlie and Ernst Zoller...made the rounds they could set 'em up on the house for a five–case note. And now what do you get for a five–caser? You meet some slimey bootlegger in a dark doorway and slip him a five–spot for pint of white mule that would make a rabbit spit at a lion.

The paper offered a more sobering headline that opening week of 1922:

> OVER 600 FIND OASIS IN DAVENPORT DESERTS IN 1921; 274 IN 1920 THOUSANDS BRAVE TERRORS OF VOLSTEAD SAHARA—ARIDITY LESS THAN IN PRECEDING YEAR, RECORDS SHOW—LIQUOR CRAZE NOT HALTED BY LEGISLATION—200 MORE 'JAGS' ARRESTED PAST YEAR THAN IN 1918 B.P.
>
> The Volstead amendment and prohibition enforcement measures adopted by the government have failed miserably, at least in Davenport, and the figures reveal that more intoxicated men have been on the streets than in the 'good old days' when saloons flourished on every corner....Illicit liquor which now un–aged and strong in fusel oil is being sold in Davenport almost direct from the still. Last year the distillate brought about $20 per gallon while now the price is sometimes as low as $3.50 for the same amount. This can be explained by the low cost of corn and grains.
>
> Any number of private homes is now equipped with stills to make liquor for the consumption of the members of the immediate family.... "Whenever a man wants prohibition he'll quit drinking and not until then," one official said.

UK cornetist Mike Durham with Jim Prockaska, owner of the former Bluebird Inn on Milan's Knoxville Road

BLUEBIRD INN

Les Swanson recalled Bix becoming infatuated with swing jazz played by local black musicians at a place called Bluebird Inn on Old Knoxville Road. Just south of Milan, the place still flourishes as Jim's Knoxville Tap.

Current owner Jim Prockaska purchased it in 1966. "I don't know when the former owner bought it," Jim said, "but I think it was back in the '20s. Before that, it was a bootleg joint."

Les' daughter lived nearby so one night they dropped in for supper. While sitting there, Les pondered those days long ago when Bix bravely introduced himself and asked the bandleader to let him sit in for a number or two.

The Bluebird employed a hot jazz band that played until the wee small hours of the morning. "I remember many nights when Bix would bum a ride to the Bluebird after we finished playing a gig," Les Swanson recalled. "Most of us had day jobs, too, that required us getting some sleep. But there were times that Bix could talk someone into taking him."

Cornetist Mike Durham, leader of UK's *West Jesmond Rhythm Kings*, visited Jim's Knoxville Tap a few years ago, and enjoyed it so much that he brought *Spike Langham & His Rhythm Boys* across the Atlantic for the first time in 2005 to play where Bix once played.

Bluebird Inn was what they called a *black and tan* club. The charm of the place is that it hasn't changed much during the past hundred years. "Oh, we've upgraded it, and moved the bar around," Jim said, "but otherwise it's pretty much the same as when Bix played here, except that the chickens are gone. They were living under the building when I bought the place," he laughed.

If asked discreetly, Jim might even talk about the rooms upstairs where ladies once sold their wares. "That was way before I bought it," Jim hastened to add. "I use the rooms for storage now, but the beds are still there. That sort of thing wasn't uncommon back then. Remember John Looney?"

While professionally a lawyer and newspaper publisher, Looney's major revenue came from a string of tri–cities gambling parlors, speakeasies and brothels run by cohorts Helen Van Dale and Emeal Davis. Davis had the Bluebird plus a couple Davenport speakeasies, and a Rock Island hotel.

11 March 1923 *Davenport Democrat–Leader*:
> Helen Van Dale, formerly queen of the Rock Island underworld, free on bond, having confessed and implicated several yet unnamed and making the cases against many of those indicted, besides agreeing to turn state's evidence and go on the witness stand....as proprietor of a hooch parlor and gambling joint, and Emeal Davis, king of the great Rock Island darktown, have told all they know.

22 December 1925:
> "Bill Gabel's murder was highly effective, considering its motive," Senator James J. Barbour of Chicago, special prosecutor in the trial of John Looney, said in the course of his closing arguments to the jury..."The evidence is that not until John Looney got out of the county jail in Rock Island, would Emeal Davis, a prisoner in the same jail on the same charge, go across the street to the state's attorney's office and give evidence against Looney, his former chief.... The rest of the morning was spent by the senator in exposing the weakness of John Looney's three alibis and tracing the course followed by the death car, as described by Emeal Davis, about the streets of Rock Island on the night of the murder.... That Emeal Davis, Fat Walker, Shorty Burns and Joe Zeringer had cleaned their guns at Looney's place before starting out to kill Gabel that night...four men and Looney and his son going down from Looney's house to kill Gabel.... Conner [John Looney Jr.] went down to Emeal Davis' place and into the room where Burns and Walker were and the murder was talked over....

Other Bix Haunts

Outing Club

In 1891 Unitarian Minister Arthur Judy and Maj. Morton L. Marks took a carriage ride with John Mason to the J. D. Brewster property on the southeast side of Central Park. The property had been vacant for years but Brewster wanted ten thousand for the thicket–tangled lot. The three men offered $8,000, bringing along $7,500 in gold coins to convince him. Brewster accepted their offer on May 28th and the Outing Club was born. Its purpose was a gathering place for Unitarian Church members and their youngsters looking to enjoy outdoor sporting activities and picnic lunches. Chicken dinners with mashed potatoes, rolls and homemade pies on the front lawn became popular after–church events. Annual membership was ten dollars.

Membership expanded beyond Rev. Judy's congregation with subscription fees going to build a band shell, bowling alley and shooting gallery. A clubhouse, built for $25,000, drew a thousand attendees to its opening July 1, 1903. It included a large dining room, smoking and billiard rooms, reading room, a ballroom with a stage and theatrical scenery.

Davenporters watched a fire consume all but the chimneys and outer walls of that first clubhouse on April 4, 1905. It was rebuilt and reopened on August 24th.

In August 1907, Club stockholders sold the grounds to a holding company which paid all indebtedness and furnished the property free of rental to club members.

The Outing Club changed the way QC society entertained. If out–of–town guests mattered enough to get a mention in the newspaper, they could count on dining at the Club. Instead of large gatherings in homes for occasions such as weddings and anniversaries, families booked their events at the club. Musical soirees, tea parties, even bridge games moved from the family parlor to the Outing Club.

Amusement Parks

Schützenpark or shooting park opened in 1870 in Davenport as a target range for rifle marksmanship. The park included an inn, dance hall, music pavilion, zoo, refreshment stand, athletic fields and picnic grounds. The

Early clubhouse at Outing Club Unitarian minister Arthur M. Judy opened Davenport's Outing Club in 1891 as a church retreat southeast of Central Park, below, renamed Vander Veer Park for an early park superintendent.

park featured the first ten-pin bowling alley in Davenport, whereas others were nine pins and all located in taverns. The Volstead Act led to bowling alleys being built in alternate venues and women's leagues began forming.

Meanwhile, anti-German sentiment during WWI restricted public gatherings among German-Americans. German-owned businesses and social groups Americanized their names. Prohibition dealt a second blow when beer concessions, the park's major source of revenue, were outlawed. The park's name changed to Forest Park and featured amusement rides including a roller coaster.

Sold in 1923, the park served awhile as a chiropractic psychopathic sanitarium, changing hands in the 1960s to the Good Samaritan Center. With the rifle club now in Princeton, Iowa, all that remains of Schützenpark is a wildlife preserve, affectionately named Das Schützenwäldchen or *the little shooting forest*. The only remaining building original to the park is a 1911 streetcar waiting shelter.

Forest Park rollercoaster and promo for Buckley's Novelty Orchestra

ROCK ISLAND WATCH TOWER
Top: band shell; right: May 1925; below: J.P. Newberg's first-ever shoot-the-chutes on the Rock River at Watch Tower

WATCH TOWER PARK was a streetcar destination. Developed originally by George Davenport's son Bailey on land that had been home to the Sauk Nation, the park is on a bluff above Rock River's Vandruff Island. Along with a band shell and formal inn where Petersen's band played regularly, it once offered amusement rides, the most popular of which was the nation's first–ever water slide, called a *Shoot the Chutes*. It plunged passengers inside flat boats down the hillside and into the Rock River. Watch Tower Inn's second–story veranda overlooked Rock River valley. After a 1916 fire, the inn was rebuilt with a second floor ballroom and a stage. The old amusement park died a slow death as automobiles replaced street cars and destinations for fun expanded beyond street car destinations. The inn was demolished in 1936, replaced by what now is the lodge at the Black Hawk State Historic Site.

HOTEL BLACKHAWK

Above: original 7-story HOTEL BLACKHAWK seen in the distance from Brady Street intersection on Third.

1921: Floors 8-11 added

Below: Gold Room

Ballrooms

Hotel Blackhawk, northeast corner of intersection at Third and Perry, opened as a 7–story building in 1915. Built for $750,000, its roof–top marquee promoted the NEW FIREPROOF HOTEL BLACKHAWK. Floors 8–11 added in 1920 which gave it 400 rooms, making it the largest hotel in Iowa at the time. The land had been used for hotels from the beginning; predecessors included the Downs Hotel, the Ackley, the Saratoga and the Commercial Hotel. The architectural firm of Temple & Burrows was a partnership between Frank Burrows, the grandson of Scott County's first settler Elisha Burrow; and Parke Temple, a Columbia Ph.D. graduate who studied in Paris and Rome before joining Frederick Clausen, architect of the Beiderbecke–Miller building. Temple & Burrows built the Davenport Hotel at Fourth and Brady in 1909, across from then–new CRI&P depot. This six–story hotel with its top floor ballroom replaced the Kimball House as Davenport's premiere hotel and was in turn out–classed by the Blackhawk.

Aggie Beiderbecke's Aunt Mary Hill attended the Davenport Business College and worked at Newcomb House, both of which occupied the building that once had been the LeClaire House, Davenport's original hotel at Second and Brady—across from Beiderbecke & Miller wholesalers.

The business college opened in 1865 and passed through several owners, becoming Brown's Business College in 1901. LeClaire House served as the first stagecoach stop in Iowa and the city's original post office. City founder Antoine LeClaire had his office on the corner of the building that later served as Martin Cigar Store.

Before the railroad arrived, before construction of the Burtis Opera House, LeClaire House was Davenport's cultural center. Well–to–do from New Orleans and St. Louis would bring their entire families, including servants north by steamboat and spend summers at the hotel. Early guests included Ralph Waldo Emerson and a relative of Napoleon Bonaparte, who stayed here while searching for a runaway French princess thought to be hiding in Wisconsin.

A vegetable garden and hothouse that supplied the kitchen at LeClaire House used to be located on the lot now occupied by the Hotel Blackhawk. Frank Downs, owner of a four–story brick hotel that preceded the Blackhawk, hosted Saengerfest visitors in 1902. His club proprietor, Oz Reynolds, was the first saloonkeeper served with an injunction during State prohibition. Davenport's 200 other saloons and the breweries that supplied them were shocked at the time because the city pretty much had always ignored prohibition law. The Saratoga bar was among several Bucktown

THE DAILY TIMES, WEDNESDAY, AUGUST 3, 1921.

PROPOSED NEW HOTEL FOR MOLINE

F. L. Cornwell of St. Louis is willing to invest $1,000,000 in a hotel in Moline of $250,000 local capital is raised and a site donated.

businesses shut down by lawsuits after Davenport was declared the *wickedest city in the nation* by Bishop Cosgrove.

Blackhawk Hotel stood empty for a time in the early '50s and then underwent a $5.5 million renovation in 1954. It came back from bankruptcy in the 1970s as a combination apartment–hotel operated by the riverboat casino owners.

Over the years, the hotel's Gold Room hosted various musical entertainers from Guy Lombardo to Jerry Lee Lewis. Among its more notable guests: Carl Sandburg, Jack Dempsey, presidents Hoover and Nixon, for whom rooms 412–414 were named the Nixon Suite; and actor Cary Grant, who was staying on the eighth floor when he died during a rehearsal for his appearance at the Adler Theater.

On the Illinois side of the Mississippi is a hotel named after Davenport's founder, Antoine LeClaire, a French–Indian agent who served as interpreter for the Sauk and Mesquakie Nations during the Black Hawk War. Construction began September 29, 1921, on the 15–story LECLAIRE HOTEL and it was completed within fifteen months at a cost of one million dollars. Laborers earned $1.25 an hour hauling sandbags up each floor to test for strength and load capacity. Fast–track construction by hundreds of workers completed the building's frame within 60 days.

The 8–foot high name on its roof had nearly 300 bulbs per letter, emitting 100,000 candlepower across its 112–foot length, the largest in the world at that time. The original lobby, decorated by Italian artist Fredrico Aquadro, featured a hand–painted ceiling with gold leaf appliqué.

The hotel had the QC's first private line phone system in each of its 330 guest rooms. The Top Hat and Sky Hi rooms on the fifteenth floor offered breathtaking views of the Mississippi River valley from encased windows on all sides. The ground floor Prime Rib Room was packed on Saturday nights and for business lunches while the Jug Tavern was the favorite watering hole after work and during breakfast hours. Famous guests of the LeClaire included John Wayne, Jack Benny, Alice Faye, Roy Rogers, and Duke Ellington. The hotel has since been converted into private apartments.

HIBERNIAN HALL

May 18, 1892 Davenport Tribune:
> THE OLD AND THE NEW
>
> A large and old–fashioned brick building on Brady street, gable to the front, between Fourth and Fifth, standing far back from the street, is labeled in large letters "Hibernian Hall." For many years

HAYNES DANCING ACADEMY OPENS NEXT TUESDAY

Mrs. Olive Haynes Will Teach Latest in Terpsichorean Art

Mrs. Olive Cameron Haynes, Davenport's pioneer dancing instructor, announces the opening of her well known dancing studio at 421½ Brady street, on Tuesday, Sept. 8.

Private lessons only will be given and Mrs. Haynes will specialize in the Charleston, waltz, one-step and fox-trot.

Assemblies will start on Sept. 20 for advance pupils only and will be held in the studio. Pupils may enroll at any time.

Mrs. Haynes who keeps herself well posted on all the latest in terpsichorean art, predicts a very good season locally. Much interest is already being shown in the Charleston and the one-step.

Hibernian Hall

Haynes' Dancing School
421 1/2 BRADY ST.
New Term Opens Sat.
Class at 7:45. Fox-trot taught: 4 Instructors. I guarantee to teach anyone to dance in one course. Social dancing at 9 o'clock
Music by
BIX BEIDERBECKE'S FIVE
For private lessons call Dav. 7641 Gentlemem taught to lead. Ladies taught to follow their partners

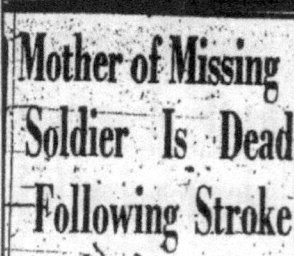

Davenport Daily Times reported on October 6, 1943, that Mrs. Olive Haynes had died from a stroke after learning that her son was missing in action in WWII. The only child of Davenport's long-time dance school owner had been stationed in North Africa and the bitter twist in this story is that he eventually returned home.

The Haynes Dance School, 421 1/2 Brady St., had operated for nearly three decades on the second floor of Hibernian Hall.

Bix played here with the Buckley Novelty Orchestra. But August 5, 1921, marked the first time he used his own name when his band, Bix Beiderbecke's Five, played for Mrs. Haynes dance academy. Bix was 18 years old at the time.

this ancient but very respectable house, right where a business block should stand, has been a source of grief to all progressive citizens. It was a church building in the marts of commerce. The money changers were all around it. Finally, a disposition was made of the property, when the congregation a short time ago erected a beautiful church building on the bluff. But, alas, in big letters on the building as successor to the Christian or Disciples congregation which had worshipped there was the brazen sign—Hibernian Hall.

Citizens then gave it up as to getting that old house out of the way. It might be a Hibernian Hall long as it was the Christian Chapel, and the first was built there in 1844, and this house erected in 1855–6, as a then costly structure. But the Hibernians are up with the spirit of the age, or with the progress of Brady street. As before noticed in the Tribune, they are erecting a large brick business house, with two store rooms, right in the expansive front yard of the old chapel, and yesterday the street walls were just beginning in their rise to obscure the high up sign of "Hibernian Hall." In a few days the old church building and hall will be but a memory, lost to sight, yet still there and in the performance of honest duty.

January 24, 1896 *Davenport Daily Leader* : TURKISH BATH NOTES

P. Prosperi has secured the services of J.C. Fuller, former manager of the Palmer house, Chicago, Turkish bath rooms, and Mr. Fuller will henceforth be found at Mr. Posperi's fine establishment in the Hibernian hall building on the East side of Brady street, between Fourth and Fifth. Mr. Fuller is an experienced and skilled operator and his advent to Davenport will be learned with pleasure by all devotees of the health–giving and refreshing system. Special arrangements have been made also for ladies, and every Thursday henceforth will be ladies day, from 8 a.m. to 9 p.m.

July 7, 1898 *Daily Leader:*

...A.A. Mallon, actor and comedian, who has been in the city for the past two or three weeks, and who was one of the members of the old joint stock companies organized here away back in the sixties was introduced. To say that the audience was delighted would be expressing it rather tamely. He gave them a program, devised on the spur of the moment that the equal of which has rarely been seen in this city.

Mr. Mallon opened with a short "actor talk" on the late Edwin Booth and then gave an imitation of Booth in the closet scene from Hamlet. It was a wonderful piece of work and those present who had seen Booth in his balmy days say that they could almost see him again before them. From this he turned to a bit of pantomime or "silent acting" from a little French drama, the plot of which is laid in Monte Carlo. It was a very clever thing and excited the applause of the audience time and again. It remained for his comic sketches however, to take the audience by storm. It was an illustration of how different people "popped the question."

...An amusing incident occurred while the actor was doing the "silent acting." The colored Light Guard band which was accompanying a colored trolley party about the three cities, stepped in front of the hall to give them a serenade. The music was not of the "shivery, deep villain" character, but drowned even the acting. Solemnly the actor turned...and in stentorian tones called out, "Mr. Stage Manager, ring down the curtain please, the orchestra is late with the overture."

DAVENPORT'S DANCING DREAMLAND

The Col Ballroom, one of the historic places where Bix often played, is owned and operated today by the Quad–Cities Mexican American Organization. They recently completed a major restoration project on the landmark building.

Soon after, the Col was featured on Iowa Public Television's popular *Living in Iowa* series. It is one of a very small number of ballrooms still in operation in the United States and has been in continuous use since 1914 when it opened as the Coliseum, at 1012 W. 4th St., Davenport.

Back in mid–1800s, Davenport's Westside had several German halls where people gathered for music, theater, and pints of beer. The City hosted their first Saengerfest or singing festival in 1858. When their turn came around again, Davenport United Singers urged local business leaders to build them an arena with 5,000 seating capacity.

Saenger Fest Halle at Fourth & Myrtle was built by George Mengel in 1898 for the 18th annual singer's festival. An estimated 100,000 people traveled by railroad to attend the four–day event. With hotel rooms filled to capacity, residents took as many as six out–of–towners into their homes.

When Mengel couldn't make money enough from special events and prize fights to cover expenses, he converted a portion of building into a warehouse. In 1906 he sold the property to plumber Leo Kerker who added a second floor and renamed it the Coliseum, *Davenport's Dancing Dreamland*, as he promoted it. A fire destroyed the original wood building October 21, 1913. Kerker built its replacement with steel and brick across the street. And it still stands to this day.

Over the years the Col has hosted well–known and lesser–known musical performers. Frank Sinatra and Louis Armstrong performed at the

First COLISEUM—original Saenger Fest Halle
Second COLISEUM, across Fourth Street from original

Interior of original COLISEUM, 1908 postcard

Interior of second COLISEUM, c. 1920

Col. So did Jimmy Hendrix and Harry James. On the walls are posters that celebrate decades of musical history from Dixieland to Rock.

Esten Spurrier, boyhood friend of Bix and himself a cornetist, told of when they were too young to go inside but stood at the open doors, drinking in the music and dreaming of the day they might play such a ballroom.

Members of the Mexican American Organization had their dreams, too, of a night of dancing but either could not afford admission or were turned away because of prejudices in those early days.

Now, in addition to hosting dances for people of all backgrounds and musical interests, the Col also serves as a community meeting place for Quad–Citians whose family roots may trace back to Bosnia as well as Germany, or to islands in the North Atlantic or the South Pacific, or villages in Africa and Asia. Whether Irish or Mexican or Vietnamese, it's proud Americans all, and the dance floor is yours.

Eagles Danceland

Founded in 1902, Davenport Aerie 235 Fraternal Order of Eagles had seventy charter members meeting in rented quarters on West Second near Harrison. With a membership of 1,600 the Davenport Lodge celebrated its new building at Fourth and Scott streets on New Year's Eve 1923. The three-story brick building with ornamental terra cotta exterior was designed by Clausen & Kruse and cost $375,000. The ground floor originally housed an automobile showroom for Galbraith Motor Co of Rock Island. Lodge meetings were held on the third floor.

The second floor and mezzanine served as an auditorium and ballroom with 90x60 feet of floor space plus a small stage. Lodge member Al Norgordt served as manager. In the fall of its second year of operation, Eagles Hall hosted Isham Jones' orchestra. Five days later, on September 18, 1925, a new name was announced for the popular ballroom: Danceland. Bill Greer's band, a mainstay at Eagle Hall had originally called itself the Danceland Orchestra, which may account for the name winning out over several hundred other suggestions from lodge members.

Paul Whiteman's orchestra played Danceland in January 1931. Bix was home at the time, having not played with Whiteman's outfit since before his stay at the Keeley Institute in the fall of 1929. Fans recalled Whiteman calling Bix up to the stage; close friends recalled how badly Bix played. Seven months later Bix was dead.

New Davenport Eagles Building is the Finest in the Middle West

NEW HOME OF THE DAVENPORT EAGLES

Opened New Year's Eve 1923

THE AUDITORIUM AND BALL ROOM

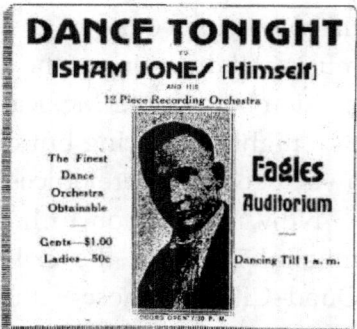

Isham Jones Ad 9-13-1925

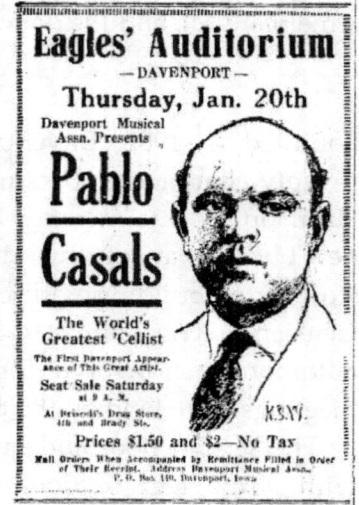

Pablo Casals Ad 1-9-1927

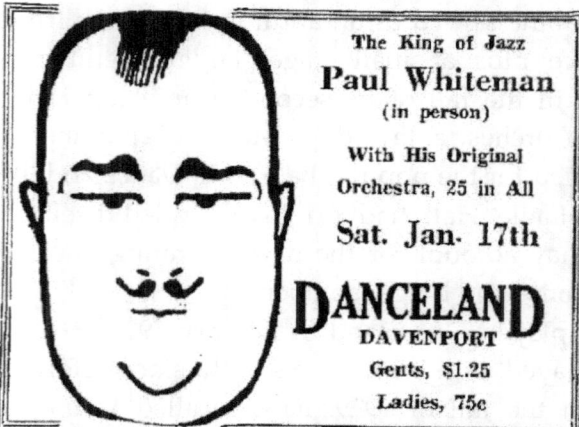

Battle Royal Ad 3-13-1927
Whiteman Ad 1-16-1931

Danceland Ballroom—501 W. 4th, Davenport exterior left and above

Moline Eagles Lodge—1404 6th Av auditorium stage, bottom left; exterior, below

WHEN BIX PLAYED KNOX COLLEGE

Old Route 150 still winds 45 miles from Moline to Galesburg past acres of verdant farmland and Illinois towns like Coal Valley, Orion and Alpha along the way. It remains a two-lane highway today, not much different than what it was in the early 1920s when Bix drove it.

Bill Marthens tells the story: "My father Ray attended Knox College in the early 1920s and played banjo with a small jazz combo. He told me that Bix used to drive down from Davenport and sit in with the band. He came several times, and Dad said Bix sometimes carried his horn in a brown paper bag.

"When Dad graduated and became an orthodontist he settled in Detroit. I think the year was 1927 or '28 when he encountered Bix again. Dad had a room on the first floor of this apartment building and whenever Bix and his musician friends returned from a gig, things got pretty wild. Dad said it was a party...a very loud party!"

Dr. Ray Marthens retired and moved to Sun City, Arizona, where he passed away in 1998 at age 96. Bill still had the banjo his dad once played with Bix.

Galesburg had its own celebrity in poet and writer Carl Sandburg, who played a pretty mean guitar, himself. He described the guitar as, "A chattel with a soul, often in part owning its owner and tantalizing him with his lack of perfection...A small friend weighing less than a newborn infant, ever responsive to all sincere efforts aimed at mutual respect, depth of affection or love gone off the deep end...."

Sandburg lived in Chicago at the time Bix was making a name for himself there. While Sandburg's musical tastes leaned toward American folk music, he appreciated the appeal of jazz, immortalizing its purveyors in *Smoke and Steel* (1920) his third published collection of poetry, which featured his poem, *Jazz Fantasia*:

> *Drum on your drums, batter on your banjoes, sob on the long cool winding saxophones. Go to it, O jazzmen.*
> *Sling your knuckles on the bottoms of the happy tin pans, let your trombones ooze, and go hushahusha-hush with the slippery sand-paper.*
> *Moan like an autumn wind high in the lonesome tree-tops, moan soft like*

you wanted somebody terrible, cry like a racing car slipping away from a motorcycle cop, bang–bang! you jazzmen, bang altogether drums, traps, banjoes, horns, tin cans—make two people fight on the top of a stairway and scratch each other's eyes in a clinch tumbling down the stairs.

Can the rough stuff ... now a Mississippi steamboat pushes up the night river with a hoo–hoo–hoo–oo ... and the green lanterns calling to the high soft stars ... a red moon rides on the humps of the low river hills ... go to it, O jazzmen.

City of the Big Shoulders:
They tell me you are wicked and I believe them, for I have seen your painted women under the gas lamps luring the farm boys.
And they tell me you are crooked and I answer: Yes, it is true I have seen the gunman kill and go free to kill again.
And they tell me you are brutal and my reply is: On the faces of women and children I have seen the marks of wanton hunger.
And having answered so I turn once more to those who sneer at this my city, and I give them back the sneer....

—Carl Sandburg, *Chicago Poems* (1916)

STORY OF STORYVILLE

The Illinois Vigilance Association released a 1922 report claiming jazz had caused the downfall of one thousand girls in Chicago alone the previous year. The report made no mention of boys like Bix Beiderbecke, expelled from Lake Forest Academy that year. Within the next four years, the City of Big Shoulders reportedly had some 2,400 jazz clubs, speakeasies and nightclubs, compared to 1,300 in the Big Apple.

So, if poet Carl Sandburg crowned Chicago the City of Big Shoulders, who dubbed New York the Big Apple?

NYC's moniker is said to have been popularized by sports columnist John J. Fitz Gerald of the *New York Morning Telegraph.* He explained its origins among jockeys in a February 1924 column, headlined: *Around the Big Apple*

...the dream of every lad that ever threw a leg over a thoroughbred and the goal of all horsemen. There's only one Big Apple. That's New York.

Before New Orleans became known as the *Big Easy,* the name was that of a dancehall recalled by New Orleans jazz man George *Pops* Foster in his 1971 autobiography:

> Music was a nice sideline to make a little change back in early New Orleans, but I never thought it would be a way to make a living. I usually had a regular job long-shoring or something...On Sunday night you might have an afternoon job at the lake [Pontchatrain] playing a picnic till six o'clock. Then you'd get on a streetcar and go way over to Gretna to play a night job [at] the Big Easy Hall and the Drag Nasty Hall.

Drag Nasty was named for its resident piano player or maybe the other way around. Back then, Pops Foster was with the Magnolia Band. He recalled sporting house piano men like Drag and Black Pete, as well as cornetist Buddy Bolden whose band played the Funky Butt dancehall. A very young Louis Armstrong sat for hours at the Funky Butt, listening and learning from Bolden. Armstrong later joined Pops Foster in Fate Marable's band on the excursion boats that brought New Orleans jazz to northern towns along the Upper Mississippi.

Foster's autobiography came on the heels of *New Orleans Times–Picayune* crime reporter Jim Conaway's novel, *The Big Easy*. Conaway claimed to have heard the phrase used among musicians in the context of finding gigs. But it was *Times–Picayune* columnist Betty Guillaud who popularized it as a nickname after responding to a new tourism campaign launched by New York City. *"If it's the Big Apple then New Orleans is the Big Easy, where everything is slower, simpler and easy–going,"* she wrote.

Beats being known as *Funky Butt Town* or the *Come Clean City*. As for Storyville, the moniker was intended to mock the New Orleans city councilman who authored the ordinance establishing *guidelines for the behavior of public prostitutes or notoriously lewd and abandoned women*.

> New Orleans Jan 26, 1897: Councilman Sidney Storey [sic] says that if you cannot eliminate prostitution, you can at least isolate it. Today, the Board of Aldermen adopted an ordinance that, in effect, legalizes prostitution in a district that centers around lower Basin Street, on the edge of the French Quarter. Jokesters are saying that the area will be called "Storyville" in honor of the congenial councilman. Open prostitution already exists in the area, where there are lavish bordellos that cater to the leading citizens and cribs or small rooms from which women beckon the not–so–leading citizens.

There's a Davenport connection here. In drafting New Orleans' vice trade ordinance, Councilman Story looked to Mississippi River ports up North for what they'd done to keep their towns from being overrun by the vice trade.

Among the reformers who influenced Story's efforts was Davenport's youngest–ever mayor, Henry Vollmer. "The scarlet woman walks the streets of every major metropolitan city," Vollmer said in his 1893 inaugural address. "Thinking men will admit that the best method of dealing with this evil is rigid regulation and control."

Vollmer was re–elected three times. Fortunately for him, Davenport's red–light district already had a name: Bucktown.

Councilman Story was as a river capitalist. He helped open Mississippi River ports, including the Quad Cities, to South American trade goods, circumventing costlier shipping routes via New York. He served as vice president of the American Foreign Commerce Association. He also lobbied for the Nicaraguan canal instead of one through Panama. But history would remember only *Storyville*.

Henry Vollmer

At the turn of the century, Davenport's east end had forty–two brothels, some forty saloons, a couple dozen dancehalls and burlesque theaters with their nefarious wine rooms, and several gambling dens. All this was within a six–block area just off the Government Bridge. This was Bucktown, Davenport's red–light district.

Sidney Story adopted Davenport's notion of a contained vice district in his city ordinance. New Orleans' Storyville encompassed sixteen square blocks. It had seven times the number of brothels and saloons as Bucktown. New Orleans' population was seven times that of Davenport in 1900.

Sanctioned or not, red light districts existed in towns and cities across the country. The original *Red Light* was a resort run by Maggie Wood in Caldwell, Kansas, where the Rock Island Line met up with the Chisholm Trail. The Red Light Resort, so named for its red lantern hanging over the entry, was a combination hotel–saloon, bathhouse, dancehall and brothel. Madame Maggie's girls supplied anything a trail–driving cowboy needed after herding longhorns for a couple months.

The Red Light Resort was popular and profitable until a city marshal was shot dead there and deputies responded by boarded up the place. Maggie obliged the townsfolk by getting out of Caldwell in 1885.

Her story got some national press and soon after reporters from Davenport to New York replaced the phrase *tenderloin district* with *red–light district*.

Red–light districts in both Davenport and New Orleans met their demise when America entered WWI. The Navy shut down Storyville. Rock Island Arsenal's commanding officer ordered the closing of saloons within a three–mile radius of his military installation. Without liquor sales as a front, Bucktown brothels retreated further into the shadows.

Iowa outlawed prostitution in 1909 with passage of the red–light district abatement law. A police sweep turned eighty women and fifty men out into the streets. But soon enough it was back to business as usual in Prohibition–era Bucktown, albeit less conspicuous.

Councilman Story never intended to rid New Orleans of its prostitutes. He did, however, hold them accountable for their impact on society. That same sense of accountability led Story to become vice president of the National Model License League, an adversary of the Anti–Saloon League. Story's group included Hugo Koehler of the Independent Brewers Co. of St. Louis. They advocated licensing and regulating liquor retailers.

Story lobbied on behalf of the liquor manufacturers and businesses that profited from liquor transportation and sales. He proclaimed the Anti–Saloon League "the most dangerous political movement this country has ever known."

Iowa was one of six to enact state–wide prohibition in the early 1880s. Davenport infamously ignored State prohibition. Except for the part about collecting mulct taxes which proved to be such a windfall that the City could forgo property taxes. It took the Volstead Act to get local officials to fully comply with the law.

BRICK'S PLACE

The *Democrat–Leader* reported that Davenport's east end after nightfall "was one blaze of lights and the sounds of revelry, of discordant orchestras, mechanical pianos, broken–voiced sopranos, and shuffling feet floated upon the night air. At Brick's pavilion, the lights burned merrily and the *bear cat*, the *Cubanola glide* and other classics were in full swing from 8 o'clock at night until 7 o'clock in the morning."

Former livery driver James A. Munro owned and operated Brick's Dance Pavilion and Summer Garden. He was known as the *King of Bucktown*. Munro's enterprises included the Palace Hotel at 111–115 Brady St, seven theaters, a pool hall, livery stable, and the city's first motorized taxi service.

W.J. Purcell wrote in his column, *Them was the Good Old Days*, that Brick Munro originated the cabaret at his pavilion and it spread over the country like wildfire.

The girls at Brick's danced with the customers—dancing being as far as it went, claimed Brick. "I have only good clean girls here."

Before achieving national acclaim as a novelist, playwright and political columnist, Floyd Dell was a beat reporter in Bucktown. He wrote about Munro's dime–a–dance emporium at Second Street and Rock Island, now Pershing Avenue:

> A wire fence divides a row of seats and tables roofed by a trellis of vines from the dancing floor, with its whitewashed pillars, wall and ceiling and in one corner bar. The liquor was only part of the operation. Tables and chairs range the sides of the room at which sit well dressed young men and girls. Over in the shade stands a special policeman, whose duty it is to see that the lads and lassies who have had too much and are getting loud leave before they have a chance to start a rough house. In the saloon the barkeep is doing a rushing business....

Various misfortunes befell Munro in later years. Lawsuits from moral crusaders led to him closing his dancehall in 1909. He then became owner of the Hollywood Inn roadhouse. But it was constantly targeted by federal

"SUNDAYING" IN DAVENPORT.

Des Moines Register's Ding Darling poked fun at Davenport's first dry Sunday on December 15, 1907, in a political cartoon showing one guy peering through the window of a boarded-up Brick's Place while others sit idle on the curb. One loiter yawns; another says, "Let's go down and look at the river." A couple more play checkers. A woman walking with her husband, one assumes, remarks: "That was a fine sermon we heard this morning." Behind them a man asks for directions to the church. "What's this dull town to me," says the guy jumping from the Hotel Davenport, now the Landmark Apartments. Before Davenport enforced the Sunday law, Brick's was known far and wide for being a 24-7 operation. Darling's illustration moved Brick's Place from its Bucktown location at 2nd & Rock Island (Pershing) streets and set it where the Davenport Public Library now stands at Fourth and Main.

prohibition agents. In his final years, Munro couldn't even pay utilities in his downtown apartment. His only light came from the flickering marquee of a nearby movie house.

The story goes that one day, while seated by the window trying to read his newspaper by the light of the flickering marquee of a nearby movie house, there came a knock at the old man's door.

A dapper man entered. "Do you remember me?" he asked. "I used to sing at your place."

Munro looked closely at him in the fading light. "I don't know," he said, "I had a lot of good performers in my day."

The dapper man smiled. "Well, I do remember that you were always smoking a cigar when I worked for you, so I brought you a box," he said, passing over a box of expensive Havanas and then departed.

The old man was touched. "He's one of the very few who was ever grateful for the break I gave him," he said. Then he opened the box of cigars. Inside, on top of the cigars was a crisp $100 bill.

The young man was Al Jolson and he had just finished filming *The Jazz Singer*.

At the peak of its popularity, Brick Munro's dance pavilion packed in more than 1,000 people a night and earned about $2,500 a week.

When Munro died in 1940, The *Daily Times* wrote that, "At the height of his career, Mr. Munro never turned down anyone who asked him for money.

Anyone with a hard luck story could obtain cash from him, and he loaned thousands of dollars to comparative strangers, most of which was never repaid." Munro put up a major share of the funds for what later became Davenport's Friendly House and annually provided them with funds to buy Christmas presents for poor children.

The *Democrat* wrote: "In his days of prosperity Mr. Munro was looked upon as the good Samaritan of the east side. The poor he helped ran well into the hundreds and not a few persons who died penniless were given decent burials at his expense."

AL JOLSON (1886-1950) Sheet music for Jolson's *Robinson Crusoe Jr.* show at Burtis Opera House on April 6, 1917; advertisements for Lew Dockstader's 1908 show; April 27, 1928 AD for *The Jazz Singer*

Thursday, October 19, 1916.

DANCES TO DISPROVE CHARGE OF INDECENCY

Burlesque "Queen" Edifies Chicago Court as She's "Walkin' the Dog."

Chicago, Oct. 18.—Judge Samuel A. Trude's court in the city hall had all the aspects of a burlesque show for five or ten minutes yesterday afternoon.

A petite brunette stepped to the judge's bench, tossed her head, flashed a smile to the jury, then threw off her heavy outer cloak, and in a trice was "Walkin' the Dog" and doing other syncopated steps about the small inclosure in a dance to a ragtime accompaniment sung by herself.

It was Miss May Mills, leading lady of the "Follies of Pleasure," dressed in her spangled costume of gold and silver, demonstrating the exhibition for which J. H. Herk is on trial on charges of keeping a disorderly house, alleged to have permitted immoral dancing and acting in the Gaiety theater, 551 South State street, of which he is manager.

"Just Walked Like This."

Miss Mills was the star witness for the defense. It is upon her interpretation that the attorneys for Herk hope to prove the charges against him groundless.

"I simply walked like this," said Miss Mills between snatches of the song, as she deftly paced the small enclosure. "I swayed like this and I waved my arms like that," demonstrating.

She pirouetted in front of the jury box, skirting the fenced enclosure, and brought up with a stamp of her foot, an appealing gesture and a toss of her head.

"Whoopee!"

"Whoopee!" cried some one in the rear of the courtroom, carried away momentarily. A stern bailiff quickly restored him to order. Then the spectators in the courtroom broke into applause, but this, too, was quickly silenced. There were some, however, who did not applaud. They were the members of the Women's Church federation, complimentary to the charge, and others allied with the prosecution.

Judge Trude at the beginning of the song and dance was seated viewing the exhibition with becoming austerity. Before it was half over, however, he was leaning back and forth behind his chair, his hands folded behind his back, his face beaming in a broad smile. His opinion of the dance, however, he refused to communicate.

No Jass Band Around.

"I'm afraid I won't do very well," said Miss Mills when called to perform. "You see, I have no music."

"Attorneys for the defense will probably whistle for the young lady," suggested Assistant City Attorney Dippus. But this they declined to do.

MAR 3, 1921

"BEE" PALMER MARRIES

(By United Press.)

Davenport—"Bee" Palmer, 22, well known actress and originator of the shimmy, today was the bride of Al Siegel, 23, New York, her pianist.

She may have originated the song but Bee Palmer did not originate the dance!

No Jass Band Around (10/19/1916)

Sept 19, 1919

Exit, the Shimmy.

Reading announcements that the shimmy is destined to pass, old-fashioned persons may have blushed and wondered what new freak of dress reform had popped up. That the American National Association of Masters of Dancing and the American Society of Professors of Dancing have decided that a certain sort of dancing is to be disapproved of really isn't startling at all.

No skill is required to learn the kind of dancing referred to, and so the dancing masters and the dancing professors have a professional interest in abolishing antics, executed to jazz music.

In all likelihood, the shimmy would have perished naturally without assault on esthetic or moral grounds. It became popular because it was daringly wicked, and it was daringly wicked because it came up into outwardly respectable society from the fetid shadows of the nether world. Slang, music and dance steps originating on levels where decency is disgraceful, are eagerly adopted by proper folk who like to play at being bad.

Wickedness is dull, after all, and the charm of what is shocking wears off very quickly.

The shimmy, and similar public squirmings, are too brazen to be seductive and too crude and ungraceful to allure for long.

BIX & THE SHIMMY QUEEN

When a Ziegfeld dancer brought her risqué vaudeville show to Davenport, Esten Spurrier and his pal Bix Beiderbecke made it their mission to be in the audience for every show.

Bee Palmer's *Oh Bee! Revue* at Davenport's Columbia Theater—part of the Orpheum circuit—from February 27 through March 2, 1921, featured the Chicago-born self-anointed *Shimmie Queen* doing her signature dance, described as "sinuous and suggestive undulation of hips and shoulders" to the accompaniment of her band, the New Orleans Rhythm Kings.

It wasn't Bee's shimmy and certainly not her singing but rather her jazz musicians that kept budding cornetists Spurrier and Beiderbecke coming back for more. Palmer's band included 17-year-old cornetist Emmett Hardy, Leon Roppolo on clarinet, Santo Pecora on trombone, drummer Johnny Frisco and piano player was Al Siegel.

Before leaving Davenport for their next gig in Peoria, Bee married her piano man in a secret midnight ceremony performed by Justice of the Peace W.W. Scott on March 3, 1921, at the Davenport Masonic Temple. Instead of a veil, Bee wore a large purple hat and on the marriage license she gave her age as twenty-three. Siegel was twenty-four but Bee actually was twenty-seven. Born 1894, Beatrice C. Palmer was the third of four children born to Swedish immigrants Charles and Anna Larsen Palmer.

A notice in *The Davenport Democrat-Leader*, picked up by the wire services, reported that Bee "evidenced all the confusion and embarrassment of the unsophisticated school-girl bride and seemed extremely happy when the ceremony had ended."

Meanwhile, Bee's stage act was getting poor reviews and, making matters worse, riling the clergy's standards of morality. To that old adage, "yeah, but will it play in Peoria," came a resounding "No!" from nervous theater managers who cancelled the show.

The band scrambled to find other work with Roppolo, Pecora, and Hardy heading back to Davenport to play with the Carlisle Evans Band aboard the steamer *Capitol*. Bee made a guest appearance with Evans' band for a short time and then returned to New York, back to Ziegfeld's Midnight Frolic.

In October 1921, Al Siegel filed suit against Jack Dempsey—also on the Orpheum circuit at the time—for alienation of affections, charging that the champion boxer lured Bee away from her marriage. Eventually Siegel dropped the suit but Bee filed for divorce on the grounds of cruelty, saying that he beat her. She told reporters, "I picked him out of the gutter. I married him at midnight on the impulse of the moment."

Siegel was accompanist for Sophie Tucker at the time he filed for divorce. But he and Bee remained married another seven years. In 1928 they officially divorced. Siegel became coach and accompanist to a former stenographer named Ethel Zimmerman. By 1930 she was on her way to stardom under the stage name Ethel Merman.

Bee Palmer and Bix would again cross career paths in 1929. Palmer recorded *Singin' The Blues* and *Don't Leave Me, Daddy* for Columbia. While music scholars debate whether or not Bix performed at the recording sessions, what is fact is that musical arranger Ted Koehler wrote lyrics for Palmer's vocal on *Singin' The Blues* to fit the solos of Bix and Frank Trumbauer on their 1927 Okeh label recording of the song.

Bee Palmer played Davenport's Columbia Theater in 1921 while Sophie Tucker made three appearances—1918, 1921 and 1924.

Red Hot Mama
Knew He Was Special

as told to Jim Arpy in 1988 for *QC Times*

I first knew Bix at Davenport High School in 1918.

I recall a school assembly when John Schmidt, associated with the Schmidt Music Co., demonstrated a variety of instruments for a firm he represented.

He played several and he was no slouch, either. But when Schmidt played a tune on a trumpet, Principal George Edward Marshall recognized it as a piece in Bix's repertoire. Marshall called Bix up on stage saying, "Let's see how you'd play that piece."

Well, Bix did and all I can say is that it was out of this world. Mr. Schmidt was flabbergasted that we had such a talent in high school.

Oh, he knew he was good, but didn't go around telling you about it.

While he was still in high school, Bix played in the orchestra at the Columbia Theater some nights and always on weekends.

When Sophie Tucker, *Last of the Red Hot Mamas*, came to town she was always the star of the show—and what an elegant lady and good sport she was.

Every time she'd come out to take her bow, she'd point out Bix and introduce him as "the greatest trumpet player in the world" and he was just a high school kid.

Whenever Sophie was on for the afternoon matinee, Bix would play hooky and always buy a box seat and sit there alone for the show. And as soon as she went off, Principal Marshall would march up to the box seat, take Bix by the ear and lead him back to school.

It happened several times and always brought down the house. I'd heard about it and a couple of buddies and I played hooky to see it. Sure enough,

Mr. Marshall took Bix by the ear. But he understood Bix and enjoyed the joke, and he was never punished.

—Rolla Chalupa, 1904–1998
Davenport Postmaster

Sophie Tucker performed at the Columbia three times: February 1918 with her Five Syncopation Kings; February 1921 with the house orchestra; and April 1924 with Ted Shapiro and Jack Carroll.

Bix's pal Esten Spurrier told of skipping school to catch the matinee show. Bix was just learning cornet the first time Sophie Tucker came to town. The Original Dixieland Jazz Band's *Tiger Rag* arrived summer 1918 in Davenport.

Strict union rules would have prevented Bix playing during Miss Tucker's 1921 show. But given Bix's ties to the Petersen family he could have wormed his way into a couple of practice jams. If the principal had caught the boys and dragged them out of the theater and it got a laugh, Miss Tucker might well have arranged for an encore performance.

Bix was touring with the Wolverines when Miss Tucker made her 1924 appearance.

Bix and Sophie did eventually appear together, at least by name when their recordings made the top seller lists—Bix with Frank Trumbauer's band in 1927–1928. By then Sophie Tucker wasn't alone in calling Bix *the greatest*.

The Columbia was built in 1914. It converted to a movie house in 1940 and was demolished in 1967 to make way for the Kahl building's off–street parking.

Davenport Democrat-Leader August 1, 1918

Kahl Building under construction in 1919; Columbia Theatre on the left

Linwood White Sulphur Springs

A DELIGHTFUL SUMMER RESORT.

Is beautifully situated on the banks of the Mississippi, six miles below the city of Davenport, Iowa, affording lovely drives to and from the city. Sail and row boats, croquet, billiards, ten pins, good hunting and fishing, in fact everything to interest and amuse the pleasure seeker. The waters possess superior medicinal qualities, having been thoroughly tested for many diseases, such as Rheumatism, Paralysis, Skin Diseases, &c. Linwood is now open for the season. Rates per day, $2.00; per week, $7.00 to $10, including baths. Special rates made to families. Parties desirous of visiting the Springs can engage rooms and learn further particulars by addressing

H. R. WOOD,
Proprietor Linwood White Sulphur Springs
Linwood, Iowa.

N. B.—Steamer leaves Davenport every day at 3 o'clock P. M. for the Springs.

LINWOOD ADS
top left: **1882**; right: **1896**; below: **1904**

LINWOOD PICNIC GROUNDS

H. R. MEYER, Proprietor.
Old 'Phone 1439 J. One.

The finest spot on the Mississippi River for private parties, Sunday Schools, Lodges, etc., etc. Reached by trains or boat.
Meals and Short Orders furnished in quick order.
Ice Cream and Soft Drinks.
H. R. MEYER, Proprietor.
Old 'Phone 1439 J. One.

OUTING AT LINWOOD.

The United Presbyterian church has decided to hold its annual church and Sunday school picnic at Linwood this year. A committee of members have visited the former summer resort and report that it is in tip top condition for a day or week's outing. The grounds have been leased by a Moline man who has built a small house and resides there with his family. He is making a good income by renting tents to camping parties, several of whom are now located on the ground. The whole place with its excellent fishing and bathing and spring of sulphur water should make a winning in the hearts of Davenport campers and excursionists.

H. R. MEYER

Linwood manager 1902-1919

Floyd Bean, Lazy Piano Man

When a young woman asked, "Who is that man playing piano who looks like a college professor?" she was answered by an elderly supper club patron: "That's Floyd Bean. He's one of the saints of jazz."

Lean and scholarly–looking with iron gray hair, Bean was the subject of a *Cedar Rapids Gazette* feature in 1963, proclaiming him among the dwindling group of musicians who had played jazz during its formative stages. At various local night spots, Bean played his style of relaxed and bluesy piano.

Born in 1904 at Ladora, about 40 miles southwest of Cedar Rapids, Floyd's dad, Ira Bean, had been the town plumber. His mother played a bit on the family reed organ but Floyd's first formal contact with music came when the family moved to Grinnell. He joined the high school band, playing on an ancient rope–tensioned bass drum. But what he loved was the piano. Floyd was introduced to jazz by way of his first piano instructor, George 'Stick' Leins who had a band called the Mississippi Six.

Bean began jobbing around with local bands and hit the road at eighteen "with a bunch of kids." They landed a summer job at the Linwood Inn on the Mississippi river, seven miles outside Davenport. Along with Bean on piano, the band included Jimmy Fritz, trumpet; Al Hamilton, banjo; Gene Hamilton, drums; and Silas Thompson, saxophone.

"A trumpet player by the name of Bix Beiderbecke used to come out from town and sit in with us," said Bean of then–19–year–old Bix. "We knew that he was a wonderful musician, but he had only a local reputation then. When our trumpet player left, we thought of hiring him, but we needed someone who could carry the lead on new sheet music, and Bix couldn't read."

In those days, new songs were introduced by the composers or *pluggers* with lead sheets passed out to band leaders who were expected to play them at least once. "Bix showed me a lot of new things about piano," said Bean, "playing tenths...I'd never heard of that before, always played octaves in the bass."

The summer at Linwood over, Bean moved on to Muscatine. "I remember that while in Muscatine I first figured out about augmented and diminished chords by listening to early pianists on a crystal radio set. Those were the days of Heine Greishenbach [a.k.a. Henry Griesenbrock] and the Club Royal orchestra, the Walter Mohnson orchestra, and the Bill Hogan orchestra, all territory bands."

By 1924 Bean was working out of Fond du Lac, WI, about three hours north of Chicago, with a band that included trumpeter Bunny Berigan.

Important in those days, as indeed it still is to any musician, was a recording date. Bean observed this momentous event in the studios of Gennett Records in 1928.

This cramped cubbyhole of a place was a hallowed hall to jazzmen, because it was here that King Oliver had muted his trumpet for the famous chorus on *Dippermouth Blues* and the New Orleans Rhythm Kings had roared through *Bugle Call Rag*, and the Wolverines with Bix Beiderbecke had recorded *Riverboat Shuffle*.

Bean was playing piano with Fred Dexter's Pennsylvanians, a band very popular with Iowans in the late twenties. With Bean on piano, they had one record released on the red Champion label, a cut–price subsidiary of Gennett. The tunes were *What's the Use*, an excellent bounce tempo ballad, and a dog tune called *Cheer Up*.

In 1930 Bean landed a job as staff pianist with WOC radio in Davenport, and did some playing and arranging for the Jimmy Hicks band. By this time Bix was a star in the Paul Whiteman band. To musicians like Bean, Whiteman was the apex of bandleaders.

From Davenport, Bean went to Chicago and a year with Eddie Niebauer's Seattle Harmony Kings and then with Jimmy McPartland at the Three Deuces.

In the spring of '39 Bean got his big break. The Bob Crosby band was casting about for a new piano man. Crosby cut four sides for Decca, including *Penthouse Serenade* and *Rose of Washington Square*.

In the fall of that year Decca produced a Chicago–Style jazz album that featured Bean with trumpeter Jimmy McPartland. Bean next worked with Eddie Howard, a young vocalist on WGN radio show with Luxor cosmetics as a sponsor. It aired two nights a week. Bean wrote all of Howard's arrangements. They cut twenty–one sides for Columbia.

In 1944 Bean joined Eddie Stone's band as a pianist and arranger. Stone, fresh from one of the Isham Jones units, was a violin–playing singer, and the band he was fronting was strictly business band playing little or no jazz.

Bean asked Stone to evaluate one of his original songs. Stone liked it, so wrote some lyrics and *I Never Thought I'd Sing the Blues* was born. Stan

Kenton recorded the tune.

In the spring of 1946 Floyd joined his cousin Carl Bean, leader of a well known Iowa territory band at Chicago's Rainbow ballroom for a recording session. This band featured Paul and Ernie Lenk, plus trombonist Art Leonard. They cut four sides including *Honeysuckle Polka*, a barn burner that featured triple–tonguing Leonard on his baritone horn. The releases were on the obscure Tower label. This was wartime, and record materials were unbelievably poor.

Blue Skies, a side that spotted some nice solo piano by Floyd, never got past the record salesmen's sample case. It had been pressed off center, causing the music to *wow*.

In 1950 Bean joined trumpeter Muggsy Spanier for his Mercury recordings, one of which was an original Bean composition. *Down Beat* magazine had printed the score and called it the *Back Room Blues*. Studio moguls listened to its languid and limpid style and melody and promptly re–christened it the *Lazy Piano Man*. And so it was issued, and the tune became a piano classic.

Bean said his influences included Earl Hines, Teddy Wilson, Art Tatum, George Shearing and Oscar Peterson. Among the classics, Bean said his favorites were Stravinksy, Debussy, and Ravel. As for the evolution of jazz and its relation to classical music, he noted, "the lines are closer now."

Bean spent his last decade playing at various jazz festivals and local clubs in Cedar Rapids.

He met his first wife, Violet Marsh of Muscatine in 1924. They spent their honeymoon on an 8–month regional tour with the Henry Griesenbrock orchestra— Griesenbrock & his wife were their wedding attendants. Floyd and Violet had one daughter, Patricia. While living in Davenport, Floyd met and married his second wife, Florence Schankle in 1937. He died of cancer in Cedar Rapids in 1974.

Floyd Bean

Linwood Inn c. 1921

LINWOOD WILL OPEN SEASON SUNDAY, MAY 1

The Linwood resort, eight miles west of Davenport, will open its season May 1, George Kettnich, proprietor, announces. The resort has been remodeled and inside washrooms and toilets have been installed. A spring well water system is also a new feature.

The dining room has been rebuilt and redecorated and the hotel rooms have been transformed into private dining rooms. A five-piece orchestra will furnish dance music each evening.

The resort has been made more easily accessible by the introduction of motor bus service between Davenport and Linwood. The bus will leave the corner of Second and Brady streets at 8 p. m. and 10 p. m. daily, beginning May 1. The resort is on the Mississippi scenic highway and the roads leading there are reported to be in excellent condition this year.

LINWOOD Spring Duck and Chicken Dinners BIG DANCE —EVERY— Saturday Tel. Dav. 1024 Dance Sunday, July 25. Music by Buckley Novelty Orchestra Have your Picnics at Linwood

1921 Season

LINWOOD RAIDS

11 June 1922: FEDERAL DRY AGENTS SPONGE UP LINWOOD IN MIDNIGHT RAIDING PARTY

Surrounding the Kettnich and Jaeger resort at Linwood last night, federal agents and Sheriff Brehmer's squad raided the biggest and perhaps the most widely known of roadhouses in this section of the country. For more than an hour and a half the raiders held the huge crowd prisoners in the establishment until they had taken sufficient alcoholic liquor for evidence.

George Kettnich and his wife were arrested and brought to the county jail where they were attempting at a late hour this morning to raise U.S. Commissioner A.G.

Bush to have a bond set so as to obtain their release from custody.

Seized by the raiding party were about twelve gallons of home brew, approximately two quarts of which were distributed into half a dozen pint bottles, a quart of gin and several bottles containing a highball mixture of ginger ale and whiskey.

The strains of the jazz band were made jazzier and jazzier as the raiders drove thru and up the road toward the resort which been rumored to be more than two years under the management of Kettnich and Jaeger, who are also owners and managers of the Grotto Café, Third and Perry streets.

Wilder and wilder the dancers were swinging to the tuneful syncopation of one of the best dance orchestras in this section of the country. A score or more prominent Davenport businessmen were enjoying the orchestra early on and had taken rooms on the second floor of the place.

The evening had just stated to get into its swing when the prohibition agents were creeping toward the place. The raiding party had been well instructed and when the signal came from the leader, Federal Agent Muhs, they opened the doors and took their stand just inside. Several of them carried revolvers openly in their hands, patrons of the place said afterward.

There was a scurry and scramble from the dance floor and the strains of the jazz band had died away while the prohibition agents announced that the place was raided and for no one to attempt to leave.

Meanwhile other raiders were making their way thru the rooms of the place confiscating all the liquor they could find and loading it into automobiles which were waiting them.

One frightened citizen said to be a business man of excellent reputation seized the first opportunity and fled thru the yard. The raider fired three shots into the air but the fleeing man refused to stop.

With the liquor in the hands of the federal investigators there was little left to drink, many thought and the road was soon filled with automobiles bound toward Davenport. Some however were not so easily discouraged, and when the jazzy orchestra again half–heartedly resumed its work, the dance floor was soon filled with shaking quivering toddlers. There was a noticeable lack of the wild abandon which characterized the dances preceding the raid.

The raid was completed at 1:30 o'clock and the sheriff's car, filled with whiskey, federal men and Mr. and Mrs. Kettnich, started for the county jail. A dozen or more auto parties which had not heard of the raid drove up to the place only to turn sadly back toward Davenport when they found that the "kick" had been removed.

12 June 1922: HOLD LINWOOD OWNERS TO THE FEDERAL JURY

The "inside story" of Saturday night's raid on Linwood Inn was not related in court today by the so–called prominent business men who were rounded up in the raid. While practically all of them gave fictitious names Saturday night, the identity of many of them was known to the raiding party and they were informed at the time that they would be subpoenaed to testify at the hearing.

...Mr. and Mrs. Kettnich both waived examination and were bound over to the federal grand jury. Mr. Kettnich was released on $2,000 bonds and his wife on $500 bonds. Harold Metcalf was their attorney. No charges were preferred against Hans Jaeger. Mrs. Kettnich today declared that she was the sole owner of Linwood and that her husband George Kettnich and Hans Jaeger had no proprietary interest in the place. According to Mrs. Kettnich, she bought out all her husband's interest last fall. Jaeger, she says, at no time had an interest. Mr. Kettnich and Mr. Jaeger are partners in the ownership of the Grotto cafe on Perry street. Saturday night both were at Linwood helping Mrs. Kettnich during the rush hours. "I am the sole owner of Linwood and am willing to take all responsibility for its management. I endeavor to conduct a first class place and have worked hard along these lines. I do not see how I can be held responsible for all the acts of my patrons," declared Mrs. Kettnich today.

19 June 1922: ASKS COURT TO FORBID LINWOOD SELLING LIQUOR

Injunction proceedings to prevent the sale of intoxicating liquors at Linwood, a summer resort located west of the city in Buffalo township, was started in district court today by Assistant County Attorney W.A. Newport. The resort was raided a week ago by federal agents and the proprietor, George Kettnich and his wife, arrested. A quantity of liquor was seized by the prohibition enforcement men.

...An attempt will be made by the county attorney's office to obtain a permanent injunction against both Kettnich and his wife and the Linwood Stone & Cement company, owners of the property.

2 Oct 1922: FEDERAL COURT STARTS ON OVERLOADED DOCKET

Tomorrow morning, promptly at 10 o'clock, the gavel in the hand of Federal Judge Martin J. Wade will resound thru the erstwhile deserted court room in the Federal building like a terrific peal of thunder on a storm tossed sea, and the monstrous wheels of the grist mill of justice will start their semi–annual grind of the more than two hundred cases on the federal docket.

Tomorrow morning the court room, the scene of many sighs, the silent listener of many pathetic tales, yielding its last breath of freedom, for terms of years to many and yet withal the cause of many a young miscreant turning on to the straight and narrow, will take on the bustling air of ponderous activity.

The docket, probably the heaviest of any that has been presented to the court for many years, contains 78 cases left over for the spring term and 108 new cases...91 are alleged violation of the Volstead act, said Prohibition Officer Roy E. Muhs, this morning. Many of these defendants are repeaters, persons who have faced the Federal Judge from one to four times before.

At 10 o'clock tomorrow morning the Grand jury will be impaneled... Then the petit jury, the pleadings of defense attorney, the sobs and sighs of those dear to those on trial, then the long anxious suspense of the dragging moments while the jury, retired, is weighing the evidence and then the verdict which means either happiness for some, a fresh start for the defendant or a blasting life with years behind the bleak, dark walls of the penitentiary.

Some of the most prominent cases to come before the Federal court starting tomorrow are...MR. AND MRS. GEORGE KETTNICH, said to be the proprietors of LINWOOD... JOHN LOONEY, JUNIOR, and Louis Pedigo, alleged bootleggers...HARRY KOEHLER and George Fahey said to be the proprietors of the PALMER INN on the Nahant road...Joe Johnston and Skimmer Hines, charged with being waiter and proprietor of the HOLLYWOOD INN, across the road from the Palmer....

[Harry Koehler, cousin of Karl Vollmer]

4 Oct 1922: ROADHOUSE PROPRIETORS ARE WORST EVIL

Declaring that the present day roadhouse or picnic grounds are the worst sort of bootlegging establishments, Federal Judge Martin J. Wade continued to dish out jail sentences to proprietors and employees of such places.... Jail sentences run from 30 days to six months. Every jail sentence was accompanied with a fine from $500 to $1,000.

[Judge] said that it was these so-called temperance picnic grounds were corrupting the morals of the younger set in the rural communities. "Things have reached such a state of affairs that the young farmer boy does not think of going to a dance without this hooch. It is the fault of you fellows who are such cowards that you will not do your bootlegging in the city, but go out into the country, then proceed to sell promiscuously." This and other statements of a like nature constituted the severe lectures which accompanied the sentences of the defendants. Pleas of hard times, of families with no means of support and the scarcity of work were of no avail.

"Considering your case and the plea of yourself and the counsel I will be lenient with you," he would say, then follow with six months in jail and fines as high as $1,000. The first one to be so disappointed was Joe Johnston, said to be a waiter at the HOLLYWOOD INN on the Nahant road. He was charged with the sale of liquor on September 4 and the possession of 74 pints of beer on September 9.

...George Fahey, alleged proprietor and HARRY KOEHLER, said to be a waiter at the PALMER house, another of the rural picnic grounds, were dealt with the severest of any of the "roadhouse magnates." This resort is located across the road from HOLLYWOOD INN. The two were charged with the sale of liquor on September 4 and with the possession of 132 pints of beer, five quarts of wine, a quantity of gin and whiskey on Sept. 9. Fahey drew a sentence of three months in jail and a fine of $1,000, none of which was suspended and KOEHLER was awarded a fine of $1,000, $800 of which is held suspended for thirty days pending a more thoro investigation. The contention of the defendants was that they had just taken the place over and that they were preparing to establish an eating house there.

KETTNICH IS LET OFF WITH $300 AND COSTS

LINWOOD PROPRIETOR SAYS GUESTS BROUGHT THEIR OWN LIQUOR

After an eloquent plea on the part of the counsel for the owners of the property

Linwood Inn
Opening

Announcement is made of the opening of Linwood Inn and picnic grounds for the season of 1923.

Arrangements for picnics and dinner parties may be made by telephoning Dav. 1979-L1.

The River Road (Mississippi River Scenic Highway) is in exceptionally good condition for this time of the year and doesn't require any apologies.

It will be the policy of the management to conduct the place in a highly respectable and lawful manner and we hope with your co-operation and support this can be done. We want to make Linwood the most popular place to go for a good, sociable time. Our meals are the best and our chicken dinners are unexcelled. Kindly give us a trial.

Refined entertainment and excellent service at all times will be our policy.

Thanking you for your patronage and co-operation in the past and trusting that the same may continue in the future.

MRS. E. KETTNICH

1923 SEASON

Linwood Inn
Eight miles west on River Road
CHICKEN DINNERS

Served in Faultless Linwood Style on our screened porch where the cool breezes from the river fan your appetite.

FEATURING DAILY

Blue Diamond Syncopators
and their
ORIGINAL "5"
Tri-Cities' Best Dance Orchestra

For reservations for Banquets and large Dinner Parties telephone Dav. 1979-L-1

Let there be no misunderstanding of the fact that Linwood is operated strictly in accordance with the 18th Amendment.

July 11, 1923

Let there be no misunderstanding of the fact that Linwood is operated strictly in accordance with the 18th Amendment

Federal "Dry" Agents Sponge Up Linwood in Midnight Raiding Party

Prohibition Officers with Sheriff and Deputies Block Entrances to Davenport's Biggest Roadhouse, while Hundreds of Patrons Seek to Flee—Prominent Business Men and Parties Held for More than an Hour by Raiders—Officer Fires Shots to Halt Flight of One Man.

above: June 11, 1922
below: June 19, 1922

ASKS COURT TO FORBID LINWOOD SELLING LIQUOR

State Files Application for Temporary Injunction Against Resort.

GEORGE KETTNICH. MRS. GEORGE KETTNICH.

on which LINWOOD INN is located, George Kettnich was fined $300 costs by Judge Wade in Federal Court when he claimed that he did not have the liquor there for sale, but that the patrons of the place had brought it with them. The arresting officer testified that when the raid on the inn was made, July 10, the defendant tried to break the bottles of liquor on the ice in the ice box. Eight pints of whiskey, four pints of gin, and ten quarts of home brew were confiscated.

Kettnich was first arraigned this morning and pleaded not guilty. Then the prosecuting attorney threatened to change the information to include his wife as co–defendant. This afternoon the plea was changed to guilty. He and the owners of the property promised to do everything in their power in the hereafter to keep the place as clean a recreation resort as possible.

8 July 1923: STATE MOVES TO CLOSE 3 ROADHOUSES CROW CREEK INN, HOLLYWOOD INN, AND HELEN VAN DALE'S RESORT SEARCHED

Closing of at least 3 roadhouses in Scott county thru injunction proceedings was forecast Saturday by county officials following a series of raids conducted the night before by state, federal and county authorities on Hollywood Inn, Palmer's Inn and Crow Creek Inn in which eight men and three women were arrested, including HELEN VAN DALE, FORMER QUEEN OF THE OLD ROCK ISLAND UNDERWORLD and reputed head of an inter–state vice ring. Considerable whiskey, wine and hooch were confiscated.

The following were arrested and later released from the county jail on $500 appearance bonds pending their preliminary hearings in Justice Merle F. Wells' court:

JAMES (BRICK) MUNRO, PROPRIETOR OF HOLLYWOOD INN, John Allen and Fred McCarty, booked as bartenders and helpers at the inn. LeRoy and Ed Gadient, proprietors of the inn at CROW CREEK, located two miles east of Bettendorf. Helen Van Dale is held as the proprietress of PALMER INN, located across the road from the HOLLYWOOD INN near Nahant. Edna Smith and W.W. Bennett, found at Helen's place, were booked as inmates. Helen's case is set for hearing on July 18th.

In addition to raiding the three road houses, the authorities also visited the river shacks of Harry Hoffman and Sabin Bray in Rockingham township...not considered roadhouses by the authorities for the reason that both buildings are mere shacks and do not enjoy the class of patronage associated with HOLLYWOOD, PALMER OR CROW CREEK INN.

That the resorts are responsible for much of the delinquency to be found among the younger girls of the city and county is claimed by State Agent Risden. He claims young girls are invited to parties in the resorts and encouraged to drink.

[Brick Munro, former Bucktown dance pavilion owner]

13 Feb 1925: MR. AND MRS. KETTNICH OPEN NEW LINWOOD ON BRADY ST. ROAD SOON

After tomorrow night's dinner and dance at beautiful Terrace Gardens, the place will be closed for the season, according to announcement made today by the

> **Terrace Gardens**
>
> **DANCING**
>
> 8 P. M. — 2 A. M.
>
> **Your Last Chance**
>
> for a good time at this popular place
>
> **Saturday, Feb. 14th**
>
> Hereafter the Gardens will be closed indefinitely
>
> **Watch for the Opening**
>
> of the
>
> **New Linwood Inn**
>
> 5 Miles North on Brady St. Road
>
> Will open on or about March 14th, the Inn now being entirely remodeled and redecorated.

management. For the closing night there will be a special program of dancing music and other attractive features. Mr. and Mrs. George Kettnich, who have operated the Gardens during the winter season, will on or about March 15 open New Linwood, five miles out on the Brady street road. Like old Linwood, it promises to become one of the most popular pleasure resorts in the community.

Recently it was announced that old Linwood west of the city had to be abandoned on account of the erection of the big cement plant on the site. New Linwood will have several decided advantages over the old place. It will have a spacious dance floor, 40x70 feet in dimension. There will be four private dining rooms and the dance floor will be surrounded by attractive latticed-in booths. The most modern and up-to-date equipment for serving the public will be installed. The grounds surrounding the inn will be parked in splendid style with flower beds, shrubbery, benches, rockers and other details for the pleasure of the guests. A superb electric lighting system and beautiful decorations will add to the attractiveness of the inn.

Farewell, old Linwood! Welcome, New Linwood!

8 Mar 1925: TO OPEN BEAUTIFUL NEW LINWOOD INN NEXT SATURDAY, MARCH 14TH

Saturday, Mar. 14, will usher in the opening of the New Linwood inn on Brady street paved road two miles north of the city limits. It will be operated by Mr. and Mrs. George Kettnich, former proprietors of the old Linwood Inn west of the city. The latter has been demolished to make place for the new cement plant. In their new location Mr. and Mrs. Kettnich have spent thousands of dollars in alterations and improvements. Their dance hall is a veritable dancing dreamland, large, airy, and beautiful. In addition to the main dining room a number of private dining rooms have been arranged. The appointments and decorations are marvels of artistic beauty. The cuisine service will be in keeping with the splendid reputation established by Mr. and Mrs. Kettnich at old Linwood.

15 Mar 1925: BIG CROWD AT OPENING NIGHT OF NEW LINWOOD

A gathering which taxed the capacity of the place was present Saturday night at the formal opening of New Linwood Inn, two miles north of the city limits on the

Brady street road.

The vast assemblage was loud in their praise of the beauty of the place, especially the interior decorations, which reflected in the credit of the enterprising proprietors, Mr. and Mrs. George Kettnich.

The large dining room and spacious dance floor were utilized to their best advantage at the opening. Flowers and good wishes greeted the proprietors on all sides. Al Knappe's Club Royale orchestra furnished an excellent musical program both for the diners and the dancers.

18 Mar 1925: STATE RESUMES LINWOOD CASE

Attorneys Carl Lambach and Alex Carroll for Mr. and Mrs. George Kettnich and Mr. and Mrs. Victor Meyer, charged with maintaining a public nuisance as the result of a raid of the New Linwood inn Sunday morning by three federal prohibition agents, the county sheriff, and three deputy sheriffs, and is declared by Justice Wells to have been one of the biggest federal raids ever made in Scott county.

No testimony or evidence of any kind was adduced at the hearing to show that intoxicating liquors had been sold by the defendants, but rather that those who were drinking and brought their own liquor.

S.E. Kronkheit of Knoxville, one of the prohibition agents, testified that he had seen more drunks at the New Linwood inn than he had ever seen before in one place. The Davenport prohibition officer testified that there were 400 people at the inn and at least a fourth of them were drunk.

Deputy Sheriff Fred Scharfenberg told of locking up with others the four people who were later fined for drunkenness, and said that there were so many drunks that "it would have taken a moving van to carry them all back to county jail."

One of the federal agents declared that Scott county is the only place in the state permitting roadhouses to operate, that all others have been closed. "We are going to close them up if it is the last thing we do while in office," he declared.

22 Mar 1925: CANCEL LEASE NEW LINWOOD; CLOSE DOORS

The bright lights of the New Linwood Inn, opened just a week ago and immediately raided by Sheriff Frank Martin, will burn no more. George Kettnich, the proprietor, announced that in order to avoid more trouble he had canceled his lease and closed the place for good. Tho Sheriff Martin has declared that the "roadhouses must go," there have been no announcements from other establishments of any intention of closing. No other roadhouses were raided last week. Mr. Kettnich first offered to close his New Linwood Inn if the injunction proceedings against him were dropped. When the sheriff's office insisted that it be pushed, however, he decided to close voluntarily.

[George & Emma Kettnich moved to California]

REMEMBERING LINWOOD
by Jim Arpy

The year: 1924. The place: Linwood Inn, a few miles down river from Davenport.

The Jack Rogers orchestra played for the dinner hour and later in the evening moved next door to provide music in a house of ill–repute. Lloyd *Bud* Hance of Rock Island remembered Linwood Inn and its bucolic landscape before quarries wiped from the face of the earth any remnant of this Prohibition–era roadhouse.

"The businessmen—bootleggers—with their *girlfriends* came over from town to spend the evening," Bud recalled. "Many times we played until three or four in the morning, grabbed a few winks, then got up and played golf."

Bandleader Jack Rogers played banjo, along with George 'Whitey' Carstens, drums; Joe Stroehle, piano; saxophonists Bill Pierce, Eddie Anderson and Bud Hance.

"I started on violin," Bud said, "played a jazz fiddle with the Carlisle Evans band on the riverboats and around the Quad Cities. Then Bill Pierce suggested that I learn the sax, so I could play triple harmony with Pierce and Anderson. I never took any formal sax lessons but learned to play with help from Bill and Eddie. I had some piano background so that helped my reading."

Bud went with the Ben Saltzman band and played all over Wisconsin. "We traveled in one car. You have to remember there were few paved roads; it was primitive to say the least. We played the lumber camp circuit—went into lumber towns where they had the tents and dance floors. The lumber companies would provide the electric power until 10 pm. One night it was too late to drive on after the dance so we went down where the lumberjacks were sleeping and said, 'Hey, roll over, we need a bed.' It was so dark you never knew who you were sleeping with. Then in the morning, the lumberjacks would get up early and go to work."

Bud traveled with a band called Kel–Harts Blue Boys, the name derived from leaders Gus Kelly and Joe Hart who played in theaters between movies and vaudeville acts.

He then spent a year in Pontiac, MI, where vaudeville troupe owner Billy Sharp needed a pianist. Band members told Sharp that Bud played piano. "I couldn't read notes," Bud said. "But the owner said all I had to do was set the tempo for the pit band so the hoofers could dance. So I tried it and was with them for three years. Later I added my sax, clarinet and violin into the act. It was a classic case of being in the right place at the right time."

He married Arline 'Pat' Renner in 1927 and she joined him on the Pantages vaudeville circuit which included the cities of Salt Lake, Vancouver, and Seattle. They traveled first class on trains and Bud became manager of the act. This continued until the talkies became popular and vaudeville began to fade. "Bud attended the demise of vaudeville," his wife Pat said, adding, "might say he helped kill it."

"Yes, I gave it a good shove," Bud said. "I told the guys they better start looking for a hotel to manage because vaudeville is done." Other performers scoffed at the idea. They had hopes of getting a little hotel of their own to manage when they retired or quit show business. "They thought I was crazy. They couldn't believe that vaudeville was through."

Old friend Leo Bahr called Bud from Dallas in the summer of 1929 to say they needed a sax man. That's how he came to join the Frank Quartell Brunswick Recording orchestra of Chicago. Later he moved to California, returning to Rock Island in 1936 to take over his dad's real estate business.

Bud's last professional job was with the Nate Marblestone band at the Crossroad Inn in Milan, IL. That was 1938. Even when Bud was not playing music, he was never out of music. He wrote barbershop arrangements for the Elks and Rotary clubs and helped his brother Monty, who also had gone into show business.

Bud's collection of more than two thousand 78 RPM records included six or eight original Bix recordings, one of which he purchased when Bix's brother Charles was running the music department at the Harned Von Maur Department store.

"As close as I came to knowing Bix was during the summer of 1928 when I was playing on the old *W.J. Quinlan* ferryboat, going between Davenport and Rock Island," Bud said. "One night a young fella sort of sat around the bandstand, then got up and talked to the leader, Tony Catalano. They chatted in a friendly manner for a while and then he walked away.

"None of us knew it was Bix, though, until Tony told us. Bix was famous then in New York and Paris, but not much locally. He was a kind of maverick in a lot of ways. He had trouble with the musicians union, so he didn't play a lot around the Tri–Cities."

Waiting on the ferry

Bud Hance of Jack Roger's Deluxe Syncopators Linwood—1924 Season

Below: Quinlan Ferry

below right: 1931 AD

QUINLAN MEMORIES
by Bud Hance (1905–1990)

To those of us who have lived many years in the Quad Cities, the great river that runs through our towns holds us in a state of awe and reverence because of its natural beauty, its great power, and sense of permanence, as well as its recreational and commercial importance. When we leave it for awhile, we miss it and are always happy to return home to the environment of the Mississippi.

The ferryboat between Rock Island and Davenport was important during those days when the river was free of ice. Our ferryboat, the *W.J. Quinlan*, was built in Rock Island at Kahlke Boatyards by Billy Quinlan. In Quinlan's navy, I belonged to special services as a non–combatant on the upper deck playing in the dance band.

Old–timers may remember that Tony Catalano's Jazz–bo Band played for the dances during the summer of 1928. We played six nights a week and also for special occasions and outings.

Dancing was a major diversion in those Volstead days. While the many winter dance hall floors were getting a new sanding and coat of varnish, the ferryboats provided summer dancing.

Tony had a six–piece band on the ferry, with himself on trumpet; Ernie Beaverbrook [sic Bieberbach], trombone; Louie Bruhn, piano; Herb Day, drums; Johnny Eberhardt and I played sax. Tony had been playing since jazz was invented and had a wide reputation.

There was great fascination to the river. Sunsets and golden paths of waves under silhouetted bridges changed into a Disneyland of thousand of lights with each light reflected on a million dancing waves. And the boat itself was outlined by white bulbs, and the dance hall was colorful with hanging Japanese lanterns of many colors. Many people came just to ride in this cool festive atmosphere.

There seemed to be a rhythm to the boat and to the river, in addition to the dance music. The great wooden drive–shaft seemed to set the basic beat

Davenport-Rock Island Ferry
sold by the Spencer family to W.J. Quinlan in 1925

as each slat of the stern–wheel slapped the water in double time. The entire boat throbbed. And at just the right time, the throaty old whistle would let patrons and shoppers know that the boat would soon be docking. This path was repeated by the clock as the pilot put the boat in a dog trot against the current, back and forth in sort of a figure–8.

Nearing the dock on the upstream loop, Lee 'Red' Bateman, with a large rope in his hand, would leap across the churning gap and twirl the rope around a large piling to stop the boat's momentum. As the current settled the boat back, Lee would re–twirl the rope and lock it by a slot at the piling top as the shiny post squeaked painfully, holding the boat secure. Bateman would then raise the restraining fence and lower the gangway.

Next, he'd race to the rear where another piling and rope would hold the boat in place while docked and act as a pivot, allowing the bow to swing out of the current when pulling away. This would require another leap from the dock to the boat.

There was great skill shown in these landings and debarkings between the pilot, the rope man, and the engineers in the boiler room who obeyed the bell signals for power, both forward and reverse. Wind, river stages, and currents kept the river alive and sometimes unfriendly.

The boat was Billy Quinlan's pride and joy. He was all over the boat during the long hours of every day. He was a trim dapper little Irishman in his naval officer blues and white cap. He ran a tight little ship with efficiency and decorum at all times. He would take tickets, relieve the pilot, sweep out peanut shells and popcorn, ink–stamp hands of dancers and perform any duty of the moment. I often thought of the ferryboat as Billy Quinlan's toy as he pushed it back and forth across his big Mississippi bathtub.

There was a romance about the ferry boat. Tourists and vacationers enjoyed riding the upper deck just for the sights and sounds of the Mississippi. Children were always thrilled to ride the ferry.

It also provided an efficient way to cross the great river in those days of downtown shopping and keen rivalry between Davenport and Rock Island merchants. At a nickel a crossing, it was a real bargain.

The final demise of the *W.J. Quinlan* is a sad memory. Dry–docked and resting on a rotting wooden cradle, deserted and stripped bare, smothered in horse weeds and nettles, she burned to the ground in 1967.

But I'll always remember those happy, smiling faces as viewed from the orchestra stand, see the Japanese lanterns, hear the paddlewheel and splashing water, the signal bells, the beckoning whistle and squeaking ropes, and picture Billy Q in complete command of his lovely toy.

TERRACE GARDENS: WHAT A GRAND PLACE

The date was Dec. 23, 1920. Terrace Gardens advertised itself as the most modern and beautiful dining and dancing room in the Tri–Cities. It occupied the lower level of the newly constructed Kahl Office Building at West Third and Ripley Streets in Davenport. Its original managers, the Maehrs brothers, owned a popular confectionary and ice cream parlor.

The *Davenport Democrat–Leader* proclaimed:TERRACE GARDENS OPENED TO PUBLIC AS MUSIC AND BEAUTY MINGLE IN MERRY FIRST NIGHT.

The paper's reporter reached into his bag of superlatives to record his first impressions: "A little bit of heaven has been transported into every nook and corner of the Terrace Gardens. The marble stairs winding down from the street are constructed in the same manner as the entrance to the Terrace Gardens in Chicago. When you first enter you wonder if you haven't suddenly stepped into the exclusive dining room of the Italian Palace, but no, there are too many tables, too many pleasant-looking serving girls, and the crowd assembled is evidently having too enjoyable an evening to compare with the icy dignity and cold splendor of a royal gathering.

"The dining room is L-shaped and takes up all the space under the office part of the Kahl Building. Along the sides is a terraced aisle. A little white fence, delicately painted, separates the main room from the tables along the wall. The tables are for two and placed beside what looks like a window, but proves to be a painting, set in a niche in the wall and surrounded by hidden lights, so as to give it the aspect of a natural landscape. Each table, finished in pale blue enamel and covered with rare Irish linens, has such a picture, hand-painted by Louis Amorossi, known internationally for his art. Even the walls of the Gardens are decorated with genuine oil paintings by this renowned artist," the reporter stated.

"A slightly elevated stage sits in the corner where the 'L' turns. Lights in the ceiling are set to throw their full force of variegated colors directly on the stage, yet are hidden from patrons of the place. At the front of the stage is a beautiful cerise velour curtain with gold fringe at the bottom 12 inches long. Seated around an Apollo grand piano is the orchestra, which has been selected by the management.

"Formalities, conventions and dignities were shed with overcoats at the entrance, and from 6:30 p.m. until midnight the first nighters dined, danced and visited to their hearts' content.

Vaudeville stars Frank Devoe and Harry Hosford, featured on the Columbia Theatre as musical comedy favorites, added the touch that put the 'pep' in the diners. Formerly with Trixie Friganzi, Mr. Devoe is known to every theatre-going person in the country, and his excerpts from prominent successes were well-received last night.

"The Deluxe Jazz Band was well-received by everyone present and all hearts were opened to this frolicking bunch of musical youngsters. Dancers applauded until their palms were red and the orchestra responded with several encores."

Also premiering at the Kahl Building was the Capitol Theatre. It possessed "the splendor of an Oriental palace and the art and charm of the chateaux of Louis XIV," according to the *Davenport Democrat-Leader*. The estimated opening attendance on Christmas day and night was 1,100 to watch the movie, *The Man Who Lost Himself*. The theater recently underwent extensive remodeling.

14 SEP 1924: GARDENS OPEN OCT. 1; MANAGER IS G. KETTNICH
POPULAR CAFE PASSES TO MANAGEMENT OF POPULAR LOCAL MAN

Terrace Gardens, one of the most beautiful cafes in the middle-west will pass to the management of Mr. and Mrs. George Kettnich, for the past four years managers of Linwood Inn, it was announced Saturday by Superintendent Wesson of the Kahl building. Arrangements for the opening of the popular dining and dancing palace are now being made by the new managers who will throw open the doors on Wednesday, Oct 1. The announcement that Mr. and Mrs. Kettnich will assume management of Terrace Gardens will be met with much favor in the Tri-Cites and their many friends will wish them success in their new venture. Mr. Kettnich announced Saturday that the Gardens will be operated in a very high class manner and that the same quality of meals that made Linwood Inn famous will be served at the Davenport café.

18 Aug 1925: The beautiful Cathay Garden in the Kahl building had the most auspicious opening last evening when an assemblage of between 300 and 400 people, representative of Davenport's business and social life, gathered there as specially invited guests of C. Chung, the manager. Mr. Chung proved a most hospitable host and was showered with compliments and well wishes for his success. The public opening of the Garden is this evening. CATHAY GARDEN, formerly TERRACE GARDEN, is without question the most elaborate and beautiful restaurant in this section of the country. It will be conducted on the American-Chinese plan by the new owners, featuring fine music and dancing...

9 JULY 1927: REMODELING OF DANCE GARDENS IS UNDER WAY

Work of remodeling the former Cathay Gardens into what is said will be the Tri-cities most beautiful ball room and which will be named "The Capitol Gardens" was started today when carpenters and decorators took possession of the Davenport's one time cabaret. ….An entire new floor, which when finished will have a capacity of more than 250 couples, will be installed.

Sept 14: The formal opening of the new Capitol Gardens, the ball room in the Kahl building, took place last night. More than 200 enjoyed the dancing on the opening night despite the extreme heat. Music for the dancing was furnished by the Capitol Gardens orchestra, under the direction of Carlisle Evans.

Sept 25: After the theater have you taken her to Capitol Gardens for lunch and dancing? Since it has been remodeled you'd hardly recognized the place, 'cuz it's so entirely different. You'll love the romantic atmosphere of Old Spain as it's reflected in the design. And that isn't all, for you'll find a floor that is smooth and fine, waxed just enough for dancers to easily glide their way thru "castles of old Madrid," picturesquely characterized on the walls. And now that there is more dancing space you'll enjoy steppin' to the music of the Capitol Gardens orchestra, under the direction of Carlisle Evans.

5 Oct 1928: NITE CLUB WILL OPEN SATURDAY ON NEW SCALE

The latest night club in the Tri–Cities, the Capitol Gardens, will usher in the indoor season of entertainment and advance indications point to a capacity crowd for the first night. William Johnson, the manager, promises a distinctly modern club with the atmosphere of the Eastern type of club. CARLISLE EVANS' ORCHESTRA will furnish the music for the dancing.

Les Swanson sat in several times with Carlisle Evans' Capitol Gardens Orchestra. "What a grand place it was," Les recalled.

But it fell on hard times during the Depression. Alternative uses for the space included a bingo parlor, headquarters for Junior Achievement, and Club Mo–Kan nightclub.

The Kahl's vacant basement is like a time capsule. Its marble steps leading from the sidewalk off Third Street are still there, but the doors that opened into the restaurant have been welded shut. Access with proper permission, is by elevator inside the lobby.

Scraps of wallpaper cling to its bare walls. The hard maple dance floor has been removed and the bandstand is gone. Taking a 90–degree turn from the dance floor, the L–shaped room continues on for several feet to what once served as a kitchen.

In a eulogy to Henry 'Hummer' Kahl, who spared no expense in building the Kahl, Davenport Mayor C.L. Barewald said, "When we, who sit here tonight, have laid ourselves down for our final and eternal sleep, when our descendants and their descendants pass up and down these familiar streets, they will look upon this building and will admire the courage and genius of Henry Kahl."

Ironic that a 17–year–old musician who failed his union exam and thus denied the opportunity to play for the opening of Terrace Gardens went on to international notoriety while its far–sighted capitalist is all but forgotten.

One other irony—offices of the Bix Society occupy the Kahl's first floor, literally steps away from the grand old Terrace Gardens.

THE GUY WHO FLUNKED BIX

Fritz Putzier probably told the story many times through the years: how the Buckley Novelty Orchestra landed the job at the opening for the Terrace Gardens Restaurant in the newly–erected Kahl Building in Davenport, and how everything looked great until word got out that they were a non–union band.

"When the union musicians learned we'd been booked for the opening, they said that if we got hired they'd never play there," Fritz said. "We either had to join the union or give up the job."

Buckley's members played well as an ensemble during their audition at the union hall, but disaster struck when union examiner Roy Kautz asked each musician to sight–read a music composition.

"Bix, of course, was in trouble," Fritz said. "I can still hear the stick crashing down on the piano as Kautz landed on him. He realized Bix was trying to play by ear.

"Bix had tears in his eyes because he knew he had loused up the whole band," Fritz recalled. The Buckley Orchestra missed out on the Terrace Garden opening. "We couldn't play it without him. He was what made it go," Fritz explained.
"We needed him for the hot licks."

So who was this Roy Kautz?

Rock Island's FORT ARMSTRONG THEATER, Third Av & 18th St. Opened in January 1921 as a vaudeville and movie house, it became part of the A.H. Blank chain in 1926. Since 1977 it's operated as Circa '21 dinner theater. CASEY JONES AND HIS JAZZ JESTERS had folks "waiting in a line a block long," according to the *Democrat-Leader* in October 1927: "Those on the outside were waiting to hear what those on the inside were applauding." Band members: Roy Kautz, piano; William Pearmann, violin; Ted Matthews & Ed Andrews, saxophones; Ed Baumgarten, clarinet; Al Woeckner & Harry LaRue, cornets; Tal Sexton, trombone; Dean Handley, bass; Henry Banderob, traps. Postcard of exterior above; interior below.

FT. ARMSTRONG POLICY PACKS HOUSE SUNDAY

Casey Jones and His Jesters Furnish Entertaining Program.

They were waiting in a line a block long at the Ft. Armstrong theater. Those on the outside were waiting to hear and see what those on the inside were applauding. —Casey Jones and his Jazz Jesters.

Manager Cummings' "New Idea" policy went over with a large bang at all the performances Sunday, and when Casey, the master of ceremonies, and his boys had finished their last encore last night, the fans and fanettes were still asking for more. Which, after all, is not a bad sign.

In the group are Roy Kautz, piano; William Pearmann, violin; Ted Matthews and Ed Anderson, saxophones; Ed Baumgarten, clarinet; Al Woeckner and Harry LaRue, cornets; Tal Sexton, trombone; Dean Handley, bass, and Henry Banderob, traps.

Orchestra sounded very well Sunday, and the patrons gave it a big hand.

Big Business Is Reported at Capitol Gardens

There were over 200 in attendance at the Capitol Gardens Saturday night, which number attests to the growing popularity of this well known amusement place in the Kahl building under the able management of John H. Davies. The guests greatly enjoyed the dance numbers to the strain of the Capitol Gardens orchestra under the direction of Carlisle Evans.

The Gardens are open to the public every night in the week except Monday, which is reserved for private parties. Hours are 9 to 1 o'clock except Saturday nights, when the Gardens are open from 9 p. m. to 2 a. m.

The man locals knew as *Mr. Show Business*, Roy E. Kautz made friends with many of the greats on the vaudeville circuit, including Will Rogers, Sophie Tucker, Jack Benny, Eddie Cantor, Bill Robinson and Ginger Rogers.

Born March 26, 1886, in Buffalo, IA, Kautz came to Davenport as a youth and studied music while attending business college. He married Frances Stapleton in 1915. He joined Local No. 67, American Federation of Musicians on Oct. 2, 1903. The same year Bix was born, Kautz got his first professional gig on Christmas day at the Columbia Theater in Davenport. Later, he led orchestras at A.H. Blank's Capitol and Orpheum theaters in Davenport, and the Rock Island Fort Theater—today's Circa 21.

In later years, Kautz gave private music lessons and taught band at the Annie Wittenmyer Home in Davenport. He died April 28, 1964, at age 78.

Vince Petersen, son of Albert Petersen and Bix's second cousin, was himself an officer of Local 67 A.F.M. He explained that union examinations hinged a lot on supply and demand. If union membership was stable, the tests became more difficult and fewer musicians would pass. Later, when memberships lagged, "we would take anyone," Vince said, laughing. Of course, that isn't the reason Kautz flunked Bix. The jazz cornetist just couldn't read music. Kautz had no other choice.

Fritz said that Kautz felt sorry Bix had failed and tried to console him. Two years later Bix was back again by way of some arcane maneuvering by his mother and Albert Petersen. Bix passed the union exam—not by playing cornet, but piano.

FRITZ PUTZIER
by Jim Arpy

Richard 'Fritz' Putzier, July 1974 at razing of Whitaker building

Richard 'Fritz' Putzier never dreamed that when he sneaked out of high school convocation to haggle with a fellow student over the sale of his cornet that he'd be making history.

But the eager young man digging into his pocket for a $15 down payment was Bix Beiderbecke and Fritz's Conn Victor horn would be his passport to musical immortality.

"It really all started when a group of us high school musicians had a summer job cleaning the calcimine walls at the high school," Putzier said. "Bix at that time wasn't far enough along to be regarded as part of the orchestra, though he used to play piano for Friday afternoon dances in the gym.

"Anyway, Capt. Percy Swain, who operated the Julia Belle Swain excursion boat out of Peoria, stopped and asked us to finish out the season playing on his boat. Well, you can imagine we threw the brushes in the air and took off for Peoria at once. Remember Bix wasn't with us.

"It was a tough job on the boat and we had to play a lot. By the time we got down around Starved Rock I was certain that I'd blown my lip. There were rumors that this could happen to horn players and they'd never play again.

"We decided we just had to get off that boat and when it docked somewhere around Starved Rock another guy and I sneaked off. We wanted

Bettendorf Town Hall as it looked when Bix sat in with Fritz Putzier's bandmates at a school dance. Both still were in high school and the gig was not all that long after Bix bought Putzier's cornet. The town hall was built in 1907 with council chambers and fire department on the ground floor; the top floor served as a dance hall when not in use for meetings. The tower had a bell to signal firefighter volunteers The building was moved a block up in 1935 when the first span of the Iowa-Illinois Memorial Bridge was built and torn down in the early 1970s to make way for the second span of what is now I-74 Bridge from Moline to Bettendorf.

to get back to school, anyway. I remember we kept our heads down and while we waited in the railroad depot for a train home we felt like escaped criminals and envisioned the captain coming to arrest us," Putzier related.

"Well, I was back in school and seated at the rear of the auditorium next to Bix while George Edward Marshall, the principal, gave the welcoming address for the new school year. Bix and I weren't listening. Instead, he was asking about the job on the boat.

"When I told Bix I was going to sell my cornet, he grabbed me by the arm and demanded, 'how much?' When I told him I wanted $35, he stood up and led me across the hall to the music room. Bix said he didn't have that much money, but could give me $15 and the rest in monthly installments. Well, we consummated the deal but you know Bix never did make the last $8 payment!"

Putzier bought a C–melody saxophone that he played in bands for several years. "I didn't see Bix for six weeks after that, but one day I was standing on the corner of Third and Brady and Bix saw me from across the street and rushed over, asking in his eager way where the band was playing that night. When I told him we were playing for a high school dance at the Bettendorf town hall he asked if he could sit in with us and I said, 'Sure.'

"I wasn't certain I'd said the right thing," Putzier recalled, "because I didn't know if he could play or not. As far as I knew, he'd never had a horn in his hands before. I learned later he had used a borrowed old one for a while, but this was his first legitimate cornet.

"I'll never forget that night. Bix arrived late, around 10:30 and he was so eager to play that instead of going around the dancers, he cut right through them, heading for the stand. We were right in the middle of a number when he took that horn out of the case and started putting a string of cute little configurations together.

"We were all just amazed. Sure there were some blue notes, but you could see right there that the boy had something. I've never been so surprised in my life," Putzier said.

Bix's progress from then on was rapid. Putzier remembered that Bix's first legitimate playing job was with Neil Buckley's Novelty Orchestra in Davenport. Putzier recalled, too, when he and Bix were hired to play with the Ralph Miedke band for the grand opening of the Moline State Trust Bank.

"It was the first time Bix had to wear a tuxedo. It was an old one that had belonged to his uncle and had been cut down for him. It was obviously still a little big and kind of green around the edges. We were supposed to play from 1 to 6 pm, but we were so excited we put on our tuxes and went downtown in Davenport a couple of hours early," Putzier related.

"I said to Bix, 'look, we may never have our tuxes on in the daytime again. Let's go in and have our pictures taken. So, we went into the Whitaker Building, where a photographer had his studio, and had them taken.

"I knew Bix, of course, before he got into the big leagues, and to me, though I greatly respected his musical ability, he was the all–American boy, pink–cheeked, enthusiastic, a fine tennis player, an all–around likeable person," Putzier said.

Putzier recalled that when the Kahl Building was nearing completion, Buckley's Novelty Orchestra, of which Bix was an important part, had been hired to open the new Terrace Gardens in the basement.

"We were a non–union band and we anticipated some trouble with the union, which wasn't long in coming. When the union musicians learned we'd been hired for the opening they said that if we got hired they'd never play there.

"We either had to join the union or give up the job. We knew we were in trouble because all of us played by ear, though the rest of us could read a little, but Bix couldn't read a note.

"But we were determined to try, so for several days we practiced with the music set up in front of us. We all met at 3rd and Brady a half hour before audition time in front of Roy Kautz, who represented the union and had the Orpheum Theatre Orchestra. Bix was more nervous than any of us.

"He said, 'let's go over to the YMCA for one last rehearsal,' so we trooped over there and set up. Then we headed for the union headquarters and very carefully set up our music. We played just as we had rehearsed and got by all right. That is, until Kautz said he wanted to take each individual and have him play separately.

"Bix, of course, was in trouble but he tried to fake it. Not knowing the melody, he picked out the notes of the piano part and tried to play along, a fraction of a second behind. I can still hear the stick crashing down on the piano as Kautz landed on him. He realized Bix was trying to play by ear. Bix had tears in his eyes because he knew he had loused up the whole band. And the thing was that we couldn't play it without him. He was what made it go. We needed him for the hot licks."

Putzier remembered when Bix came back to Davenport after leaving Whiteman's band. "We sat in my car outside his house and talked for a long time. Bix didn't look much different physically, but he seemed pensive and wanted to talk about old friends we'd known. He didn't talk much about having to leave the band. But the old spark and enthusiasm seemed to be missing. He wasn't quite the same."

Putzier had gone on to the University of Iowa where he played with a fraternity band. Out of school, he played a short stint at the LeClaire Hotel roof garden, but his heart wasn't in it. Eventually, he sold his home and, following his father's advice, entered the investment business. He moved to California in 1927.

A favorite memory of Bix was the time when their band was coming home after playing in Sabula, Iowa. Bix had gone to sleep next to a window and as the coal–burning train rolled along his face became covered with soot. "Bix was so sleepy when he got off the train that he lay right down in a sunny spot in a vacant lot and went to sleep. He was so likeable that anything he did seemed funny. He was just Bix and that was all there was to it," Putzier said.

"I lived in Blue Grass and stayed many nights with Bix in his home on Grand Avenue. We would talk nothing but music all the time I was there, way into the night. I always had a high regard for his family. They were nice people. Bix would be up in the morning and at the piano before he left for school.

"He had a little phonograph next to the piano and would put on Dixie records and slow the music way down. Then he'd sit there and with one finger pick it all out perfectly. I always thought that's where he got some of his later ideas, listening to those records note by note."

Putzier said the end of the cornet he sold to Bix came when it got dropped on a New York railway station platform. "He apparently bent something so that it was almost impossible to get the right tone out of it but nonetheless he went on with it that way and managed to sit in with the Original Dixieland Jazz Band, who were his idols at the time, though they liked his piano playing better."

Looking back, almost to the beginning, Putzier recalled that, "it was true Bix was no scholar. I sat two seats behind him in study hall and we worked out a way of communicating by tapping two pens on the inkwell, telling each other what we were thinking in that noisy way.

"The tapping," Putzier grinned, "was done with a jazz beat."

ORCHESTRA FROM BLUE GRASS TO HAVE LAWN FETE

Special to The Democrat

Blue Grass, Ia., Aug. 4.—On Saturday evening of this week, a lawn party will be given at the J. F. Putzier home by the Blue Grass Community orchestra. The new paved road to Blue Grass will be opened entirely by this time, and the Putzier home is right at the end of the pavement.

The event is for the benefit of the orchestra which will shortly enter upon its fall program. The girls of the Phi Omega club have offered to do the serving for the social. The spacious lawn of the Putzier home will be decorated and lighted by Japanese lanterns. Refreshments will be served and the public is invited to attend. Music thruout the evening will be given by the orchestra.

Arrangements are being made for a community banquet to be given during the latter part of September, partly in celebration of the opening of the paved road. The event will also mark the observance of the fifth anniversary of the building of the Community house. A meeting will shortly be announced to which all community organizations will be asked to send representatives to make arrangements for the banquet. It is expected that a large number of people from Davenport will be present.

Those who compose the orchestra are William Bettendorf, leader and saxophone; Fritz Putzier, saxophone; Harold Bendixen, saxophone; Herbert Metcalf, piano; Robert Bedford, violin; Francis Gordon, banjo; and John O'Donnell, traps.

Richard 'Fritz' Putzier, 1921 photo; top left is a 1925 news clip. July 1917 commentary, music critic R.C. Brown got it when he wrote: *jazz had to be heard to be understood.*

While the ague of ragtime still shivers through the musical veins of America, a new disease is making its symptoms apparent. It is a particularly spasmodic form of cholera known as *jazz* among its victims.

Like most American slang, jazz may be used as a noun, adjective or verb. One may put jazz into a rendition of Dvorak's *Humoresque*; there are jazz bands, and the ability to jazz is a prime recommendation for one seeking employment in a café orchestra.

Any ordinary ragtime piece can be jazzed. Of course one might not be able to recognize the piece during or after the rendition.

Jazz is a riotous blare of sound, a slam-bang, knock-em-down-and-drag-em-out confusion of noises. The instruments work one against the other in frantic endeavor to excel in insulting the ear that has been accustomed to harmless, modest ragtime.

Jazz is a brazen, screaming, banging, tin-panning, moans and groans from a saxophone. The saxophone runs wild and does things that cannot be written in music. The wilder it runs the better. If the player should become completely insane instead of partly, he would be considered a genius.

Jazz musicians are not expected to stick to the score. They wander off on independent excursions of their own, each trying to drown his knowledge of music in instrumental dissipation. The fascination of *jazz* music is in its wild barbarity. It must be heard to be understood and even then, no one who has heard it can explain it in any definite manner.

Bix's most famous portrait was not taken in Davenport in 1921 but rather 1924 in Cincinnati at Doyle's Dancing Academy, same time as group portrait of the Wolverines, shown here L-R: Vic Moore, drums; George Johnson, sax; Jimmy Hartwell, clarinet; Dick Voynow (standing), piano; BIX, Al Gandee, trombone; Min Leinbrook, brass bass; and Bob Gillette, banjo.

On the Hunt For a Bank and a Band

The date was August 30, 1921. Ralph Miedke's orchestra played for the grand opening of the Moline State Trust and Savings Bank. Did the bank hire a photographer to cover the event? Perhaps, somewhere deep in their dusty archives there could be found photos of the Miedke Orchestra with Bix playing in the bank lobby. Barbara Sandberg, a Moline city historian, said that the bank archives we were searching for, if they existed, are in the bank located on the southwest corner of Fifteenth Street and Fifth Avenue, just across the street from the original Moline State Trust and Savings Bank.

When a very nice lady named Julie was told of our mission, she smiled and sadly informed us that the photographs didn't exist. The bank's archives, not unlike Mother Hubbard's cupboard, were bare. But Julie surprised us when she said the very bank we were standing in was the Moline Trust and Savings Bank where Miedke played in 1921.

Wait a minute! The building across the street had *State Trust and Savings Bank* embossed on its top facade. "Yes, that was the original bank building," Julie said, noting the lobby, even after several remodeling projects still retained its high ceilings and many of its original decorations. "Bix would probably recognize it if he came here today," she said.

Next on our search list was Ralph Miedke. We knew he was a musician, but didn't know what instrument he played. The Ralph Miedke Society Orchestra performed all around the QC. Miedke also made appearances with the Romance and Rhythm Orchestra and on WOC with the Bernie Schultz Orchestra.

Ralph was born in Moline. He married the sister of Warren Giles, president of the National Baseball League. They had a son, Warren, whom we tracked down in Houston, TX.

He passed along a photo of his father's band. Bix is not in it. Warren said his father originally played the saxophone but later changed to banjo. After Ralph left the music business he and his wife became managers of the Algona Country Club in Kossuth County, IA.

The club's golf professional, Jack Canning, burned to death in a fire that completely destroyed the clubhouse in 1947. In 1950, the Miedkes moved to Neenah, WI, where Ralph was running Valley Inn at the time of his death March 10, 1967.

Ralph Miedke on banjo with the Miedke Orchestra at the Coliseum Ballroom, c.1920s. Below: Eagles (Danceland) Ad, May 1924, and obit 1967

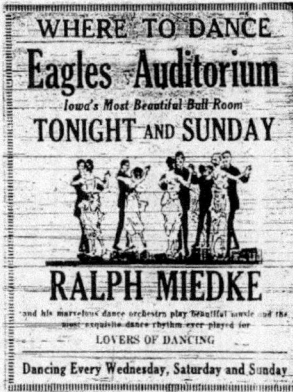

Above: Postcard of Moline State Bank as it looked in 1921 when Bix played with Ralph Miedke Orchestra for bank's grand opening

Right: Chase Bank
      501 15th St, Moline

Thelma's Valentine

She was the cute gal working in a department store. He was the snappily-dressed young man in a straw hat.

She was Thelma Griffin, newly-named assistant buyer at a department store in downtown Davenport. He was 18-year-old Leon Bix Beiderbecke, an up-and-coming musician.

It was 1921, Valentine's Day. Romance was in the air. Thelma Griffin would never forget that day. "I'd just come from Tipton, Iowa, to be an assistant buyer at Harned Von Maur. One of my duties was to model clothes in the style shows. Bix played in the show's orchestra.

"He was always dressed well and wearing that straw hat. He would come into the store every day. Oh, and he had a certain walk. The way he would swing up the stairs!" Thelma recalled.

"Bix and some of the other musicians and I used to have jam sessions at places like Griffin's chocolate shop on Davenport's Third Street. I'm a pianist myself and listeners tell me I have a different style. It's one that Bix taught me, how to play *Somebody Stole My Gal*, with a beat at the end where he'd come in on cornet.

"Bix was just a wonderful guy. I can't believe some of the things they say about him today. He and I were just friends, even if the Valentine I've kept all these years does say, *To my sweetheart*. He was friendly, but shy."

How shy? He left the elaborately decorated Valentine on her desk at work and slipped away. She wasn't even there at the time. It was simply signed, *Bix*.

Thelma held the old Valentine tenderly as she remembered. "I never dreamed that Bix would reach the status he did. I moved to Springfield about the time he started on his road to the top bands. We corresponded for a time, but I didn't save his letters. Sometimes I wish I had, now that he's famous."

Scandal Finds Bix

Bix was a third–generation American who never knew his German–born grandfather but deeply loved his Oma Beiderbecke. He especially loved playing her piano and teaching her tunes popular among his friends.

In the span of a decade, Davenport's German–Americans went from being celebrated for their contributions in commerce and culture to being suspected terrorists.

> This memorial stone shall teach our children that we can be good American citizens without being ashamed of the race from whence we have descended and its many thousand years of glorious history—Henry Vollmer, Franco–Prussian memorial ceremony at Washington Square Park, 1907

Davenport's Washington Square was replaced in 1940 by an entrance ramp to the Centennial Bridge. Gone the *Sachsen Wald* oak trees donated in 1898 to the citizens of Davenport by Prince Bismarck. Two memorial stones—one for Schleswig–Holstein veterans and one for the armies that defeated Napoleon III in the Franco–Prussian war, thus ushering in the German Empire—erased from the landscape.

German ancestral pride became tantamount to treason in America during WWI. The Davenport Patriotic Committee called for erecting a scaffold at the Commercial Savings Bank at Third and Main. They intended to chip away the word *German* carved in stone above the entrance of the Commercial Savings and Loan, formerly the German Savings Bank. Davenport's Bismarck Street was renamed Concord and Schuetzen Park became Forest Park.

Davenport attorney C.A. Ficke was asked by the local Council of Defense to remind the German–speaking musicians that only English was allowed at symphony rehearsals. Even with his wife heading up local Red Cross work and his son serving in France, Ficke was the subject of rumors—among members of his own church, no less—that he had been arrested by the Secret Service and had to post $80,000 in bail.

In May 1918, Iowa Governor William L. Harding banned all foreign language and made English the official state language. It became known as Iowa's Babel proclamation.

SEVEN HUNDRED GERMAN FAMILIES HEADED FOR CITY

We clip the following paragraph from the columns of the Daily Pennsylvanian of the 1st inst.

"Seven hundred German families are now on the way to Davenport, Iowa, as the first of the spring emigration. This will prove a valuable addition to the population of Iowa."

Glad to hear it, for there is no place in the west which offers so great inducements to German or any other respectable class of immigrants as Davenport and surrounding country. The selection of this point shows conclusively that they are persons of good discrimination. There is room yet for seven hundred families more.—The Democrat, June 8, 1857.

German Americans went from being welcomed with open arms in 1857 to being vilified as enemies of the United States, as illustrated in November 1917 by syndicated political cartoonist Jay 'Ding' Darling of Sioux City, IA, who later earned two Pulitzers and helped form the U.S. Fish and Wildlife Bureau under President Franklin D. Roosevelt.

The law led to the arrest of five Scott County farm wives overheard chatting in German on a telephone party line. They were fined $225.

When Congress established the Selective Service Board, *slacker* became the word for anyone who failed to register for the draft or shirked his military duty. One of the nation's largest slacker drives was held in Davenport where factory jobs had drawn thousands of new tri–cities residents, many from Mexico.

On August 1, 1918, five hundred federal agents, local police and sheriff's deputies began a systematic canvas of draft–age men, arresting those not carrying their draft cards. Young men exiting the theaters had badges shoved in their faces with orders to show a draft card or get hauled off to jail. Twenty–two men were taken from the Davenport YMCA before they could finish

Pioneer Davenport City Builder is C.A. Ficke, Example to Youth Who Would Carve Out Success

C. A. FICKE.

Far enough north of St. Louis; far enough south of St. Paul; far enough west of Chicago; far enough east of Omaha—that's Davenport.

A simple lesson in geography. On the map for all to see, and Davenport's history is preciously sprinkled with the names of men who did see it and learned from it an axiom of success. But all of them perhaps "saw" it just in terms of distance — and few of them expressed it that way.

On this, then, C. A. Ficke for four decades and longer, laid the foundation of his life's plan. It has adhered to it thru all the years—as confident now of its verity as in the days when the most optimistic of Davenport's boosters raised a doubting eye at the news that Ficke had bought another frontage in the business belt. Nor were his purchases then always in the business belt. He bought Third street property—the site of the Kahl building—when farsighted investors doubted it ever Davenport would grow quite that big.

Today the Ficke interests hold more than 1,000 feet of frontage in the business district. Nearly four blocks of property, it consolidated, and values have increased more than tenfold.

Mr. Ficke, however, has been a builder—a developer of Davenport; his purchases have not been made with sole desire to enjoy an unearned increase of valuation. Improvements, business blocks, new stores, new buildings have marked the extension of the Ficke holdings. They have been of value to the city as much for their balancing effect, their inspired spirit of confidence in Davenport's future, as for the dollar-and-cents investment.

A Ficke buy in real estate has meant the early trend of business into that field. When Third street was "just off" town and seemingly destined always to remain "outside," the northeast corner of Third and Ripley streets was purchased. Sagacious investors openly doubted the wisdom of such a move. Then the old American theater rose and business plunged into West Third street. It grew and bigger business came to Third and then finally the master stroke, with the erection of the Kahl building which established it as the heart of Davenport's business area.

This same story may be written and repeated with some minor changes of much of the Ficke holdings.

Born in Germany.

The lifestory of C. A. Ficke is the story of a pioneer, too. A native of Mecklenburg, Germany, he was born April 21, 1850. His father, a merchant, came to America in 1852 and afterward established residence on a Scott county farm. Mr. Ficke's early education was in the rural schools and his early years spent on a farm but this soon became too narrow and at 12 he entered a Lowden store and the next year, working other hours, managed to support himself and attend the Davenport schools. In conserving his earnings he fitted himself for a business course. He obtained employment in the United States assessor's office, working there until 1868, when he entered the Davenport National bank. Thru intermediate positions he rose to discount clerk but fired with an ambition to become a lawyer he spent his spare hours studying in the office of H. R. Claussen. He resigned from the bank and in 1875 entered the New York law school in Albany, graduating the next year.

Six months were spent in traveling abroad and upon his return to Davenport he entered active practice. His success seemed to come immediately. His practice grew and Mr. Ficke soon became an outstanding figure of the bar and one of the representative members of his profession.

He displayed a keen interest in public affairs and this led to his position of importance in county and congressional committees of the Republican party with which he was then affiliated. In the Cleveland campaign he became a supporter of his candidacy in 1886, and six years later was elected county attorney. In 1890, against his protest, he was nominated and elected mayor of the city. Accepting the choice he devoted himself with a faithfulness to the office and so successfully that the following year he was renominated by acclamation and received the largest majority ever accorded a mayoralty candidate.

A World Traveler.

Mr. Ficke, however, has not permitted business to crowd all else from his life. Since his first six months abroad, just before he entered the legal field here, he has been a traveller—a world traveller. Each succeeding voyage has taken him into new fields, new scenes, new lands. His journeys have been planned on the scale of trips around the world.

With these journeyings into far fields he carried the spirit of the lover of the arts. His home is filled with treasures from every land; the Academy of Sciences has attained its enviable position in the Mississippi valley in no small measure thru the beneficences of the Ficke donations—and a greater gift even awaits the city and has awaited it two years because the treasure is so rich that the municipality has not yet been able to solve the proper housing and care of the art gallery which has been offered.

In this gallery, which fills rooms and halls at the Ficke home and crowds the attic, are 339 canvases, some of them 500 and 6,000 years old; of a value estimated as high as half a million dollars. One painting, a Van Dyke, 4½x8½ feet, is valued at $50,000. The collections represent 30 years given over to its assembly. Here are Blakelocks, Inness, Thomas and Ed Moran canvases; 30 famous American artists are in the catalog, which lists nearly all the painters of the American school; 11 British; 60 Dutch; 28 French; 34 Flemish; 67 German; 62 Italian; 26 Spanish and scores not classified, make up this gift to the city.

"The collection has given me a great deal of pleasure," said Mr. Ficke at the time of the offer of the donation, "and I hope to be able to share that pleasure with every citizen of Davenport." Nor has a two-year delay in acceptance of the gift changed his attitude. "Everything I have I owe to Davenport—this is my way of expressing my appreciation. This gift won't be lost to the city, no matter what happens," he concluded.

Arthur Davison Ficke, known thruout American literary circles as a poet and a leader in the modern school, is a son of Mr. Ficke, carrying into the realm of the literary world the paternal love of the arts.

The elder Mr. Ficke was married March 24, 1882, to Miss Fannie Davison, daughter of a well known attorney of this city. Three children have been born to them.

C.A. Ficke 1850-1931
Mayor 1890-1892
Ficke home, 1208 Main St
38-room mansion built in 1892 by J. Monroe Parker, partner in firm of Cook-Sargent-Parker with banks in Davenport, Rock Island and Omaha; mansion sold in 1978 to Palmer College's Delta Sigma Chi.

Far enough north of St. Louis; far enough south of St. Paul; far enough west of Chicago; far enough east of Omaha— that's Davenport. ~Charles August Ficke

eating supper. A circus crew posting bills around town seemed puzzled when asked about draft cards. They were hauled off to the courthouse.

Mexican–American workers, stopped at the factory gates as they exited from their work shifts, were arrested by agents. Because of the language barrier they had difficulty understanding what law they had broken.

Some 1,700 men had been arrested by the end of the day. They'd been pulled off factory lines, from streetcars and inbound trains, rounded up from parks and saloons.

With the Quinlan ferry being patrolled and the Government Bridge under guard, Rock Islanders faced a night in the Davenport jail for not having their cards. Several escaped across the Crescent railroad bridge downstream.

The prospect of having to fight their own kin led some German–Americans to stage anti–draft rallies. They woke the next morning to find their front doors painted yellow.

Also painted yellow was the Schleswig–Holstein memorial stone at Washington Square; the Prussian memorial had already been voluntarily removed. A replacement stone for the Schleswig–Holstein memorial recently was rededicated by Davenport's German–American Heritage Society. The Franco–Prussian memorial is all but forgotten.

Fred Vollmer, brother of former Davenport mayor and U.S. Congressman Henry Vollmer, was one of five local men imprisoned under the Espionage Act for attending an anti–draft rally.

The Espionage Act expired at war's end. Ethnic bigotry did not.

Philadelphia grocer Preston Ivens had moved to Davenport to attend Palmer Chiropractic School. His wife and three children—two boys, ages ten and nine, and a five–year–old daughter—lived on Iowa Street while Ivens lived on Grand Avenue, several blocks north of the Beiderbeckes.

According to Bill Roba, a professor at Scott Community College, Mr. Ivens had lost a brother in the war. That and Ivens staunch advocacy for the *One–Hundred Percent Americanism* policy is what Roba believes may have led to an accusation in 1921 against Bix Beiderbecke for the vilest of crimes.

Americanism called for conformity with mainstream culture. Proponents wanted more from immigrants seeking citizenship than just dropping their hyphenated identities and learning to speak English. They insisted citizenship required forgoing ethnicity in one's food, clothing, even in one's lifestyle. Festivals that celebrated foreign ancestry were seen as disloyal to America.

Bix's German ancestry may or may not have had anything to do with anything. The fact remains that the name of Leon Beiderbecke appears sixth on a list of seven arrests entered into the Davenport police blotter on April 22, 1921.

One arrest was for peddling, one for assault and battery, three for disturbing the peace, one for intoxication, and one arrest for lewd and lascivious act with a child.

The latter charge is why Bix was bound over to the grand jury on a $1,500 bond. The *Democrat–Leader* reported a similar case the following year, in which the defendant was found guilty. Conviction carried a maximum fine of $500 and three years in the state reformatory.

Up till then, Bix had only a fine for speeding. It would remain the only thing on his record after charges were dropped in State of Iowa vs. Leon B. Beiderbecke. County Attorney John Weir filed the memorandum for District Court criminal docket #4188. Dated Sept. 26, 1921, it stated: *"No Bill" filed.*

"No bills were found in 16 of the cases investigated, owing to lack of evidence to establish the crime charged, or punishment in a previous criminal action," reported the *Daily Times* on September 26.

Both Davenport newspapers published names and charges in cases that went before the September 1921 Grand Jury. They listed dismissed cases as well as indictments. Bix's name does not appear. His arrest was not reported in the *Times* nor the *Democrat*, both owned by the Lee Syndicate.

In tracking down descendants of Preston Ivens, Gerri Bowers learned the family had moved to Texas and that Ivens left without having completed his studies at Palmer. His descendants were unaware of the 1921 incident.

Despite efforts by the Beiderbecke family to keep the incident a secret, other Bix biographers published court documents. They are included here for context as to the names appearing in these documents.

YOUNG SPEEDER GETS FINE AND COURT LECTURE

L. B. Beiderbecke, a youthful speeder, received a lecture by Magistrate Metcalf and paid a $25 fine following his plea of guilty to a charge of speeding preferred by Officer Dietz this morning.

Young Beiderbecke was arrested on West Fourth street after he had attempted to burn up the pavement with a stripped down Ford. He paid the $25 almost cheerfully.

Daily Times, above, and *Democrat-Leader*, below, reported Bix's speeding arrest January 22, 1920

AGE SAVES HIM FROM JAIL

The fact that he was but 17 years old is all that saved L. B. Beiderbecke, a Davenport high school student, from being sent to jail by Police Magistrate Metcalf this morning. Beiderbecke was arrested by Patrolman Pat Dietz last night on a charge of violating the auto speed ordinance. Beiderbeck pleaded guilty to the charge and drew a $25 fine. The court informed the defendant that his age had saved him from jail.

April 22 Davenport Police Report:
Leon Beiderbecke—Lewd & Lascivious Act with Child
    He was accused by Sarah Jane, 5 years old, 1700 Iowa Street, of putting his hands on her

person outside of her dress in Goddard's garage, Locust & Grand Ave, where he took the girl out of the rain. They were in an auto in the garage and he closed the door on the girl and she hollered and attracted the attention of James L. Duncan, 1330 E. 10th and Mahlon Bailey, 1105 Oneida Ave, who were working across the street and they went over and the girl went home. He waived preliminary hearing before Judge Scott and held to G.J. on $1500 bond.

Affidavit of Preston R. Ivens, State of Iowa vs. Beiderbecke

Preston R. Ivens being first duly sworn on oath says: I live at 3030 Grand Ave. Davenport, Scott County, Iowa. I am a student at the Palmer School. On April 22, 1921 my little girl came home, told me that a man took her in the garage, said some awful things to her. I ran up to the garage, then called up the police but could get no clue. Next day I saw 2 boys whom I had seen when I went to the garage. I asked if they saw a man take a little girl into the garage the day before. They said yes & told me it was the Dft. My little girl told her story to me & later to the chief of police & the County Attorney. She said he asked her to show herself. The little girl is 5 years old. In consideration of the childs age & the harm that would result to her in going over with this case I would request that no action be taken by the grand jury. I consulted with Dr. Eliot & Dr. B. J. Palmer & Dr. Craven & they all besides with Mr. C. H. Murphy thought it best to drop the case for the betterment of the child. Signed: Preston R. Ivens

The garage belonged to Frank Goddard, a purchasing agent for the Bettendorf Axle Works Company. His wife Ella was a cousin of Robert Ficke—the neighbor whose son loaned his cornet to Bix. The Goddards joined First Presbyterian Church the same year Bix was confirmed there; Bix and Austin had been classmates since kindergarten.

Mahlon Bailey, age 18, was an apprentice machinist at the Bettendorf Axle Works. James Duncan, 16, was the son of an accountant. Both lived in the neighborhood.

According to the police report, Bix was arrested the same day as the alleged incident. Yet Ivens' signed affidavit states that it wasn't until the following day he talked to the boys who identified Bix as being in the garage with his daughter.

When time came for the case to go before the Grand Jury, Ivens requested it be dropped. Named as having advised him in this decision, B.J. Palmer owned the chiropractic school Ivens attended. Another named advisor, Frank W. Elliott, was the school's business manager. He had convinced Palmer to purchase a broadcasting license and operate the first radio station west of the Mississippi River. Elliott oversaw WOC—the call letters stand for World of Chiropractics—where Bix and others in his family had been on–air performers. Elliott later became president of the National Association of Broadcasters. John H. Craven, also named by Ivens, was a PSC instructor and a Methodist minister. He moved to Seattle in 1926.

C.H. Murphy was a curious advisor, given that he was a criminal defense attorney at the time of State of Iowa vs. Beiderbecke. Conrad Murphy had done some prosecuting in his career. District Attorney is an elected post and Murphy, active in Scott County's Republican Party, had served a couple terms as Assistant D.A. In 1906, he helped prosecute the County's first case under a new law barring unlicensed medical practice. The defendant was D.D. Palmer, founder of chiropractics and father of B.J. Palmer. The elder Palmer was convicted and chose to serve out his jail term rather than pay the fine.

Murphy could always be counted by the local newspapers for good copy, whether in or out of the courtroom, as in the following excerpts from newspaper stories:

March 2, 1904 *Davenport Daily Leader:* HOT WORDS ENSUED BETWEEN ATTORNEY AND OFFICERS WHICH ALMOST ENDS IN A FISTIC ENCOUNTER

> There was a lively scene at the police station this morning and the usual quiet routine was varied by a little excitement that came near ending in blows. The cause of the commotion was the trial of F. Gordon who was arrested for being an inmate of a house of ill fame...There was much conflicting testimony, but the judge concluded that the prosecution had the stronger case and Gordon was fined $10 and costs. Attorney C.H. Murphy, who appeared for the defense, at once gave notice that he would appeal the case and stated that the bond for the young man would be filed before the evening and he would be responsible for him until that time. He stated that this matter was going to be fought out to the end and stated that some lively times might be looked for. In the meantime the row started when Attorney Murphy began questioning Officer Sanford. The attorney asked some things which Mr. Sanford took as an insult and the court had to call for order before things quieted down. It was evident that it was not all over yet, however, and as soon as court had adjourned the attorney and the officer met in the police room. Clenched fists and white faces were good evidence that the temper of both men was quite riled and the other officers were compelled to intervene to stop the racket. Hot words flew back and forth at this and but for the time presence of the chief

Bottom photo is Palmer School of Chiropractic on Brady St. Hill in 1910. Left is original office of D.D. Palmer's Chiropractic Cure, corner of Putnam building on Brady & Second, next door to Beiderbecke & Miller Wholesalers.

WOC Radio Station, c. 1921

left: studio where Bix played piano

below: station tower

Call letters stood for "World of Chiropractics"

there might have been a battle royal where one would least expect it. Things quieted down finally, but there was no very amiable parting and the dark cloud still hangs in the horizon.

September 29, 1925 *Davenport Democrat–Leader*: HARSH WORDS HURLED BY ATTORNEY AND FEDERAL OFFICER IN KAHL BLDG. INNUENDOES AND OPEN INSULTS RESULT IN PHYSICAL ENGAGEMENT IN CORRIDOR AS RESULT OF PARLEY OF OFFICERS WITH WITNESS IN BOOZE CASE—JUSTICE OF THE PEACE RESTORES QUIET.

Tenants of the Kahl building within three stories of the seventh floor, and passengers on the elevators this morning thought a murder was being committed. But it isn't true. It was only a verbal battle and an incipient physical clash between Attorney Conrad H. Murphy and Federal Prohibition Officer Roy Muhs. The combatants were separated by Justice of the Peace Ralph G. Smith in the corridor outside his offices before any bodily harm had been done. The argument started when Muhs summoned from the office of Justice Smith, L.E. Morris…charged with the possession of intoxicating liquor with intent to sell on September 26, on information sworn out by Deputy Sheriff Fred Scharfenburg. He was also charged with bootlegging…a large group of persons stood in the office and awaited the appearance of the county attorney or his assistant as presenting counsel. Muhs and Scharfenberg stood in the hall. Muhs opened the door and asked Morris to step out into the hall. "You'd better go out and find out what they say to him," Attorney Murphy said to Morris' wife, who was also in the office. "They aren't his friends, you know."

Muhs evidently heard Attorney Murphy thru the transom, opened the door and remarked: "Con, I'm not trying to frame anybody." Attorney Murphy's reply came before Muhs had finished speaking. Words were passed back and forth regarding "framing witnesses," and Attorney Murphy said something to Muhs about framing his own brother–in–law. Muhs then grabbed Attorney Murphy by the shoulder and pulled him out into the hall. It looked for a minute as if there might be blows, but the attorney did not falter. He called Muhs substantially a big young brave man for attacking a smaller man 70 years of age. At this juncture, Justice Smith called for peace, altho Deputy Scharfenberg said something about letting them "have it out."

During Prohibition, Murphy represented a client charged with having a disorderly house after police found "a quantity of moonshine" and several intoxicated guests at the client's residence. Murphy told the judge that "breaking off the drink habit with persons that drank all of their lives was quite a bit like trying to make a man quit chewing tobacco after he had chewed all his life. He is liable to take a chew when he thinks nobody is looking," said Murphy. "It is hard to teach an old dog new tricks and if you fine this man, you are taking money from his want and not from his plenty." The police magistrate levied the homeowner a fine of $55.35.

Murphy defended a school principal charged with beating a crippled student, punishment for bad behavior. When the not guilty verdict was read, parents who had packed the courtroom shouted out their disgust. Murphy responded to the angry parents with what in today's vernacular amounted to "get over yourselves."

Community outrage again greeted Murphy after winning acquittal on an animal cruelty charge. His client was a teacher who killed a puppy by tossing it out a third-floor classroom window.

Over the years Murphy had his share of juvenile defendants. In the case of an 11-year-old boy who had shot at a neighbor, Murphy advised the boy's single mother to take her son to Sunday school. The *Tri-City Star* reported he *"preached a rattling good sermon, telling Mrs. H– that no mother can expect to raise good boys and girls who does not throw around them moral influences."*

A lawyer as tenacious as C.H. Murphy would have relished a case involving the son of a prominent family. But Murphy didn't represent the plaintiff. That job belonged to John Weir, the County prosecutor. So, why would Preston Ivens seek advice from a criminal attorney?

He probably didn't. More likely Murphy's involvement was as legal counsel for Bix. The Beiderbecke family would have hired a lawyer when their son was arrested. He would have been there for the bond hearing. And in preparation for the case, he would have talked to the arresting officers, and deposed witnesses.

A lawyer of C.H. Murphy's caliber would have quickly sized up the evidence and any discrepancies in the plaintiff's story. Makes sense that a criminal defense attorney would advise his client's accuser to drop the case.

Had a client's parents voiced concern over a public scandal and what it would mean to their son's future, it's not so far a stretch of the imagination as to the sort of advice a man like Conrad Murphy would have offered. He'd likely have told them the boy ought to be applying himself in school, getting his grades up instead of hanging out at jazz joints.

September 26, 1921 *Davenport Daily Times*: FOURTEEN MEN WERE INDICTED BY GRAND JURY RETURN 18 TRUE BILLS AFTER INVESTIGATING 36 CRIMINAL CASES

The report of the September term grand jury filed in the Scott county district court this afternoon, shows that a total of 18 true bills were returned against 14 men in the 36 cases that were investigated during the term session. No bills were found in 16 of the cases investigated, owing to lack of evidence to establish the crime charged, or punishment in a previous criminal action. Two cases were referred to the next grand jury because of the evidence to be presented was not complete at the close of the session.

One of the cases in which no bill was returned was against Dan Drost, publisher–manager of the Rock Island News, now serving a term in the Scott county jail on a charge of criminal libel. According to the county attorney, evidence from Drost's trial was presented to the grand jury for consideration of a perjury charge, but was found to be insufficient to form a definite charge.

Defendants in the criminal cases in which indictments were returned will probably be arraigned Monday to take pleas in the district court. The list of cases and indictments is as follows: Harry Blessing, one bill charging arson, in connection with the alleged incendiary fire at the Miller hotel building; Joe Herring, indicted in three bills for separate charges of indecent exposure; Joseph Brown, alias Francis Jones, two bills charging robbery; Oldrich Hendrych, one bill charging defendant with having received stolen goods; LeRoy Quick, Ray C. Gartz and Benney Wells, one indictment against the three defendants on charge of breaking and entering. Emil Fevery, three true bills charging defendant with having received stolen property; Arthur Quick, one true bill on charge of larceny; George Wren, one true bill on charge of lewdness; Marion Sisk, one true bill on charge of obtaining money under false pretenses; John Carroll, one true bill on charge of larceny; Joe Sanchey, one true bill on charge of larceny; Joseph G. Bolte, alias Glenn Dale Gearhart, two true bills charging embezzlement and concealing mortgaged property; Benney Wells and LeRoy Quick, one true bill charging larceny.

No bills were returned against Jose Sabala, Harry Connell and Thomas Hines, Robert Burlingame and Gene Seiffert, both of whom paid fines of $50 and cost in police court, Fred Mills, Aaron Strong and B. Kinney, Steve Mitoff, James Jessen, Irene Parks, Roy Brady, who is serving 30 days on a police court sentence, Agnes Smith and Wm. Smith, Minnie Foster, Raymond Gartz and Roy Quick, Dan Drost, Elmore Bascom, Thomas Hines and Tracy W. Robertson.

September 26, 1921 *Davenport Democrat–Leader*: 14 DEFENDANTS HELD BY JURY; 16 DISMISSED 19 INDICTMENTS RETURNED BY GRAND JURY IN FINAL REPORT TO COURT

Nineteen true bills or indictments, holding 14 defendants to trial

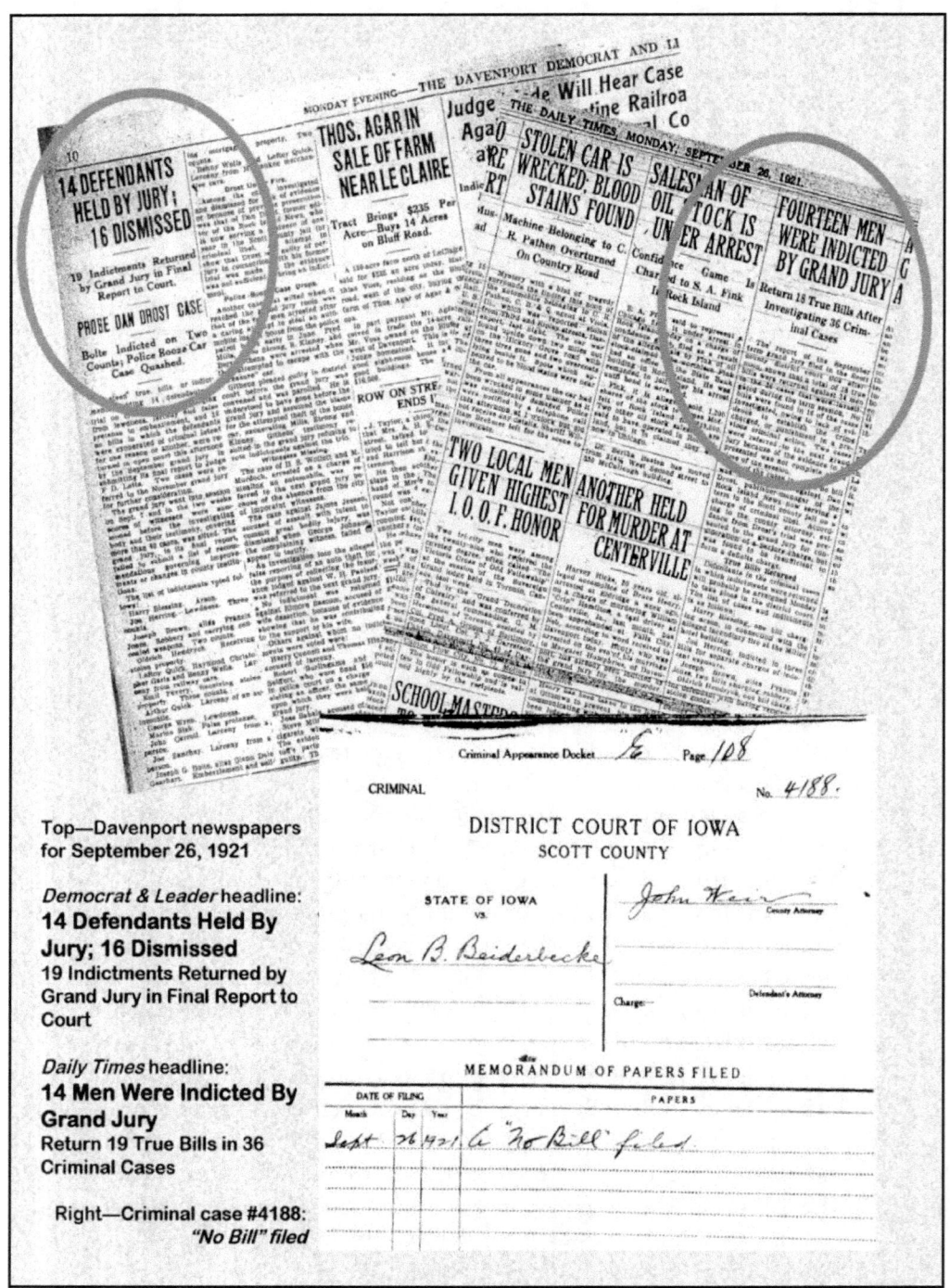

Top—Davenport newspapers for September 26, 1921

Democrat & Leader headline:
14 Defendants Held By Jury; 16 Dismissed
19 Indictments Returned by Grand Jury in Final Report to Court

Daily Times headline:
14 Men Were Indicted By Grand Jury
Return 19 True Bills in 36 Criminal Cases

Right—Criminal case #4188: "No Bill" filed

on criminal charges ranging from lewdness, larceny and false pretense to embezzlement, and 16 no bills in which the defendants were exonerated of criminal intent for one reason or another, were returned in open court this afternoon by the September grand jury in submitting its final report to Judge F.D. Letts. Two cases were referred to the November grand jury for further consideration.

The grand jury went into session on Sept. 7 and in the two weeks scores of witnesses were summoned before the investigating body and their testimony, covering more than 40 cases, was sifted. The grand jury in its final report, failed to submit a list of recommendations governing improvements or changes in county institutions. The list of indictments voted follows: Harry Blessing, Arson; Joe Herring, Lewdness, Three counts; Joseph Brown, alias Francis Jones, Robbery and carrying concealed weapons, Two counts; Oldrich Hendrych, Receiving stolen property.

LeRoy Quick, Raymond Christopher Gartz and Benny Wells, Larceny from railway cars; Emil Fevery, Receiving stolen property, Three counts' Arthur Quick, Larceny of an automobile; George Wren, Lewdness; Marion Sisk, False pretense; John Carroll, Larceny from a person; Joe Sanchey, Larceny from a person; Joseph G. Bolte, alias Glenn Dale Gearhart, Embezzlement and selling mortgaged property, Two counts; Benny Wells and LeRoy Quick, Larceny from Milwaukee merchandise cars.

Drost Under Fire

Among the cases investigated and dismissed for lack of evidence or because of previous prosecution was that of Dan Drost, former editor of the Rock Island News, who is now serving a sentence of one year in the Scott county jail for criminal libel. An attempt to show that Drost was guilty of perjury in connection with his former trial was made but the evidence was not sufficient to bring an indictment.

Police Booze Case Drops

Another case that wilted when it reached the grand jury room was that of the four men arrested after a daring attempt to steal an automobile load of booze from the police patrol barns in early June. Fred Mills, Aaron Strong, B. Kinney, and Bert Githens were arrested when they attempted to escape with the "Treasure" car. Githens pleaded guilty in district court before the grand jury was convened and was paroled. He is understood to have gone before the grand jury and assumed the blame for the attempted theft of the booze car, exonerating Mills Strong and Kinney. Githens' testimony resulted in the grand jury refusing to vote indictments against the trio.

WITNESSES MISSING

The case of H.S. Wollett and M. Murdock, arrested on a charge of stealing an automobile, was referred to the next grand jury because of the absence from the city of important witnesses.

The case against James Jessen, accused of assault with intent to commit great bodily injury, was dismissed when George Johnson, the complaining witness, failed to appear to testify.

An investigation into the alleged false reporting of an auto theft for the purpose of collecting the insurance lodged against W.H. Paulsen was referred to the next grand jury.

No indictment was returned against Elmore Bascom, accused of wife desertion, because of evidence showing that he was contributing to the support of his wife.

Others against whom no indictments were voted were: Harry Connell and Thomas Hines, accused of larceny; Robert Burlingame and Gene Seiffert, who were fined $50 each in police court on a charge of resisting an officer, the same offense upon which they were held to the grand jury; Jose Sabala, accused of larceny; Steve Mittoff, accused of selling cigarettes without a state license. The evidence showed that Mittoff's partner was the one really guilty. The partner paid a fine of $100 in district court before the grand jury convened. Irene Parks, accused of larceny; Roy Brady, who has served a 30–day sentence for larceny; Minnie Foster, accused of shoplifting; Agnes Smith and William Smith, accused of a conspiracy in connection with the obtaining of a marriage license for a Rock Island boy under age; Thomas Hines, stealing tires; Tracy W. Robertson, accused of stealing an auto, Robertson's partner, Ralph Yorick, of Muscatine, pleaded guilty several months ago and was paroled.

Some already familiar with the 1921 documents wondered why Bix's complexion was stated as dark on the police blotter. In those days, Caucasians were categorized not so much by skin tone as by hair color. If Bix had been blond– or auburn–haired, he'd have logged in as light–complexioned. His brown eyes and dark brown hair account for the blotter entry.

The more pertinent question is what the two witnesses would have testified to under oath had there been a trial. The only accounts came from Preston Ivens and the officers who recorded his complaint. Those familiar with this chapter in Bix's life continue to debate its implications.

Putting it into context, Bix was playing music with Neal Buckley's Novelty Orchestra that spring of 1921. A couple months before the arrest, he had given a valentine to Thelma Griffin. She wasn't his girlfriend, just a

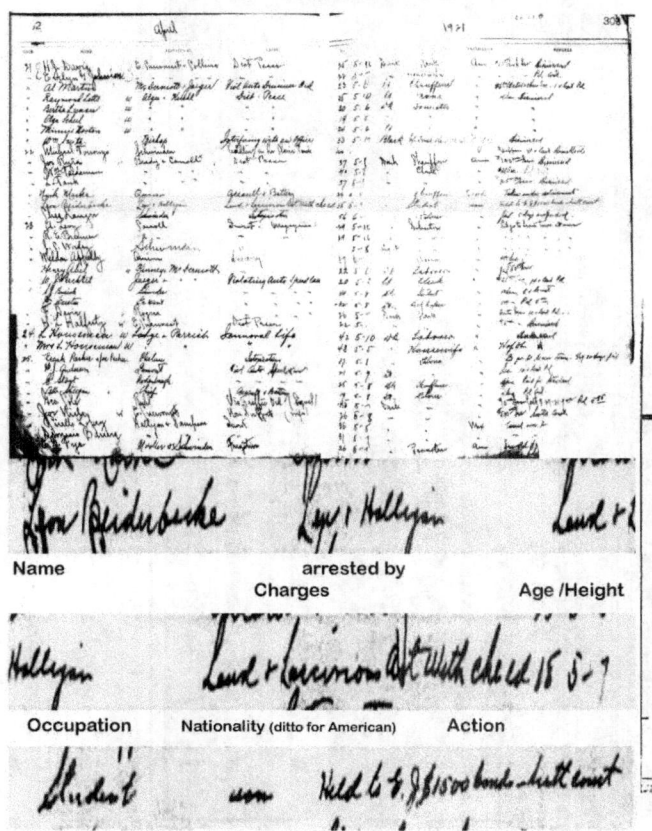

Arrest Report April 22, 1921

Ivens affidavit September 1921

APRIL 1921 Davenport Police Blotter

fellow musician who thought Bix a sweetheart of a guy.

Bix turned eighteen that March. The 1921 DHS Blackhawk yearbook noted an offer from the senior class: *To Bix Beiderbecke, a comp. at Rothermel's hair dressing parlor, so the Juniors can save their money.* John Rothermel's barbershop at 1507 Harrison was just a few doors up from Moetzel's Drug Store. Bix's fellow juniors at Davenport High had made a running joke of dropping coins in his locker to pay for a haircut.

After school let out for the summer, Bix got work aboard the excursion boats. The local musician's union ended his riverboat career but in August Bix put together his own band, the Bix Beiderbecke Five, for a gig at Haynes Dance School. Later that August Bix performed with Ralph Miedke's orchestra for Moline State Bank's grand opening. All the while looming over him was that September grand jury. When they took up the case of State of Iowa vs. Beiderbecke, Bix had already transferred to Lake Forest Academy.

LAKE FOREST ACADEMY 1921

BIX AND THE FUTURE FOOTBALL HALL OF FAMER
1988 interview with Jim Arpy

I first really got to know Bix when we were freshman at Davenport High School and both belonged to the same high school fraternity.

The big thing about him that sticks out in my mind is that three or four times a year we'd have a fraternity dance at the Davenport Outing Club with a hired orchestra.

And every time there'd be Bix talking them into letting him sit in on the piano. The minute he got in there, the music got terrible. It was absolutely no good, as far as we were concerned. We told Bix several times to quit sitting in, and when he wouldn't we just blacklisted him from the fraternity.

But he knew more about what he was doing than all of us put together. He was just so far ahead of his time we didn't understand what he was doing on the piano.

I can't say I was too friendly with him. His butting-in on the music was one reason. Another was that he was bumming around with some fast company, some pretty tricky guys. He seemed to drift toward people like that. We were concerned about Bix, but there was no way to stop him.

This was the time when the legendary Elmer Layden—later one of the four horsemen of Notre Dame—was playing football at Davenport High. He and a friend of mine, Karl Vollmer, were both in line to become captain of the team. Karl thought he might get the job if he could recruit some new players. He talked me into it, but I got knocked around so much the first time on the field that I knew football wasn't for me.

Then he convinced Bix to go out for the team and told me to give Bix my new football shoes. I said I wouldn't give them to him, but would sell them to him for eight dollars—just what I'd paid.

He said Bix probably wouldn't have any money, and he was right, but Bix promised to pay me, so I gave him the shoes. Well, I never did get paid. He still owes me.

—Chet Salter (1903–2000)
Mississippi Valley Fair, former president

LAKE FOREST

Imagine the scene: Settling into bed for the night, Aggie shows Bismark her copy of *Harper's* magazine and just before he turns out the lamps, she reads to him from the ad for Lake Forest Academy: *Small classes, individual attention without coddling. Definite preparation for entrance examinations of Yale, Princeton, Harvard, Mass. Tech, etc. Graduates admitted without examination to all certificate universities. The school life is non–military, the relationship of the masters with the boys being one of friendly guidance rather than antagonistic regulation…. Spacious campus with fine old oaks on a bluff overlooking Lake Michigan. The town itself, one hour north of Chicago, is a residential center of beauty and culture—without saloons.*

There in the darkness, whispers of other possibilities for their youngest child at a school that could encourage both his musical and athletic inclinations while preparing him for an Ivy League school. If–when Aggie and Bismark considered the proximity to Chicago, the thinking likely would have been based on their daughter's educational experience, not the speakeasies and roadhouses that would become Bix's preferred venues for extracurricular activities.

Bix's passion for music may have come from his mom but he inherited a love of sports from his dad. From the *Davenport Sunday Leader*, Aug 5, 1900:

BASEBALL NOTES
A RATTLING GAME YESTERDAY AFTERNOON —
ANOTHER THIS AFTERNOON

There was a rattling game of ball yesterday afternoon at the Fairgrounds between the employees of the Beiderbecke and Miller company and the Van Pattern & Marks company. The interesting feature of the game was the extraordinary precautions the umpires took to protect themselves.

The umpires were W.R. Wier and Fred White. They have been umpires before and when approached for this game they employed an able attorney and had an agreement drawn which specifically provided that they be treated with such courtesy as would preclude the use of baseball bats as implements of warfare; that their decisions were not to be overruled with any more force than was absolutely necessary and that they be given safe passport and a clear right of way off of the fairgrounds after the game. This agreement was signed, sealed and delivered into the hands of an innocent third party in the presence of witnesses. The result of the game was 10–11, in favor of Van Patten and Marks.

John Van Patten and Morton L. Marks were partners in a wholesale grocery store at 119 E. Second, erected one year after Beiderbecke–Miller opened their new building at 109 E. Second. These guys competed in business and sport. Van Patten was 67 and Charles Beiderbecke 65 when their ball teams played one another for bragging rights. On September 16, 1900, the *Davenport Daily Leader* reported:

A HOT GAME

Saturday afternoon the Beiderbecke & Miller and Van Patten & Marks baseball teams played a hot game of ball to judge from the report handed in. After reading the following, which evidently was written by a sympathizer, it is likely that the Van Patten & Marks people will be forthcoming with another account of the game.

The B.M.company clearly demonstrated their superiority this afternoon in a game of baseball with the Van Patten & Marks team at the Forester's Gun Club grounds. Although the game was a very one-sided affair, as the score goes to show, the defeated struggled hard to the bitter end.

One of the many features of the game was the remarkable fielding of Charles Beiderbecke. Bix Beiderbecke also displayed his good qualities as a ball player, but the main feature of the game was the pitching of Roberts, who compelled nearly all the Van Patten players to relinquish their rights as a runner before reaching first base.

The line up was as follows:

BEIDERBECKE MILLER COMPANY

Roberts, p; McCormack, c; J. Kahler, 1b; B. Beiderbecke, 2b; F. Kahler, 3B; Denkmann, ss; C. Beiderbecke, lf; Woolf, cf; Johnson, rf. The Van Patten & Marks team players were too much disgusted with the outcome of the game to give their names to the reporter. [Jacob] Strong, of the Van Patten & Marks team, pitched a good game, not withstanding his poor support. It was plain to see that Van's players are fast becoming too old to be ball players, but they still retain forlorn hopes of once more rising from their recent defeat. The score was 6–12 in favor of the Beiderbecke & Miller team.

That's Bismark Beiderbecke at second base and Opa Charles in left field. Leon Bix carried on that Beiderbecke tradition, playing baseball for the fun of it but with a competitive spirit.

It was during a friendly game with Austin Goddard and other neighborhood boys that Bix chipped a front tooth. Doc Davis made him a crown. Without it, Bix couldn't play the cornet. The story goes that he developed a nervous habit of wiggling the crown, so much so that over time it loosened and often fell out while Bix was playing.

He'd then scramble around on the floor in search of it. Bandmates would be down on their hands and knees with him, searching through the peanut shells and spit–soaked sawdust.

Hoagy Carmichael remembered Bix losing the tooth in the snow.

from the *Daily Leader* Sports pages
left: 9-16-1900
right: 8-5-1900

below:
Almost Persuaded
c. 1916

Bix, front row center, with 1922 Lake Forest Academy varsity baseball team; below: June 1927 with Goldkette saxophonist Red Ingle

Jazz is the product of a buoyant spirit. It is exuberant America expressing itself in sound. It is music that one must expect from a country that loves baseball and builds sky–scrapers. It is the folk music of America.   ~Outlook Magazine, Oct 5, 1924

"We searched frantically with matches burning our fingers—so he could play that night. No tooth, no music," wrote Hoagy in his 1947 memoir, *Stardust Road*.

Another tooth story, this one from Bix's Goldkette days, involved a ballroom owner presenting Bix a large wooden tooth. Bix got a kick out of the joke. His sense of humor was as legendary as his athletic prowess.

During his stint on the Camel Pleasure Hour in 1930, Bix played outfield and pitched baseball for a team of New York–based musicians, including the Dorsey brothers. Sonny Greer, drummer for Duke Ellington's Cotton Club outfit, said: "I remember one game that Bix pitched against us. Man, we didn't score a run. He shut us out!"

CHARLES BURNETTE BEIDERBECKE, third from left in the back row, played right tackle for Davenport High School's football team. From the December 1913 DHS Bulletin: *Beiderbecke and Duley have been the best pair of tackles the school has had representing it. Bix, in fact, is considered the best line-man on the team by Coach Nixon, being both a good defensive and offensive player. Duley has been a big help to his side of the line and in many games has played a stellar role. Beiderbecke may be in school next year, but Duley graduates in June.*

Bix was said to have palled around with Babe Ruth. But it wasn't only baseball. Bix loved tennis and football, too.

In a letter dated Oct 22, 1921, Bix wrote his mom from Lake Forest: *Notre Dame Freshmen had one of the best teams I ever saw & we beat them 22–0 you can imagine the team—all or most all the boys 2 & 3 & 4 yr men & all stars individually. Tell Burnie to bring on his alumni team & watch his old ball game go.*

Burnie had played varsity football in high school. Sibling rivalry showed through when Bix wrote home boasting of the three baskets he scored against Great Lakes Naval Training School's basketball team. Final score: 40 –3. He played all of ten minutes.

Bix's coach at Lake Forest was Ralph Jones. He came from the University of Illinois same year Bix enrolled at the academy. Coach Jones led the Chicago Bears to their first NFL league championship in 1932.

Even a coach of that caliber couldn't sway Bix from his true passion. In a letter to Sis, Oct 30, 1921, he bragged of a five-piece band he and classmate Sid Stewart organized: *I got an orchestra that is the best that has ever been at the Academy...they all say it was the best music they ever heard let alone at the 'Cad'. I can say it's the best band I have ever played with. People are still raving about it and we sure made a hit with the ferries. [Ferry Hall Girl's Academy] Even Big Dick* [Headmaster John Wayne Richards] *came around with a smile on his face and said that we must expect to play all the dances as it was the best music 'Cad' had ever had which certainly was nice of him.*

In a letter Nov 7, 1921, Bix asked his dad to write a permission note allowing him to leave campus so he could go with a classmate who had arranged for Bix to play with other musicians in Flint, MI. Bix's sign-off showed him to be adept at being both dutiful son and keeping dear old dad wrapped around his finger: *...Well pop if you have a moment to spare answer this because your letters sure are encouraging & make one want to do well. Give my love to mam & mes hermanos & also to Oma and Aunt Tillie & the whole family. L.B. Beiderbecke P.S. Herr Koepke wants to teach me piano (he is a wizard) He says I'm wonderful. Maybe it's because my name is Beiderbecke.*

Bismark likely hoped some German-style discipline from Koepke would rub off on his boy. But Bix had already made a habit of sneaking out after curfew and heading to Chicago's Southside where jazz men honed their craft in after-hours jam sessions.

When Burnie took up the saxophone, Bix must have envisioned a brother act like Harold and Orey Oerman. He wrote on Nov 16, 1921: *Great guns Burnie have you actually got an orchestra? you guys?, hell fire reserve me a position will you? I won't take any jobs Burnie if you people don't want me to but that don't mean to not play with my own gang here at LFA does it? In Dubuque I mean? I'll bet you felt like a bill poster at the grand that night. In regard to music have you heard Saturday? Emaline? Why Dear? Well if you haven't lend me your ears and Ill teach you some real numbers. I hear from V.L.C. every now and then and she continually speaks about you or has something to say about you.*

V.L.C. is Vera Cox. Bix mentioned her often in letters, not as his girlfriend but by way of playing cupid for his brother. In a letter a week later to his mom and dad, Bix wrote: *Tell Burnie that Vera's nuts about him that he's not to* [sic] *old to get a date with her.* At the time, Sis Beiderbecke was dating Vera's future husband, Ferd Korn.

When Bix got back to Lake Forest Spring 1922, he was on academic probation. He wrote his mom the day before she turned 52, nine days before his 19th birthday:

Mother Dear—

This is one day mam old boy that I wish I could be home. I don't know why it is that I should feel that way but I do and understand that I'm present in spirit & soul if not physically. Let's see your 42 now aren't you or is it 32. I've forgotten.

...Mr. Richards called me into his office and told me that it was custom that whenever anyone was down in their work in two subjects that they were put on a parole to make them work and if they don't they are put on limited parole and then if they don't work they are campused and the next step is dismissal.

We had a good talk—he sure is a peach—he told me that I had guts and brains and that I had done much better in my studies and holding myself down than he had expected I would due to my handicap in being a musician. He said that he thought I'd be a girl snip and a social butterfly, judging from my D.H.S. record but he said that it was a "misled prejudice", he said that if I came back next year I'd make something of myself athletically and scholastically as he thought that this school had made me sit up & take notice and was the place for me.

I just thought I'd say this to convince you that I have something in me, which surprises me as much as it does you....

On May 20, Bix got caught sneaking back into his dormitory via the fire escape after curfew, having played for a fraternity at Northwestern. The Academy faculty voted to expel him and Headmaster Richards sent a telegram informing Bix's parents that he was being sent home by train out of Chicago. Instead Bix headed to Michigan City to play piano at a beach hotel.

The headmaster wrote Bismark that Bix's "influence upon other boys has deterred them from work and has upset them in the matter of conduct."

He went on to say "that certain parents have objected strenuously to their sons' association with him."

Bismark wrote back: "May I ask you to state the nature of his conduct which aroused the parents' objection?"

Headmaster Richards responded with the full details of Bix's expulsion in a letter that arrived a week later: *At the time he left we were not absolutely dead sure as to his part with regard to liquor around the School. Since then we have definitely learned that he was drinking himself and was responsible, in part at least, in having liquor brought into the School....The more we have found out concerning him since he left, the more we regret the things he did and are sorry that he was in the School at all. Bix is a very clever excuse–maker, and I think he sometimes fools even himself in a way.*

The Beiderbeckes were told their son could return to campus to take his make–up exams but then had to leave "without mixing or meddling around the School." Not such a peach after all, that headmaster.

Given that Prohibition turned otherwise law–abiding citizens into criminals, Bismark Beiderbecke may have been ambivalent about Bix's drinking. But he would have insisted his son either be in school or be gainfully employed. Bismark went to Chicago to find Bix. By the time he got there, Bix had a job at the Sheridan Beach Hotel on Lake Michigan. His dad brought him home to Davenport and put him to work as an errand boy at the coal company. Burnie worked there, too, as a bookkeeper.

With both his sons on the payroll, Bismark may have given thought to organizing a company baseball team. But with Bix always riding that train to Chicago, he acquiesced to his youngest son's chosen career path. As for baseball, perhaps a game of catch now and then.

After his expulsion from Lake Forest, Bix worked at his dad's coal company. Among his duties, he had to collect money from the clients.

Nebraska cornetist CHARLES HAROLD TROMBLA (1905-1983) combined Bix's love of baseball and music in a caricature that he drew for a note to Bix. Trombla, who played for Ross Gorman and Ted Fio-Rito while Bix was with Whiteman, considered himself a *"gut-bucket cornetist whereas Bix was an artist."*

A fuel bill to Frank Boyler, dated January 11, 1922, included a handwritten note: *Do your utmost to get this settled this month as per agreement. BIX*

That would be Bix Sr., and as Richard K. Boyler tells it:

"My father, Frank W. Boyler, owned a blacksmith shop in the Village of East Davenport near the East Davenport Fuel Co. where Bismark Beiderbecke worked and managed. The Fuel Co. office was a two-story wooden building located on the south side of River Drive. The upper portion was where workers and their families lived. The company's lumber yard was located across the street on the north side of River Drive.

Office of the East Davenport Fuel Co can be seen to the right of the streetcar, stopped on River Drive between Spring and Mound streets. Ad below is from 1922 when both Burnie & Bix worked for their dad.

TELEPHONES DAV. 444, 443 AND 3511

East Davenport Fuel & Lumber Co.

Lumber, Building Material, Shingles, Roofing, Sewing Pipe and Drain Tile

LIME, CEMENT, PLASTER, LATH, STONE, BRICK, SAND, GRAVEL

ALL KINDS OF FUEL

2023 EAST RIVER STREET.   DAVENPORT, IOWA

"My father bought supplies such as smithing coal for the forges from the fuel company and he, in turn, would shod their horses or make repairs to their wagons.

"As a teenager in the '20s, I went on errands for my father that included going to the fuel company and I vividly remember walking up the wide steps that led into the office where a large high counter stood toward the back of the room. Behind that counter sat Bismark Beiderbecke. He always was properly attired in a white shirt and suit. His manner was abrupt and not friendly, or so I remember, and I always felt intimidated. Evidently he was a very good manager and was aggressive in collecting delinquent accounts."

"Do your utmost to get this settled this month as per agreement. Bix" reads the note with underlined words from BH Beiderbecke on the Jan 1922 bill to blacksmith Frank Boyler from East Davenport Fuel Co.

Boyler's is the brick building with the truck parked out front in this 1922 photo. The building still stands at 11th St & Jersey Ridge Rd in the village of East Davenport, serving as a history museum.

Is Jazz the "Devil's Own Music?"

Why Many Think the Strange Melodies and Rhythms Now So Popular Are to Blame for the Spirit of Undress, Immodest Dances and Other Evils of the Present Day

Jazz should be stamped out, said Dr. Florence Richards, medical director at the William Penn High School for Girls. *Jazz sets aside control and restraint in the years when they are most necessary...Dancing, in the real meaning of the word is, of course, impossible with jazz. Its broken rhythm and its tom-tom count make any real poetry of motion out of the question.*

The CLOSE-UP PREVENTER, which has been suggested to make dancers keep safely within the bounds of modesty. Below, on the left, one of the objectionable dance attitudes which the PREVENTER would make quite impossible.

By and large, jazz has always been like the kind of a man you wouldn't want your daughter to associate with. ~Duke Ellington

Six Weeks in Syracuse

The 1920s hadn't yet been labeled *roaring* when parents started worrying over the music popular among their children. *Ladies Home Journal* in August 1921 featured a lengthy essay titled: DOES JAZZ PUT THE SIN IN SYNCOPATION?

> Ragtime quickens the pulse, it excites, it stimulates; but it does not destroy...Jazz disorganizes all regular laws and order; it is harmful and dangerous, and its influence is wholly bad.

If that didn't give pause, the *Journal's* December issue that same year ran an article quoting dance instructors and ballroom owners who proclaimed: UNSPEAKABLE JAZZ MUST GO!

> Jazz dancing is a worse evil than the saloon used to be! ....It lowers all the moral standards. Unlike liquor, a great deal of its harm is direct and immediate. But it also leads to undesirable things. The jazz is too often followed by the joy–ride. The lower nature is stirred up as a prelude to un–chaperoned adventure. ... The road to hell is too often paved with jazz steps.

Rock Islander Wayne Hostetter, a classically trained violinist, worried his folks when he started taking jazz clarinet and saxophone lessons at Bowlby Music Shop. His dad, a piano tuner, had arranged a try–out with the Tri–City Symphony. Wayne skipped the audition.

Instead, he played violin in a jazz combo at local dances while taking classes at Palmer School of Chiropractics. An automobile accident in the summer of 1922 left Wayne with severe cuts on his hands from the shattered windshield. By the time he'd healed enough to get back on the music scene, his original bandmates had scattered.

So Wayne signed on with Moline drummer Mervin *Pee Wee* Rank for a six–week gig in Syracuse, NY. Rank had secured the job while in Peoria. Since he couldn't get his own guys to agree to an extended engagement so far from home, Rank made some phone calls to line up other musicians.

Along with Hostetter, he recruited fellow Moliner and saxophonist Johnny Eberhardt. When he asked around about horn players, Rank learned Bix was back in Davenport, working at his dad's coal office. Bix had played with Rank aboard D.W. Wisherd's *Majestic* excursion boat briefly the year before. Bix jumped at Rank's offer, finding paid gigs hard to come by without a union card.

He packed some clothes and his Conn Victor cornet. Hostetter brought along his chiropractor's table. That table, patented by B.J. Palmer, was manufactured at the Adams Suit Case Factory in Davenport. It weighed about eighteen pounds but could hold up to 1,600 pounds. The legs folded inside the frame with its lower section providing storage room for toiletries, eliminating the need for an extra traveling bag.

The tri-cities foursome traveled to Chicago where they picked up a 17-year-old banjoist with two years professional experience under his belt. Like Bix, Indiana-born Eddie Condon did not read music. His first bandleader, Hollis Peavey, had called in some favors to get Condon his union card in Waterloo, IA.

Peavey's Jazz Bandits played the dancehall circuit in Iowa, Wisconsin and Minnesota. He regularly scouted for musicians aboard excursion boats on the Upper Mississippi. That's where Peavey found trombonist Lyle 'Tal' Sexton, although they'd known each other previously at Iowa's Camp Dodge during World War I.

A correspondent reported to Peavey's hometown newspaper in 1918 that Peavey "made a big hit with the saxophone…a musician of much ability, he ragged popular favorites until the fellows made him exhaust his repertoire."

Sexton played in Iowa's Company K band at Camp Dodge before hooking up with Tony Catalano and Carlisle Evans.

Peavey, who later became mayor of a Los Angeles suburb, told historian Phil Evans he'd recruited Bix aboard the Steamer *Capitol*. "He was engaged to come to work for me but the trumpet player I was letting go went to the owner of the ballroom and cried on his shoulder," Peavey said. When the owner wouldn't let him replace his horn man, Peavey said Bix "was okay about it and said he was going to study up and learn what the third valve was for on his cornet."

Eddie Condon told the story differently in his 1947 autobiography *We Called It Music: A Generation of Jazz*, which he dedicated to Bix. He claimed that after returning from Syracuse and rejoining Peavey, he bugged the bandleader until finally getting him to offer Bix a job based solely on Condon's praise for Bix's musicianship. Having heard him play, Peavey wouldn't have needed any convincing about Bix's talent. The issue came down to what Peavey was willing to pay for that talent.

According to Condon, Bix's response, via postcard, was that he wanted

PEAVEY'S JAZZ BANDITS at the Roseland ballroom in Winnipeg, Manitoba, from Dec 1923-April 1924. Saxophonist Hollis Peavey, standing center, and his second wife Doris Yenney Peavey, with accordion. Other identified band members include banjoist Eddie Condon, seated left of Doris and seated to bandleader Peavey's right: drummer Harold Cranford, trumpet player Louis Arndt, and trombonist Tal Sexton. Bix was recruited to join this band but wanted more money than Peavey was willing to pay, according to Condon.

Left: 1923 sheet music for original song by Doris & Hollis Peavey

$75 a week. "Originally he had put down sixty–five," Condon claimed. "There was a smudge where he had erased the six, but it was still plainly visible under the seven. Peavey handed me the card and watched me fidget. 'I don't think I want him in my band,' he said."

Considering Bix still didn't have a union card, it's understandable that Peavey would balk at his salary demand. Maybe it wasn't inflated ego but instead a lesson learned by Bix after Syracuse of what it cost to keep a roof over his head and food in his stomach.

Condon wrote that they were paid $45 a week for the engagement at the Alhambra Dance Academy. Proprietor Harry E. Morton apparently had no qualms with jazz. He made fifty cents per dancer, ten cents from those in the balcony listening to the band.

No explanation for the band's name, *Royal Harmonists of Indiana*. No names recalled for the three other musicians who made up Pee Wee Rank's eight–piece band. Among its known players, Condon was the youngest and Rank the senior member at twenty–one. Bix was nineteen.

In his memoir, Condon wrote nothing of the music they played. He mostly focused on the off–stage shenanigans of Bix and Hostetter, whom Condon called *Doc* because he practiced spinal adjustments on bandmates, whether or not they wanted or needed them. At the time, Wayne still had another year of courses to complete to earn his chiropractic degree.

"Hostetter had charts of all the parts of the body, including a blow–up of the eye," Condon wrote. "This he folded and took with him when we visited strange speakeasies. After the first drink he put it on the bar and studied it."

Condon wrote that inevitably a bartender would ask about the eye diagram. Hostetter claimed it showed him how to read fortunes. When the bartender asked for a demonstration, Hostetter would stare closely in his eyes and then nonchalantly say that he'd had a social disease. "That was the end of the examination; we got drinks on the house for the rest of the night," Condon wrote.

Those who knew Eddie Condon said he never let facts get in the way of a good story. Nevertheless, he came up with the most quoted line describing Bix's sound.

He wrote it in recalling the train out to Syracuse. They'd just passed Cleveland and Condon started in playing tunes with Eberhardt. As hoped, Bix took out his cornet and joined them. Condon finally got to hear what everybody back in Chicago had been raving about. "He put it to his lips and

SEP 23, 1922

blew a phrase," Condon wrote. "The sound came out like a girl saying yes"

After Syracuse, Hostetter took Bix to New York City to hear the Original Dixieland Jazz Band. Hostetter headed home from there but Bix stayed over in Scranton, PA, where Harry Morton had arranged for him to fill in for a band there.

Back in the tri–cities, Wayne told Fritz Putzier that the Conn Victor horn he'd sold Bix had its tuning slide dented when it got dropped as they rushed to catch the train. He also told Fritz that Bix had played that horn with the one and only Nick LaRocca.

Bix already had a style all his own, LaRocca later recalled. "I showed him the fingering and how to put his lips to the mouthpiece." As for piano, "Bix played more on the order of the great composers," LaRocca said.

He had let Bix crash a couple days at his hotel room. "I began worrying about this time and had to send him home as I could have been charged with harboring a minor," he said, adding, "This boy was a perfect gentleman and a brilliant musician."

Chalk up both the manners and the musicality to Bix's close–knit family. His parents loved him unconditionally, no matter what others would have us believe. His whole life Bix was moving toward something, not away. While working in Syracuse, he got word that his grandmother had passed away. No better example of what family meant to Bix can be found than in a letter addressed to his dad at the coal company office:

Tuesday–Wednesday
Nov 1/22

Dearest Dad:

    Received sis's sweet letter containing the sad news but of course which seemed inevitable in the near future at least. And pop on top of Oma's death my sorrow was heighten by the fact that I couldn't be home but even if I wasn't there personally I was in thought because I didn't realize how much Oma meant in my young life until she died. It's kind of hard to write a letter of this kind home because in our happy home I have nothing to write but stories of good times that I've had and of those I'm going to have with a feeling that everything as usual is O.K. at home but it happens in the best regulated families and we've got to take it as it comes but Dad I can see your part of it. Of all the troubles that I can imagine and that are bound to come in time the trouble I dread worse is to have the time come when mother and you & all of course must go and I sometimes feel I'd as soon not live to see the time.

    Well I'll check this as I know it isn't making you feel any better but just between you and me Dad I think that we can say that when Oma was living we had the best mothers in the world, am I right?

    Last night we played a hallowe'en masque ball and really that was the first time my mind was off Oma and home really I never did see so many funny costumes and such a variety. This is a dam good job pop and I am finishing up here as I promised in a bout a week and a half then the boss wants me to go to Scranton Pennsylvania to open up with a good band for just a week or two until they get a cornet player. Syracuse is a real town about as big as Des Moines but is about 300 miles from N.Y.C. while Scranton Pa. is only 100, so I may go if you let me. Only for a week to save carfare to N.Y.C. cause I sure hate to leave without putting my foot on Broadway. The boss was going to take us up but he can't for at least a month and I wont be here so that's the dope. I'm going to Scranton and then ease into N.Y.C. and come straight home 'cause I want to come so I'm there to stay when I get there.

    Just send my mail to the Alhambra dancing academy Syracuse

N.Y. & I'll get it—the place is the best in town, as big as the coliseum only a better class of people. I had a letter all written to you folks but when I got sis's I didn't send it so pardon the delay. I really haven't much time but I'll write more now on.

I'll try to send some 'do' but I'm afraid New York will all about break me but I'll go easy and save some I now have 30 bucks saved.

Well pop I'll have to close and get in a tux to play so grease aunt Lutie and Aunt Tillie & Uncle Tallie and extend to them my heartiest sympathies.

      Love to mom & Sis & Burnie

Bixie

If I get enough 'do' while in Scranton I'm going to send for mom as G. City* isn't far from there.

Grove City was the birthplace of Aggie's mother, Carrie Hill Hilton. Aggie's Aunt Emily would have been nearly eighty. Bix's second cousin, Edwin Harshaw, was a prominent banker in Grove City. The two younger Hill brothers, Wallace and Addison, had farms about an hour north of Pittsburgh. They would have been in their seventies.

CHICAGO JAZZ

BENNY GOODMAN

Benny Goodman remembered being all of fourteen and still wearing knee pants when he first met Bix Beiderbecke aboard a Chicago excursion boat in 1922. Goodman walked in with his clarinet case and stumbled over a heap of horns. "Bix looked me up and down. He mistook me for a meddlesome brat and threatened to pull my ears if I didn't go back to my mama," recalled Goodman. Instead he took out his licorice stick and blew a lively rhythm, rich in tone. Bix approved.

"Bix knocked me out the way he played his horn," Goodman said. "I figured listening to him that I could play the trumpet, too. I was third trumpet with

CUT OUT JAZZ, IS ADVICE OF DANCE MASTER

J. LOUIS GUYON SHOWS WAY TO CLEANER DANCING

Above: Guyon's Paradise dancehall, 1926 Benny Goodman got his first job here before joining Bix Beiderbecke aboard an excursion boat in 1922.

Frank Teschemacher and Wild Bill Davison were hired to play at the Paradise, February 1932 but the night before they started Tesch died in an auto accident with Davison at the wheel.

Right: Mr. & Mrs. J. Louis Guyon demonstrate proper dancing on the roof of their dance academy. Guyon's comments on jazz reported in a UP wire story printed in the QC on June 13, 1921.

"Let's cut out jazz music. People don't dance indecently to good music. I tried an experiment at my academy by playing jazz music. In sixty seconds the dancers were wiggling and twisting in indecent positions—doing everything but dancing. It had the same effect as five big drinks of whisky."

Guyon allows nothing but the old fashioned dances in his academy.

Ben Pollack's band back in those early days in Chicago. I'm on a few of Pollack's records playing trumpet but not much—maybe four notes or so.

"Jimmy McPartland was a marvelous trumpeter and laughed at what I was doing," Goodman said. "I knew I couldn't be Bix, anyway, so I stayed with my clarinet."

James Duggald McPartland—named for his Scottish grandfather—and his brother Rich started out playing in Chicago's west side Austin High School band. Their father had taught them to box and to play violin. It was the rough stuff they liked most.

Until one day their local hangout, the Spoon & Straw soda fountain, got a phonograph and some records. "We heard the New Orleans Rhythm Kings' *Farewell Blues* and *Tin Roof Blues*. This was jazz," said McPartland. "A record by King Oliver and Louis Armstrong came out, I think *Dipper Mouth Blues*. We loved that. Then we heard the Wolverines and Bix Beiderbecke and we flipped. Bix had a beauty of tone and phrasing that made you feel the emotion. He had sort of an affectionate tone, a nice round full tone. It's what we tried to emulate." Jimmy had a more aggressive style.

"We started playing fraternities. One time a guy said, 'your music stinks.' Rich said to me, 'You know what to do, don't you, Cocky?' I hit two or three guys so fast my brother didn't even have to get up. It happened again, and that time Rich had to help me knock some of them down. After that, word got around: if you don't like our music, don't say anything. That's why we were called a gang."

Jimmy's brother Rich had a banjo. Bud Freeman, who lived two blocks from the McPartland clan, took lessons on a C-melody sax from Jimmy's dad. "Jim Lannigan, who married my sister, got a bass. He had a piano at his house, so we'd practice there. Dave North played the piano. We met Frank Teschemacher at school. He wanted to play clarinet. We could all read music. We all played violin."

His junior year at Austin High, Jimmy got a wire from the Wolverines. Bix was leaving to join Jean Goldkette's band. Would he come replace him at the Cinderella Ballroom in New York for $87.50 a week? Testing whether it was a joke, McPartland wired for traveling money. He was sent $35 for a train ticket. McPartland quit school.

At first rehearsal Bix stood in the back, listening. "I like you kid," Bix told McPartland. "You sound like me but you don't copy me." Bix was 21 and Jimmy 17.

They roomed together briefly while Bix taught two or three songs a day to his replacement. Bix also took Jimmy to a music store and picked him out

WOLVERINES in NYC, 1924. Bix, seated on right, trained Jimmy McPartland to be his replacement before joining Jean Goldkette's band only to be fired due to his inability to read music. He would rejoin Goldkette after Trumbauer's tutelage.

Bix once told me, "I don't feel the same way twice. That's one of the things I like about jazz, kid. I don't know what's going to happen next. Do you?"
~Jimmy McPartland

Austin High School Gang, 1922, L-R: Frank Teschemacher, Jimmy & Rich McPartland, Bud & Arnold Freeman

a new cornet like his own that Jimmy admired. The cost was deducted from his salary. Within two years McPartland became the Wolverine's bandleader, bringing on his old Austin High Gang including saxophonist Bud Freeman.

In a 2000 profile by Max Jones, Freeman shared another side of his musical hero:

> Bix was not only a master of his instrument but an artist who loved the theater, loved to read, loved the aesthetic life. When I played with Ben Pollack in New York's Little Club in '28, Beiderbecke came down to tell me that John Barrymore was back from England with the English company that had been playing *Hamlet*. He told me they were going to do *Hamlet* on radio that night and I went with him to hear it. I remember being gone an hour and a half or more and missing the next set. Pollack was furious, but Bix and I were great friends from then on.

In a 1939 interview for a WPA oral history on Chicago jazz, cornetist Joe 'Muggsy' Spanier told of putting on his brother's long pants to get into the jazz clubs:

> I met Bix at the Friar's Inn where the New Orleans Rhythm Kings were and we both came down to listen to them. We met in a funny way, sort of unconscious. We'd sit around and listen to the boys and then one day Bix said, "I'm a cornet player." And I said, "I'm one, too." After that we went out to the south side together and there was one place we dropped in at where there was a piano and a drum and we sat in with our two horns and we played together so well we decided we'd be a cornet team. Always we met at Friar's Inn and then we'd knock around together....

Guitarist George Barnes never met Bix but he was interviewed for that same WPA oral history project. Sam Ross spoke to Barnes at Chicago's famed Three Deuces and later in his rented hotel room. Ross wrote:

> He played some Beiderbecke records and wished to hell those cymbals would be thrown out of the orchestra, for they cluttered up the beauty of Beiderbecke's tone. There was one spot in the recording of *Singin' the Blues* where Beiderbecke takes a terrific break, and right after that Beiderbecke goes into a savage attack. Barnes' face sparked up. "Listen to that break. You can just feel how big a bang he got of it the way he attacks the next phrase." At the end when Beiderbecke goes into a very restrained high phrase, Barnes said, "That's beautiful, isn't it? That's beautiful." And he would interrupt the record spin and play the sections over and over again.

"...I liked swing. I always liked it even when I didn't know what it was. I felt it like this. I knew Guy Lombardo was bad. But I didn't know what swing really was until I heard Bix Beiderbecke on records. He has been my big influence. I don't think anybody playing today has not been influenced by Bix. I understand he was a great guy, everybody who ever worked with him thought he was great.

Another of Bix's admirers was a 22-year-old Chicago bandleader who recalled playing to a crowd of big-wig politicians at one of Capone's clubs the night of the Dempsey-Tunney fight. Capone wanted to impress his guests so he asked to take the baton for a rendition of Gershwin's *Rhapsody in Blue*. "Since my favorite pastime was breathing, I said yes to Big Al," said Julius 'Jule' Styne, "and I must say he did very well. He really knew the whole piece."

Styne had been a piano prodigy, playing with the Chicago Symphony at age nine. But when a teacher said his hands were too small for certain classical pieces, Styne veered off into jazz. "I learned to be a popular songwriter by playing the joints with guys like Bix, George Wettling, and Benny Goodman," Styne said.

"All my early songs were two-beat blues but like Bix that classical background kept creeping in," Styne said. He recalled "doodling with the second movement of a Ferdinand Hiller piano concerto."

Out of it came *Sunday*, Styne's first hit song recorded by Bix with the Goldkette band. Styne went on to compose some 1,500 songs for Broadway and Hollywood shows including *Gentlemen Prefer Blondes, Gypsy*, and *Funny Girl*. He got an Oscar for *Three Coins in the Fountain*.

Around Chicago the story circulated about reedman Milton Mesirow, a.k.a. Mezz Mezzrow going at it with Capone's younger brother Mitzi for putting the moves on one of the girls in his show. Big Al laughingly said "the kid's got plenty of guts," and with that, tensions eased and the band played on.

Mezzrow learned to play jazz as an inmate at the Illinois Pontiac Reformatory. In his 1946 book, *Really the Blues*, Mezz wrote that he earned his PhD in "more creep joints and speakeasies and dancehalls than the law allowed." He later became a record producer and concert promoter and briefly managed Louis Armstrong. Mezz held such affinity for black musicians that he listed himself as a Negro on his jail records, cabaret license, even his selective service card.

Southsider George Wettling idolized drummer Warren 'Baby' Dodds.

Summer 1926

L-R: Charles 'Pee Wee' Russell (1906-1969), Mezz Mezzrow (1899-1972), T. Sonny Lee, standing (1904-1975), Bix, George Wettling (1907-1968), Eddie Condon (1905-1973) grouped on a replica train platform in this tattered souvenir shot at White City when Bix, Pee Wee & Sonny were in Frank Trumbauer's outfit.

Chicago's White City Amusement Park at 63rd and South Park

He'd hop the train from his Irish neighborhood where he attended Calamus High School and ride to the Chicago Loop. There he joined Bix and other jazz-crazed youngsters, courtside for King Oliver and Prince Armstrong. Wettling recalled Capone showing up at the Triangle Club with seven or eight henchmen in his entourage. They locked the doors, nobody allowed in or out. "We saw these rods come out—and ducked. The boss was shot in the stomach but we kept working," Wettling said.

Capone sent up his song requests to the bandstand, along with hundred dollar tips for the musicians, Wettling said. Heady times for tyro musicians perfecting their musical chops while playing to customers not so much interested in the band as in drinking Big Al's Prohibition hooch. Paid gigs were hard to come by in those early days, recalled Wettling. "We didn't care," he said. "We had the music and didn't need bread."

In 1935 he followed Eddie Condon to New York and established his reputation with the likes of Artie Shaw, Bunny Berigan, Muggsy Spanier, even Paul Whiteman. Still, he preferred drumming in small combos and particularly was proud of his trio sessions with Jess Stacy and Bud Freeman.

In later years Wettling and trombonist Sonny Lee expanded their artistic expressions beyond jazz, both becoming students of modernist painter Stuart Davis, famous for his abstract landscapes.

Texas–born Thomas Ball 'Sonny' Lee got his big break with Billy Lustig's Scranton Sirens. Lee was a replacement for the Pennsylvania territory band when Lustig took the group to New Orleans on an extended engagement.

Lustig organized his outfit in 1918 and disbanded it in 1928. Several future jazz greats got their start in the Scranton Sirens. Among the alumnus: Tommy and Jimmy Dorsey, Russ Morgan, Wingy Manone, and another Texas trombonist, Jack Teagarden.

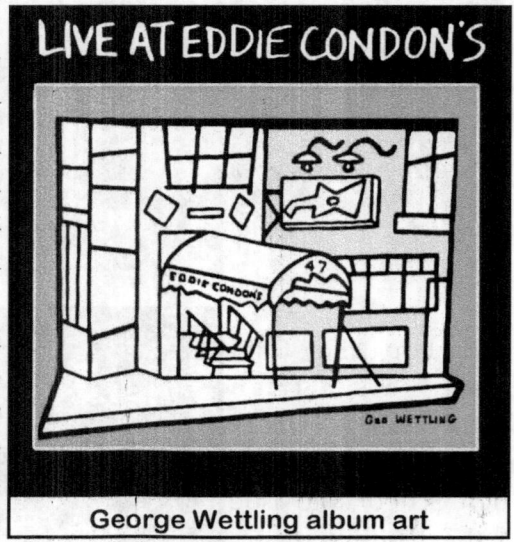

George Wettling album art

Sonny Lee was playing in Charlie Creath's riverboat band when Frank Trumbauer recruited him for his St. Louis outfit. Lee recorded with Creath and later with Isham Jones and subsequently with Woody Herman when Jones handed over the reigns in 1936.

Charles 'Pee Wee' Russell came from a family of musicians; his father a violinist and his mother a pianist. At fourteen Russell got caught sneaking out of the house to play on the riverboat. His dad then enrolled him at Western Military Academy in Alton, IL. Bix's Uncle Max Von Binzer had been on the faculty at WMA but died two years before Russell attended.

Russell held first chair–clarinet in the academy band. After graduating he returned to the riverboats before joining Trumbauer. During the two years that he and Bix were bandmates, Russell said they never were apart "day, night, good, bad, sick, well, broke, drunk."

HERE HE IS, GIRLS— THE PERFECT MAN.

As promised two weeks ago, Homade Hooch is presenting today the male American Beauty of Davenport. The American Beauty is the composite citizen pictured above, whose features and various excellencies have been culled from a score of local sheiks and Meighanites.

The features incorporated into the picture were selected from thousands of suggestions emanating the male-worshipping sex. Here they are:

Curl in hat brim: Adapted from Realff Ottesen and Bert Frahm.
Mustache: Merle Wells.
Eyebrows: Bob MacGregor.
Hair: Dean Handley.
Sideburns: Edwin Lindsay.
Nose: Erwin Swindell.
Complexion: Judge Letts.
Teeth: Tony LeClaire.
Lips: Albert Block.
Smile: Bix Beiderbecke.
Neck: Ralph Blank.
Eyes: "Doc" Cody.
Chin: No. 1, Urban Ott; No. 2, Harry Mann.
Eyelashes: Ray Nelson.
Ears: Tad Martin.
Forehead: Merle Skolley.
Head posture: Harry McCullough.
Shoulders: Ed Stafford.
Wing collar: "Lefty" Miles.
Bow tie: Jack Teegan.
Sartorial unity: A. F. Petersberger.
Shirt: Robert Wain.
Chest: Jack Isaacson.
Photographability: Ralph Blank.
Strut: Willie Engel.

Democrat-Leader
April 11, 1924

The perfect man has the smile of Bix Beiderbecke...

But which Bix?

Leon Bix was on the road with the Wolverines; they'd yet to release a record.

Papa Bix was friends with several men whose winning attributes made the list. These guys ranged in age from 20 to 40, some single, others married.

More likely that perfect smile belonged to the Bix who also went by the nickname of Burnie.

He wasn't yet married and it wouldn't be until mid-summer that he took over Harned Von Maur's record department but Burnie was a very popular guy in Davenport and handsome even by the standards of *People* magazine's annual 'sexiest man alive' issue.

WHEN THE GREAT GERSHWIN PLAYED THE COL
by Jim Arpy

While Bix was at Indiana University with the Wolverines on May 23, 1924, the Paul Whiteman Orchestra arrived by train in his hometown. That evening George Gershwin was at the piano in the Coliseum ballroom and audience members paid one dollar to $2.50 to hear him.

This was Whiteman's famous *Experiment in Modern Music* concert, introduced February 12, 1924, at Aeolian Hall in New York City. Gershwin accompanied Whiteman's orchestra on an 18-day tour that included Davenport.

Gershwin had been working as a Tin Pan Alley piano pounder when Whiteman commissioned the twenty-six year old to write a jazz piece for the white-tie trade. Gershwin admitted years later that he'd actually forgotten about the commission until he read a notice in the newspaper one day that he was working on a jazz rhapsody. He got to work and turned out the song in ten days.

Whiteman's orchestra also featured celebrated pianists Ferde Grofe and Phil Bouteje. Grofe had worked with Gershwin on the orchestrations for *Rhapsody in Blue*. Davenport newspapers advertised the presence of three Chickering grand pianos, favored by Franz Liszt, and Norwegian composer Edvard Grieg.

The Chickering piano was chief rival of the Steinway. Jonas Chickering founded the company in 1823 and continued it until 1908 when it merged with the Knabe Company to form American Piano Company.

Gershwin's name appeared in a pre-concert news story but oddly did not appear in the promotional advertisements. He had penned the hit song *Swanee* in 1919 and music for Broadway's *Scandals of 1920*, including the tunes *Somebody Loves Me* and *Stairway to Paradise*. But Gershwin really never became famous with the general public until he and his brother Ira became a songwriting team in Hollywood. Gershwin lived only to the age of 38 but his *Rhapsody in Blue* survives to this day as proof, as Whiteman said, that jazz has something to say.

Life is a lot like jazz...it's best when you improvise. ~George Gershwin

1924

14 May 1924 *Davenport Democrat–Leader*:
WHITEMAN HAS FINE PROGRAM FOR CONCERT
NOTED ORCHESTRA LEADER WILL SHOW STRIDES JAZZ HAS MADE

In arranging his program for the concert at the Coliseum May 23, Paul Whiteman works out a novel idea which will show the great advances made by composers of popular music.

"Some ten years ago a blatant method of treating music was introduced to the American public which came to be known as jazz," says Mr. Whiteman.

"This program proposed to indicate the tremendous strides which have been made in modifying this treatment, proving that the term jazz, tho still applied to the melodious music of today, is a misnomer.

"The greatest single factor in the improvement of American popular music has been the development of the art of arranging the music for orchestra in accordance with the best musical traditions. Paul Whiteman was the first musician to prepare special arrangements (or scores as they are technically called) for his orchestra and play the music according to said scores. Since then a staff of arrangers has become a necessary adjunct to the personnel of every modern American orchestra.

"As a result there are thousands of young people scoring, arranging and composing; they are creating most of the American music of today. They are not influenced by any foreign school; on the contrary their own influence is spreading abroad. Paul Whiteman has issued a general invitation to these musicians to compose special works for his orchestra and he intends that it shall be the vehicle for their endeavors. Thus, in the second part of this program four serenades by Victor Herbert written especially for Paul Whiteman's orchestra are presented, and George Gershwin's "Rhapsody in Blue," recognized by New York critics as the first serious effort in musical composition in the American idiom."

The Program
I.
True Form of Jazz
(a) Dixieland—One–Step …..LaRocca
An early American discordant jazz tune
(b) Medley—One–Step…A similar tune
made less blatant by clever scoring
Contrast—Legitimate vs. Jazzing
Selection in True Form—"Whispering," Schonberger
The forerunner of the modern type of American music

Same selection with Jazz treatment...How this beautiful
number may be ruined by jazzing
Comedy Selections
Origin of a well known melody...Frank appropriation of
themes from Handel's "Messiah."
"So This Is Venice" from "Carnival of Venice" Thomas
Imitating by musical instruments sounds depicting
emotions or noises is as old as music itself
Soloist: Ross Gorman
Popular Compositions with Modern Score
"Limehouse Blues"...Brahm
"What'll I do" — Waltz ....Irving Berlin
"Shanghai Lullaby"..Isham Jones
"Wonderful One" — Waltz.......................Paul Whiteman
"Linger Awhile" Michael Pingatore (soloist) Vincent Ross
Example of simple melodies far removed from the original jazz
Adaptation of Standard Selections to Dance Rhythm
"Pale Morn"................Logau
"To a Wild Rose"...McDowell
"Chausonette"................Friml
Many standard selections owe their popularity with the general
public to dance arrangements by Paul Whiteman
Flavoring: A Selection with Borrowed Themes.
"Russian Rose" based on the "Volga Boat Song....Ferde Grofe
II.
A Suite of Serenades.....Victor Herbert
(a) Spanish
(b) Chinese
(c) Cuban
(d) Oriental
These numbers are Victor Herbert's first compositions
for the modern American orchestra
Rhapsody in Blue....Geo. Gershwin
Geo. Gershwin (piano) and Orchestra
This is the first Rhapsody written for solo instrument
and the modern American orchestra

In a 1927 *Democrat–Leader* article, Crescent Orchestra bandleader and former Whiteman trumpet player Bernie Schultz wrote:

This is an age of jazz. It is little understood and indiscreetly discussed—yes, mostly cussed by the so–called 'lover of music.' *An Experiment in Modern American Music,* New York City 1924, proved significant. The concert was offered as a serious contribution to the arts, and consequently opened the discussion and one question remains: Will jazz serve as the foundation for true American music?

In considering jazz for such an important role in the development of a purely American school of music, one can admit only those works that display originality and understanding.

To a concert given some time ago by Paul Whiteman, Victor Herbert contributed *Suite of Serenades*, one of his last compositions. The so-called jazz orchestra presented the Herbert number and others, not in fox trot rhythm but with symphonic comprehension. There was no evidence of wailing saxophones—there were saxophones—clarinets did not shriek, nor was there a bombardment of drummer's dishpans and other such freak noises as disturbed the atmosphere when the average five-piece dance band of some five or ten years ago was in action.

No, there was distinct melody and harmony and sufficient rhythm resulting in an orchestral affect worthy of place on the program of the most dignified symphony orchestra.

KINGS OF JAZZ

Alabama-born James Reese Europe was playing piano at a Harlem cabaret in 1905 while outside on the curb sat seven-year-old George Gershwin. Europe's 125-member orchestra played Carnegie Hall three times during the decade before Gershwin introduced his *Rhapsody in Blue*. Gershwin explained that Jim Europe set himself apart from contemporaries like John Phillip Sousa with his syncopated rhythms—what they called *ragging* the standard march time. Europe laced his compositions with extended reed notes and muted brass chords. They called it *jazzing*, Gershwin explained.

Europe's 1913–1914 recordings for the Victor Talking Machine Company were not marketed as jazz. They also were not the first recordings of ragtime. They were the bridge between.

As musical director for husband-and-wife dance team Vernon and Irene Castle, Jim Europe's rendition of W.C. Handy's *Memphis Blues* set off the foxtrot dance craze. After returning from France a decorated WWI veteran, Europe and his Hell Fighters Band went on a national tour. It ended tragically with Europe's jugular severed by his drummer's knife during an argument. Newspaper headlines proclaimed: *The Jazz King Is Dead*. Europe was buried with full military honors at Arlington Cemetery the same year Denver-born Paul Whiteman brought his nine-piece band to New York.

MAY 11, 1919.

"KING OF JAZZ" WHO CAPTIVATED EUROPE, IS SLAIN

BOSTON, Mass., May 10.— Jimmy Europe is dead. The black master of syncopation, sometimes known as "King of Jazz," whose rag-time band made the feet of royalty misbehave and almost caused Marshal Foch to hitchy-koo, was stabbed by one of his own drummers last night.

Europe's band was giving a concert here—starting a world tour—when Europe, standing behind the scenes, was stabbed in the neck and died shortly afterward. Herbert Wright was arrested, accused of doing the stabbing when Europe reprimanded him for disobeying orders.

Lieutenant Jimmy Europe was leader of the 369th infantry band—the "hell fighters." It was he who introduced real ticklefoot rag-time overseas, astonishing the foreigners, and it was claimed his jazz helped win the Argonne forest victory.

Lieutenant Jim
EUROPE'S HELL FIGHTERS 369th U.S. Infantry JAZZ BAND
is now making records EXCLUSIVELY for

No Needles to Change

Jim Europe's Jazz Band Played Trombones or Machine Guns and Beat Everything Except a Retreat.

Lieut. James Reese Europe, 369th Infantry, the Harlem bandmaster who led his 100-strong jazz unit thru France and helped to break the Hindenburg Line.

Lieut Noble Sissle
cornetist, singer and drum major

Play slowly until you can catch the swing. ~Scott Joplin

WOLVERINES-SUMMER '24 ABOVE, seated: George Johnson, tenor sax; Bob Gillette, banjo; Bix, cornet; Vic Burton, drums; standing: Jimmy Hartwell, clarinet/sax; Min Leinbrook, brass bass; Dick Voynow, piano

ANGELA'S RING

Researching Bix has led down some surprising paths. One came by way of an obituary in the local newspaper back in 1996. In an all-too brief account of the life of Angela Kelly, it was noted that, *Prior to her marriage to James Kelly, she was engaged to the legendary trumpet player Leon Bix Beiderbecke.*

Angela's obituary got filed away in a drawer and there it remained for a decade. It surfaced again while preparing this book. A search of telephone listings led to Angela's son, Tony Kelly, who works as a photographer in Evanston, IL. His photography has been featured on PBS and ABC, and in magazines including *Life, Newsweek, Smithsonian, Ebony, Vogue,* and at fine art galleries in NYC and Chicago. He has taught at Columbia, American University, Notre Dame, and Northwestern University.

When asked if his mother was once engaged to Bix, Tony answered, "Yes!"

Then he added: "In fact, my sister still has the ring!"

Wow!

Tony's sister Cinda Graham is an artist, sculptor, and printmaker whose work has been shown in New York galleries. Her husband John Graham heads the string department at Eastman School of Music in Rochester, NY.

Cinda and Tony filled in the details about their family's special connection to Bix.

First, some background on the Searle family. Angela's grandfather, Elhanan Searle, had migrated to Rock Island County from Ohio with his family in 1837 when he was two. He graduated from Northwestern University and apprenticed for attorney John L. Beveridge—later the governor of Illinois. In 1859 Searle became an associate of Abraham Lincoln in the law office of Lincoln and Herndon in Springfield. While living in Springfield, he met and married Cassie R. Pierce in 1863.

Searle served with distinction as a lieutenant colonel in the Civil War, organizing the Arkansas troops and later served as Justice of the Arkansas Supreme Court and a founding trustee of the University of Arkansas.

After retiring in 1887, Judge Searle returned to Rock Island and purchased the Rodman House. General Thomas Jackson Rodman, founder and commandant of the Rock Island Arsenal was famous for designing the Civil War era cannon named after him. Rodman died in 1871.

Judge Searle fathered six children but only two survived his death in 1906—Blanche Searle Eckart, Angela's mother, and C. J. Searle, a second-generation Rock Island judge. C.J. Searle officiated preliminary court appearances in the John Looney trial before a change of venue moved proceedings to Galesburg.

Five generations of Searles had lived in the Rodman House, including Tony's children. The house had been listed as the Rodman-Searle House in 1987 on National Register of Historical Places, but is gone now, destroyed by a fire. Tony said his oldest son dug through the rubble and found the old marble fireplace mantle, taking it back to Evanston where it is now in his home there.

Angela lived about six blocks from her uncle's Rock Island home. Bix's cousin, Victor Stibolt lived in the same neighborhood—known now as Rock Island's Broadway Historic District. Like Davenport's Gold Coast, Broadway is noted for its stately Victorian homes.

Victor, oldest son of Ottilie Beiderbecke Stibolt, was married to Helen Davis, granddaughter of Frederick Denkmann of the Weyerhaeuser-Denkmann lumber dynasty. Victor was vice president of the Rock Island Plow Company.

Being among Rock Island's upper crust, the Searles and Stibolts likely socialized. But they may not have commiserated over one another's

Judge C. J. Searle

Rodman-Searle House c. 1880

wayward sons. In the Searle family that would have been Angela's cousin and Bix's pal Charles Searle Jr.

Cinda noted that her uncle had quite the reputation. "He was what you might call, *a man about town*, who liked music and hung out with musicians," said Cinda.

The *Davenport Democrat–Leader* reported in June of 1924 that Charles Searle Jr. had to go to court in Scott County for a hit and run after damaging a parked car on Davenport's Main Street. "Charles was a boozer and a crazy guy," Tony said. "After a wild Christmas party, he and Bix decided to go to Iowa City and enrolled at the university there.

"They joined a fraternity—the one that the football players and drinking guys joined. Well, Charles and Bix got into some kind of brawl and the University ended up suspending the whole fraternity. Instead of returning home, Charles and Bix went to Chicago where my mother was studying."

Angela and her cousin graduated together from Rock Island High School in 1922. She later graduated from the same teacher's college that Bix's sister Mary Louise attended. Angela returned to Rock Island where she taught in Rock Island's first kindergarten class, Cinda said. "She was told that the aim of teaching was to break the will of the students!"

Bix may have given Angela the ring after his time in New York with the Wolverines before joining Goldkette in 1924. Tony said his mother didn't talk much at all about Bix and when she did, she talked in generalities.

His sister agreed. "Mother was not a storyteller," Cinda said, laughing, "So, I don't have many stories to repeat..." She did recall her mother describing one date with Bix at a dance in Iowa City. "Bix was playing in the band so she was left on her own. She had been so excited that she had forgotten to eat during the day leading up to the event. She fainted on the dance floor.

**Angela Searle
Rock Island High School**

"Mother said that, contrary to some

Kelly-Searle Wedding, Rock Island, Surprise to Friends

Announcement is made of the marriage of Miss Angela Searle, daughter of Mr. and Mrs. James B. Eckert, of 2532 Eighth and a Half avenue, Rock Island, to James A. Kelly, son of Mrs. Driscoll Kelly of 220 East Fourteenth street, Davenport, the wedding having been a quiet ceremony of Thursday afternoon at 4 o'clock.

Plans of the young couple were known only to immediate relatives and the wedding comes as a great surprise to their many friends who had not been taken into the secret of the wedding date. The bridal couple went to the office of Judge C. J. Searle, the uncle of the bride, who read the marriage service. There were no attendants.

The bride was in a white sport ensemble of blue and white print dress, and white top coat, and she carried a bouquet of sweet peas and roses.

Mr. and Mrs. Kelly left immediately after the ceremony on a northern motor trip and they will be at home on their return at Hotel Blackhawk, Davenport. Both come of well known families in the Tri-Cities.

The bride graduated from Ward Belmont college, Nashville, and also attended the National Elementary Kindergarden college at Evanston, Ill. For the past year she has taught the kindergarten in the Audubon school, Rock Island.

Mr. Kelly, after graduating from St. Ambrose college attended the Art Institute, Chicago, and later he was with the New York Tribune as manager of that big daily's art department. He has been active in the work of the local Art League, especially before going to New York and since returning has been in charge of the art department of the L. W. Ramsey Advertising company of Davenport.

MRS. JAMES A. KELLY
nee Angela Searle

Left: July 20, 1928; below: 1996 obituary; Bix's ring worn by Cinda Kelly Graham

Angela Searle Kelly

Angela Searle Kelly, 91, Rochester, N.Y., formerly of Rock Island, died Monday, June 24, 1996, in Rochester.

The former Angela Searle was born the daughter of James Eckart and Blanche Searle. She married the late James Anthony Kelly in 1933, who later became prominent as a magazine illustrator in New York City.

Prior to her marriage to James Kelly, she was engaged to the legendary Davenport trumpet player, Leon Bix Beiderbeck.

She attended Ward Belmont College in Nashville, Tenn., and went on to study at the National Kindergarten and Elementary College in Chicago in 1925. Upon graduation, she returned to Rock Island to teach in the city's first kindergarten class.

In earlier years, she was a reporter for a New York fashion magazine called The Breath of the Avenue.

Her teaching career ended with her marriage because the marriage of teachers was not in accordance with the educational policy of that era.

Until her marriage in 1933, Angela lived with her parents and her brother, Robert Eckart, in the historic Rodman House, Rock Island. Blanche Searle was the daughter of a Judge of the Rock Island Circuit Court, Elhanan Searle, who had apprenticed in law with Abraham Lincoln. James B. Eckhart was a prominent Rock Island realtor.

Survivors include a daughter, Cinda Graham, Rochester, N.Y.; a son, Tony Kelly, Evanston, Ill.; four grandchildren; and three great-grandchildren.

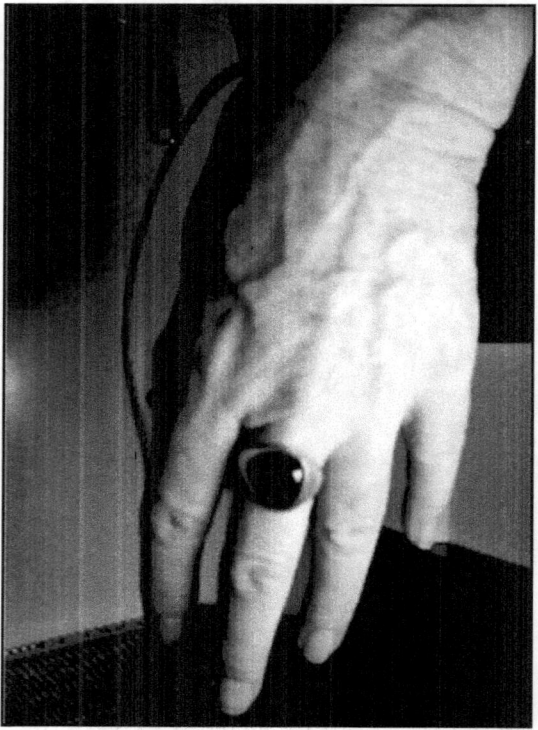

comments she had read, Bix had been a sharp dresser. My mother was a keen dresser and would not have gone out with anyone who was not clean and neat. She later worked for a New York fashion magazine called *The Breath of the Avenue*."

Angela's keepsake from her former beau is now in Cinda's possession. "The ring that Bix gave my mother was his class ring. It is gold with a red stone. I still have it."

Tony remembered his Grandmother Blanche telling their mother, "Of all the young men that called on you, Bix was the most polite and considerate."

In July of 1928 Angela married Davenport artist James Kelly. The *Democrat–Leader* reported that their secret ceremony, performed by C. J. Searle in his Rock Island law office, came as a surprise to the couple's friends and family.

The Kelly family moved to Queens, NY, where James Kelly worked as a magazine illustrator for such publications as the *Saturday Evening Post*. He had previously been manager of the art department at the *New York Tribune* but moved to Davenport and was working for the L. W. Ramsey Advertising Company when he and Angela married.

"Father also knew and liked Bix," Tony said, "and when my parents

L-R: BLANCHE SEARLE ECKART, ANGELA KELLY, JIM ECKART, BABY TONY AND BOB ECKART

moved to New York City, Bix contacted them to get together. To my parent's regret, the meeting with Bix never happened," Tony added, noting his parents learned of Bix's death soon after.

When Tony was a reporter in Davenport his editor assigned him an interview with trumpeter Harry James, who was staying at the Blackhawk Hotel. "So I went over there and talked with Harry," Tony said.

"He was very congenial, so I asked if he knew that Bix was born and buried here. Harry said that he knew, then added, 'you know, when I was growing up there were only two horn players worth listening to: Bix and Louie,' admitting he favored Armstrong's style. 'I followed Louis because I like to play those high notes. But Bix was in a class of his own. Nobody, nobody, has really heard Bix until they hear him play at one o'clock in the morning!' James added."

Harry James, of course, dubbed Kirk Douglas' trumpet playing in the 1950 movie, *Young Man with a Horn*, based on the novel of the same name, inspired by the life of Bix Beiderbecke and co–starring Hoagy Carmichael.

IOWA CITY

> From the society column of the *Iowa City Daily Press*, June 7, 1920: *Armand Shiley was pleasantly surprised by a few of his high school friends yesterday on the occasion of his sixteenth birthday. The young people had been out motoring when one suggested that they go to Reich's for refreshments. As the entered they beheld a table tastefully decorated in pink and white, and upon which a delectable luncheon was served. The guests who enjoyed the 'surprise' were Misses Gertrude Grant, Julia Dondore and Gretchen Swisher; and Lovell Sulser, Cecil Huntzinger and Armand Shiley.*

Birthday boy Armand Shiley was a piano prodigy, graduating in 1921 with honors from Iowa City High School with pals and fellow musicians Lovell Sulser and Cecil Huntzinger.

But it was another piano prodigy whose musical path crossed those of Sulser and Huntzinger, casting their lot with his into the annals of jazz.

While Shiley pursued classical studies at the University of Iowa, Sulser and Huntzinger put together a band they called the Iowa Collegians. Lovell played alto sax and violin; Huntzinger played piano. A dozen or so university boys filled the ranks for fraternity dances and local society gatherings.

During winter break in 1924, bandmate Chet Ogden lined up a gig for the Collegians in his hometown of Davenport at the Garden Theater. They were booked among several vaudeville acts for New Year's Eve and throughout the run of the silent film version of J.M. Barrie's *Peter Pan*.

At some point during the Collegian's Davenport engagement, Bix dropped by to see Ogden, whom he had replaced aboard the *Majestic* three years earlier. Ogden had to leave the riverboat due to an illness in his family but he was soon back working excursion tours that season aboard the *Capitol* with Carlisle Evans. He left Evans band to enter college and was replaced by Harold Oerman, a high school classmate of Bix, who had what Bix did not at the time—a union card.

Oerman had since gone off to school at the University of Illinois and Bix was giving serious consideration to entering Iowa when the winter term started back up again. In a 1964 interview with historian Phil Evans, Huntzinger said that Bix asked if, "we could use him if he decided to come to Iowa U. to study. The boys were flabbergasted. Bix had just come off playing with the Wolverine Orchestra, who had a growing following due to their records."

Lovell Sulser was the elder son of C. Merton and Lillian Metzinger Sulser. His father was a carpenter who made violins as a hobby. Cecil lived with his aunt and an uncle who worked as a printer at the local newspaper.

"The band was a partnership between Bromo and myself," Huntzinger told Evans, describing Lovell—not his father Merton, as previously misidentified—as a personable front man with a great jazz moniker. "He was a matinee idol type that attracted the girls." Sulser's nickname of *Bromo* was a nod to his name sounding similar to Dr. Emerson's patented headache salts.

Sulser would later play with New York's Smith Ballew Band. It's not clear whether or not Sulser was with the band when Bix stayed with Ballew bassist Rex Gavitte in New York. Gavitte introduced Bix to a relative who helped him get the apartment in Queens where he died.

Back in Davenport that winter of 1924, Bix reconnected with several musician pals, including Rock Island banjoist Lou Black, who played New Year's Eve with Carlisle Evans at the Coliseum ballroom.

The Collegians played the Garden from December 28 through January 3. When they went back to Iowa City, Bix joined in on some of their weekend gigs.

Democrat–Leader Ads for Garden Theatre New Year's Eve 1924 *Peter Pan* with Bromo Sulser and His Collegians Dec 28, 1924 to Jan 3, 1925

IOWA COLLEGIANS c.1924 LOVELL 'BROMO' SULSER stands left of center; fourth from right at the piano is CECIL HUNTZINGER

SMITH BALLEW BAND c. 1931 BROMO SULSER, far right; REX GAVITTE, standing third from left

The late Einer C. Johnson, a dentist from Eagle Grove, IA, said he met Bix for the first time while playing brass bass with Sulser and His Iowa Collegians in the Quad Cities. "Bix didn't play that night, but came to visit one of the guys in the band. Later, he joined us in Iowa City where he had just enrolled as a freshman. Bromo told him he could only pay him $7 a night, but Bix said, 'that's good enough for me.'"

At age 84, Dr. Johnson proudly claimed, "I believe I'm one of a few surviving Iowans who actually played in a band with Bix."

Johnson recalled, "Bix's playing surprised us...he was so far ahead of the rest of us that his music didn't appeal to us at first. After he'd played with us for a while, though, he worked in pretty well."

Bix enrolled at the university on Feb. 2, 1925. University records show that he was signed up for classes in Freshman English, Philosophy—Religion and Ethics, Music Theory, Music History—Romantic and Modern periods, and Piano for a total of thirteen semester hours.

Without a high school diploma, his university enrollment was on conditional basis, meaning he had to complete specific course work before officially enrolling as an undergraduate.

Prior to enrolling at the university, Bix went to Indianapolis where he met up with Hoagy Carmichael. Hoagy then drove him to the Gennett Studio in Richmond where Bix had pre-scheduled a recording session with a band he dubbed Bix Beiderbecke and His Rhythm Jugglers. The others who performed at those sessions included Tommy Dorsey, trombone; Tommy Gargano, drums; Paul Mertz, piano; Don Murray, clarinet; and Howdy Quicksell, banjo. Mertz wrote out the lead sheets for an original composition by Bix. The other musicians named the song in honor of Bix's hometown. It became *Davenport Blues*.

Back again in Iowa City, Bix pledged Alpha Beta Chapter of Beta Theta Pi, same fraternity that his older brother Burnie had joined while a student at Iowa State University in Ames.

Bix's name is one of fourteen signed on a paddle that was presented to their pledge master, Carlyle Fairfax *Andy* Anderson.

Anderson's son presented that paddle to the Bix Beiderbecke Memorial Society. In a letter accompanying his gift, Robert G. Anderson wrote, "Both my mother and father were at the University of Iowa at this time, and both remember hearing Bix play. They said they never heard anything so beautiful in their lives as the sound that Bix made. My mother remembers him playing on the back of a flat-bed truck that toured around the campus.

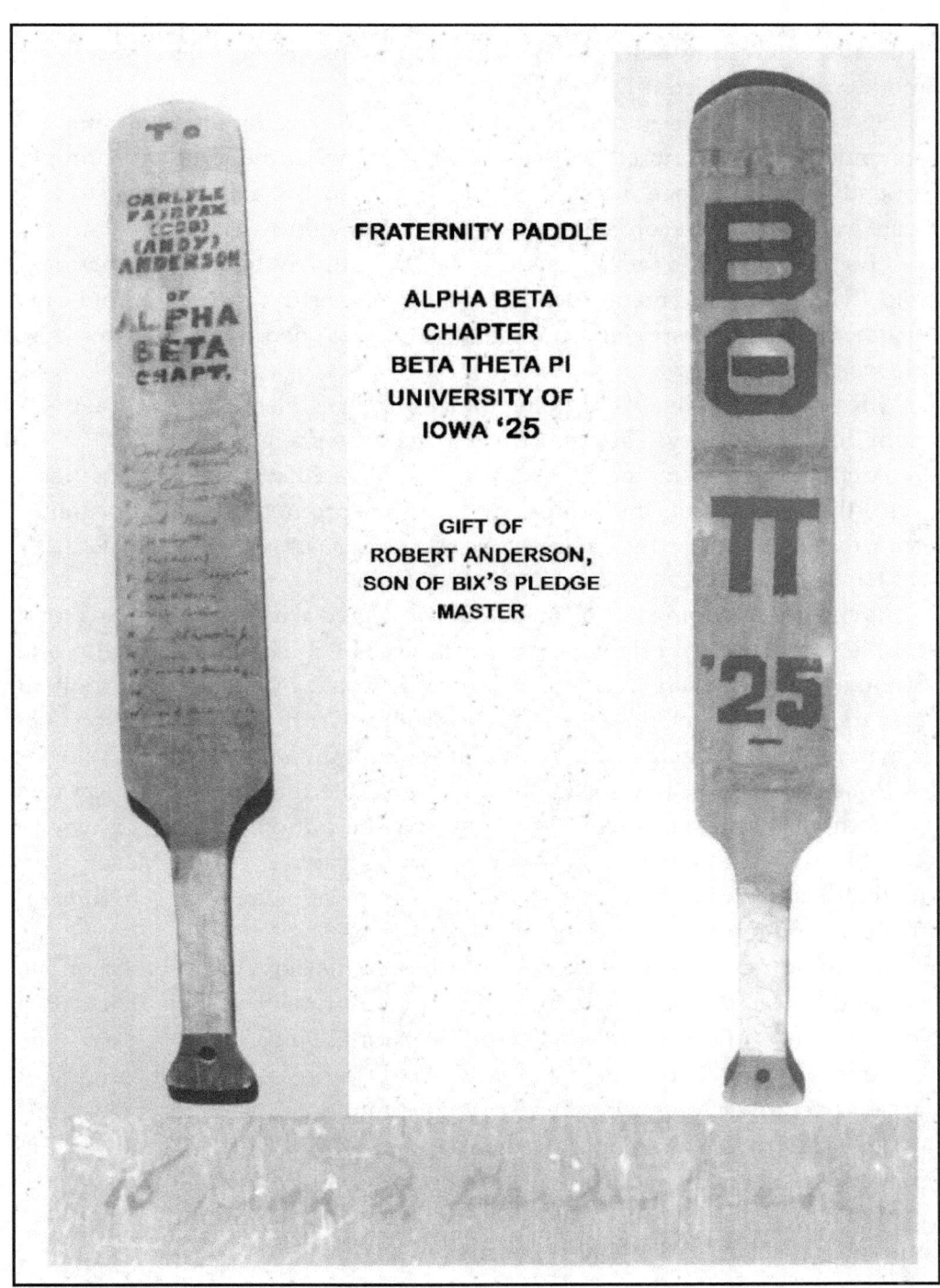

FRATERNITY PADDLE

**ALPHA BETA CHAPTER
BETA THETA PI
UNIVERSITY OF
IOWA '25**

**GIFT OF
ROBERT ANDERSON,
SON OF BIX'S PLEDGE
MASTER**

It is also interesting that she went to summer camp with Bix's sister. My mother was from Cedar Rapids."

Spotty attendance and refusing to take more freshman requirements, combined with a rumored participation in a brawl at the local café brought an end to Bix's college days. Huntzinger claimed Bix and another student were expelled. The records indicate only that he withdrew on Feb. 20th.

"Bix was already a familiar sight in campus student haunts," Huntzinger told Evans. "And he made friends quickly, a cheerful figure in an old blue sweater... He was especially popular with the women, you could see that. He was a killer that way.

"In those days, they were doing dances like the 'Flea Hop' and that was right down Bix's alley. They just loved the way he played.

After the Collegians performed for the Lion's Charity Ball at the men's gym, the *Daily Iowan*, the campus newspaper, promoted Bix's appearance with the band under the tagline: A SENSATION AT THE CHARITY BALL LAST NIGHT: BEIDERBECKE, TRUMPETER EXTRAORDINARY!

Even after dropping out of school, Bix appeared with the Collegians for a couple more weekend dances at the Burkley Hotel's Blue Goose ballroom. Huntzinger told Evans the dances were promoted by a couple of football players, one of them the team captain Tubby Griffin. Hobe Dawson, sax player for the Collegians also was on the football squad.

Robert Anderson wrote, "It is entirely possible that this *other fellow* was my father, as I do remember him saying that he put on dances as a way to pay his way through the university. He was captain of the Mason City football team, and although he didn't play at Iowa, he had some friends on the team and this would fit."

Bix could never have imagined that a future master's thesis based on his life and music would come from a graduate student at Beta Theta Pi's founding institution: Miami University in Oxford, Ohio.

James Robert Grover created a 19-part radio series that originally broadcasted over Miami U's WMUB radio station. Grover presented a full set of tapes to the Davenport Public Library during the 1971 Bix tribute celebration that launched the Bix Beiderbecke Memorial Jazz Festival.

Grover's *Life and Music of Leon Bix Beiderbecke,* aired to a national audience in 2003 for Bix's 100th birthday.

Iowa Student To Play In Orchestra for Prom

Bix Beiderbecke, who will play first trumpet with Jean Goldkette's orchestra at the 1925 Junior Prom here May 1, is a student at the University of Iowa, Iowa City, Ia., when not touring the country filling contract engagements with the musical organization. During an appearance at the University of Michigan J-Hop Feb. 27, he was acclaimed by many critics at the Wolverine school as the best cornet player in the United States.

Beiderbecke will be remembered on the campus here as the "sock" artist who played for several dances with the Wolverine orchestra last year. This band, with which the versatile cornet player appeared last year, is in Bloomington this week-end to play for two formal dances.

Bix lasted only 18 days at the University of Iowa but two months after dropping out, an Indiana headline told a different story—maybe with intent to make him more respectable in the eyes of the university administrators there.

The last graph's mention of *sock artist* is a reference to the jazz style Bix and Hoagy first picked up from the New Orleans Rhythm Kings at the Friars Inn, Chicago, in 1922. Sock-time delineated jazz's evolution from ragtime to swing with its heavy accent on the first beat, less so on the third; dancers of the 1920s favored its smoother rhythm.

Jan 26, 1925—Bix & His Rhythm Jugglers in the studio, L-R: Don Murray, clarinet; Howdy Quicksell, banjo; Tom Gargano, drums; Paul Mertz, piano; Bix, cornet; and Tommy Dorsey, trombone. Hoagy was with them during this session when they recorded Bix's *Davenport Blues*.

I Am Not a Swan

Bixophiles will recognize the title of this piece in connection to Bill 'Monk' Moenkhaus, Hoagy Carmichael's Indiana University classmate.

In his 1947 memoir, *Stardust Road*, Carmichael described Monk as a guy "who made straight–As in a bored sort of way." Monk's dad was a zoology professor at Indiana University, where Bix and the Wolverine's played several dances. Bix played there with Frank Trumbauer's Orchestra, also.

"I remember trying to put Bix together with Monk, so that he would see him and hear him and feel him the way I did," Carmichael wrote. "It was like the telling of a vivid dream and knowing that it wasn't making sense."

Hoagy introduced Bix to Monk, hoping they all might be friends. But Bix first had to answer six questions posed by Monk:

1. Spell Wheatena in four different directions
2. What horse when it rained
3. Define freight luner and amelia
4) Tell all you know about vetter
5) Tell all you know about the defeat of New Mexico
6) Write a short diary about skates. Leave out page three.

For you younglings, Wheatena was a breakfast cereal—Bix preferred shredded wheat. The so–called Wheatena Test was *hogwash*, as was Moenkhaus' nickname for Hoagland Carmichael, a.k.a. Hoagy—Hogwash. Monk, who had a knack for surrealist poetry and satire, posed his six questions simply to see how Bix's mind worked. Their friendship clinched on Bix's five–word response, *I am not a swan*.

So, how does a high school drop–out match wits with a college egghead? I'll be a monkey's uncle if it doesn't have something to do with the uncle of Bix's neighbor and the sister–in–law of Bix's Uncle Carl. Together they made up two of three Spectrist poets and one of literature's great hoaxes.

Spectra: A Book of Poetic Experiment, published in 1916, was a satirical send–up to the avant–garde poets. The poems were composed by Davenport attorney Arthur Davison Ficke (1883–1945) and his Harvard pal Witter Bynner. Moline socialite Marjorie Allen Seiffert (1885–1970) contributed additional Spectra poems.

It all started with a booze–filled weekend in the Tri–Cities when Ficke and Bynner wrote their original batch of poems. By way of introduction, Ficke composed a *Spectrist manifesto*, a convoluted treatise that, in part, claimed: *It is the aim of the Spectric group to push the possibilities of poetic expression into a new region, to attain a fresh brilliance of impression by a new method not so wholly different from the methods of Futurist Painting.* A sampling of lines from this so-called new school of poetry:

>Asparagus is feathery and tall,
>And the hose lies rotting by the garden-wall
>
>***
>
>If I were only dafter
>I might be making hymns
>To the liquor of your laughter
>And the lacquer of your limbs

Ficke and Bynner were flabbergasted when their spoof on modernism was received as serious poetry. Clueless magazine editors clamored for more. To perpetuate the hoax Ficke locked his friend Marjorie Seiffert in her bedroom, refusing to let her out until she had satisfied their quota for more poems. She came up with such gems as:

>You are a raisin, but I am a nut!
>What meat there is to you
>Can be seen at a glance—
>
>***
>
>Madame, you are ever retreating,
>But are never gone—
>Some day I shall pursue you
>Hoping to see you
>Vanish.
>
>***
>
>If castor oil removes a boil
>And Oscar rows a goat
>Don't use your feet on
>Shredded wheat
>Inhale it through a boat

Oops, that last one's a ringer. It actually was penned by Bill Moenkhaus. The professor's kid with his nimble mind and coyote howl didn't mock modernism. He embraced it. The Spectrists would have applauded when Monk proclaimed, *"This is for minds keyed to vistas beyond the horizons of so-called rational thought,"* and then recited:

>Blooters, thou knowest no Heaven,
>Blooters, thou knowest only us.

> Bugs, men, tarts and fowls—
> They are the Children of Heaven. The end.

Satire is fun when you're in on the joke. Monk was. If only his poetic high jinks had been around a couple years earlier, he too might have joined the Spectra league.

By the time Bix had learned to play *Tiger Rag*, the Spectra Hoax had been revealed and its perpetrators reviled. Bix learned Nick LaRocca's tune on a borrowed cornet from Arthur Ficke's nephew. At the time, Arthur was serving as an Army Ordnance officer in France, having volunteered when Americans joined the Allied Forces in WWI.

Ficke and his *Spectra* allies had used pseudonyms and refused all invitations for public readings thus keeping their identities a secret. Later, after the hoax had been revealed, Ficke told of a superior officer pulling him aside one day and asking what he, a legitimate and published poet, thought of the Spectra poems. When Ficke dismissed them as jokes, his superior patted his back and in a hushed voice took credit for having authored Ficke's poems. Ficke later described their conversation as "one of the most deliriously happy hours I have ever spent."

Before the Spectra Hoax, Ficke had published ten volumes of poetry. He still worked at the time in his father's Davenport law firm. He also had published two scholarly books on Japanese art, having gained an appreciation through world travels with his dad, Charles August Ficke.

The nucleus of collections both for the Quad Cities' Figge and Putnam museums came of the art and antiquities that Arthur and his dad brought home from their travels—everything from Japanese woodcuts to Chinese porcelain to Peruvian pottery and Mexican paintings, even a mummy from Cairo. When other buyers became enamored with impressionists, C.A. Ficke snapped up works by Europe's old masters, particularly German and Flemish paintings. Along with his paintings, Charles Ficke willed his extensive library to his hometown. He died the same year as Bix, 1931.

Arthur's ties to Bix's family go back to a loan made to Aggie's Aunt Mary when she had a millinery shop. At a time when other Davenport lenders charged ten percent interest plus commission, Arthur's terms were eight percent with no commission.

As for Marjorie Seiffert, parlor poetry and chamber music—what Bix's Uncle Carl called *chamber pot* music—was a typical evening's entertainment at the home she shared with her husband Otto Seiffert. The poets that Bix loved to read: Keats, Byron and Shelley were read aloud in Marjorie Allen's parlor.

Among Tri-Cities upper crust, the Ficke and Seiffert families were the alamode to our apple-dumpling Beiderbeckes. Otto Seiffert took over his dad's lumber business in 1919, essentially becoming Bismark Beiderbecke's boss. Otto Seiffert's sister, Adele, was the wife of Carl T. Beiderbecke.

Marjorie Allen Seiffert grew up in an elegant Moline estate called Allendale. Located on 11th Avenue between 16th and 17th streets, Allendale was donated to the Moline School District and now serves as its administrative building.

Otto Seiffert

Marjorie studied music composition at Smith College. When she performed her original songs for Arthur Ficke, he dismissed the music but said her lyrics made for some pretty good poems. So Marjorie submitted verses to magazines, eventually becoming a regular contributor to the likes of the *New Yorker*. The first of her three volumes of poetry came out around the time of her tenth wedding anniversary. While Bix was in St. Louis playing with Frank Trumbauer's band and dating Ruth Shaffner, Marjorie was riding a wave of notoriety as the Tri-Cities grand dame of poetry.

Marjorie Allen Seiffert

> 26 Oct 1925, *Democrat–Leader*:
> Mrs. Otto Seiffert (Marjorie Allen Seiffert) of Moline, the well known Mid–West poet, gave "An Afternoon of Poetry" as an informal talk before the Art and Literature department of the Davenport Woman's club for its first meeting of the fall at the Chamber of Commerce…Mrs. Seiffert spoke more especially on the manner in which the poet approaches his work, the subject matter, and something of the technical side of poetry and its fashioning, and she pointed out that while poetry is most appealing in its possession of the richly inspirational, it should fall easily into certain lines and conform to certain principles, unobtrusive, yet most essential in the creation of really good literature. Mrs. Seiffert read a number of her own poems to the great enjoyment of the listeners.

Marjorie and Otto were patrons of the Tri–City Symphony Orchestra; Otto served as symphony board president. As for her own musical compositions, "They lie packed away, not quite completely finished," Marjorie remarked in later years, adding "I feel toward them as I should toward a dead child."

A psychiatrist once told Marjorie that "women do *no* service to their families and communities by pursuing self–centered creative outlets such as music and poetry." Marjorie ignored him.

A couple weeks each year she left the hubby and the kids at home to pal around Manhattan in the company of her poet friends. They'd do dinner, the theater, and top off the night at a speakeasy. Marjorie picked up the tab. She opened her pocketbook to writer friends short on rent money or in need of a patron for some start–up literary magazine.

Physician–poet William Carlos Williams recalled Marjorie taking him to Eugene O'Neill's *Desire Under the Elms* and leaving him there just before the second act because she had plans to meet up that same night with someone else.

O'Neill's play was staged by the Provincetown Players, an amateur theater group founded by Davenport couple George Cram Cook and Susan Glaspell. She won the Pulitzer Prize the year Bix died.

Others in the Provincetown Players included Davenport's Floyd Dell, poet Edna St. Vincent Millay and journalist John Reed, whose story was told onscreen in Warren Beatty's Oscar–winning *Reds*.

Arthur Ficke abandoned law after returning from France and taking up with Millay. Back when Arthur practiced at his dad's law firm, his clients included Bix's grandfather. C.A. Ficke served on the board of directors of the Iowa National Bank when Bix's granddad was president. Arthur clerked

Arthur Ficke wrote as Anne Knish and Witter Bynner as Emanuel Morgan for *Spectra*, a 1916 spoof on modernism.

Arthur Davison Ficke, seated, with Edna St. Vincent Millay and her husband Eugen in New York 1926.

on several of the bank's real estate dealings. Arthur's cousin, Robert Ficke, was a senior partner in the family law firm. Robert and his wife Madeline Spelletich Ficke lived with their son Robert Jr. at 2020 Grand Avenue.

Bobby Ficke attended Tyler School where his mom was active in the school district's first PTA. Bob Ficke did not attend Davenport High, graduating instead from an Eastern preparatory academy and from there entered Princeton. He got his Master's in chemical engineering. During the 1930s, Bob spent summer breaks traveling through Europe and playing in a jazz band before going to work for DuPont Co. What is it with chemists and jazz? Perhaps Albert Haim, webmaster of the most extensive online site for all–things Bix might have some insight on that.

Bob Ficke's maternal grandfather, Michael Spelletich, was a Hungarian exile who lost titles and land after peasants waged a war for independence from Austria in 1848. Iowa's Kossuth County on the Minnesota border is named for exiled Hungarian president Lajos Kossuth. Ficke's grandfather was among those exiled immigrants to Iowa where he rebuilt the family fortune with farmland, organizing the Scott County Farmers Association.

Although preferring jazz, Bob Ficke inherited his grandfather's mandolin and learned to play traditional Bohemian folksongs from his Uncle Kalman Spelletich. Uncle Kalman, who also headed the symphony board several seasons, became president in 1928 of Gordon–Van Tine, a Davenport building supplies company formerly at Federal and River Drive.

Gordon–Van Tine was a major dealer in kits for prefab houses and farm buildings. The company supplied materials for Sears & Roebuck's house kits, and sold their own GVT architectural designs under the Montgomery Wards label. They had government contracts for prefab bungalows in factory towns where large influxes of workers created housing shortages during WWI. Thousands of GVT homes were built in the Quad Cities on both sides of the Mississippi. Many still stand.

The Gordon–Van Tine Co. was liquidated in 1947, same year Bob Ficke designed his own house on Long Beach Island—a summer resort made famous by the movie *Jaws*. The movie and book were based on a series of shark attacks off the Jersey Shore in 1916. That was *no* hoax.

As for the *Spectra Hoax*, its perpetrators lost ground career–wise but gained immortality as artistic rebels. *"Art is the revolt of the heart against the tyranny of the brain,"* Arthur Ficke later claimed.

Monk Moenkhaus would have agreed. But while he had taken well to formal musical training, it was Bix who seemed in a *revolt of the heart* with formality of any sort. When the two met, Monk was just joining the revolution while Bix had been in its vanguard.

Hoagy wrote in his 1965 memoir, *Sometimes I Wonder* that Bix looked bad, detached, and indifferent to life...but he had heard Isham Jones' recording of *Stardust* and said, *'Hey, that new tune of yours is pretty good.' I smiled at Bix. It was the second time he had given me a compliment.*

That was March 1931. Isham's *Stardust* went to #1 on the record charts. Monk had died earlier that year. Bix was gone before Bing Crosby recorded his version of *Stardust*, which hit #5. Next month, Frank Trumbauer released *Georgia On My Mind*. It made it to the top ten. A year earlier, Bix had played with Hoagy on his original recording of *Georgia*. Turned out to be Bix's last recording, far as anyone knows.

Three lines of a poem Arthur Ficke wrote for Edna Millay may suffice as a swan song to Hoagy's pals:

> *...robs the heavens of their glory*
> *And moves with stately grandeur*
> *Into the vast inane...*

Sunday Morning, January 30, 1916

Blues Is Jazz and Jazz Is Blues

She leaned across the table while the waiter slunk away and in a pleading voice said something to the Worm.

The Worm was her husband. You may have guessed this before. Anyway what she said was this.

"Orlus," she murmured, looking into his tired eyes, "if you don't kick trot with me shortly, I shall bring suit for divorce. Our life cannot go on this way."

"Don't I give you clothes—all you want?" the Worm returned. "Huh? Don't I now? Don't I love—you—"

"Stop!" she cried, deathly white. "You don't understand me. Clothes—bah—! Coverings for the soul. Love—a mockery! You do not realize that I have a soul—that I have two feet—that I want fox trotting?"

"You know I can't dance. Why last wee—"

"Enough!" she cried imperiously, drawing a veil over her snow white shoulders which always appear in scenes like this. "You have failed me in the fox trot—I cannot go on—"

She stopped. The music had started. Suddenly from above the thread of the melody itself came a harmonious, yet discordant wailing, an eerie mezzo that moaned and groaned and sighed and electrified, a haunting counter strain that oozed from the saxophone.

The Worm stopped. His eyes shone with a wonderful light—the light that lies in the eyes of a man who has had two around the corner. His mouth moved convulsively. The years fell away from his shoulders leaving only his frock coat.

The Worm had turned—turned to fox trotting. And the "blues" had done it. The "jazz" had put pep into the legs that had scrambled too long for the 5:15.

What mattered to him now the sly smiles of contempt that his friends had uncorked when he essayed the foxy trot a month before? what mattered it whose shins he kicked?

That is what "blue" music is doing for everybody; taking away what its name implies, the blues. In a few months it has become the predominant motif in cabaret offerings its wailing syncopation is heard in every gin mill where dancing holds sway.

Its effect is galvanic. Cripples take up their beds and one-step; taxi drivers willingly suffer sore feet because of it; spring halt becomes St. Vitus's dance in its grip.

Maybe you, poor soul, in your metropolitan ignorance, do not gather just what the "blues" are. Worry not; neither does the average person that plays them,

and it was only after weeks of toiling that the true definition was obtained.

The first sortie after the definition was made in a song publisher's arena, where beautiful actresses try their voices and the manager's nerves.

"Halt," cried the seeker after the definition, fixing a dark-haired piano player with a relentless eye, "What are the blues?"

The young man recoiled and shuddered, "I don't know," he said, "All I can do is play 'em. A kind of a wail you might call it. Still I couldn't tell you positively. But, say, I can take any piece in the world and put the blues into it. But as for a definition—don't ask me."

At the next place a young woman was keeping "Der Wacht Am Rhein" and "Tipperary Mary" apart when the interrogator entered.

"What are the blues?" he asked gently.

"Jazz!" the young woman's voice rose high to drown the piano.

A tall young man, with nimble fingers rose from the piano and came over. "That's me," he said, and then he unraveled the mystery of the "blues."

"A blue note is a sour note," he explained. "It's a discord—a harmonic discord. The blues are never written into the music, but are interpolated by the piano player or other players. They aren't new, They are just reborn into popularity. They started in the South half a century ago and are the interpolations of darkies originally. The trade name for them is 'jazz.'

"There's a craze for them now. People find them excellent for dancing. Piano players are taking lessons to learn how to play them."

Thereupon Jazz Marion sat down and showed the bluest streak of blues ever heard beneath the blue. Or, if you like this better, Blue Marion sat down and jazzed the jazziest streak of jazz ever.

Saxophone players since the advent of the "jazz blues," have taken to wearing "jazz collars," neat decollete things that give the throat and windpipe full play, so that the notes that issue from the tubas may not suffer for want of blues—those wonderful blues.

Try it some time—for that tired feeling—the blues.

—Chicago Tribune.

Callouts (annotations pointing into the article):

- Suddenly from above the thread of the melody itself came a harmonious yet, discordant wailing, an eerie mezzo that moaned and groaned and electrified, a haunting counter strain that oozed from the saxophone.

- "What are the blues?"
  "...I don't know," he said, "All I can do is play 'em..."
  "...I can take any piece in the world and put the blues into it. But as for a definition—don't ask me."

- "The blues...aren't new. They are just reborn into popularity.... They started in the South half a century ago...The trade name for them is *jazz*."

- The Worm had turned—turned to fox trotting. And the *blues* had done it. The *jazz* had put pep into the legs...

❖ ❖ ❖ ❖

Jass is music crying out against being murdered.
—1907 news filler, earliest mention in tri-cities press

"THE DAVENPORT BLUES" IS LATE POPULAR PIECE

Composed by "Bix" Beiderbecke of This City; Recently Recorded.

Very prominently displayed on one of the most recent releases of the Gennett Record Co., is "The Davenport Blues", a recent blues number composed by Leon "Bix" Beiderbecke of Davenport, and recorded by his own orchestra, "Bix And His Rhythm Jugglers."

"Bix", a pianist and trumpet artist who has a musical history which would occupy pages and pages to do justice to, is a Davenport product and in deciding on a name for his latest hit, chose that of his old home town. Besides directing his own orchestra he is also in the ensemble of "Jean Goldkette's Victor Recording Orchestra" of Detroit.

Any of the Gennett records made by "Bix" and his orchestra or any of the Goldkette Victor records can be heard at the Harned & Von Maur victrola department, which is managed by C. B. Beiderbecke, who proudly boasts that he is "Bix's" older brother.

LOCAL BOY IS RECORDING FOR VICTOR CO.

Tomorrow a new Victor Record which many local people will be more interested in than usual will be placed on sale at Harned & Von Maur's Victrola Parlors.

It is a record of the dance piece —"Honest and Truly" and was recorded by the famous Gene Goldkette Orchestra of Detroit, of which L. B. ("Bix") Biederbecke is a member.

Mr. Biederbecke has been engaged as cornetist by Gene Goldkette. This is a great compliment to the ability of the local boy for only the most expert are acceptable to the Goldkette Organization. Local people are invited to visit Harned & Von Maur Victrola Parlors and hear this new record tomorrow.

NEWS OF THE NEW!

A Native Son Did It!

Yes! Bix Beiderbecke, that nationally known cornet player, and a home town product, has composed a wailing, syncopating blue-y fox trot, and named it Davenport Blues. It's out on OK record, and we predict it'll be a riot. Miff Mole's Molers play it. 75c.
—Balcony

After becoming record department manager at Harned Von Maur, Burnie Beiderbecke promoted his brother's recording career, beginning with Goldkette's 1924 *Honest and Truly*. Bix got fired his first time round with Goldkette but was back in the studio in early 1925 to record his original tune, *Davenport Blues*, with his Rhythm Jugglers. Burnie ran several ads for it and the *Democrat Leader* did a feature story March 5, 1925

Jazzmania Inspires Goldkette Musician To Write Harmonies

Bix Beiderbecke, Trumpet Player Composed "Davenport Blues."

Where is the person, who at some time in his life has not been ambitious to be a composer? Who has not tried to "pick out" a melody on some instrument? To the normal individual, what supernatural genius must be contained in one who is able to "think a tune" easily? Imagine the relative difference between the labor involved in the placing of the basic notes, and that of the final arrangements.

Last February, in a little studio in Indianapolis, Bix Beiderbecke, trumpet player with Jean Goldkette's orchestra, concocted one of the cleverest hits of the year. Written in deference to that fickle goddess, Jazzmania, the piece carries with it the spirit of the age. If syncopation expresses American life, the "Davenport Blues" is a current history. All the arrangements for his four colleagues were turned out the same afternoon. The record was made and is obtainable at music dealers.

The Junior Prom-goers will witness another high point in the bringing of musical organizations to the Indiana campus when they hear Jean Goldkette's Victor Recording orchestra. Following the latest development in modern music, this band uses the full-note harmony, emphasized so much by Whiteman, Biese, and other great orchestra leaders. Goldkette's personnel of 13 men will be used in the principal numbers, but to the half dozen composing Bix's group, will be left the task of presenting jazz to the Hoosiers.

Feb 18, 1924: WOLVERINES at Gennett Studio; they returned in May to record *Riverboat Shuffle* by Indiana U's Hoagy Carmichael.

May 1, 1925: After recording *Davenport Blues*, Bix played Indiana U's senior prom with the Jean Goldkette orchestra

April 16, 1926: Bix identified as assistant director in Frank Trumbauer's orchestra when they played Indiana U's junior prom; makes a specialty of Charleston time, promo noted.

THE INDIANA ALUMNUS

WILL PLAY AT JUNIOR PROM

FRANK TRUMBAUER'S ORCHESTRA.

Frank Trumbauer's eleven-piece orchestra, of St. Louis, will play for the 1926 Junior Prom in the Men's Gymnasium on the night of April 16. The orchestra makes a specialty of Charleston time as well as other types of music with which Hoosiers are familiar. The Charleston will be permitted in the gymnasium during the Prom, it is announced.

BIX & HIS RHYTHM JUGGLERS
L-R: Howdy Quicksell, banjo; Tom Gargano, drums; Paul Mertz, piano; Don Murray, clarinet; Bix, cornet; Tommy Dorsey, trombone

Back again with Goldkette in 1926

A great jazz musician is no different from a great artist in any of the arts. If he hadn't been a player he would have written a poem or acted in a play or painted a picture. How many times we heard musicians say: 'I couldn't make a living so I got out of the business? A real artist couldn't have said that. He has to play as he has to breathe.

~Bud Freeman

Dancing Coliseum
SAT., SUN., THURS.
TONIGHT
BIG CHARLESTON CONTEST
$30.00—In Cash Prizes—$30.00
10 Dollars for Winners, Each—5 Dollars for the Second Team, Each
COMING SUNDAY, DEC 13—DRESSER AND TILLSBURY

COMING—THE
—RAVENS—Something New
10——PEOPLE——10

DANCE CRAZE AT COLISEUM HAS MUCH INTEREST

Charleston Contest Tonight; Chicago Couple Here Dec. 13.

Owing to the success of the Charleston contest at the Coliseum last Sunday, the Coliseum Company will stage another contest tonight with a cash prize of $30 as the sidelight.

Mrs. Haynes local Charleston dancer, assisted by her two dancing partners, will act as judges. Their selections pleased the crowd which witnessed the contest between Galesburg and Davenport.

Arrangements have also been made by the management to have Leroy Dresser and Constance Pillstrum appear at the Coliseum on Dec. 13. This Chicago team has made a great hit with its performance of the intricate dance.

The Charleston Is Destined to be Popular and Lasting, Says Local Dance Instructor

Nov 1925

STEP up lively, young and old, and learn to dance the Charleston if you want to be in vogue. This eccentric terpsichorean maneuver has come to stay, at least for several reasons, declares Olive Cameron Haynes, well known local dancing instructor. Mrs. Haynes says:

"The Charleston has swept the country like wild fire, contrary to the predictions of most dancing teachers, altho they must now admit that it is the dance of the season. At its start most instructors prophesied that it would die a very sudden death, if indeed, it ever gained the prominence of a ballroom dance. But they erred in their prediction, as all realize now.

"In 1923 Ned Wayburn, the New York dancing master, introduced the Charleston on the stage of the New Amsterdam theatre in New York City in "Shuffle Along," but at that time it did not catch the popular fancy. It was left to Bee Jackson, who claims to have regenerated it after watching the darkies of Charleston North Carolina, to make it popular. Whether she originated it or not, and she has many disputants who make the same claim, she has certainly popularized it, until now a dancer who is not familiar with its peculiar, restless rythmic figures is considered behind the times.

"There are many variations of the Charleston, but they are all centered around one basic step, and a dance is not a Charleston without it. There must also be a continuous vibration up and down —up and down, which has caused some comment, but the dance is much to be preferred to a great deal of the dancing indulged in during the past few years.

"In order to dance the Charleston properly, the leader must hold his partner at least a foot away from him, which is a decided improvement over the close position, which has up to the present been used by many dancers. "Necking" is impossible while dancing the Charleston.

"If nothing but the Charleston were danced on a ballroom floor, the people who now object to dancing as a pastime would sanction it."

Mayor and Chief O. K. Charleston if Kicks Are Low

Waterloo Ia., Nov.26.— If you kick higher than six inches off the floor when you Charleston, you will have another kick coming.

Police Chief E. A. Leighton and Mayor A. E. Gnagy viewed the Charleston proper last evening, stripped of the sordid motions seen at various times at Waterloo dances, and decided it to be a graceful dance.

The complete ban on the Charleston is off, they said, but the addition of other shakings, shiverings and shufflings to the original dance will bring about one's removal from the floor and a probable appearance in municipal court.

Columnist Elson Irwin wrote that man has *beat his feet* on the banks of the Nile and in the soft ooze of the Mississippi mud. Nobody thought to call any specific era of time the *dance craze* until just before WWI. This was rag–time, jazz–time and everybody was doing it.

Doing What? Turkey trot. Cake walk. Castle walk. Charleston—the only one that stayed long enough for the populace to learn it and that wasn't until around 1925. Ten years earlier Mr. and Mrs. Vernon Castle attempted to take the crudeness out of early jazz steps and introduced the first refinements into ballroom dancing. In 1925 Arthur Murray, more of a rewrite man than originator, imported the Lambeth Walk from the British Isles, originally an old English folk step performed in the Limehouse district of London. Ah, the Limehouse district! Remember *Limehouse Blues*? The Brits had it even then.

FRANK TRUMBAUER'S BAND—KINGS OF CHARLESTON MUSIC

Frank Trumbauer's orchestra, popularly known as "The Voice of St. Louis," has established the reputation as being one of the "hottest" bands in the country. One of his main henchmen is the assistant director, Bix Beiderbecke, who made his debut on the Indiana campus several years ago with the Wolverines and returned last year to play the Prom with Gene Goldkette. Critics have pronounced him as being the most efficient exponent of "dirty" trumpet playing in jazz circles. Trumbauer's orchestra is made up of artists from many headliner bands. Frank himself performs on the saxophone.

Above: Bix with Tram's outfit in 1927.

Artist Miguel Covarrubias' 1926 Whiteman caricature with a few notes from original Charleston tune.

All That Jazz

When Bix rejoined Goldkette, Newell 'Spiegle' Willcox occupied the seat vacated by trombonist Tommy Dorsey. Willcox previously had replaced Dorsey in the California Ramblers; they did a lot of recording sessions but never traveled.

Like Bix, Willcox's dad was in the coal fuel business. Unlike Bix, Spiegle opted for the family business and a family instead of a musician's life on the road.

Born the same year as Bix, Spiegle grew up playing alongside his dad in their hometown band in upstate New York. Papa Willcox taught him the valve trombone but Spiegle switched to slide at Manlius Military Academy. After two years at the academy he joined a Syracuse band and passed through other upstate combos before joining the Ithaca–based Bob Causer's Big Four.

After Paul Whiteman became bandleader, he expanded the Big Four's roster and renamed the group Paul Whiteman Collegians, which would become the world–famous Whiteman Orchestra.

Before emigrating from France to the U.S. in 1911, Detroit–based Jean Goldkette had trained as a concert pianist in Greece and Russia. He rivaled Whiteman's popularity and had many of the same top jazzmen under his baton.

Bix and Willcox toured New England in the fall of 1926 under the Goldkette banner and cut several records together, including reedman Don Murray's arrangement of Gershwin's *Sunny Disposish*.

Willcox claimed their recordings hardly did justice to the Goldkette band's live performances. "They're just a shadow, just a hint," he said, adding "Bix? Well, you can't begin to imagine listening to those records what his tone really sounded like. You had to be there."

Bix's posthumous fame garnered Spiegle new generations of fans when he began accepting invites to jazz festivals. He especially enjoyed annual trips to Bix's hometown, making his last Davenport appearance the summer before his death at age 96.

NEWELL LYNN *SPIEGLE* WILLCOX
1903-1999

Spiegle Willcox, seated, playing trombone during final appearance in Davenport at 1998 Bix festival

Close-ups of Spiegle, left, and Bix, right, from 1926 Goldkette Tour

Jean Goldkette Fall Tour 1926
Still images from amateur film shot by tour manager Charlie Horvath, seen below on lower left against the wall with Bix and Goldkette bandmates serenading boa constrictor held by a Bronx zookeeper. Above images show Bix playing his horn & carrying his cornet case—no paper bag in sight! Bandmates, clockwise round Bix: Howdy Quicksell, banjo; Ray Ludwig, trumpet; Irving Risken (piano); Don Murray, clarinet; Steve Brown, bass; Spiegle, trombone; Tram, sax; Fred Farrar, trumpet

DER——NOVEMBER 23, 1927

Davenport Boy Will Tour World With Paul Whiteman's Orchestra

L. "Bix" Beiderbecke, son of Mrs. B. H. Beiderbecke, 1934 Grand avenue, composer of many popular numbers and regarded as the finest cornet player of popular selections in the country, will tour the world with Paul Whiteman during the late winter, spring and summer.

Whiteman's orchestra is now playing at the Tivoli theater in Chicago after completing engagements at the Chicago and Uptown theaters. Next week the organization moves on to Pittsburgh and then to New York for six weeks at the Paramount theatre.

Off for Europe.

Then the orchestra will sail for Europe, where concerts will be presented in London, Paris, Berlin and other large cities. The itinerary will continue thru southwestern Europe and Asia, the plans calling for a circling of the globe before the return to American shores.

It is expected that at least eight months will be spent in the globe tour.

Tho only 24 years old, "Bix" Beiderbecke, as he was always known to his local associates and as he is known today in musical circles, is an artist with the cornet. He was for a long time associated with Gene Goldkett's celebrated orchestra.

Known as Composer.

He is also known as a composer and recording artist. The Okeh records company has just issued his latest composition, "In a Mist," played by Mr. Beiderbecke himself at the piano. One of his compositions which attained considerable popularity was "Davenport Blues."

Paul Whiteman and Players Please Big Auditorium Crowd

While Paul Whiteman and his greater concert orchestra proved just as delightful as ever, in their concert at the auditorium Tuesday night it was the concensus of opinion that the maestro of jazz has fallen off a little, in weight, since his last Atlanta appearance.

Of course that hasn't got anything to do with his baton wielding or the playing of his orchestra, but when such an internationally known figure as Paul comes to town everyone is more or less interested in the "figure" part of the personality.

That Paul's personality has a whole lot to do with his occupation of the top pinnacle in that American musical contribution, jazz, is incontrovertible. Not only the infectious grin, the boyish camaraderie that he diffuses over the footlights, but the spirit that he instills into every one of his players, the art that he packs into every moment of every number produced, are the things that have made him so great.

Orchestra Changes Little.

There is little change in his orchestra with the passing years. One or two old faces are missing, and there are a few new ones here and there, but there has been no loss in the charm of performance by the changes made inevitable by time.

The program was a typical Whiteman offering. A few new and daring steps forward along the path which American composers are blazing in this new field of musical composition; a few novelties that no one except Whiteman would have the originality to dream or the courage to realize, and a lot of the snappy, peppy, jazzy tunes that are historically associated with his name.

Perhaps the most important item on the list was the new Gershwin composition, "Concerto in F," for pianoforte and orchestra. This is an ambitious thing, going beyond even the famous "Rhapsody in Blue" by the same composer. Like the Rhapsody, it probably will grow on us as we have further chances of hearing it. Last night it was intensely interesting and magnificently done, but its complications are the type which we like to study by repeated hearings before finally closing it as a real favorite or not.

Piano Work Superhuman.

Roy Bargy, the piano soloist, displayed an almost superhuman technique of the keyboard.

The accolade for most applause of the evening must go to the saxophone solo by Chester Hazlett, "Valse Inspiration." It is one of the minor tragedies that Mr. Hazlett hasn't an available encore.

Finishing off the first half of the program was "Melancholy Baby," which, personally, proved as delightful a thing as any of the evening.

"Metropolis," by Ferde Grofe, was another modern novelty that opened the second half. This was a syncopated, blaring, blasting tone picture of the modern great city with its strange, discordant, yet beautiful soul.

Other remembered highlights were "Tiger Rag," "Chiquita," "Liebestraum" (in fox trot tempo) and "American Tune."

Vocalists Shine Unnamed.

Vocalists numbered three and unfortunately the program didn't name them, so proper acknowledgment for their big contribution cannot be made.

Wilbur Hall repeated his success of former days with his comedy playing on a foot pump, a violin and trombone and was assisted wonderfully by another—name again not given.

Then, never forget the little fat man with the gilt derby, singing and dancing that perpetual "Weakness" song.

The concert was the first of the current season, presented by the Southern Musical bureau. An interesting announcement was made with the programs, that the American Opera company, the organization of young American singers that set New York and Chicago wild with their modernized presentations of grand opera in English, is coming for four performances at the Erlanger theater, November 5, 6 and 7.

—RALPH T. JONES.

Democrat-Leader announced Bix had joined Whiteman in 1927; he grew a moustache on advice from a couple of Whiteman's boys that it would improve his embouchure. Above: The *Atlanta Constitution*, 10-24-1928; Bix's sister Mary Louise, living in Atlanta at the time, hosted a party after the show for Paul and a handful of Bix's bandmates. She got a thrill when the guys sang, *I Can't Give You Anything but Love.*

January 1928 promotions from the *Democrat-Leader*, left, and *Daily Times*, right, for a nationwide broadcast on Jan 4th that included Bix performing a solo on the Bill Challis' arrangement of *Changes*.

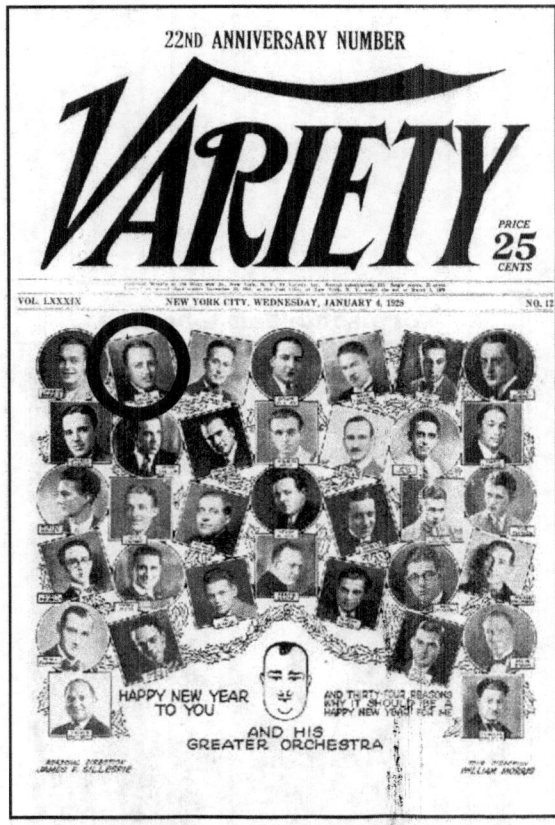

For Bix, 1928 started with a featured solo under the baton of Paul Whiteman during a coast-to-coast broadcast that his family listened to on WOC radio. Besides Whiteman's band, the January 4th program included Will Rogers from Hollywood and Al Jolson from New Orleans.

Closest Whiteman's 1928 tour got to Bix's hometown was a stop in Clinton, Iowa.

Big entertainment news that year was the dance marathon fad sweeping the nation. The *Democrat–Leader* declared: "If you've ever told a girl that you could dance on with her forever, she may call your bluff now that this marathon dancing craze is with us."

JAN 16: LOCAL COUPLE WINS MARATHON DANCE AT COLISEUM

Dancing continuously for 27 ½ hours from 10 o'clock Saturday night to 1:40 Monday morning, Miss Ora Jurgens, 1608 Elm street, and Henry Bert Willis, 319 Sturdevant street, won the marathon dance contest and the $100 cash prize offered by the Coliseum. At 1:39 a.m. John Lange and Dorothy Langwith were forced out of the contest when the male part of the team weakened...leaving a clear field and the $100 to Miss Jurgens and Mr. Willis.

The lucky couple did not train for the marathon and both looked capable of going on for hours longer. Miss Jurgens was out late Friday night and worked up to 8 o'clock Saturday night. Following the contest, she was given an alcohol rub and today she is perfectly well. She is a telephone girl. Mr. Willis, who works in Silvis and is a well-known musician, was none the worse for wear.

NOW THAT THE MARATHON DANCE IS OVER—

JAN 22: All those who paid nickels to see the couples trying to out-dure the endurance contest last Sunday at the Coliseum might have gotten their money's worth. The dancers looked as if they were in the contest on a dare. Youth will be served, no matter in what manner.

FEB 12: There was considerable discussion in regards to the marathon dance

DANCING COLISEUM

Starting Tomorrow Nite

Big Marathon

Endurance Dance Contest

How Long Will They Dance?

Dancing for All!

Gents 50c Ladies 25c

Jan 13, 1928 AD

Marathon winners Feb 7, 1928

Terpischorean Champs

MR AND MRS E. P WILLIAMS

Moline Couple Shatters World's Marathon Record by Dancing Over 52 Hours

By dancing continuously from 10 o'clock Saturday night to 2:53 this morning, Mr. and Mrs E P Williams, 2907 Sixteenth street Moline, shattered the world's marathon dance record in the Iowa-Illinois contest at the Coliseum. They had danced for 52 hours and 53 minutes. They won a cash prize of $100.

contest... Many insisted that such a thing should be barred by city ordinance because of the possibility—even probability—of injuring the health of the participants. Others held the view that it was a yokel demonstration. Still others claimed it was asinine. Regardless of what it was, the fact remains that the Marathon event attracted more attention than any contest ever held here. The telephone girls will vouch for that.

SEP 27: YOUNG FATHER AND MOTHER SEE HOPES OF HOME VANISH AS THEY CEASE MARATHONING

Hopes of winning a little home for their family went glimmering for Mr. and Mrs. Marion Cowman of Des Moines when the tired wife dropped out of the marathon dance at the Coliseum at 6:30 o'clock Wednesday evening.

Their two youngsters, Raymond, 5, and Mildred, 3, were coming to Davenport Saturday to see Daddy and Mother dance but now the party's over for them. Three hundred and twenty-eight hours for nothing and the $1,000 that they had hoped to stake them to a home will be the coveted reward to another couple, days and perhaps week hence. "But it might have been worse," is Mrs. Cowman's cheerful attitude this morning. "We'll try again and will start our training right away. We're booked for the St. Louis marathon beginning December 4."

"It was a tough break," is her young husband's rejoinder. "But I'm glad she dropped out when she did. I wouldn't have anything happen to her for a million dollars."

Mrs. Cowman had been dragging thru the dance throughout the day, half supported by her husband, and at times, with the nurse accompanying her. Excitement buoyed her up and she was not the one to suggest her quitting. The nurse, however, ordered her off the floor as she was running a temperature.

Other marathoners rallied to the rescue at the evening performance. It was a way they have at the marathon performances in the larger cities. Merle McWilliams of Davenport gave a solo dance and I.A. Neeley of Harvey, Ill, sang "Coquette." Then the money came jingling into the ring. The contribution for the down and out couple amounted to $17.59.

Mr. Cowman is 26 years old and his wife, 24. Until this summer he had been employed as a machine operator. When he was laid off, he tried unsuccessfully to get other employment then he and his wife set out in search of a foothold. They went to Peoria first but were too late to enter the marathon there. Hearing of the marathon in Davenport, they set out on foot for this city, arriving two days before the dance started. We'd like to stay to see the finish," Mr. Cowman said today, "but we're anxious to get back home to see the children....Five couples are still shuffling.

OCT 2: NEW WORLD'S MARATHON DANCE RECORD IS MADE AT DAVENPORT COLISEUM

At 4 o'clock this afternoon the Marathon dancers at the Coliseum had completed 468 hours of shuffling. In so doing, the five remaining couples have shattered all previous world records for marathoning under the rules which govern the local contest. The previous record was 368 ½ hours....The contest may last throughout the week or it may end any day...Betting on the prospective winners is now a favorite pastime.

OCT 16: MRS. NEELEY, HEAVYWEIGHT WOMAN OF MARATHON,
DROPS OUT AFTER 800 HRS DANCING

But for her feet giving out, Mrs. Jess Neeley, 180 pound contestant in the marathon dance which has been in progress at the Coliseum for the past 34 days, might still be shuffling. But at noon today those feet, supporting the 180 pounds of avoirdupois, refused to longer function, and after completing 800 hours of dancing, Mrs. Neeley gave up. Her husband–partner, much smaller in size, retired with her.

The 802 hour period of dancing was reached at 2 o'clock this afternoon with three couples remaining in the ring. They are: Mr. and Mrs. Earl Waldron of Chicago; Lester Scheef and Elizabeth Meyers, Davenport; James 'Benny' Solomon, Rock Island, and Evelyn Fries, Peoria.

Elizabeth Meyers was reported to be in bad shape today. She had a tooth extracted this morning, the second since the contest started, and is suffering intensely from neuralgia...she is liable to pass out at any moment.

Her partner, Lester Scheef, who lost a hand in an accident several years ago, appears in good shape.

All three couples now dancing will come in for a share of the money. First prize is $1,000; second prize $350 and third prize $150. And it won't be long now.

OCT 17: TWO MARATHON COUPLES NOW WEAKENING

Mrs. Elizabeth Meyers of Davenport passed a bad night after having her third tooth pulled Tuesday and was keeping on the floor thru sheer force of will power today. Earl Waldron of Chicago shows signs of nervous strain and is expected to be out of the running at any moment...

The remaining dancers are still going strong after 826 hours.

Miss Evelyn Fries of Peoria and Benny Solomon of Rock Island compose the couple now with the best chance of winning the marathon prize.

Each has lost a partner during the long shuffle and joined forces. Mr. Waldron's partner is his wife and Mrs. Meyers' partner is Lester Scheef of Davenport.

DER —— OCTOBER 31, 1928

Marathon Ends at 8 A.M. as Dancers Establish New World Record, Passing 1156th Hour

Everybody's going to get some sleep!

The marathon dance at the Coliseum closed at 8 o'clock this morning after going 1156 hours for a new world's record, exceeding the record made at Hammond, Ind., under more lenient rules by two hours.

Lester Scheef and Mrs. Elizabeth Meyers, both of Davenport, have $1,000 to split between them as a result of winning first place, when Benny Solomon, Rock Island, entrant and partner of Mrs. Earl Waldron of Chicago, failed to return to the ring as the rest period ended.

Mr. Solomon and Mrs. Waldron will get second prize money of $250.

Third prize of $150 was captured several days ago by Mr. Waldron and Miss Evelyn Fries, Peoria, when they dropped out after a split-up.

Contrasting sharply with the long drawn out days of shuffling with 15 minutes of rest out of every hour was the end which came eight hours after the announcement of new rules at midnight Tuesday.

New Rules Made.

According to the new rules the two remaining couples agreed to dance continuously for four hours, before taking any rest. They were then to be allowed five minutes relaxation and five more minutes to get back on the floor.

At the end of the first four hour period all showed the strain. At the end of the second all walked off the floor vowing they'd return. But at 8:05 Mr. Solomon failed to show up and the Davenport couple were declared winners.

MRS. ELIZABETH MEYERS. LESTER SCHEEF.
Winners of first prize.

NOV 1: RESOLUTION OF PROTEST; WILL ASK CITY COUNCIL TO TAKE ACTION

Resolved. By the Davenport Woman's Missionary alliance, widely representative of a cross section of the homes of our city that we denounce both the principle and the practice of so–called marathon dances, and furthermore petition the city council to enact such an ordinance as shall hereafter prohibit such an exhibition within our city.

Melody Maker, June 1928

PARLOPHONE
NEW RECORDS OF MODERN DANCE MUSIC.
ALL 10-inch BLUE LABEL RECORDS, 3/- EACH

NEW WONDER RECORDS
FRANKIE TRUMBAUER
AND HIS MARVELLOUS ORCHESTRA
with Bix, Lang, Venuti, Rollini and Schutt

R 105 — KRAZY KAT. (Tone Poem in Slow Rhythm (Morehouse & Trumbauer.)
THREE BLIND MICE. (Rhythmic Theme in advanced Harmony). (Morehouse & Trumbauer.)

FRANKIE TRUMBAUER
King of all Saxophone Players
and the greatest figure in
Modern Music.

JOE VENUTI'S BLUE FOUR

R 109 — PEN PEACH BLUES. (Venuti-Lang).
FOUR STRING JOE (Venuti-Lang).

THE GOOFUS FIVE
With ADRIAN ROLLINI AND LES REIS.

R 108 — BLUE BABY, WHY ARE YOU BLUE? Fox-Trot.
WHERE THE COT-COT-COTTON GROWS, Fox-Trot.

The Jazzologist Supreme.
BOYD SENTER, Clarinet
Acc. by ED. LANG, Guitar, ARTHUR SCHUTT, Piano.

R 107 — BEALE STREET BLUES.
DOWN HEARTED BLUES.

SOPHIE TUCKER SINGS

R 100 — THE MAN I LOVE / MY PET
R 3455 — WHAT'LL YOU DO? / THERE'LL BE SOME CHANGES MADE
R 3413 — BLUE RIVER / THERE'S A CRADLE IN CAROLINE
R 3353 — I AIN'T GOT NOBODY / AFTER YOU'VE GONE
R 3342 — FIFTY MILLION FRENCHMEN CAN'T BE WRONG / ONE SWEET LETTER FROM HOME

SOPHIE TUCKER
With Ted Shapiro's Orchestra
and Miff Mole's Molers
only on Parlophone Records.

ONLY FOR
PARLOPHONE RECORDS

Insist on hearing these wonderful Records at your nearest stores or dealers.
THE PARLOPHONE COMPANY, LTD., 85, CITY ROAD, LONDON, E.C.1

WHITEMAN'S BOYS

Bandleader Paul Whiteman (1890–1967) fined his musicians $25 each time they were late on the job. "Bix Beiderbecke was the worst offender," Whiteman recalled in a 1947 interview:

"One day in Texas, Bix awoke late and discovered the band already had left by train for the next concert. He had already set himself back nearly $100 so to avoid another fine, he hired a car—only he misdirected the driver who set off in the opposite direction. When Bix discovered the mistake, he chartered a plane and arrived in the city four hours before the train did. He checked into a hotel to wait for the arrival of the rest of the band. Then he dozed off and didn't wake up until an hour after the concert was over."

Whiteman was quoted as saying, "America's flaming youth is not nearly as hot as it looks," in the February '28 issue of *Smart Set* magazine:

Bix and Frank Trumbauer on tour with Whiteman in 1928

> The rotund bandsman, who rode to fame on the post–war wave of jazz, has been watching his band with one eye and the younger generation with the other these several seasons past, in ballrooms, nightclubs and other spots where youth is popularly supposed to be found at its wildest. "Most of the current furor is a result of the older generations taking the younger generations too seriously." Youth wants to appear much wilder than it really wishes or dares to be, he points out, and

That's Bix under the baton of Paul Whiteman; below in a publicity photo with his Whiteman bandmates.

PAUL WHITEMAN AND HIS GREATER CONCERT ORCHESTRA

Jazz tickles your muscles, symphonies stretch your soul. ~Paul Whiteman

the automobile, jazz and other accessories of the speed age give it the opportunity. "Young people always did want to show off," opines Mr. Whiteman. "They want speed; that's natural enough. But at the same time they want the world to see it. If they drink, they want someone to know it. They would like to have you think they are just a little daring and a little shocking...Our fathers and mothers, grandpas and grandmas would have done the same things in their day with the same opportunities."

In a May 1928 interview for Princeton University's student newspaper, Whiteman addressed the criticism that jazz corrupted the morals of the young: "People speak of jazz, crime, and booze all in the same breath. How do they get that way? Jazz is music, beauty of sound. It is the greatest rhythm yet discovered.

"To most people it's a tonic. Millions of people listen to it every day through various mediums. Jazz bands are among the most popular attractions in the show business. And jazz has nothing more to do with drinking than the soft waltz of the little German band at a Turnverein picnic has to do with the number of kegs of beer which are consumed during the festivities."

Later that year, Whiteman saxophonist Frank 'Tram' Trumbauer recorded in his diary: Dec 2. Bix still gone. Stayed in Cleveland with DTs. I spent 4 years with him to no avail.

Bix first met Trumbauer when the Benson Orchestra played Davenport's Coliseum in April of 1923. Trumbauer had studied violin, piano, trombone and flute but made his fame with the C–melody sax. He had his own band in 1917 before joining the Navy in WWI.

Bix was playing with the Wolverines when Trumbauer first took note of his remarkable musicianship. He invited Bix to join his band at the St. Louis Arcadia ballroom where Tram tutored Bix in sight reading enough so he could get back into the Jean Goldkette band in Detroit.

Bix and Tram joined Whiteman's outfit together in Indianapolis on Oct 27, 1927. On December 27th, the two of them were featured in the *Cleveland Press* when the Whiteman orchestra was in town. Bix sent a tear sheet from the newspaper home to his family with a hand–written note: *They got me sketched good looking & Tram hideous how about the mustache?*

Bix and Tram

In carefully selected spots on this page the eager reader will find sketches of Bix Biederbeck [sic] and Frank Trumbaur, [sic] known wherever musicians gather as leading exponents in the field of ultra

—modern dance music. They are with Paul Whiteman, now appearing at the Allen.

Whiteman's orchestra also includes two other musicians of equal caliber in the Dorsey brothers.

Bix has only one recognized rival as a trumpet or cornet player: Red Nichols. Tram is in a class by himself on the saxophone.

They have been identified with the leading bands such as Goldkett's [sic] and Ray Miller's for several years but are at their best when a small combination such as Fran Trumbaur's orchestra, composed of this pair, Eddie Lang on the guitar and piano (played by Art Schutt, we believe).

They have recorded numerous records under almost as many names.

However, "Three Blind Mice," "Krazy Kat," Singing the Blues," "For No Reason at All in C," "Trumbology," "Way Down Yonder in New Orleans," and "I'm Coming Home, Virginia," all have been under the name of Frank Trumbaur and recorded for Okeh.

[Bix marked following graph and handwrote: *get a load of this*]

To our way of thinking, no child should be started in life without being brought up on this kind of music.

Tram and Bix were turned loose only for a moment in Whiteman's early week program. Each had a short chorus in "Under the Moon."

Singin' the Blues, first recorded by the Original Dixieland Jazz Band, was a big hit for Frankie Trumbauer and His Orchestra featuring Bix on cornet in 1927. Fifty years after its release the Bix & Tram version of the song would be inducted into the Grammy Hall of Fame.

After Bix's death, Trumbauer remained another five years with Whiteman and then had his own band until becoming a B–25 bomber test pilot with the Civil Aeronautics Administration in Kansas City. He died in Kansas City in June 1956.

Whiteman was playing in Chicago at the Edgewater Beach Hotel when Bix died. He went from there to Denver in August 1931 to marry his fourth wife, actress Margaret Livingston. They'd met in Hollywood while Whiteman was there filming *King of Jazz*.

As Whiteman's own musical career ebbed, he snagged a $5.2 million contract to host a radio show, largest syndication sell in broadcasting history at the time. He later hosted a summer variety show on television.

Whiteman once said the future of jazz depended on the public taking it seriously. He also said, "Jazz tickles your muscles, symphonies stretch your soul."

As to the changing musical tastes of the American audience, Whiteman stated: "What killed the big bands? Over a period of ten years they taught people to listen to the singers instead of dancing."

When he died of a heart attack at age 77, Whiteman was retired and living in Bucks County, PA, where he and Margaret had a house they called Coda Cottage. Earlier that year he had played his old viola for his youngest daughter's wedding. The song he performed was the only one he ever wrote, *Wonderful One*.

Bix & Red

When Red Nichols and His Five Pennies played Davenport's Danceland in October 1928, Bix was in Alabama with Red's one-time boss, Paul Whiteman.

Bix had been on the road with Whiteman a year by then. They played Atlanta, GA, on October 23. In the audience were Bix's sister Mary Louise and brother-in-law Ted Shoemaker. The Shoemakers hosted an after-party for Whiteman and a handful of Bix's bandmates. One of the musicians recalled to jazz historian Phil Evans that Bix's sister kept asking him to sing, *I Can't Give You Anything But Love*.

At the time, Sis and Ted had two children, two-year-old Ted Jr. and eight-month-old Charles Bix. Sis would give birth to twins, a daughter who died and their third son, Julien, born in Atlanta in March of 1931.

Ten years earlier Sis had been shipping baked cookies to her kid brother at Lake Forest Academy. That's also when the up-and-coming Iowa cornetist first crossed paths with Utah cornetist Ernest Loring 'Red' Nichols (1905–1965) in Chicago.

After recording *Davenport Blues* with his Rhythm Jugglers in January 1925, Bix went to New York. He stayed in Nichol's hotel room and sat in with the California Ramblers, which included Nichols on cornet, Tommy Dorsey on trombone, and Jimmy Dorsey on clarinet.

Bix and Red were guests at the Dorsey family home. "Their mother cooked the dinner," Nichols recalled. Tommy had played with Bix on those Gennett Records in Richmond, IN. Along with Bix's original composition they recorded *Toddlin' Blues* and two other songs that were rejected, the masters destroyed.

Nichols said his own drinking was pretty heavy in those days and he needed Bix to get him through his gigs. "I asked Bix to go along with me and help me out. In return I would split the money with him. He agreed. Who this was for I will probably never know because it was a case of the blind leading the blind."

In May 1925 Bix was back in Chicago, playing with the Charlie Straight Orchestra. This time around Nichols crashed with Bix. Red was wooing

Straight's band singer, Hannah Williams. Apparently, Hannah's mother put an end to Nichols' hopes for a romance.

Nichols eventually married dancer Willa 'Bobbi' Stutsman. In a 1960 interview with historian Phil Evans, Bobbi said she had talked by phone with Bix on August 4, 1931. He had called for Red, said Bobbi, keeping her on the line awhile in the hope that her husband would arrive home while they talked. "I can so clearly remember Bix wanting to talk about family life and how he felt that Red was so lucky to have a wife and daughter," Bobbi told Evans. She added that her husband tried to call Bix back the next day but couldn't reach him. The following day Bix was found dead in his Queens apartment.

Davenport Democrat Leader
October 10, 1928 AD

> *I am basically deep in my heart a jazz musician, Dixieland jazz. In my early life I was buying all the Red Nichols records, the things by Miff Mole, Bix Beiderbecke, Frankie Trumbauer, right down the line. It's my favorite type of music. I tried to play jazz when starting out in my career but prairie audiences didn't dig it. ~Lawrence Welk*

Bix & Bing—Songbirds of a Feather!

Look at an old payroll of the Paul Whiteman Orchestra in the 1920s and see who made fifty a week more than Bing Crosby.

Surprise! It's Leon Beiderbecke.

Despite his renown, Bix never got into the big bucks as did other musicians of his era, Louis Armstrong and Hoagy Carmichael for example. Those who knew Bix say he was usually broke soon after payday.

Bing Crosby's later recording contracts, movies and television appearances made him a flood of money and continued to do so for the heirs to his estate. Meanwhile, Bix's earnings tapped out at $1,408.28 from Robbins Music Corporation for song royalties, recorded in the assets of Aggie Beiderbecke when Bix's brother, Charles, served as executor of their mother's estate in March 1940.

Bix's legacy has little to do with money but there's a wealth to be found in his influence on the careers of others. Crosby's rapid rise to stardom, for one, came after he changed the way he sang. And who was responsible for the change in how he sang?

The answer once more is Bix Beiderbecke!

Bix would hit a phrase clean and then feather it off in little ripples and liquid fragments. You can hear him do it on *Because My Baby Don't Mean Maybe*. And then Bing does the same thing with his voice.

In 1987, Larry Kart, a Chicago writer and editor, echoed what others close to both men claimed when he wrote that "The man who had the most profound effect on Bing Crosby's development, both as an influence and an example, was Crosby's one-time roommate in the Whiteman Orchestra, Bix Beiderbecke."

Crosby and his college pal Al Rinker had joined Whiteman in 1926 and were teamed up with Harry Barris—uncle of Gong Show's Chuck Barris—to form a novelty trio known as the *Rhythm Boys*. They contributed the *vo–dee–o–doh* interludes to several Whiteman recordings. Barris also wrote songs, including *Wa–da–da (Everybody's Doin' It Now)* recorded by Bix Beiderbecke and His Gang in 1928.

Chicago columnist Tony Weitzel recalled stories shared with him by State Street old timers from the era of speakeasies and Capone. It was 1928.

RHYTHM BOYS in Hollywood after leaving behind their vo-dee-o-do days with Paul Whiteman; Bing is flanked by Al Rinker, left, and Harry Barris, right.
Right: 1939 newspaper promo with Bing, wife Dixie Lee and sons—twins Dennis and Phillip, youngest son Lindsay and eldest Gary. Ad copy reads in part: *Crooners come and go but Bing Crosby is still very much a central figure as popular entertainer and no doubt he will be in demand long after his singing voice is passé.*
Before becoming a singer, Bing played drums with a band back home in Tacoma, WA.

A kid from Tacoma, Harry Lillis Crosby, tagged along with Bix to an after-hours session at Three Deuces. "When I got to Chicago years later, they were still talking about that night the *Man with the Horn* and the *Bing with the Rhythm* let it all hang out."

In *Bix: Man & Legend* by Sudhalter and Evans, the friendship of Bix and Bing is said to have been there from the start. "They appeared to share an easy-going approach to most of life's tribulations, as well as a fondness and awesome capacity for bootleg gin.

"But the making of music was something else; both took it seriously and Bing often confessed himself in awe of Bix's absorption and knowledge of the world of concert music."

Larry Kart noted that in Crosby's early years, he "was an accomplished Louis Armstrong-style *scat* singer. *Some of These Days*, recorded with Joe Venuti has a delightful wordless chorus from Bing. But it was on the romantic ballads that Bing really found himself, applying Bix's less-is-more lyrical lessons."

That less-is-more attitude seems to have defined Bix's financial sense, too. Still, there is no less pride among those who can claim blood kinship to Davenport's immortal jazzman.

AN INTERVIEW WITH BIX'S OLD FLAME

In September, 1983, Bix fan Jedge Daniel of Huntsville, AL, was preparing a trip to St. Louis to take his dad to a Cardinal's baseball game. Re-reading *Bix, Man & Legend* for the umpteenth time, it dawned on Jedge that maybe Bix's old flame, Ruth Shaffner, might still be in the area.

Bix historian Phil Evans confirmed that, yes, Ruth resided there. "Excitedly, I phoned her to see if she was agreeable to chat with a stranger from Alabama. Indeed she was." Here's Jedge's account of their visit:

It was a little like going back in time as I entered the older, but well-maintained apartment building at 4616 Lindell Boulevard. The decor and self-service elevator were straight out of the '30s, at least my perception of that era. It set the mood perfectly for my first meeting with Bix's sweetheart from his St. Louis days.

My knock at apartment 312 was answered by a petite, well-groomed, attractive 78-year-old woman. Let me repeat that, a *very* petite woman. If Ruth was five feet tall, she was probably in heels. After a few minutes of awkward pleasantries, we sat down at her kitchen table to talk.

In absolute awe of the setting and the moment, I forgot to turn on the cassette recorder I had brought. What a shame, because I just sat there with my mouth open and my brain in neutral, too excited to file away many particulars from our conversation. I do remember that she enjoyed a good marriage to Mr. Sweeney, who had passed away some time before. But when she spoke of Bix her entire countenance changed.

I could sense her love for him even after half a century. I also learned that she liked baseball and that her favorite Cardinal player was Andy Van Slyke. When asked why she liked Van Slyke, she grinned and said, "because he's cute." I couldn't argue with that kind of logic.

Ruth's sister Estelle dropped in, as she lived in the same building. When she learned that I was a Bix fan, she treated me like a brother–in–arms. She reminisced of the times she and Bing Crosby and Ruth and Bix double–dated when the Whiteman band played St. Louis. Estelle said that Bing's eyes made him "almost too pretty to be a man." Dating Bix and Bing was obviously a high point in the Shaffner sisters' lives. Ruth signed my copy of *Bix, Man & Legend* and we promised each other to keep in touch.

From '83 to '87 Ruth and I exchanged occasional letters and Christmas cards. It wasn't until September 1987 that I was able to get to St. Louis again. On this occasion, my wife accompanied me, although her taste in music runs more to country than jazz. We planned to take Ruth out for a nice meal but as her health was declining we opted for an evening at her apartment.

She was *dressed to the nines*–where does that come from?—when we arrived. [Origin: Old English *thyn eyenes* or *thine eyes*, thus dressed to be visually appealing.] Ruth and my wife took to each other like they were old friends. The presence of another woman must have made Ruth feel comfortable, as she was more relaxed and talkative than on our first visit.

Eventually, the conversation turned to Bix and, as before, the gleam in her eyes was unmistakable. As she talked of the Arcadia Ballroom, the after–hours clubs, and the early morning breakfasts with Bix, she seemed to be not just telling but re–living the events.

I am unable to accurately convey the way her face lit up and whenever she talked of Bix. Her eyes became misty and it was obvious that although she had gone on with her life after Bix, her heart had never let him go.

She bristled at the notion that Bix was unkempt. "He took as many baths as the next fellow and always smelled nice, even after being on the bandstand all night, she insisted.

I asked her what she remembered most about Bix. She paused and then said, "two things: his sense of humor and the way he seemed to laugh with his eyes. He would just look at me and I'd melt."

She still had a bow tie and handkerchief that Bix had left at her apartment during the Whiteman tour stop in St. Louis. Call me a male groupie, but I got all fuzzy holding items that my hero had actually worn. Ruth must have sensed my reverence and she asked if I would like to have them and her old Bix 78s when she passed away. I said, "I would be honored but don't make it anytime soon."

The Shaffner sisters, L-R: Estelle, Ruth, and Bess

Jedge Daniel in 1987 with Bix's St. Louis gal, Ruth Shaffner Sweeney (1904-1990)

The last letter I received from Ruth was in November 1989. She wasn't feeling well and had a heart condition. She had lost both sisters—Estelle in '86 and Bess in '88, and missed them, but promised that she wasn't getting senile.

I wrote back but didn't hear from her again. Five months later, I received a short letter from a relative of Ruth's, saying that she had passed away, peacefully, in her favorite chair. Bix was in all ways a gentleman and it seems only fitting that the one woman in his life was truly a lady.

San Francisco Postmark: June 10, 1929/2 PM—Mr. B.H. Beiderbecke East Dav. Fuel Co. Davenport, Iowa   Just crossed desert in shöne [German *schöne*=beautiful] Cal. hope to see you later trip marvelous I feel the same Love to Mom Burnie Cork & Mary [Burnie's son & wife] & yourself—Bix

THE OLD GOLD — PAUL WHITEMAN SPECIAL
EN ROUTE FROM NEW YORK TO LOS ANGELES

Broadcasting from coast-to-coast the Old Gold — Paul Whiteman Hour, sponsored by P. Lorillard Company, makers of Old Gold cigarettes.

BIX IN HOLLYWOOD

While visiting Bix in California in the summer of 1929, Aggie Beiderbecke became concerned about his health. Hoagy Carmichael recalled that she tried, "to coax him back to Davenport for a more protracted period of recovery."

Hoagy was in Hollywood at the time to pitch his own music compositions to movie studios. He'd been doing arrangements for clarinetist Ernie McKay, whose band at the time was performing at Roscoe 'Fatty' Arbuckle's Plantation in Los Angeles. McKay, who'd roomed together with Bix in Detroit, told of running into Bix in the company of his mother. Bix still walked with a cane, McKay reported.

Carmichael said Bix saw his mother only once while she was in town. "It wasn't something he wanted to discuss, and I didn't feel right bringing it up. I think there was conflict between them, despite their close attachment."

Meanwhile script work for *King of Jazz* was going nowhere fast. Whiteman's boys spent their free time making the rounds as the house band for parties hosted by Hollywood celebrities, among them actor Richard Barthelmess, whose guests included Charlie Chaplin, Douglas Fairbanks and Mary Pickford.

Bix impressed the gathering with his cornet solo on *Sweet Sue* but Whiteman trombonist Bill Rank said the boys mostly enjoyed Carmichael's antics. "Hoagy was dancing with every female star and starlet in the place," Rank said. "That was some party, all right."

Perhaps among those actresses Hoagy twirled with on the dance floor was Rock Island's Helen Mack or Peggy Montgomery, maybe Bettendorf's Hazel Keener.

Helen Mack co-starred with Barthelmess in *Four Hours to Kill*. Born Helen McDougall in Rock Island, she attended New York's Professional Children's School where Ruby Keeler also got her start. Far more than a starlet, Helen Mack was an entertainment industry pioneer whose career spanned the emergence of Broadway and the final days of Vaudeville, the evolution of motion pictures, the transition to *talkies*, the Golden Age of Radio, and the early years of television.

In New York, she acted on screen with Gloria Swanson and Clara Bow and appeared in D. W. Griffith's final film. When movie-making shifted from the east coast to the west, Helen made the transition from child actress to Hollywood contract player. She made 44 films before turning to scriptwriting and producing/directing for radio and television.

Rock Island-born Margaret 'Peggy' Dorothy Montgomery was a classmate of Angela Searle—the girl who had kept Bix's class ring as a token of their broken engagement. Rocky's Watch Tower yearbook named Peggy Montgomery "the prettiest girl in the sophomore class." That was the year Bix went with Karl Vollmer and Vera Cox to the Rock Island High School's senior class play. Peggy caught the acting bug in high school and after graduating she moved to Hollywood.

She got her start as a movie stunt double and went on to acting roles in thirty silent films, mostly westerns between 1924 and 1929. She married in 1930 and left the movie business.

Film websites mistakenly credit silent era child star *Baby Peggy* for the adult Peggy Montgomery's movies. While Baby Peggy's dad, Jack Montgomery, had been a Hollywood stuntman, it sure wasn't Baby Peggy thrilling movie-goers as the spunky heroine who rode horses, swam rapids, climbed mountains and out-witted villains in films such as *Prisoners of the Storm*, *Arizona Days*, *Two Guns of the Tumbleweeds* and *The Sonora Kid*.

At the time Bix was in Hollywood, Peggy Montgomery would have been 26 years old, same age as Bettendorf's Hazel Keener. Hazel had abandoned her studies at the University of Iowa to pursue an acting career. She got her first Hollywood audition after winning the *Chicago Tribune's* national beauty contest. In 1922 she played opposite Wesley 'Freckles' Barry in the screen adaptation of Booth Tarkington's *Penrod*.

Later that summer the Iowa-born brunette won the Miss Hollywood pageant. But she lost out to an L.A. blonde whom the judges selected instead to represent southern California in Atlantic City's Labor Day weekend pageant. That was the year the world was first to hear the title: Miss America.

Hazel was in the stands in 1925 when Davenport's Elmer Layden of Notre Dame's Four Horsemen scored four touchdowns against Stanford to win the Rose Bowl. "She surely is a dandy girl," Layden said of Hazel, his date at that night's victory celebration in Pasadena. "Davenporters will be glad to know that she is rapidly winning her way to the top of the movies," Layden told the folks back home.

**STARTS TOMORROW
SON OF KONG**
How does he feel toward the men who captured his father, Mighty King Kong?

Return to Kong's Island for amazing, thrilling adventures—with a climax that will leave you breathless and applauding.

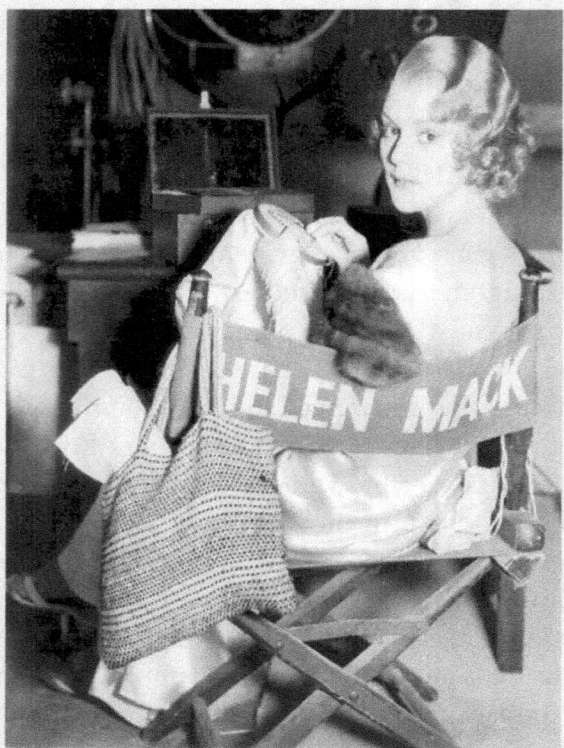

Clockwise from top left: HELEN MACK in 1929 (no, that's not Lassie); on the set of *Blind Adventure* 1933; with George Raft in *All of Me*, 1934; with Richard Barthelmess in *Four Hours to Kill*, 1935; *Son of Kong* Ad 1934.

Above: two of sixteen movies PEGGY MONTGOMERY made in 1927. Below: Fellow Rock Islander HELEN MACK as a 1935 *St. Louis Post Dispatch* paper doll with outfits from her movies

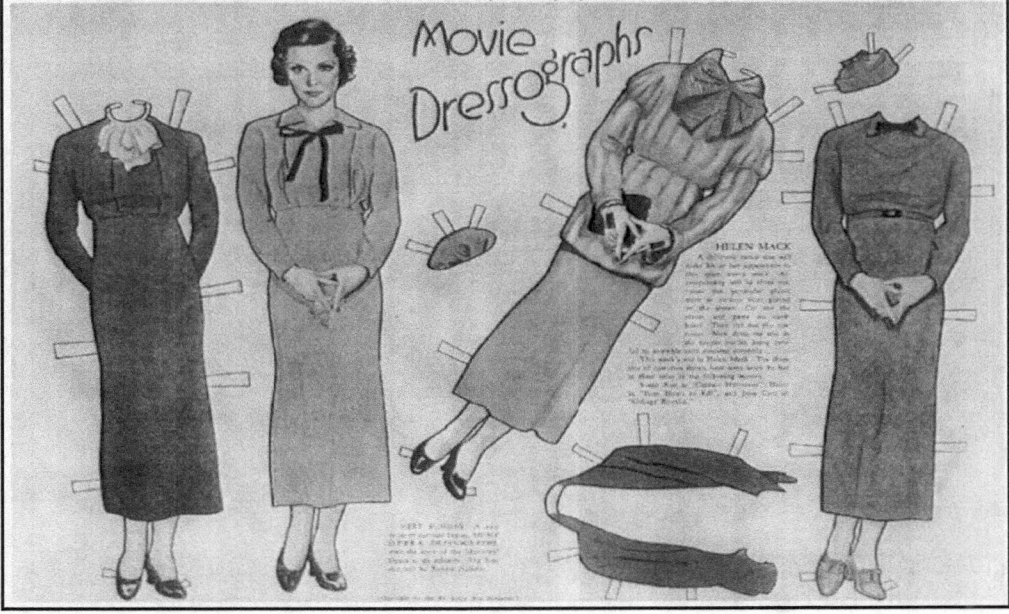

ROCK ISLAND GIRL STARRED IN GARDEN FILM

Peggy Montgomery Seen in Billie Dove's "Sensation Seekers" Here Today.

The Title: "Sensation Seekers."
The Stars: Billie Dove, Peggy Montgomery, Huntley Gordon.
The Type: Dramatic Romance.
The Locale: America.

When the "Sensation Seekers" film opens at the Garden theatre this afternoon, appearing in the cast is Miss Peggy Montgomery of Rock Island who plays the role of Margaret Todd. Of her the following notice appears:

Peggy Montgomery was born in Rock Island, Ill. A typical screen-struck girl, she came to Hollywood with her parents three years ago and secured a part in "The Thief of Bagdad." Her early experience was gained doubling for stars in dangerous scenes. She played opposite Harry Langdon in "There He Goes" and opposite House Peters in "Prisoners of the Storm."

A new dramatic team, equalling the comedy team of Reginald Denny, star, and William A. Seiter, director, has sprung up on the Uni-

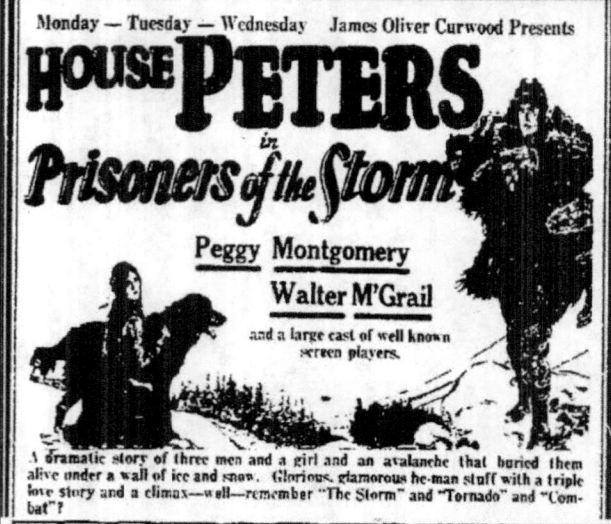

Do You Recognize Her? Well It's Our Own Hazel Keener as She Appears In First Movie

YEP, it's Hazel Keener—our own Hazel—and Wesley (Freckles) Barry, as they appear in "Penrod." Miss Keener, who is a Bettendorf girl, as you all know, won the beauty prize of $1,000 and a chance to go on to the movies. She displayed such unusual talent that she was given a place in the cast of "Penrod," supporting the youthful Wesley Barry. "Penrod" comes to the Garden soon.

The Stage and Screen

HAZEL KEENER
Photograph by Frank Free

THIS is the picture that put Hazel Keener on the map. This week she appears in our city in her first moving picture.

Let us make a special picture for you for the Des Moines Register beauty contest. An ordinary picture will not answer the purpose.

F. A. FREE
"STUDIO ON THE HILL."

Starts Today · Starts Today

10th Anniversary Week
Sept. 22-1915   Sept. 22-1925

Celebrating a Decade of Success With Laughter

Harold Lloyd
in
The Freshman
ASSISTED BY HAZEL KEENER and JOBYNA RALSTON

NOTE—Miss Keener, Davenport's own beauty prize winner, has her first real role in this picture.

ADDED ATTRACTIONS
SEARS AT THE ORGAN

Democrat-Leader.
HAZEL KEENER in *Penrod*, Jan 31, 1922; Free Studio AD Feb 19, 1922; Garden Theater AD Sep 20, 1925

ELMER LAYDEN TO APPEAR IN VAUDEVILLE

Announced in last Issue of "Variety," a Theatrical Publication.

Our own Elmer Layden of Notre Dame fame is to appear in vaudeville along with the other three horsemen. Announcement of the fact appears in the March 4th, issue of "Variety," a theatrical publication, and reads as follows:

Elmer Layden, Harry Stuhldreher, Don Miller, and Jim Crowley, commonly termed football's "Four Horsemen" will make their vaudeville debut in May via western vaudeville.

Ed Keough is responsible for recruiting the Notre Dame gridiron battlers as an act, which will be a singing, dancing and musical turn.

Jimmy Co...
ton univers:
moleskin lu

Hazel Keener, Iowa's $1000 Beauty Prize Winner, Who Had to Put Out a Sign to Keep Aloof Would-Be Husbands, Lovers and Cranks.

Top Left: Elmer Layden, second from left, in famous Four Horsemen pose.
Top right: *Davenport Democrat,* Mar. 8, 1925.
Center: Notre Dame's star fullback and Hazel Keener a.k.a. Barbara Worth.
Left: Publicity shot of Bettendorf's Hazel Keener published in newspapers across the country in 1923.

Indeed, Hazel had a couple dozen films under her belt when she co-starred that same year in Harold Lloyd's comedy, *The Freshman*. The following year she was cast with then–eighteen Douglas Fairbanks Jr. in *Broken Hearts of Hollywood*.

She went by the name Barbara Worth for that movie. She'd first worked as Barbara Worth in 1923's *An Old Sweetheart of Mine*. She would use the name through much of the 1930s, mostly in low budget westerns—a couple with Olympic gold medalist Jim Thorpe.

Thorpe had his own QC connection. In the waning years of his athletic career he played a season for the Rock Island Independents professional football team.

Elmer Layden turned down an offer to play for the Indees. Eventually he took a coaching job that led back to Notre Dame, where he replaced Coach Knute Rockne.

Bix was home when Notre Dame won the Rose Bowl and he surely would have been rooting for his former Davenport High football teammate. As for any actresses with ties to Bix's hometown, his interest at most was as a fan of their movies. He was said to have told his friend Larry Andrews: "After you play behind the Follies, where they pick the most beautiful girls out of thousands, then you ride on a train from New York to California with them, you get so that the girls don't interest you much."

Bix missed out on his own chance to be immortalized in film. By the time Hollywood got around to making *King of Jazz* in late 1929, Bix was recuperating at home.

King of Jazz came to Davenport's Uptown Theatre on Harrison Street in 1930. Bix bought a ticket and sat in the darkened theater watching his Whiteman band mates on the silver screen.

DER—APRIL 25, 1928

Jazz Trumpeter and Soloist of Whiteman's Orchestra Is Former Davenport Lad

LEON "BIX" BEIDERBECKE.

Above: Fox Movietone newsreel from May 12, 1928, shows Whiteman with his back to the camera and Bix, standing behind the string section, playing his horn.

Left: *Democrat-Leader,* April 25, 1928

Below: Clinton's Lafayette Hotel where Bix performed with the Whiteman orchestra before a hometown crowd on November 23, 1928

"BIX BEIDERBECKE, perhaps the finest trumpeter in the country, will now play for you his own composition, 'In a Mist.'"

This simple announcement in the Paul Whiteman orchestra broadcast in the midnight program over the national networks from New York Tuesday night electrified the Davenport Bixophile, and most of all a little family group in the B. H. Beiderbecke home, 1934 Grand avenue. Their son, Leon, was that same "finest trumpeter."

But six months ago he joined Paul Whiteman's orchestra after repeated requests from that famous jazz leader. His reticence was due to the fact that he played by ear and scarcely knew one note from another. Now he is a soloist and a composer, this latter with the aid of a fellow musician who wrote the score as he played it. "In a Mist" he played on the piano in this featured broadcast.

"Bix" as he was known by the gang, and there always was a gang of 'fellers' with him in his boyhood days, has displayed his jazz tendencies since earliest youth. He went to the local schools, went 2 years to the Davenport high school and one year to the Lake Forest academy at Lake Forest, Ill. He was known as a jazz artist in every school he attended but beyond that school had little appeal and he had no inclination to go on to college.

Music lessons, too, were too much like a grind. He took piano lessons for a time from two local instructors, not more than a score in all. He had wonderful promise, his teachers said, but he veered away from the labor of learning. What was the use of droning "one, two, three, four" when you could rattle off the latest jazz tune thru a magic sense entirely apart from mathematics? So ran his youthful reasoning.

He exhibited the same attitude toward a business career. During the summers he assisted his father in his coal office, but for a life work he had other plans.

For the past three years he has been cornetist with the Jean Goldkett orchestra of Detroit, and it was on one of the musical tours with that organization that Paul Whiteman heard him play. He is now 25 years old.

"We can always tell when Bix's horn comes in," says his mother. "We know every time Paul Whiteman's orchestra is on the air and Leon knows we'll be listening in. The air is carried by the other cornetist but the sudden perky blare and the unexpected trills, those are the jazz parts and they are Leon's."

LAFAYETTE HOTEL CLINTON IOWA ON THE LINCOLN HIGHWAY

BIX TAKES THE CURE

Paul Whiteman brought his cross-country tour to Bix's home state of Iowa in the fall of 1928. They made three stops, none in Davenport.

Saxophonist Frank Trumbauer noted in his diary for November 19th that the orchestra performed in Sioux City and wrote: *Bix day all the folks were there and lauded long and loud. I wish he would straighten up.*

By other accounts, friends and family from Davenport did not travel across state but instead saw Bix perform in Clinton, just up river from Davenport on the 23rd. The one other Iowa stop was the night before in Cedar Rapids.

At Clinton, Paul Whiteman put on two shows at the Lafayette Hotel. Bix's brother Burnie and sister-in-law Mary brought along Bix's new nephew, Charles Hilton Beiderbecke to see Bix perform in Clinton.

Davenport trumpet player and jazz historian Wayne Rohlf recalled that the matinee audience was small, only about forty.

The evening show had less than a hundred and most of them were from Davenport. The crowd wasn't much bigger than the orchestra!

"After the intermission, the curtain went up and the band started to play a big symphonic introduction," Wayne said.

"The first trumpet blew some awfully foul notes. He quit playing, looked his trumpet all over and finally found that his A-slide had been pulled out during the intermission.

The band almost broke up, they laughed so hard that Whiteman got redder than a spanked baby's butt.

The band continued playing the number right to the end. I heard later Bix was the guy who pulled the slide."

A week later Bix had to be hospitalized in Cleveland, Ohio, having passed out during a performance there.

Whiteman sent him home to Davenport that winter of 1928 to recuperate.

EXCERPT FROM BIX'S LETTER TO TRAM IN EARLY 1929:

>...I am writing this flat on my back as I have been since my arrival home. The rest is sure making a new man out of me, I'm in good shape, all but my knees. It seems I had a touch of pneumonia at one time and that our doctor thinks it wasn't discernable because

of its slightness. He also said that because of the wonderful doctor and care that Paul arranged for me in New York, the pneumonia didn't get a chance to show itself. But here at home, he noticed a slight infection in the lower right lobe of my lung. It seems that after all this trouble, the poison in my system has settled in my knees and legs—I guess I am a minus quality. I have never suffered so continually without a letup in my life. The doctor says the heart and everything is okay, but I am not worth a dime. My knees don't work. I try to stand and fall right on my face. I am taking walking lessons and I am improving every day, but with great pain. I haven't had a drink for so long I'd pass on one. I'm strictly gleaming above the boys on the big wagon and I am sticking there....

Sure doesn't read like a Bix letter. Sobriety may account for the clarity of thought but it doesn't explain his dramatic improvement in spelling and grammar. More likely that he dictated the letter, possibly getting his cousin Otie Stibolt Hass to be his secretary. Bix was said to have escaped to her Spanish motif house when boredom set in from staring at the same old walls on Grand Avenue.

The Beiderbecke family's last known photograph of Bix shows him and Tram during a stop on the train trip back to New York in 1929. The photo was staged to make Tram look larger by having Bix stand on lower ground. Fritz Putzier had seen Bix just before the train left Los Angeles on Aug 28th and he remembered Bix walking with a cane.

November 1929, *Melody Maker*:
> Bix Beiderbecke needs no introduction. He has been mentioned time and again in the MELODY MAKER. He is still with Whiteman and I am sorry to say still far from fit. His recent illness has had a serious effect on his work and he will need all his will power to pull himself together. Everybody will join in wishing him a complete recovery.

Bix's grandfather, a banker and businessman, had experienced first–hand the national panic over federal gold reserves. Paper currency was a promise. Gold was the real deal. Dr. Leslie E. Keeley traded on that perception of gold as the standard for authenticity, touting his *double chloride of gold* formula as a cure for addictions to alcohol and drugs. Keeley's first patients were doctors who had lost their practices due to their own addictions. Many of them were then hired to staff Keeley facilities. With their medical credentials backing him, Keeley withstood charges of quackery.

By the time Bix sought treatment for his alcoholism, the gold cure had become simply the Keeley Cure. A *Davenport Democrat–Leader* ad in 1929 showed a guy on the golf links and a promo that read:
> ONE OF THE STRIKING FEATURES OF THE KEELEY INSTITUTE IS AN ABSENCE OF RESTRAINT. PATIENTS LIVE IN PLEASANT, WHOLESOME ATMOSPHERE. THERE ARE GOLF, TENNIS AND OTHER FACILITIES FOR SPORTS. SPLENDID OPPORTUNITIES FOR GOOD COMRADESHIP. NO EMBARRASSMENT. NOWHERE IS IT POSSIBLE TO SPEND A MORE BENEFICIAL OR ENJOYABLE PERIOD FOR THE TREATMENT OF DRUGS OR LIQUOR.

So Bismark Beiderbecke's youngest child finally would get some much needed rest and maybe even get in a few rounds of golf and play some tennis—activities his *Bickie* loved as a boy.

That alone would have been worth the $18–a–week treatment charges. That, and knowing Bix would be somewhere safe from distractions and negative influences.

Burnie drove Bix the 140–so miles east from Davenport to Dwight, IL. Dwight was home to the Keeley's flagship facility, first among some 200 around the country. Bix checked in there on October 14th.

Medical records from Dwight are now in the possession of the Illinois State Historical Society. Bix's file includes his admission intake, physical examination, and release notes from the attending physician, as well as invoices and correspondences.

The admission form noted Bix suffered from loss of appetite, memory lapses, dizziness, accelerated heart rate, shortness of breath, and insomnia.

Comparison of Bix's signature from 1922 when he worked at his dad's coal company office and the signature on his 1930 admission form at the Keeley Institute. While under treatment Bix stayed at the Lodge in Dwight, shown in this 1930 postcard.

Bix reported having had pneumonia and delirium tremens—a.k.a. the DTs, a symptom of alcohol withdrawal—in December 1928. He had noticed pain in his feet around that time, also. Bix admitted to having drunk liquor *in excess* for the past nine years—so, a heavy drinker since high school—his daily consumption over the last three years amounted to three pints of *whiskey* and twenty cigarettes.

Those who hung out with Bix said he drank gin. Whisky takes time to age. Gin could be made quickly and easily in any large container—thus bathtub gin—by mixing raw alcohol with juniper extract and whatever flavorings were readily available.

Prohibition gin's poor quality gave rise to cocktails in which mixers disguised the taste. Stories of Bix drinking bootlegged liquor straight from the bottle pretty much indicate he was beyond being bothered by the taste, whiskey or gin, or whatever.

Bix got a complete examination at the Keeley Institute. His chart indicated symptoms of chronic alcoholism: neuropathy or nerve damage in his legs—probably malnutrition which alcoholics are prone to because their bodies are not metabolizing nutrients; and hand tremors, typical during withdrawal. The examiner also noted *mild delirium and harsh breath sounds*, possibly bronchitis from heavy smoking.

Leslie Keeley reported the highly addictive nature of smoking as far back as 1894: *"It is difficult to cure a cigarette smoker of the habit, said Dr. Keeley who professes to have a specific cure for alcoholism. He confesses that he is powerless to cure a man of inebriety who has become addicted to the cigarette."*

The so-called *Keeley Cure* secret formula turned out to be a mixture of atropine, strychnine, arsenic, and cinchona, all plant derivatives with glycerin used as a solvent. Atropine still is used to alleviate withdrawal symptoms and as an analgesic. Strychnine, in controlled dosages, counteracts nerve damage from alcohol. Arsenic and cinchona are also analgesics.

Keeley patients like Bix were administered a dram of the concoction every two hours along with their daily liquor allotment to help ease them through the withdrawal stage. Gradually the alcohol intake would be decreased. The treatment plan also would have included a regimen of healthy eating, fresh air and daily exercise, and a regular sleep routine.

After a five-week stay at the Keeley Institute, Bix returned to Davenport to continue his recovery. His release form, mailed to his mother, noted Bix reported no craving for liquor. There remained "a considerable tremor in

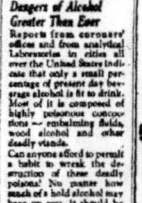

extended fingers and a lack of stability while standing" but Bix's overall condition was stated as satisfactory and he was judged to have been a cooperative patient. The treatment invoice totaled $332.80. A lot of money, considering Bix's treatment at Keeley came in the wake of the Stock Market Crash in October 1929.

Bix's pal Fritz Putzier saw positive improvements to Bix's health after he had sobered up. Earlier that summer, Fritz had seen Bix in Hollywood as Whiteman's train was preparing to take the band east. When they met up again in Davenport that winter, Putzier noted that Bix no longer had to use a cane to walk.

1930 wire story published in the *Davenport Daily Times*:

NUMBER OF KEELEY CURE PATIENTS HAS ALMOST
TREBLED SINCE PASSAGE OF PROHIBITION LAW

Dwight, IL. Apr 28—If the prohibition law has cut down the amount of heavy drinking that goes on in America, the news hasn't yet reached the Keeley Institute headquarters here.

...It is doing such a big business that its present quarters are too small. The one building it now occupies is to be replaced by three new ones just as soon as they can be made ready.

...Figures compiled in the office of Dr. James Henry Oughton, president of the institute show that the number of patients has steadily increased since prohibition until it now tops the average for pre–prohibition years.

...The institute is not getting any more women patients than it used to, and the average age of its patients hasn't changed since prohibition. If flaming youth is drinking more than it used to, it at least isn't taking the cure any oftener.

The average age of the patients is still what it used to be—41 years.

"There's one peculiar thing," says Dr. Oughton. "A greater proportion of our alcoholic cases now show mental disturbances than was the case in the old days.

This may be because the quality of the liquor now is worse or it may be because men get drunker now than they used to, I don't know.

"I do know this: Men who have taken the cure, gone home and then resumed drinking heavily so that they have had to come back to us for another course of treatments, tell me it's harder to lay off of liquor now than it used to be.

They're offered more.

The whole business of drinking is done differently.

"Men carry booze with them now, whereas before prohibition they rarely did. Consequently it's always accessible."

March 1931, *Melody Maker*:
>Paul Whiteman called a rehearsal for his band at the Granada Café, in Chicago. Paul appeared late, looking very sad and dejected. "Boys," he said, "I've just heard some bad news. BIX BEIDERBECKE was found wandering about the streets of New York yesterday, completely out of his mind. He's in a hospital now." Naturally everyone took this news with dismay, and several of the boys shook their heads sadly, and remarked what a shame it was.
>
>Just then, the door burst open, and who walked in but Bix, looking as well as ever.
>
>"Hello, fellows!" he called to the dumbfounded crowd, "How's everything?"
>
>Just now, Bix is in New York for a few days, considering a couple of offers.

American music scene news appeared a month out in the British–based *Melody Maker*. Bix had spent what would be his last Christmas and New Year's with his family, playing gigs with friends Larry Andrews and Les Swanson.

He'd been home again since having blacked out during a solo on a live broadcast of the Camel Pleasure Hour on October 8, 1930.

Bix slipped out of town without telling anyone in February 1931.

Through Joe Stroehle, Les Swanson learned why.

Turned out that Bix had gone on a three-day bender and ended up at Roxie's place where Henry 'Roxie' Auerochs recognized the cornet player from his performances at Danceland. A former cohort of tri-cities gangster John Looney, Auerochs had a broken nose from a stumble he took down the stairs at Danceland on New Year's Eve.

He operated out of his West Second flat between Ripley and Scott. At any sign of trouble the barkeep poured the booze down a funnel in a hole in the floor where a tube ran to the cellar. It was what they used to call a *blind pig*, not the kind of Prohibition saloon where folks came to hear jazz.

Speakeasies were too high-falutin' or *-verlooten* as Auerochs would have said. Roxie's catered to a hardcore clientele. But the barkeep took pity on Bix and got him sobered up before sending him home.

Bismark and Aggie must have found out anyway, because Bix was still apologizing when he wrote from New York on March 4, 1931: *"Dear Folks— you probably will tear this up before you read it because you must be disgusted with me, but I'll take a chance and write anyway...."*

He blamed a bout of tonsillitis for not writing his mom on her 61st birthday, March 1st. March 16th he wired birthday greetings and money to his dad: SPEND THIS ANYWAY YOU LIKE, AS LONG AS YOU TURN IT INTO BIRTHDAY GLADNESS. WARMEST CONGRATULATIONS. BIX.

Bix, himself, had turned 28 on March 10th. It's unknown how he celebrated what turned out to be his last birthday. Only work he was getting was some fraternity gigs with Benny Goodman and the Dorsey brothers.

"Poor Bix, he was going fast by then and we didn't realize it," recalled Dick Turner, who had been a fan since Bix's Wolverine days. They double dated when Ruby Keeler was Bix's date, Turner claimed.

Looking back to those final days, Turner told jazz historian Phil Evans: "Bix was a genius and a dying man and dedicated to getting something out of his soul that could only be expressed while he had that cornet in his face."

Jazz Is Captivating World, Says Previn

Radio Conductor Sees New Art Developing Here

CHARLES PREVIN

"JAZZ is captivating the entire world and we Americans far from being ashamed of it, should be proud of the remarkable development of this new and fascinating idiom."

This is the belief of Charles Previn, noted leader of the Camel Pleasure Hour orchestra, and regarded generally as one of the leading interpreters of syncopated music on the air.

"Passing completely from its elementary oompah and thump, thump stage, jazz has achieved the rank of an art," said Previn. "And a thoroughly distinctive, original art—a wholly American achievement."

OCTOBER 10, 1930

Great for Dancing

Indian Love Call
Huguette Waltz
    RUDOLF FRIML
        No. 22540, 10 in.
High Powered Mama
In the Jail House Now—No. 2
    JIMMIE RODGERS
        No. 22523, 10 in.
Sing Something Simple—Fox Trot
Lucky Seven—Fox Trot
    LEO REISMAN AND HIS ORCHESTRA
        No. 22538, 10 in.
Love is Like a Song—Fox Trot
Say "Oui," Cherie—Fox Trot
    LEO REISMAN AND HIS ORCHESTRA
        No. 22531, 10 in.
African Serenade—Fox Trot
I'll Be Blue, Just Thinking of You—Fox Trot
    NAT SHILKRET AND THE VICTOR ORCHESTRA
        No. 22529, 10 in.
I Don't Mind Walkin' in the Rain—Fox Trot
I'll Be a Friend "With Pleasure" —Fox Trot
    BIX BEIDERBECKE AND HIS ORCHESTRA
        No. 23008, 10 in.

Bix's last steady work came under the baton of CHARLES PREVIN, conductor of the *Camel Pleasure Hour* orchestra. The radio program premiered June 4, 1930. Previn later moved to Hollywood and became musical director for Universal Pictures; his German-born cousin, Andre Previn won four Oscars for his screen scores, including the film version of George Gershwin's *Porgy & Bess*. An October 1930 ad for Bix's recording of Maceo Pinkard's *I'll Be a Friend "With Pleasure"* includes releases by Victor Records orchestra conductor NAT SHILKRET. Besides getting Bix the radio job, he released Gershwin's first-ever recording of *Rhapsody in Blue*.

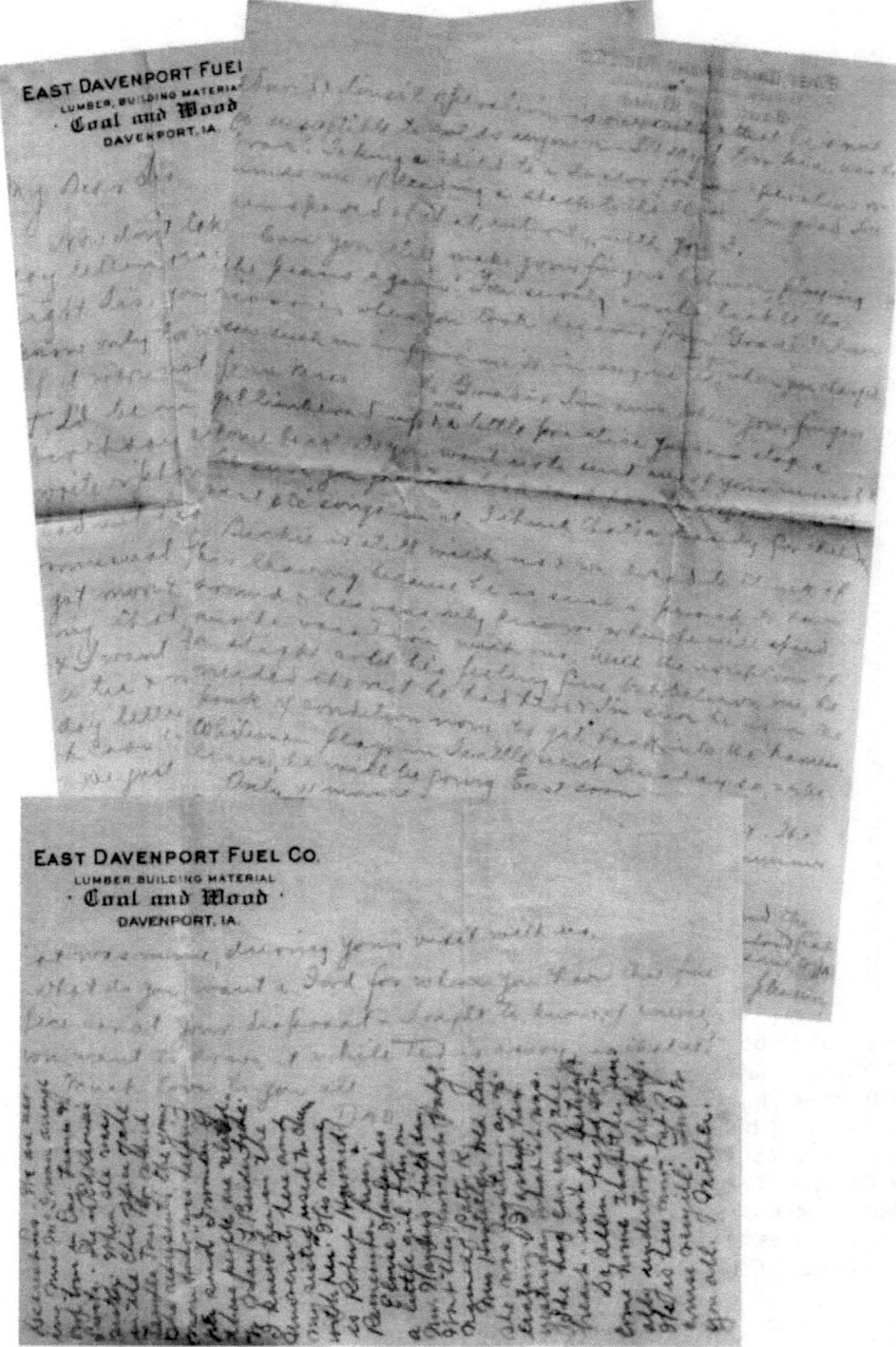

Transcript of Letter to Sis

Apr. 4 '30

My Dear Sis

Now don't take it so serious about having birthday letters reaching us just on the dot. That's all right Sis, you inherited that from your Dad. I know only too well how easily it can be overlooked. If it were not for my "calendar", Mother & Aunt T., I'd be in one h... of quandary every time a birthday came around, of those whom I should write or phone my congratulations to. But we had not heard from Mch. 3rd & being unusual for you to keep mum for so long, we got more & more nervous from day to day, thinking that perhaps you were sick. All is well now & I want to thank you & Ted for just my taste of a tie & mothers B.V.D's & also your dandy birthday letters & the one written on Mc.D Const. Co. letterheads (no date).

We just devour your descriptions of your darlings & their cute prattle. Thank the lord the water Bix spilled all over himself was not boiling — whew! What a close ___. If Ted slipped a pillow in a case, he can do more than I can. I'll give a lot to see and hear Bix saying big words, like minuet and Mother Goose rhymes & Ted singing in Sunday school. I hope both are entirely over their croups & am very glad that darn adenoid & tonsil operation is over with & that he is not so susceptible to colds anymore — I'll say! Poor kid. Was he brave? Taking a child to a doctor for an operation reminds me of leading a sheep to the block. I'm glad I've been spared of that, entirely, with you 3.

Can you still make your fingers behave playing the piano again? You certainly could tickle the ivories when you took lessons from Gradi(?) I never saw such improvement in anyone as in you when you changed from Mrs.— to Gradi. I'm sure when your fingers get limbered up with a little practice you can stage a "come back". Do you want us to send any of your music? Be sure you get that book that has "an elephant to the city went, etc." songs in it. I think that's a dandy for children.

Bickie is still with us & we dread to think of his leaving because he is such a peach to have around & heaven only knows when he will spend another vacation with us. With the exception of a slight cold he's feeling

fine but believe me, he needed the rest he had here & I'm sure he is in the pink of condition now get back into the harness. Whiteman plays in Seattle next Tuesday so, we believe he will be going East soon.

Only 11 more days & we leave Davenport. The time is dragging on just as it did last summer when we expected you & family.

Yesterday I raked the leaves from around the porch & under them I found 3 blocks, the celluloid fish, one green wooden marble & a wooden handle (off some toy) & I became real sentimental & thought back of the extreme pleasure that was mine during your visit with us.

What do you want a Ford for when you have that fine office car at your disposal—I ought to know, of course, you want to drive it while Ted is away, is that it?

Much love to you all,

DAD

New York Passenger Lists, 1820-1957

Name: **Adele Beiderbecke**
Birth: 25 Aug 1873 - Iowa
Departure: Hamburg, Germany
Arrival: 11 Aug 1930 - New York, New York

Name: **Agatha Beiderbecke**
Birth: 1 Mar 1870 - Iowa
Departure: Hamburg, Germany
Arrival: 11 Aug 1930 - New York, New York

Name: **Bismarck K Beiderbecke** *
Birth: 16 Mar 1868 - Iowa
Departure: Hamburg, Germany
Arrival: 11 Aug 1930 - New York, New York

Name: **Carl Beiderbecke**
Birth: 24 Dec 1864 - Iowa
Departure: Hamburg, Germany
Arrival: 11 Aug 1930 - New York, New York

* data base reads the H as a K

Passenger manifest of the S.S. Cleveland, docking in New York from Hamburg, Germany on August 11, 1930. Bismark & Aggie visited Bix in New York while he was performing on the Camel Pleasure Hour radio program; Carl and Adele, Bix's uncle and aunt, disembarked at Boston.

Dearest Sis—We are using Mrs. McGowan arranging tour in Eng, France & Switz. She is Ed Krouse's sister. When she was in the Chi office of the ___ Tour Co which she represents, the young man who was helping her said "I wonder if these people are related to Mary L. Beiderbecke—I knew her in the University here and my sister used to chum with her." His name is Robert Howard. Remember him?

Elvie Hanley had a little girl born on Mrs. Hanley's birthday. Won't they love that baby? Named Patty K.

Mrs. Hostetler told Dad she was fighting an operation. I asked her yesterday what it was. She has cancer of the heart—isn't that pitiful.

Dr. Allen begged so to come home that they finally undertook the trip. He is here now but of course very ill. Love to you all. Mother.

The BIX referred to here is Charles Bix Shoemaker, Mary Louise's middle child. Bismark still called his own son BICKIE. McD Const is McDougall Construction, the company in Atlanta where Ted Shoemaker worked before the Great Depression left him out of work and having to move the family to Davenport to live with his in-laws.

Bismark's and Aggie's references to their upcoming trip abroad seem to indicate they planned to visit Sis before departing for Europe. On their return via New York City in August they visited Bix while he was engaged with the Camel Pleasure Hour radio orchestra.

Mrs. Hostetler is Eugene Hostetler's wife Ella; cancer of the heart was a euphemism for breast cancer. Dr. Allen is William Allen, a retired surgeon who had been chief of staff at Davenport's St. Luke Hospital. In 1899, he invested his own money in getting the City's first electric streetcar line on the Brady Street hill.

The Government Bridge between Rock Island and Davenport before and after electric street railway line. This was the third bridge, built in 1896 and still standing to this day. Davenport was second only to Richmond, VA, in having electric streetcars, thanks to city benefactor W.L. Allen.

DOWN MEMORY LANE

A gold card member of the American Federation of Musicians, Leslie C. Swanson held the distinction of being the last surviving Quad City musician who played with both Bix Beiderbecke and Louie Bellson, fellow AFM Local #67 members.

Les played piano with the Trave O'Hearn Orchestra when Ronald *Dutch* Reagan worked for WOC radio, doing live remotes from the Blackhawk Hotel ballroom. When Reagan's career took him to California and eventually to the White House, the two men kept in touch through letters and holiday cards. They reconnected in 1992 when President Reagan visited his birthplace in Tampico, IL.

Les' friendship with Bix came during the last couple years of the cornetist's life. Many jazz scholars and Bix biographers sought Les out for insights on the man and his music. His own writing career began at the copy desk of the former *Davenport Daily Times.* He later published his writings on Americana. Topics included steamboat calliopes, river canals, old mills and covered bridges.

A book on riverboat gambling, published in 1991 when Les was in his 80s, coincided with Iowa's sanctioning of gaming boats. He was interviewed on national television by ABC's *Good Morning America* crew and played the calliope aboard Bettendorf's *Diamond Lady* for its inaugural cruise.

Seven decades as a professional musician began for Les while still in high school. Back then he played organ for silent movies at the Strand Theater in East Moline. Les learned to play ragtime from Evar Lofgren, who played at Moline's Avoy Theater. That was in 1918.

In the 1940s, Les played calliope and piano nightly aboard the *W.J. Quinlan* ferryboat. "We played while the boat was in motion but stopped when it docked."

He got his start on the riverboats in 1928 when Clarence *Heavy* Elder, purser and bandleader aboard Streckfus Line's *Washington*, contacted the local musicians union for someone to play the calliope. "I signed a contract but it was almost misrepresentation," Les said. "I knew nothing about playing a calliope. In fact, I had never even seen one."

His introduction to the steam piano came while the *Washington* still was in its winter dock at Nahant Harbor on the southwest outskirts of Davenport.

Les got a two–week crash course from former whopper Louie Bruhn of Rock Island. He quickly learned that ragtime and jazz tunes didn't work on a steam piano, producing only unintelligible rumbles. He had to stick to waltzes and foxtrots.

When his *Washington* contract ran out, he took a job with the Art Biddinger band in LaSalle, IL. But three months in Les bowed out. "Those road trips were murder," he said, adding that plenty enough job opportunities could be found right at home.

"In the '20s, there were forty to fifty local places that bands could play for dances on Saturday nights," he said. Among those where Bix played was Crow Creek Inn, a small nightclub in Pleasant Valley just outside Bettendorf.

"Every Saturday night for six years I played the Blackhawk Hotel. Prohibition was still on because I remember everybody bringing in a half pint and spiking Kingsbury beer."

Bix played some of those dates with him, Les said. He remembered their first gig together in December 1929. "I'd worked five or six years by then with the Trave O'Hearn Band at the Blackhawk Hotel in addition to my job as news reporter for the *Daily Times*.

"O'Hearn told us that Bix would be playing with us for our next fraternity dance. We were all amazed and thrilled. Bix didn't even bother to come to our rehearsal, but showed up with his horn and sat right there on the second trumpet chair.

"We didn't use any arrangements and he'd never heard us play before. I was amazed at how he could just follow along. This was after he'd been sent back by Paul Whiteman to recuperate.

"At Bix's invitation, I went to his parents' home on Grand Avenue. We compared notes on piano playing and then I drove him around town to some of the old spots where he'd played when he lived here.

"The next week we went to a movie together. I got to his house early and Bix wasn't ready so I talked to his mother who was the essence of culture and refinement. "Bix called down from upstairs and said, 'Play something on the piano, Les.' I played *In a Mist*, which Bix composed. Just about the time I finished, he came down and muttered something like 'very good,' but I don't think he was too impressed with my rendition."

When Les asked Bix to play the tune the way he intended it, Bix needed no further coaxing. "I noticed he was inserting a lot of new wrinkles to the whole thing. When he finished, I said to Bix 'it seemed that you were straying a little from the script in spots.' He laughed and replied, 'that's me...I never play anything the same way twice.'"

Bix went with Les to a couple prize fights at Wharton Field House. "Actually, I was covering them for the newspaper so we had front row seats. Bix really got into the action. He was yelling and carrying on. He enjoyed himself immensely.

"We went to Danceland one night to see Krazy Katz and His Kittens, a big-name band in those days. Of all the times I'd been with Bix, I'd never heard him mention anything about drinking, but that night some of his friends brought us a couple of drinks. I think it triggered what happened later while driving Bix home.

"We were nearing the Blackhawk Hotel and he started shivering and grabbing out and yelling, "I have to have it! I have to have it!"

"Pull over. I'll tell you in a minute," Bix said. There was a bootleg joint in the next block. He was back in five minutes with a sack.

"Bix pulled out a half pint of alcohol and said he was going to take it to bed with him. I kept that story a secret for 60 years."

Poppy Gardens was one of the places Bix recalled for Les from earlier days. The popular roadhouse stood on the banks of Green River just across

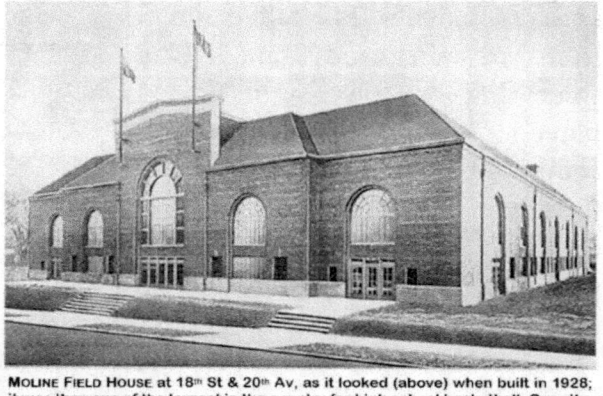

MOLINE FIELD HOUSE at 18th St & 20th Av, as it looked (above) when built in 1928; it was then one of the largest in the country for high school basketball. Over the years it hosted visiting entertainers, Easter sunrise services, Deere & Co.'s 100th anniversary, and professional wrestling watched by Les Swanson and Bix Beiderbecke. Renamed Wharton Field House in 1941 for the man who spearheaded its financing, the facility served in the late 1940s as home court for the Tri-City Blackhawks (now NBA's Atlanta Hawks)

Les Swanson with his *Tin Lizzy* in Sep 1929

1929
DEC 28 & 29 ⇒

BATTLE OF MUSIC
TONIGHT
15 — MUSICIANS — 15

Jimmy Hicks Orchestra — Danceland BALLROOM — Tony's Iowans

GENTLEMEN, 75¢   LADIES, 35¢

DANCING SUNDAY
Don't Fail to Hear "BIX"

⇐ **ROCK ISLAND ELKS DANCES**
'29 NEW YEAR'S EVE
'30 VALENTINE'S DAY

1930
JAN 1 – FEB 4 ⇓

DANCING TONIGHT
Danceland BALLROOM
JIMMY HICKS AND HIS ORCHESTRA
— Featuring —
"Bix" Beiderbecke
Hottest Trumpet Player in the Country
Gentlemen, 50¢   Ladies, 25¢

DEC 10 ⇒

Former Whiteman Soloist to Play At Eagles Dance

Bix Beiderbecke, former cornet soloist of Paul Whiteman's orchestra, will appear with Trave O'Hearn's band at the Moline Eagles hall Wednesday night. O'Hearn's orchestra is opening at the Eagles hall after a successful engagement by Jimmy Hicks and his orchestra.

Beiderbecke whose home is in Davenport, has returned to the tri-cities for the holidays. Since leaving Whiteman, Beiderbecke has been directing his own orchestra, which has filled many dance, radio and recording engagement in New York.

Right: Dec 23, 1928 Bix played several gigs with O'Hearn

Left: Crow Creek Bix played in 1929 with Jack Rogers

Jan 24-25, 1931 Bix with Cliff Mandy

March 1-9, 1930: Bix with Bob Tyldesley

Has Conducted Orchestra 61 Weeks at Hotel

TRAVE O'HEARN

Acclaimed as one of the leading orchestras of the vicinity, Trave O'Hearn and his musicians are entering on their sixty-first consecutive week at the Roof Garden of the LeClaire Hotel. This is the same orchestra which is heard over Station WOC every Tuesday, Wednesday, Thursday and Friday nights from eleven o'clock until midnight.

Mr. O'Hearn, the leader, has announced that the orchestra has been signed by the Columbia Phonograph Company to start recording in 1929. Among the first records to be made will be "Some Little Some-One," the number which they have made very popular here.

Previous to coming to the Tri-Cities Mr. O'Hearn and his players were in the Golden Pheasant, Cleveland; Nixon Cafe, Pittsburgh; Abraham Lincoln Hotel, Springfield, Ill., and at Joyland Park, Lexington, Ky.

The personnel of the orchestra is Chester Shaw, bass and voice; Tot Ensminger, drums; James Noble, piano; Ed Sidebotham, trumpet and melaphone; Warren Gregory, saxophone; John Schultz, saxophone, and Trave O'Hearn, saxophone.

the Burlington Railroad tracks at the south edge of Colona, Illinois. Poppy Gardens was *the* place to dance or listen to real jazz. The featured band there was Carlisle Evans.

Poppy Gardens sprang up around 1920. The roadhouse had a brief run of about three years and then came to a fiery finish in the summer of '23 when a blaze leveled the structure. Later that fall the Evans band showed up at the Friend's Circle Club in Moline's Old Towne.

"I played with practically all of Evans' guys in later years, but never had the pleasure of playing at the Poppy Gardens since I was still in high school," said Les. "I did see the place during its heyday while on a trip to Geneseo in 1922."

Besides the Trave O'Hearn band, Les played with Jack Willets, Ken Dick, Ken Paulson, Hi Morgan, and Jimmy Chase. Louis Bellson was Chase's drummer back then. Les also played with Pee Wee Hunt at the Col Ballroom when Hunt's piano player got sick.

"I remember Marian McPartland at the Flamingo with her trumpet-player husband Jimmy. The Horseshoe in Rock Island featured musicians like George Shearing, Father Hines and Jack Teagarden."

Les recalled St. Patrick's Day in 1930 when he played the Rock Island Elks with Bix. "After Bix got back from New York, we got a call from bandleader Jimmy Hicks. He said there was a job for a small four- or five-piece band in downtown Rock Island. I went down not knowing who was going to be there and waited around.

"I heard someone trolling up the stairs and there was Bix carrying some drums. I thought he was lugging them for the drummer so I asked him who was on drums. 'I am,' he answered. 'Did you ever play drums?' I asked. He answered, 'No.'

"We had Andy Anderson on sax, Bob Struve, the best trombone player around this area, Esten Spurrier on cornet, and Bix on drums. Bix wasn't too flashy, better than some guys I played with, and he could hold a tempo. On the last dance, Bix asked if he could play piano, so I ended up messing around on drums."

Neil Whiteside once told Les about what might well have been Bix's last public performance in the Quad Cities. "Neil was a member of the Cliff Mandy band in 1931 when Bix came up to the bandstand and asked to sit in for a number or two. Three hours later he was still there, apologizing because his lip wasn't stronger. During intermissions Bix spent the time doodling on the piano with his intricate spread chords. Shortly after that appearance Bix left Davenport and died five months later in New York."

The dates for Minnesota's Cliff Mandy Orchestra at the Col Ballroom in early 1931 were Saturday, January 24th and Sunday, the 25th. The band had an extended stay at the Col later that summer.

While recuperating from a virus in 1991 at St. Anthony's in Rock Island, Les crossed paths with reedman Leo Bahr (1908–1999) and as would be expected the two old friends reminisced about Bix. Bahr was with the Jimmy Hicks band at Danceland in 1931 and was on hand the night that Paul Whiteman's touring orchestra took the stage.

Midway through the program, Whiteman announced that Bix was in the crowd and asked if his old friend would come to the bandstand to take a bow. "Bix ignored Paul's summons," Leo said, "because he was too busy dancing with my wife Cheryl." Bix did make it to the bandstand later, he added.

After Leo Bahr passed away, Les became the sole remaining QC musician who had played with Bix. When folks gathered in 2003 to celebrate Bix's 100th birthday, Les was there and played a couple of numbers on the piano at Davenport's Blackhawk Hotel.

He was in a wheelchair and on oxygen because of a recent bout of pneumonia. But he had been determined not to miss the party. His daughter Vicki Wassenhove said Les told the doctor, "I'm going no matter what happens!"

Less than a month later, Les Swanson joined the band of the Great Beyond.

LES SWANSON at the piano with the Lee Johnston Band aboard the *Quinlan* ferryboat. That's Johnston on drums. Les' caption for this photo: This band was so hot they came equipped with a fire extinguisher. Les played aboard the *Quinlan* three seasons with these guys; the ferry was put in dry dock in Nov 1945.

Les Swanson
1905-2003

SATCHMO TOOTS BIX'S HORN

Bix's Vincent Bach Stradivarius cornet, along with the black pouch in which it was carried, is now in safe–keeping at Davenport's Putnam Museum. The cornet was purchased in May 1927 at the Hans Bach music store in New York. Actually, Bix bought two cornets. The one at the Putnam is Serial #0620, bell mandril #106, made of French brass and gold–plated.

This was the horn Aggie brought back with Bix's other personal belongings from the apartment in Queens where he died. The Bach horn eventually wound up with Bix's sister, Mary Louise Shoemaker, who showed it to Louis Armstrong when he visited her family while in Boston. *Boston Traveler* magazine published Matt Clark's account of Armstrong's visit for its January 17, 1958 issue: *He lovingly fingered the stiff keys of the tarnished old cornet. On the bell of the horn were engraved the words, "Bix, 1927."*

Mary Louise entrusted that cornet to Robert Mantler with the understanding that he would get it restored to working order. Instead Mantler, who worked for Victor Records, kept the horn. Several years passed until finally the Shoemakers had to get a court order for the horn's return in 1976.

Mary Louise's son Charles Bix Shoemaker sold Bix's cornet to Eva and Bob Christiansen of California in 1992 with a stipulation that it be returned after five years to Bix's hometown. The Christiansens made good on that

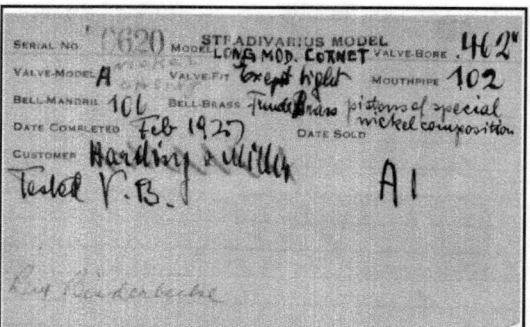

Date on the sales card indicates when the cornet was made. Bix purchased it in May 1927 while touring with Goldkette band. The horn & pouch are now at the Putnam Museum.

Leo Bahr holds Bix's Bach Stradivarius cornet while posed between Les Swanson and Bob Christiansen, who bought the horn from Bix's nephew, Charles Bix Shoemaker. As promised Bob returned the horn to Bix's hometown in 1997.

agreement in 1997 during the annual festival held in Bix's honor in Davenport.

Bix's brother Burnie had another of Bix's cornets, a JW Pepper Surprise model, Serial No. 38774 that he had retrieved from a Davenport pawn shop. The same year that Armstrong visited his sister Mary Louise, Burnie gave away their brother's Pepper model cornet to 8-year-old Gene Gast Jr., who pulled weeds for him at Oakdale Cemetery where he was the caretaker.

Gene's dad owned a music store in Bettendorf and was a cornet player in a local band. Gene Jr. said he had been turned on to Bix by Peter Maeller, a clarinetist in his dad's band.

The younger Gene said Burnie gave him Bix's horn because he was so impressed by young Gene's knowledge of his brother. He added that he plans to donate the JW Pepper Surprise cornet to the community. It will be added to the Beiderbecke collection at the Putnam.

J.W. Pepper Surprise model No. 38774. The cornet is owned by Gene Gast of Bettendorf and was given to him by Bix's brother Burnie.

Fritz Putzier, who had sold Bix his Conn Victor cornet, told of the time he and Bob Struve rode the train with Bix for a gig they had with Bill Greer's band in Sabula, IL, about 45 miles north of the Quad Cities. "Bix was sort of curled up on one seat, his head toward the window, probably propped on his CORNET CASE. The window was wide open and he was sound asleep with soot all over his face."

Despite this and several other references to Bix's cornet case and despite the existence of that pouch with the Bach cornet, stories persisted that Bix always carried his horn in a brown paper bag. Amateur film shot during the

Bix's image isolated from the Rhythm Jugglers group shot at Gennett Studio, where they recorded *Davenport Blues* on January 26, 1925

ABOUT BIX'S HORNS

Anytime Bix's name is mentioned some kind of controversy seems to arise. One we feel needs clearing up concerns the type of horn he played. As is well known, Bix's first horn was a short model cornet of either Wurlitzer or Carl Fischer make.

The cornet Bix was frequently photographed with was a Conn Victor long model cornet. This horn was given to him by Richard Putzier and was the horn he played all through his years with the Wolverines.

Mr. Vincent Bach states in a letter that Bix had acquired a Stradivarius model cornet. This was a short model. Mr. Bach at that time recommended and built for Bix a long model cornet that for nearly all of the rest of Bix's career, with few exceptions, was the horn he played through the Whiteman years, and during his last years in Davenport.

To clarify the picture a bit and to explain some of the differences, a short model cornet has a large bend in the lead pipe just beyond the third valve, with the tuning slide usually to the front of the horn. The long model cornet has the same basic dimensions and physical characteristics of a trumpet, making it a bit more brilliant in tone, as compared to the small model. This is the easiest way, we feel, to explain the differences.

The whereabouts of Bix's Bach long model cornet still remains a mystery.

Sincerely,

Don O'Dette
President, BBMS

bixiana
2225 West 17th St.
Davenport, Iowa 52804

After leaving Fred Waring, trumpeter Dude Skiles joined Jack Teagarden. He owned a San Antonio record store in '46.

1955

Around the Plaza
By RENWICKE CARY

At his next Sunday jam session at Club Hurricane, Dude Skiles will perform with a cornet which once belonged to the fabulous Bix Beiderbecke. The horn was a wedding present to Skiles in 1939 from a member of the Fred Waring orchestra, with which Skiles was playing at the time. Beiderbecke played the cornet when with the Paul Whiteman orchestra.

Dude Skiles, a trumpeter who went from the very bottom to the very top in less than two years, and who was here the other day on vacation from the Fred Waring band, heralds Emory Hammer of San Antonio as the finest tenor saxophonist in the South.

1936-37

Two San Antonio boys, by the way, are traveling in some very fast swing company in the West. They are Dude Skiles, trumpeter, and Bobby Skiles, guitarist, who played on the radio in a family band here for years. The Brothers Skiles were

heard last week with the famous Tommy Dorsey and others in the Los Angeles swing jam session.

1941
Dude Skiles Plays At Mountain Top Saturday Night

Dude Skiles and his orchestra have been engaged to play for

DUDE SKILES
Here with orchestra

dancing Saturday night at the Mountain Top Dinner club.

Dude, a San Antonio boy, plays the trumpet, and originally was with Bob Skiles and his Haywire orchestra.

In recent years, Dude crashed the big time dance business. For 2 1-2 years he played with Fred Waring's Pennsylvanians, and was heard in radio broadcasts with Johnny Green's orchestra for another two years.

This summer Dude is headquartering in San Antonio.

1926 Jean Goldkette tour, clearly shows Bix carrying a cornet case. Still, the paper bag myth lives on.

As with all legends, this one started with an actual event. George Crowe of Rock Island recalled the story to Jim Arpy in 1988:

"Those of us who were in bands were in the habit of meeting at Maehr's Confectionery, a downtown Davenport ice cream parlor. We were there one night while we were waiting for two or three cars to pick us up to take us to an engagement out in Northwest Davenport. Our instruments were piled up on the curb.

"The cars arrived rather hurriedly and we all piled in. But when we got where we were going and were ready to play, Bix discovered he didn't have his cornet.

"Well, Bix frantically caught a ride back downtown and looked all over for his horn, but it was gone. You can imagine how he felt, how much a part of his life that horn was to him. Bix was very forgetful. But he was very lucky. The next day he learned that someone had found it, evidently recognized it as Bix's horn, and had turned it in at the Martin Cigar store."

Another story shared with Jim Arpy in 1988, this from Moline musician Cy Churchill:

"Bix and I were the same age. I played in the Moline High School band at the same time he was in the Davenport High band and we'd occasionally see each other.

"Later, when I was playing professionally, Bix would come and sit in with us once in a while. I remember that he was doing a lot of drinking then. The local musicians weren't always impressed when Bix sat in with them. He played a very different style and didn't read music as most of them did.

"He'd just suddenly appear and sit in. That story about him carrying his horn in a paper sack is true. I saw him do it a couple of times, even into the LeClaire Hotel ballroom.

"And even though local bands weren't always thrilled to have Bix sit in because of his unusual style, they did know that he'd played with some pretty good musicians like Hoagy Carmichael and with Paul Whiteman's Orchestra for a while.

"But none of us ever imagined that Bix would become a legend. Such a thing never entered our minds."

Where Crowe recounted a specific event, Churchill provided more of a character sketch. He's all over the place time–wise. Bix didn't play in Davenport High's band because he couldn't read at that time. He did, however, play at Lake Forest Academy. Rather than pick at the details, consider the broad strokes in Churchill's story. He wasn't the only one to admit to feeling resentment and jealousy toward Bix. Check out Chet Salter's *Bix and the Future Hall of Famer* elsewhere in this book.

Facts and truth are not the same. Case in point: Louis Armstrong wasn't always accurate with the facts. Still, he never wavered in his true feelings toward Bix. Back to that *Boston Traveler* story from 1958:

> When I was playing at the Sunset in Chicago, he'd come in with his horn. When all the cats left we'd lock the door and jam all night. Our styles were different but he was one of the greatest. That's all I can say. Bix always played fresh. He had changes in his mind and knew where he was going all the time. A real serious kid, you know. Kids today don't dig that. Take that solo in *From Monday On*, with Whiteman. Just 16 bars of the most beautiful thing I ever heard.

Only two years older, Armstrong's image of Bix remained that kid musician, never aging even as his legend grew.

Les Swanson recalled an afternoon spent with Armstrong and His All Stars band in May 1950. They were in town that week to play Rock Island's Horseshoe nightclub. All that remains of the former club is a horseshoe embedded in the sidewalk on Rock Island's Second Avenue.

But Les managed to capture and preserve history in a photo of Armstrong and bandmates: Jack Teagarden, trombone; Arvell Shaw, bass; Earl 'Fatha' Hines, piano; Barney Bigard, clarinet; and Bill 'Cozy' Cole, drums.

A commercial photographer, Les had a studio in Rock Island where he specialized in weddings and children's portraits. He grabbed his camera

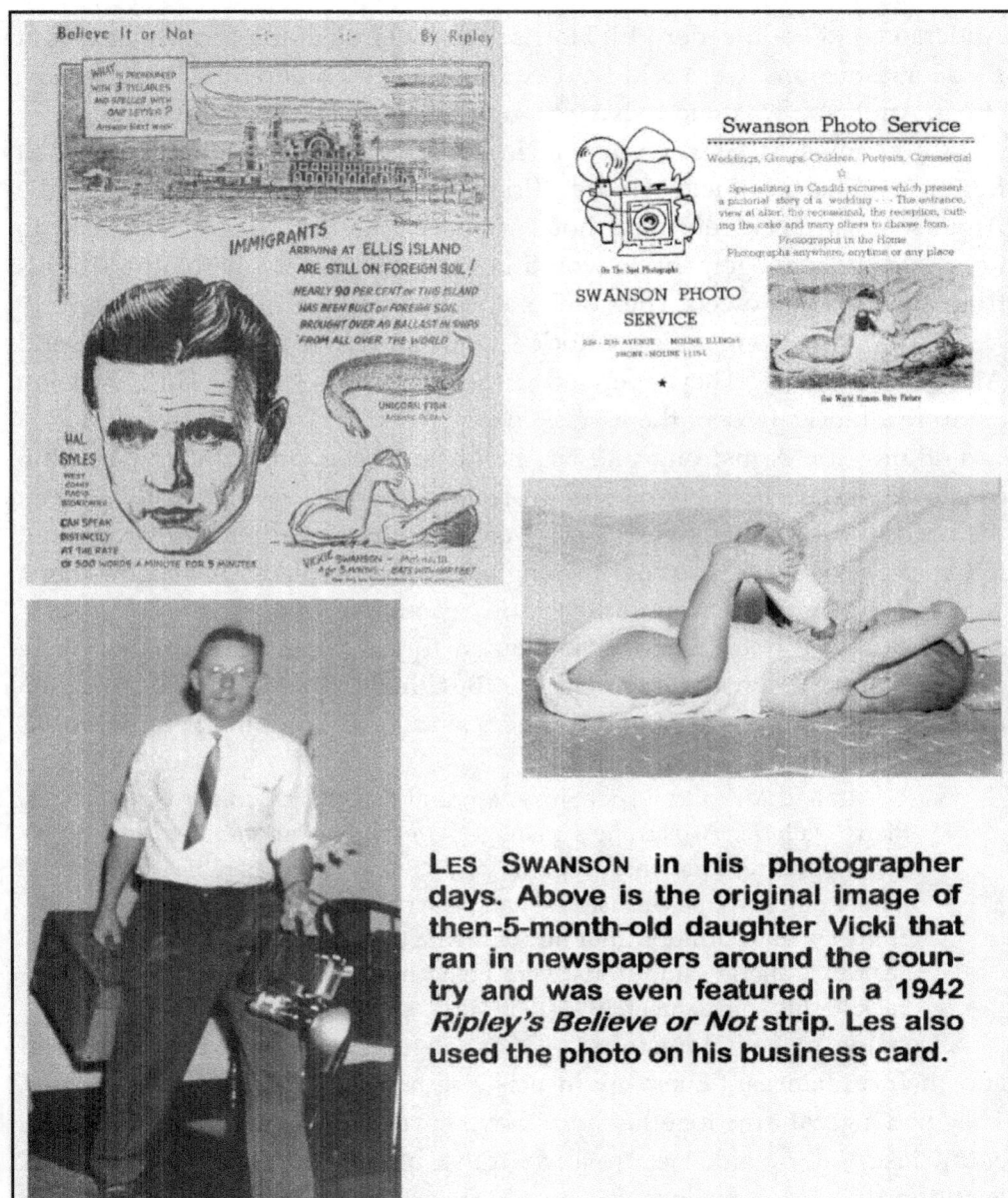

LES SWANSON in his photographer days. Above is the original image of then-5-month-old daughter Vicki that ran in newspapers around the country and was even featured in a 1942 *Ripley's Believe or Not* strip. Les also used the photo on his business card.

and "accompanied Satchmo's group across the river to Davenport to radio station WOC where the band performed and Louis was presented the Key to the City."

A *key to the city* did not necessarily open hotel doors back in 1950. Or so that's the story as it involves Jack Benny's sidekicks Eddie 'Rochester'

Anderson and bandleader Phil Harris. They went looking for Armstrong at the Horseshoe and were told he'd be found at the funeral parlor down the street. Anderson was said to have thought the worst had happened.

Jack Benny's All Star Revue was in town for a one–night appearance at Moline's Wharton Field House. Prior to their QC appearance, Eddie Anderson had been refused a hotel room in Missouri. Benny was said to have told the management he would not stay at a hotel where others in his troupe were not allowed. The hotel relented and gave Anderson a room.

During Armstrong's gig in Rock Island, he was a guest of George and Alysine Nicholson. They operated a mortuary in a century–old mansion about five blocks west of the Horseshoe.

Lodging for Armstrong and his band had been pre–arranged by club owner Al Barnes. Possibly he was protecting the musicians. Possibly, he felt the need to protect his investment. A couple months earlier Armstrong had left Spokane, WA, without performing after being denied hotel rooms there. Newspapers here and around the country ran the wire story.

The Spokane hotel manager explained to the press: "He said we were discriminating against colored people. But that's not true. He wanted ten rooms and we simply did not have them since he did not make reservations for the entire band."

> Mr. and Mrs. Orvil [sic] Shaw, Mr. and Mrs. Barney Bigard and Pierre Tallerie, Armstrong's manager, were given rooms because they had reservations. Bigard and Shaw are members of Armstrong's troupe. Armstrong had been booked to play at a dance at the Spokane armory…but he boarded a train and headed back to Seattle…Tallerie said efforts were being made to bring 'Satchmo' back for his engagement. [3–4–1950 UP]

According to Les, Armstrong's QC engagement pleased both the band and their audiences. "Every night was one big jam session for this group. They had a great time together and I have never witnessed such hilarity and enthusiasm," Les said. He drove the guys back from Davenport to Rock Island in time for their opening show. "The place was packed with a crowd of 200 or more waiting for some great jazz and I'll tell you right now, they were not disappointed! The old Horseshoe fairly rocked. Extra seating was added, yet people were standing five and six deep around the bar. Unfortunately, I didn't catch the act more than a few times since we had small children then that curtailed night–clubbing."

Les sent *Holiday* magazine rep Charlie Barnett a group shot of him and Armstrong's band at the WOC studio. The photo was published by the

ALL STARS, L-R: Jack Teagarden, Earl 'Fatha' Hines, Charlie Barnett of Curtis Pub, Louis Armstrong, Cozy Cole, Barney Bigard and Arvell Shaw

June 1950 issue of *Holiday* magazine, seen in above publicity photo shot by Les Swanson at Radio Station WOC

Saturday Evening Post. Both the *Post* and *Holiday* magazines were owned by Curtis Publishing Co of Philadelphia, which also owned *Ladies Home Journal* and the children's magazine *Jack and Jill*.

Armstrong requested and received a couple dozen copies of the photo, now a historic image that has been widely circulated but without Les getting photo credit.

A BIT OF THE MACABRE

Jack Teagarden was dumbfounded one summer night when Bix suggested they visit, of all places, the grim Bellevue morgue in New York City.

That was the last place Teagarden wanted to show up, even at high noon, but Bix wheedled and persisted and at last the two set out for the place. He later recalled: "it must be the most gruesome morgue in the world that place. But there we were.

"Bix slipped the night caretaker a $5 bill to let us through and in we went."

Though some have since surmised Bix might have had a fascination with death, or a premonition of his own approaching early death, Bix had a more matter-of-fact reason for the visit. He told Teagarden his brother Burnie had written from Davenport that he was going into the cemetery business and Bix wanted to do some independent research for him.

Bix also loved a lark and a practical joke, and likely just wanted to scare the trusting Teagarden. But the joke was on Bix because as it turned out Teagarden managed to survive with his stomach contents intact. Bix did not.

BIX TRIED TO GET ME UP THERE

27 June 1959: SPOLETO, Italy—Louis 'Satchmo' Armstrong appeared to have rallied Thursday from a grave attack of pneumonia and was chuckling over telegrams of good cheer that lined the wall above his bed at the civic hospital here Friday.

Watched over by Dr. Giovanni Coata and English-speaking nurse Anna Venturini, Armstrong told U.S. television star Ed Sullivan over the telephone: "Yesterday was the rough day. But now I think Pops is in the clear."

Sullivan had called to wish Armstrong well before leaving this central Italian town where he had been taping performances at the Two Worlds Festival. Organized by maestro Gian-Carlo Menotti, the festival was to have featured a performance by Armstrong.

The jazz king was told by Sullivan that American soprano Eileen Farrell had filled in for him, performing "Sunny Side of the Street" with Armstrong's band during a taped segment that will be featured on Sullivan's television show next month.

Maestro Menotti, whose Christmas opera 'Amahl and the Night Visitor' premiered in 1951 on the NBC television network, has twice received the Pulitzer award for his original operas.

The festival being held in his home town featured an international cast of musicians, singers and dancers....

Reporters, who were admitted to Armstrong's room today, were told that the hospital's famous guest had rested well overnight and was feeling much better. As if to prove it, Armstrong held his wife Lucille's hand and hummed, 'On the Sunny Side of the Street,' and said, "I can still play that."

When asked about his illness, Armstrong told the reporters: "I ain't never been an invalid—sick like this—before."

He then joked with them that, "Bix tried to get me up there to play first horn," referencing late trumpeter Bix Beiderbecke who died of pneumonia almost three decades ago. As if to make the point that he didn't plan on booking a gig with Bix any time soon, Armstrong pulled himself up and sat on the edge of the bed with his legs dangling over the side. He was wearing lightweight cotton shorts and a shirt with Hawaiian designs. "I'm feeling stronger than ever," he said.

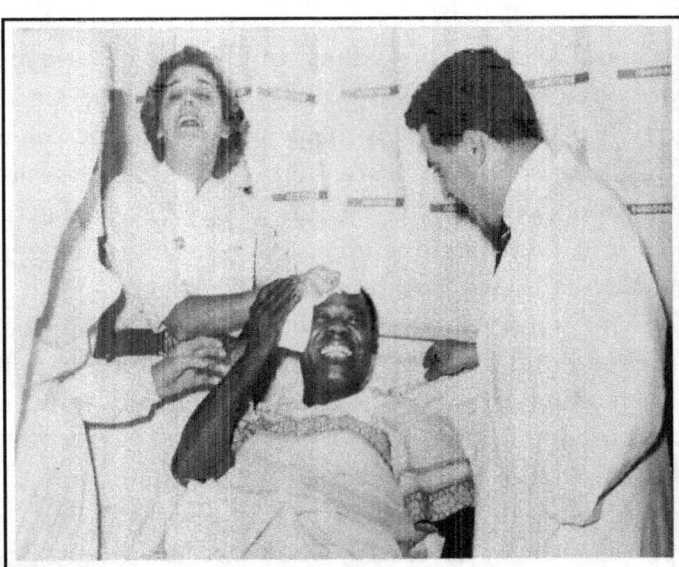

June 1959—hospitalized for pneumonia, Armstrong said, "Bix tried to get me up there to play his first horn." Right: with his personal physician in a wire photo that ran in the *Democrat-Leader*. Below: Opera singer Eileen Farrell launched her pop career with Armstrong's band in Italy.

SADLY, THE FORTUNETELLERS WERE RIGHT

When a celebrity dies young, myths true or false are certain to follow. Some are obvious concoctions; others perhaps true, or with a grain of truth, but devilish to track down many years after the celebrity's demise. Certainly this holds true with Bix Beiderbecke. His legends are legion.

Among the many legends about Bix is the one about him and Don Murray, both 19 at the time, encountering some gypsies while playing a gig at Northwestern University near Chicago.

The gypsies supposedly were roaming about the campus telling fortunes for food and lodging. But when Bix and Don approached them and asked for readings, the gypsies shook their heads, murmured, "No, no, forget it," and tried to leave.

This only intrigued the young men more and they followed the gypsies, pressing them to reveal what the future held in store for them. Finally bowing to their insistence, the gypsies reluctantly agreed and, as Bix and Don supposedly repeated to friends later, murmured something like: "We see that both of you will suffer early deaths. We cannot tell you more. And remember that we did not tell you this."

Bix and Don had a good laugh over the prediction. But one wonders if the prophecy came back to Bix seven years later when, in 1929, he read the newspaper headline that told of Don Murray's sudden death in California.

On the boardwalk in Atlantic City, 1927
Bix playfully chokes pal Don Murray

Murray had gone to Hollywood with the Ted Lewis Band to do a film, ironically titled: *Is Everybody Happy?* After production wrapped, Murray supposedly had been standing on the running board of a car and for reasons unknown, possibly from having been drinking, he toppled backwards and struck his head on the curb. He died later in the hospital.

Bix's interview on jazz, published Feb 10, 1929, in *Democrat-Leader* while he was home recuperating from a break-down the previous November in Cleveland, OH.

December 1929 ad for the movie featuring Bix's pal Don Murray, who died shortly after shooting wrapped; Bix learned of his death while enroute to California with Whiteman.

Don Murray held a special place in Bix's heart. They had bonded through shared experiences in their musical careers. In particular, they had witnessed history in the making by being in the studio when Jelly Roll Morton recorded with the New Orleans Rhythm Kings—first known interracial recording session.

When Don's movie played at Davenport's Garden Theater, Esten Spurrier went with Bix to see it New Year's Day of 1930. Spurrier said Bix asked him along because he didn't have it in him to watch it alone.

Later that day, Bix visited Ferd and Vera Cox Korn at her parents' home. Vera was now mother to a 15-month-old son. She and her husband had seen Bix the night before when he played at the Rock Island Elks New Year's Eve dance. They invited Bix to come see their boy and he showed up with a bag of peanuts as a gift for him.

A decade or so later Vera was introduced to a jazz historian by Fred Flick, a one-time banjo player with the Carlisle Evans Band. Flick's mother Alvina was a highly regarded pianist who played in several local orchestras and taught piano in Moline.

The historian introduced by Flick was Belgian artist Robert Goffin, then on an American cross-country trip to collect material for his French-language *History of Jazz* book. At the time of Goffin's visit, Moline had the second largest Belgian population in America and its own Belgian consulate's office.

Flick had arranged for Vera to meet with Goffin at Moline's LeClaire Hotel. As they chatted, she opened up to him about her last time seeing Bix. Maybe it was that Goffin was writing for a European audience, whatever the reason Vera opened up to him about the man behind the legend.

She told how on that New Year's Day back in 1930 Bix had seemed melancholy, maybe even bitter about how things had turned out, Goffin wrote in his book. He quoted Vera as saying that Bix contemplated a different life, maybe a better one had he been a husband and a father.

In his later autobiography, Goffin wrote that Vera admitted to him that she and Bix had briefly been engaged, but she said she would not talk about it because of her husband's jealousy.

Bix missed his chance with Vera, as he had with Angela and Ruth. By the time he met Helen or Alice, whoever it was in that photo his mother found among his things in his New York apartment, Bix was on course to fulfill what had been foretold by gypsies.

That is, if one is inclined to believe in fortunetellers. And if so, does one

(July 30/31) Thursday —

Dearest Falko: —
By now you have Alexis picture — what do you think of her? We're together constantly — I dragged her in and of those photo-studios on B'way — for a buck we had that made + enlarged. The little sweetheart framed it, packed it, and sent it to you — given she knew you wanted it —

Bickie's letter, never finished

A 25901

STATE OF NEW YORK
Department of Health of The City of New York
BUREAU OF RECORDS
STANDARD CERTIFICATE OF DEATH 5304

1 PLACE OF DEATH: Queens
No. 4330 – 46th St
Character of premises (tenement, private, hospital or other place, etc.): Apartment House

2 FULL NAME: Leon Bix Beiderbecke

3 SEX: M
4 COLOR OR RACE: W
5 SINGLE, MARRIED, WIDOWED, OR DIVORCED: Single
15 DATE OF DEATH: Aug. 6, 1931

5A WIFE / HUSBAND OF: —
6 DATE OF BIRTH: March 10, 1903
7 AGE: 28 yrs.

8 OCCUPATION: Musician

9 BIRTHPLACE: Davenport, IA
(9A) How long in U.S.: Life
(9B) How long resident in City of New York: 3

10 NAME OF FATHER: Bismarck
11 BIRTHPLACE OF FATHER: Davenport, IA
12 MAIDEN NAME OF MOTHER: Agatha Hilton
13 BIRTHPLACE OF MOTHER: Davenport, IA

16 I hereby certify that the foregoing particulars (Nos. 1 to 14 inclusive) are correct as near as the same can be ascertained, and I further certify that I attended the deceased from Aug 4 1931 to Aug 6 1931, that I last saw him alive on the 6 day of Aug 1931, that death occurred on the date stated above at 9:30 P.M., and that the cause of death was as follows:

Lobar Pneumonia

duration yrs. mos. 3 ds.
Contributory (Secondary):

Witness my hand this 7 day of Aug 1931
Signature: John J. Haberski, M.D.
Address: 4330 46th St, Sunnyside L.I.

FILED AUG 8 1931

17 PLACE OF BURIAL: Oak Dale Cemetery, Davenport, Iowa
DATE OF BURIAL: August 10th, 1931

18 UNDERTAKER: Michael J. Kimmel
ADDRESS: 39-44-58 , Woodside, L.I.
#1608

5304

TO PHYSICIANS

1. The attending physician must furnish a certificate to the Department of Health within 36 hours after death, and where death has resulted from infectious or contagious disease a certificate must be furnished by him **forthwith** (Sanitary Code, Sections 33 and 90).

2. All physicians practicing in The City of New York (including those in public institutions) must be registered in the Bureau of Records (Sanitary Code, Section 218).

3. If a person dies from **criminal violence** or by a **casualty** or by **suicide**, or **suddenly while in apparent health**, or when **unattended by a physician** or in prison, or in any **suspicious or unusual manner**, it shall be the duty of any citizen who may become aware of the death of any such person to report such death forthwith to the office of the chief medical examiner, and to a police officer who shall forthwith notify the officer in charge of the station house in the police precinct in which such person died. Any person who shall willfully neglect or refuse to report such death or who without written order from a medical examiner shall willfully touch, remove or disturb the body of any such person, or willfully touch, remove, or disturb the clothing, or any article upon or near such body, shall be guilty of a misdemeanor. (Inserted by Laws 1915, Chapter 284, Section 2. In effect January 1, 1918.)

4. **Certificates will be returned for additional information** which give any of the following diseases, without explanation, as the sole cause of death:

Abortion,	Hemorrhage,	Meningitis,	Phlebitis,
Cellulitis,	Gangrene,	Metritis,	Pyaemia,
Childbirth,	Gastritis,	Miscarriage,	Septicaemia,
Convulsions,	Erysipelas,	Peritonitis,	Tetanus.

(Any one of these may be the result of an injury, and thus be a subject for investigation by a Medical Examiner. If it is not, the certificate should make that fact plain.)

5. No certificate giving "**Heart failure**," "**Dropsy**," or other mere symptom as the sole cause of death will be accepted, unless accompanied by a satisfactory written explanation.

6. **Statement of Occupation.**—Precise statement of occupation is very important, so that the relative healthfulness of various pursuits can be known. The question applies to each and every person, irrespective of age. For many occupations a single word or term on the first line will be sufficient, e. g., *Farmer* or *Planter, Physician, Compositor, Architect, Locomotive Engineer, Civil Engineer, Stationary Fireman*, etc. But in many cases, especially in industrial employments, it is necessary to know (a) the kind of **work** and also (b) the nature of the **business or industry**, and therefore an additional line is provided for the latter statement; it should be used only when needed. As examples: (a) *Spinner*, (b) *Cotton Mill*; (a) *Salesman*, (b) *Grocery*; (a) *Foreman*, (b) *Automobile Factory*.

TO UNDERTAKERS

1. No burial permit can be obtained without a proper certificate.

2. Certificates must be written throughout in black ink.

3. No certificate will be accepted which is mutilated, illegible, inaccurate, or any portion of which has been erased, interlined, corrected or altered, as all such changes impair its value as a public record.

I hereby certify that I have been employed as undertaker by *Agatha Biederbecke* (NAME) the *Mother* (RELATIONSHIP) of deceased. This statement is made to obtain a permit for the burial or cremation of the remains of deceased *Leon Biederbecke*.

Signature *Michael J. Kimm*

also give credence to the tale told by Larry Andrews in *Storyville* magazine in 1967?

Bix's pal since their days at Tyler School, Andrews learned of Bix's death from reading about it in the newspaper. At the time Andrews was working for an insurance firm in Storm Lake, Iowa. He claimed to have met the medium by happenstance while calling on a client. The medium had a message for him from Bix which supposedly was *"tell Helen that he couldn't understand why that had to happen now."* Andrews insisted he didn't know anyone named Helen associated with his friend Bix. Nevertheless, the medium insisted, he said, that the message be passed along to Bix's folks.

On a list Aggie made of cards that came with the funeral flowers—no doubt to send thank-you cards later—there are entries for the Weiss Family of New York and Alice O'Connell of New York.

Researchers have hunted in vain for this mystery woman from Bix's final days. Hoagy Carmichael recalled spending an evening with Bix and a woman Bix introduced as Helen Weiss. Prior to that Bix had written home about his engagement to Alice O'Connell in a letter dated June 16, 1931. He wrote the letter while recuperating at the New York home of Rex Gavitte, bassist for the Smith Ballew Orchestra—the band Bix played with at Princeton, just before his death in a rental flat in Queens. According to the building's landlord, Helen Weiss secured the apartment for Bix.

Hoagy claimed it was Helen Weiss who gave him the handkerchief and a pair of mismatched cufflinks that Bix wore during the Princeton gig, according to the letter accompanying these items donated by him in the early '60s to the jazz museum in New Orleans.

Given the doggedness of Bix Beiderbecke researchers, it is quite a feat for anyone associated with Bix to have carried her secret to the grave.

CROWD SCANT AT BIX'S FUNERAL

Kenneth Peterson of Bettendorf played piano at Bix's funeral. "I was working for the Hill & Fredericks Funeral Home," he recalled, "I was just 21 years old and had been with them about 10 months."

The former chapel at 13th and Brady Streets in Davenport today houses an assortment of radio stations and offices. Peterson remembered the interior of the chapel: "The main entrance was off Brady Street and as you entered there was an aisle leading to the front, with rows of seats on both sides. The casket was placed on a pedestal in the front and center of the room. The music room was to the front left of the chapel, with windows placed so the pianist could see both the minister and the audience. We always played hymns back then. I'm sorry but I don't remember which hymns the family requested, but I do remember that the minister was Presbyterian and the burial was private," he added.

1920s ad for mortuary that handled funeral services for Bix, his brother, both parents and Oma Louise Beiderbecke

Below: as it looked when Aggie died. Today it is home to Cumulus Quad Cities Radio

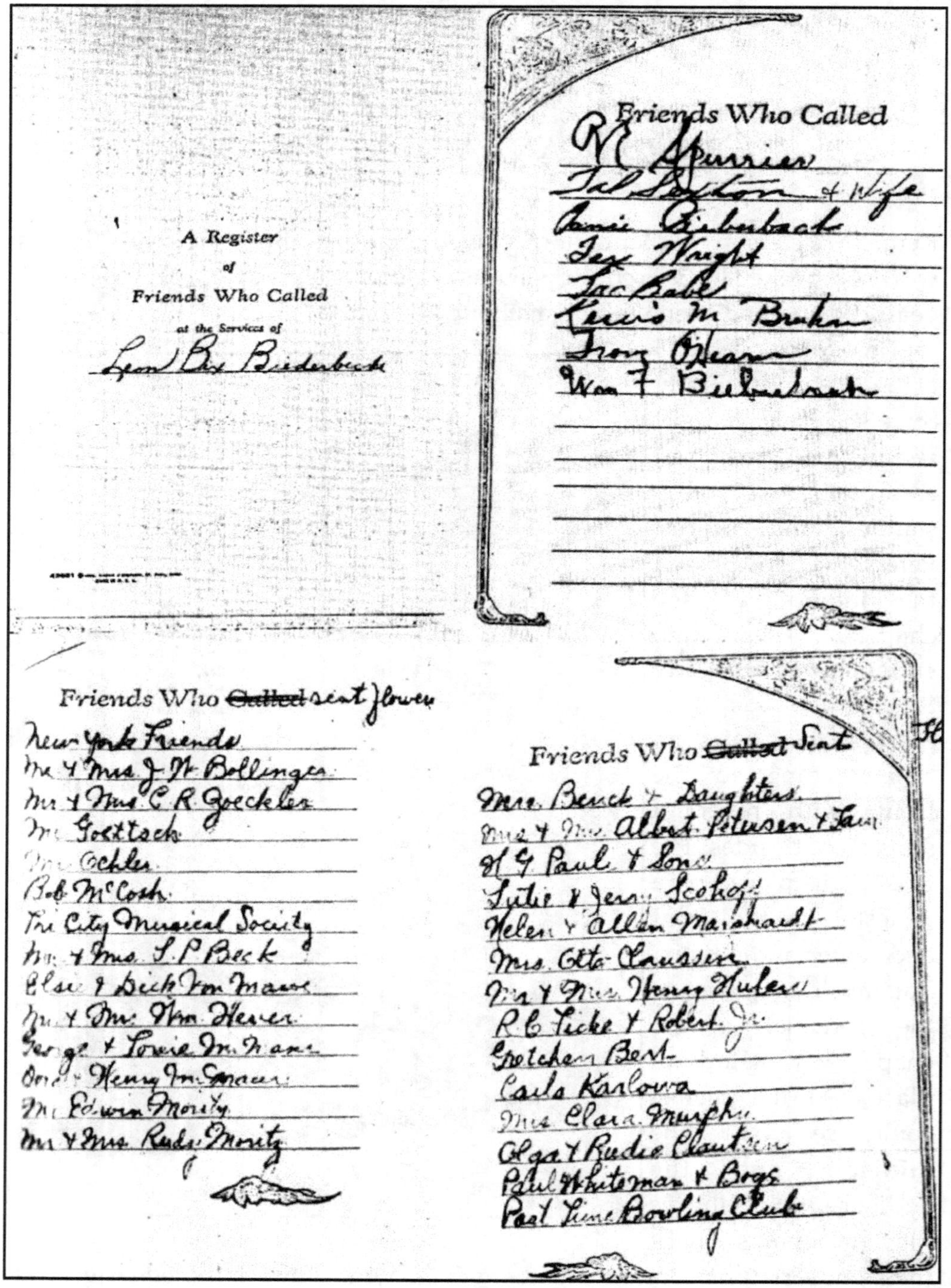

A Register
of
Friends Who Called
at the Services of
Leon Bix Beiderbecke

Friends Who Called

- M. Spurrier
- Ted Sexton & Wife
- Amie Biebenbach
- Tex Wright
- Jac Rabel
- Lewis M Braken
- Tony O'Hearn
- Wm F Biebenbach

Friends Who ~~Called~~ sent flowers

- New York Friends
- Mr & Mrs J N Bollinger
- Mr & Mrs C R Goeckler
- Mr Gottsch
- Mr Ochler
- Bob McCosh
- Tri City Musical Society
- Mr & Mrs S P Beck
- Elsie & Dick Von Maur
- Mr & Mrs Wm Heuer
- George & Lorrie Von Maur
- Dr & Mrs Henry Von Maur
- Mr Edwin Moritz
- Mr & Mrs Rudy Moritz

Friends Who ~~Called~~ Sent

- Mrs Beuck & Daughters
- Mr & Mrs Albert Petersen & Fam
- H G Paul & Sons
- Lutie & Jerry Scokoff
- Helen & Allen Maischaedt
- Mrs Otto Claussen
- Mr & Mrs Henry Huber
- R C Ticke & Robert Jr
- Gretchen Bert
- Carlo Karlova
- Mrs Clara Murphy
- Olga & Rudie Claussen
- Paul Whiteman & Boys
- Pastime Bowling Club

When asked if he was aware then who Bix was in the music world, Ken laughed and replied, "No, I didn't know who he was," then added, "and considering that just one-third of the chapel was filled that day, evidently the people of Davenport didn't know who he was either."

Peterson was 93 at the time of this interview, still plying his trade at Runge Mortuary and Crematory in Davenport. "Thus far, I've played for 23,000 funerals," he said, "and since 1960 I've kept a log of every song I've played. Funeral music has changed through the years. So now if I play for one of every three I'm lucky. Today families bring in CDs or taped favorites of their departed loved ones."

Had he ever played or listened to any of Bix's piano compositions? He replied that he hadn't but would be willing to give them a try. Then he added with a grin, "You're never too old to try."

In a 1985 letter to the Class of '23 alumni, Warren Postel wrote that Fritz Putzier, Wayne Rohlf, and Esten Spurrier should have been Bix's pallbearers "but were not asked for some reason or other by the family. There were no jazz musicians. My father sent me a clipping from the Davenport Democrat and the only mention that associated Bix with this new art form was a mention that Paul Whiteman had sent a 6 foot tall cornet done in roses."

Harold Oerman attended the visitation and noted the huge floral display with its tag "From Paul Whiteman and the boys." He also recalled, *"Bix was laid out clad in a light gray tweed suit with a colorful necktie, the first time I had ever seen a corpse clothed in anything other than somber black. It was most befitting."*

Bix's Funeral Book—People Who Called:
Esten Spurrier—childhood friend of Bix, and noted cornetist in his own right
Tal Sexton and his wife—trombonist with Catalano and Evans
Ernie Bieberbach
Tex Wright—probably Foster Wright, another musician
Joe Rabe—family friend
Lewis M. Bruhn—pianist with Jimmy Hicks Orchestra
Trave O'Hearn—local band leader
Wm F. Bieberbach

Friends* Who Sent Flowers:
Mr. & Mrs. H.O. Seiffert
Mrs. A.J. (Ottilie) Stibolt
Mrs. M. (Lutie) Von Binzer

Oakdale

Alice O'Connell, N.Y. [Bix wrote that he and Alice were engaged]
Weiss Family, N.Y. [Bix introduced Helen Weiss to Hoagy Carmichael]
Sis & Ted Shoemaker
Theda & Robert Wagner [Tri–City Symphony board president]
Mrs. Isaac Deutsch [Rebecca, wife of former ad man for Burtis & Grand theaters]
Mrs. Arthur Cassling [Helen Tefft, wife of Augustana College vocal dept head]
Mrs. C. Baker [Lillian, wife of dentist Charles Baker]
Mrs. J.H. Hass [Emma, mother–in–law of Otie Stibolt Hass]
Clara 'Lalle' Kruse [wife of architect Walter Kruse; sister–in–law of Otie Stibolt Hass]
Mr. & Mrs. James Bollinger [district court judge]
Charles & Margaret Zoeckler [banjo player & stationer]
Arthur Goettsch [E. Dav. Coal clerk]
Adolph Ochler [Seiffert Lumber clerk]
Bob McCosh [E. Dav. Coal salesman]
Tri–City Musical Society [local musician's union]
Mr. & Mrs. Louis P. Best [son of Paul Best; grandson of Louis Best]
Elsie & Dick Von Maur [son of Charles & Mary; cousin of George]
Mr. & Mrs. Wm. Hubers [Rock Island Fuel Co.]
George & Lorie Von Maur
Dorothy & Henry Von Maur [parents of George]
Edwin Moritz [Hub Men's Clothing]
Mr. & Mrs. Rudy Moritz [Hub Men's Clothing]
Mrs. [Clifford] Busch & daughter [Mabel and Eunice, neighbors]
Mr. & Mrs. Albert (Carrie) Petersen & Family
H.G. Pauli & Sons [florist]
Lutie & Jerry Seehof [cousin]
Helen & Allen Marquardt [cousin]
Mrs. Otto Claussen [Evaline; husband owned Brammer Mfg, home appliances]
Mr. & Mrs. Henry Hubers [wife Adele; son of William & Clara Hubers]
R.C. Ficke & Robert Jr. [neighbors]
Gretchen Best [sister of Louis Best]
Carla Karlowa [widow of Robert Karlowa]
Klara Murphy [daughter of Paul Karlowa]
Olga & Rudie Clausen [daughter & son of architect Fred Clausen]
Paul Whiteman & Boys
Past Time Bowling Club [Burnie's bowling league]

*Spelling corrected from original and errors made later by someone tracing over faded registry.

GRAND PLAYERS WILL ARRIVE IN CITY NEXT WEEK

"Why Men Leave Home" to Be First Opening Here on Sept. 19.

"Why Men Leave Home" will be the first offering of the Berkell Players when that organization reopens the Grand theater on Sunday, Sept. 19. The play is a comedy by Avery Hopwood and scored a decided hit when it was presented by the company at Indianapolis during the summer season.

Members of the Berkell Players will arrive in Davenport early next week following the close of the season at Indianapolis Saturday. William Bieberbach will be director of the orchestra which will be known as the Grand theater orchestra. Mr. Bieberbach will direct and play the cornet. Willard Newark will play the piano, Richard Moeller, drums, Ernie Bieberbach, trombone, Bud Hance, saxophone and violin, and Leo Barr, saxophone and clarinet.

W. F. Bieberbach Dies; Funeral Is Thursday

Tuesday, July 20, 1965

William F. Bieberbach, 67, of 723 Taylor St., Davenport, who formerly was a supervisor with the Rock Island Arsenal, died Monday evening in the Davenport Nursing Home.

A life resident of the city, Mr. Bieberbach had retired from the Arsenal two years ago.

Formerly he had played the trumpet for local dance bands.

He had never married.

A veteran of World Wars I and II, Mr. Bieberbach was a member of the American Legion Post No. 26, the Knights of Columbus No. 532, and the 40 & 8.

He is survived by a brother, Ernest A., of Davenport.

Funeral services will be at 10 a.m. Thursday in St. Mary's Catholic Church, with burial to be in Holy Family Cemetery.

Visitation will be after 7 p.m. today in Halligan-McCabe Funeral Home, where the Rosary will be recited at 8 p.m. Wednesday.

Above: 1926 announcement of Grand Theater orchestra staff; right: Ernie Bieberbach's 1928 wedding announcement; far right: obits for William & Ernie Bieberbach; below: 1949 obit for father of William & Ernie

Bride of June 27

MISS ANNA E. MURPHY

Mr. and Mrs. Charles Murphy of 742 Charlotte avenue announce the engagement and approaching marriage of their daughter Anna Elizabeth to Ernest Bieberbach, son of Mr. and Mrs. Wm. Bieberbach of 725 Taylor street. The wedding will be a ceremony of June 27 taking place at the early morning mass in St. Mary's church. The Rev. R. J. Renthan will read the service and celebrate the mass. Miss Helen Donohue cousin of the bride groom and George Crowe will attend the couple as bridesmaid and best man.

There will be a wedding breakfast after the ceremony and the couple will leave shortly afterward on an eastern trip. Mr. Bieberbach, who is a well known young musician of the Tri-Cities, is with the Dart Troubadours and his bride will accompany him on the tour of the east which will offer a series of engagements of the summer months.

Both are graduates of the local schools Miss Murphy attending the Immaculate Conception academy. She is a supervisor with the Northwestern Bell Telephone company.

Mr. Bieberbach is a graduate of St. Ambrose college and also attended Browns Business college.

A number of parties are planned as preequisite in honor of the bride to be.

Riverboat Trombonist, E. A. Bierberbach, Dies

TIMES-DEMOCRAT Tuesday, July 1, 1969
Davenport-Bettendorf, Iowa

Ernest A. Bieberbach, 66, 723 Taylor St., Davenport, Mississippi riverboat trombonist, was found dead in his home Monday night by a neighbor.

Dr. R. M. Perkins, Scott County medical examiner, said death was due to an apparent heart attack. It appeared Mr. Bieberbach died sometime Sunday night, Perkins said.

Services will be at 10 a.m. Thursday at St. Mary's Catholic Church, Davenport. Burial will be in Holy Family Cemetery.

Visitation will begin at 7 p.m. today at the funeral home, where the Rosary will be recited at 8 p.m. Wednesday

Mr. Bieberbach and his brother Bill played with such riverboat bands as Minnie Fitzgerald and her Tropical Jazz Band, and the Burke-Leins Novelty Orchestra on the excursion steamer, the Capitol. Bill Bieberbach, a professional trumpet player, who was often host to Bix Beiderbeck, died in 1965.

Ernest Bieberbach was born in Davenport and lived here his entire life. He began his musical career in 1925, six years after his brother began to play professionally. He never married.

Mr. Bieberbach was later employed at the Rock Island Arsenal and the Aluminum Company of America, Davenport works, until his retirement.

Survivors include several nieces and nephews.

E. A. BIEBERBACH

Funerals

WILLIAM BIEBERBACH.

William Bieberbach, Sr., 78, 723 Taylor street, died in his home at 10 p. m. Sunday following a months' illness.

Funeral services will be held at 2 p. m. Wednesday in the Halligan funeral home followed by burial in Holy Family cemetery. Born in Germany, Mr. Bieberbach had lived in Davenport the last 56 years, and was employed by the Northwestern Bell Telephone Co. 16 years, retiring in 1936. He was married to Julia Kinney Nov. 3, 1896 in St. Mary's church. Active in musical circles here for many years he was an honorary member of the Tri-city Musical society.

Surviving are the widow; two sons, William F. and Ernest A. Bieberbach, both of Davenport, and a brother, Fred Bieberbach, New York City. A daughter, Mrs. Lolita Scott, a brother and a sister preceded him in death.

THOSE BIEBERBACH BROTHERS

Blame it on Julie Craighead! That multi-talented whippersnapper who, while doing research on Bix Beiderbecke, discovered an item on microfilm that listed the Bieberbach Orchestra playing for a 1918 Knights of Columbus dance. It's just a misprint, she was told.

Julie coyly smiled and answered, "I found a Bieberbach name in an old city directory that was listed as a cigar manufacturer."

Months passed and the Bieberbach issue lay dormant. Then Jean Pierre Lion, the French author of *Bix: The Definitive Biography of a Jazz Legend*, e-mailed to ask: who were these Bieberbach people who signed the book at Bix's funeral?

The list contained eight names—nine counting Tal Sexton's wife.

Two of the names were Ernest and William Bieberbach. Ernie, as he signed the book, turned out to have played trombone in riverboat bands, including Minnie Fitzgerald and Her Tropical Jazz Band, and the Burke–Leins Novelty Orchestra.

Like Bix, Ernie was born in 1903. He died in 1969. He worked at the Rock Island Arsenal, later at the Alcoa plant from which he retired.

William 'Bill' Bieberbach was a veteran of both world wars. His obituary states he never married. He played trumpet and also worked at the Rock Island Arsenal, from which he retired. Bill played the riverboats and with area dance bands. He was director and cornet player for the Grand Theater orchestra in 1926; musicians included his brother Ernie, trombone; Bud Hance, saxophone and violin; Leo Barr, saxophone and clarinet; Willard Newark, piano, and Richard Moeller, drums.

The brothers' parents were William and Julie Kinney Bieberbach. Their father, a musician in Albert Petersen's orchestra, came to Davenport from Germany at age twenty. He was married here. Census records show he first worked as a cigar maker, which accounts for that city directory entry Julie Craighead uncovered. He later worked sixteen years for Northwestern Bell Telephone Co, retiring after sixteen years.

Alfred Bieberbach, uncle of Ernie and Bill, played French horn and had his own band in Davenport. There was one other uncle, Fred Bieberbach who lived in New York City.

Bill and Ernie had one sister, Lolita Katharine Bieberbach Scott. Her husband worked for the railroad. Lolita played piano and worked as a private secretary for a Rock Island Arsenal colonel.

Ernie's obituary states that he never married; an engagement appeared in the *Democrat–Leader* June 7, 1928:

> Mr. and Mrs. Charles Murphy of 742 Charlotte avenue announce the engagement and approaching marriage of their daughter Anne Elizabeth to Ernest Bieberbach, son of Mr. and Mrs. Wm. Bieberbach of 723 Taylor street. The wedding will be a ceremony of June 27...the couple will leave shortly afterward on an eastern trip. Mr. Bieberbach, who is a well–known young musician of the Tri–cities, is with the Dart Troubadours and his bride will accompany him on the tour of the east which will offer a series of engagements of the summer months....

The announcement stated both worked for Northwestern Bell Telephone Co. A later story told of a party thrown for the bride–to–be by phone company co–workers.

Ernie's obit noted that he was survived by nieces and nephews. His sister's 1922 obituary stated she was survived by her husband, parents and two brothers—no mention of children.

German origins for the Bieberbach and Beiderbecke families account for both similarities and differences in the spelling of their names. Bieberbach is a combination of two words: beaver–*bieber* and stream–*bach*. Beiderbecke translates to *by the brook*—a fitting name since Bix's hometown of Davenport is on the Mississippi and his early musical awakening came of hearing music from the riverboats.

The Bieberbach patriarch did not arrive here until the late 1800s, but the Mighty Mississippi could have been called *beaver stream*. Long before jazz came up stream, millions worth of beaver pelts went down stream to St. Louis, Davenport and surrounding towns being major fur trading posts at the dawn of the 19th century.

Ernie's obituary states that his brother Bill *hosted* Bix Beiderbecke while playing in area dance bands. That may just be a way of saying Bill Bieberbach talked a bandleader or two into allowing Bix to sit in, possibly before he had any established credentials. The Bieberbach and Petersen families had close ties. Art Petersen Jr. served as a pallbearer at the funeral for Ernie's and Bill's dad.

Tri–City Musician's Union

Local #67 of the American Federation of Musicians celebrated its centennial in October 1997. Serving residents of the Quad–Cities area from Muscatine to Dubuque and Illinois' Rock Island, Henry, Mercer and Carroll counties, the Tri–City Musical Society was chartered on Oct. 27, 1897.

For sentimental reasons, it still keeps *Tri–City* in its name and includes in its roster of nationally prominent members drummer Louis Bellson, whose family operated Bellson Music store at 1711 5th Avenue in Moline. Bellson joined in 1940 and received an honorary gold card in 1972.

Along with Bellson memorabilia, union headquarter walls display the account sheet for Bix Beiderbecke. He flunked his initial entrance exam as a cornetist but later got his union card playing piano. His account sheet shows that he joined October 1, 1923, and paid quarterly dues of two dollars.

The national musician's union was formed a year before the local chapter on October 19, 1896, in Indianapolis. National's first president, Owen Miller, signed the charter of the Tri–City Musical Society, which also hangs on the wall at Local #67 headquarters at 304 E. 3rd Street, Davenport.

When the Kahl building opened, union members had a meeting hall there but later located to the Davenport Eagles building, home to Danceland Ballroom. Its current building, purchased in September 1978, originally was a Standard Oil gas station.

Arthur Petersen, long–time principal cellist of the Tri–City Symphony, was president of Local #67 for 35 years. His grandson Vince Petersen—Bix's second cousin once removed—is on the union's executive board.

QC CHANTEUSE

...I met Bix when he was recording for Gennett Records in 1924 and 1925, with a six–piece orchestra which included Hoagy Carmichael (the composer of *Star Dust*) at the piano and Tommy Dorsey, one of the famous Dorsey brothers, on trombone.

At the conclusion of a 43–week tour to the Pacific Coast and back with my singing single vaudeville act, I signed a one–year contract with the New York studios of the Gennett Record Company (the main office was in Richmond, Indiana.) The accompaniment for the

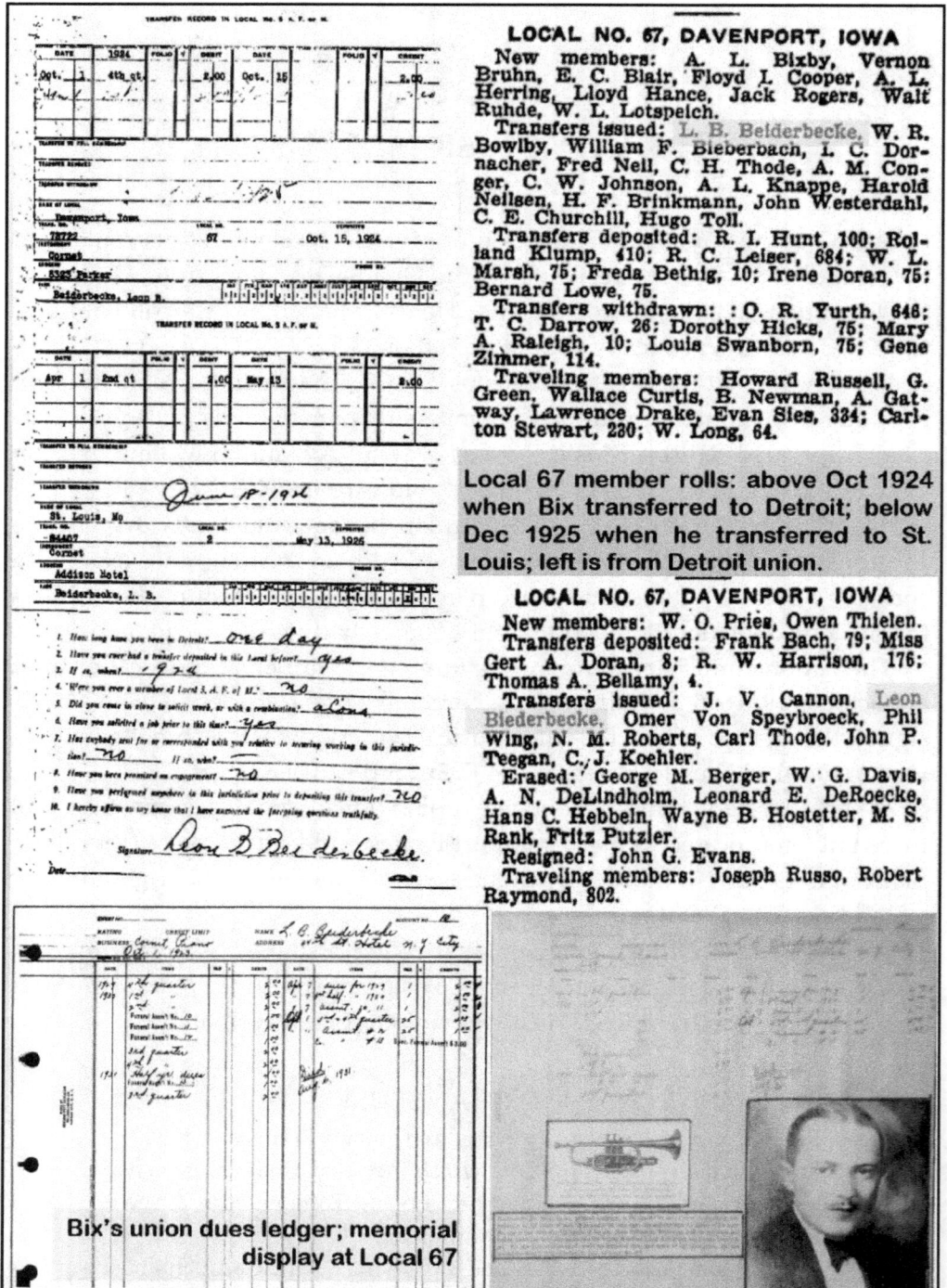

LOCAL NO. 67, DAVENPORT, IOWA

New members: A. L. Bixby, Vernon Bruhn, E. C. Blair, Floyd I. Cooper, A. L. Herring, Lloyd Hance, Jack Rogers, Walt Ruhde, W. L. Lotspeich.

Transfers issued: L. B. Beiderbecke, W. R. Bowlby, William F. Bieberbach, L. C. Dornacher, Fred Neil, C. H. Thode, A. M. Conger, C. W. Johnson, A. L. Knappe, Harold Neilsen, H. F. Brinkmann, John Westerdahl, C. E. Churchill, Hugo Toll.

Transfers deposited: R. I. Hunt, 100; Rolland Klump, 410; R. C. Leiser, 684; W. L. Marsh, 75; Freda Bethig, 10; Irene Doran, 75; Bernard Lowe, 75.

Transfers withdrawn: O. R. Yurth, 646; T. C. Darrow, 26; Dorothy Hicks, 75; Mary A. Raleigh, 10; Louis Swanborn, 75; Gene Zimmer, 114.

Traveling members: Howard Russell, G. Green, Wallace Curtis, B. Newman, A. Gatway, Lawrence Drake, Evan Sies, 334; Carlton Stewart, 230; W. Long, 64.

Local 67 member rolls: above Oct 1924 when Bix transferred to Detroit; below Dec 1925 when he transferred to St. Louis; left is from Detroit union.

LOCAL NO. 67, DAVENPORT, IOWA

New members: W. O. Pries, Owen Thielen.

Transfers deposited: Frank Bach, 79; Miss Gert A. Doran, 8; R. W. Harrison, 176; Thomas A. Bellamy, 4.

Transfers issued: J. V. Cannon, Leon Biederbecke, Omer Von Speybroeck, Phil Wing, N. M. Roberts, Carl Thode, John P. Teegan, C. J. Koehler.

Erased: George M. Berger, W. G. Davis, A. N. DeLindholm, Leonard E. DeRoecke, Hans C. Hebbeln, Wayne B. Hostetter, M. S. Rank, Fritz Putzler.

Resigned: John G. Evans.

Traveling members: Joseph Russo, Robert Raymond, 802.

Bix's union dues ledger; memorial display at Local 67

Local #67 American Federation of Musicians union officers
standing, left-right: Esten Spurrier, Roy Kautz, Dean Handley, Jack Willett, John Peschinski
   seated, left-right: Chester Schaeffer, Arthur A. Petersen, Al Woecknee, Ray Otto.

below: Local #67 Union Office, 304 E. Third St., Davenport, IA

first six records I made for them was played by the staff orchestra — the groups in which Bix was on trumpet.

On the first record, *Where the Lazy Daisies Grow*, Bix came through beautifully and equally as well on the flip side, a comedy song, *Mindin' My Business*. Fortunately I have the six recordings on which he played. The masters have long since disappeared.

— June 1972 *Music Journal*, Maureen Englin: *Bix Beiderbecke Remembered*

She shot pool with W.C. Fields and Walter Winchell, played piano with George Gershwin and Liberace, and sang at the famed London Palladium. These names are the top echelon of the entertainment world and Maureen Englin claimed her place among them.

Born in Rock Island, IL, on August 13, 1891, Maureen was singing and dancing on stage by age four. She joined the Pantages Theatre Circuit, performing vaudeville shows throughout North America. Eventually she made her way to Broadway.

Maureen at 15

The stage where she performed was part of an entertainment complex built for Oscar Hammerstein (grandfather of the songwriter) in 1895. It featured two large auditoriums, a smaller concert hall and a roof garden ballroom. Within the complex also was a café, bowling alley, billiards room, even a petting zoo.

In 1912, Florenz Ziegfield's *A Winsome Widow* starring Mae West performed there. During the show's run, the venue was renamed the Moulin Rouge. Three years later, part of the property was purchased by the Loew's Theater chain. CBS took over one of the theaters for its radio shows and eventually produced television programs there, including the Ed Sullivan Show. Known today as the Ed Sullivan Theater, it is home to the *Late Show with David Letterman*.

During Maureen's two years there, she hobnobbed with Broadway's best. "At that time Paul Whiteman and his orchestra were appearing upstairs with George Gershwin and Ferde Grofe at two pianos," Maureen recalled. "And across the street at Giolitto's Italian Restaurant a then–unknown Rudolph Valentino worked as a busboy." Maureen said she and *the Sheik* became very close friends. She even confessed to owning a lock of his hair.

She lived at New York's Vaudeville Artist's Club. Also in residence were

Rock Island's Charlie Correll and his partner Freeman Gosden, better known as radio's *Amos 'n' Andy*. Other artists who had rooms at the club included Jack Benny, Bob Hope, Walter Huston, George Burns, Judy Garland, Sophie Tucker, Buster Keaton, Burt Lahr, and a young Archie Leach who later changed his name to Cary Grant. He died in Davenport, following a cerebral hemorrhage on November 29, 1986, while preparing for an appearance at the Adler Theater.

When Maureen performed at the famed London Palladium, her show broadcast live over the BBC, which led to her doing shows in Paris, Berlin, Barcelona, Warsaw, Brussels, and Naples.

Her photograph appeared on sheet music throughout the 1920s and '30s and she co–wrote eleven songs. But the stock market crash of '29 wiped out her life savings.

She eventually found work again, singing with the Fred Waring Orchestra. She then got a featured spot in Milwaukee's Pilsner Club. There, she met a 17–year–old pianist who convinced her to let him play for her show. The young pianist was Liberace. He went on to national fame.

Maureen moved back to Rock Island and joined Local #67 AFM. She then went to work at the Fort Armstrong Theater before opening her own nightclub on Twelfth Street, aptly named Club Maureen. The club prospered through the big band era but lost favor when musical tastes turned to bebop and rock 'n' roll. Maureen spent her later years writing for magazines in the U.S. and Canada. She passed away at age 87 in 1979.

TED FIO RITO PRESENTS

Burnie Beiderbecke recalled to Phil Evans in 1962 that his brother Bix had played several times in 1923 with the Russo–Fiorito orchestra. The former Detroit band debuted at the Edgewood Beach Hotel that year. The previous year, Fiorito's *Toot, Toot, Tootsie* had been a top seller for Al Jolson. In 1924, Bix recorded Fiorito's *I Need Some Pettin'* with the Wolverines.

Many remarkably talented performers got their professional starts with the Ted Fio Rito Orchestra, including St. Louis–born singer Betty Grable and Moline drummer Louis Bellson. Born Luigi Balassoni in Rock Falls, IL, in 1924, Bellson's family moved to the QC where his dad opened a music store in downtown Moline. All eight Bellson kids learned to play several instruments. While still in grammar school, Louie played banjo in a street–corner band with two of his four brothers. "Mom disapproved until one day we brought home five dollars given us because people liked our music."

Top right: Chicago's Edge Beach Hotel & WEBH radio tower in 1923 when Bix played with the Dan Russo-Ted Fio Rito Oriole Orchestra, shown in above sheet music.

Davenport Democrat-Leader 1929
SONG WRITER TO BRING HIS ORCHESTRA HERE SUNDAY, APRIL 21

Ted Fiorito, illustrious composer of song hits and debonair dispenser of jazz music, is bringing his sparkling dance orchestra of 11 pieces to the Tri-cities and will play at Danceland Sunday evening, April 21.

For many years Mr. Fiorito was co-director of the famous Oriole orchestra, which made an enviable reputation of nation-wide fame with Mr. Fiorito at the piano. Through the Orioles' radio performances from Station W-E-B-H at the Edgewater Beach Hotel of Chicago, Mr. Fiorito gained an enthusiastic national following which has seldom been equaled. Later, it was this orchestra which was selected to open the gorgeous Aragon ballroom, and even more recently the opening of the new Piccadilly theater, also in Chicago. Now Mr. Fiorito is leader of his own organization. Melodies fairly drip from the instruments, counter themes dazzle the listener, odd syncopated bits magnetize the feet, and outstanding above all are Mr. Fiorito's nimble gymnastics on the piano keys.

A Ted Fiorito arrangement and rendition of a popular number makes something altogether different and delightful of an ordinary song. His sense of public taste combined with musical talent enabled him to write such songs as the lovely "Dreamer of Dreams," and "Meadow Lark," as well as such song hits as "Charlie, My Boy," "I Need Some Pettin'," and the peppy "Toot, Toot, Tootsie."

Louie recalled that besides drums, he gave lessons on trumpet and trombone at his dad's store. "I had to know every aria from every opera. I had to learn the symphonies as well as the basic drum techniques." At

Left: Capitol Theater AD
June 2, 1949

Louis Sr. & Jr. at Bellson Music Store, 1713 5th Av, Moline ; below: Louie with his mom Carmen and new bride Pearl Bailey in Chicago, Jan 1953

LOUIS BELLSON

fourteen, he was playing drums at a Rock Island tavern. "I had to have a guy sit there with me, like a guardian."

In high school, Louie designed a double bass kit to suit his ambidexterity. "I write with either hand, kick a football with either foot...I'm a switch-hitter in baseball. I had to have two base drums."

Bellson was still in high school when he first heard Buddy Rich in concert. Rich was on tour then with Tommy Dorsey. Bellson later toured with Dorsey, doing a show at Davenport's Capitol Theater in 1949.

His start in big bands came with Ted Fio Rito. He had gotten the bandleader's attention during his senior year at Moline High. That was 1942 and Louie had beat out 40,000 other drummers in Slingerland's Gene Krupa International Drum Contest.

"Shortly after I joined Ted Fio Rito, his girl singer quit so I suggested June Stovenour as a replacement," Louie said. "After listening to June sing, Ted liked what he heard and hired her."

Louie moved on to Benny Goodman's band. After a three-year stint in the Army, he joined Dorsey, then Harry James and briefly with Count Basie before moving on to the Duke Ellington orchestra. "The first time I met Duke was when his band played at the Illinois Theater," Louie said. "I feel ashamed to tell this, but they wouldn't let the band stay at the hotel. They had to sleep in their bunks on the train. Duke offered to pay for the whole floor of the hotel. They still wouldn't let him stay there."

As for the girl singer named June, she used her stepfather Bert Haver's name onstage. June Haver was born Beverly Jean Stovenour in Rock Island in 1926. She was the middle of three sisters; the eldest Dorothy and youngest Evelyn. Their mother Marie was an amateur actress. Their father Fred, the son of a minister, was a composer and former piccolo player for John Philip Sousa.

At age eleven, June hosted her own radio program on WHBF at their studio in Rock Island's Harms Hotel. The program showcased talented kids from around the tri-cities area. Louie Bellson had been one of June's featured guests.

Thanks to Bellson getting her the job with Ted Fio Rito, June Haver made her way to Hollywood and her first onscreen appearance with Fio Rito in *Skyline Serenade*, a musical short for Universal Studios. Three more musical shorts followed, including *Trumpet Serenade* with Tommy Dorsey. She then became a contract player for Twentieth Century-Fox and was soon on a career course to rival that of Betty Grable.

1947: R.I. Mayor Mel McKay gets a kiss from June while setting her footprint in cement at Fort Armstrong Theater

June and her sisters

Below: first husband Jimmy Zito

JUNE HAVER

June & Fred on Rock Island riverfront

Haver and Grable co-starred in The *Dolly Sisters*, Twentieth Century-Fox's 1945 biopic of twin-sister vaudeville dance team Rosy and Jenny Deutsch.

In 1953, with only fifteen feature films to her credit, June quit the business. The full story, Hollywood-style: Gal meets guy. Gal and guy elope. Gal gets annulment after three months. Gal enters convent. Leaves after seven months. Marries other guy. Lives happily ever after. Roll credits.

June's first husband was trumpeter Jimmy 'Zeets' Zito. He came from a Chicago Italian family of seven kids. June and Jimmy met when both were teenagers and touring with Ted Fio Rito.

June's second husband was Kankakee IL-born saxophonist and actor Fred MacMurray. They first met as co-stars of the 1945 release, *Where Do We Go From Here*. A bit of a step-down for MacMurray, who gave a memorable performance the year before in the multiple-Oscar-nominated *Double Indemnity*. But it would be the only film he and his future wife appeared in together. They married in 1954.

June and Fred played themselves on the 1958 *Lucy Finds Uranium* episode of the *Lucy-Desi Comedy Hour*. TV acting turned into a 12-year commitment for MacMurray when he took on the role originally turned down by Rock Island-born Eddie Albert—that of the widowed father in Desilu studio's *My Three Sons*.

MacMurray's original co-star, William Frawley, had, of course, come off of ten years as Fred Mertz on *I Love Lucy*. A vaudeville veteran from Burlington, IA, Frawley had introduced audiences to the song, *My Melancholy Baby*. He made more than a hundred films, including *Rose of Washington Square* with Al Jolson, *St. Louis Blues* with Hoagy Carmichael, *Rhythm of the River* and *Going My Way* with Bing Crosby, and the immortal *Miracle on 34th Street*.

Rock Islanders June Haver and Eddie Albert both died in 2005. Albert, born in 1906, made some 85 films, including *Oklahoma, Roman Holiday*, and *The Heartbreak Kid*, earning Oscar nominations for the latter two. Besides *My Three Sons*, he also had turned down the lead on TV's *Mister Ed*. When asked why he had taken the *Green Acres* role Albert said, "Everyone gets tired of the rat race. Everyone would like to chuck it all and grow some carrots."

June Haver's ex-husband had his own TV career. After Ted Fio Rito, Jimmy Zito joined Tommy Dorsey's band and recorded Frank Sinatra's 1942 RCA album. Zito also played on Dorsey's extended version of *Fascinatin' Rhythm* for the 1943 soundtrack of Mickey Rooney's *Girl Crazy*, and with Harry James on the soundtrack for *Young Man with a Horn*. In 1957 he played on *Pacific Jazz Presents: Hoagy Sings Carmichael*. But his biggest gig came by way of Doc Severinsen's orchestra on the *Tonight Show with Johnny Carson*.

"They offered me a job, steady," Bellson said, "but I was on the road with Pearl." Pearl, of course, being his wife, Pearl Bailey. She was a singer with Duke Ellington's band when Louie met her in 1952. Four days later, they were married.

After Pearl's death in 1990, Carson sent Louie tapings of her on the *Tonight Show*. And just before Carson ended his run as *King of Late Night*, Louie was a guest on the show and announced his engagement to second wife Francine.

Bellson recalled Carson, Severinsen, and Ed McMahon came regularly to the Hollywood club where he played after they'd finish taping their Thursday shows. "They'd close the door and John would stay after hours and play the drums."

Bellson credited Carson with keeping jazz and big band music alive on network television, and for providing steady work for a lot of great musicians for three decades. Carson, by the way, was an Iowa native, having been born 1925 in Corning, IA, on the Nebraska border.

Given Carson's Nebraska ties, Bix Beiderbecke remains Iowa's most acclaimed native son. Well, maybe there's a case to be made for Winterset's John Wayne, but that's a discussion for another day.

Music Goes Round and Round

As a guest columnist for Walter Winchell in 1938, Tommy Dorsey wrote:
> Since swing music became the thing, we've heard a lot of jive from the ickies. The hepcats—and I'm proud to be one—sometimes laugh at this jive and sometimes cry. You take an average icky: maybe he thinks Dixieland is just noise, or maybe he thinks my gates just play rhythm. Now I'm not denying that solid, sending rhythm is the basis of hot jazz. But there's a lot more to it than that. In fact, that's just the beginning. The main thing is riding out: giving the alligators that out–of–this–world chill with a lowdown Dixieland. What does it mean to ride out? Even a lot of the cats are in the dark about this matter. It means when a gate picks up his

licorice stick or gitbox and hits a couple of riffs and gutbucket. Now a gate has to be pretty good to do this. He can't play by the paper; he's got to be hot enough to make up his own improvisations as he goes along. When a group of cats get together and get off in the groove we call it a jam session. Obviously these musicians have to be way above par to compose simultaneously five or six of them playing simultaneously and all making up melody as they go along and yet harmonizing perfectly.

How do they do it? It's mostly instinct. Some of the best sidemen like Sidney Bechet, one of the few who plays a soprano sax, can't even read music. Louis Armstrong, the king of hot trumpet, couldn't read music for many years. It's just something that's in your blood and you have to get it out. Some gates can make it come out right when they blow and the others just press the first valve down and the music goes round and round and when it comes out, it's just noise.

...Many times we are giving out a beautiful melodic breakdown and everybody is paying too much attention to the rhythm. ...Of course a stomp tune or a killer–diller is okay but my favorite kind of swing is gentler, softer kind. That's the kind Bix Beiderbecke used to play and he was the greatest for pure swing. They tell me some woman has just written a novel about Bix's life. Well, they should write a dozen novels about this gate's life. You almost want to cry when you listen to one of his cornet choruses, they're so full of pathos.

Bix, of course, died in 1931 but he left the best part of himself on records. Many have been reissued within the last two years and every alligator who wants to hear swing at its purest should hear these records.

Bix & Tommy Dorsey

Early Dixieland jazz musicians referred to one another as *gates*, short for *gator* which was shortened from *alligator*; thus, the saying: *See ya later, alligator*....

Besides his better known nickname—*Satchmo* for satchel mouth—Louis Armstrong also was affectionately known as *Gate Mouth*. Eventually all jazz devotees became known as *gates*. Those who disliked jazz were called *ickies*. Fans of swing jazz were *hepcats*. Dorsey neglected to mention the *jitterbugs*: swing fans of the can't–sit–still variety.

Gutbucket was a style of music associated with the brothels of Storyville, memorialized in the tune, *Gutbucket Blues*. A *licorice stick* is a clarinet, *gitbox* a guitar. In the lexicon of jazz, Bix contributed *clam*, slang for hitting a bad note.

F. Scott Fitzgerald immortalized the flapper's bobbed hair and rolled chiffon stockings, doing the Charleston at a time when *boyfriend, sugar daddy*, and *red hot mamma* came into popular usage. And while popular among Bismark Beiderbecke's peers in the Gay '90s, *23–skidoo* had lost vogue before Bix turned five. His peers would have said: beat it!

During an epidemic of *"so's your old man"*, Bix had his dad's habit of using *peach* as slang for a *sweet guy*, as in: *We had a good talk—he sure is a peach*, writing home of the headmaster at Lake Forest.

Bickie is still with us & we dread to think of his leaving because he is such a peach to have around & heaven only knows when he will spend another vacation with us.

Bismark wrote those lines in a letter to Mary Louise early in 1930 while Bix was home following his stay at the Keeley Institute. At the time, Bismark and Aggie were preparing for their European vacation. On the return trip, Bix's parents stopped by the New York studio where he performed on the Camel Pleasure Hour. Bix was back in Davenport the following October, having blacked out during a solo on the live radio show.

His grandfather's generation had a slew of slang for drunkenness: cockeyed, pie–eyed, woozy, canned, fried, oiled, plastered, stewed, tanked—all in common usage in the Civil War era. Opa Beiderbecke was of a time when *booze,* from the Low German *buizen*, meant drinking to excess.

Hooch found its way into the language of Bismark's generation; Bix's generation added *blotto*. They also added bathtub gin and rot–gut whisky.

But back in kindergarten Bix would have been reciting poems Miss Robinson taught her students under state–mandated abstinence education.

> Oh! Let us shun these poisons—
> Rum, brandy, gin and beer;
> Drink liquor brewed from heaven,
> That we may never fear
> The dreadful fate of drunkards—
> The drunkard's fearful fall,
> That robs of food and clothing,
> Health, honor, heaven—all.

Temperance proponents touting water as the alternative to intoxicating beverages had a hard sell among immigrants. Long before science proved parasites and bacteria, folks knew alcohol made water fit to drink. Brits trusted their gin. Scots and Irish had their whisky; Swedes their vodka.

French had their wine. Germans trusted beer.

Around about 1901 Water Wagon Clubs popped up everywhere. Membership required pledging abstinence. If someone *fell off the wagon* he was out of the club. Railroad companies and factories like the Bettendorf Wagon Works signed up their entire workforce in hopes of decreasing accidents caused by on–the–job drinking.

It all was prelude to national Prohibition. Enacted in January 1920, the Volstead Act wasn't repealed until more than a year after Bix died. Only time Bix seriously had been *on the wagon* was during that stay at Keeley.

One journalist described the *Keeley Cure* as "an inebriate's theory for the cure of inebriates." During Prohibition, Keeley doctors made out like bootleggers. Fitzgerald wrote:

> The honest citizens of every class who believed in a strict public morality, and were powerful enough to enforce the necessary legislation, did not know that they would necessarily be served by criminals and quacks...so when this attempt collapsed our elders stood firm with all the stubbornness of people involved in a weak case, preserving their righteousness and losing their children.

That's an excerpt from Fitzgerald's *Echoes of the Jazz Age*. When he wrote it in March 1931, Bismark and Aggie were settling into their sixties. Bix had turned twenty–eight. He'd be dead before the essay appeared in the November *Scribner's Magazine*.

The Jazz Age, as Fitzgerald defined it, began with 1919's May Day Riots and ended with the '29 Stock Market Crash. He chronicled the decade in stories such as *Bernice Bobs Her Hair* and *The Great Gatsby*.

> Sometimes, though, there is a ghostly rumble among the drums, an asthmatic whisper in the trombones that swings me back into the early twenties when we drank wood alcohol and every day in every way grew better and better.

Fitzgerald saw jazz as a metaphor for the era. Bix was its poster boy. Following Fitzgerald's lead, newspaper columnists wrote eulogies to jazz like the following, published locally May 26, 1931:

> That insanity, fever or whatever it was which was summed up under the word jazz, seemed, like so many other problems to have been a by–product of the war. For nearly a decade it appeared that the country had taken syncopation for its permanent rhythm; that there would nevermore be quiet, decorum, dignity or peace.
>
> Today there are signs—faint, but unmistakable—that the jazz era has reached its apogee and is now in the decline. Beautiful and musical melodies are germinating from the seeds of jazz.

> Jazz is a disease of youth, like measles and infantile paralysis. It reached its epoch in raccoon coats, rumble seats, the hip–pocket flask, necking and petting, all that youthful exuberance. Jazz hasn't gone but it is going. And the tempo of the future, while rapid, will no longer be quite so jerky.

Melodic, not jerky? Bix had that. He sold *Flashes* and *In the Dark* to Robbins Music Company in April 1931. The money from these original compositions and his other song royalties pretty much was his only income as the Great Depression made jobs few and far between.

Like the era Fitzgerald wrote about, Bix was *on borrowed time*. Years of bad liquor had sealed his fate. Shortly after he died, a reporter posed the question: "Is Jazz Dead?" Several Hollywood and radio stars responded, among them:

BING CROSBY: "Jazz dead or dying? I should say not! It may decline slightly from its zenith of popularity, but it will always have its place in entertainment."

MILLS BROTHERS: "Jazz Dead? Our kind of jazz dead? No sir!" exclaimed a full chorus of first and second tenor, baritone and bass.

KATE SMITH: "Jazz will never die. It remains a symbol of our time, although historians probably will refer to it as syncopation."

CAB CALLOWAY: "Jazz can't die, because its appeal to humanity is more basic than any other musical type. As long as human emotions respond to rhythm, jazz will continue."

>   I blow thru here
>   The music goes 'round and around
>   Whoa–ho–ho–ho ho–ho
>   And it comes out here
>   I push the first valve down
>   The music goes down and around
>   Whoa–ho–ho–ho ho–ho
>   And it comes out here
>   I push the middle valve down
>   The music goes down around below
>   Below, below, deedley–ho–ho–ho
>   Listen to the jazz come out
>   I push the other valve down
>   The music goes 'round and around
>   Whoa–ho–ho–ho ho–ho
>   And it comes out here

William Harold 'Red' Hodgson (1908–1988) made a total of $13,800 on his hit tune, *The Music Goes 'Round and Around*. He'd have been a millionaire if only he'd copyrighted the song back when he originated it in Galesburg, IL, in 1931.

Five years later, you couldn't turn on a radio without hearing Red Hodgson's song. *Billboard* magazine noted that not since 1923's *Yes, We Have No Bananas* had a popular song fired the imagination and enthusiasm of the public. Folks on the streets whistled it and sang it as greeting to one another.

It remained #1 on the Lucky Strike Hit Parade radio program for much of 1936. Columbia Pictures rushed a B–movie to theaters based on the song that had sold a million copies of sheet music and about that many records here and abroad.

Les Swanson remembered having played the song *ad nauseam*. "Those of us who worked both the theaters and nightclubs played the darn thing on request a dozen times a day." He and his fellow keyboardists breathed a collective sigh of relief when Hodgson's tune finally wore out its welcome.

The Music Goes 'Round and Around came along at a time when commercial sales of jazz records had gone flat. Still, the jazz clubs thrived. Audiences showed up for the live shows because that's where they'd hear musicians playing in the style of the late great Bix Beiderbecke—improvised solos, never the same way twice. *You had to be there or be square.*

Hodgson was playing with the Ernie Palmquist band in Bix's old stomping grounds around the Quad Cities when he introduced the tune that ushered in America's swing era. "It started out as a novelty number," Hodgson said in a 1968 interview. "I didn't sit down and write it. I just developed it as I went along.

"I'd get out front to sing and the band would be playing *Dinah* behind me. Ernie would come over and say that I wasn't supposed to sing during the trombone solo. He'd hand me an orange and say, 'Here. Keep yourself busy.' I'd make faces at the audience and peel the orange and stuff the peelings in my mouth.

"When my mouth was full of peelings, Ernie would come to me again and say, 'Now is your time to sing.' But I couldn't sing because my mouth was full. Then I'd get rid of the peelings as gracefully as I could and he'd say, 'Well, if you can't sing—play.'

"I'd play a few bars and he'd stop me and say, 'That's terrible. If you can't do better than just tell the people how the music goes.' Then I'd go into the song."

Hodgson used a mellophone for what he originally called, *The Orange Song*. In later years his trumpet served as prop when club patrons requested the song. He'd long since abandoned the orange routine.

Hodgson joined Earl Burtnett's band at Chicago's Drake Hotel in 1933. His novelty song remained part of his repertoire but the comic bantering was done with Burtnett's singer, Ruth Lee. When she quit the band and moved to New York City, she shared the song with Onyx Club's trombonist Mike Riley and trumpeter Ed Farley. They liked it. Since Hodgson hadn't copyrighted it they did, with an added prologue:

> One night while playing in the band
> A girl came up; she said, you're grand
> So I replied in words low–down
> Now this is how the music goes 'round

Riley and Farley claimed the song came about after Riley bought an old flugelhorn. Their story was that one night a tipsy club patron asked if the odd-looking horn was hard to play. Farley was said to have overheard Riley explain the instrument and remarked, "There's a song in there, partner."

Regulars at the Onyx became so fond of the song, they began wearing *Round and Round Club* pins—spiral paperclips ordered by the caseload from a factory in Cleveland. "Gloria Vanderbilt wore a necklace of round-and-round paperclips," Riley bragged to a reporter.

Back in Chicago, Hodgson was unaware of what was happening with his novelty tune. Then one day he got a phone call from New York's Select Music Publishing Company. Stan Hickman, a singer with the Ted Fio Rito band, tipped them off that the Riley-Farley song they were about to publish had been written by his friend Red Hodgson.

Irving Berlin had praised the New York duo, proclaiming they'd "bucked the trend of mechanized songs produced by industry hacks who had nothing by way of originality."

Hodgson said: "I could see that Riley and Farley had me over a barrel." So he settled for one-third royalties and credit as lyricist with composer credit going to the New Yorkers. Each man got an initial $10,000 royalty fee.

After Riley and Farley played the song on Rudy Vallee's New Year's radio broadcast, Select Music sold 102,000 copies in one day, compared to 10,000 sheets for their previous best seller according to a company representative.

With the song's popularity skyrocketing, Hodgson sued for copyright. The case got more complicated when bandleader Palmquist filed suit, claiming he had ownership rights to the song. Burtnett had died of appendicitis in '36. Otherwise, he might have wanted his piece of the action.

"The case went to federal court and wasn't scheduled to be heard for over a year," Hodgson said. "I could see that lawyer fees were

Mike Riley & Ed Farley

Red Hodgson

going to eat up most of the profits so all of us agreed to an out-of-court settlement." In the end, song rights went to the publishing company and ASCAP. Hodgson said he might have come out better if he'd gone ahead with his lawsuit. "I had 85 affidavits from musicians and friends saying I'd written the song."

Hodgson remained in Chicago, playing trumpet until his death at age 80. His song topped the charts for Tommy Dorsey, Louis Armstrong and Ella Fitzgerald. Danny Kaye sang it in *The Five Pennies,* Hollywood's film version of that other trumpeter named *Red*, Bix's friend Red Nichols.

> *They call it jazz, swing, they change the name. It's ragtime.*
> —cornetist Willie G. 'Bunk' Johnson

"I don't really like Dixieland. Never did," Jimmy McPartland said in a 1982 interview. "It's two beats to the bass drum. When we were in high school, we made it four beats to the bass drums and called it *swing*. Benny Goodman liked that word."

McPartland called Bix Beiderbecke the quintessential *swingman*.

Paul Whiteman, who featured Bix's solos in his symphonic jazz orchestra, claimed *swing* was nothing more than musicians ad-libbing some heavy rhythms. "This always happens in the last hour of any dance band's engagement," Whiteman said in a 1936 interview.

"We arrange the score up to the time where the players take off. Then the swingman is on his own. Nobody knows where he's going. Not even the swingman himself. He feels his way. Not cautiously but with abandon."

When asked his definition of *swing*, Tommy Dorsey—who once played trombone in Whiteman's band—said, "It's like love. It just happens."

Benny *King of Swing* Goodman claimed in that 1936 newspaper feature that the new jazz was what the old jazz started out to be before it lost its way.

That *way* is said to have started with New Orleans' cornetist Buddy Bolden. He arrived on the scene around the time that Bix's brother Burnie was born in Davenport.

By the time Bix was blowing out five candles on his cake, Bolden was in an insane asylum—schizophrenia some said, but another theory is tinnitus—same as believed to have caused Van Gogh to whack off an ear.

Jazz musicians said Bolden blew his brains through his cornet. He died same year as Bix.

Back in Bolden's day, bands put a big tin can painted with the word

LOUIS 'SATCHMO' ARMSTRONG 1901-1971   DOMINIC 'NICK' LA ROCCA 1889-1961

BOLDEN BAND C. 1905   CHARLES 'BUDDY' BOLDEN 1877-1931

Jazz will endure just as long people hear it through their feet instead of their brains.
~John Philip Sousa

SUGAR out on the floor where the dancers spun by. When the band kicked into gear, the dancers showed their approval by throwing money into the can.

In July 1918 Nick LaRocca took a sugar can and his Original Dixieland Jazz Band to Manhattan's Reisenweber Saloon. The can went empty their opening night. Soon, though, ODJB won over the jeering Manhattan crowds to their strange new rhythms. By the next month the band had a hit.

"Jazz lost its way," said Goodman, "when it got written down."

Pacific Stars and Stripes columnist Elson Irwin agreed.

He wrote that Paul Whiteman didn't know much about jazz but got credit for discovering it. "Whiteman did much to give bad jazz a good name...all written down on clean, white sheets of paper. Real jazz was written down in the soul and only those who knew it could blow it."

Goodman claimed that by the end of the Great War jazz had become so symphonized, so pasteurized that nothing of its original spirit remained. He believed swing recaptured that lost spontaneity and free expression—all that Bix made great.

Goodman's band, including trumpeter Bunny Berigan, Jess Stacy on piano and drummer Gene Krupa—the original *king of swing*—tossed aside their orchestrated arrangements and worked from the charts of Harlem composer Fletcher Henderson.

Fans swarmed the bandstand at LA's Palomar ballroom, nearly causing a riot.

They came to hear the music.

The claim goes that no true jazz aficionado would anymore dance to a swing band than a symphony listener would perform a minuet during Mozart.

Whiteman would later claim the big bands died when audiences stopped dancing.

When he heard that Goodman was packing them in at Chicago's Urban Room, Whiteman shrugged and said, "He has tremendous technique and can sit in on anybody's symphony."

Careful, now...somebody's about to come out swinging!

Whiteman Visits Davenport Grave

Davenport, Ia. —(P)— Paul Whiteman, famous orchestra leader, who is appearing at a theater here, Wednesday placed a wreath on the grave of Leon "Bix" Beiderbecke in Oakdale cemetery. Beiderbecke played with Whiteman's band as a trumpeter for several years.

1939 Iowa State Fair Ad; Whiteman stopped off in Davenport with his swing band on July 29th before heading to Des Moines to play the fair; photographed at Bix's grave May 23, 1940, while in Davenport to play at the Capitol Theater.

Paul Whiteman and his CBS orchestra head into the midwest next week for a two-months' tour, including stops at Rochester, Minn., Des Moines and Burlington from Aug. 28 to Sept. 2. While in Iowa, Paul and his crew are to place a marker on the grave of Bix Beiderbecke in Davenport. Charley Teagarden will sound taps during the ceremony. Bix, rated as the greatest trumpeter of his time, was playing with the Whiteman aggregation at the time of his death.

NBC Radio news, FEB 15, 1939: Hoagy Carmichael, who has written some of Tin Pan Alley's most poignant and appealing ballads, will be Tommy Dorsey's guest on WEAF at eight pm. Tommy will dedicate the whole broadcast to the playing of Carmichael's music, with the exception of one tune. The song that will not be from the Carmichael pen is *Davenport Blues*, written by Bix Beiderbecke. It was during a recording session 15 years ago that Hoagy dropped in on a small pick-up band that included both Tommy and the famous Bix. The band was recording *Davenport Blues* and between choruses Hoagy played over for the boys two melodies that had been running through his head. One he had already named *Washboard Blues*—one of Tommy's most successful recordings. The other strain had no name but would later become *Stardust*, one of the more popular tunes of American music and the composition for which Hoagy is best known.

Hoagy's Tribute

In a letter responding to Don O'Dette's invitation to attend the Bix jazz festival, Hoagy Carmichael gave his wholehearted support for a hometown tribute to Bix, his great friend and fellow musician. But ill health and a serious eye problem prevented him from coming to Davenport.

Carmichael later sent O'Dette, president of the Bix Beiderbecke Memorial Society, a recording of *Piano Pedal Blues*, written shortly before his death in 1981. He said he composed it for Bix as a creative debt since many of his own songs "tried to catch the influence of Bix's genius."

"Hoagy sent the song to me on a home disc," O'Dette said in a 1988 interview. "I'm sure it has great musical significance, though I've never mentioned it to any musical researchers."

Sheet music for the tune, perhaps Carmichael's last, is available on the Hoagy Carmichael Collection web site. It was featured during a Carnegie Hall presentation of more than half a century of his work. Carmichael, 80 at the time, joined a pianist on stage in a performance of *Piano Pedal Rag*.

At that time, he confessed, "I wrote more no-hits than hits." It's not clear in which category *Piano Pedal Rag* landed.

"The influence of Bix is evident in it, as it is in *Stardust*. Hoagy, himself, told me he had been strongly influenced by Bix's style when he wrote both tunes," O'Dette said. Bix also influenced Carmichael's 1924 *Freewheeling*, by changing its name to what jazz fans now know as *Riverboat Shuffle*.

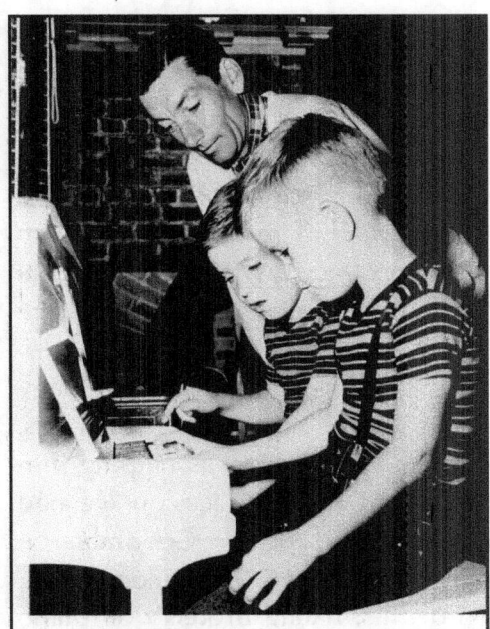

Hoagy Carmichael with his sons, Randy and Hoagy Bix

Hoagy on hearing Bix for the first time: I got up from the piano and staggered over and fell on the davenport.

Hoagy as Smoke, the piano player in *Young Man With A Horn*

Carmichael recalled for O'Dette the days in which he and Bix played together and cut records. "You just had to be there and hear his tone and attack and sheer brilliance to appreciate what Bix was doing for music. It was all so amazing. And remember, we recorded on wax discs. But you had to hear Bix in person to appreciate how extraordinary he was."

Gloria O'Dette, Don's widow, said she could not recall the disc from Carmichael. "While Don was president of the Bix Society, he received letters from so many music celebrities. So many years after his death, it would be difficult to find much of anything," she said.

Bud Freeman recalled their recording sessions shortly after Hoagy arrived in New York with his Indiana law degree and a stack of tunes. "Hoagy got a contract from Victor Records and Bix, who was helping him get the musicians, highly recommended me. At the first session we had Tommy Dorsey on trombone, Jimmy Dorsey and Benny Goodman on clarinet, Bubber Miley on trumpet, Bix on cornet, Joe Venuti on violin, Harry Goodman on bass, Gene Krupa on drums, Irving Brodsky on piano and me. We did a recording of *Stardust*. Of course it became a classic and Hoagy became a millionaire but we played it at the wrong tempo. Everybody in the band said, get rid of that stupid tune and we threw it out. Six months or a year later, Isham Jones recorded it as a ballad."

1938 BOOK REVIEWS

YOUNG MAN WITH A HORN by Dorothy Baker is a sure antidote for that bored feeling. It's the kind of book that won't be put aside until the final page is turned.

Mrs. Baker says that the late Leon "Bix" Beiderbecke inspired her novel but adds, "the inspiration has been the music, not the life of a great musician."

Man or music–inspired, Mrs. Baker has turned in a first–rate book. The story is ordinary enough in substance. It is an account of Rick Martin, born with music in his soul and a genius to express it.

Rick's rise to international renown as a hot trumpet player and his equally swift decline to oblivion is told in rhythmic, episodic sequence—a story of too much genius, liquor, and the wrong woman.

But it is the sheer beauty of Mrs. Baker's writing, her sparkling patter that makes the book. Hers is a free, unrestrained style—a style that almost matches the superlative tones of Rick Martin's trumpet.

Mrs. Baker sidesteps any attempt to be technical in her passages on music, she frankly admits her ignorance in this field, but relies for the most part on a sincere and probing characterization.

* * *

Bix Beiderbecke to most readers is the most outstanding portrayal of American youth. You don't have to like jazz to sympathize with Bix, to whom swing music spells life's drama, philosophy and enchantment. *Young Man With a Horn* proves the extraordinary ability of an author who was rewarded a Houghton Mifflin Fellowship to write this novel. It is an exquisitely turned–out story, not too long, smoothly readable, definitely slated for the top of the reading list.

After the success of Dorothy Baker's novel, Hoagy Carmichael approached Broadway producer Vinton Freedley in 1939 about doing a play that wove together Baker's novel and the *real* Bix. It was announced in late December of that year that the show would soon hit the boards with Burgess Meredith in the role of Bix, directed by Charles MacArthur. Carmichael was working on tunes for the play with the idea that Meredith would act out the horn performances while a professional cornetist played off–stage. Stories soon were being circulated about Meredith actually learning to play trumpet.

The recent career of young Burgess Meredith sounds like an ad for mail order music lessons. A few months ago he was a' bindle stiff on a California barley ranch. Today he is rich and successful –and all because he learned to play the trumpet.

But it's all in fun. The bindle stiff was a role in Of Mice And Men, the film version of the John Steinbeck story; and Meredith is practising hot licks on his trumpet for the leading part in Young Man With A Horn, the play from the Dorothy Baker novel which narrates the life of a jazz musician strongly resembling the late, great Bix Beiderbecke.

Buzz (which is what everybody calls him) also does a string of radio shows—a three letter man in the world of make believe if there ever was one! Visitors to his apartment these days find him amidst strange antics.

He interrupts any social call to look for his trumpet, and, after a few experimental trills and scales, he really can bring forth a professional rendition of St. Louis Blues.

"That's just a straight chorus," he then explains, "wait until you hear me send it—right out of this world." A confirmed hep cat!

December 31, 1939

Second Chorus 1940 l-r: Charles Butterworth, Fred Astaire, Paulette Goddard, Artie Shaw, and Burgess Meredith

Burgess Meredith Set For Biederbecke Film

Burgess Meredith, young stage star, will have the lead in Jed Harris's film version of "Young Man with 'a Horn" Dorothy Baker's biographical novel of the great swing trumpet player, Bix Biederbecke. . . John O'Hara, the novelist, is writing the screen play, and Harris is on the West Coast now to find a director. Meredith reported this week at Metro for "Spring Dance," Philip Barry college story.

November 1938

Burgess Meredith, star of the first Cavalcade program, is equally at home in the entertainment worlds of stage, screen, and radio.

His next Broadway role will be that of Bix Beiderbecke in Vinton Freedley's "Young Man With a Horn" to open soon with Charles MacArthur directing the production.

January 4, 1940

. . . Burgess Meredith, who was to have appeared on Broadway in "Young Man With a Horn," which was shelved, now toots a trumpet, along with Fred Astaire, in "Second Chorus." Neither actor can play the instrument. . . .

August 20, 1940

Jan 4, 1940: *Visitors to [Meredith's] apartment these days find him amidst strange antics. He interrupts any social call to look for his trumpet, and after a few experimental thrills and scales, he really can bring forth a professional rendition of 'St. Louis Blues.' "That's just straight chorus," he then explains, "wait until you hear me send it right out of this world."*

A confirmed hep cat!

By late summer 1940 the play had been shelved and Meredith had moved on to playing trumpet onscreen with Fred Astaire in *Second Chorus*. "Neither actor can play the instrument," an entertainment columnist reported.

Young Man With a Horn was made into a movie in 1950. Kirk Douglas starred as Baker's fictitious horn player Rick Martin. Hoagy co-starred as Smoke, Rick's piano-playing friend.

Despite a failed stage production, Carmichael walked away with a new song he titled, *Bix Lix*. Published in 1942 with lyrics by Johnny Mercer, the song had been re-titled: *Skylark*.

This One's About Pete Kelly

NEW YORK, 1954—So Jack Webb has become fascinated by the short, strange life of Bix. It figures. Most of us have.

When I say most of us, I mean jazz buffs and when I say Bix I mean Leon Beiderbecke, a cornet player. When I say Jack Webb, all of you say dum-da-dum-dum.

The word has come from the coast that jug-eared, hard-working Webb is going to take a breather from the cold fury of *Dragnet* shortly to produce a movie based on Bix's life. Naturally, Webb, who is by way of being an aficionado himself, will play Bix—a figure of such monumental tragic stature, that looking at it one way, it dwarfs *Hamlet*. For one thing, Bix was real.

The news of Webb's movie plans stirred up a mess of talk here in the big town. It has been 25 years or more since Beiderbecke played his cornet and raised h— in Manhattan, but the old-timers tell me their memory of him remains green. It's just as if he had stepped off the stand for 10 minutes and gone around the corner for a quick one. For instance, if you sit Eddie Condon down in a dark recess of his Greenwich Village saloon, he will set aside his guitar with the rubber strings and talk for hours on end of the things Bix did and the music he played.

What Bix was, was a musician. He played popular music and he made good money and he drank too much. His life ended quickly and there are a dozen stories of why and how. On the surface there was nothing to distinguish him from a hundred other jazzmen who went the same way—a few years in the spotlight, a thousand gin bottles, a lot of pretty girls and then one day, the dark stranger.

However, Bix, they tell me, was a little different. In his innards was artistry. He would wipe off the mouthpiece of his horn and when the time came for him to take his 12-bar solo, he would point the cornet down and play.

Tinny little songs. Trifles. *I'm Coming Home Virginia*. It came out a dozen ways—rough, easy, sad, happy...all the ways men feel. The songs were cheap. The music was timeless. Even if jazz bored you or grated on you—when Bix played, there was an urgency, a poetry, a sweep to it that made you stop and listen.

...Toscanini led an orchestra that way. The difference is he had Brahms or Debussy for handmaidens, so to speak.

Bix was lost in a sea of smoky night clubs, noise, cut liquor, hoodlums, sugar-and-water women, the uneasy rumble of cut-rate life. I'm being a little high-flown but I cannot help it; Bix was, as far as I can judge, an artist painting on a postage stamp.

All that is left of him now along Broadway are a few re-pressings of his old records, piled on dusty shelves in the backs of music stores...And, oh, yes—an out-of-print book called *Young Man With a Horn*, written in 1937 on a Houghton Mifflin fellowship by Dorothy Baker who, like Jack Webb, became fascinated by the short strange life. Mrs. Baker's hero was called Rick Martin, but forget it. He was Bix.

I wish Webb luck but I wonder. The movies tried to do Mrs. Baker's book a few years ago and it came out trash with Harry James' syrupy trumpet and Kirk Douglas' overacting dismaying Bix's friends. The music must be honest, the story sad, the confusion utter—ah, it will be like trying to pick up a drop of mercury....

—Mel Heimer

Webb never made the Bix movie. Instead he produced, directed, and starred in 1955's big screen version of his *Pete Kelly's Blues*. Webb originally played Pete Kelly in a 12-episode NBC radio crime drama that aired over WOC in the summer of 1951. The series showcased 1920s jazz over plots that centered on the title character's dealings with gangsters, gun molls and FBI agents. William Conrad played various mob bosses.

On film, Edmond O'Brien played the villain. The rest of the cast included Peggy Lee, Ella Fitzgerald, Lee Marvin, Andy Devine, and Janet Leigh. Peggy Lee's performance as a gangster's moll earned her an Oscar nomination.

The radio series didn't get picked up after its initial run because radio execs were holding Webb to his *Dragnet* contract. But the movie spawned a

TV series and two albums—a soundtrack and an instrumental, *Pete Kelly Lets His Hair Down*, showcasing musicians from the series.

Matty Matlock and His All Stars supplied the music for the fictional Pete Kelly's Big Seven. Besides Matlock playing clarinet and scoring the arrangements, the band featured Dick Cathcart playing the Pete Kelly cornet parts. Other musicians included Moe Schneider, trombone; Eddie Miller, tenor sax; Ray Sherman, piano; George Van Eps, guitar; Jud DeNaut, bass; and Nick Fatool, drums.

Considered among the best arrangers of Dixieland jazz, Matty Matlock [1907–1978] also scored the music for Bing Crosby's radio show before moving on to television as a studio arranger. Matlock was born in Fate Marable's hometown of Paducah, Kentucky. His start in music came as a replacement for Benny Goodman in Ben Pollack's band in 1929. Matlock went on to record with many top-notch musicians, including Wingy Manone, Vic Berton, Bob Crosby, Bunny Berigan, Jack Teagarden, and Red Nichols.

Jack Webb
Intrigued by Bix's story

Dragnet's Jack Webb was such a fan of Bix, he wanted to make a movie about his life but instead brought his radio crime drama *Pete Kelly's Blues* to theaters in 1955.

Davenport Democrat-Times   Sept 6, 1955

Harry James coaching Kirk Douglas for *Young Man With a Horn*, loosely based on the life of Bix Beiderbecke

BIX LIVES

Aggie Beiderbecke was still living when Bill Wundram, wrote the following for the *Davenport Democrat–Leader*, published July 24, 1949:

18 YEARS AGO BIX BEIDERBECKE BLEW HIS LAST SPARKLING NOTE, BUT HIS FAME GOES MARCHING ON

Bix Beiderbecke blew his last sparkling note 18 years ago this month. That stubby cornet of his that he sometimes carried around in a paper bag has been stilled since 1931, when this Patron Saint of Jazz joined up to play duets with the Angel Gabriel. Yet, thru the years since Bix punched out his last note, his stature as a Titan among the greats of jazz giants has been growing in volume, instead of diminishing. His horn and tone are now sacred things. Bixiana is now a cult. A legend among musicians and disciples to this figure, whose impact on jazz is approached by no other.

The word Bix itself is jazz. They are synonymous words for Davenport's contribution to modern music. He is one of music's all–time greats. He is the one who set down the very standards of the hot music which we know today. Altho dead for 18 years he is still the Gabriel of the jazz world. There is no one to deny it.

And so, this is a story about that intriguing and lovable character Bix, who died when only a young man. It is a yarn of the roaring '20s when Beiderbecke was lipping out Dixieland with the Dorsey brothers; when Paul Whiteman was calling him "my greatest musician," and when Bix himself was taking solos thru the most baffling passages that audiences had ever experienced. They would burst into cheers and sometimes spasms over his playing.

There's a story that Paganini fiddled in such a way that imaginative ones believed the devil was guiding his arm. There were some who thought Bix, too, was doing better than any human ought to do.

BORN IN DAVENPORT

The Bix story begins March 10, 1903, in Davenport when Leon Bix Beiderbecke was born to Mr. and Mrs. B.H. Beiderbecke. Bix, when a toddler, showed signs of musical talent. He plinked at the piano, picking out little tunes when he could hardly reach the keyboard. He was always coming home with oranges and cookies, which neighbors gave him for playing. The Beiderbeckes were a musical family and little Bix received encouragement from his mother, who still lives in Davenport at the Mississippi hotel, and his brother, C.B. Beiderbecke, superintendent of Oakdale cemetery. His parents hired him a teacher, who agreed that Bixie was something of

Bix is Jazz's #1 Saint and any attempt at rational analysis of his talent usually invokes the bitterness of a theological dispute. ~Benny Green, jazz critic

Bill Wundram, *Democrat-Leader* 1949

Merrill Blosser strip, c. 1950

a prodigy. "I don't know whether or not Bix practices his lessons much but he plays them perfectly," the teacher said.

Bix grew up in Davenport. He liked tennis and played on a softball team. Somewhere along the time he borrowed a cornet, and with a phonograph taught himself to play. But what Bix started to play was something different than "Carnival of Venice." His records were of a new music sensation. They called it jazz, and the scratching disks crackled forth...and Bix imitated the style. Then improvised and improved upon it. He was going to Davenport high school in those days and was courting a young lassie, Miss Vera Cox, now Mrs. Ferd Korn of Davenport. The more jazz Bix heard, the more he played it. Music was starting to make an indelible impression on Bix's thoughts. What to do? His parents decided to send him to a private school, Lake Forest Academy, to take his mind off music.

CHICAGO...AND JAZZ

This move didn't exactly bring about the desired results in the eyes of Papa and Mama Beiderbecke, for Bix didn't pay too much attention to his studies. Lake Forest was near Chicago and in those days Chicago was jazz. Bix was nightly excursioning into the Windy City to hear that King Oliver man. Bix was forming his own little combos to play for dances and eventually he gave up his studies entirely. He and his band, the now–famous Wolverines, toured the middlewest and immediately young Bix's horn was established as its brightest star. Jazz followers detected the boy's talent; his fellow musicians did, too. In a short time, Beiderbecke was becoming the idol of every musician who carried a union card.

Tall and good–looking, Bix was a personable lad whose mop of brown hair stayed in place for only a few minutes at the start of a playing session. He wasn't much of a woman's man. Bix never gambled or went nuts over blondes. His tastes in music, for a jazz man, were something out of the ordinary. But Bix was not an ordinary guy. The modernism of Stravinsky and Debussy's shimmering impressionism appealed to him. Like Ellington of today, Bix wore out such Debussy recordings as Afternoon of a Faun and Clair de Lune.

BLOWIN' IN THE CORN

Thruout the life of Beiderbecke are sprinkled anecdotes about his individuality, personality and willingness to pull anything for kicks. Among the best Bix yarn spinners is Hoagy Carmichael (the Stardust man) and one of the late musician's best friends. Carmichael named one of his sons Bix, and has a number of Beiderbecke mementos: his mouthpiece, cuff links, original manuscripts, etc. Carmichael tells the story of how one wintry night when and Bix were riding from Chicago to Richmond, Ind., for a recording date, Beiderbecke suddenly got a yen to play. Bix stopped the car, grabbed his horn and at 3 a.m. in the morning in a cornfield started playing Way Down Yonder in New Orleans. He handed the horn to Carmichael who ripped off a chorus. Then Bix took it up again to play one of his greatest performances. After finishing, Bix said: "You weren't bad, Hoagy."

JOINS TRUMBAUER

Bix jobbed around for a short time after the Wolverine's band and then went to Charley Straight's orchestra in Chicago. He spent a year in St. Louis with Frankie Trumbauer, and then joined the big Jean Goldkette outfit in Detroit. Bix was 24 years old those days, and recognized as just about the best in the business. He was also happy, for he had the chance to alternate between sweet and hot music.

At this time, there was coming into prominence one Paul Whiteman, who scouted Bix, hired him and featured him in the small hot section with his orchestra. The young zealots clamored for Beiderbecke, and soon his fame was nationwide. Whiteman hired over 800 musicians in the last quarter of a century, many of whom later assembled their own bands or became great solo men. Of all those, Whiteman states definitively that Beiderbecke was the greatest.

As a tribute to the almighty Beiderbecke, Whiteman says that Bix's sheet of the score to be played bore only the notation "ad lib." This was in deference to Bix's genius for improvisation. "He created his choruses as he played them," Whiteman said, "and each sounded as tho Gabriel was guiding his fingers."

Bix did not read music with great ability. Once he stuck a pulp magazine on his rack to make it look good. He was unethical in his approach to music, which was far ahead of his time. As Wayne Rohlf, Davenport trumpet player puts it:

"Bix was probably the greatest improviser the world has ever known—his style of licks, chords and progressions were years ahead of their time. Altho he couldn't readily read music until the last couple of years on earth, he played in perfect pitch. Even today, Bix's playing is considered very modern. He didn't bother to practice very much and subsequently his range was limited. Except for an occasional scream, Bix rarely went out of the staff.

"There are many men better than Bix who can play ten times as much cornet as he could. But there isn't a man, living or dead who can improvise the beautiful solos for which Bix is noted. Technically, he wasn't a great musician, but my God, what glorious music he played!"

MISSES TRAIN, TAKES PLANE

With Whiteman, Bix was at his greatest height. He played his best horn and had his best licks. Once he missed a train to a concert in Houston, Whiteman recalls. "This was in 1926, when plane travel was an event. We'd been enroute for about three hours when suddenly we heard the zoom of an airplane overhead. It dove to a low altitude, circled our train, and we knew it was Bix and that he would get to the Rice hotel hours ahead of us so he could catch up on his sleep.

"He did, but too well. He overslept at the hotel, missed the concert and the fee that went with it. Besides, he was out $75 for the plane. Another time he overslept; when he woke up he slammed his self-locking trunk shut with the key inside. A banjo man shoved an overcoat over Bix's pajamas and rushed him to the train. There he borrowed clothes from some of the boys.

"I was often sore at his irresponsibility—until he began to play. I shall never forget the exhilarating grandeur of his playing."

HE LIKED CORNET

Bix, in those days, was making about $300 a week, besides sizable royalties from his recordings. (His mother still receives royalties from his records.) He had absolute disdain for a trumpet, giving away several of them to pals after they had been presented to him by manufacturers. He preferred the mellow, throatier notes of the cornet to the shrillness of a trumpet.

As long as Bix could play that horn of his he was happy. After a night's toil with his regular band he would retire to some café with a few other musical cohorts and jam out until morning. There is a story that Bix and Louis "Satchmo" Armstrong, regarded in the present era of jazz as the best of hot trumpeters, once hooked up in a horn blowing duel. Musicians tell that Bix and Louie got together for their blowfest late one night after a Chicago theater had emptied of its evening crowd. Only a few musicians heard the duel of horns. In the semi–darkness of the auditorium, Bix stood in the balcony, horn to his lips. Poised in the opposite balcony was Armstrong. First Bix would blow. Then Armstrong would answer him. Like two Gabriels sounding from opposite mountain tops. They blew into the night. Finally, Louie, collapsing in ecstasy, tossed his horn aside and bellowed: "You win, Bixie. I can't play as good as you, and nobody else can either."

BIX STARTS TO CRACK

He was only 26 years old when he began to slip. Bix was working too hard in the fast–living fraternity. Other things piled up. Ferde Grofe's work—Whiteman's arranger—bewildered Bix. Demands of the band became greater and greater—recordings, radio shows, and strictly commercial music. It was a headache for Bix, who found himself buried in a complicated musical maze from which he couldn't fight himself out. His health began to fail, and the great Bix began to crack. Whiteman sent him back to Davenport for a rest.

In 1931, a recovered but mixed–up Beiderbecke returned to New York; however he didn't feel up to rejoining the Whiteman band. He played a few radio dates, jobbed with roadhouse bands and made a few records, but mostly he plunked out tunes on the piano in his little hotel room. In the summer of 1931, Bix caught a bad cold and was forced to take to his bed. On a July afternoon a musician came to him with the news: "We've a date at Princeton University, but they want you or we don't get the job." Jobs were scarce in those days, and the likeable Bix wasn't one to let his friends down. He hauled himself out of bed and went to Princeton with the boys. Bix returned to his hotel room a very sick guy.

HE DIES

It was a hot night and he had a fever. Sometimes Bix didn't use his head. He didn't that night. He went to sleep in front of an electric fan. Two days later, the doctor said that Bix's condition was critical. Frankie Trumbauer called Davenport, convincing Bix's mother and brother to come to New York right away. Bix had pneumonia. They left immediately but didn't make it in time. Bix died that night, August 6, 1931.

It is important for history to properly record the authentic origin of the Bix Beiderbecke memorial.

Many years ago, Doctor David Palmer and his wife called upon Bix Beiderbecke's brother who was at that time custodian of Oakdale Cemetery; telling him he wanted to start a fundraising memorial for Bix. His brother's main quote heard by Dave and his wife was: "You'll never get it off the ground".

Dave started a memorial fund by his own donation in escrow at a Davenport bank. The result was that Doctor David Palmer planned a memorial service at the gravesite of Bix at Oakdale Memorial Gardens Julie McDonald, Lucille Mauget, Esten Spurrier and his wife and Jimmy O'Dette, Sr. and his young son were among the attendants, which perhaps did not exceed ten people. Jimmy O'Dette, Sr. called his small son to meet Mrs. Palmer. As the little boy came from behind the tombstone to shake her hand he was only half her height, so was quite young, and probably doesn't remember. Paul Ives was also there.

Jimmy O'Dette, Sr. played "Nearer My God to Thee" on his accordian, after someone gave a eulogy. It cannot be recalled at this time who it was. Dave called upon Esten Spurrier to play taps on his cornet as a closing tribute to Bix Beiderbecke.

Living witnesses: Julie McDonald

Mrs. D.D. (Dr. Agnes) Palmer

Lucille Mauget

DAVID D. PALMER

LA's KFI began annual Bix tribute programs thanks to Larry Andrews & David Palmer, seen below third and second from right.

AT TECHNICAL COUNCIL SESSION—Among leaders at the dinner meeting of the Quad-city Technical council in the Masonic temple Wednesday night were (left to right) A. F. Burleigh, American Society of Civil Engineers; C. W. Anderson, executive secretary of Associated Industries of Quad-cities; B. D. Kent, vice president of the technical council; W. L. Lawrence, of the RCA promotion department, speaker; Hans I. Hansen, president of the Quad-city Technical council; Larry Andrews, president of the Quad-city Radio Technicians association; Dr. Dave Palmer, vice president of the Tri-city Broadcasting Co., and R. G. Stearns, chairman of the technical council.

March 1954

Beiderbecke Program

The memory of Bix Beiderbecke, the late great trumpeter from Davenport, Ia., will be commemorated on KFI from 10 to 11 p.m. today on the American Popular Music program.

March 1955

Beiderbecke Tribute on KFI at 9:30 p.m.

A 90-minute tribute to the late jazz artist Bix Beiderbecke is set for 9:30 p.m. today on radio station KFI on "America's Popular Music" show.

Beiderbecke Memorial Week is an observance originated and celebrated each year by the citizens of the jazz artist's home town, Davenport, Iowa.

March 1956

Program to Honor Jazz Trumpeter

An hour and a half birthday tribute to trumpet and cornet player Bix Beiderbecke will be broadcast by Andy Mansfield for the fourth consecutive year at 9:30 p.m. today on radio station KFI.

Mansfield will do Bix's life story in records from the first with his own little band, to his last where he played a small role with Paul Whiteman and his orchestra.

In a short span of 4 years, Beiderbecke rose to great heights in the jazz field. He died an untimely death at the age of 31.

The regular world was not overly startled at his death. Newspapers carried only a few inches on his obit, but the music world was crying. Walter Winchell decried the apathy of the public toward the Beiderbecke death, describing him as one of music's "all time greats."

And so they buried the almighty Bix in Oakdale cemetery. His grave is a shrine for the jazz world, and is visited more than any other in the cemetery...some of his pals came to Davenport on an anniversary of his death and played jazz over his grave...It may sound irreverent to some but Bix would have liked that perfect tribute. All he would have asked was that the boys play it with unfettered imagination, letting it ride joyously into the air, as free and easy as the air itself.

Text of undated letter about the 1949 Bix memorial service:

It is important for history to properly record the authentic origin of the Bix Beiderbecke memorial.

Many years ago, Doctor David Palmer and his wife called upon Bix Beiderbecke's brother who was at that time custodian of Oakdale Cemetery; telling him he wanted to start a fundraising memorial for Bix. His brother's main quote heard by Dave and his wife was: "You'll never get it off the ground".

Dave started a memorial fund by his own donation in escrow at a Davenport bank. The result was that Doctor David Palmer planned a memorial service at the gravesite of Bix at Oakdale Memorial Gardens. Julie McDonald, Lucille Mauget, Esten Spurrier and his wife and Jimmy O'Dette, Sr. and his young son were among the attendants, which perhaps did not exceed ten people. Jimmy O'Dette, Sr. called his small son to meet Mrs. Palmer. As the little boy came from behind the tombstone to shake her hand he was only half her height, so was quite young, and probably doesn't remember. Paul Ives was also there.

Jimmy O'Dette, Sr. played "Nearer My God to Thee" on his accordion, after someone gave a eulogy. It cannot be recalled at this time who it was. Dave called upon Esten Spurrier to play taps on his cornet as a closing tribute to Bix Beiderbecke.

- DAVID D. PALMER (1906–1978) was the grandson of the founder of the chiropractic profession and became the third president of Palmer College and head of Palmer Broadcasting Co. after his father, B.J. Palmer, died in 1961. He served as president of the Davenport Chamber of Commerce at the time the original Bix memorial was held.
- AGNES PALMER, nee Agnes Mae High (1913–1998) married David Palmer in 1943. Besides graduating from Palmer and operating her own successful chiropractic practice, Agnes was an accomplished sculptress. She did the busts of her husband and her mother–in–law, Mabel Heath Palmer, for the college's Brady Street Heritage Wall. She also sculpted busts of Robert F.

Kennedy, and Lee Enterprises president/*QC Times* publisher Philip D. Adler, whose name is now attached to the former RKO Orpheum Theater in Davenport and he was a classmate of Bix.

- JULIE MCDONALD, a long-time QC reporter, recalled having signed this letter in the early 1970s but said she was *not* present at that early graveside gathering.
- LUCILE MAUGET (1904–2002) was David Palmer's administrative secretary and associated with Palmer Corp for 57 years, retiring in 1985.
- JIMMY O'DETTE (1897–1963) played in a local band billed as *America's Biggest Little Band* and played with Esten Spurrier at the Blackhawk Hotel in the 1920s where the show aired live on WOC; Bix sat in with them in 1929.
- DON O'DETTE (1929–1988) helped organize the 1971 graveside tribute with New Jersey's Bix Beiderbecke Memorial Band; he then became founding president of the Bix Beiderbecke Memorial Society.
- PAUL IVES (1905–1998) was the program manager at WOC radio, and former theater manager for the Capitol and Family theaters. He and the Palmers were members of Trinity Episcopal Cathedral in Davenport.
- ESTEN SPURRIER (1905–1980) is likely the author of the letter. Gloria O'Dette said the storytelling style sounds like him, including *remembering* either of Jimmy O'Dette's sons—Don or his brother Jim as *small boys*. Jim Jr. was six years older but Don was the bigger

of the two and already playing professionally at the time of that graveside gathering, she said. Spurrier enlisted the help of TV personality Dave Garroway in 1952 to attempt again for an annual Bix tribute. His belief in Bix's capacity to draw a crowd, even in death, was proven in 1971 when 1,500 people showed up for the graveside musical tribute by a New Jersey band.

4 March 1953 *Davenport Times*: TO REVIEW LIFE, MUSIC OF NOTED JAZZ COMPOSER

The many achievements of the late Leon (Bix) Bismark Beiderbecke will be reviewed in special memorial program Tuesday in Davenport, his birth and burial place, by the Beiderbecke Memorial Committee, George A. Cooke, chairman, of

Chicago, announced today.

Local members of the committee include Dave Palmer, vice–president of the Palmer enterprises and president of the Davenport Chamber of Commerce, and Esten Spurrier, chief civil deputy in the Scott county sheriff's office and well–known Quad–City musician. Both men are making arrangements for the Davenport memorial programs, which will include special radio and TV broadcasts with members of the national committee attending.

A special graveside service will be held Tuesday morning at Bix's grave in Oakdale cemetery.

Beiderbecke was born and reared in Davenport before he gained fame as one of the greatest figures in the jazz world. He died in 1931 while still a young man of 28, with the music world at his feet.

The music world never forgot the Beiderbecke cornet, his rare composing talents and his impression on Music Americana, Palmer said. "It is only fitting that his home honors the man who has left such a deep impression on American music," Palmer added.

Today, 22 years after his death, Beiderbecke is more renowned and more revered than he was while still alive. His name is known the world over with special festivals held in his honor in England and sections of the United States. Bing Crosby, in a special article in *Saturday Evening Post* this week paid special tribute to his old show partner, Beiderbecke.

Members of the Memorial committee who are scheduled to participate in the Davenport programs include Dr. John Steiner, research chemist and recording studio owner of Chicago; Fosdick Goodrich, advertising executive of Popular Science magazine; C.E. Powell, Peoria lumber executive, William Priestly, industrial architect.

10 Mar 1953 *Davenport Times*: HONOR MUSICIAN'S MEMORY

Members of the National Beiderbecke Memorial Committee today paid tribute to the young Davenporter who made music history during his brief and colorful career—Bix Beiderbecke.

In simple graveside services this morning in Oakdale cemetery a large floral piece was placed on the grave of the great cornet player who died in 1931 at the age of 28.

Attending the services were Dave Palmer, president of the Davenport Chamber of Commerce and member of the committee; Esten Spurrier, chief civil deputy in the Scott county sheriff's office and well–known musician, and other members of the committee from Chicago.

The Chicago group included Dr. John Steiner, research chemist; George A. Cooke, chairman of the national committee; Fosdick Goodrich, magazine advertising executive; C.E. Powel, Peoria lumber company executive; and William Priestly, industrial architect.

Also at the graveside services was C.B. Beiderbecke, brother of Bix and secretary–treasurer of the Oakdale Cemetery association.

Davenport was the center for the national memorial services for Bix as over 400 radio stations throughout the nation aired special programs featuring records of Bix and his cornet.

Dave Garroway, emcee of the NBC television show "Today" featured a special section of the program with scenes of Davenport and conversations with Esten Spurrier and Frank Trumbauer, one of Bix's old bandmates who arrived in Davenport Monday.

Local radio stations are planning evening programs which will feature discussions by members of the committee as some of Bix's records are played. The committee will appear on WOC–TV at 6 p.m. in a special memorial program.

Davenport Times (3-10-53)—attending the Bix Beiderbecke memorial services today in Oakdale cemetery were members of the National Beiderbecke Memorial committee. Shown at the grave, standing, L-R: Dave Palmer, George A. Cooke of Chicago; Larry Andrews, Radio Station KMFA; C.B. Beiderbecke; kneeling, L-R: Esten Spurrier, John Steiner of Chicago, Rex Kleinhen, vice president of Davenport Chamber of Commerce

The committee will meet tonight to organize plans to establish a Beiderbecke Memorial in Davenport. The idea of the memorial has been discussed in previous years. However, adequate funds for such a project have not been available.

6 August 1971, *Davenport Democrat*:

Jazz buffs and musicians wearing *Bix Lives* buttons toasted the jazz immortal Bix Beiderbecke, with early morning champagne and the *Davenport Blues*—the song he wrote for his hometown—over his grave at Oakdale Cemetery today. More than 1,500 people gathered before the simple headstone in the Beiderbecke family plot to honor the trumpeter and composer on the fortieth anniversary of his death at age 28 on August 6, 1931.

7 August 1971 *Des Moines Register*:

A floral tribute from the Musician's Union, placed behind the tombstone, reads: Bix Lives—Our Most Famous Member. The band is composed of, from left: Joe Ashworth, Skip Strong, John Schober, Jay Duke, Bill Taggart, John Gill, Bill Barnes and William Donohoe, who is out of picture. The musicians are all from the East.

Leon (Bix) Beiderbecke would have felt right at home.

The jazz band was playing his own *Davenport Blues* and later there were his favorites, *Louisiana*, and *At the Jazz Band Ball*.

"He lives on through his music," said cornetist Bill Barnes, 36, of Smithtown, N.Y., a member of the Bix Beiderbecke Memorial Jazz Band.

The band and some 1,500 persons gathered at the cemetery Friday to pay tribute to the jazz great in an unusual memorial service.

Rev. C.H. Meyer, pastor of St. Mark Lutheran Church gave the eulogy. "Today, we thank God for the life of Bix Beiderbecke...His memory and his music belong to the ages."

As the service ended, the crowd—many of them elderly and middle-aged men and women, but composed too of long-haired youths and young parents with children—began clapping in time to *When the Saints Go Marchin' In*.

"We felt the finest tribute we could give to Bix would be to play jazz at his grave," said Esten Spurrier of Davenport, who played in bands with Beiderbecke. "I'm proudest of being able to take the stigma out of playing jazz in a cemetery with a tasteful service like this."

Bix's brother, Charles Beiderbecke, 75, of Davenport, was there, as well as old friends of the beloved jazz musician.

"People called here from all over the country asking about the date of the service," said Mr. Beiderbecke, who said he was never a musician. "Music is in me, but I never got it out of me...My brother, he got it all out."

Doc Ryker, now 73, of New York City, was there, too. Ryker had played first saxophone beside Beiderbecke as a member of the Jean Goldkette orchestra in 1926-27. "It must have been very hard for him to play with the rest of us, who weren't as good as he," said Ryker. "He was so good, when he took a chorus, I'd sit and listen and forget to come back in when I was supposed to..."

The memorial jazz band members are part of a growing group on the East Coast who meet regularly to celebrate the memory of the late jazz great. Annually, a Bix Beiderbecke Memorial Stomp is held at the home of E. William Donohoe, Long Valley, N.J., a data processing executive.

Donohoe, who played the washboard in the band Friday, said the group has talked about coming to play at Bix' grave for years, deciding to do it on the fortieth anniversary of his death.

"This is Mecca to us...Bix was the greatest," he said. "All the greats—Hoagy Carmichael, Gene Krupa, the late Louis Armstrong—said Beiderbecke was the greatest genius of the jazz world." Donohoe admits Bix is an obsession to him—and the other members of the cult. Donohoe's kitchen clock is stopped at 9:30 a.m., the time Beiderbecke died.

The band moved on to a program at the Davenport Library, went out to play on a river excursion boat in the afternoon, visited some of Beiderbecke's old haunts and took part in a public concert Friday night.

Pg 3 photo ID: Gravel-voiced Bill Barnes of Smithtown, N.Y., sings the Dixieland tune, *When the Saints Go Marchin' In* **over the grave of Leon (Bix) Beiderbecke Friday in Davenport.**

Barnes doesn't try to imitate Beiderbecke on the cornet, saying, "Nobody can get the same tone—round and pure—that Bix had. But the real thing about him was his harmonics, the way he played the chord changes.

"Had he lived, he would have been one of the originators of modern jazz."

Des Moines Register, July 1977:

Davenport, IA—Donald O'Dette is a Davenport electrician, known by many people for his handiwork with wiring and the like. O'Dette is content to squeeze his money-making work around his life's primary interest: the music of Bix Beiderbecke.

That love of his consumes about half his time during the year, and its most visible outlets are the Bix Beiderbecke Memorial Society, which O'Dette helped to found and which he leads today, and the music festival the society sponsors annually in Bix's memory.

O'Dette, a rotund man of 49 years, has been president of the society since it was formed in 1971 following an unusual musical memorial service at Bix's grave here in Oakdale Cemetery on the fortieth anniversary of the musician's death.

...O'Dette's enthusiasm for the famed cornetist began during his childhood, he said. His father Jimmy, himself a professional musician, was an acquaintance of Bix's and Don recalls spending many hours as a young man in Davenport listening to Bix's style of music being played by Beiderbecke's friends.

O'Dette started to follow his father's musical footsteps but he gave up a career as a professional musician when he discovered that there wasn't enough *ham* in him and that he would rather please himself with the music he played, rather than the paying public.

"Hell, I just like to play," he said. "I had many opportunities. Nobody stopped me." One of O'Dette's musical mentors, Esten Spurrier of Davenport, said there is no question of Don's musical abilities.

"He's top-notch. If Don would practice and play, he would set any cornet player on his ear." Spurrier played for many years with Jimmy O'Dette before he realized what Don later was to discover. "There isn't much money in the music business. You play till you get it out of your system."

O'Dette has been playing musical instruments for 35 years. He's at home with

1971 Memorial Gathering

An Anniversary Blast for Bix

Jazz Band Performs at Bix Beiderbecke's Grave

'When the Saints...'

Library Gets Tapes

Jim Grover, right, representing Miami University Radio, presents Robert Kellenberger, chairman of the Davenport Public Library Board of Trustees, original tapes of 19 half-hour radio shows, including interviews with many musical greats who knew and admired Bix Beiderbecke. Grover says the programs will soon be aired on national radio networks. [Staff Photo]

the cornet, bass horn, bass fiddle, trombone and drums, and he said he plays "damn little piano and much less guitar. And my clarinet is despicable."

Don left the professional music career behind in the early 1960s, but he still picks up the cornet and plays in the Davenport Jazz Band, a six-member group of musical hobbyists who limit their performances primarily to an occasional party.

ABOUT THAT BIX BUST

Eight years passed before the Bix festival produced enough extra revenue to make a permanent memorial to Davenport's legendary son. That happened on July 24, 1980, when the bust and large stone court and backdrop was formally dedicated with Davenport Mayor Charles Wright presiding.

Don O'Dette

LeClaire, IA, sculptor Ted McElhiney was commissioned to create a bronze bust, portraying Bix as the public knows him with his slicked-back hair parted in the middle, ears slightly protruding, and jaunty bow tie in place. The bust was sculpted in clay, and then cast at the Paragon Foundries in nearby Oregon, Illinois. It's two feet high and weighs 140 pounds. Few probably know that a twin bust was made for the Putnam Museum. McElhiney was later commissioned by the *Quad-City Times* to create a full-body bronze statue of Bix for their memorial park at the confluence of River Drive and Fourth Street.

The LeClaire Park bust sits on a five-foot stainless steel pedestal just north of the band shell. When the river hits its 15-foot flood stage the water spills into the park, reaching 20-foot depths in spots. On at least two occasions flood waters have reached Bix's bow tie, but never covered his head. Needed repairs were made in 2006, including bronze plaques that replaced the original plastic-lettered panels honoring Bix and Don O'Dette, founding president of Bix Beiderbecke Memorial Society.

Over the years, thousands of visitors have had their pictures taken with Bix, sometimes even adorning him with their own headgear.

BIX BEIDERBECKE MEMORIAL
LeClaire Park on the Davenport Levee
Below: Flood of '93

BIX MURAL painted in 1988 by Loren Shaw-Hellige on a former parking ramp at 2nd &Perry.

Bix and his *Davenport Blues* got sopped in the Flood of '93 and torn down to make way for the Radisson Hotel, built in 1995.

Without music, life would be an error. ~Friedrich Nietzsche

Appendix

Charles & Louise Beiderbecke Estates

Points of Interst Then & Now

Bix Kin

Image Index

Coda

Bix Meets Louis

INSTRUCTION. — The appraisers in making their appraisement must affix a value to each item of property separately, as the same appears in the list.

APPRAISERS' BILL.

Estate of **Chas. Beiderbecke** Deceased.

STATE OF IOWA, SCOTT COUNTY, ss.   IN DISTRICT COURT.

An Appraisement Bill of the Goods, Chattels, and Personal Estate of **Chas. Beiderbecke** late of said County, deceased, so far as the same have come to our sight and knowledge; which appraisement has been made by us by virtue of the annexed warrant from the District Court of said County, we having been first duly sworn as required by law.

When the deceased leaves a widow, all personal property which in his hands as the head of a family would be exempt from execution, after being inventoried and appraised, shall be set apart to her as her property, and be exempt in her hands as in the hands of the decedent.— Code 1897, page 1260, Chapter 3, Section 3315.

[Read carefully the printed instructions at the head of this page before making any entries here.]

Copy of list of property subject to appraisement, as shown by the inventory filed by the **Executors** of said estate.

LIST OF PROPERTY LEFT IN HANDS OF WIDOW, EXEMPT FROM EXECUTION.

ARTICLES	Dollars	Cts.
Reception Hall. 1 Music Stand, 1 Piano and 2 stools, 3 Rugs, 2 Stands, 2 Chairs, 2 Rockers, 1 Settee, 1 Desk, 1 Pillow, 1 Silk Curtain, 1 Desk Lamp, 4 Small Pictures, 1 Clock, 1 Bust of Schiller, 1 Card Receiver, 1 Paper Basket, 1 Guitar.	181	35
Library. 1 Screen, 1 Couch, 4 chairs, 1 Rocker, 1 Table, 1 Book Case, 1 Clock, 1 Music Stand, 1 Work Basket, 1 Flower Table, 3 Pictures, Fire tongs Shovel and stand, 1 Rug, 1 Mirror, Curtains, Bric a Brac.	41	35
Dining Room 1 Table, 1 Clock, 9 Chairs, 1 High Chair, 1 Rug, 4 pair Curtains, 1 Tea Table, 1 flower stand, 1 Screen, 1 pair Fire Dogs	29	00
Parlor Carpet, 2 pr. curtains, 2 pr. Portiers, 1 Settee, 5 chairs, 1 Arm chair, 1 Foot Rest, 1 Table, 1 Stand, 1 Tabourette, 4 Pictures, 1 Bisque Plaget, 1 Mirror		

LIST OF GENERAL ASSETS OF SAID ESTATE.

ARTICLES	Dollars	Cts.
1 Pedestal and Urn, 1 pair Candelabras, 1 Clock, 1 large vase, 1 small vase, Bric a Brac and Books, 4 Pillows	144	50
Vestibule. 1 pr. Curtains, 1 Iron Flower Stand and Urn, 1 Hall chair, 1 Hat Rack.	17	50
Bedding to the value of about $150.00	150	

Sewing Room. 3 Pictures, 1 Table, 2 Chairs, 1 Dresser, 1 Sewing Machine, 1 Lamp, Matting on the floor.	5	00
Upstairs Sitting Room. 3 chairs, 1 Arm chair, 1 Couch, 1 Desk, 2 Tables, 1 Stand, 1 pair Curtains, 2 Pictures, 3 Vases, Carpet.	14	75
Man Servants Bed Room. 1 Wardrobe, 1 Bed, 1 Wash Stand, 1 Small Table, 2 chairs, 1 Mirror.	6	75
Linen Closet. Blankets and Linen. all Bedding see Bedding	1	50
Stair Landing. 2 pair Curtains.	2	
Upstairs Hall. 1 Table, 1 Rocker, 1 Sofa, 1 Rug, 1 Lamp, 1 Jardinere, 1 Picture.	6	00
Sitting Room. 1 Mirror, 2 pair Curtains, 2 pr. Portiers, 1 Sofa, 2 Rockers, 2 Tabourettes, 2 chairs, 1 Table, 1 Cabinet, 1 Lamp, (Piano), 1 Revolving Book Case, 1 Book Stand, 1 Smoke Stand, 4 Pictures, 1 Rug, 1 Iron Flower Stand, Bric a Brac.	63	00
China Closet. Dishes, Table Linen, Glasses.	20	00
Kitchen. 3 chairs, 1 Range, 1 Table, 1 Clock.	4	50
Kitchen Pantry. Cooking Utensils.	2	50
Back Hall. 1 Hat Rack, 1 Towel Rack		85
Laundry. 1 Gas Stove, 1 Laundry Stove, 1 Table, 1 Kitchen Cabinet, 2 Chairs, 1 Floor Brush, 1 Ice Box	8	70
Cellar. 1 Billard Table and belongings, 3 chairs, 2 Cabinets, 20 tons hard coal, 10 Bushels soft coal.	226	
Servant Girls' Room. 1 Bed, 1 Wash Stand, 1 Stand, 3 chairs, 1 Mirror.	4	25
Barn Sleigh, 1 Coupe, 1 Surry, 1 Phaeton, 1 Lawn Mower, 1 Horse, 3 Sets Single Harness, 15 bu. Oats, No. bu. Oats, ½ ton Hay, 7 Garden Benches, 8 Garden Chairs, 1 Table, 1 Hose Reel, 100 feet Hose, 2 Fur Robes, 1 Plush Robe, 1 Ladder, 2 Light Robes, 1 Lawn Roller	302	60
S. W. Bed Room. 1 Bed, 1 Dresser, 1 Table, 1 Carpet.	12	25

S.E. Bed Room 1 pair Porters, 1 pr. Curtains, 3 chairs, 1 Rocker, 1 Bed, 1 Medicine Chest, 1 Carpet, 6 Pictures (Family) 1 Dresser, 1 Table. ... 40.00

Bath Room 1 Medicine Chest, 1 Chair, 1 Mirror ... 1.25

East Bed Room 1 Picture, 1 Bed, 1 Table, 2 Chairs, 1 Wash Stand and belongings, 1 Bureau. ... 11

Total ... 1445.10

General Assets.

Item	Rate	Value
Certificate of Deposit Iowa National Bank	1500.00	1500
20 Shares Merchants and Mechanics Loan and Building Association	@ 20.00	400
Dpt. Shooting Association (Note)	100.00	000
5 Shares Hawkeye Electric Mfg. Co.		000
25 " German Savings Bank		4375
1 share Davenport Co-Operative Bank		250
825 Shares Beiderbecke-Miller Co.	@ 75.00	61875
21 " First National Bank	125.00	2625
22 " Citizens National Bank	130.00	2860
1 Share Lincoln County Land Co.		750
29 Shares Iowa National Bank	120	3480
Gustave Donald Note	50.00	00
Salary at Iowa National Bank		00
11 Shares Davenport Mills Co.		00
4 " Northern Cremation Society		00
8 " Davenport Fair and Exposition		00
5 " Bettendorf Axle Co.	@ 60.00	300
10 " Davenport Safety Deposit Co.	@ 15.00	150
2 " Davenport Foundry + Machine Co.		00
20 " Masonic Temple Association	23.50	470
Herman Lohmeyer Note	Mch. 4000.00	00
Balance in Scott County Savings Bank	948.95	948.95
" " German Savings Bank	831.58	831.58
Mortgage C.S. Ackley and wife	2700.00	2700
" " James F. Hall	3500.00	3500
Balance due at Beiderbecke-Miller Co.	1706.23	1706.23

Total. 90166.86

Certified to by us, this third day of December A.D. 1901.
We also certify that we attended and served _____ day — each in appraising said property.

F. Dyyer
H. Leiffert   } Appraisers
Chas Fircke

II. GENERAL ASSETS.

Exempt Property, Continued.

NO. | **ARTICLE.**

1. Medicine Chest. 1 Carpet. 6 Pictures (Family) 1 Dresser, 1 Table,
Bath Room 1 Medicine Chest. 1 Chair, 1 Mirror.
East Bed Room. 1 Picture, 1 Bed, 1 Table, 2 Chairs, 1 Wash Stand and belongings. 1 Bureau.

General Assets.

Certificate of Deposit Iowa National Bank.	1800.00
20 Shares Merchants and Mechanics Loan and Building Association.	
Sgt. Shooting Association (Note)	100.00
5 Shares Buckeye Electric Mfg. Co.	
25 " German Savings Bank	
1 Share Davenport Co-Operative Bank.	
825 Shares Biederbecke Miller Co.	
21 " First National Bank.	
22 " Citizens National Bank.	
1 Share Lincoln County Land Co.	
29 Shares Iowa National Bank.	
Gustave Donald Note	50.00
Salary at Iowa National Bank.	
11 Shares Davenport Mills Co.	
4 " Northern Cremation Society.	
8 " Davenport Fair and Exposition.	
5 " Bettendorf Axle Co.	
10 " Davenport Safety Deposit Co.	
2 " Davenport Foundry & Machine Co.	
20 " Masonic Temple Association.	
Herman Sohmeyer Note	Mark. 4000.00
Balance in Scott County Savings Bank.	948.95
" " German Savings Bank.	831.58
Mortgage C. S. Aspley and Wife.	2700.00
" " James J. Hall	8500.00
Balance due at Biederbecke Miller Co.	1706.23

IN THE DISTRICT COURT OF THE STATE OF IOWA,
IN AND FOR SCOTT COUNTY.

IN THE MATTER OF THE
   ESTATE OF
LOUISE BEIDERBECKE, Deceased.

REPORT OF EXECUTORS OF RECEIPTS AND DISBURSEMENTS FOR THE PURPOSE OF ALLOWANCE OF CLAIMS, EXPENSES, EXECUTORS' COMPENSATION AND ATTORNEYS FEES TO THE END THAT THE SAME MAY BE DEDUCTED IN ASCERTAINING FEDERAL ESTATE TAX AND IOWA INHERITANCE TAX DUE FROM THIS ESTATE.

TO SAID COURT:-

    Come now Carl T. Beiderbecke and Bismark H. Beiderbecke, and state to the Court that they are the duly appointed and legally qualified Executors of said Estate.

    That said Louise Beiderbecke died October 27-1922.

    That these Executors gave notice of their appointment, as directed by this Court, and that the year of administration will not expire until November 3rd-1923.

    The Executors state that this report is made at this time for the purpose set forth in the title of this report.

    The Executors state that under an order entered by this Court on the 22nd day of December, 1922, they made partial distribution of the assets of said estate, as follows:

  32 Shares Stock American Commercial & Savings Bank
  32   "   "   Iowa National Bank
  Cash $10,000.00

    The Executors state that the persons interested in said estate have distributed in kind the household furniture, automobile

- 2 -

and jewelry among themselves to their mutual satisfaction, and, therefore the same are no longer treated as assets of said estate.

A detailed statement of the receipts and disbursements of the Executors is as follows:-

RECEIPTS

Received	deposit in Savings Account, American Commercial & Savings Bank,	$2723.94
"	deposit in checking account in American Commercial & Savings Bank,	129.82
"	deposit in Savings account in Iowa National Bank	645.50
"	Interest on Savings accounts,	15.49
"	principal note of C. T. Beiderbecke,	2000.00
"	Interest on same,	87.10
"	principal note, C.T.Beiderbecke,	110.00
"	Interest on same,	5.25
"	principal note B. H. Beiderbecke,	5075.00
"	Interest on same,	197.71
"	principal note B. H. Beiderbecke,	279.13
"	interest on same,	11.82
"	principal V. A. Stibolt note,	1000.00
"	interest on same,	180.00
"	for War Savings Stamps,	50.00
"	four dividends of $129.00 each-First National Bank	516.00

Total,...... $13026.76

DISBURSEMENTS

Item No.		
1	Claim - Henry Claussen,	$ 10.00
	plumbing prior to October 27-1922.	
2	Claim - Mrs. A. J. Stibolt,	27.21
	Sundry household expenses prior to Oct. 27-1922	
3	Claim - H. E. Ross Electric Co.,	1.00
	Electrical services prior to Oct. 27-1922	
4	Claim - Otis Elevator Co.,	37.50
	Elevator Inspection, etc., prior to October 27-1922.	
5	Claim - Schlegel's Drug Stores,	4.85
	For merchandise prior to Oct. 27-1922.	
6	Claim - J.H.C.Petersens Sons,	5.48
	Merchandise prior to October 27-1922.	
7	Claim - Louis Chanez,	2.00
	Cleaning incident to death.	
8	Claim - N.W.Bell Telephone Co.,	5.00
	For services prior to October 27-1922.	
9	Claim - L. F. Cawiezel,	10.00
	prior to Oct. 27-1922.	
10	Claim - Lorenzen Bros.	12.55
	Milk and cream prior to Oct. 27-1922.	

Item No.		
11	Claim - Worley Laundry, ...	5.00
	Washing incident to death	
12	Claim of Mid-West Grocery Co., ...	12.09
	Groceries prior to Oct. 27-1922.	
13	Claim - Peoples Light Co., ...	25.26
	Light bill prior to Oct. 27-1922.	
14	Claim - H. O. Seiffert Lumber Co., ...	14.08
	Merchandise prior to Oct. 27-1922.	
15	Claim - Henry Detlefsen, ...	4.10
	Merchandise prior to Oct. 27-1922.	
16	Claim of Weir & Meier, ...	48.00
	Insurance bill prior to Oct. 27-1922.	
17	Claim of Henry Braunlich, ...	45.00
	Medical services to deceased.	
18	Claim - Mutual Insurance Association, ...	29.77
	Assessments due prior to October 27-1922.	
19	Claim of Hill & Fredericks, ...	479.00
	Funeral expenses.	
20	Collector - Dubuque, Iowa, ...	233.70
	Income Tax Louise Beiderbecke for period January 1-1922 to October 27-1922.	
21	Collector, Dubuque, Iowa, ...	3.50
	Income Tax for Estate for period October 27-1922 to January 1-1923.	
22	Henry Vollmer, ...	25.00
	For services in making address at funeral of deceased.	
23	Paid B. H. Beiderbecke, ...	2500.00
	partial distribution December 23-1922.	
24	Paid Lutie von Binzer, ...	2500.00
	partial distribution Dec. 23-1922.	
25	Paid Ottilie Stibolt, ...	2500.00
	partial distribution December 23-1922	
26	Paid Carl T. Beiderbecke, ...	2500.00
	partial distribution December 23-1922.	
27	Paid Schicker Marble Co.	72.00
	Marker for grave of deceased,...	

Total, ... $11112.09

Total Receipts, ... $13,026.76
" Disbursements, ... 11,112.09

Balance on hand, ... $ 1,914.67

REMAINING ASSETS

43 Shares of stock of First National Bank of Davenport, Iowa.

Liberty Bonds, par - - - - $2150.00
  together with accrued interest.
German Legacy appraised at - - - 5.00
Cash - - - - - - 1914.67

    The Executors now ask that the Court approve of all of the disbursements shown by the foregoing report, and state that they have personal knowledge of the correctness of the same.

    The Executors further ask that the Court now fix and determine their compensation as Executors, and the allowance to Cook & Balluff for legal services rendered in the administration of said estate, which shall include the services of both for closing administration upon said estate.

Carl T. Beiderbecke
Bismarck H Beiderbecke
EXECUTORS.

STATE OF IOWA) SS:
SCOTT COUNTY)

We, Carl T. Beiderbecke and Bismark H. Beiderbecke, being duly sworn, on oath state that we are the Executors named in the foregoing report; that we have read the same, know its contents and that the statements therein contained are true, as we verily believe.

Carl T. Beiderbecke
Bismarck H. Beiderbecke

Subscribed in my presence by the said Carl T. Beiderbecke and Bismark H. Beiderbecke and by each of them sworn to before me this 15th day of October, 1923.

Walter M. Balluff
Notary Public in and for Scott County, Iowa.

IN THE DISTRICT COURT OF THE STATE OF IOWA,
IN AND FOR SCOTT COUNTY.

IN THE MATTER OF THE ESTATE
OF
LOUISE BEIDERBECKE, DECEASED.

FINAL REPORT OF EXECUTORS

TO SAID COURT:

Comes now Carl T. Beiderbecke and Bismark H. Beiderbecke, and state to the Court:

That they are the duly appointed and legally qualified Executors of the Last Will and Testament of Louise Beiderbecke, deceased.

The Executors state that on November 1?, 1?1?, a? Final Report to this Court on all matters relating to said Estate, except the item designated "German Legacy". That this item relates to a legacy of one Eibe Pieper to said Louise Beiderbecke.

That said Eibe Pieper died a resident of Hamburg, Germany, on April 25, 1916, and that said Louise Beiderbecke was the residuary legatee of her estate.

That in 1916 Germany was at war, and that the collection of the balance of the Estate due said Louise Beiderbecke was not determined during her lifetime.

That when the United States entered the War against Germany all of the property of non-residents of Germany was taken in charge by the Alien Property Custodian of Germany, among which was the assets of the Estate of Eibe Pieper, deceased. That after the close of the War an agreement of settlement between the Republic of Germany and the United States was consummated, under which the claims of American citizens were to be paid out of the funds in the hands of the Government of the United States, which were the proceeds of the sale of the property of German citizens in the United States.

That the Mixed Claims Commission of the United States and Germany, which passed upon said claims, made an award to these Executors as follows:

250 Marks of the new German Redemption Bonds, with drawing rights.

And also an award to be paid in cash, of the sum of Three Thousand Five Hundred Ninety-five and 21/100 ($3595.21) Dollars, with interest.

That the bonds were disposed of by these Executors, less charges for their sale, and that they realized therefrom the sum of One Hundred forty-three and 75/100 ($143.75) Dollars, net. That they received for the cash award, with interest, the sum of Five Thousand Five Hundred Seventy-three and 43/100 ($5573.43) Dollars.

That they contracted with Whitman & Knauth, of New York City, for a collection charge of fifteen per cent on the amount received as their fees, which amounted to $836.01.

That a detailed account of receipts and disbursements relating to the above matter is as follows:

RECEIPTS

Received from sale of Bonds---------------------------------$ 143.75
Received from cash award, $3595.21, and interest, $1978.22-- 5573.43

                              Total Receipts---------$5717.18

DISBURSEMENTS

Paid to Whitman & Knauth, collection charge
as per contract----------------------------------$836.01
Paid Henry Vollmer attorneys fees for services in "Legacy" matter during life
of deceased-------------------------------------- 25.00
Paid Cook & Balluff for their legal services in the matter of the handling of this claim from the date of the death of Louise Beiderbecke to the date of final payment------------- 150.00
Paid Court costs to close estate---------------- 2.50

                       Total Disbursements----------$1013.51

               Balance on hand for distribution$4703.67

The Executors state that they have disbursed the foregoing balance by paying to each of the heirs entitled thereto their share thereof.

STOCKS

43 Shares of the Capital Stock of the
First National Bank, of Davenport, Iowa,
Organized under Federal Law
Par Value $100.00 per share.
Certificate 375 for 20 Shares
" 412 " 21 "
" 430 " 2 " 10750.00

32 Shares of the Capital Stock of the
American Commercial & Savings Bank,
of Davenport, Iowa,
(Formerly German Savings Bank) an Iowa Corporation,
Par Value - $100.00 per share.
Certificate 302 for 7 shares
" 11 " 25 " 12800.00

32 Shares of the Capital Stock of the
Iowa National Bank, of Davenport, Iowa,
Organized under Federal Law.
Par Value $100.00 per share.
Certificate 659 for 3 Shares
" 634 " 29 " 9600.00

4 Shares of the Capital Stock of the
Davenport Cremation Society
an Iowa Corporation.
Par Value - $25.00 per share.
Certificate 137 for 4 Shares.   0

199 Shares of the Capital Stock of the
Shaw Land & Timber Co.
an Iowa Corporation.
Par Value - $100.00 per share.
Certificate 257 for 33 Shares
" 179 " 33 "
" 142 " 33 "
" 27 " 50 "
" 26 " 50 " 4975.00

This Company is in process of liquidation.

Distribution of principal has been made as follows:

Nov. 6-1919 - 25 per cent
Sept. 2-1920 - 20 " "

(The Stock of the Shaw Land & Timber Co. is
inventoried subject to the following explanation and claim that same is not subject to tax:)

On September 2-1920 the distribution of principal of the
Shaw Land and Timber Company was received by the four
children of deceased, as follows:

   Carl T. Beiderbecke - $995.00
   Bismark H. Beiderbecke - 995.00
   Ottilie Stibolt - 995.00
   Lutie L. von Binzer - 995.00

The value on October 27-1922 of such distribution is as follows, with interest at 6% from Sept. 2-1920:

Bismarck H. Beiderbecke	-	$1123.35
Carl T. Beiderbecke	-	1123.35
Ottilie Stibolt	-	1123.35
Lutie L. von Binzer	-	1123.35

That shortly after November 6-1919 and after liquidation of Shaw Land and Timber Company was begun, and long prior to September 2-1920, said deceased presented to her above named four children, in equal shares, the balance then remaining unpaid on the stock of the Shaw Land and Timber Company, and said children claim that the dividend received by them in distribution September 2-1920 in cash, as above stated, and the balance still to be paid on said stock in liquidation, are not part of the estate of said deceased, and are not liable for either Iowa Inheritance Tax or Federal Estate tax.

BANK DEPOSITS

Savings Account 43810 in American Commercial & Savings Bank, of Davenport, Iowa, amounting with interest to October 27-1922 to - - $2723.94

Savings Account #515 in Iowa National Bank, of Davenport, Iowa, amounting with interest to October 27-1922 to - - - 645.50

Checking Account in American Commercial & Savings Bank, of Davenport, Iowa, Balance October 27th-1922 - - 129.82

NOTES

Note - C.T.Beiderbecke   2000.00
  Dated February 1-1917
  Due on Demand
  With 5½% Interest from Mar 1-1922   - 72.10

Note - C.T.Beiderbecke   -110.00
  Dated February 1-1922
  Due on Demand
  With 6% Interest from date   - 4.35

Note - B.H.Beiderbecke   5075.00
  Dated April 1-1912
  Due on demand
  With 5½% Interest from April 1-1922- 160.50

Note - B. H. Beiderbecke   279.13   279|13
   Dated April 1-1922
   Due on Demand
   With 6% Interest from April 1-1922 - 4.88   4|88

Note V. A. Stibolt   1000.00   1000|00
   Dated July 1-1922
   Due on Demand
   With 6% Interest from July 1-1922 - 19.50   19|50

WAR SAVINGS STAMPS

Certificate 42659719 - Series A
10 Stamps of $5.00 each
     Par $50.00
     Due January 1-1923   46|90

UNEXPIRED INSURANCE

Policy	Company	Amount
B.T.C. 21659	Federal Surety Co.	.55
No. 10272	Home Insurance Co.	14.27
No. 13396	Hartford Insurance Co.	3.45
No. 4239	Royal Insurance Company	4.30
No. 6923	Milwaukee Mechanic's Ins. Co.	3.90
No. 634	Girard Fire & Marine Ins. Co.	8.12
No. 385114	National Fire Ins. Co.	4.63
No. 628	Girard Ins. Co.	36.94
No. 4533	Royal Ins. Co.	55.44
No. 14864	Insurance Co. of N. America	36.90
No. 66107	Phoenix Insurance Co.	30.80
No. 767556	Security Fire Insurance Co.	11.83
No. 766422	Security Fire Insurance Co.	26.95
No. 1240	Glens Falls Insurance Co.	8.99
No. 766417	Security Fire Insurance Co.	16.83
No. 67219	Farmers Fire Ins. Co.	27.73
No. 458	Norwich Union Ins. Co.	55.47
No. 12892	Aetna Ins. Co.	55.47
No. S.B. 231742	Maryland Casualty Co.	12.93
No. 7620	National Liberty Ins. Co.	42.65
No. 5348691	Fire Association	85.33
No. 11527	Home Insurance Co.	46.65
No. 192126	Scottish Union Ins. Co.	9.58
	Total	$599.67

599|67

HOUSEHOLD FURNITURE, ETC.

Qty	Item	Value
1	Old Clock	5 —
1	Mahogany Bed	1 —
1	" Dresser	50
1	Small Rug	30 —
	Brass Andirons and enclosure	1 —
1	Black Walnut Bed	25 —
1	" " Dresser	10 —
1	" " Stand	1 —
1	" " Wash Stand	4 —
1	Brass Stand	50
1	Oak Rocker	3 —
1	Maple Desk	5 —
1	" Chair	1 —
2	Wicker Rockers (damaged)	2 —
1	Medicine Chest	2 —
1	Oak Screen	50
1	Oak Medicine Chest	50
1	Black Walnut Chair	50
1	" " Mirror	10 —
1	Mahogany Dresser	10 —
2	Walnut Chairs	2 —
1	Plush Settee (Damaged)	1 50
1	Wicker Stand	50
1	Marble top table	2 00
3	Billiard Chairs	3 —
1	Green Plush couch (old)	1 —
1	Sewing Machine	75
1	Walnut Chair (damaged)	1 —
1	Wardrobe	50
1	Wash Stand	50
1	Stand (nest)	50
2	Electric Fans	10 —
1	Piano Lamp (damaged)	2 —
1	Oak Settee	2 —
1	" Hall Chair	1 —
1	Black Walnut Hat Rack	2 —
2	Mahogany Chairs	5 —
1	" Rocker	2 —
1	" Settee	5 —
1	" Music Cabinet	5 —
1	Wrought Iron Stand	3 —
1	Electrolier	2 —
1	Beethoven Bust	4 —
1	Incense Burner	50
1	Cut Glass Vase	3 —
1	Blue Plush Arm chair (damaged)	3 —
1	Cherry Stand	2 —
1	" Chair (Broken)	3 —
1	Wicker Chair	4 —
1	" Couch	5 —
1	Walnut panel mirror	1 50
1	Porcelain plaque	2 —
1	Overstuffed hassock	2 —
4	Silk cushions	6 —
1	Set firearms	6 —
1	Brussels Rug	10 —
1	Gold Mirror	10 —
1	Walnut Table	5 —
1	" Sofa	5 —
1	" Armchair	6 —
3	" Chairs	4 —
1	" Rocker	1 —
1	" Foot stool	50
1	" Magazine Rack	2 —
1	Cherry Music Stand	1 50
1	" Tabouret	2 —
1	Metal Pedestal	1 50

Qty	Item	Value
2	Mahogany Chairs	8 —
1	Tapestry screen	13 —
1	Large Gardinere	3 —
2	Wicker Ferneries	4 —
1	Velvet Rug	15 —
1	Oriental Rug (damaged)	2 —
1	Book case and books	20 —
1	centre table (damaged)	8 —
4	Walnut Chairs	8 —
1	Black Stand	1 —
1	Oak Rocker	1 —
1	Electrolier	8 —
2	Mahogany Candle Sticks	10 —
1	Brown Rug	3 —
1	Oak Dining Table	1 50
1	" Arm Chair	8 —
8	" Chairs	2 —
1	Tea Table	7 —
2	Glass Candelabra	10 —
1	Punch Bowl (damaged)	3 —
1	Set Andirons and enclosure	2 75
1	Set China Dishes	3 —
1	" Stone "	1 —
3	Kitchen Chairs	1 —
1	" Clock	700
1	Set Kitchen Cooking Utensils	15 —
1	Garage Bed	3 —
1	" Wash Stand	2 —
1	" Stove	1 —
1	Electric Car (2½ years old)	2 —
1	Rectifier	10 —
1	Set Garden Utensils	2 —
1	Oak Wardrobe	2 —
1	Walnut Wash Stand	15 —
1	Old Single Bed	10 —
1	Steamer Trunk	15 —
1	Hat Trunk	25 —
3	Trunks (Large)	25 —
2	Cots	4 —
2	Stands	1 —
2	Sets Porch Furniture	30 —
1	Old Desk	7 —
1	Brass Bed	2 —
1	Mahogany Chiffonier	15 —
1	" Dresser	50 —
2	Chairs	15 —
2	Pictures	6 —
1	Oriental Rug	9 —
1	Velvet Rug	16 —
1	Stair Carpet	2 —
1	Dining Room Rug	4 —
1	Silver Tea Set	5 —
2	Dozen Silver Forks	30 —
1	" Knives	1 50
1½	" odd spoons	10 —
10	Table spoons	10 —
1	Dozen Coffee spoons	20 —
1	Plated Serving Tray	
1	Silver Mirror and brush	
1	Lot small trinkets	
1	Mantle clock and candelabra	
1	small desk clock	
1	Jewelry case	
1	Lot Knicknacks	
	Sundry Pictures	
	" Linens	

```
Sundry Curtains ─────────────────────────────
1  Ring ──────────────────────────────────────      10 —
1  Ring ──────────────────────────────────────      60 —
1  Ring ──────────────────────────────────────      25 —
1  Ring ──────────────────────────────────────      75 —
1  Old Bar Pin ─────────────────────────────────    10 —
1  Pearl Pin ───────────────────────────────────     6 —
1  Diamond Cross ───────────────────────────────    25 —
1  Anchor & Chain ──────────────────────────────   200 —
1  Ladies Watch (old) ──────────────────────────     3 —
1  Piano, 27 years old. ────────────────────────   100 —
```

German Inheritance from Eibe Piper,
    Hamburg, Germany - 30,000 Marks.   500

Total Value of Schedule B - - - - - - - - - - - $5975 98

(If more space is needed attach additional sheets)

RESIDENCE OF CHAS BEIDERBECKE

534 West Seventh—Beiderbecke Inn

THEN: Charles & Louise house at 4th & Scott (right of fire station)

NOW: Central Fire Station, 331 Scott (addition)

THEN: Turner Hall and Grand Theatre

NOW: Heritage Senior High Rise, Third & Scott

THEN: Columbia Theatre, 406 Third St

NOW: Corner of Ripley & West Third

THEN: Iowa National Bank
NOW: Harrison Street Parking Ramp

THEN: Masonic Temple

Third & Main

NOW: Wells Fargo Drive-Thru Bank

**THEN: Whitaker Building　　　Brady & Third
NOW: First Midwest Bank**

THEN: Rock Island Elks Club
NOW: Blue Cat Brew Pub

18th St & First Avenue (Highway 92), Rock Island, IL

THEN: Moline LeClaire Hotel & Theatre
NOW: LeClaire Apartments

19th St & Fifth Avenue, Moline

1012 West Fourth, Davenport

THEN: Harned Von Maur
                    NOW: Figge Art Museum

THEN: Beiderbecke & Miller Wholesalers

NOW: vacant
Second & Brady, one block west of Radisson Hotel

THEN: Burtis Opera House 1867-1921

NOW: Tri-City Electric, 415 Perry St.

THEN: Outing Club in 1906

NOW: Outing Club, 2109 Brady Street

First Presbyterian

Iowa & Kirkwood

THEN

&

NOW

THEN: No. 9—Tyler School

NOW: Tyler Park

1934 Grand Avenue before & after renovation

Name (spouse)	Relationship to Leon Bix (lineage)
Beiderbecke, Adele Seiffert	aunt, wife of Carl T
Beiderbecke, Sophie Becker	great grandmother
Beiderbecke, Aggie Jane Hilton	mother
Beiderbecke, Bismark Herman	father
Beiderbecke, Bix Alexander	great-grandnephew (Charles Hilton)
Beiderbecke, Carl Thomas	uncle
Beiderbecke, Charles Burnett	brother
Beiderbecke, Charles Hilton (Eileen)	nephew
Beiderbecke, Charles Michael (Susie)	grandnephew (Charles Hilton)
Beiderbecke. Charles–Carl	grandfather
Beiderbecke, Christopher Bix	grandnephew (R. Bix)
Beiderbecke, Friedrich–Fritz	granduncle
Beiderbecke, Friedrich Wilhelm	great granduncle
Beiderbecke, Johannes Herman	granduncle
Beiderbecke, Heinrich Christof	great grandfather
Beiderbecke, Henry–Heinrich	granduncle
Beiderbecke, Louise Piper	grandmother
Beiderbecke, Margarita Hahn	wife of granduncle Heinrich
Beiderbecke, Maria Carolina	grandaunt
Beiderbecke, Mary Dennison Neelans	sister–in–law
Beiderbecke, Richard Bix (Arlene) (Judith Andrews)	nephew
Beiderbecke, Stephen Richard (Angela)	grandnephew (Charles Hilton)
Beiderbecke, Troy Marcus	great grandnephew (Charles Hilton)
Beiderbecke, Wilhelmina Johanna	grandaunt
Besse, Helen Petersen	second cousin
Besse, Ira Dale	husband of second cousin
Braren, Emma Beiderbecke	first cousin once removed
Braren, Howard	second cousin once removed
Braren, Kenneth	second cousin once removed
Braren, Ralph	second cousin
Braren, Warren	second cousin once removed
Buch, Wilhelmine–Minna C. Beiderbecke	grandaunt
Caddes, Polly Washburn (Scot)	first cousin twice removed (Gertrude)
Cavanaugh, Margaret Anne Daugherty	second cousin
Cavanaugh, Daniel P.	husband of second cousin
Chapman, Bill	first cousin twice removed
Chapman, Linda	first cousin twice removed
Chapman, Mike (Lesley)	first cousin twice removed
Chapman, Patricia–Patsy Washburn	first cousin once removed (Gertrude)
Chapman, Sam	husband of first cousin once removed
Chapman, Steve	first cousin twice removed (Gertrude)
Cummins, Dorothy Petersen	second cousin twice removed (Arthur)
Curra, Janet Noel Shoemaker	grandniece (C. Bix)
Curra, Ruthann	great–grandniece
Curra, Warren	husband of grandniece

Name (spouse)	Relationship to Leon Bix (lineage)
Curra, Warren Jr.	great grandnephew
Dery, Amy Louise Shoemaker	grandniece (C. Bix)
Dery, Eli McConnell	great grandnephew
Dery, Sammie Bix	great grandnephew
Dougherty, Edward	second cousin
Dougherty, Fannie Hilton	first cousin once removed
Dougherty, William	husband of first cousin once removed
Dunphrey, Anne Louise	great–grandniece
Dunphrey, Laura Shoemaker (Ray)	grandniece (Julien)
Dunphrey, Kyle David	great–grandnephew
Edmondson, Anne Marquardt (James)	first cousin once removed (Helen)
Fletcher, Sarah Washburn (Greg)	first cousin twice removed (Gertrude)
Hellmers, Elisabeth	great great–grandmother
Harshaw, Emma–Emily Hill	grandaunt
Harshaw, Edwin	first cousin once removed
Harshaw, William James	husband of grandaunt
Hart, Carl	husband of grandniece
Hart, Elizabeth Anne Beiderbecke	grandniece (R. Bix)
Hart, Lauren	great–grandniece
Hart, Olivia	great–grandniece
Hass, Otie Stibolt	first cousin
Hass, Elenora	first cousin once removed
Hass, Leon	husband of first cousin
Hass, Peter	first cousin once removed
Hill, Adam	great great–grandfather
Hill, Adam M.	great grandfather
Hill Addison	granduncle
Hill, Amanda Blair	wife of granduncle David
Hill, Carrie	first cousin once removed (Nelson)
Hill, Clarence	first cousin once removed (David)
Hill, David	granduncle
Hill, George	first cousin once removed (Nelson)
Hill, Jane	first cousin once removed (Nelson)
Hill, Edward	first cousin once removed (David)
Hill, Ida	first cousin once removed (David)
Hill, John	granduncle
Hill, Mary	grandaunt
Hill, Nelson	granduncle
Hill, Sarah A.	wife of granduncle Nelson
Hill, Wallace	granduncle
Hilton, Anna L.	first cousin once removed (Edmund)
Hilton, Beriah L.	maternal grandfather
Hilton, Caroline Hill	maternal grandmother
Hilton, Edmund James	granduncle
Hilton, Fannie Mason	great grandmother

Name (spouse)	Relationship to Leon Bix (lineage)
Hilton, Helen	grandaunt
Hilton, James	great–grandfather
Hilton, James R	first cousin once removed (Edmund)
Hilton, Mary Gertrude	first cousin once removed (Edmund)
Hilton, Rachel King	wife of granduncle Edmund
Kennedy, Alexander	husband of grandaunt Sarah
Kennedy, Benedict	husband of grandaunt Jane
Kennedy, Jane Hill (Benedict)	grandaunt
Kennedy, Sarah–Sallie (Alexander)	grandaunt
Kennedy, Emma	first cousin once removed (Jane)
Kennedy, Jane	first cousin once removed (Jane)
Kennedy, Sarah	first cousin once removed (Sarah)
Kennedy, William	first cousin once removed (Sarah)
Kidd, Lizzie Hill	grandaunt
Kidd, Blanche	first cousin once removed
Kidd, Frank	first cousin once removed
Lewandrowski, Callum Bix	great–grandnephew
Lewandrowski, Suzanne	grandniece (C. Bix)
Lewandrowski, Natasha	great–grandniece
Larson, Katie Washburn (Dick)	first cousin twice removed (Gertrude)
Marquardt, Allen (Natalie)	first cousin once removed
Marquardt, Clayton	first cousin twice removed
Marquardt, Helen Seiffert Beiderbecke	first cousin
Marquardt, R. Allen	husband of first cousin
Murdoch, G. Donald	husband of first cousin
Murdoch, Gretchen–Gay Beiderbecke	first cousin
Petersen, Albert Alexander (Ana Garcia–Nunez)	second cousin once removed (Arthur)
Petersen, Albert	husband of first cousin once removed
Petersen, Antoinette Moetzel	wife of second cousin Ceno
Petersen, Arthur	second cousin
Petersen Caroline–Carrie Kennedy	first cousin once removed (Sarah)
Petersen, David	second cousin twice removed (Arthur)
Petersen, Donald G.	second cousin once removed (Arthur)
Petersen, Dorothy E. Griffin	wife of second cousin Arthur
Petersen, Dorothy Swan	wife of second cousin Harry
Petersen, Harry	second cousin
Petersen, Howard	second cousin twice removed (Arthur)
Petersen, James (Sue Schwarte)	second cousin once removed (Victor)
Petersen, Jerald J.	second cousin twice removed (Victor)
Petersen, Joseph	second cousin twice removed (Arthur)
Petersen, Michael	second cousin twice removed (Arthur)
Petersen, Rebecca	second cousin thrice removed (Victor)
Petersen, Scott	second cousin twice removed (Victor)
Petersen, Victor	second cousin
Petersen, Vinceno	second cousin

Name (spouse)	Relationship to Leon Bix (lineage)
Petersen, Vincent (Winnifred Tyerman)	second cousin once removed (Ceno)
Petersen, Violet Hirl	wife of second cousin Victor
Phillips, Jennie Sheldon	second cousin
Pieper, Adolph	granduncle
Pieper, August	great-grandfather
Pieper, Caroline Hellmers	great-grandmother
Pieper, Eibe Vollmer	step great-grandmother
Piper, Catarina Maria Dorothea Sass	great great-grandmother
Piper, John Peter	great great-grandfather
Rush, Ann Weir Beiderbecke (Scott)	grandniece (Charles Hilton)
Rush, Erik Paul	great-grandnephew
Rush, Kristin	great-grandniece
Sasse, Dorothea Voss	great-great-great grandmother (Piper)
Sasse, Julius David Hans	great-great-great grandfather (Piper)
Seager, Gretchen Marquadt (David)	first cousin once removed (Helen)
Seehof, Jack (Jerri)	first cousin once removed
Seehof, Jerome	husband of first cousin Lutie
Seehof, Lutie Seiffert Beiderbecke	first cousin
Seehof, Ted (Lois)	first cousin once removed
Seehof, Tom (Jean)	first cousin once removed
Sheldon, Anna Hilton (Lemuel)	grandaunt
Shoemaker, Adam	grandnephew (C. Bix)
Shoemaker, David	grandnephew (Julien)
Shoemaker, Charles Bix (Barbara)	nephew
Shoemaker, Charles Bix Jr.	grandnephew
Shoemaker, Fredrick Warren	grandnephew (C. Bix)
Shoemaker, Julien (Marti)	nephew
Shoemaker, Julie	grandniece (C. Bix)
Shoemaker, Kevin	grandnephew (C. Bix)
Shoemaker, Lisa	grandniece (Ted)
Shoemaker, Linda	grandniece (Julien)
Shoemaker, Mary Louise Beiderbecke	sister
Shoemaker, Peter	grandnephew (Ted)
Shoemaker, Ted Jr.	nephew
Shoemaker, Ted Sr.	brother-in-law
Stibolt, Albert	husband of Aunt Tillie
Stibolt, Carl (Martha Morse) (Donna)	first cousin
Stibolt, Helen Davis	wife of first cousin Victor
Stibolt Ottilie Beiderbecke	aunt
Stibolt, Richard	first cousin once removed (Victor)
Stibolt, Thomas	first cousin once removed (Victor)
Stibolt, Victor Albert	first cousin
Stibolt, Victor Davis	first cousin once removed (Victor)
Von Binzer, Carl	first cousin
Von Binzer, Friedel	first cousin

Name (spouse)	Relationship to Leon Bix (lineage)
Von Binzer, Lutie Beiderbecke	aunt
Von Binzer, Max Moritz Carl Wilhelm	husband of Aunt Lutie
Von Binzer, Werner (Alma Barman)	first cousin
Washburn, Gertrude–Trudel Beiderbecke	first cousin
Washburn, William D.	husband of first cousin Gertrude
Washburn, Robert (Suzanne)	first cousin once removed
Washburn, Tom (Carmen)	first cousin once removed
Wolfman, Katie Murdoch (Ron)	first cousin once removed (Gretchen)
Woodward, Mary Kennedy (J.W.)	first cousin once removed (Sarah)

IMAGE INDEX

Adams, Dorothy 689
Aebersold, Jamey 278
Alford, Clarence 233
Allen, William 556, 562
Anderson, Carlyle F. 'Andy' 499
Andrews, Larry 208, 212, 217, 218, 632, 636
Arpy, Jim 689
Armstrong, Louis 273, 292, 579, 581, 617
Arsenal Bridge 3, 4, 562
Ashworth, Joe 639
Astaire, Fred 623
Bach, Vincent 571–572
Bahr, Leo 572
Bailey, Mahlon 453
Baker, Charles & Lillian 588
Ballew, Smith 497
Barnes, Bill 639
Barnett, Charlie 579
Barris, Harry 535
Barthelmess, Richard 542
Bean, Floyd 405
Beeson, Judith Ann 178, 210
Beiderbecke, Aggie 38, 41, 42, 45, 46, 84, 110, 120, 154–155, 157, 158, 160, 205, 262, 556, 558, 560–561, 587; Bismark 38, 41, 42, 44, 45, 47, 205, 214, 221, 458, 481, 556, 560–561; Burnie 41, 43, 48, 124, 132, 134, 139, 205, 460, 481, 511, 632, 636; Charles Hilton 132; Mary Neelans 128, 132; Richard Bix 132; Carl T. & Adele 28, 205, 560–561; Charles 16, 18, 19, 20, 21, 28, 66, 67, 236, 458, 644–647;

Louise 16, 18, 25, 28, 204, 205, 218, 236, 250–251, 648–659; Henry & Margarita 67, 68, 71; **LEON B.** 41, 43, 139, 141, 157, 163, 178–198, 205, 208, 212, 214, 231, 263, 332, 349, 356, 433, 442, 453, 454, 459, 463, 476, 481, 488, 497, 499, 501, 502, 511–513, 515, 517–519, 521, 526–528, 539, 546, 548, 552, 557, 567, 574, 582–583, 585–587, 598, 609, 637
Beiderbecke & Miller 5, 10, 21, 150, 216, 443, 671
Beiderbecke Five 378
Beiderbecke Inn 660, 692
Bellson, Louis 604
Berber, Ed 691
Berkell, Charles 247
Bernhardt, Sarah 239
Besse, Helen Petersen 104, 251
Best, Gretchen 590; Louis 20; Louis P, 590
Bettendorf Town Hall 428
Beyer, Theresa Evans 281
Bieberbach, Ernie & Wm 560, 594
Bigard, Barney 579
Bix Beiderbecke Orchestra 557
Bix Memorial Band 639
Black, Louis 271, 278, 280, 295
Blackhawk Hotel 374
Blank, A.H. 229
Bluebird Inn 368
Bolden, Buddy 617
Bollinger, James 590
Booth, Edwin 239
Bowers, Gerri 689

Bowlby, Wallace 339
Boyler, Frank 465
Braren, Howard 691
Braunlich, Henry 20
Brown, Steve 293
Bruhn, Lewis M. 'Louie' 590
Brunies, George 293
Bucket of Blood, 217, 366
Buckley Novelty Band 287, 372
Burke–Amidon 265
Burtis/Kimball House 4, 236
Burtis Opera House 4, 247, 672
Burton, Vic 488
Busch, Mabel & Eunice 590
Capitol Theatre 8, 604, 626
Carmichael, Hoagy 178, 502, 512, 621; Randy & Hoagy Bix 621
Carlson, Vic 339
Casals, Pablo 384
Casey Jones Jazz Jesters 425
Cassling, Arthur & Helen 588
Castle, Vernon & Irene 216
Catalano, Tony 271, 289, 290
Central Fire Station 661
Cervantes, Michael 692
Challis, Bill 518
Chappell, Ben 690
Christiansen, Bob 572
Clausen, Frederick 5, 20; Olga & Rudie 590
Claussen, Otto & Eveline 590
Cleveland Steamer 560–561
Cody, Buffalo Bill 7
Cole, Cozy 579
COL–Coliseum 381, 382, 433, 512, 522, 524–525, 568, 669, 692
Columbia Theatre 395, 398–399, 401, 663
Commercial Club 214
Condon, Eddie 469, 479, 480
Conger, Hal 331
Cook, Bob 690
Cooke, George A. 636
Correll, Charles 9
Cosgrove, Bishop Henry 6
Covarrubias, Miguel 515
Craighead, Julie 689
Craven, John H. 453
Credit Island 266
Creole Band 273
Crosby, Bing 535, 539
Crow Creek Inn 566

Daniel, Jedge 539
Darling, Jay 'Ding' 393, 439
Davenport, George 3
Davenport High School 149
Davenport Malting Co 358
Davis, John L. 146
Davison, 'Wild' Bill 474
DeFaut, Voltaire 'Vollie' 293
Deutsch, Isaac & Rebecca 588
Dodds, Johnny 273
Dockstader, Lew 395
Donohoe, William 639
Dorsey, Tommy 501, 513, 604, 609
Douglas, Kirk 626
Duke, Jay 639
Duncan, James 453
Durham, Mike 368
Eagles Danceland 384, 385, 433, 533, 567, 603
Eagles, Moline 385, 567
East Davenport Fuel Co 464–465, 558
Eckart, Blanche Searle, James & Bob 493
Ed, Carl 322
Eipper Drug 324, 326; August 325; Helen 327
Elder, Clarence 'Heavy' 275
Elks, Rock Island 567, 667
Elliott, Frank W. 453
Englin, Maureen 600–601
Europe, James Reese 487
Evans, Carlisle 271, 278, 280, 281, 283, 297, 305, 306
Evans, Phil & Linda 690
Farley, Ed 615
Farrell, Eileen 581
Fay, Romelle Alford 229, 233, 235
Ficke, Arthur 508; Charles A. 20, 440; Robert & Robert Jr. 590
Figge Art Museum 670
Fio Rito, Ted 603
First Presbyterian 144, 674
Fitzgerald, F. Scott 612
Flindt, Emil 289
Forest (Schuetzen) Park 372
Fort Armstrong 425–426, 606
Foster, Wade 332
French, Alice 5,
Freeman, Bud & Arnold 476
Gandee, Al 433
Garden Theatre 229, 544–545, 582

Gargano, Tommy 501, 513
Gast, Gene 573
Gavitte, Rex 497
Gerswhin, George 483, 557
Gill, John 639
Gillette, Bob 433, 488
Giordano, Joe & Vince 691
Glaspell, Susan 5,
Goddard, Austin 186, 217; Frank 186, 453; Ella Ficke 186
Goettsch, Arthur 590
Goldkette Band 501, 511–512, 513, 517–518
Goodman, Benny 473, 474
Gosden, Freeman 9
Grade, Charles 263, 556
Graham, Cinda Kelly 492
Grand Avenue House 47, 676
Grand Theatre 247, 248, 251, 657
Griesedieck, Bud 362
Griffin, Thelma 217, 437
Griggs Piano 565
Griswold College 4
Grover, James R. 639
Guyon, J. Louis 474
Hahn, Hugo 71
Haim, Albert 691
Hance, Bud 417
Handley, Dean 599
Hardy, Emmett 278, 280
Harned Von Maur 189, 511, 670
Harold Teen 321–322
Harris, Grant 331
Harshaw, Emily 116
Hart, Elizabeth Beiderbecke 691
Hartwell, Jimmy 433, 488
Hass, Leon 50; Otie Stibolt 48, 50, 205; J.H. & Emma 588; Nora 139
Haver, June 606
Haynes, Olive Cameron 378, 514
Heath, Laura 692
Henry, Alfonso 181
Hibernian Hall 4, 378, 691
Hicks, Lloyd J 'Jimmy' 531, 562, 603
Hill, Addison 116; David 89, 110, 114; John 89, 107, 109; Mary 87, 109, 114, 120, 154–155, 157; Nelson 92, 116
Hill & Fredericks 589
Hill Tavern 358
Hines, Earl 'Fatha' 579

Hilton, Beriah L. 84; Carrie Hill 84, 85
Hodgson, W.H. 'Red' 615
Horst, Rich 691
Hostetler, Eugene & Ella 559
Hostetler, John & Roger 217
Howe, Mervyn 'Bus' 341
Hubers, William 590; Henry & Adele 590
Huntzinger, Cecil 497
Illinois Theater 351
Ingle, Ernest 'Red' 459
Iowa National Bank 5, 10, 664
Ivens, Preston 453
Ives, Paul 632
James, Harry 626
Johnson, Chic 345
Johnson, George 433, 488
Jolson, Al 347, 395, 520
Jones, Isham 384
Judy, Arthur 371
Julia Belle Swain 338
Kahl Building 401, 426
Karlowa, Carla (Robert) 590; Klara Murphy 590; Paul 20
Kautz, Roy 424–426, 599
Keeler, Ruby 347
Keeley Institute 552, 554
Keener, Hazel 545–546
Kellenberger, Robert 639
Kelly, Angela Searle 491–493; Tony 491
Kettnich, George & Emma 410
Kindt, Charles 247
King, David 285
Kleinhen, Rex 636
Knappe, Al 413
Koehler–Lange 358
Korn Bakery 353
Korn, Ferdinand 355; Vera Cox 208, 212, 348, 349, 352, 356
Kramer, Bill 281
Krause, Robert 20,
Kruse, Clara 'Lalle' 50, 588
Lafayette Hotel, Clinton 548
Lake Forest 454, 456
Lang, Eddie 526
Langtry, Lily 239
LaRocca, Nick 400, 617
LaRoque, Dennis & Pam 692
Lasher, Louis and Nora 218
Layden, Elmer 546

LeClaire, Antoine 3
LeClaire Hotel 376, 568, 668
LeClaire Park 364, 641
Lee, Thomas 'Sonny' 479
Leinbrook, Min 433, 488
Lewis, Ted 582
Liberty Theatre 214
Licata, Curly & Paul 329
Lillard, Henry 6
Lindbergh, Charles 9, 285
Linwood 402, 406, 410, 412, 413, 417, 688
Lion, Jean Pierre 692
Lischer, Henry 20,
Lloyd, Harold 545
Local 67 AFM 598–599, 639
Lorenzen, Jens 20
Looney, John 7, 366
Luscombe, Don 355
MacCosh, Bob 590
Mack, Helen 542–543
MacMurray, Fred 606
Maehr Co. 575
Maennerchor 21
Mandy, Cliff 568
Mansfield, Richard 239
Marable, Fate 277, 289, 292
Marathoners 522, 524–525
Mares, Paul 293
Marks, Morton L. 10, 458
Marquardt, Helen & Allen 33, 205, 590
Martin Cigars 150, 328, 575
Masonic Temple 665
Mauget, Lucile 632
McCalister, Rev J.R. 84
McCandless, Marlene 692
McDonald, Julie 632
McElhiney, Ted 637
McKay, Mel 606
McPartland, Jimmy & Frank 476
Meikel, Ed 229, 231
Mekar, E.R. Muri 235
Meredith, Burgess 623
Mertz, Paul 501, 513
Meyers, Elizabeth 525
Mezzrow, Milton 'Mezz' 479
Miedke, Ralph 435
Millay, Edna St. Vincent 508
Miller, Frank 14
Mississippi Hotel 46
Mister Dooley 259

Moetzel Drug Store 323, 324
Moline State Bank 435
Monocoupe Aeroplane 355
Montgomery, Peggy 545–546
Moore, Raymond 250–251
Moore, Vic 433
Morgenstern, Dan 691
Moritz, Edwin & Rudy 590
Morton, Jelly Roll 272, 273
Munro, Brick 7, 393
Murphy, Conrad H. 453
Murdock, Gretchen 33, 139, 205
Murray, Don 501, 513, 517–518, 582–583
Nichols, Ernest L. 'Red' 533
Neal, Myron 271, 278, 280
New Orleans Rhythm Kings 293
Oakdale 592, 619, 636, 688
Ochler, Adolph 590
O'Connell, Alice 585, 588
O'Dette, Don 574, 640; Jim Sr. 632, 634
Oerman, Harold 297, 300, 305, 319; Orey 300, 305
Offerman, Emma Doering 123
O'Hearn, Trave 568, 590
Oliver, Joe 'King' 273
Olsen, Ole 345
Original Dixieland Jazz Band 400
Otto, Ernst 160, 216, 226
Otto, Ray 599
Outing Club 371, 673
Palao, Jimmie 273
Palmer, Bee 396, 398
Palmer College 445–446
Palmer, Agnes 632; B.J. 6, 453; Daniel D. 443; David D. 632, 636
Pariser Garden 216
Peschinski, John 599
Pauli, H.G. & Sons 590
Peavey, Hollis 469
Pelote, Vincent 691
Perhonis, John Paul
Petersen, Albert 94, 224, 373, 590; Arthur A. 599; Carrie Kennedy 94, 590; Ceno 101; Jim 223
Pieper, Adolph 64, 66; August 64
Pinkard, Maceo 557
Pollack, Ben 293
Poppy Gardens 283, 306
Postel, Warren 337
Previn, Charles 557

Prockaska, Jim 368
Putzier, Richard 'Fritz' 427, 432
Quicksell, Howdy 501, 513, 516
Quinlan ferry 416, 417, 418, 570
Rabe, Joe 590
Raft, George 542
Rank, Mervin 'Pee Wee' 332
Reagan, Ronald 'Dutch' 563
Renwick, William 146
Reuter, Florizel 261
Rhythm Jugglers 501, 513
Richardson, J.B. 221
Riley, Mike 615
Rinker, Al 535
Riverboaters 689
Robinson, Alice 210
Roddewig, Louis 285
Rogers, Jack 568
Rogers, Will 520
Rohlf, Earl 265; Wayne 265, 339
Roppolo, Leon 278, 280, 293
Ross, James 339
Royal Harmonists of Indiana 471
Russell, Charles Edward 9
Russell, Lillian 254
Russell, Pee Wee 479, 512, 515
St. Katharine's 146, 148
Saengerfest 6, 20, 21
Sandburg, Carl 387
Sandke, Randy 691
Sandow, Eugen 239
Sandstrom, Claud H. 285
Schaeffer, Chester 599
Scheef, Lester 525
Schleswig–Holstein memorial 6
Schmidt–Gobble, Amalia 263
Schober, John 639
Schroder, Ernie 689
Schultz, Bernie 339
Searle, Charles 490
Sears, Glenn 217, 342
Seehof, Lutie Beiderbecke 33, 48, 205: Lutie & Jerry 590
Seiffert, H.O. 27, 28, 588; Otto & Marjorie Allen 506
Sell, Vic 331
Sexton, Lyle 'Tal' 271, 280, 425, 469, 590
Shaw, Artie 623
Shaw, Arvell 579
Shaw–Hellige, Loren 642
Shaw, Rev William E. 45

Shears, Ed 231
Sheppard, John 331
Shilkret, Nat 557
Shoemaker, Charles Bix 132, 556; Julien 132; Mary Louise 41, 43, 124, 132, 134, 136, 138, 139, 141, 205, 519, 556, 588; Ted 138, 139, 556, 588; Ted Jr. 132, 556
Siegel, Al 396
Siemon, Rome 332
Soesken, John H. 285
Simpson, Charles 218
Sinatra, Frank 346
Skiles, Dude 574
Spurrier, Esten 590, 599, 632, 636
Stacy, Jess 287
Steiner, John 636
Stewart, Samuel 'Sid' 231
Stibolt, A.J. & Ottilie 28, 205, 588; Carl 48, 50, 205; Victor 48, 50, 205
Stitzel, Mel 293
Strasser, Jacob 225, 226
Streckfus, John 268, 270; Joe, John Jr., Roy & Verne 270
Streckfus Lines 266; *Capitol* 290, 292, 331; *J.S. Deluxe* 268, 290, 292; *President* 290; *Sidney–Washington* 267
Stroehle, Joe 329
Strong, Skip 639
Struve, Bob 319, 332
Sulser, Lovell 'Bromo' 496–497
Sunday Laws 76, 393
Swanson, Les 277, 566, 570, 572, 577, 579, 690
Sweeney, Ruth Shaffner 537
Swindell, Erwin 227
Taggart, Bill 639
Tanguay, Eva 242
Teagarden, Jack 319, 362, 579
Terrace Gardens 412, 420
Teschemacher, Frank 474, 476
Thompson, Chester 285
Tripilas, Gus 690
Trombla, Charles H. 463
Trumbauer, Frank 512, 515, 517–518, 526–530, 550
Tri-City Symphony 483
Tucker, Sophie 398–399, 526
Turner Hall 662
Tyldesley, Bob 568
Tyler School 210, 675

Uptown Theatre 547
Valentine, Jim 690
Van Patten, John 10, 458
Van Patten & Marks 10, 456
Van Speybrock, Omer 331, 334
Vander Veer (Central) Park 371
Venuti, Joe 526
Victor Animatograph 213
Vollmer, Henry 390; Karl K. 217, 349, 356, 362; Karl Sr. 217
Von Maur, George & Lori 590; Henry & Dorothy 590; Richard & Elsie 590
Von Binzer, Lutie 52, 148, 205, 588; Max 53, 148, 205; Werner 58, 205
Von Reuter, Florizel 261
Voynow, Dick 433, 488
Wagner, Robert & Theda 588
Washburn, Gertrude 'Trudel' 33, 185, 205, 349
Wassenhove, Vicki Swanson 577
Watch Hill Park 373
Watson, Bobby 331
Webb, Byron 331
Webb, Jack 626
Weir, John 450
Weiss, Helen 585, 588
Wernentin, Leon 204
Wettling, George 478, 480
Weyerhauser–Denkmann 26
Wharton Field House, Moline 566
Whitaker Bldg 426, 666
White City 479
Whiteman, Paul 384, 483, 515, 519–521, 528, 530, 539, 547, 548, 590, 619
Willcox, Newell 'Spiegle' 517–518
Willett, Jack 271, 280, 599
Winecke, W.F. 216,
Wisherd, D.W. *Majestic* 332
WOC 8, 446, 520, 563, 579
Woecknee, Al 599
Wolverines 433, 476, 488, 512
Woodyatt, Al 332
Wright, Foster 'Tex' 590
Wrixon, Albert 'Doc' 331, 335
Wunder, Art 339
Wundram, Bill 628
YMCA, Davenport 328
Zito, Jimmy 'Zetes' 606
Zoeckler, Charles & Margaret 590

Coda

As a historian, I've been fortunate through the years to discover formerly unknown details about Bix Beiderbecke that excited me, but who could I share them with?

Well, there was Bill Saunders who lives in New Jersey or Albert Haim, a New Yorker no less.

But mention Bix to my wife Gail and she just smiles and turns on the TV. And while my kids have helped tremendously with tech support on the computer, they never were all that interested in the details of my research.

Finding something new about Bix has always been like opening a Christmas present with no one around to see my excitement.

That is until I was blessed with two wonderful fellow researchers, Julie Craighead and Gerri Bowers. Since joining with me in this incessant search for all things Bix, Julie and Gerri experienced their own gentle ostracizing from family and friends.

"You're going down to that library again?"

"Who is this Bix guy anyway?"

"Oh, no, not Bix again!"

Well, folks, it's as somebody said, once you've heard Bix play a few notes you're never the same! Like children mesmerized by the seductive rhythms of the Pied Piper of Hamelin, we traipsed through graveyards, snooped around musty abandoned buildings, not-so-abandoned backyards and spent hour after hour scanning old newspapers on microfilm at the library.

You can bet your best Gennett 78 that with each freshly unearthed find, we'd hurriedly called one another excitingly exclaiming, "Hey, guess what I've found!"

In March 2004, I wrote an article on Bix's maternal grandfather, B.L. Hilton, and asked for help in tracking down family records. That's when Gerri Bowers went beyond being a fan of Bix's music to creating a 700-page genealogy for the Beiderbecke–Hilton–Hill clan.

The fruit of Gerri's labor is the framework for BIX: THE DAVENPORT ALBUM. Many of the stories and anecdotal materials in this book appeared first in columns written by me and my dear friend Mr. Jim Arpy, a retired newspaper reporter who continues to edit the Bix Society's newsletter. While Jim and I argued over details of Bix's life, Gerri tracked down the facts.

There's still so much more to be investigated. But my book editor gave me a deadline and so we'll just have to leave it to others to discover all there is still to be learned about Bix.

As for me, these many years devoted to all things Bix can be summed up in a moment during the QC's celebration weekend commemorating Bix's 100th birthday in 2003.

While taking a break from playing onstage with the *Riverboaters Jazz Band* at the Blackhawk Hotel, I was called over by the late Les Swanson, sharp-witted still at age 97. "You are sitting in the exact spot where Bix sat when he played with us in 1929." It gave me the goose bumps.

Rich J. Johnson
March 2008

ROUND OF APPLAUSE

Elizabeth Beiderbecke Hart, Julien Beiderbecke, Howard Braren; Julie Craighead, Ray & Muriel Voss, Bill Wundram, Bill Perry, Staff, *Davenport Public Library Special Collections*; Bob McCue, *Davenport School Museum*; *German–American Heritage Society*; *Rock Island County Historical Society*; *Maquoketa Historical Society*; Don Southwood, *First Presbyterian Church*; Deb Williams, *Oakdale Cemetery*; Ernie Schroder, Dorothy Adams, *Buffalo Historical Society*; John Smith, *Davenport Radisson*; Pam LaRoche, *Beiderbecke Inn*; Marlene McCandless, *Beiderbecke Grand Avenue House*; Laura Heath, *Trash Can Annie's*; Jedge Daniels, Jim Weerts, Linda Meadows, Karen Anderson, Don Dussliere, Phil Pospychala, Ken Kline, Lewis Shaw, Tom Pletcher, Jim Grover, *Life and Music of Leon Bix Beiderbecke*; Linda Evans and the late Phil Evans, Bill Saunders, Albert Haim, Jean Pierre Lion, Trevor Rippengale, Warren Miedke, Marie Giltner Smith; Tony Kelly and Cinda Kelly Graham; John Van Speybroeck, Jean Oerman Yelle, Vicki Swanson Wassenhove, Annie Peart, *Bix Beiderbecke Memorial Society*; Catfish Jazz Society, Josh Duffee, Gail Johnson, Kent Bowers, Sara Toliver, Kent Richard

Boone, Stephaine Erin Armbrust; Bj Elsner and Terri Wiebenga, *Mississippi Valley Writers Colony*; and the Kay & Gary Durham Memorial Fund, England.

FRONT MAN

RICH JOHNSON, Moline, has been into jazz from when he first played his dad's 78 rpm records on the family Victrola. He plays rhythm guitar, but started out on the clarinet and sax in school bands. He received the Purple Heart and Bronze star for WWII service in the South Pacific. He attended college on the GI Bill, graduating Augustana College in Rock Island with a bachelor's degree in music. After 37 years as a senior planner and plant photographer for American Air Filter Co, he retired and devoted his energy to championing his musical hero, Bix Beiderbecke. He served as photographer and festival music director for the Bix Beiderbecke Memorial Society. He received the Jean Goldkette Award in 2005 and the Society's first *Bix Lives* bronze statue in 2007. He co–founded the Catfish Jazz Society. And he continues to play traditional jazz regularly with fellow QC musicians. He also co–founded a QC writers group that was the genesis of the Mississippi Valley Writers Colony. He is a regular contributor for the *Mississippi Rag*, *BixNotes* and the Catfish Jazz Society newsletter. Publishing credits include four Quad–Cities books Arcadia's *Images of America* series; *Rock Island: Yesterday, Today, and Tomorrow*, edited by Bj Elsner; and *With Pen In Hand: QC Notable Writers of the Past*. Rich and his wife Gail are parents to daughter Jackie and son Jeffre; grandparents to Cori, Christopher, and Sean; and great–grandparents to Jackson.

SIDEMEN

JIM ARPY graduated Drake University and began as a feature writer for the Davenport Times in 1951. After retirement from full–time reporting in the 1990s, he continued as publicity chair for the Bix jazz festival and served as vice chairman of the Bix Jazz Society. His QC Times feature columns remain popular among Iowa and Illinois historians, genealogists and Americana collectors. His series on gangster John Looney, *The Lawless Looney Years*, was published as a QC Times special edition in 1979. He also authored *The*

Magnificent Mississippi: Legend of Our Land (1983, Sutherland) previously published as Legends of Our Land (1968, Davenport), and co-authored *Quad–Cities: Joined By A River* (1982, Lee Enterprises). He is editor of *BixNotes*, the official newsletter of the Bix Memorial Jazz Society. He and his wife Barb live in Moline, IL.

GERRI BOWERS, Davenport, started her own family genealogy in 1989. Spending so many hours in the Special Collection Department at the Davenport Public Library led to her volunteering as a part-time library staffer in Special Collections. She now enjoys helping others with their genealogy research. After reading in the Bix Society newsletter that Rich Johnson was hoping someone could help him find Bix's relatives on his mother's side, Gerri got to work and researched marriage and death notices, property deeds, census records and much more. She then introduced herself to Rich by handing him a stack of documents. She and Rich have been close friends ever since. She is a board member of the Bix Beiderbecke Memorial Society and historian for the Catfish Jazz Society. She and husband Kent have been married 52 years and have three daughters and three grandchildren.

COVER SOLO

WARD OLSON hasn't been able to break the habit since his first *Bix fix* doing the cover art for the *QC Times* 1980 jazz festival edition. Olson has done a dozen Bix portraits and related watercolors. Les Swanson proclaimed them the best paintings of Bix that he had ever seen. Renowned for his versatility in design and illustration, Olson's portrait work and regional nostalgia paintings have won numerous awards. He has a special fondness for working in acrylic and watercolor mediums and a knack for developing representational works from odd bits and scraps of materials, often found on frequent antiquing excursions. Olson attended the Frederic Mizen Academy of Art in Chicago and the Minneapolis Institute of Art. His early career was interrupted by military assignment where he put his artistic talents to use aboard the Navel destroyer Samuel N. Moore. Olson's roots are deep in the Quad Cities area. He and his wife Beverly enjoy dancing and travel. Ward also enjoys architecture, interior design and natural landscape sculpture.

Above: Genealogist GERRI BOWERS at the Hilton family gravesite in Oakdale Cemetery

L-R: Ernie Schroder and Buffalo Historical Society president Dorothy Adams with JULIE CRAIGHEAD and JIM ARPY at Linwood quarry

Riverboaters, c. 1999
seated: Gus Tripilas, Bob Cook; back, L-R: Rich, Jim Valentine & Ben Chappell

Phil & Linda Evans in 1998

Rich with Les Swanson in 2000

Top, L-R: Rich Johnson, Albert Haim, Vincent Pelote, Vince Giordano, Dan Morgenstern, Ed Berber, Randy Sandke, Joe Giordano, Rich Horst and Howard Braren.
Below, L-R: Elizabeth Beiderbecke Hart; Rich Johnson, Albert Haim

Top: Michael Cervantes, manager of Col Ballroom

Left: Jean Pierre Lion with Laura Heath, owner of Trash Can Annie's at Hibernian Hall

Top: Marlene McCandless, Duea Films office manager at the Bix Beiderbecke House on Grand Avenue

Left: Dennis and Pam LaRoque, owners of Beiderbecke Inn, former home of Bix's grandparents

Background by Ward Olson

BIX MEETS LOUIS

On a postcard dated 7–11–21 to his mom, Bix wrote: *Just arrived in Quincy from Louisiana, Mo, on an all day excursion and are staying a couple hours so thot I'd drop a line. Tomorrow we take an excursion from Quincy to Louisiana & back then Wed from Burlington to Ft. Mad. & back home Friday—having a wonderful time—good food etc plenty of sleep—good band. With love to all—LBB*

In a lengthy letter from Lake Forest to Burnie & Sis, postmarked 9–19–21, Bix wrote: *I sure had a wonderful time in Chi & in regard to the music you heard. That's Faite Maribores bunch who use to be on the St. Paul—the talk of the river—why I tried to tell you about them—I heard em in Louisiana, Mo.*

Bix misspelled Fate Marable's name but in identifying Louisiana, Missouri, just downriver from Hannibal, where he heard Marable's band, he nailed down what Louis Armstrong could not: when they met.

Bix was aboard the *Majestic* and Armstrong on the *St. Paul*. Two ships passing in the night. Bix and Louis found solid ground for their friendship in Chicago.

Bix's letter from Lake Forest, responding to his brother Burnie about Marable's band in Davenport probably refers to Marable's Kentucky Jazz Band that played aboard the Streckfus Steamer *Sidney*, rechristened the *Washington* in 1921.

The *Washington* did excursions around Davenport early and late in the season on the Upper Mississippi River. All the Streckfus excursion boats moored at Davenport's Nahant Harbor off Credit Island in the winter months. Only the *Capitol* operated year–round.

During peak summer months, the *Washington* worked the Ohio River, the *St. Paul* and *J.S. Deluxe* traveled between St. Louis and New Orleans, and the *Capitol* traveled the Upper Mississippi, between St. Louis and St. Paul, MN.

Images of the *Washington* sternwheeler's interior are familiar to riverboat buffs and jazz fans from the 1921 publicity shots of Marable's band in the remodeled ballroom of the *Washington*. That would be the last season of river excursions for Armstrong, drummer Warren *Baby* Dodds, and banjoist Johnny St. Cyr.

Confusion as to which bands were on which boats comes from the multiple names they used, depending on where they played and what style of music they played.

Setting the record straight: Louis Armstrong did not play in the Kentucky Jazz Band. No one from New Orleans did. Marable put together his first jazz band with professional musicians recruited from his hometown of Paducah, KY. The Kentucky Jazz Band worked for Streckfus Lines beginning in 1918.

"They played real nice but did not compare to those New Orleans boys," Marable said in a 1945 interview with Beulah Schacht of the now–defunct *St. Louis Globe Democrat.*

With the 1919 season, Marable introduced St. Louis audiences to authentic New Orleans jazz musicians with a band that performed under the names: Fate Marable and the Cotton Pickers, Fate Marable's Society Syncopators, and the Metropolitan Jaz–E–Saz Orchestra

Besides Armstrong, St. Cyr and Baby Dodds, other featured New Orleaners included George *Pops* Foster on bass; Bill Ridgeley, trombone; Paul Dominguez, violin; Sam Dutrey, clarinet; Norman Mason, trumpet; and Davey Jones, who played various instruments but was famous for the *mellophone,* a brass band instrument similar to a French horn but with coils and a big bell.

Jones, whom everyone called *Professor,* tried to teach then–18–year–old Armstrong to read music, a requirement Marable made of all his musicians. "Louis, you can blow and you can swing because it's natural to you," Jones said. "But you'll never be able to swing any better than you already know how until you learn to read. Then you can swing in ways you never thought of before!"

Armstrong quit, some say he was fired, over artistic differences with Marable. Others who came and went over the years seemed ambivalent about Marable's management style. Demanding of his musicians and noted at times for being cruel to them, Marable nevertheless got them union memberships, often based on his own reputation.

Armstrong and Bix both had the talent to get through the door. What kept Armstrong from being kicked to the curb was that union card.

While the other Streckfus boats were moored for the winter, Marable and the New Orleans musicians worked the Lower Mississippi aboard the *Capitol*. In May, they switched back to the *St. Paul* and music director duties aboard the *Capitol* were turned over to Tony Catalano for excursions between St. Louis and St. Paul, MN.

Marable and Catalano had been bandmates aboard the original *J.S.* excursion boat before Streckfus enacted a policy of segregated bands on its riverboats.

Since Armstrong mentioned several times that he had played with Marable aboard the *Sidney/Washington*, it's likely he is referring to the months when the *Capitol* was undergoing extensive remodeling. Major renovations were done in Keokuk, IA, and finishing touches completed in Davenport in time for the 1920 season.

June 13, 1920—Dubuque *Telegraph–Herald*:
STEAMER CAPITOL HERE NEXT WEEK
MOST MAGNIFICENT ON UPPER WATERS

On Saturday and Sunday next, the new steamer Capitol will make her debut on the Mississippi at Dubuque.

...There has been so much interest displayed in regard to the first voyage of the Capitol that there will be undoubtedly a capacity attendance to see the new steamer for the first time here and to inspect the fixtures and decorations that have given her the name and reputation of being the most magnificent and wonderful excursion steamer on inland waters. More than 2,000 electric lamps alone are used to illuminate the dancing deck through the medium of the remote system and the effects are varicolored, giving the semblance of a beautiful ballroom. The steamer carries an excellent jazz band under the direction of Tony Evans, of Rock Island. [Tony & Evans Capitol Jazz Band]

...Following the four excursions here next Saturday and Sunday of the Capitol, the new steamer will continue on her way north where she will start the return trip from St. Paul. It is expected that the Capitol will make excursions from Dubuque all summer at regular intervals of about two weeks. The St. Paul and the J.S. (Streckfus' two side–wheel excursion steamers), will operate out of St. Louis all summer and the Sidney (the other sternwheeler excursion boat in addition to the Capitol), will continue at New Orleans.

www.ingramcontent.com/pod-product-compliance
Lightning Source LLC
Chambersburg PA
CBHW060306240426
43661CB00059B/2678